Modern Scandals

1904-2008

Great Events from History

Modern Scandals

1904-2008

Volume 2
1972-1998

Editor
Carl L. Bankston III
Tulane University

SALEM PRESS
Pasadena, California   Hackensack, New Jersey

Editor in Chief: Dawn P. Dawson

Editorial Director: Christina J. Moose	*Research Supervisor:* Jeffry Jensen
Development Editor: R. Kent Rasmussen	*Design and Graphics:* James Hutson
Project Editor: Desiree Dreeuws	*Layout:* William Zimmerman
Acquisitions Editor: Mark Rehn	*Research Assistant:* Keli Trousdale
Production Editor: Andrea E. Miller	*Editorial Assistant:* Dana Garey
Photo Editor: Cynthia Breslin Beres	

Cover photos (pictured clockwise, from top left): (The Granger Collection, New York); Duke and Duchess of Windsor. (Hulton Archive/Getty Images); (The Granger Collection, New York); Jean-Bédel Bokassa. (AP/Wide World Photos); (AP/Wide World Photos); (©iStockphoto.com/Mark Sauerwein)

Library of Congress Cataloging-in-Publication Data

Great events from history. Modern scandals / editor, Carl L. Bankston III.
   v.   cm. — (Great events from history)
   Includes bibliographical references and indexes.
   ISBN 978-1-58765-468-8 (set : alk. paper) — ISBN 978-1-58765-469-5 (v. 1: alk. paper) — ISBN 978-1-58765-470-1 (v. 2 : alk. paper) — ISBN 978-1-58765-471-8 (v. 3 : alk. paper)
   1. Scandals—History—20th century. 2. Scandals—History—21st century. 3. Scandals—United States—History—20th century. 4. Scandals—United States—History—21st century. 5. History, Modern—20th century—Anecdotes. 6. History, Modern—21st century—Anecdotes. 7. United States—History—20th century—Anecdotes. 8. United States—History—21st century—Anecdotes. I. Bankston, Carl L. (Carl Leon), 1952- II. Title: Modern scandals.

D422.G74 2009
909.82—dc22
                                                                                        2008054757

First Printing

CONTENTS

1970's *(continued)*

1980's

CONTENTS

1990's

Keyword List of Contents

KEYWORD LIST OF CONTENTS

li

Modern Scandals

1904-2008

July 25, 1972
NEWSPAPER BREAKS STORY OF ABUSES IN TUSKEGEE SYPHILIS STUDY

Journalist Jean Heller reported that an agency of the U.S. government was still conducting a study, begun forty years earlier, to determine the effects of untreated syphilis in African American men without informing them about either their disease or the nature of the study. In response, the U.S. Congress enacted a law that mandated institutional review boards to supervise and approve all federally funded projects using human subjects. Also, all federal agencies established strict rules on informed consent.

ALSO KNOWN AS: Tuskegee experiment; Tuskegee Study of Untreated Syphilis in the Male Negro

LOCALES: Washington, D.C.; Macon County, Alabama

CATEGORIES: Medicine and health care; racism; civil rights and liberties; human rights; publishing and journalism; government

KEY FIGURES

Jean Heller (fl. 1970's), reporter with the Associated Press

Taliaferro Clark (fl. 1970's), head of the venereal (sexually transmitted) diseases division of the U.S. Public Health Service

Eunice Rivers (fl. 1970's), African American nurse who worked on the project

Peter Buxton (fl. 1970's), lawyer, former researcher for the Public Health Service

Fred Gray (b. 1930), Alabama civil rights attorney

SUMMARY OF EVENT

The Tuskegee syphilis study had its beginnings in 1929, when the U.S. Public Health Service (PHS) was awarded a Julius Rosenwald Foundation grant to investigate the prevalence of syphilis among African Americans and to explore the possibilities of

mass treatment. Taliaferro Clark, head of the venereal (sexually transmitted) disease division of the PHS, was fascinated by a 1928 Norwegian study that included 473 patients with syphilis who had the disease for more than twenty years without treatment. The study found that 27.9 percent of the patients had undergone a "spontaneous cure." The director of the study, Emil Bruusgaard, estimated that 70 percent of all syphilitics would never suffer serious inconvenience from the disease, although he warned about the dangers of untreated syphilis for the other 30 percent.

Because the Norwegian study had used only white patients, Clark and his associates wanted to compare its results with a study using patients of African ancestry. Their initial goal was to determine whether the disease had different effects on the two racial groups. After conducting a survey of several Alabama counties, they chose Macon County because it had the largest concentration of syphilitics. No funds were available for treating the patients. Apparently researchers did not consider the lack of treatment to be unethical, in large part because the best treatments of the time, Salvarsan and other arsenic-derived drugs, were frequently ineffective and had extreme side effects. Also, the treatments were so expensive that they were unaffordable for an estimated 80 percent of the American people during the Great Depression. From the perspective of the PHS, the study would neither harm nor benefit the patients, and they hoped it would result in significant medical knowledge.

Beginning in 1932, the study examined the condition of 412 men who had the disease, as well as another 204 unaffected men who served as study controls. Physicians at the Tuskegee Institute at Tuskegee University in Alabama, and other local physicians, cooperated with the PHS in the study. An African American nurse, Eunice Rivers, was especially active in recruiting the men and transport-

A staffer with the U.S. Public Health Service draws blood from a partici-pant in the Tuskegee Syphilis Study in this undated photograph. (NARA)

ing them to see the cooperating physicians. Most of the men were sharecroppers; all were quite poor and uneducated. To encourage participation, they were promised free meals, a $50 death benefit, as well as experimental treatment for "bad blood," which re-ferred to a variety of medical conditions in the local dialect. At that time, the procedures used in the study did not directly violate any established ethical principles of informed consent, although most phy-sicians recognized an obligation for truth-telling. PHS officials originally planned for the study to continue for a year or less, but they later decided to continue it to trace the long-term consequences of the disease.

Even after the antibiotic penicillin had become widely recognized as an effective cure for syphilis by 1945, the PHS continued its Tuskegee study without any major changes in policies. No evidence exists to show that any PHS physician considered the possibility of using the new treatment. Perhaps they assumed that penicillin would not benefit long-infected persons, especially those with latent syphi-lis. At least until the 1950's, however, some of the men were young enough to be sexually active, and an uncertain percentage of them probably remained

contagious. Many critics of the study argue that had the patients been middle-class whites, it is highly likely the PHS would have informed them of their disease and recommended treatment. In 1965, a doctor in Detroit, Michi-gan, read a published report of the study. He became the first mem-ber of the medical profession to write to the PHS expressing con-cern about the study's ethics. PHS officials did not respond to the letter.

Peter Buxton, a PHS researcher, was distraught when he read about the Tuskegee study. On Novem-ber 6, 1966, he filed an official protest, asserting that the study was similar to the medical experi-ments of the Nazis that were con-demned at the Nuremberg Trials after World War II. PHS physicians attempted but failed to convince Buxton that his concerns were unjustified. Two years later, Buxton, now a lawyer, wrote a stronger protest, warning about "the thinking of Negro mili-tants that Negroes have long been used for medical experiments." Responding to the second protest, the PHS in 1970 cooperated with the U.S. Centers for Disease Control and Prevention (CDC) in hold-ing a blue-ribbon panel. Only one of the participants argued that the surviving patients should be given treatment. The majority of the panelists, however, concluded that treatment would not help the pa-tients and that continuation of the study was war-ranted.

Angry about the panel's decision, Buxton leaked information about the Tuskegee study to Edith Lederer, a journalist in San Francisco, California. Lederer's supervisors insisted on research by a journalist in the East, so she contacted her friend, Associated Press (AP) reporter Jean Heller. Heller interviewed CDC officials, who provided her with frank and straightforward information. Her article, "Syphilis Patients Died Untreated," was picked up by the Washington *Evening Star* and published on

July 25, revealing the study to the general public. The story broke nationally the following day.

IMPACT

Although overshadowed by events relating to that year's presidential election, Heller's story attracted nationwide attention. Merlin Duval, an assistant secretary at the U.S. Department of Health, Education, and Welfare (HEW; now Health and Human Services), was "shocked and horrified" to learn of the Tuskegee study, and he appointed an ad hoc panel to investigate the matter. Based on the panel's recommendation, HEW ordered an end to the study on November 16, 1972. A few months later, Democratic U.S. senator Edward M. Kennedy, chairman of the Senate committee on health, held hearings on the scandal. Participants in the study were brought to Washington, D.C., to tell of their experiences. Kennedy called the study "an outrageous and intolerable situation."

The federal government, however, did not voluntarily offer monetary compensation to the surviving patients. In July, 1973, African American lawyer Fred Gray filed a lawsuit for $1.8 billion against the government. In his brief, Gray asserted that the government had failed to treat the men, had not informed them that they had syphilis, had led them to think they were receiving appropriate medical treatment, and had failed to obtain their consent to be part of a study. Two years later, Gray and the government agreed on an out-of-court settlement for $10 million, including $37,500 for each living syphilitic and $16,000 for each person used as a control.

Reacting to the Tuskegee study, HEW reviewed its regulations on human experimentation and made fundamental changes in its procedures. The study was one of the major reasons that Congress enacted the National Research Act of 1974, which mandated institutional review boards to supervise and approve all federally funded projects using human subjects. Publicity about the study also was a major factor in leading all federal agencies to establish strict rules on informed consent by the late 1970's.

As early as 1965, the Tuskegee Institute became a national historic landmark. In 1997, U.S. president Bill Clinton apologized on behalf of the government in a ceremony attended by Gray and eight survivors of the study. Clinton declared, "To our African American citizens, I am sorry that your federal government orchestrated a study so clearly racist. That can never be allowed to happen again."

—*Thomas Tandy Lewis*

FURTHER READING

Gray, Fred D. *The Tuskegee Syphilis Study: The Real Story and Beyond*. Montgomery, Ala.: NewSouth Books, 1998. A look at the study by the prominent civil rights lawyer who represented the patients in a successful suit against the government.

Jones, James H. *Bad Blood: The Tuskegee Syphilis Experiment*. 1981. New ed. New York: Free Press, 1993. A pioneering work that is highly critical of PHS doctors, based on exhaustive archival research that was utilized by Fred D. Gray for his book and by subsequent writers.

Marks, Harry M. *The Progress of Experiment: Science and Therapeutic Reform in the United States, 1900-1990*. New York: Cambridge University Press, 1997. Includes much information about the historical development of ethical standards in medicine and science and informed consent.

Reverby, Susan M. "More than Fact and Fiction: Cultural Memory and the Tuskegee Syphilis Study." *Hastings Center Report* 31 (September-October, 2001): 22-28. Focusing on how preconceptions have influenced memories and interpretations, Reverby acknowledges the limitations of treatment before the late 1940's and observes that some patients eventually received treatment.

_____, ed. *Tuskegee's Truths: Rethinking the Tuskegee Syphilis Study*. Chapel Hill: University of North Carolina Press, 2000. Excellent collection of scholarly writings, some of which argue that the study was based on blatant racism, while others insist that no intentional harm was done to the patients.

Uschan, Michael V. *Forty Years of Medical Racism: The Tuskegee Experiments*. Farmington Hills, Mich.: Lucent Books, 2005. A relatively short account that is primarily for young readers, twelve years and older. Part of the Lucent Library of Black History series.

Washington, Harriet. *Medical Apartheid: The Dark History of Medical Experimentation on Black Americans from Colonial Times to the Present.* New York: Doubleday, 2007. A scholarly but somewhat sensationalized history about how African Americans have been studied by the medical profession without their knowledge or consent.

SEE ALSO: Mar. 21, 1928: Alberta Government Sterilizes Thousands Deemed Genetically and Mentally Unfit; July, 1961: Psychologist Stanley Milgram Begins Obedience-to-Authority Experiments; Sept. 19, 1988: Stephen Breuning Pleads Guilty to Medical Research Fraud; Nov. 26, 1997: Canadian Health Commissioner Releases Report on Tainted Blood; Mar. 4, 1999: Quebec Offers Support for Abused Duplessis Orphans; Sept., 2000: American Scientists Are Accused of Starting a Measles Epidemic in the Amazon; Jan. 30, 2001: Liverpool Children's Hospital Collects Body Parts Without Authorization; Aug., 2002: Immunologist Resigns After Being Accused of Falsifying Research; May 12, 2006: Scientist Is Indicted for Faking His Research on Creating Stem Cells.

July 31, 1972
THOMAS F. EAGLETON WITHDRAWS FROM VICE PRESIDENTIAL RACE

The withdrawal of U.S. vice presidential candidate Thomas F. Eagleton from the 1972 Democratic ticket because of a history of mental illness was the controversial beginning of the end for Senator George McGovern's presidential campaign; he lost in a landslide against incumbent president Richard Nixon.

ALSO KNOWN AS: Eagleton affair
LOCALE: Washington, D.C.
CATEGORIES: Politics; government; psychology and psychiatry; social issues and reform

KEY FIGURES
Thomas F. Eagleton (1929-2007), U.S. senator from Missouri, 1968-1987
George McGovern (b. 1922), U.S. senator from South Dakota, 1963-1981

SUMMARY OF EVENT
"One rock in the landslide" is how U.S. senator Thomas F. Eagleton described his contribution to the overwhelming defeat of Senator George Mc-

Govern in the 1972 presidential race. This political episode was so momentous that Eagleton's later significant legislative achievements were overshadowed by his removal after eighteen days as the vice presidential nominee in 1972. He was removed by presidential nominee George McGovern after revelations that Eagleton had received psychiatric treatment, including electroshock therapy, for depression in 1960, 1964, and 1966.

The 1972 scandal had an inauspicious beginning. Eagleton was a last-minute selection for vice president on the Democratic ticket. As Eagleton would later reveal, he was so far down the list of potential candidates that even Theodore Hesburgh of the University of Notre Dame was considered a more viable choice. Although not unusual for its time, choosing a vice presidential candidate so late in a campaign was further exacerbated by the failed courting of the reluctant Senator Ted Kennedy of Massachusetts. After the Kennedy option was closed, McGovern's campaign staff had to scramble to find another choice.

Campaign staff sought the advice of several pro-

Democratic presidential candidate George McGovern, left, announces the withdrawal of his running mate Thomas Eagleton from the campaign. (AP/Wide World Photos)

spective candidates on the approved list, one being Gaylord Nelson, U.S. senator from Wisconsin. Nelson refused the offer but told McGovern's staff that there was no more attractive candidate than Eagleton of Missouri.

Initially, Eagleton was thought to be an unlikely choice for vice president. He was only forty-two years old and in his first term as senator. In addition, he was an early supporter of Senator Edmund Muskie of Maine in the Democratic primary and criticized McGovern for supporting "amnesty, abortion and the legalization of pot." There also were rumors of an alcohol problem, which were later found to be untrue. Eagleton posted sixth on the list of potential candidates.

After further consideration by the McGovern campaign staff, Eagleton was considered an attrac-

tive candidate—Irish Catholic, young, bright (Amherst College and Harvard Law School), witty, handsome, and, as shown during his tenure as attorney general of Missouri, firm on law and order. He was known as a Franklin D. Roosevelt liberal with the solid support of labor and was a staunch opponent of the Vietnam War.

During the late afternoon of July 13, McGovern called Eagleton and offered him the number two position on the ticket. Before McGovern could finish his sentence, Eagleton said, "George, before you change your mind, I accept." Campaign staffer Frank Mankiewicz then took the phone and asked Eagleton if there was anything in his background that might embarrass the campaign. Eagleton said there was nothing.

The media began investigating Eagleton's back-

1970's

ground, revealing that three times he had been hospitalized for depression and had twice received electroshock therapy. McGovern staffers, through anonymous tips, became aware of this issue shortly after the Miami Democratic convention but did not tell McGovern. Mankiewicz and Gary Hart, later U.S. senator from Colorado, met with Eagleton to discuss the problem and, after a frank and full airing of the affair, Eagleton offered to resign. Mankiewicz said no, that McGovern must be told and McGovern must decide.

On July 25, Eagleton was asked by reporters about rumors that he had a history of mental illness. In fact, the media began to report that he had a "nervous condition." Eagleton responded that he had been treated for "nervous exhaustion" in the past and was frank and forthcoming when asked about specific treatments, acknowledging that they included psychiatric counseling and electroshock therapy. The treatments worked, he said, and his mental illness "was like a broken leg that healed." Since those early episodes of depression he learned to pace himself and became successful in his political career, which included positions as St. Louis City solicitor, Missouri attorney general, lieutenant governor, and U.S. senator. Doctors had given him a clean bill of health, and his professional effectiveness was never questioned.

McGovern responded to these revelations by announcing that he was "1,000 percent for Tom Eagleton," telling the press that Eagleton was "fully qualified" to be vice president and, if necessary, president. Critics, however, charged that in a nuclear age, the nation could not afford to have someone with a history of mental illness decide if and when to use nuclear weaponry. It certainly did not help that Eagleton's depression was referred to as a "nervous condition" by the media. In addition, mental illness carried a heavy social stigma. Even supporters of Eagleton worried that the voting public would never accept him in such a leadership role. Pressure from within the campaign, especially from campaign manager Hart, according to Eagleton, as well as pressure from major donors, led McGovern to force Eagleton to withdraw from the ticket. Eagleton withdrew on July 31 and said he did so for

"party unity." No later accusation would bother Eagleton more than the one claiming that he deceived the McGovern campaign.

Showing great grace and courage, Eagleton campaigned hard for the newly formed McGovern ticket with Sargent Shriver. His efforts were to no avail, as the Democratic ticket did not carry Missouri or any other state except Massachusetts. Richard Nixon won his second term in a landslide victory. McGovern supporters blamed the scandal for the magnitude of the loss. After leaving the ticket, Eagleton received sympathy and support from political colleagues as well as one prominent foe. On August 2, Nixon sent a personal, handwritten letter to Eagleton's thirteen-year-old son, Terry. In the letter, Nixon praised the senior Eagleton's "courage, poise and just plain grits he showed against overwhelming odds."

McGovern's handling of the Eagleton affair hurt his campaign; however, how much so is difficult to measure. That Eagleton's personal background was not properly vetted led to charges of campaign incompetence. For some critics, McGovern's decision to remove Eagleton smacked of insensitivity, at best, and called into question McGovern's image as a person of decency. In an April, 2006, interview, McGovern said that if he had to do it over again, he would have kept Eagleton on the ticket. He admitted that little was known about mental illness in 1972, and that a lack of information and understanding about depression led to a mistake in his judgment.

Eagleton survived the controversy and went on to serve with distinction in the Senate for eighteen years. He was a leading sponsor of the original 1974 War Powers Act (although he ultimately voted against a watered-down compromise version), the first Clean Air and Clean Water Acts, and the 1973 Eagleton amendment halting the bombing of Cambodia, which effectively ended the Vietnam War. It is the latter he regarded as his top legislative achievement.

Upon his retirement from the Senate in 1987 he received the highest praises from both his Democratic and Republican peers, and was referred to often as "the conscience of the Senate." He served the remainder of his life as teacher and mentor to students at Washington University in St. Louis and as a partner in the St. Louis law firm of Thompson-Coburn.

IMPACT

The Eagleton episode led to microscopic vetting of potential running mates in U.S. politics. No longer are vice presidential candidates selected without a thorough background check. Personal, professional, social, and medical histories are now scrutinized by campaign staff long before the names of potential running mates are leaked to the press. It is also possible that the Eagleton affair put more focus on the vice presidency as a significant and powerful office, for no other reason than being "a heartbeat away" from the presidency. Vice presidential running mates are now chosen not simply for adding electoral appeal to a party's ticket but also for the possibility that they might serve as president.

Mental illness, especially depression, received added attention after the Eagleton episode as well. At the time, mental illness still carried a heavy social stigma, leaving few sufferers, especially politicians, willing to talk about the disease. Mental illness is now more understood by the American public, discussed more in public, and revealed as a part of the life of celebrities and other public figures, which has had the effect of releasing some of the social stigma surrounding the disease.

Whether or not Eagleton or, for that matter, someone such as former U.S. president Abraham Lincoln, who also suffered mental illness, would be shunned as a potential running mate remains a question for debate. Some still argue that mental illness, unlike other diseases, uniquely disqualifies a person from holding the vice presidency or presidency. Others argue that given what is now known about mental illness and given medicine's ability to treat and manage the disease, one should no longer be disqualified from high political office simply because they suffer from, or have suffered from, depression or other types of mental illness.

—*Steven Richard Neiheisel*

FURTHER READING

Miroff, Bruce. *The Liberals' Moment: The McGovern Insurgency and the Identity Crisis of the Democratic Party*. Lawrence: University Press of Kansas, 2008. Political scientist Miroff argues that McGovern's handling of the Eagleton affair damaged his reputation as competent and decent. McGovern's presidential image was one of compassion, thoughtfulness, and of not being Richard "Tricky Dick" Nixon.

Novak, Robert D. *The Prince of Darkness: Fifty Years of Reporting in Washington*. New York: Crown Forum, 2007. Longtime Washington reporter Novak reveals controversial secrets from sources inside the 1972 McGovern-Eagleton campaign. From notes taken during the Democratic presidential primary of 1972, Novak discloses that Eagleton was a forceful critic of McGovern. Novak had disclosed Eagleton's negative comments about McGovern in 1972 but not the source.

White, Theodore H. *The Making of the President, 1972*. New York: Atheneum, 1973. From the dean of political journalists, White offers insightful commentary on the political implications of the "buffoonery of the Eagleton affair." White casts a generally sympathetic view of Eagleton, describing the McGovern campaign staff's handling of the situation as confused, rushed, and incompetent.

SEE ALSO: Sept. 23, 1952: Richard Nixon Denies Taking Illegal Campaign Contributions; Mar. 1, 1967: Adam Clayton Powell, Jr., Is Excluded from Congress; May 9, 1969: Supreme Court Justice Abe Fortas Is Accused of Bribery; June 13, 1971: *New York Times* Publishes the Pentagon Papers; June 17, 1972-Aug. 9, 1974: Watergate Break-in Leads to President Nixon's Resignation; Oct. 10, 1973: Spiro T. Agnew Resigns Vice Presidency in Disgrace; Oct. 11, 1979: Senate Denounces Herman E. Talmadge for Money Laundering.

1970's

August 19, 1973
CHEATING SCANDAL SHOCKS SOAP BOX DERBY

Engineer Robert Brookings Lange, Sr., encouraged his fourteen-year-old nephew, Jimmy Gronen, to install an electromagnet and battery in his soap box derby car. The addition of such a device violated race regulations and provided Gronen, the derby's overall winner, with an unfair advantage. When questioned, Lange justified his actions by claiming that there had been extensive and consistent cheating by other derby participants in other races. Gronen's title was stripped and he lost a $7,500 scholarship.

LOCALE: Akron, Ohio
CATEGORIES: Corruption; sports; families and
   children; popular culture

KEY FIGURES
Jimmy Gronen (b. 1959), soap box derby racer
Robert Brookings Lange, Sr. (1925-2000),
   engineer, inventor of ski boots, and Jimmy
   Gronen's uncle
Bobby Lange (b. 1958), Robert Lange's son and
   1972 derby winner

SUMMARY OF EVENT
On August 19, 1973, 138 youths between the ages of eleven and fifteen years gathered to compete in the thirty-sixth annual All-American Soap Box Derby at Derby Downs in Akron, Ohio. The participants, all winners in local community races, were excited yet nervous about their performances in this major race. Regulations required the racers to have built their own vehicles, with some guidance from adults if necessary. The event was intended to instill in children a sense of pride and accomplishment in their craftsmanship, but this year's seemingly wholesome children's activity was fraught with scandal. The first-place winner quickly lost his standing, stories of cheating emerged, and the outrage that followed tarnished the event for years to come.

   As with other sports, derby-racing rules existed for creating uniformity. Derby regulations required

that race cars not exceed specific dimensions, that the total weight of the car and driver not exceed 250 pounds, that cars use specific derby wheels and axles, and that welded material was not permitted in making the car. The policy, however, did not specify particular materials for the car body, which allowed for some flexibility in design. Throughout the years of racing, derby cars had become more sophisticated and the races more intense. With these advanced models came vague rumors of cheating, but the speculations had not been taken seriously—until after the race of 1973.

   Racer Jimmy Gronen slid into his derby car, and the metal starting plaque was dropped. His car made a fast leap away from the starting line and down the course of 953.75 feet toward the finish line. Spectators immediately began to speculate about his unusually fast start. Because gravity was technically the only means of propulsion in a soap box derby race, Gronen's quick jump ahead of the other competitors raised questions. His finishing time in the heat also drew speculation: Gronen won by a large margin in derby racing, 20/100th's of a second.

   Rumors began circulating that Gronen had buffed his wheels, a prohibited activity, which led authorities to replace his wheels. Officials also drilled into the car to remove excess weight. Later, after the final run of the day, onlookers puzzled over yet another phenomenon. They wondered why Gronen's race speed decreased in each of his three derby heats. Considering that race car tires normally heat up with each race, the expected result in successive runs was increased momentum, not reduced speed. It was odd that Gronen's pace decreased with each successive run. Despite the suspicions, Gronen was named the official champion of the 1973 derby. His winnings included a trophy, a championship jacket, and a $7,500 scholarship. As Gronen received his first-place award, some spectators booed in protest.

   Race officials then examined Gronen's car and noticed prohibited alterations. A physical inspection revealed a button or switch that could be activated by pressing it with a driver's helmet. Follow-up X rays conducted at Goodyear Aerospace proved that an electromagnet in the front of the car likely pulled Gronen's car forward as the metal starting plate was dropped at the beginning of each run. Locating this mechanism helped explain Gronen's quick lead at the start of the races and also showed that his decreasing running speed was the result of a draining battery caused by the electromagnet's use. Two days after the race, on August 21, Gronen was disqualified.

The sophistication of the device hidden in Gronen's car left no doubt that an adult helped in its design. Gronen's uncle and legal guardian, Robert

Jimmy Gronen holds up his championship trophy for winning the national soap box derby on August 18, 1973. He lost the trophy the next day for cheating. (AP/Wide World Photos)

Brookings Lange, Sr., a former derby participant himself, admitted that he had encouraged his nephew to install the apparatus. Lange argued that other cheating had become commonplace at the derby and continued without repercussions, and he saw no reason why this case was different. A follow-up investigation by the district attorney's office in Boulder County, Colorado (Gronen's place of residence), revealed that at least thirty derby cars had, for example, illegal axles.

The race and subsequent scandal shocked derby fans and triggered questions about other possible cheating incidents. The grand marshal of the 1973 race, Gronen's cousin, Bobby Lange, had won the 1972 race with a similarly designed car. Some people thought that Bobby might have used the same device in his car, while others wondered if his car was the same used by Gronen for the 1973 race. Robert Lange denied claims that the apparatus had been used previously, but the suspicious disappearance of the 1972 racer left room for doubt. Deceit and unethical practices in an all-American children's sport were unconceivable to many. Just when the derby was seeking a new corporate sponsor, the scandal erupted, nearly ruining the event's future.

IMPACT

The 1973 soap box derby scandal affected the confidence level of participants, spectators, supporters, and sponsors. The derby was known for its fairness and justice, but the scandal destroyed this assumption. Already in 1972, the automaker Chevrolet had withdrawn as the derby sponsor (but it financed the 1973 winner's scholarship). Furthermore, the Akron Chamber of Commerce, which had sponsored the 1973 event, decided to end fiscal and managerial connections with the derby.

Robert Lange was charged with contributing to the delinquency of a minor. He was ordered to donate two thousand dollars to the local boys' club and to issue a formal apology, directed specifically at youth. He also was banned from the derby for two years. Gronen had already been disqualified from the race and stripped of his $7,500 scholarship and championship coat.

The derby scandal and Lange's rationale that cheating was ubiquitous at the derby brought the attention of the media. News reports compared the derby with the great political scandal of the time: Watergate.

Obtaining a new sponsor for the All-American Soap Box Derby was the main focus of derby organizers. The Akron Jaycees took up the challenge to rebuild enthusiasm for the event and immediately set out to tighten regulations. Racers were issued race-approved wheels and their cars were carefully scrutinized before the start of each derby. Drivers were asked questions to verify that they built their own cars. New starting blocks were created, too.

By 1974, the number of derby contests had dropped dramatically, but despite a general disillusionment with the sport, the competition was kept alive for the 1975 race by generous contributions from local businesses. Novar Electronics agreed to sponsor the derby officially in November, 1975, saving it from certain ruin. Novar remained the main sponsor until 1988. The All-American Soap Box Derby rebounded from its 1973 scandal, but the blemish remains.

—Cynthia J. W. Svoboda

FURTHER READING

Gibson, Gwen. "Watergate on Wheels." *Ladies Home Journal*, August, 1974. Gibson reviews the events of August, 1973, providing a general overview of the history of the soap box derby. Also looks into the derby's aftermath.

Lidz, Franz. "It's All Downhill: Gravity Rules When the U.S.'s Fastest Kids Roll into Akron for the Unsinkable Soap Box Derby." *Sports Illustrated*, August 4, 2003. Thirty years after the scandal in 1973, the author provides a retrospective of the annual soap box derby in Akron.

Payne, Melanie. *Champions, Cheaters, and Childhood Dreams: Memories of the Soap Box Derby*. Akron, Ohio: University of Akron Press, 2003. Covers the history of the derby from 1934 and provides a detailed account of the 1973 scandal, including its fallout.

Rosenthal, Sylvia A. *Soap Box Derby Racing*. New York: Lothrop, Lee & Shepard Books, 1980. A history of the derby written especially for younger readers.

Telanger, Rick. "Running the Gauntlet of Grownups." *Sports Illustrated*, August 12, 1974. This article discusses adult interference in the designing, building, and construction of derby cars.

Woodley, Richard. "How to Win the Soap Box Derby." *Harper's*, August, 1974. Reviews the 1973 scandal and discusses Lange's involvement with the 1972 and 1973 winning cars.

SEE ALSO: Aug. 27, 2001: Little League Baseball Star Danny Almonte Is Found to Be Overage; Feb. 11, 2002: French Judge Admits Favoring Russian Figure Skaters in Winter Olympics; Sept. 13, 2007: New England Patriots Football Team Is Fined for Spying on Other Teams.

October 10, 1973
SPIRO T. AGNEW RESIGNS VICE PRESIDENCY IN DISGRACE

Spiro T. Agnew was indicted for accepting bribes from contractors while he was Baltimore County executive, governor of Maryland, and U.S. vice president. The specific charges included conspiracy, extortion, bribery, and tax fraud. To avoid a trial, he pleaded no contest to one charge of income tax evasion and resigned as vice president. Agnew's resignation set in motion, for the first time in U.S. history, the provisions of the Twenty-fifth Amendment to the U.S. Constitution.

LOCALE: Baltimore County, Maryland
CATEGORIES: Corruption; government; politics; law and the courts

KEY FIGURES
Spiro T. Agnew (1918-1996), vice president of the United States, 1969-1973
George Beall (b. 1937), U.S. attorney, district of Maryland
Elliot Richardson (1920-1999), U.S. attorney general
Richard Nixon (1913-1994), president of the United States, 1969-1974

SUMMARY OF EVENT
In 1973, the U.S. Attorney's Office in Maryland, headed by George Beall, began investigating political corruption in Baltimore County, which had been experiencing the serious problem since 1963. In 1963, A. Gordon Boone, Democratic speaker of the Maryland House of Delegates, had been convicted of mail fraud involving a savings and loan scandal. During the mid-1960's, several Baltimore County employees and asphalt suppliers were caught on payoff charges. In 1972, former U.S. senator Daniel Brewster was convicted of taking a bribe.

Beall's investigation initially targeted Democrats Marvin Mandel, Spiro T. Agnew's successor as governor of Maryland, and Dale Anderson, who followed Agnew as county executive. Beall assured U.S. Department of Justice (DOJ) officials

that the probe would not involve Agnew. Beall's attorneys interviewed numerous Baltimore County employees and contractors and subpoenaed many documents. Prosecutors learned that Baltimore County employees received kickbacks from contractors who provided public services. The contractors secured their work by paying cash to those county agencies, usually around 5 percent of the value of a job. The contractors concealed the cost of the bribes by recording phony bonuses to employees. Faced with certain prosecution for income tax evasion, bribery, and tax fraud, Maryland engineering and architectural executives began cooperating with Beall's office in exchange for leniency.

In May, 1973, the Attorney's Office discovered that Agnew had accepted substantial bribes while he was a Baltimore County executive, Maryland governor, and U.S. vice president. Agnew was not wealthy before assuming office and considered his salary too low. He believed that his public position required him to adopt a standard of living beyond his means and that his political ambitions compelled him to build a financially strong political organization.

I. H. Hammerman III, a Baltimore real estate developer and investment banker, and other witnesses, told prosecutors about Agnew's involvement. The Attorney's Office said it had evidence of cash arriving to Agnew under disguised names of "papers" and "information," of a representative's signal for payments by offering "congratulations," and of a kickback-splitting arrangement with two of his closest friends. One contractor delivered ten thousand dollars cash in a sealed white envelope to Vice President Agnew. Agnew received bribes from consulting engineers, including Allen Green and Lester Matz, in exchange for business contracts. A financial institution gave him lucrative state bond issues.

In June, Beall gave newly appointed attorney general Elliot Richardson a preliminary report of

Vice President Spiro T. Agnew, center, leaves court in Baltimore, just before resigning his office. (AP/Wide World Photos)

the allegations against Agnew. Richardson encouraged Beall to pursue the investigation regardless of politics, government position, personal concerns, or professional apprehension. He was dismayed by the investigation's implications after learning the amount of evidence the Baltimore prosecutors had against Agnew. They then told Richard Nixon what they had found. Nixon wanted Agnew confronted with all the evidence and at least twice asked the vice president to resign.

Beall hand-delivered to Agnew a confidential letter dated August 1, warning the vice president that he was under investigation for conspiracy, extortion, bribery, and tax fraud and gave him an opportunity to explain his actions to the U.S. attorney. The letter detailed how Agnew had collected graft from contractors as a county executive, governor, and vice president. Agnew refused to cooperate with Beall's office, denouncing the investigation

and proclaiming his innocence. He did not expect to be indicted and vowed not to resign.

Richardson, who assumed command of the probe, believed that Agnew's misconduct warranted a prison term and realized that Agnew stood only a heartbeat from the presidency. Richardson could have demanded prison time but opted to clear the line for the presidency. The Agnew scandal came amid numerous public charges of political misconduct against the Nixon administration. Nixon's own income tax returns were contested. The tide of the Watergate scandal surrounding Nixon rose amid public disclosures on national television before the Senate Judiciary Committee. Grave accusations of criminal misconduct dogged Nixon's former legal counsel. Some of Nixon's closest former aides were indicted, while two former cabinet members faced trials on criminal charges. The U.S. Supreme Court ordered Nixon to hand over the tapes of conversations dealing with many disputed points in the Watergate criminal scandal. After the tapes were released, Nixon resigned in August, 1974.

With Nixon's future clouded, Richardson plea-bargained with Agnew to prevent him from becoming president. The DOJ and the Internal Revenue Service had gathered incontrovertible evidence that Agnew evaded paying $13,551.47 in federal taxes in 1967. On October 10, Richardson released in federal district court a forty-page document citing overwhelming evidence that Agnew had accepted more than $100,000 in bribes and kickbacks. Agnew's attorneys and DOJ officials worked out a plea agreement for Agnew's resignation. Agnew reluctantly accepted the terms and resigned as vice president the same day. His decision appeared based on personal rather than political or historical considerations. Nixon considered Agnew's plea bargain advisable "to prevent a protracted period of national division and uncertainty." Several of Agnew's coconspirators received prison sentences. Federal prosecutors later indicted and convicted Baltimore County executive Anderson, Anne Arundel County executive Joseph Alfino, and Maryland governor Mandel on related corruption charges.

Also on October 10, Agnew walked into a federal courtroom in Baltimore and pleaded guilty to income tax evasion. Judge Walter Hoffman fined Agnew ten thousand dollars and sentenced him to three years unsupervised probation. Agnew vehemently refuted the government's allegations, except income tax evasion, but wanted to avoid a prolonged struggle before the courts or U.S. Congress. He firmly believed that the public interest required swift resolution of the case. Agnew denied accepting cash kickbacks from contractors while serving as county executive, governor, and vice president, and he insisted that Maryland state contracts were issued only to those qualified to perform the work. He denied that payments influenced his official actions or that he had enriched himself at public expense.

On October 15, Agnew told a national television audience that he resigned to restore confidence and trust to the vice presidency and insisted that he had done no wrong. Agnew blamed Nixon for his downfall, claiming the president sacrificed him to appease his Watergate critics. Agnew's resignation set in motion, for the first time, the provisions of the Twenty-fifth Amendment to the U.S. Constitution, under which the president needed to nominate a successor subject to a confirmation by a majority vote of both houses of Congress. Nixon named Republican representative Gerald R. Ford of Michigan as Agnew's replacement.

Agnew withdrew from politics, resided in Rancho Mirage, California, and Ocean City, Maryland, and brokered business deals for an international clientele. He continued to live and travel in style, seemingly flaunting the plea bargain terms and exhibiting no remorse. In May, 1974, the Maryland Court of Appeals disbarred Agnew. Seven years later, he was ordered to pay the state of Maryland $268,482 to cover the illegally earned kickbacks and interest. A civil court in 1981 determined that Agnew had solicited $147,000 in bribes while county executive and state governor, $17,500 of which he received as vice president.

IMPACT

Agnew became only the second U.S. vice president to resign and the only vice president forced out of office because of legal problems. John Calhoun had resigned the vice presidency in December, 1832, because of a political split with President Andrew Jackson. The Agnew case proved that no U.S. citizen, including the vice president, is above the law. It also added fuel to the fire that was the Nixon administration, ensuring, in a way, his boss's demise as well. The Nixon case, too, proved that no U.S. citizen is above the law.

—David L. Porter

FURTHER READING

Agnew, Spiro T. *Go Quietly . . . or Else*. New York: Morrow, 1980. Agnew's memoir, in which he continues to press his innocence. The book's title reportedly is a reference to a comment made by Alexander M. Haig, Nixon's chief of staff, who Agnew said had planned to assassinate him if he refused to resign. Haig allegedly told him "to go quietly . . . or else."

1970's

449

Beall, George. "A Prosecutor Remembers: Agnew's Fall." *Baltimore Sun*, August 3, 2003. The U.S. attorney who prosecuted Agnew discusses his role in the case against the vice president.

Cohen, Richard M., and Jules Witcover. *A Heartbeat Away: The Investigation and Resignation of Vice President Spiro T. Agnew*. New York: Viking Press, 1974. An excellent study of Agnew's fall from grace, relying on clear, pointed recollections of numerous firsthand witnesses.

Richardson, Elliot. *The Creative Balance: Government, Politics, and the Individual in America's Third Century*. New York: Holt, Rinehart & Winston, 1976. Richardson, the U.S. attorney general during the Agnew affair, discusses his role in the plea bargain that led to Agnew's resignation.

Witcover, Jules. *White Knight: The Rise of Spiro Agnew*. New York: Random House, 1972. An excellent, authoritative biography of Agnew by a veteran Washington, D.C., newspaper correspondent. Written before Agnew's resignation.

SEE ALSO: Jan. 23, 1904: Senator Joseph R. Burton Is Convicted of Bribery; Oct. 22, 1923: U.S. Senate Begins Hearings on Teapot Dome Oil Leases; May, 1930: Postmaster's Division of Airmail Routes Creates a Scandal; May 22, 1939: Kansas City's Boss Pendergast Pleads Guilty to Income Tax Evasion; Nov. 16, 1951: Federal Tax Official Resigns After Accepting Bribes; June 25, 1956: President Truman's Appointments Secretary Is Convicted of Tax Conspiracy; May 9, 1969: Supreme Court Justice Abe Fortas Is Accused of Bribery; June 17, 1972-Aug. 9, 1974: Watergate Break-in Leads to President Nixon's Resignation; July 31, 1972: Thomas F. Eagleton Withdraws from Vice Presidential Race; May 14, 1974: *Washington Post* Reveals That the Nixons Received Jewelry Gifts; Oct. 11, 1979: Senate Denounces Herman E. Talmadge for Money Laundering; Aug. 5, 1994: Kenneth Starr Is Appointed to the Whitewater Investigation; July 1, 2005: Federal Agents Raid Congressman Randall Cunningham's Home.

April 15, 1974
KIDNAPPED HEIR PATTY HEARST HELPS ROB A BANK

Two months after her kidnapping by members of the Symbionese Liberation Army, Patty Hearst was photographed inside a bank holding a gun and helping her captors carry out the robbery. By all appearances, she seemed to have voluntarily joined the revolutionaries and was thereby considered to be "thumbing her nose" at the privileged echelons of society in which she was raised. The case also brought to light the Stockholm syndrome, a psychological phenomenon in which a hostage develops an affinity with his or her captors.

LOCALE: San Francisco, California
CATEGORIES: Violence; law and the courts; psychology and psychiatry; social issues and reform; politics

KEY FIGURES

Patricia Hearst (b. 1954), heir to Hearst fortune
Donald DeFreeze (1943-1974), leader of the Symbionese Liberation Army
Camilla Hall (1945-1974), member of the Symbionese Liberation Army
Patricia Soltysik (1950-1974), member of the Symbionese Liberation Army
Nancy Ling Perry (1947-1974), member of the Symbionese Liberation Army

SUMMARY OF EVENT

Patricia Hearst, heir to the fortune of the famous California newspaper magnate William Randolph Hearst, was kidnapped on February 4, 1974, from the Berkeley, California, apartment she shared with her fiancé, Steven Weed, who was beaten during

A security camera catches Patty Hearst robbing a bank in San Francisco, California. (AP/Wide World Photos)

the abduction. The kidnappers were members of the Symbionese Liberation Army (SLA), an urban terrorist group formed in 1973 with the goal of freeing a broad range of persons of the American "underclass" (including African Americans, prison convicts, women, military draftees, and others they believed victimized by corporate America).

Initially, after her abduction, Hearst was kept in a dark closet. After several weeks, however, it seems that she began to identify with her captors' ideology, even to the point of releasing tapes that espoused some of their radical ideas.

The bank robbery itself was preceded by weeks of elaborate planning. According to Hearst, the "action," as it was called by the group, had three distinct purposes: to obtain much-needed funds that would support future SLA revolutionary activities;

to demonstrate to the rest of the world that Tania (Hearst's adopted nickname) had truly renounced her privileged upbringing and wholeheartedly joined the SLA, actively supporting and taking part in even its most violent activities; and to show the world that the SLA revolutionaries were strong, resolute, and unafraid. Hearst would later say that she believed she would die either in a shoot-out with police or at the hands of the SLA group leader himself, Donald DeFreeze, a convict who had escaped from prison in March, 1973.

In a tape-recorded message released to the media on April 3, 1974, Hearst said,

> I have been given the choice of one: being released in a safe area, or two: joining the forces of the Symbionese Liberation Army and fighting for my freedom and the freedom of all oppressed people. I have chosen to stay and fight.

Hearst's parents believed their daughter had been brainwashed by her captors.

At 9:45 A.M. on April 15, 1974, two cars arrived at the Hibernia Bank on Noriega Street in the Sunset district of San Francisco, California. (Ironically, this bank had been founded by the grandfather of one of Hearst's closest childhood friends.) Four veteran SLA members, including DeFreeze, Camilla Hall, Patricia Soltysik, and Nancy Ling Perry, headed for the bank entrance, preceded by Hearst. Before entering, Hearst was knocked in the face by the front door released by a customer ahead of her. Now in the bank, the robbers took out rifles they had concealed beneath their coats and ordered everyone in the bank to drop to the floor. One of the bank guards later reported that Hearst did not appear nervous at this time. Rather, the guard said, she seemed to know what she was doing and appeared ready to use the gun if necessary. There are reports that she threatened to blow the head off anyone who moved, but Hearst herself remembers only pointing her gun at those on the floor in front of her.

The bank manager saw the entire operation from his office on an upper level. He set off a silent alarm that activated the bank cameras. The manager noted that all aspects of the robbery were carried out with great precision and that the SLA members seemed

451

to have a solid working knowledge of the bank's floor plan. He also said that Hearst directly threatened the customers with her rifle. The entire robbery lasted only four minutes. The robbers fled in the two cars with $10,960, but not before two of them (excluding Hearst) shot their weapons and injured two passersby. Back at their apartment, the euphoric SLA members spread all the stolen bills on the floor in front of them. The robbery would generate an enormous amount of media coverage.

Using her nickname Tania, Hearst later released several tapes that indicated her sympathy with SLA goals and her commitment to the movement. She disappeared from public view and the law but was arrested on September 18, 1975, in San Francisco; she was tried and then convicted on March 16, 1976, for her role in the bank robbery. Her primary lawyer, F. Lee Bailey, unsuccessfully argued that his client had been brainwashed by the SLA. He also cited the effects of the Stockholm syndrome, a phenomenon in which a hostage not only develops a positive relationship with his or her captors but also becomes protective of them and actively identifies with their cause. The Stockholm syndrome is significant in this case because the Hearst abduction and her participation in the bank robbery would become synonymous with the syndrome.

The Stockholm syndrome was named after a hostage-taking incident in which a victim, held in a Stockholm bank, told rescuing police that he would not let them harm his captor. In the aftermath of another hostage incident, a flight attendant who had been held at gunpoint continued to visit and bring gifts to the incarcerated hijacker. One explanation for this phenomenon involves the hostage's rational calculation that if he or she develops a personal relationship with his or her captors, the latter may find it harder to follow through on threats to kill the hostage. Key to preserving a hostage's life is meeting the demands that the captors are making to authorities. On a more subtle, subconscious level, however, the Stockholm syndrome is also, in part, a reflection of the helplessness of a victim in the face of a hostage taker who may also be a killer, even if demands are met. The hostage is infantilized and, in response, unconsciously adopts the attitudes of the captor.

Many believe that Hearst's attorney did not bring out the infantilization aspects of this syndrome sufficiently at the trial. Hearst was sentenced to a seven-year prison term but actually served less than two years following a commutation by U.S. president Jimmy Carter in 1979. She received a full pardon from U.S. president Bill Clinton in 2001. She later married one of her bodyguards and moved to Connecticut.

IMPACT

The Hibernia Bank robbery was in many ways the quintessential act of social defiance on the part of the Symbionese Liberation Army. It was undertaken to establish each participant's identity as a confirmed and committed revolutionary "soldier," a stance from which, apparently, there was no return. That Hearst was featured so prominently in this robbery, photographed several times holding a rifle and using expletives in her orders to bank patrons, underlines the class differences the SLA wanted to highlight. The image of Hearst, heir to a fortune and a child of the privileged, robbing a bank is permanently etched in the American psyche. Hearst, in those four minutes, became at once a symbol of self-loathing and, from the SLA's viewpoint, an exemplar of how even America's most privileged elite can be inwardly disgusted with the class disparities in the United States.

Hearst's motivations and her state of mind during the bank robbery were the subject of detailed analyses during her trial. Debate continues over whether she was forced into joining her captors or whether she was a willing participant in the crime. Jurors in her trial concluded, however, that even after experiencing extreme situations (having been kidnapped) and even if affected by the Stockholm syndrome, people should be held accountable for their actions. If they violate the law, they must accept responsibility and pay the price. Ultimately, this episode in American criminal history serves as an affirmation of the basic moral principles and expectations as well as the integrity of the American legal system.

—Eric W. Metchik

FURTHER READING

Alexander, Shana. *Anyone's Daughter: The Times and Trials of Patty Hearst*. New York: Viking Press, 1979. A prominent American journalist's detailed account of every phase of Hearst's trial.

Hearst, Patricia Campbell, with Alvin Moscow. *Every Secret Thing*. New York: Doubleday, 1982. Hearst's retelling of her kidnapping, life with the SLA, arrest, and trial.

Isenberg, Nancy. "Not 'Anyone's Daughter': Patty Hearst and the Postmodern Legal Subject." *American Quarterly* 52, no. 4 (2000): 639-681. Exploration of the Hearst kidnapping and trial through a lens stressing the strategic political manipulation of her gender.

Third, Amanda. "Nuclear Terrorists: Patty Hearst and the Terrorist Family." *Hecate* 28, no. 2 (2002): 82-99. Analyzes the Hearst kidnapping in the light of the ideological and sexual undertones of terrorism and its relationship to the role of the nuclear family in modern society.

Weed, Steven, with Scott Swanton. *My Search for Patty Hearst*. New York: Crown, 1976. A comprehensive account of events leading up to the Hearst trial, from the viewpoint of her former fiancé.

Wilson, Theo. *Headline Justice: Inside the Courtroom—The Country's Most Controversial Trials*. New York: Thunder's Mouth Press, 1996. Informal but informative view of the Hearst trial proceedings, written by a veteran trial reporter.

SEE ALSO: July 23, 1978: Utah Millionaire Is Murdered by His Grandson; Mar., 1990: Menendez Brothers Are Arrested for Murdering Their Parents.

1970's

May 14, 1974
WASHINGTON POST REVEALS THAT THE NIXONS RECEIVED JEWELRY GIFTS

Although the U.S. Constitution and the Foreign Gifts and Decorations Act forbids U.S. government officials and their families from accepting gifts from foreign rulers without permission from Congress, President Richard Nixon's wife and daughters received more than $100,000 worth of jewelry from the Saudi Arabian royal family. The Nixons received about 3,500 gifts from foreign officials, most of which they kept after Nixon's resignation in 1974.

LOCALE: Washington, D.C.

CATEGORIES: Politics; publishing and journalism; ethics; international relations; government

KEY FIGURES

Richard Nixon (1913-1994), president of the United States, 1969-1974

Pat Nixon (1912-1993), First Lady of the United States, 1969-1974

Tricia Nixon Cox (b. 1946), Nixon's eldest daughter

Julie Nixon Eisenhower (b. 1948), Nixon's youngest daughter

Maxine Cheshire (b. 1930), syndicated columnist for *The Washington Post*

Faisal (c. 1905-1975), king of Saudi Arabia, r. 1964-1975

Fahd (1922 or 1923-2005), half-brother of King Faisal and later king of Saudi Arabia, r. 1982-2005

Sultan bin Abdul Aziz al-Saud (b. 1928), half-brother of King Faisal and later crown prince of Saudi Arabia, r. 2005-

SUMMARY OF EVENT

Article 1, Section 9 of the United States Constitution prohibits federal officials from accepting gifts from the heads of foreign states. Also, the Foreign Gifts and Decorations Act of 1881 (amended in

1966) details procedures for handling such gifts to keep from offending foreign leaders, and it expanded the prohibition to include the families of federal officeholders. Jewelry and any other gifts with a value greater than $100 automatically become the property of the U.S. government. The purpose of the ban was to prevent foreign countries from bribing or otherwise influencing U.S. office holders in hopes of receiving preferential treatment for business contracts or foreign policy.

The relationship between Richard Nixon and the Saudi Arabian royal family began before Nixon became president. Adnan Khashoggi, a billionaire Saudi Arabian businessman with ties to the Saudi royal family, gave about $60,000 worth of jewelry to Nixon's daughters and made a $1 million campaign contribution to Nixon in 1968. However, the law in question did not apply at that time, because Nixon and Khashoggi were both private citizens, and candidates were not required to disclose campaign contributions. Nixon's youngest daughter, Julie, married David Eisenhower, grandson of former U.S. president Dwight D. Eisenhower, on December 22, 1968, but Nixon was still only the president-elect at this time, so the law did not apply to any of the Nixon-Eisenhower wedding gifts.

Nixon was inaugurated president of the United States on January 20, 1969. In October of 1969, Prince Fahd, half-brother of King Faisal of Saudi Arabia, gave First Lady Pat Nixon a parure—a matching set of emerald and diamond jewelry consisting of a necklace, bracelet, and ring, and a pair of earrings and a brooch. The set was appraised at $52,400 by Harry Winston, one of the most famous jewelers in the world, in 1970. In May of 1971, King Faisal gave the first lady a pair of marquise diamond and cabochon ruby shoulder-length, dangling earrings and a strand of pearls possibly worth as much as $100,000. The Nixon's oldest daughter, Tricia, wore them at a 1972 reelection fund-raiser. In July, 1972, Prince Sultan bin Abdul Aziz al-Saud, another half-brother of King Faisal, gave the first lady a diamond bracelet, gave Tricia a diamond and sapphire pin, and gave Julie a diamond and ruby pin. On another occasion, Faisal gave the first lady a diamond-studded platinum watch, using Winston

as an intermediary. When Tricia married Ed Cox in 1971, the shah of Iran gave her a diamond and emerald brooch, and the emperor of Ethiopia, Haile Selassie, gave her a silver vase. No appraisal was ever done on the latter gifts, and the three women wore the jewelry from the Saudi Arabian royal family at several official White House social functions. The record-keeping for gifts in the Nixon White House was very poor.

In 1970, *Washington Post* columnist Maxine Cheshire received a tip that the shah of Iran had given the first lady diamonds and emeralds worth millions of dollars. Cheshire checked to see if the jewels were turned over to the U.S. government, as the law mandates; there was no record that the jewels existed at all. Her inquiries eventually led to a member of Betty Ford's staff. Betty Ford's husband, Gerald, became vice president of the United States following the resignation of Spiro T. Agnew in 1973, and her staff member confirmed that the jewelry existed. Cheshire then found a disgruntled former employee of the White House Gifts Unit, who also confirmed the existence of the jewelry. Unfortunately, neither was trained in appraising jewelry, nor could they be 100 percent certain that the Nixons were not wearing costume jewelry on those occasions. The second source also disputed that the gift-giver was the shah, insisting that the person who provided the gifts was an Arab.

Cheshire then went to the head of the White House Gifts Unit and, to her surprise, found the woman in charge of the unit quite cooperative. The employee agreed to provide a photograph of the jewelry given to the first lady by Prince Fahd. Cheshire discovered that the jewelry was kept in a wall safe in Nixon's White House bedroom until March, 1974, in violation of the 1966 law. On the recommendation of White House attorney Fred Buzhardt, the jewelry was transferred to the custody of the chief of protocol in the executive office building. Cheshire reported on May 14 that the jewelry from the Saudi Arabian royal family had not been officially recorded until March 8. Deputy press secretary Gerald Warren denied any impropriety and said that the first lady and her daughters always planned to leave the jewelry in federal custody when Nixon left office.

When Nixon resigned the presidency because of the Watergate scandal later that year, the Nixon family turned over to the U.S. State Department 824 gifts that were given to them by foreign officials. However, 2,632 gifts were kept by the Nixons on the grounds that they were given by foreigners who were not government officials. Among the gifts retained by the Nixon family were a silver tray from Pepsi-Cola bottlers of Japan; a gold centerpiece from the Philippine sugar industry; a pair of gold cuff links from the former head of Mitsui, a Japanese conglomerate; and an oil painting and fifteenth century jewelry from the chairman of Lepetit Chemical Company of Milan, Italy.

A 1978 probe by the U.S. General Services Administration concluded that all the gifts received by the Nixon family during his presidency were accounted for. Tricia Nixon Cox was allowed to keep two wedding presents: the vase from Haile Selassie and a rare temple carving from South Vietnam's president.

IMPACT

At the time, the gifts scandal was considered minor compared to Watergate, but considering that foreign policy, specifically regarding the Middle East, could have been jeopardized, the gifts scandal was found to be more significant than first realized. No legal action was taken against Nixon or members of his family. After Nixon resigned on August 9, 1974, the jewelry was placed in the custody of the federal government. Any violation of the law became moot after the new president, Gerald Ford, fully and unconditionally pardoned Nixon for any crimes he may have committed while president. Furthermore, no evidence existed showing that Nixon changed his Middle East policy because of those gifts. In fact, he had infuriated King Faisal when he asked the U.S. Congress for a $2.2 billion aid package to Israel in 1973.

That the Nixons were exposed by *The Washington Post* led many elected officials to take notice and reveal the gifts they, too, had received from foreign leaders. Most notably, former vice president

Agnew and Senators Hubert Humphrey and J. William Fulbright began relinquishing gifts they had received from foreign officials.

The Nixon Gift Collection is stored at the National Archives and Record Administration in College Park, Maryland, and items from the collection are periodically lent to museums around the United States. Most of the jewelry from the Saudi Arabian royal family is on permanent display at the Nixon Library in Yorba Linda, California.

—Thomas R. Feller

FURTHER READING

"The Case of the Diamond and Emerald Parure." *Time*, May 27, 1974. Contemporary account of the jewelry scandal that implies the scandal was trivial.

Charlton, Linda. "Gifts of Jewels to Nixons from Saudis Disclosed." *The New York Times*, May 15, 1974. Contemporary account of the scandal that includes a photograph of the jewelry from Prince Fahd and another of Pat Nixon wearing the earrings and necklace.

Cheshire, Maxine, with John Greenya. *Maxine Cheshire: Reporter*. Boston: Houghton Mifflin, 1978. One-third of Cheshire's autobiography is devoted to her pursuit of the jewelry scandal.

Lippman, Thomas W. *Inside the Mirage: America's Fragile Partnership with Saudi Arabia*. Boulder, Colo.: Westview Press, 2004. History of the close relationship between the governments of the United States and Saudi Arabia.

Summers, Anthony, with Robyn Swan. *The Arrogance of Power: The Secret World of Richard M. Nixon*. New York: Viking, 2000. This critical biography of Nixon recounts allegations of immoral and illegal activity made against the disgraced president. Includes discussion of the jewelry scandal.

SEE ALSO: Sept. 23, 1952: Richard Nixon Denies Taking Illegal Campaign Contributions; June 13, 1971: *New York Times* Publishes the Pentagon Papers; June 17, 1972-Aug. 9, 1974: Watergate Break-in Leads to President Nixon's Resignation; Oct. 10, 1973: Spiro T. Agnew Resigns

1970'S

May 20, 1974
FRENCH CARDINAL DANIÉLOU DIES IN A PROSTITUTE'S HOUSE

The mysterious death of Roman Catholic theologian and scholar Jean Daniélou in the house of a prostitute led to a scandal in the popular press and among colleagues. His life and work suggested several possible explanations for his death, including the possibilities that he was assassinated by philosophical enemies, that he died while ministering at the brothel, or that he died following an intimate encounter with a prostitute.

LOCALE: Paris, France

CATEGORIES: Murder and suicide; prostitution; sex; publishing and journalism

KEY FIGURES

Jean Daniélou (1905-1974), French theologian and scholar

Alain Daniélou (1907-1994), Hindu scholar and brother of Jean Daniélou

Mimi Santoni (b. c. 1950), dancer and friend of Jean Daniélou

SUMMARY OF EVENT

Jean Daniélou's background and achievements were impressive. Educated at the Sorbonne and the University of Lyon, he held doctorates in both letters and theology. Entering the Jesuit order as a young man, he was ordained priest in 1938. In 1969, he became an archbishop, and the same year his personal friend, Pope Paul VI, made him a cardinal. As his reputation grew, he was invited to lecture internationally, notably at the University of Notre Dame in the United States in 1950. At the Institute Cat-

holique de Paris, he was professor of primitive Christianity from 1943 to his death, serving as dean in the last decade of his service there. He founded study circles and edited numerous publications. Honored as a Chevalier of the Legion of Honor, he was also a member of the French Academy.

Daniélou told his friends numerous times that, "I am naturally a pagan, and a Christian only with difficulty." As he entered his sixties, he confided his fear that opponents in his church were plotting against him. However, he arrived at the last day of his life seemingly without premonition. On that Monday, May 20, 1974, he arose as usual, said mass, worked at his desk, and received a few visitors. At noon he lunched at a favorite restaurant and talked by phone with a Sorbonne University colleague. He then collected some mail and returned briefly to his residence, before departing again at 3:15 P.M., leaving word that he would return by 5 P.M.

Thirty-eight minutes later, an emergency call was received by the police, from Madam Santoni, who lived on the upper floor of a building in Rue Dulong, which was in a disreputable quarter of Paris. According to Santoni, Daniélou had hastened up the steps to her flat, collapsing at the top. Fearing she would be charged with his death, she quickly summoned help and tore his clothes apart in an unsuccessful attempt to revive him.

Church dignitaries, including the apostolic nuncio, the Jesuit provincial of France, and the superior of the Jesuits in Paris, along with nuns called in to tend the body, quickly arrived on the scene. Reporters from *France Soir* also arrived, but they were cautioned to maintain discretion. The press was informed that the cardinal had died in the street or in the stairway. Reporters quickly discovered that Santoni, who called herself Mimi, was a married woman, well known to the police as a bar host and a cabaret and striptease dancer. Allegedly, she also ran a brothel with her husband, who at the time of Daniélou's death was in jail for pimping.

Daniélou was known for his wit and urbanity. There was something slightly bohemian about him, according to friends, a tendency to seek out social rejects. Mary Magdalene, the reformed harlot of the Bible, especially intrigued him. Possibly through sympathy with the open sexual orientation of his brother Alain, he held regular masses for gays and lesbians. With his disheveled appearance, knowledge of cinema, and his secular friends, he often resembled a new wave film critic more than a Catholic cardinal. *The National Review* observed that he "looked as if he had been drinking very black coffee for fifteen years in a sidewalk café with [French philosopher and feminist] Simone de Beauvoir." He lived simply at his Paris residence, without a secretary or an automobile, yet his life was not an open book.

In earlier years, Daniélou had been identified as a Catholic progressive. He read the books of the controversial Jesuit paleontologist Pierre Teilhard de Chardin and seemed to make common cause with innovative Dutch and Belgian churchmen. The best known exponent of this "new theology" was Swiss professor Hans Küng. Küng's early admiration of Daniélou, however, would change when, with the pontificate of Paul VI, Daniélou became increasingly conservative and a staunch defender of papal infallibility. Küng came to believe that raw ambition drove Daniélou to pander to the pope to become a cardinal. When the circumstances of his death were later reported, Küng, along with other church liberals who already suspected Daniélou of expediency, put the most scandalous interpretation on the event.

Daniélou wrote voluminously, both scholarly and popular works on religious history, philosophy, ethics, and theology. Some scholars regarded him as the standard authority on the early Christian church. He explored the newly discovered Dead Sea Scrolls, outlining parallels between the teachings of the people who produced them and early Christianity. He also was an expert in Greek patristics and Hellenistic culture. His writings were characterized by both learning and clarity.

Christianity, Daniélou believed, must be actively applied. Early in his career he had been sympathetic to the French worker-priest movement, which was later disbanded. His explorations in world religions, perhaps in part stimulated by the career of his brother Alain Daniélou, led him to conclude that, while Christianity was the lighted path, elements of useful truth could be found in all traditions. With this tolerance, not common in his milieu, he pursued dialogue not only with Protestant scholars but also representatives of all religions. He founded the Fraternity of Abraham, an interfaith group composed of Jews, Christians, and Muslims, and was a strong supporter of Catholic initiatives in appointing more African and Asian cardinals.

Jean Daniélou, c. 1920. (Hulton Archive/Getty Images)

Daniélou's family background may shed light on his curious death. The Daniélous were a distinguished Breton family. The father, Charles, a politician who held numerous French ministerial posts, usually was absent from the family scene. The dominant influence was the mother, Madeleine Clamorgan Daniélou, descended from Norman nobility, deeply religious, and committed to female education. The institutions she founded to educate devout women took priority over her family of four sons and two daughters. Two of her sons would receive international recognition. Alain, the cardinal's younger brother by two years, converted to Shaivite Hinduism, becoming a classical dancer, musicologist, and authority on Indian music.

The death of Alain's brother remained a mystery, yet Church officials rejected requests for an official inquiry. Cardinal Daniélou was buried with full honors in a Jesuit cemetery. The Daniélou family accepted the Church's explanation that he had died of a heart attack during a pastoral visit to a woman he had previously consoled. The three thousand francs found in his pocket was said to be bail money for Santoni's husband. A Jesuit spokesperson pronounced that this was a most appropriate way for a man of God to die, on a mission of mercy to a social outcast.

Not surprisingly, leftist anticlerical newspapers took another interpretation. *Le Canard Enchaine*'s investigation suggested that the cardinal had been paying regular visits to Mimi for some time. His body, the paper alleged, had been hurriedly dressed, and the money in his pocket was intended payment for her professional services.

Further explanations were advanced by others. Daniélou had once referred to the liberal school of Catholic theologians as "assassins of the faith," and some believed that this group had framed or possibly even murdered him. Another scenario, worthy of the so-called Da Vinci-code theorists, was that Daniélou had run afoul of secret societies, specifically the Grand Lodge of France.

IMPACT

The immediate reaction to Daniélou's death was scandalous titillation in French popular newspapers

and beyond. American publications relished the irony of a prince of the Church dying on the steps of a brothel. The cardinal's theological enemies, who believed that he had betrayed the renewal movement in the Church, took the circumstances of his death as evidence of his hypocrisy and self-serving indulgence. Admirers, colleagues in the Jesuit order, and his family saw in his death a Christ-like ministry to the dejected of society. The mystery has never been conclusively solved.

The scandal had more far reaching repercussions. For some, it was a wake-up call, heralding the major sex scandals that would rock the Catholic Church in the last decades of the twentieth century. For Church reformers, Daniélou's questionable death seemed further confirmation of the need for married and female priests.

The circumstances of Daniélou's death, however, did not diminish the cardinal's importance as a scholar, and his books continue to be widely read. His patristic writings would serve as foundation for other scholars, while his more popular books on the Dead Sea Scrolls, angels, and Christian approaches to non-Christian religions would have special relevance to the increasingly diverse populations of Europe and the United States. He would also be honored as an important pioneer in Christian ecumenism and interfaith dialogue.

—*Allene Phy-Olsen*

FURTHER READING

Boysson, Emmanuelle de. *Le Cardinal et L'Hindouiste*. Paris: Editions Albin Michel, 1999. The most thorough examination of Jean and Alain Daniélou, within the context of their family, written by their great niece. In French.

Clinton, Farley. "The Jesuit Confrontation." *National Review* 26 (October 11, 1974): 1162-1164. A perceptive examination of Daniélou's mysterious death and its relevance to the modern Catholic Church.

Daniélou, Jean. *God and the Ways of Knowing*. 1957. Reprint. San Francisco, Calif.: Ignatius Press, 2003. Daniélou wrote that this book "is not to record what I say of God, but what God has said of Himself." This work places religions and philosophies "in their proper relationship with the knowledge of God." A good starting point for any serious study of Daniélou and his theology.

Küng, Hans. *My Struggle for Freedom: A Memoir.* Translated by John Bowden. Grand Rapids, Mich.: William B. Eerdmans, 2003. A discussion of innovative movements in the Catholic Church, with a harsh judgment of Daniélou's opposition to those movements.

SEE ALSO: Mar. 26, 1922: Hindemith's Opera *Sancta Susanna* Depicts a Nun's Sexual Desires; May-June, 1926: Evangelist Aimee Semple Mc-Pherson Claims She Was Kidnapped; Mar. 9,

1956: British Conductor-Composer Is Arrested for Possessing Pornography; Oct. 29, 1965: Moroccan Politician Mehdi Ben Barka Disappears in Paris; May 6, 1992: Irish Bishop Eamonn Casey's Romantic Affair Leads to His Resignation; Aug. 16, 1996: Belgian Media Reveal How Police Bungled Serial Murder Case; Dec., 2000: Sexual Abuse of Children in France Leads to the Outreau Affair; June 30, 2001: Korean Religious Teacher Jung Myung Seok Is Charged with Rape; Jan. 6, 2002: *Boston Globe* Reports on Child Sexual Abuse by Roman Catholic Priests; July 9, 2007: Senator David Vitter's Name Is Found in D.C. Madam's Address Book.

Summer, 1974
DALKON SHIELD CONTRACEPTIVE IS REMOVED FROM THE MARKET

The Dalkon Shield was an intrauterine device marketed as a safe and effective form of birth control. Soon after the device became available, however, women suffered infections and infertility, and some died. A. H. Robins Company continued to market and sell the device until 1974 but eventually went bankrupt under the weight of lawsuits.

LOCALE: Washington, D.C.
CATEGORIES: Medicine and health care; business; women's issues; law and the courts

KEY FIGURES
Hugh J. Davis (1927-1996), gynecologist and coinventor of the Dalkon Shield
E. Claiborne Robins, Sr. (1910-1995), chairman of A. H. Robins Company
Robert Merhige, Jr. (1919-2005), U.S. federal judge, 1967-1998

SUMMARY OF EVENT
By the early 1970's, intrauterine devices, or IUDs, had been used safely and effectively as a form of

birth control for decades. An aggressive marketing campaign by the distributor of one such IUD, the Dalkon Shield, placed profit over safety. Close to three million women in the United States were using the Dalkon Shield at the height of sales. The shield, sold by the A. H. Robins Company, was developed by Hugh J. Davis, a gynecologist, and Irwin Lerner, an engineer. The shield was three-quarters of an inch in size, had prongs on either side to prevent expulsion, and had a tail to aid in its removal. Unlike other IUDs, the Dalkon Shield's tail was made with multifilament fiber encased in a nylon sheath, which became a vehicle for bacteria. Other IUDs used monofilament fiber. The Dalkon Shield's design elements caused a majority of the health issues that arose.

A Centers for Disease Control report in 1983 showed that pelvic infection was five to ten times more likely in women who used the Dalkon Shield over other IUDs. The success of the deceptive marketing campaign, combined with the poor design features of the shield, led to the eventual injuries, illnesses, and deaths. There were also many cases of sterility caused by the shield.

A physician associated with Johns Hopkins University, Davis had tested the new shield on 640 patients. Traditionally, no less than 1,000 subjects are used for clinical trials to be considered statistically valid. In Davis's test, controls were poorly implemented, which skewed the results favorably to establish the marketability of the shield. Also, many of the test subjects used other forms of birth control during the study, and not all used the shield for the entire length of the study. In the end, Davis concluded that the birthrate for those using the shield was 1.1 percent, which was less than the birthrate for those taking the birth control pill. Davis had received revised results after publishing his report, which put the birthrate at more than 5 percent, but he failed to amend his study.

Because they are considered devices and not drugs, IUDs do not fall under the purview of the U.S. Food and Drug Administration (FDA). Davis and Lerner founded the Dalkon Corporation in 1970 and started to sell the shield on their own. Davis, by then a recognized expert in contraception, spoke before a U.S. Senate subcommittee about the dangers of the birth control pill and the need for safer alternatives. He failed to note that not only was he marketing just such an alternative but also owned the company that would produce the devices. Sales did not reach hoped-for levels, however, so the Dalkon Corporation sought the backing of a larger company.

A. H. Robins Company was one of the four hundred largest companies in the United States and could distribute products worldwide. The company, run by E. Claiborne Robins, Sr., lacked experience with contraceptive devices and so based its purchase of Dalkon Corporation on Davis's flawed study. Furthermore, Robins bought Dalkon despite learning that actual pregnancy rates were nearly five times Davis's published result. Robins also had no data on the safety of extended use. Robins paid $750,000 for the right to distribute the shield.

Robins began an aggressive marketing campaign and used Davis's original study to promote the shield. Robins ignored its own medical advisory board and marketed the shield, beginning in early 1971, to general practitioners instead of obstetricians and gynecologists exclusively. The company took the additional step of marketing beyond the medical field as well to further promote sales.

High-ranking officials at the company, as well as E. Claiborne Robins, received a warning from Lerner as early as 1970 about a potential "wicking effect" caused by the use of the multifilament tail. Because the tail was open at both ends, bacteria could easily travel between the filaments and past the protective cervical plug into the normally sterile uterus. This fact was confirmed by the company's own quality control department. The department suggested heat sealing both ends, but the design change would have slowed production, so the alteration was never made. The sheath over the filaments also had a tendency to break down over time. The damaging effects of the wicking and the breakdown of the sheath were made worse by the decision to include in the sales literature information that the shield could be left in place for five years or more. The sales literature contradicted the recommendation made by the company's own medical board, which warned that the device should be changed every two years. Because of Robins's aggressive marketing, the shield outsold all other IUDs combined from 1971 to 1973.

Reports of high pregnancy rates and infections came in from field reports from medical consultants within the first month of release, but the company disregarded the reports. The first reports of septic abortions—abortions caused by infections in the uterus—came in soon after. The prongs also caused perforations of the uterus in pregnant women. The reports of the first two deaths occurred in May of 1973. Two women died within three days of detection. In response to the deaths, Robins merely printed new labels on the shield's packaging that recommended removal of the shield during pregnancy. It was not until the company received notice of a forthcoming article in the *American Journal of Obstetrics and Gynecology* that it chose to send letters to 120,000 physicians, stressing the urgent need to remove the device from women who were pregnant. These letters came a full two years after the same recommendation was made by the company's own consultants.

By 1973, the company was facing several hundred lawsuits. The first suit came to trial in December of 1973. Connie Deemer's uterus had been perforated by the shield while she was pregnant, leading to lifesaving surgery. The prosecuting attorney in the case was the first to discover Davis's financial stake in the shield. He also found the memo to company directors outlining the misleading birthrate statistics, which proved the company deliberately withheld the information, and that they most likely did so to increase sales. Because of the large number of lawsuits, cases were combined first at the state level in Minnesota and later on a national level at the federal court in Virginia under Judge Robert Merhige, Jr.

One of the most important issues discovered in trial was that Robins added copper and copper sulfate to the design. Had this been known by the FDA, the shield would have then been placed under the stricter federal guidelines and faced years of testing. Robins, however, never reported the addition of the copper sulfate to the FDA. It was at this time that the FDA requested that Robins withdraw the shield from the market, and by summer, 1974, Robins stopped further distribution of the shield. During trial, the wicking tests of the tail string that Robins performed also were confirmed, and it was determined that the company willfully destroyed incriminating documents. In December, 1987, Merhige ordered Robins to create a trust fund of $2.48 billion for women affected by the Dalkon Shield.

Two women protest outside the courtroom in Richmond, Virginia, where A. H. Robins Company was ordered to set up a $2.48 billion trust fund for women harmed by the Dalkon Shield. (Bettmann/Corbis)

IMPACT

The stigma surrounding the harmful health effects of the Dalkon Shield caused a downturn in the entire IUD market, with sales of IUDs dropping off by two-thirds over the ten years following its initial release to the market. The large numbers of national lawsuits led to the establishment of a $2.6 billion trust fund to cover damages and to try to restore the fertility of women affected by the shield. More than 200,000 women received financial compensation from the trust. The scandal and litigation was large enough that by 1985 it bankrupted one of the largest companies in the United States.

Furthermore, in 1976, the FDA first began to require the testing and approval of all medical devices, and not just drugs, in part because of the Dalkon Shield case. Medical device amendments were added to the Food, Drug, and Cosmetic Act of 1938.

—*James J. Heiney*

FURTHER READING

Breslin, Catherine. "Day of Reckoning." *Ms.*, June, 1989. A personal account of harm caused by the Dalkon Shield. Examines the impact of the A. H. Robins bankruptcy proceedings on women who

461

were harmed by the device. Also discusses the efforts of various organizations formed to protect the rights of women who claimed harm.

Hawkins, Mary F. *Unshielded: The Human Cost of the Dalkon Shield*. Toronto, Ont.: University of Toronto Press, 1997. Focuses on the history of the Dalkon Shield, from its development to the years of litigation. Contains little discussion, however, of the "human cost" of the shield and its effect on the women who used the device.

Kimble-Haas, Sheila L. "The Intrauterine Device: Dispelling the Myths." *Nurse Practitioner* 23, no. 11 (1998). An exploration of the positive aspects of IUDs on the market and how the Dalkon Shield case damaged the reputation of IUDs in general.

Mintz, Morton. *At Any Cost: Corporate Greed, Women, and the Dalkon Shield*. New York: Pantheon Books, 1985. A comprehensive account of the acquisition and marketing of the Dalkon Shield by Robins and of the lawsuits. Contends that A. H. Robins officials were aware of the po-

tential danger of the device from the beginning but were driven by the profit motive.

Perry, Susan, and Jim Dawson. *Nightmare: Women and the Dalkon Shield*. New York: Macmillan, 1985. Traces the saga of the Dalkon Shield through early 1985, using material gleaned from examination of thousands of documents. Focuses in particular on the lawsuits that arose in Minnesota.

Sobol, Richard B. *Bending the Law: The Story of the Dalkon Shield Bankruptcy*. New York: Notable Trials Library, 1996. A study of the litigation process, from the beginning lawsuits to the establishment of the trust fund. Also explores the bankruptcy of A. H. Robins.

SEE ALSO: Mar. 21, 1928: Alberta Government Sterilizes Thousands Deemed Genetically and Mentally Unfit; Sept.-Oct., 1937: Prescription Elixir Causes More than One Hundred Deaths; 1956-1962: Prescription Thalidomide Causes Widespread Birth Disorders.

October 7, 1974
CONGRESSMAN WILBUR D. MILLS'S STRIPPER AFFAIR LEADS TO HIS DOWNFALL

A U.S. representative from Arkansas and powerful House committee leader, Wilbur D. Mills was an alcoholic who reportedly was having an extramarital affair with stripper Fanne Foxe. Foxe was found by police in the Tidal Basin in Washington, D.C., having either fallen or jumped in the water following a traffic stop of Mills's car. Mills's activities became a public scandal and led to the end of his government career.

ALSO KNOWN AS: Tidal Basin incident

LOCALE: Washington, D.C.

CATEGORIES: Government; politics; sex; public morals

KEY FIGURES

Wilbur D. Mills (1909-1992), U.S. representative from Arkansas, 1939-1977, chairman of the House Ways and Means Committee, 1957-1975

Fanne Foxe (Annabel Battistella; b. 1936), Argentine-born stripper

SUMMARY OF EVENT

Wilbur D. Mills, who was first elected to the U.S. Congress in 1938, was only twenty-nine years old and the second-youngest member of Congress in U.S. history when he took office. He eventually became one of the most powerful leaders in the House of Representatives as chairman of the House Ways and Means Committee. At one point he was rumored to be under consideration for an appointment to the U.S. Supreme Court. He was the nation's most respected fiscal authority and was a candidate for president in 1972 but was defeated in the primaries by George McGovern. Had McGovern defeated Richard Nixon in the November general election, Mills likely would have become the secretary of the Treasury Department.

Within two years of his run for the presidency, the respected Mills was a much maligned alcoholic who was widely assumed to have been cheating on his wife. He became a national laughingstock after he met Fanne Foxe, a striptease dancer who had come to the United States from Argentina.

At 2:00 A.M. on October 7, 1974, the U.S. Park Police in Washington, D.C., stopped a car in which Mills and three women were riding. The car was stopped because it was traveling at an unreasonable speed and it did not have its headlights on. In an apparent attempt to protect the intoxicated Mills from being discovered by police, Foxe leaped from the car, ran, and ended up in the water in the adjacent Tidal Basin. Foxe, also intoxicated, was pulled out of the water by police and taken to a nearby hospital for treatment.

Initially, Mills denied news reports that he had been in the car. However, he admitted guilt in an October 10 article in *The Washington Post* after finding out that a television news crew filmed part of the incident. Ten days later, Mills finally told voters that he had done "something that he shouldn't have done." He attributed his earlier denials to miscommunication with his staff. In early December, he appeared on stage with Foxe to stem the innuendos about their relationship; they claimed to be just "very close friends." He told the press that had he been having a clandestine relationship, he would not have been so careless. He also claimed in a newspaper interview that Foxe was a friend of his wife. Six months later, he blamed the entire incident on a combination of pain pills (for a sore back) and alcohol.

As chairman of the House Ways and Means Committee, Mills was extremely influential. The

Wilbur D. Mills. (Library of Congress)

committee met in secrecy. In addition to dealing with bills on taxation and trade, it also determined who served on congressional committees. The general view among his colleagues in Congress was that Mills was a despot who ruled Congress by giving out favors for those who voted as he did and for doling out punishments to those who voted against him. He often could get tax bills passed without amendments. (Floor amendments often turn general tax bills into loopholes for special interest groups. Mills would not give special interest groups an opportunity to get an amendment added to a bill.)

Throughout his job as chairman, Mills never lost a tax bill on the floor of the House. Thus, it seems that Mills used a combination of both the "carrot" and the "stick" in his approach to getting tax bills passed. Following the demise of Mills, tax bills that passed did so because they offered tax benefits to everyone, and not because they represented sound legislation, resulting in a complex mass of tax laws and a system lacking internal stability.

IMPACT

Mills was reelected to Congress less than one month after his relationship with Fanny Foxe became public knowledge. He was fortunate that 1974 was a good year for Democrats, and he won with nearly 60 percent of the vote. About a month after the 1974 election, Mills, again drunk, appeared on stage at a Boston strip club called the Pilgrim Theater, where Foxe was performing as the Tidal Basin Bombshell. Mills's behavior further embarrassed Congress, leading his peers to urge him to resign from his leadership position. House Speaker Carl Albert assured voters that Mills would not return as chairman of the House Ways and Means Committee.

In January, 1975, a few weeks after the Boston incident with Foxe, Mills stepped down from his position with the committee and acknowledged that he was an alcoholic. He joined Alcoholics Anonymous and checked himself into a hospital to get away from alcohol. He did not seek reelection in 1976. In 1977, he returned to Washington, D.C., as a lobbyist on tax matters.

Another lasting impact of the Foxe scandal was a change in the way congressional committee members are selected. In December, 1974, the Democratic caucus voted to strip the Ways and Means chairman of the power to appoint congressional committee members. The greatest impact of Mills's downfall, however, was the effect it had on income tax law in the United States. All revenue bills, which include all changes in the tax laws, must originate in the Ways and Means Committee. Mills was known for carefully editing every tax bill so that it meshed with existing tax law. Because of Mills, the Internal Revenue Code was well organized, internally consistent, and stable throughout his eighteen-year tenure as chairman. After he resigned, his successors lacked either the ability or the motivation to carefully monitor the tax laws.

In effect, the downfall of Mills led to a loss of a clear source of order and constraint and opened up the tax agenda to special interest groups. Tax law soon became a hodgepodge of miscellaneous provisions that complicated life for taxpayers and tax preparers. Thus, many believe that today's tax loopholes and "exceptions to the exceptions" in the In-ternal Revenue Code can be attributed to the Foxe scandal of 1974. Twenty years later, following the 1994 election, the newly elected chairman of the Ways and Means Committee, Republican William Archer of Texas, stated at a press conference that he wanted to conduct the affairs of the committee "as Wilbur Mills did." For a Republican chairman to make such a statement about a Democratic predecessor simply underscores the impact that Mills had on the Ways and Means Committee and federal tax law.

—*Dale L. Flesher*

FURTHER READING

Barnes, Fred. "Congressional Despots, Then and Now." *Public Interest*, Summer, 1990. This article considers Mills a near-sovereign of a powerful fiefdom. The author attributes a decline in the power of the House Ways and Means Committee to the Fanne Foxe scandal.

Battistella, Annabel, with Yvonne Dunleavy. *Fanne Foxe*. New York: Pinnacle Books, 1975. Foxe's mass-market autobiography written shortly after the Tidal Basin incident, most likely to capitalize on the publicity.

"Democrats: Wilbur's Argentine Firecracker." *Time*, October 24, 1974. A newsmagazine article published shortly after the Foxe scandal erupted that covers the story as it unfolded.

Manley, John F. *The Politics of Finance: The House Committee on Ways and Means*. Boston: Little, Brown, 1970. An entire chapter is devoted to Mills. The author considers Mills one of the "most influential committee chairmen in recent years, if not in history."

Zelizer, Julian E. *Taxing America: Wilbur D. Mills, Congress, and the State, 1945-1975*. New York: Cambridge University Press, 1998. Analyzes the work of Mills and provides insights into the evolution of income taxation, Social Security, and Medicare during Mills's tenure as committee chairman.

SEE ALSO: Feb. 7, 1960: President Kennedy's Romantic Affair Links Him to Organized Crime; July 18, 1969: Senator Edward Kennedy's

Driving Accident Kills Mary Jo Kopechne; May 23, 1976: *Washington Post* Exposes Congressman Wayne L. Hays's Affair; Sept., 1976: Jimmy Carter Admits Committing Adultery in His Heart; Jan. 26, 1979: Former Vice President Nelson Rockefeller Dies Mysteriously; July 20, 1982: Conservative Politician John G. Schmitz Is Found to Have Children Out of Wedlock; July 20, 1983: Congress Members Censured in House-Page Sex Scandal; Jan. 17, 1998: President Bill Clinton Denies Sexual Affair with a White House Intern; Apr. 30, 2001: Washington Intern Chandra Levy Disappears; Sept. 29, 2006: Congressman Mark Foley Resigns in Sex Scandal Involving a Teenage Page.

October 25, 1974
Evangelist Billy James Hargis Resigns College Presidency During Gay-Sex Scandal

Christian conservative evangelist Billy James Hargis, who founded a number of organizations, including American Christian College, preached antigay and antisex sentiments. He was forced to retire from the college and his ministries after he was accused of having sex with both male and female students and pressuring them to keep silent about the relations.

Locale: Tulsa, Oklahoma

Categories: Sex; religion; public morals; education

Key Figures

Billy James Hargis (1925-2004), Christian evangelist

David A. Noebel (b. 1936), conservative Christian author and academic

Anne Constable (fl. 1970's), reporter for *Time* magazine

Summary of Event

The McCarthy era saw the rise of anticommunist attitudes throughout the United States. Right-wing fundamentalist Christians, including Billy James Hargis, stood at the forefront of those opposed to communism, particularly the official atheism of the Soviet Union. Originally ordained by the Disciples of Christ, Hargis founded the Christian Crusade in 1950 and his own ministry, the Church of the Christian Crusade, in 1966. He had gained fame in 1953 for his effort to send God to the Soviets by sending Bible quotations in balloons. However, the U.S. Internal Revenue Service disapproved of his political involvement and revoked his organization's tax-exempt status. Hargis would gain even more fame in 1974, when he become embroiled in a sex scandal, but not just any sex scandal: He was accused of having homosexual sex.

In 1971, Hargis had founded American Christian College in Tulsa, Oklahoma, with the aim of teaching youth how to avoid communist values through fundamentalist Christianity. His college's choir, All American Kids, traveled around the country, performing for host churches. His doctrine opposed rock music, popular culture, and sex education in schools, all of which, he argued, led to a decline in public morality. His solution, much like that of the emerging Religious Right, was a return to biblical values. Indeed, Hargis's Christian Crusade was a predecessor of the Christian conservative movement that became influential in the United States in the second half of the twentieth century.

Scandal erupted after Hargis was accused of having had sex with a couple (students at the college) after their wedding ceremony, a ceremony he had conducted that day. The couple brought their accusation to college vice president and Hargis follower

David A. Noebel, who was horrified at the news. Noebel's next action is truly significant. After two weeks of internal debate, he believed the students. Had he chosen to deny the accusations, the incident likely would have remained secret, but with his decision to support the couple's accusations came confessions from three more students, all men, claiming to have had sexual trysts with Hargis.

According to the three male students, the sex occurred in several places, including Hargis's office and home and in hotel rooms during tours with the All American Kids choir. Hargis reportedly justified these affairs by referring to the biblical friendship of David and Jonathan as one that was homoerotic. Typical of many molesters, he had threatened the young men, warning them against revealing the relationships.

Noebel took the case to the college board, which joined him in supporting the students. On October 25, Noebel and two board members met with Hargis and his lawyers. According to Noebel and one of the other officials, Hargis confessed to the affairs. Even though he was married, Hargis blamed his biological makeup for his behavior and agreed to resign from the college presidency and leave his leadership position at other Hargis ministries. However, he left only after being offered an annual stipend of twenty-four thousand dollars and seventy-two thousand dollars from a life insurance policy the college had to protect their interests in him. Hargis's disgrace would not last. He immediately denied the allegations and the confession. Four months after his resignation from the college presidency, in February of 1975, he attempted a return to the job. However, the college board supported Noebel, who by this time was serving as Hargis's successor.

Hargis's ministries, however, suffered financially in his absence. His charisma and speaking skills had charmed supporters, who donated large sums of money to the ministries. In his absence, donations decreased. By September, his former ministries, except the college, were willing to forgive his actions and accept his return. Even though his popularity would never again reach its pre-1974 heights, he had regained his empire.

In 1976, *Time* reporter Anne Constable learned

of the scandal, which had been kept from the public eye. Her story brought the affair to national attention and led to questions about Hargis's integrity. Constable's story drew special attention to a letter Hargis penned after his return to power, a letter in which he urged Christians to disavow images of homosexual men in popular culture. Hargis continued to deny culpability, blaming Noebel and internal school politics for his ouster, but the organizations that welcomed his return concentrated on his penitence (and their own near-bankruptcy), rather than on attempts to claim his innocence. The college and other Hargis ministries severed ties with each other, which presented the college with a new financial problem. Hargis had the address lists of all the donors, and he refused to share those lists. By 1977, the college's doors would be closed forever, while Hargis's other ministries would continue to flourish.

IMPACT

The scandal, in the short term, exposed Hargis as a hypocrite, while his departure from the presidency of American Christian College fueled that institution's demise. The scandal certainly reduced Hargis's fund-raising abilities, but not to the point that his ministries collapsed upon his return one year after the scandal broke. More to the point, however, the scandal drew national attention to the potential for hypocrisy in Christian fundamentalism. Hargis, in his autobiography *My Great Mistake* (1985), denied all accusations against him and focused his discussion on those same Christian values he had been accused of violating. The charismatic Hargis was good at making people forgive his own deviance (while denying any wrongdoing) while simultaneously preaching his antigay doctrine.

In the long term, analysts of the scandal argue that Hargis was part of a trend of outwardly conservative religious and political figures who behaved contrary to what they pronounced. As antigay politics consumed the U.S. Congress during the early 1980's, and as the Religious Right, along with its flagship organization, the Moral Majority, influenced many on the subject of homosexuality, several well-known antigay activists, such as Congressman Robert E. Bauman, were embroiled in their own homosexuality-related scandals. Other fundamentalists also would stand accused of violating their self-professed sexual codes. For example, Jim Bakker, the charismatic leader of the PTL (Praise the Lord) ministries, had a sexual affair with his secretary, Jessica Hahn, during the 1980's. Thus, Hargis's behavior stands with other religious leaders and conservatives who failed to practice what they preached.

—Jessie Bishop Powell

FURTHER READING

Allyn, David. *Make Love Not War: The Sexual Revolution—An Unfettered History*. Boston: Little, Brown, 2000. Includes chapters about the connections of clergy, sexuality, and gay and lesbian rights. Chapters cover most of the twentieth century and include Hargis's era.

Danforth, John C. *Faith and Politics: How the "Moral Values" Debate Divides America, and How to Move Forward Together*. New York: Viking Press, 2006. Argues the conservative Republican Party must move away from fringe issues to unite. Contrasts with the views of the Religious Right. Danforth was a well-known conservative politician.

Hargis, Billy James, and Cliff Dudley. *My Great Mistake*. Green Forest, Ark.: New Leaf Press, 1985. Hargis's take on the controversy surrounding his bisexuality, which he adamantly denied. Slanted toward the resurrection of his ministerial career.

Martin, William C. *With God on Our Side: The Rise of the Religious Right in America*. New York: Broadway Books, 1996. History of the Religious Right, including its rise during the Hargis era and its impact on politics in the United States.

Miller, Brett A. *Divine Apology: The Discourse of Religious Image Restoration*. Westport, Conn.: Praeger, 2002. Analyzes religious figures accused of sexual misconduct. Includes a section on fundamentalist preacher Jimmy Swaggart, whose scandalous dalliance with a prostitute, Debra Murphree, was covered closely by the national media.

"Reviewing the Fundamentals." *Christianity Today*, January, 2007. Focuses on the biblical teachings of the New Testament on sex and sexuality. Cites the book of James, which states that Christian leaders are placed under strict moral standards.

SEE ALSO: 1970: Study of Anonymous Gay Sex Leads to Ethics Scandal; Jan., 1977: Singer Anita Bryant Campaigns Against Lesbian and Gay Rights; Aug. 4, 1978: British Politician Jeremy Thorpe Is Charged with Attempted Murder; Sept. 3, 1980: Congressman Bauman Is Arrested for Liaison with Teenage Boy; Mar. 19, 1987: Jim Bakker Resigns as Head of PTL Television Network; Feb. 21, 1988: Evangelist Jimmy Swaggart Tearfully Confesses His Adultery; Sept. 19, 2000: Ex-gay Leader John Paulk Is Photographed Leaving a Gay Bar; Aug. 19, 2004: Blog "Outs" Antigay Congressman Edward Schrock; Dec. 6, 2005: Spokane, Washington, Mayor Recalled in Gay-Sex Scandal; Nov. 2, 2006: Male Escort Reveals Sexual Liaisons with Evangelist Ted Haggard; July 11, 2007: Florida Politician Is Arrested for Soliciting an Undercover Male Police Officer.

1970's

November 20, 1974
BRITISH POLITICIAN JOHN STONEHOUSE FAKES HIS SUICIDE

John Stonehouse was a Labour Party member of Parliament who falsified records of his business and then attempted to flee by faking his suicide and taking on another identity. He had hoped to start a new life in Australia with his mistress. He was discovered, extradited, and sentenced to seven years in prison.

LOCALES: London, England; Melbourne, Australia

CATEGORIES: Government; politics; sex

KEY FIGURES
John Stonehouse (1925-1988), British Labour government minister, 1964-1970
Sheila Buckley (b. 1948), Stonehouse's secretary, mistress, and second wife
Harold Wilson (1916-1995), prime minister of Great Britain, 1964-1970, 1974-1976

SUMMARY OF EVENT
John Stonehouse was for a time a high-flying politician in Prime Minister Harold Wilson's Labour Party government. When the Labour Party was defeated in the 1970 election in the United Kingdom, Stonehouse pursued various business interests that soon became mismanaged. Stonehouse attempted to fabricate the business accounts but finally realized he was going to be investigated for fraud. This led to his desperate attempt to escape and start his life again under a new name by faking his own death.

Stonehouse had been educated at Tauntons School, Southampton, the city where his mother later became mayor. After a period in the Royal Air Force during World War II, he attended the London School of Economics, graduating in 1951. While there, he had been chairman of the Labour Society, and after graduating he became involved in the co-operative movement, a socialist retail and political movement. He served the co-op in Africa, becoming its manager in Uganda (1952-1954). He re-turned to work with the London Co-operative Society and became its president (1962-1964).

Stonehouse maintained an active interest in politics, contesting two elections in 1950 and 1951 before finally being elected member of Parliament (MP) for Wednesbury in the West Midlands in 1954, as a Labour and Co-operative Party candidate. He continued to hold this seat until it was abolished in 1974. He then won the new Walsall North constituency.

When the Labour Party came to power under Wilson, Stonehouse gained his first government position as parliamentary secretary to the minister of aviation (1964-1966). He quickly moved up the ladder to the office of postmaster-general, a cabinet post, in 1968. He reorganized the British postal system and then became minister of posts and telecommunications until the Labour government was defeated in 1970.

Though Stonehouse was reelected, he was not appointed to the shadow cabinet, and he could see his political progress was blocked. He turned to setting up various business ventures, many connected to his colonial and overseas experience, with his nephew Michael Hayes and businessman James Charlton. In the end, these totaled twenty-three different companies, which soon ran into trouble. Stonehouse began transferring funds from one company to another, then asset-stripping some of them. Some of these moves were fraudulent, designed to trick his accountants and investors, and he came to the attention of the British Department of Trade and Industry (DTI).

Aware of the likely repercussions, Stonehouse hatched a plan with his long-time secretary and mistress, Sheila Buckley, to fake his own death. He discovered that two of his constituents, who had been about his own age, had died recently. He applied for passports under their names once he had obtained their birth certificates from their widows. The planning took several months. In late November, 1974, he planned a business trip to Miami, Florida, with

Charlton. While staying at the Fontainbleu Hotel on Miami Beach, he left his clothes on the beach and took a plane to San Francisco, California, using one of his fake passports. He was soon reported missing, his clothes were found, and it was presumed he had drowned while swimming. Buckley told police that Stonehouse was a strong swimmer, but he preferred swimming alone. The U.S. Coast Guard and local police mounted an intensive search, even digging up a car park. They found a body, though it was not his. The news of his disappearance was overshadowed in Britain by several bomb atrocities committed by Irish terrorists and subsequent anti-terrorist legislation.

Stonehouse's wife, Barbara, was in shock. No body was washed up on shore at the beach but, nonetheless, he was declared dead. Stonehouse, in fact, had journeyed to Australia under the surname Markham and then left the country again. He traveled back to Europe, met Buckley in Denmark, and saw how his alleged death had been reported. He then returned to Australia using his other alias, Donald Clive Muldoon, and rented a house in a beach area of Melbourne, Victoria. The Australian police were tipped off both by British contacts and the banks that Stonehouse was moving his money. The police thought, however, they were looking for Lord Lucan, another prominent figure who had also disappeared following the mysterious death of his children's nanny.

On December 24, the Australian police arrested Stonehouse for illegal entry into Australia. He confessed to document tampering but because he was a British MP it was not clear whether he broke any law. MPs were exempt from certain entry requirements. After being held briefly, he was released.

Stonehouse claimed he had fled Britain because he was being blackmailed, and Buckley supported the story. He said his fake suicide had been a result of a "brainstorm." His wife, who knew nothing of his involvement with Buckley, flew out to be with him. Stonehouse sent a telegram to the prime minister to apologize, stating he wished to stay in Australia. Immediate speculation was that he was involved in spying, though the British authorities soon squashed such speculation. Others had believed his death had been a result of a Mafia hit.

At a personal level, once Barbara Stonehouse had been faced with the truth, she divorced him in 1978. John Stonehouse married Buckley in 1981 and they had a son. He had two daughters and a son with Barbara. More immediately, he was charged on twenty-one counts of fraud, theft, forgery, conspiracy to defraud, causing a false police investigation, and wasting police time.

Stonehouse's trial began in the summer of 1976 and lasted sixty-seven days, the longest fraud trial in British history through that year. He conducted his own defense. He was convicted on eighteen counts and sentenced to seven years in prison. In prison, Stonehouse suffered three heart attacks and needed open-heart surgery. He was released from Wormwood Scrubs Prison in 1979, after serving

John Stonehouse, far right, returns to England in July, 1975. He was soon indicted for fraud, conspiracy, and forgery after faking his own suicide in 1974. (Hulton Archive/Getty Images)

three years only. Buckley also was sentenced to two years, which was suspended. Stonehouse occasionally appeared in public and continued to write, mainly fiction. He had another heart attack and died in 1988.

IMPACT

The Stonehouse affair was a major embarrassment to the Wilson government, which had just been reelected in 1974 with the slimmest of majorities. Stonehouse's absence meant the party was basically managing with a majority of one. He returned to his position as a Labour MP. He then resigned from the Labour Party during his trial and joined the English National Party, an anti-immigrant right-wing party.

The British press, with no other crisis on hand, did a good deal of investigating, discovering the Buckley connection and the fraudulent business dealings, especially with the Anglo-Bangladesh Trust. The DTI and the fraud squad later established that Stonehouse had illegally obtained about £2 million. Immediate calls for his resignation from Parliament came to nothing. The British authorities eventually had enough evidence to apply for his extradition, which was finally granted after six months of legal wrangling. Meanwhile, Stonehouse had applied unsuccessfully for asylum status to Sweden and Mauritius.

When Stonehouse finally resigned his seat after his conviction on August 28, 1976, the Conservative Party opposition won the seat in the subsequent by-election. He also had to resign as a privy councillor, one of only three councillors to have done so in the twentieth century.

—*David Barratt*

FURTHER READING

Adut, Ari. *On Scandal: Moral Disturbances in Society, Politics, and Art.* New York: Cambridge University Press, 2008. A comprehensive analysis of scandals of all types. The author explores the contexts in which "wrong-doings generate scandals and when they do not." Focuses on how people experience scandals emotionally and cognitively.

Stonehouse, John. *Death of an Idealist.* London: W. H. Allen/Virgin Books, 1975. A personal confession by Stonehouse of his fall from grace. Includes discussion of the 1974 fake-suicide scandal.

_____. *My Trial: My Blow-by-Blow Account and Psychological Reaction to Trial and Verdict from the Old Bailey Dock.* London: Star, 1976. Stonehouse's own account of his trial.

SEE ALSO: May, 1915: British Government Falls Because of Munitions Shortages and Military Setbacks; June 22, 1922: British Prime Minister David Lloyd George Is Accused of Selling Honors; Oct. 25, 1924: Forged Communist Letter Brings Down British Government; May 20, 1936: British Cabinet Member Resigns After Budget Information Leak; Mar. 9, 1956: British Conductor-Composer Is Arrested for Possessing Pornography; Mar. 2-Sept. 25, 1963: John Profumo Affair Rocks British Government; June 22, 1972: Police Arrest Architect John Poulson for Bribery and Fraud; 1985-1986: Westland Affair Shakes Prime Minister Thatcher's Government; Jan. 12 and May 11, 1987: Media Reports Spark Investigation of Australian Police Corruption.

February 3, 1975

HONDURAS'S "BANANAGATE" BRIBERY SCANDAL LEADS TO EXECUTIVE'S SUICIDE

The U.S. Securities and Exchange Commission's investigation of Eli M. Black's suicide led to the discovery of a system of corporate bribes and the downfall of Oswaldo López Arellano, the president of Honduras.

LOCALES: New York, New York; Tegucigalpa, Honduras

CATEGORIES: Murder and suicide; business; corruption; banking and finance; colonialism and imperialism; trade and commerce

KEY FIGURES

Eli M. Black (1921-1975), president of United Brands Company

Oswaldo López Arellano (1921-1996), president of Honduras, 1963-1971, 1972-1975

SUMMARY OF EVENT

On February 3, 1975, Eli M. Black, former rabbi and the chief executive officer of United Brands Company, began his day in a seemingly routine manner. He packed his briefcase, received the morning papers, and left his Park Avenue apartment in New York City to meet his driver, James Thomas, for his usual ride to work. Upon arriving at his office, Black locked the doors to the reception area and to his own office, both from the inside. He then used the briefcase, filled with heavy books rather than the usual working papers, to break the window of his forty-fourth-floor office in New York's Pan Am building. He cleared away some shards of glass from the broken window, tossed the briefcase through the window, and watched it fall to the street. Moments later, at 8 A.M., he climbed through the window and jumped to his death onto Park Avenue.

In the meantime, Black's driver parked the car and returned to Black's office, finding the doors locked. Black did not answer his phone, so Thomas

broke into the office. He immediately went to the broken window and looked down upon the body of his employer, whom he identified for the police. Black was only fifty-three years old, apparently happily married with two grown children. He left no suicide note. His family had not noticed anything unusual in his behavior the day before his death. Early responses to his death suggested that the stress of working in the corporate world led to his suicide.

United Brands, however, had been low on cash and was under pressure to sell one of its enterprises to increase liquidity. Black had successfully negotiated the sale of Foster Grant to a West German chemical company, a sale announced the day after his dramatic plunge. In 1968, Black had bought a significant number of shares of the United Fruit Company. In 1970, he took control of the company and merged it with his other holdings, American Seal-Kap and John Morrell meatpacking, to create United Brands. He soon discovered that he had overpaid for his stock and that the company was in deep financial trouble.

United Fruit had a long protectionist history of meddling in the politics of the sovereign nations of Central America in particular. In 1911, United Fruit sponsored an invasion of Honduras, whose government had blocked the company's development efforts. The most egregious political act of the company was its support for the Central Intelligence Agency-sponsored overthrow in 1954 of the democratically elected president of Guatemala, Jacobo Árbenz Guzmán, plunging that country into decades of civil unrest. Árbenz Guzmán had intended to purchase fallow lands at a low price to distribute to landless peasants, but United Fruit owned much of the land to be redistributed. The company came to be known as El Pulpo, or the Octopus, because its "arms" reached into the affairs of banana republics, small unstable nations—most often in Central

America—that depend on a limited crop such as bananas.

In 1973, seven Latin American nations created the Union of Banana Exporting Countries and demanded a tax of one U.S. dollar on every box of bananas. Though the tax plan was not implemented, in part because Ecuador declined to enact the tax, Honduras did enact a tax of fifty cents per box in 1974. The money from the banana tax was intended to support economic development in Honduras and more agrarian reform, but the new fees would have cost United Brands millions of dollars. In 1974, Hurricane Fifi destroyed 70 percent of United Brands's Honduran banana crop.

Black's suicide triggered an investigation of his company by the U.S. Securities and Exchange Commission (SEC). Such an inquiry was standard practice in the case of an unusual death. The SEC uncovered evidence of a $2.5 million dollar bribe of Honduran president Oswaldo López Arellano to lower the per-box tax. The president reduced the tax to twenty-five cents with future incremental increases. (Of the bribe money, $1.25 million had been paid to a Swiss bank account prior to Black's suicide and the remaining $1.25 was never paid.)

The SEC charged United Brands with concealing the $2.5 million dollar bribe as well as paying over $750,000 to Italian officials beginning in 1970 to prevent restrictions on imports of bananas to Italy. United Brands initially denied the existence of a bribe, then admitted it but asked the SEC to keep the bribes secret to avoid harm to stockholders and the company. The company law firm even requested intervention by the U.S. State Department, arguing that the investigation would harm the relationship between United Brands and Honduras. The State Department declined and the investigation went forward. In Honduras, the United Brands branch office announced that it had no knowledge of the bribe. A special commission of the government of Honduras prohibited middle- and high-ranking officials from leaving the country during the investigation.

President López Arellano was removed from office on April 22, 1975, by military coup. Abraham Bennaton Ramos, his minister of economy, was

Eli M. Black. (AP/Wide World Photos)

charged with negotiating, and perhaps receiving, the bribe and was likewise removed from office. A number of United Brands stockholders sued the company in an attempt to force reimbursement of the money lost in the bribes. Public trading of United Brands stock was suspended.

IMPACT

Black's suicide signaled the end of an era of corporate influence that had begun during the late nineteenth century with the happy marriage of Minor C. Keith's banana plantations and his construction of railroad lines to ship them. Founded in 1899, Keith's United Fruit Company—then United Brands—was a symbol of U.S. imperialism, and the company exercised its influence on the politics and economics of the countries where it had holdings. Its influence extended to U.S. policy as well.

To protect its assets and forward company interests, United Brands financed the invasion of Honduras, assisted with the Bay of Pigs invasion, supported the overthrow of Árbenz Guzmán of

Guatemala, provided favorable media coverage for Honduras in its war with El Salvador, and bribed the head of state of the sovereign nation of Honduras. It also bribed government officials of Italy and, perhaps, Costa Rica, Panama, and Germany.

Although no one from United Brands was incarcerated as a result of the SEC investigations, the company's stock value plummeted along with its reputation. In its earlier history, United Brands could count members of the State Department as friends and supporters. In 1975, William D. Rogers, U.S. assistant secretary of state for inter-American affairs, rejected the company's plea for assistance with the SEC, noting that multinational conglomerates must be good citizens and not interfere with the affairs of other nations. Black's suicide caused an international scandal that led to a sea change in the public's view of corporate behavior and responsibility.

—Linda Ledford-Miller

FURTHER READING

Chapman, Peter. *Bananas: How the United Fruit Company Shaped the World*. Edinburgh, Scotland: Canongate, 2007. Originally published as *Jungle Capitalists*, this work begins with Black's suicide then investigates the power plays and deceits of a company that affected policy and politics in several countries. Argues that United Fruit's (Brand's) actions contributed to the rise of the powerful and the downfall of governments.

Cole, Robert J. "More Stockholders Suing United Brands on Bribery." *The New York Times*, April 12, 1975. Newspaper report on the continuing financial problems of United Brands that was published shortly after Black's suicide.

Kilborn, Peter T. "Suicide of Big Executive: Stress of Corporate Life." *The New York Times*, February 14, 1975. An analysis of Black's suicide that seeks to answer the question of why business professionals would take their own lives. Argues that career stress is the trigger.

McCann, Thomas. *On the Inside: A Story of Intrigue and Adventure on Wall Street, in Washington, and in the Jungles of Central America*. Rev. ed. Boston: Quilan Press, 1987. Part memoir of the author's years in public relations, part history of United Fruit/Brands, and part travelogue.

Soluri, John. *Banana Cultures: Agriculture, Consumption, and Environmental Change in Honduras and the United States*. Austin: University of Texas Press, 2005. History of the banana industry and its effects on local, national, and international politics. Includes discussion of the Black and the Bananagate scandal.

SEE ALSO: Feb. 25, 1977: Film Producer David Begelman Is Found to Have Forged Checks; Aug. 6, 1982: Banco Ambrosiano Collapses Amid Criminal Accusations; Nov. 13, 1986-May 4, 1989: Iran-Contra Weapons Scandal Taints Reagan's Administration; Feb. 28, 1995: Former Mexican President Carlos Salinas's Brother Is Arrested for Murder; May 28, 2007: Japanese Politician Charged with Corruption Hangs Himself.

1970's

October 31, 1975
BUDDHIST TEACHER ORDERS HIS STUDENTS TO REMOVE THEIR CLOTHES

The Vajrayana Buddhist teacher Chögyam Trungpa, founder of the Naropa Institute in Boulder, Colorado, was a controversial leader whose life and practices came to a head at a three-month educational retreat. Trungpa instructed his students to strip their egos, which included stripping their clothes, at a Halloween party, but two students, poets W. S. Merwin and Dana Naone, refused. The resulting scandal symbolized for some the behavioral extremes of the counterculture movement in the United States during the 1960's and 1970's. For others, Trungpa's methods reflected a different form of Buddhism.

LOCALE: Snowmass, Colorado
CATEGORIES: Public morals; religion; cultural and intellectual history

KEY FIGURES
Chögyam Trungpa (1939-1987), Tibetan Buddhist monk and teacher
W. S. Merwin (b. 1927), American poet
Dana Naone (b. 1949), American poet

SUMMARY OF EVENT

Chögyam Trungpa was born in Tibet and trained as a Buddhist monk. Displaced from his homeland at the time of the Chinese invasion of Tibet in 1959, he spent time in India, England, and Scotland before coming to the United States in 1970. By this time he had gained considerable renown as a teacher and religious leader. In 1974, he founded the Naropa Institute (now Naropa University) in Boulder, Colorado, the first Buddhist school of its type in the United States. He was also a focus of controversy for his behavioral extremes, which included heavy drinking, womanizing, and the heavy-handed treatment of his followers.

In the fall of 1975, Trungpa began a three-month intensive-training program for advanced students in

Vajrayana Buddhism at the Eldorado Lodge in Snowmass, Colorado. In contrast to other forms of Buddhism, Vajrayana practice focuses on a direct approach to achieving enlightenment, an approach often involving a complete surrender of adherents to the influence of their teacher. Among the participants were poets W. S. Merwin and Dana Naone.

Merwin at this time was well established in his career. He had published his first collection of poems, *A Mask for Janus*, in 1952 and won a Pulitzer Prize for *The Carrier of Ladders* in 1971. He had came to Naropa in the summer of 1975 to study Buddhism under Trungpa and to teach poetry. With close to one dozen years separating Merwin and Trungpa in age, however, and coming from very different cultural backgrounds, the older Merwin's scholarly, intellectual propensities from the outset seem to have run counter to Trungpa's so-called crazy-wisdom approach to imparting Buddhist teachings. Nonetheless, Merwin was eager to participate in the three-month program, and Trungpa, who was impressed with Merwin's poetry, allowed him and Naone to attend.

An area of difference between Trungpa and Merwin soon surfaced when Merwin refused to take part in the violent and angry chanting that was a part of Vajrayana training. Other conflicts arose as well, and involving not only Merwin. Trungpa's Vajrayana security guards were armed with peashooters that they used to attack recalcitrant participants. Some participants initiated violent counterattacks against the guards and Trungpa. At one point a pitched battle broke out between the opposing groups using ice snowballs. On another occasion, Trungpa's room was ransacked and his liquor stolen when he failed to appear for a scheduled lecture.

The climactic incident involving Merwin and Trungpa took place at a Halloween party that participants were required to attend. The event, for Trungpa, offered an opportunity for individuals to strip themselves of their superficial egos, and as the party progressed, this involved stripping their clothes as well. Several people either had their clothes pulled off or voluntarily stripped and were carried around naked by Vajrayana guards. Trungpa himself had stripped earlier in the evening but temporarily left the party. When he returned—intoxicated—and discovered that Merwin and Naone were not present, he ordered the Vajrayana guards to find them.

Finding the door to Merwin and Naone's room locked, the guards attempted to break in. A number of other people joined the guards outside the room as well. Some of the guards tried to get in the room through a glass door on the balcony. Merwin, who was known for his strong pacifist beliefs, nevertheless called out from inside the room that if anyone broke through either of the doors he would attack them. A lengthy period of negotiation followed, with those outside relaying messages from Trungpa that attendance at the party was required. Merwin shouted back that he considered the party to be beyond the limits of the seminar he was attending.

Eventually, at about midnight, the guards broke through the glass door and entered the room. Merwin defended himself and Naone by attacking and cutting several guards with a broken beer bottle. He was overpowered and with Naone was forced downstairs to the party. A loud verbal altercation took place between Trungpa and Merwin and Naone. The argument between Trungpa and Naone was particularly vicious. During the course of the exchange he accused her of being a slave to a white man (she was of Hawaiian background) and she called him names such as "fascist," "bastard," "Hitler," and "cop."

Trungpa once again ordered them to remove their clothes, and when they refused, he ordered the guards to strip them. After they had been forcibly stripped, the rest of those present undressed as well, and the whole assemblage danced. The next day, Merwin and Trungpa met and discussed the incident. Trungpa informed Merwin that he was free to leave the seminar if he wished. Merwin, however, elected to stay. He continued to attend Trungpa's lectures but refused to participate in any of the other activities. Another party was announced two days

before the end of the program. Slides taken at the Halloween party were set to be shown. It was at this time that Merwin and Naone left Snowmass.

While the scandalous incident at Naropa was well known within Buddhist and literary circles, the story became much more widely known a few years later with its retelling in a 1979 *Harper's* magazine article by Peter Marin ("Spiritual Obedience: The Transcendental Game of Follow the Leader"). Two small-press publications—*The Party: A Chronological Perspective On a Confrontation . . .* (1977) and *The Great Naropa Poetry Wars* (1980)—also documented the incident.

IMPACT

The Naropa scandal added to the growing controversy surrounding Trungpa's lifestyle and religious practices. His detractors saw the scandal as further evidence of wild and uncontrolled behavior that was at odds with the messages of self-control and compassion that lay at the heart of Buddhist teachings. Others saw his actions falling within the tradition of highly eccentric Tibetan Buddhist saints from centuries before—for example, the eleventh century saint Marpa Lotsawa or the fifteenth century saint Drukpa Kunley. These saints engaged in brutal domination of their disciples and practiced a kind of "crazy wisdom" in their own lives to bring themselves and others to enlightenment.

For others the incident stood as an example of the final stages of the 1960's and early 1970's counterculture, during which the idealistic dreams of the early phase of the movement came to an end in a tragic mix of self-indulgence and disillusionment. Sadly, of course, Trungpa's behavioral extremes, and especially his drinking, contributed to his relatively early death twelve years later at the age of forty-seven.

—Scott Wright

FURTHER READING

Butler, Katy. "Encountering the Shadow in Buddhist America." In *Meeting the Shadow: The Hidden Power of the Dark Side of Human Nature*, edited by Jeremiah Abrams and Connie Zweig. Los Angeles: Jeremy P. Tarcher, 1991.

1970's

475

Offers a Jungian perspective on Trungpa's message and other outrageous aspects of American Buddhism during the period.

Feuerstein, Georg. *Holy Madness: The Shock Tactics and Radical Teachings of Crazy-Wise Adepts, Holy Fools, and Rascal Gurus.* New York: Paragon House, 1991. Places Trungpa within the so-called crazy wisdom tradition, both in Tibetan Buddhism and in the broader dimensions of spiritual practice.

Marin, Peter. "Spiritual Obedience: The Transcendental Game of Follow the Leader." *Harper's,* February, 1979. A retelling of the Naropa scandal in which the writer uses letters to stand for Merwin and Naone. Their real identities quickly became known to knowledgeable readers.

Mukpo, Diane J., with Carolyn Rose Gimian. *Dragon Thunder: My Life with Chögyam Trungpa.* Boston: Shambhala, 2006. The autobiography of Trungpa's Western-born wife, whom he married in 1970 and who remained with him until his death in 1987. Provides useful, if sometimes biased, insights into the complexities of the person as well as his life at the time of the Naropa scandal.

Paine, Jeffery. *Re-enchantment: Tibetan Buddhism Comes to the West.* New York: W. W. Norton, 2004. A popular history of Tibetan Buddhism in the United States that discusses Trungpa's place within its development and offers a brief discussion of the Naropa scandal.

SEE ALSO: May-June, 1926: Evangelist Aimee Semple McPherson Claims She Was Kidnapped; Aug. 14, 1963: Madame Nhu Derides Self-Immolation of Vietnamese Buddhists; Oct. 23, 1985: Guru Bhagwan Shree Rajneesh Is Indicted for Immigration Fraud; June 30, 2001: Korean Religious Teacher Jung Myung Seok Is Charged with Rape.

1976
PEACE CORPS CONCEALS MURDER OF VOLUNTEER IN TONGA

The brutal murder of Peace Corps volunteer Deborah Gardner in Tonga became a scandal because the Peace Corps and the U.S. State Department tried to keep the murder from tainting the organization's reputation. Dennis Priven, whom Gardner identified before she died as the one who stabbed her, was found not guilty by reason of insanity by a Tongan jury. He returned to the United States and was soon freed from custody.

LOCALE: Nuku'alofa, Tonga
CATEGORIES: Murder and suicide; corruption; law and the courts

KEY FIGURES
Deborah Gardner (1953-1976), Peace Corps volunteer

Dennis Priven (b. 1952), Peace Corps volunteer accused of Gardner's murder
Mary George (b. 1929), director of the Peace Corps program in Tonga, 1975-1976
Emile Hons (b. 1949), Peace Corps volunteer and friend of Priven and Gardner

SUMMARY OF EVENT
Late at night on October 14, 1976, Deborah Gardner, a twenty-three-year-old high school teacher and Peace Corps volunteer, was attacked in her home in Tonga, an island nation in the South Pacific. Abundant physical evidence—a knife, a flip-flop, a broken pair of glasses—as well as Gardner identifying her assailant led to the eventual arrest of another volunteer, Dennis Priven.

The Kingdom of Tonga is an archipelago of 169 islands. The Peace Corps had been sending volunteers to Tonga since the early 1960's, mostly to serve as high school teachers, writers, and engineers. A poor nation with a limited agricultural economy, Tonga relied on American aid and, as events would show, was willing to accept American promises at face value to preserve good relations with the United States.

Born and raised in New York, Priven had been a volunteer in Tonga since 1974 and had a reputation as a brilliant although emotionally and mentally disturbed individual. According to Philip Weiss, author of the book *American Taboo* (2004), an account of the scandal, Priven had warm friendships with male volunteers but was bashful around attractive women. He had odd personal habits. He was rarely seen without his diving knife, an intimidating weapon with a six-inch blade. Weiss notes that Priven carried the knife to class when teaching mathematics and science classes in the Tongan high school where he was assigned.

Less well known to others was that sometime in 1975, Priven developed vague stomach pains and had to be evacuated to Hawaii for medical care. In Hawaii he was given Darvon (propoxyphene), a commonly prescribed narcotic analgesic during the early 1970's. Chemically similar to methadone, Darvon is addictive and was prescribed during the mid-1970's often for pain associated with opioid withdrawal and stomach cramps.

Priven, agnostic and cynical, loved to mock what he considered the repressed attitudes of the Tongan people, whose culture blended folk beliefs in spirits and magic with evangelical Christianity. He was judgmental of volunteers who tried to participate in Tongan culture. As one might expect, Priven was no more able to get along with his supervisors in the Peace Corps. As Weiss describes, he was frequently contemptuous of Mary George, the country director for the Peace Corps in Tonga.

By late 1976, Priven, who hated Tonga and Tongans, was applying for an extended tour of duty; he reacted violently when his application was denied. He had fallen in love with Gardner and thought he could make her love him. Throughout 1975 and into 1976, he tried to cajole and manipulate her into dating him, and he eventually began stalking her.

Gardner, who joined the Peace Corps as a teacher in early 1975, was remembered as a woman of exceptional beauty and spirit, a caring friend, and a devoted teacher. Later, in 1976, a combination of personal disappointments, frustration with cultural double standards, and a fear of Priven made Gardner depressed and desperate to escape.

As several writers noted, there was no shortage of people eager to go out with Gardner; the few men she fell in love with, however, ended up disappointing her. For whatever reason, none of the relationships worked, and Gardner became increasingly frustrated and felt more and more alone. Adding to her frustration were the cultural double standards she and other women were expected to follow.

As Weiss notes, the Peace Corps expected volunteers to follow local customs. Behaviors that would not have raised an eyebrow in the United States were deeply shocking to Tongan mores. For instance, Gardner loved to go bicycling alone or with a boyfriend and she dated several men. In Tonga, young women were not supposed to do these things. George, the country director in Tonga, advised Gardner to change her behavior and ordered her to take cultural sensitivity courses. Gardner, according to Weiss, stated that she would rather die than live a life in which she could not do what she wanted, when she wanted.

Matters came to a head in mid-October, 1976, when a group of new volunteers was set to arrive in Tonga. Priven had recently been denied an extension and was simmering with anger. Gardner was depressed and her behaviors were flamboyant. She had too much to drink at a party for new volunteers and made a scene, falling twice and eventually lying down on the dance floor. She was escorted out of the dance by Emile Hons, a close friend of both Gardner and Priven. Hons and Gardner had been having a discreet romantic affair, and they spent the night together after the party, unaware that Priven had been spying on them.

On October 14, Priven surprised Gardner while she was getting ready for bed. He overpowered her and stabbed her more than twenty times. Hearing her cries for help, Tongan neighbors startled Priven, who fled in a panic, leaving behind at the scene his eyeglasses, a flip-flop, and the murder weapon: his diving knife. Later that night, Priven turned himself in to police, showed them several self-inflicted wounds on his wrists, and told them he had tried to kill himself.

In the wake of this vicious murder, an informal conspiracy developed to shield Priven from the consequences of his crime. The conspiracy included volunteers who were friends of the accused; they withheld evidence of his guilt because they believed he needed medical and psychological treatment, not conviction and execution. The conspiracy included Peace Corps supervisors who decided to defend Priven yet keep the matter as quiet as possible, largely to protect the agency's image. The Peace Corps paid for a top-notch defense attorney and a psychiatrist to testify that Priven was insane when he stabbed Gardner to death.

IMPACT

After Priven was found not guilty by reason of insanity, members of the U.S. government stepped in to negotiate his release. The Tongan government was promised that Priven would be committed to a psychiatric facility in the United States until he was no longer a danger to himself or others. Later, Weiss notes in his book, members of the Tongan government were lied to. They were told that Priven was shot, by a member of Gardner's family, when he stepped off the plane that brought him home.

In fact, the terms of the negotiated agreement between the Tongan and U.S. governments were unenforceable. In the United States, it took pleading by friends and the threat of a poor letter of reference to convince Priven to go to a private hospital in Washington, D.C. An examination of him found no evidence of insanity. The psychiatrist explained the

murder as a situational psychosis that was unlikely to recur. Priven could not be held against his will legally, and he walked free with a new passport and a clean letter of reference from the Peace Corps. He worked for the U.S. government until he retired in 2003. In 2005, federal prosecutors, who had been asked by a U.S. representative from Gardner's home state of Washington to review the murder case for possible retrial, concluded that Priven could not be retried by a U.S. court because the murder happened outside the United States.

—*Michael R. Meyers*

FURTHER READING

Lipez, Richard. "A Killer Among Us." *The Washington Post*, June 27, 2004. A review of Weiss's book, *American Taboo*, written by a former Peace Corps volunteer.

Murphy, Dave. "Not So Peaceful." *San Francisco Chronicle*, December 17, 2004. An interview with Emile Hons, friend of Gardner and Priven, about the murder and its aftermath.

Weiss, Philip. *American Taboo: A Murder in the Peace Corps.* New York: HarperCollins, 2004. A book-length account of Gardner's murder, Priven's freedom, and the scandal's repercussions.

_____. "Stalking Her Killer." *New York Magazine*, May 24, 2004. A feature-length article about author Weiss's confrontation with Priven in New York City.

SEE ALSO: Mar. 13, 1964: Kitty Genovese Dies as Her Cries for Help Are Ignored; Mar. 21, 1976: Actor Claudine Longet Kills Ski Champion Vladimir Sabich; June 12, 1994: Double Murder Leads to Sensational O. J. Simpson Trial.

1976-1977
U.S. CONGRESS MEMBERS ARE IMPLICATED IN KOREAGATE SCANDAL

The events later known as Koreagate were exposed publicly during the administration of U.S. president Jimmy Carter. The South Korean government had feared that Carter—and Richard Nixon before him—would withdraw a substantial number of U.S. troops from the region. To ensure that U.S. politicians would favor South Korea, large amounts of cash were distributed by South Korean businessman Tongsun Park to at least one-third of the members of the U.S. Congress, leading to the convictions of dozens of lawmakers.

ALSO KNOWN AS: Operation White Snow
LOCALE: Washington, D.C.
CATEGORIES: Corruption; international relations; government; human rights

KEY FIGURES

Tongsun Park (b. 1935), Korean business executive
Jimmy Carter (b. 1924), president of the United States, 1977-1981
Richard T. Hanna (1914-2001), U.S. representative from California, 1963-1974
Donald M. Fraser (b. 1924), U.S. representative from Minnesota, 1963-1979
Park Chung Hee (1917-1979), president of the Republic of Korea, 1961-1979
Sun Myung Moon (b. 1920), founder of the Unification Church
Carl Albert (1908-2000), U.S. representative from Oklahoma, 1947-1977, and Speaker of the House, 1971-1977

SUMMARY OF EVENT

In 1970, South Korean president Park Chung Hee authorized Operation White Snow, under which the Korean Central Intelligence Agency (KCIA) provided between $500,000 and $1 million per year to enhance his influence in Washington, D.C. At about the same time, U.S. president Richard Nixon

had intimated that he might cut the U.S. defense commitment to South Korea from 60,000 to 40,000 soldiers, and indeed that reduction occurred in 1971. Moreover, in 1974, sentiment at the United Nations for an end to the stationing of U.S. soldiers in South Korea approached a majority in the U.N. General Assembly.

The impact of such a dramatic reduction in the U.S. military's staff commitment to South Korea was viewed in Seoul, South Korea's capital, as a possible signal to North Korea that the United States was less interested in defending the south in case of attack. Moreover, Koreans doing business around U.S. military bases in Korea suffered losses.

Members of the U.S. embassy in Seoul soon found out about Operation White Snow and warned the Korean government against influence peddling. Two U.S. ambassadors in Seoul, who warned visiting members of the U.S. Congress of the illegal activity, were transferred to other diplomatic posts, thereby keeping them quiet. South Korean army personnel were fighting alongside U.S. troops in Vietnam, so the U.S. Defense Department did not want a scandal to jeopardize the supply of troops. Nevertheless, the State Department complained to the Korean embassy in Washington, D.C.

In Washington, meanwhile, rumors spread about nondescript white paper envelopes stuffed with about $20,000 in $100 bills that were being handed out to members of Congress by Korean business executive Tongsun Park, who was secretly a KCIA agent. Park, a charming host at many lavish parties in Washington who had many friends dating from his days as a student at Georgetown University, had arranged a clandestine deal with Congressman Richard T. Hanna to use commissions on the sale of one million tons of Louisiana rice to South Korea from 1966 to 1976 as bribe money. Hanna and others pocketed $200,000 or more apiece. Park also encouraged the hiring of beautiful young women for employment in congressional offices.

479

Park was even more successful when Korean-born Suzi Park Thompson became legislative aide to Speaker of the House Carl Albert. On her own, Thompson arranged entertainment for those being bribed, and Albert received several gifts while on trips to South Korea. The KCIA also gave money to Reverend Sun Myung Moon's Reunification Church to promote a positive image of South Korea.

Korean critics of President Park in the United States, some of whom were under KCIA surveillance, quietly confirmed the existence of Operation White Snow to Congress. Some four hundred or more Korean business executives, students, and professors in the United States were paid for undercover jobs, such as threatening dissidents to keep them quiet. In 1976, word leaked out that the Federal Bureau of Investigation (FBI) and other federal agencies were investigating the affair. A federal

grand jury began its investigation as well by the fall. *The New York Times* began reporting on the U.S. government investigations on October 1. On November 30, the House Ethics Committee made public its request for help from the Justice Department to look into the possible bribing of Congress members.

Also in November, Jimmy Carter was elected U.S. president. One of his campaign promises was to reduce the number of U.S. troops in South Korea from 40,000 to 14,000 as a way of signaling his dissatisfaction over human rights problems in the regime of President Park, who was arresting dissidents and suppressing trade union activity. Carter also threatened to reduce economic aid to South Korea. With a critical U.S. president in office, Operation White Snow's mandate expanded: it now had to prevent Congress from approving the partial

South Korean businessman Tongsun Park, left at table, gave cash gifts to as many as one-third of the members of the U.S. Congress. (Hulton Archive/Getty Images)

withdrawal of U.S. troops from Korea, to maintain economic aid to South Korea, and to stop congressional criticism of human rights violations in South Korea. After Koreagate became public, however, Carter cut U.S. troop levels in South Korea by only 4,000.

The South Koreans in the United States then doled out even more money. Congress members who were implicated included Representative Charles Wilson of California, who married a Korean woman during this period. He received a $1,000 wedding gift from Tongsun Park that was duly recorded on the list of wedding gifts, one of the few records of a payment from Park to a member of Congress. In 1977, Park fled the United States before he was charged with thirty-six counts of conspiracy, bribery, mail fraud, failure to register as a foreign agent, and making illegal political contributions.

Congress initially was fearful of looking into the matter, which eventually implicated at least one hundred of its members. Nevertheless, Representative Donald M. Fraser, on April 4, 1977, announced that congressional hearings were set to begin on U.S.-Korea relations, with particular attention to the possible influence-peddling of Tongsun Park, the role of the KCIA in the United States, as well as the suspicious activities of the Reverend Moon.

The term "Koreagate" entered the lexicon around this time, as Fraser's hearings drew wide publicity. The committee heard key testimony from a retired State Department diplomat and then from Park, who was subpoenaed by the committee and federal grand juries to testify under immunity from prosecution. His admission that he distributed cash to thirty members of Congress led to ethics investigations and criminal prosecutions of those members.

Later in 1978, Fraser's subcommittee published a report, primarily recommending prosecution of the Reverend Moon. The House Ethics Committee found that at least ten members of the House had received slush funds, often during trips to Korea. However, most funds were earmarked to cover the legal expenses of the wives of the Congress members.

IMPACT

The House and Senate passed a strict ethics reform bill in 1977. The House Ethics Committee took disciplinary action after an investigation of its own. Representative Wilson was reprimanded by the House in 1978, censured for financial misconduct in 1980, and left Congress after his term expired. Other reprimanded Congress members were Representatives John McFall and Edward Roybal. Another, Otto Passman, was seriously ill and was not disciplined. Edward Patten was exonerated. The statute of limitations had run out on three others. Hanna was prosecuted in federal court, found guilty, and sentenced to six to thirty months in prison.

Although Park testified under immunity for prosecution in 1977, he continued gift-giving while traveling between Korea and Washington, D.C. In 2005, he received an illegal $2 million from Iraq and was sentenced to prison for five years in 2007 for giving false testimony to the FBI regarding his role in the oil-for-food scandal involving the United Nations and Iraq.

Foreign influence on U.S. elections continued to be an issue in later elections, with donations from abroad considered suspect. Indeed, the chief counsel to the Ethics Committee who investigated recipients of Park's bribe money played the same role in the investigation of the Iran-Contra affair one decade later.

Reverend Moon, who had claimed that his church was a nonprofit organization exempt from taxes, was found guilty of tax evasion because of his involvement in politics. Subsequently, the U.S. Internal Revenue Service began to crack down on churches that claimed tax exemption while engaging in political advocacy.

—*Michael Haas*

FURTHER READING

Boettcher, Robert. *Gifts of Deceit: Sun Myung Moon, Tongsun Park, and the Korean Scandal.* New York: Holt, Rinehart & Winston, 1980. The definitive account of the scandal by the staff director of the House subcommittee chaired by Representative Fraser.

Lee, Byeong-cheon, ed. *Developmental Dictatorship and the Park Chung-hee Era: The Shaping of Modernity in the Republic of Korea.* Paramus, N.J.: Homa & Sekey Books, 2005. Twelve noted Korean social scientists examine the relationship between the economic miracle under Park's rule and his social repression.

Lee, Chae-jin. *A Troubled Peace: U.S. Policy and the Two Koreas.* Baltimore: Johns Hopkins University Press, 2006. A comprehensive analysis of U.S.-Korea relations and U.S. policy toward North and South Korea, with a chapter on Koreagate.

Moore, Robin, and Gene Zack. *Suzi: The Korean Connection.* Westport, Conn.: Condor, 1978. A self-serving account of Koreagate as told by Suzi Park Thompson to Moore and Zack.

SEE ALSO: May 14, 1974: *Washington Post* Reveals That the Nixons Received Jewelry Gifts; Feb. 4, 1976: Lockheed Is Implicated in Bribing Foreign Officials; Feb. 2, 1980: Media Uncover FBI Sting Implicating Dozens of Lawmakers; Late July, 1980: President's Brother, Billy Carter, Registers as a Paid Agent for Libya; Nov. 13, 1986-May 4, 1989: Iran-Contra Weapons Scandal Taints Reagan's Administration.

February 4, 1976
LOCKHEED IS IMPLICATED IN BRIBING FOREIGN OFFICIALS

A U.S. Senate committee heard testimony that implicated Lockheed and other major American manufacturers for bribing foreign government officials and other key figures overseas to secure sales contracts. Those accused maintained that such payoffs, although considered unethical in the United States, were essential for success in business dealings in some countries around the world.

LOCALE: Washington, D.C.

CATEGORIES: Corruption; business; trade and commerce; government; space and aviation; international relations; law and the courts

KEY FIGURES

Carl Kotchian (fl. 1970's), president of Lockheed
Kakuei Tanaka (1918-1993), prime minister of Japan, 1972
Frank Church (1924-1984), U.S. senator from Idaho, 1957-1981, and chairman of congressional panel investigating Lockheed
Bernhard, Prince of Lippe-Biesterfeld (1911-2004), prince consort of the Netherlands

SUMMARY OF EVENT

On February 4, 1976, the U.S. Senate Subcommittee on Multinational Corporations announced that it had found that Lockheed Aircraft Corporation had bribed Japanese government and corporate officials and intermediaries. The committee, chaired by Senator Frank Church of Idaho, had been formed in 1972 by the powerful Senate Committee on Foreign Relations to investigate so-called slush funds used by American corporations to finance the campaigns of political candidates they favored. The committee was tasked with looking into two cases: the Watergate burglary by henchmen of the Richard Nixon administration and the subsequent cover-up, and the involvement of International Telephone & Telegraph (now ITT Corporation) in the overthrow of the democratically elected government of Salvador Allende in Chile. The investigative committee also focused on subterfuges that corporations employed to siphon funds to the Republican National Committee. What the committee found fueled its interest in learning about other possible under-the-table transactions, including the Lockheed bribes, which flouted laws regarding corporate financial behavior.

Reports and rumors of corporate bribery of foreign purchasers led the committee to question Carl Kotchian, the president of Lockheed, the largest defense contractor in the Western world. Kotchian, on February 6, was asked about the payment of bribes and the purchase of twenty-one L-1011 Tri-Star Lockheed planes by the Japanese-government-controlled All Nippon Airways. The alleged arrangement was for Lockheed to add the bribe amounts to the price of the airplanes. Kotchian defended Lockheed's payouts by noting that they constituted but a small portion of the total price of the business deal, and that the profit to Lockheed translated into income for its employees and their families and communities, and for stockholders. He admitted that Lockheed was desperate when it began negotiations in Japan. The company was on the verge of bankruptcy because of cost overruns on government contracts in the United States. Kotchian resigned on February 13.

The major Japanese political figure involved in the illegal transaction was Prime Minister Kakuei Tanaka, who had been elected to the Diet, the Japanese national legislature, and served for sixteen terms that stretched more than forty-three years. Tanaka's career was marked by several missteps, none of them significant enough to detour him on the road to political power. In 1948, he was convicted of accepting bribes from the Fukoaka mining interests in exchange for a vote against a bill that sought to nationalize the industry. The conviction was overturned on appeal. In 1974, he was implicated in a scandal in which he used a geisha to camouflage his investments in shady land deals.

Lockheed had paid an intermediary, Yoshio Kodana, a regular fee and sizable percentages that ultimately totaled seven million dollars, for taking care of the details of bribery transactions. Kodana, it turns out, had strong ties to organized crime. Another intermediary had approached Prime Minister Tanaka on behalf of Lockheed, requesting that he use his influence to swing the deal to Lockheed from a competitor. For doing so, Tanaka was paid $1.7 million.

Tanaka was subsequently arrested and charged with bribery and violating Japan's Foreign Ex-

change Control Law. It took seven years, until 1983, before the court returned a guilty verdict and imposed a fine and a four-year prison sentence. Neither penalty would be exacted, however. Tanaka's appeal dragged on until his death in 1993. Meanwhile, he was reelected to the Diet by landslides until he retired in 1989 because of ill health. In the United States, Lockheed pleaded guilty to defrauding the Internal Revenue Service by falsely listing the bribes as "marketing costs."

Lockheed also was implicated in an episode that involved the payment during the early 1960's of more than one million dollars to Bernhard, Prince of Lippe-Biesterfeld, the Netherlands, for his assistance to the company in the sale of 138 F-104 fighter jets to the Dutch air force. Testifying before a Dutch investigatory commission, Bernhard maintained that he no longer remembered his dealings with Lockheed. National affection for Bernhard's wife, Queen Juliana, who threatened to abdicate if Bernhard were jailed, along with concern over creating a political crisis, induced the commission to treat Bernhard lightly. He was made to apologize to the Dutch people and to resign from the board of directors of more than three hundred companies. He also was stripped of his position as inspector-general of the Dutch armed forces. In an interview published after his death in 2004, Bernhard had told a reporter, "I have accepted that the word Lockheed will be carved on my tombstone."

In the wake of the revelations before the congressional committee, the Securities and Exchange Commission in 1976 held its own extensive investigation of overseas bribery transactions involving American corporations. Some four hundred companies confessed to spending $300 million to bribe foreign officials and to finance overseas political campaigns to facilitate sales contracts. In addition to Lockheed, the roster included Bell Helicopter, Exxon, General Tire & Rubber, and Gulf Oil. U.S. president Jimmy Carter expressed the nation's moral outrage when he labeled the acts of bribery "ethically repugnant."

For its part, Lockheed admitted to having paid two million dollars in bribes to Italian authorities during the late 1960's for their assistance in a deal for the purchase of $100 million worth of aircraft. Lockheed also admitted to making similar kinds of arrangements during the 1970's involving "commissions" of at least $202 million with officials in Germany, South Africa, Turkey, Greece, Nigeria, Mexico, and Spain.

IMPACT

The bribery scandals involving Lockheed and other companies illustrated how major reforms typically are put in place only after serious episodes of wrongdoing galvanize public outrage and pressure lawmakers to take action. The Lockheed bribery scandal led to the enactment of the Foreign Corrupt Practices Act (FCPA) in 1977, which prohibits individuals and businesses from offering, promising or authorizing either directly or indirectly the payment of anything of value to any foreign official, government employee, or person acting on behalf of these entities. The act also penalizes the failure of an organization to keep accurate financial records. There are two major loopholes in the law, however. One allows payments for promotional expenses, such as travel and lodging for foreign officials visiting the United States to view domestic products. The second permits payments to a foreign official if such payments are lawful in their respective country.

Corporate representatives criticized the FCPA because, they claimed, it made it more difficult to compete with enterprises from other nations that do not have similar restrictions. They maintained that "greasing" was essential in some countries to obtain business deals.

Lockheed did not learn its lesson. In 1995, the company, at this time called Lockheed Martin, was fined $24.8 million after a guilty plea for making unlawful payments of $1.2 million to an Egyptian legislator. The vice president of Lockheed Martin's Middle East and North Africa regions, after evading capture for almost a year, was arrested and served an eighteen-month prison sentence, the first person to be imprisoned under the FCPA. Lockheed Martin paid the bribes to persuade the Egyptians to purchase three of its C-130 military transport planes.

—*Gilbert Geis*

484

FURTHER READING

Bialos, Jeffrey P., and Gregory Husisian. *The Federal Corrupt Practices Act: Coping with Corruption in Transnational Economies.* Dobbs Ferry, N.Y.: Oceana Press, 1997. Two Washington, D.C., attorneys examine the antibribery provisions of the FCPA, its requirements for disclosure, and the practices of foreign corporations.

Boulton, David. *The Lockheed Papers.* London: Jonathan Cape, 1978. Examines overseas bribes by Lockheed from the 1950's to 1977. Published in the United States as *The Grease Machine* (1978).

Brancato, Carolyn Kay, and Christian A. Plath. *Corporate Governance Best Practices: A Blueprint for the Post-Enron Era.* New York: Conference Board, 2003. A study that examines corporate leadership, ethics, and responsibility at a time of increased public awareness of corporate fraud and mismanagement.

Brown, H. Lowell. *Bribery in International Commerce.* St. Paul, Minn.: West, 2003. Provides details on the FCPA as well as other U.S. laws and international covenants and agreements concerning bribery in commerce.

Hunt, G. Cameron. *The Tanaka Decision: Tanaka Kakuei and the Lockheed Scandal.* Hanover, N.H.: Universities Field Staff International, 1983. A short but incisive review of the conditions surrounding the bribery of Prime Minister Tanaka by Lockheed interests.

Hunziker, Steven, and Ikuro Kamimura. *Kakuei Tanaka: A Political Biography of Modern Japan.* Los Gatos, Calif.: Daruna International, 1994. Considers the personal and political background that played a part in Tanaka's role in the Lockheed case.

Jacoby, Neil H., Peter Nehemkis, and Richard Eells. *Bribery and Extortion in World Business: A Study of Corporate Political Payments Abroad.* New York: Macmillan, 1977. Explores the historical role of bribery and extortion in cultures around the world and suggests possible remedies.

SEE ALSO: Jan., 1913: British Prime Minister's Staff Is Investigated for Insider Trading; 1932:

Insull Utilities Trusts Collapse Prompts New Federal Regulation; Feb. 8, 1960: U.S. Congress Investigates Payola in Pop Music Industry; Mar. 29, 1962: Billie Sol Estes Is Arrested for Corporate Fraud; Nov. 28, 1967: Investor Louis Wolfson Is Convicted of Selling Stock Illegally; May 14, 1974: *Washington Post* Reveals That the Nixons Received Jewelry Gifts; 1976-1977: U.S. Congress Members Are Implicated in Koreagate Scandal; Feb. 2, 1980: Media Uncover FBI Sting Implicating Dozens of Lawmakers; Oct. 9, 1980: Bendix Executive Resigns Amid Rumors of an Affair; Oct. 19, 1982: Car Manufacturer John De Lorean Is Arrested in a Drug Sting; June, 1988-June, 1989: Insider-Trading Scandal Rocks Japanese Government; Mar. 23, 1989: Scientists' "Cold Fusion" Claims Cannot Be Verified; Dec. 23, 1998: Prominent Belgians Are Sentenced in Agusta-Dassault Corruption Scandal.

March 21, 1976
ACTOR CLAUDINE LONGET KILLS SKI CHAMPION VLADIMIR SABICH

American professional skier Vladimir Sabich was killed by his girlfriend, French entertainer Claudine Longet. The prosecution's case was hampered by serious mistakes by local police. As a result, Longet was tried and found guilty of misdemeanor negligent homicide, instead of murder, spent thirty days in jail, and paid a twenty-five-dollar fine.

LOCALE: Starwood, Colorado
CATEGORIES: Drugs; law and the courts; murder and suicide

KEY FIGURES
Vladimir Sabich (1945-1976), American
  professional skier
Claudine Longet (b. 1942), French pop singer,
  showgirl, and actor

SUMMARY OF EVENT
The exclusive ski town of Starwood, near Aspen, Colorado, was turned into a media circus on March 21, 1976, when French entertainer-actor Claudine Longet was arrested for the murder of her boyfriend, international ski celebrity Vladimir "Spider" Sabich. Rumors of alcohol and drug abuse, combined with talk of the couple's imminent separation, surrounded the trial, while key blunders made by the Aspen Police Department damaged the prosecution's case.

Sabich was born on October 1, 1945, in Sacramento, California, to Vladimir and Fran Sabich. His father, a California Highway Patrol officer, nicknamed him Spider shortly after his premature birth because the boy's gangly arms and legs looked like an arachnid. Spider grew up in the remote mountain town of Kyburz, near Lake Tahoe, California. The family, consisting of three children (Spider was the middle child), grew up with a great appreciation for education, physical activity, and the outdoors. Spider began skiing at a very early age, winning tournaments throughout his childhood, and he earned a scholarship to attend the University of Colorado. While at Colorado, Spider met Coach Bob Beattie. With fellow skiers Billy Kidd and Jimmy Huega, Spider went on to place fifth in the slalom at the 1968 Olympics, emerging as America's premier skier.

In 1972, Spider turned professional and won the professional tour that year and in 1973. His good looks, along with the increased popularity of skiing, led to several product endorsements and magazine covers. His popularity also attracted the beautiful Longet. Longet, born on January 29, 1942, in Paris,

Claudine Longet and her daughter, Noelle, at a ski event in Aspen, Colorado, days before the murder of Longet's boyfriend, champion skier Vladimir Sabich. (Hulton Archive/Getty Images)

France, had married American singer Andy Williams in 1961 and enjoyed a mildly successful singing and acting career herself. Longet and her three children (from her marriage to Williams) moved in with the ski star.

After two years together, rumors began to spread that the celebrity relationship was turning sour. Spider had confided in family and close friends that he wanted Longet to move out, but he adored her three children. While dressing after a shower, Longet, who had been seen drinking in a local bar all afternoon and was rumored to be distraught over the impending break up, allegedly entered the bathroom and shot Spider once with a .22 caliber pistol. (The pistol had been purchased by his father for his younger brother in Europe, while Spider was competing there in the Olympics.) Spider bled to death in the back of the ambulance from a single gunshot wound to the abdomen. Longet was at his side in the ambulance.

On April 6, 1976, Longet was charged with reckless manslaughter, defined by the presiding judge in the case as "consciously disregarding a substantial and unjustifiable risk." If convicted, Longet could be sentenced to ten years in prison and receive a

maximum fine of thirty thousand dollars, or both. The trial became a celebrity event in the sleepy town of Aspen, with Longet's former husband Williams beside her throughout the ordeal. Because of the celebrity status of Longet and Spider, the jury selection process was extensive. More than three hundred prospective jurors were placed on standby and sixty two more were questioned by the prosecution and defense before the final twelve jurors and two alternates were selected. Longet hired a top defense team that argued the shooting was accidental, maintaining that the firearm accidentally discharged while she was asking Spider to teach her how to use the gun.

The prosecution's case was hindered by three main obstacles: First, the police had obtained Longet's diary without a warrant while she was in the ambulance with Spider. The diary contained passages expressing concerns and desperation over the possibility that Spider would leave her. Because the diary was obtained illegally, the key information it contained could not be used in court. Second, blood and urine samples, taken from Longet the day of the shooting, showed traces of cocaine and alcohol. These samples could not be admitted at trial because the tests on them were performed unlawfully. Third, the murder weapon found at the crime scene had been wrapped in a towel by someone at the scene and stored in the glove compartment of a police officer's car for several days. It should have been handled by a firearms expert and properly stored as evidence. Because the weapon was mishandled, the defense was able to claim evidence tampering.

On January 14, 1977, Longet was found guilty of misdemeanor negligent homicide, "a gross deviation from the standard of care that a reasonable person would exercise" and a crime that carried a maximum sentence of two years and a five thousand dollar fine, or both. Longet, however, was given two years probation, ordered to spend thirty days in jail beginning on a date of her choosing, and fined twenty-five dollars. Her defense team argued for straight probation, claiming that the singer was not a threat to society. Longet pleaded with the judge to have mercy on her because she had children, but the judge insisted she serve the time, stating there would be public outrage if she spent no time in jail. Upon receiving her sentence, Longet, maintaining her innocence, said of the killing, "there is not really very much to say. Only that I have too much respect for living things to do that. I'm not guilty."

IMPACT

While several people in the Aspen community supported Longet, believing the killing was accidental and that Longet should not be imprisoned, many more people believed that she had gotten away with murder. The rumors of drug abuse and emotional instability surrounding the trial added to the outrage many felt when Longet received her sentence.

As with most celebrity crimes and trials, the murder became a part of American popular culture. Spider brought competitive skiing to the American conscience and his good looks and charismatic personality ensured his celebrity. Claudine Longet was a beautiful and frail actor and singer that had been welcomed into American homes regularly through Andy Williams's Christmas specials. The trial became a media flurry, involving youth, beauty, fame, and murder, and Americans watched attentively. The NBC (National Broadcasting Company) late night comedy show *Saturday Night Live* took advantage of the trial's popularity with the skit "The Claudine Longet Invitational," which parodied a downhill skiing competition wherein the participants were accidentally shot by Longet during their ski runs.

The Sabich family later filed a civil suit against Longet for $1.3 million. The case was settled out of court, and Longet signed a confidentiality agreement promising to not speak publicly about her relationship with Spider or about the murder. Longet also had to agree to never publish a book about her life and the trial.

Longet remained in Aspen after her release from prison but was harassed. She adhered to the confidentiality agreement and other stipulations ordered by the court in the civil suit. She never again performed in show business.

—Sara Vidar

FURTHER READING

Coleman, Annie Gilbert. *Ski Style: Sport and Culture in the Rockies*. Lawrence: University Press of Kansas, 2004. A look at the effects skiing has had on American culture through the lifestyles, triumphs, and tribulations associated with the sport.

Doonan, Simon. *Whacky Chicks: Life Lessons from Fearlessly and Fabulously Eccentric Women*. New York: Simon & Schuster, 2003. This entertaining book explores the lives of eccentric and notorious women, including Claudine Longet.

Fry, John. *The Story of Modern Skiing*. Lebanon, N.H.: University Press of New England, 2006. A comprehensive exploration of the contributions Spider Sabich and others made to American professional skiing. The book also delves into the circumstances surrounding Spider's murder.

SEE ALSO: July 27, 1917: Millionaire Socialite Dies Under Suspicious Circumstances; Jan. 1, 1924: Film Star Mabel Normand's Chauffeur Shoots Millionaire Courtland S. Dines; Apr. 4, 1958: Actor Lana Turner's Daughter Kills Turner's Gangster Lover; Sept. 5, 1967: Socialite Nancy Wakeman Shoots Her Politician-Husband; 1976: Peace Corps Conceals Murder of Volunteer in Tonga; July 23, 1978: Utah Millionaire Is Murdered by His Grandson; Apr. 18, 1979: Actor Lee Marvin Is Ordered to Pay Palimony to Former Lover; Mar. 10, 1980: Scarsdale Diet Doctor Is Killed by His Lover; Mar., 1990: Menendez Brothers Are Arrested for Murdering Their Parents; May 19, 1992: Amy Fisher Shoots Mary Jo Buttafuoco; June 12, 1994: Double Murder Leads to Sensational O. J. Simpson Trial.

1970's

April 4, 1976
WEST POINT CADETS ARE CAUGHT CHEATING ON EXAMS

The discovery that a number of cadets at the U.S. Military Academy had collaborated in completing a take-home examination revealed widespread problems with the academy's honor code. The revelation was followed by outside reviews of the institution's academic programs and its punishments for honor code violations. In the end, the academy began to place greater emphasis on ethics education.

LOCALE: West Point, New York
CATEGORIES: Corruption; education; military; ethics

KEY FIGURES

Sidney B. Berry (b. 1926), lieutenant general, U.S. Army, superintendent of the U.S. Military Academy, 1974-1977

Walter F. Ulmer (b. 1930), brigadier general, U.S. Army, commandant of cadets at the U.S. Military Academy, 1975-1979

Martin R. Hoffman (b. 1932), secretary of the U.S. Army, 1975-1977

Frank Borman (b. 1928), astronaut, airline executive, and U.S. Military Academy graduate

Andrew J. Goodpaster (1915-2005), former U.S. Army general, superintendent of the U.S. Military Academy, 1977-1981

SUMMARY OF EVENT

On March 3 and 4, 1976, the Electrical Engineering Department at the U.S. Military Academy, also known as West Point, issued a homework assignment to more than eight hundred cadets in a required junior-level class with the stipulation that they could not seek help in completing the work. The course was unpopular among cadets, who found it difficult and of little practical value; most simply wanted to complete it with as little work as possible. Nevertheless, instructors assumed cadets would complete the assignment as directed, given

they were bound by a simple, but strict, honor code: "A cadet will not lie, cheat, steal, or tolerate those who do." The penalty for an honor violation was severe: immediate expulsion from the academy.

One instructor reviewing completed assignments discovered a note from a cadet who admitted receiving help on his work. After his interest was piqued, the instructor began examining other submissions, noting remarkable similarities (including identical numerical transpositions and misspellings). The department launched a review of all submissions, which led to the identification, on April 4, of 117 cadets as possible cheaters.

Because West Point had a long-standing tradition of allowing cadets to investigate honor violations themselves, the names of suspected cheaters were turned over to the cadet honor boards for review. By the end of April, honor boards recommended fifty cadets for dismissal. Two cadets resigned before appearing before the honor boards. The fifty who were recommended for dismissal by their peers appealed the decision to Lieutenant General Sidney B. Berry, the academy superintendent, who was authorized to dismiss or retain cadets chosen for dismissal by the honor boards. At the same time, news of the cheating scandal made it to *The New York Times*, which immediately began covering the story.

Public exposure of cheating at the academy could not have come at a worse time for West Point. The academy's handling of honor code violations had been the subject of the 1975 television film *The Silence*, which portrayed a cadet forced to suffer recriminations from others who disagreed with punishment meted out for an honor violation. Concurrent reports of harassment directed at a new cadet who had been retained by the superintendent after being found guilty of an honor violation had painted the Corps of Cadets as a group of vindictive martinets. Many outsiders felt a cadet accused of an honor violation was considered guilty until proven innocent, and that officers were content to let cadets

West Point Cadets Are Caught Cheating

purge their ranks of those they judged unworthy of remaining at West Point. Furthermore, the institution had been in the news because it was preparing for its first class of women in the institution's history—over the vocal objections not only of the current all-male student body but also many active duty and retired officers, some assigned to the West Point faculty and staff.

General Berry realized the magnitude of the situation concerning the cheating cadets. As accused cadets began making their appeals, the scope of the scandal began to widen. More than three hundred cadets were named either as cheaters or as persons who knew of the cheating but failed to report it to superiors. If all were found guilty, the class of 1977 would be decimated. Worse, from Berry's point of view, was that attorneys assigned to West Point's Department of Law, who had been appointed to represent cadets filing appeals, were exposing widespread disdain throughout the Corps of Cadets. The cadets believed the honor system had become corrupted into a method for dealing with petty offenses such as violating curfew or failing to complete the most trivial tasks.

Berry's response was to replace the cadet honor boards with panels consisting of officers and upperclassmen who he believed could provide more mature judgment of individual cases while protecting the institution's ability to police its own ranks. He held all juniors at the academy for weeks during the summer of 1976 so cases could be processed expeditiously. Meanwhile, the commandant of cadets, Brigadier General Walter F. Ulmer, took an active role in the investigations, urging boards to reach their conclusions rapidly. Unfortunately, many involved in representing accused cadets, especially military lawyers assigned as counsels, began suggesting publicly that their careers were being jeopardized because they were being too zealous in mounting their defenses. General Ulmer was frequently singled out as one who was bent on punishing those who stood in the way of swift justice for the guilty.

To counter charges that the academy was not handling the investigations evenhandedly, Berry petitioned Secretary of the Army Martin R. Hoff-

man to appoint an external board to conduct an independent inquiry into the incident. Hoffman declined to do so, preferring to let the academy deal with the problem internally. The constant attention given to the scandal by the media, however, soon led others within the government to act. One U.S. Congress member conducted an investigation while the academy was still pursuing these matters. By the summer of 1977, Congress was calling for the secretary of the Army to step in and take action directly. At that point, more than one hundred fifty cadets had either resigned or been separated as a result of the cheating accusations.

Hoffman responded by offering two proposals that would meliorate the short-term ill effects on current cadets and provide some long-term assurances that situations such as this would be less likely to recur. First, he decided that all cadets dismissed as a result of this cheating scandal would be allowed to apply for readmission to the academy. While this policy did not sit well with some, it made sense to many who had come to believe there were so many flaws in the administration of the honor code that something had to be done to recognize the culpability of the academy and the Army in the problem. Eventually, ninety-two cadets were readmitted and graduated from West Point.

Hoffman's second action was to appoint two commissions. One focused on problems in the legal system employed to handle honor violations. The second, chaired by academy graduate and astronaut Frank Borman, was tasked with examining both the honor code and the broader issue of life at West Point. The Borman Commission's recommendations, issued on December 15, 1976, would serve as the foundation for a number of significant changes that would shape the Military Academy's future both as an academic institution and a training ground for the Army's leaders.

IMPACT

The revelation of widespread cheating at West Point, and reports of the Army's heavy-handed methods of dealing with accused cadets, further reduced the prestige of the military in the eyes of many Americans disillusioned with the military and its role in the Vietnam War. The public already was conditioned to believe that officers and public officials were apt to lie, cheat, and protect individual reputations and institutional traditions at all costs. In this scandal, the public found further evidence that the military was out of touch with modern society and quickly becoming irrelevant as an institution serving the nation's needs. Nevertheless, steps taken by the secretary of the Army proved to have long-term positive impact.

The academy adopted recommendations for changes to procedures for dealing with honor code violations that replaced the single penalty for infractions (expulsion) with an array of disciplinary measures that gave the superintendent and other senior officers more latitude in dealing with cadets who may have committed minor violations of the code. One immediate change proved important as well. When General Berry left the academy in 1977, he was replaced by General Andrew J. Goodpaster, who had been Supreme Allied Commander for the North Atlantic Treaty Organization until his retirement in 1974. Recalled to active duty, the scholar-soldier gave credibility to efforts aimed at showing how West Point was as concerned with educating future officers ethically as it was with honing their military skills. Under his leadership, many of the Borman Commission's recommendations for curriculum changes were implemented, as the academy gradually reduced some of the pressures on cadets and placed greater emphasis on ethics education.

—Laurence W. Mazzeno

FURTHER READING

Betros, Lance. *West Point: Two Centuries and Beyond.* Abilene, Tex.: McWhiney Foundation Press, 2004. Discusses the impact of the scandal on various academic departments at the Military Academy, especially the Department of Law.

Hansen, Richard P. "The Crisis of the West Point Honor Code." *Military Affairs* 49, no. 2 (April, 1985): 57-62. Brief history of the scandal and its aftermath written by a person who was at the academy when news of the cheating incident was first made public.

Janda, Lance. *Stronger than Custom: West Point and the Admission of Women.* Westport, Conn.: Praeger, 2002. Discusses the influence of the cheating scandal on the first class of women to enter the academy in 1976.

Jorgenson, John H. "Duty, Honor, Country, and Too Many Lawyers." *ABA Journal* 63 (April, 1977): 564-567. Assessment of the legal environment in which investigations and hearings were conducted at West Point to determine the fate of cadets accused of cheating.

"What Price Honor?" *Time*, June 7, 1976. Summarizes the events occurring in the spring of 1976 and comments on conditions at the Military Academy that led to the scandal.

SEE ALSO: Apr. 28, 1994: U.S. Naval Academy Expels Midshipmen for Cheating; Jan. 2, 2003: E-mail Message Prompts Inquiry into Air Force Academy Sexual Assaults; June 22, 2005: U.S. Air Force Investigates Religious Intolerance at Its Academy.

May 23, 1976

WASHINGTON POST EXPOSES CONGRESSMAN WAYNE L. HAYS'S AFFAIR

Elizabeth Ray, hired as a secretary to Ohio representative Wayne L. Hays even though she had no skills to perform the job, exposed her romantic affair with the Congress member in an article in The Washington Post. *Hays initially denied the story but eventually admitted their relationship and resigned from Congress.*

LOCALE: Washington, D.C.
CATEGORIES: Politics; sex; publishing and
   journalism; government

KEY FIGURES

Wayne L. Hays (1911-1989), U.S. representative
   from Ohio, 1949-1976
Elizabeth Ray (b. 1943), Hays's secretary

SUMMARY OF EVENT

By the time Wayne L. Hays was elected to the U.S. Congress, he had been an Ohio officeholder since 1939. He served on the state's board of education, was mayor of the small town of Flushing, and was a state senator. A portion of his service in the former two offices overlapped so that he actually held two elective offices at the same time. After a hiatus in private life during the mid-1940's, Hays was elected to Congress in 1948 from Ohio's economically depressed blue-collar eighteenth district.

Hays was returned to office for the next twenty-eight years, during which time he steadily rose in the congressional ranks to become chairman of the House Administration Committee. He also served on the Foreign Affairs Committee and as two-term president of the North Atlantic Treaty Organization Parliamentarians Conference. Although a liberal on many domestic issues such as civil rights, he was a hawk on military matters, avidly supporting the war in Vietnam and vehemently denouncing antiwar protesters. His comments after the Kent State University shooting tragedy in 1970 were widely con-

demned. He is reported as having scoffed that the violence arose among one bunch of draft dodgers (the students) facing another bunch of draft dodgers (the Ohio National Guard soldiers).

It was in his role as House Administration Committee chairman that the abrasive Hays began to amass significant political power. Historically a minor committee overseeing congressional housekeeping details, it grew under his chairship into a major committee that made him one of the most feared and disliked politicians in Washington, D.C. He supervised the distribution of monies to members and committees of Congress for travel, office expenses, and staffing; controlled parking; and oversaw some seven hundred employees. Another center of power for Hays was his leadership of the Democratic Congressional Campaign Committee.

Hays's perceived arrogance, vindictiveness, and intransigence in the exercise of power made him widely disliked among his colleagues, at least one of whom called him the meanest person in Congress. His storied pettiness was demonstrated when he ordered the removal of the operator seats in congressional elevators because he did not want the operators to be able to sit while he had to stand. When he became annoyed with the House barbershop, he mandated a no-tipping policy for the shop.

The beginning of the end of his autocratic reign came on May 23, 1976, with the publication of the article "Closed Session Romance on the Hill" in *The Washington Post.* The article accused him of having kept a woman on his payroll solely for sexual services. Elizabeth Ray, who aspired to an acting career, claimed that she was hired as a secretary even though, as she was famously quoted in the article, "I can't type, I can't file, I can't even answer the phone."

Apparently, the accommodating thirty-three-year-old Ray had willingly been involved with other Congress members before. The North Caro-

491

lina native, born Betty Lou Ray, may have been naïve but she was reportedly far from innocent. For a time, she occupied a luxurious office but did little or no actual secretarial work while being paid $14,000 a year of taxpayers' money. She was, in other words, Hays's mistress. Although it was widely reported that Ray was forty years younger than Hays, their age difference, although substantial, was thirty-two years.

The affair was well underway when Hays married his second wife; he had been married to his first wife for thirty-eight years. Ray quoted him as having assured her that the affair could continue after his marriage if she "behaved herself" and that she should come into the office for at least two hours a

Elizabeth Ray, former lover of Representative Wayne L. Hays, announces the publication of her book, The Washington Fringe Benefit, *which details the scandal.* (AP/ Wide World Photos)

day to allay suspicions. He feared that a prominent journalist, possibly Bob Woodward, was interested in doing an exposé on him.

Ray stated that she had grown afraid of Hays and that he had threatened her if she ever revealed their affair. She said that he had made a reference to troublemakers being thrown six feet under into the Potomac River, a claim he denied. Hays admitted to the affair, but not after first disputing the allegations. In an apparent effort to save himself, he resigned his chairship and fired Ray, but it was too little, too late, and he resigned his congressional seat on September 1.

The timing of Hays's resignation was undoubtedly affected by the pending investigation by the House Committee on Standards of Official Conduct. Hays also was being investigated by the House Ethics Committee, which called off its three-month probe upon his resignation. He also faced a grand jury indictment. Also, there was some question about his ability to win reelection. In the June Democratic Party primary that took place in his Ohio district shortly after the scandalous *Washington Post* article appeared, a practically unknown opponent garnered almost 40 percent of the vote.

Hays returned to private life and to temporary disgrace. Following disclosure of his relationship with Ray, he had taken an overdose of sleeping pills but denied it was a suicide attempt. Along with his other problems, he was the subject of an investigation by the Federal Bureau of Investigation (FBI) not only for possible misuse of public funds to keep his mistress on the congressional payroll but also improper expenditures while on overseas trips.

Two years later, in 1978, he staged a mild political comeback by gaining a plurality of the votes in a race with multiple candidates and won election as an Ohio state representative. He was, however, defeated upon his reelection bid in 1980. Hays remained active in Democratic state politics and was still supported by many of his former constituents for the economic benefits he brought to them during his years in Congress. Among those benefits was the awarding of pensions for black lung disease, a common coal miner's ailment. He also was remembered for such legislation as the Fulbright-Hays

Act, which fostered cultural exchanges between U.S. citizens and citizens of other world nations.

Ray faded into obscurity, her name a mere footnote in the history of political scandals. Describing the time of her brief notoriety, one commentator said that her celebrity status was somewhere between that of "mob girl" Virginia Hill and the notorious disease carrier Typhoid Mary.

IMPACT

The public was particularly attuned to political scandals as a result of the Watergate affair and U.S. president Richard Nixon's resignation in 1974. The Hays scandal was reminiscent of the highly publicized debacle when Arkansas Democrat Wilbur D. Mills was caught carousing with stripper Fanne Fox, also in 1974. Like Hays, he had been a powerful committee chairman who had been forced to resign his House seat. The Hays scandal only added to the public's cynicism and distrust of Washington politicians. The FBI investigation of Hays's activities led to discovery of similar questionable arrangements, one involving a Texas congressman.

On a personal level, Hays's aspirations to higher office ended, a textbook case of how far the mighty had fallen. He planned to run for reelection to Congress and possibly as an Ohio favorite son in the 1976 presidential election. He reportedly also had his eye on the Ohio governorship in 1978. Although Hays was elected to a state office in 1978, he never sought public office again after his subsequent defeat. Ironically, the person who defeated Hays for his state representative seat in 1980 was Republican Bob Ney, who later became a congressman as well. Like Hays, Ney was forced to resign his seat for financial corruption; he had been linked to the Jack Abramoff scandal in 2006.

—*Roy Liebman*

FURTHER READING

Apostolidis, Paul, and Juliet A. Williams, eds. *Public Affairs: Politics in the Age of Sex Scandals.*

Durham, N.C.: Duke University Press, 2004. A study of politics and political culture in the context of sex scandals.

Clark, Marion, and Rudy Maxa. "Closed Session Romance on the Hill." *The Washington Post*, May 23, 1976. The news story that broke the scandal.

"Ex-Rep Wayne L. Hays of Ohio." *Los Angeles Times*, February 11, 1989. A telling obituary of Wayne L. Hays.

Moore, Robin. "Kissers and Tellers, I've Met Them All." *Oui*, December, 1981. A magazine article about women, including Elizabeth Ray, who brought down prominent men.

"Wayne L. Hays of Ohio Dies at 77; Scandal Ended Career in Congress." *The New York Times*, February 11, 1989. A lengthy obituary of Wayne L. Hays.

SEE ALSO: 1927: President Warren G. Harding's Lover Publishes Tell-All Memoir; Early 1928: Joseph P. Kennedy Begins an Affair with Gloria Swanson; July 10, 1934: Sex Scandal Forces Resignation of Alberta Premier Brownlee; May 3, 1950: U.S. Senate Committee Begins Investigating Organized Crime; Feb. 7, 1960: President Kennedy's Romantic Affair Links Him to Organized Crime; May 19, 1962: Marilyn Monroe Sings "Happy Birthday, Mr. President"; Oct. 7, 1963: Vice President Lyndon B. Johnson Aide Resigns over Crime Connections; Oct. 7, 1974: Congressman Wilbur D. Mills's Stripper Affair Leads to His Downfall; Jan. 26, 1979: Former Vice President Nelson Rockefeller Dies Mysteriously; Dec. 7, 1980: Rita Jenrette's "Diary of a Mad Congresswife" Scandalizes Washington; Mar. 30, 1991: William Kennedy Smith Is Accused of Rape; Dec. 11, 1997: HUD Secretary Henry Cisneros Is Indicted for Lying to Federal Agents; Jan. 17, 1998: President Bill Clinton Denies Sexual Affair with a White House Intern.

1970's

September 1, 1976
FORMER BEATLE GEORGE HARRISON LOSES PLAGIARISM LAWSUIT

George Harrison, formerly of the British rock-pop band the Beatles, lost a plagiarism lawsuit brought by the publishers of the song "He's So Fine," originally recorded by the Chiffons in 1963. Harrison's melodic adaptation, "My Sweet Lord," included on his 1970 album All Things Must Pass, *was deemed "unconscious plagiarism" by a judge. The case raised concerns of artistic creativity and doubts about the integrity of songwriters and composers, including Harrison, and affected him deeply.*

LOCALE: New York, New York
CATEGORIES: Cultural and intellectual history; law and the courts; music and performing arts; plagiarism

KEY FIGURES
George Harrison (1943-2001), British singer, guitarist, and composer
Billy Preston (1946-2006), American musician
Richard Owen (b. 1922), U.S. federal court judge
Allen Klein (b. 1931), music industry executive

SUMMARY OF EVENT
On February 10, 1971, Bright Tunes, Inc., filed a lawsuit against rock-pop star and songwriter George Harrison and his companies Harrisongs Music, Inc. (United States), and Harrisongs Music, Ltd. (United Kingdom), for his use of several musical phrases from a tune originally written by Ronald Mack and recorded by the Chiffons. The Chiffons' song, "He's So Fine," had been a pop hit in 1963 in the United States, although

most critics agree that the tune was not well known in Great Britain. Both Harrison and American soul musician Billy Preston, who would collaborate with Harrison on the new version of the song, agreed that they were familiar with the original.

Harrison's version of the song, "My Sweet Lord," was not released until the end of 1970 and was on his album *All Things Must Pass*. In December, the song became the most popular selling single in the United States by a former member of the Beatles, and it reached the top of the charts in Great Britain the following month. "My Sweet Lord" was rereleased in 1976 on another album, *The Best of George Harrison*, and again in 2001 on a new release of *All Things Must Pass*. Harrison rerecorded the song.

After leaving the Beatles, Harrison assembled another group of musicians, including Preston. One evening in 1969, while the group was in Co-

George Harrison. (AP/Wide World Photos)

penhagen, Denmark, Harrison and Preston whiled away the time waiting for a press conference to begin by playing some random chords on their guitars. Harrison, who had recently returned from a religious pilgrimage to India, began to sing the phrase "my sweet lord" over and over as a mantra. Eventually, he settled on a tune and repeated the words "Oh, my Lord, My sweet lord," "Hallelujah," and "Hare Krishna" as he picked on the guitar strings. Preston picked up the phrasing and began to play on his own guitar. The notes finally coalesced into a "G-D-C" phrase, followed by a G-A-C-A-C phrase.

After a number of revisions, the addition of several grace notes, and a rearrangement of the notes to suit the words, the song "My Sweet Lord" was written down as sheet music. At a later time, the song was then recorded in a studio, perhaps played by Preston, and was added to Harrison's new album *All Things Must Pass*. The album began to sell well, and Bright Tunes, the owner of the copyright for "He's So Fine," filed suit in U.S. federal court, accusing Harrison of plagiarizing the original song's melody for "My Sweet Lord."

During court proceedings in the case of *Bright Tunes Music v. Harrisongs Music*, Harrison was asked directly by U.S. federal district judge Richard Owen, who was knowledgeable in music as well as law, whether he had knowingly plagiarized. Harrison said that he had not, but agreed that the melodies of the two songs were similar, although to his ear they were not identical. Owen, a 1950 graduate of Harvard Law School, was a gifted composer of a number of operas. He tried to determine if there had been conscious plagiarism by Harrison. Accordingly, the judge sat down with Harrison and together they sang the phrases of the two songs to see if they were indeed identical. Harrison revealed as much as he could remember about how the song was composed. Even such intensive

UNINTENTIONAL PLAGIARISM

In this excerpt from the decision, the judge in the case of Bright Tunes Music v. Harrisongs Music *(1976) reflects on how it is that a composer crafts a musical work. In composing the song "My Sweet Lord," the judge concluded, Harrison chose a particular combination of sounds—those sounds that make up the essence of the song "He's So Fine"—thus plagiarizing the work, albeit unintentionally.*

Seeking the wellsprings [sic] of musical composition—why a composer chooses the succession of notes and the harmonies he does—whether it be George Harrison or Richard Wagner—is a fascinating inquiry. It is apparent from the extensive colloquy between the Court and Harrison covering forty pages in the transcript that neither Harrison nor [Billy] Preston were conscious of the fact that they were utilizing the "He's So Fine" theme. However, they in fact were, for it is perfectly obvious to the listener that in musical terms, the two songs are virtually identical except for one phrase. There is motif A used four times, followed by motif B, four times in one case, and three times in the other, with the same grace note in the second repetition of motif B.

What happened? I conclude that the composer, in seeking musical materials to clothe his thoughts, was working with various possibilities. As he tried this possibility and that, there came to the surface of his mind a particular combination that pleased him as being one he felt would be appealing to a prospective listener; in other words, that this combination of sounds would work. Why? Because his subconscious knew it already had worked in a song his conscious mind did not remember. Having arrived at this pleasing combination of sounds, the recording was made, the lead sheet prepared for copyright and the song became an enormous success. Did Harrison deliberately use the music of "He's So Fine?" I do not believe he did so deliberately. Nevertheless, it is clear that "My Sweet Lord" is the very same song as "He's So Fine" with different words, and Harrison had access to "He's So Fine." This is, under the law, infringement of copyright, and is no less so even though subconsciously accomplished.

scrutiny did not make for an easy disposition of the case.

Efforts to determine authorship might be understood by looking at an example: the Bach-inspired Ave Maria by composer Charles Gounod. Gounod had set his Ave Maria to a melody from Johann Sebastian Bach's *Well-Tempered Clavier* (1722). Such a use is not considered plagiarism because the composer attributed Bach as his inspiration for the

495

work. A case becomes especially difficult when a composer borrows only a few notes of an earlier work. In effect, plagiarism can be vexing in cases in which a composer uses less, not more, of an original work and does so without attribution. However, as in Harrison's case, that "use" without attribution was not necessarily conscious or intentional.

On September 1, 1976, Owen reached his decision: Plagiarism did occur, but it was "unintentional" because Harrison had so internalized the music that it had become part of his unconscious. Thus, he had not been completely aware of what he was humming when he began to sing the words "my sweet lord." In other words, he did not know he was humming the tune from "He's So Fine."

The court next had to determine damages. This second phase of the trial was scheduled for February, 1981, because after the first phase of the suit ended, Bright Tunes sold its copyright of the song to ABKCO Industries, owned by Allen Klein, a former business manager of the Beatles and Harrison's manager at the time the suit was filed in 1971. The purchase of Bright Tunes complicated the case, making it difficult to determine who should receive the money and how much should be awarded. Also, by this time, Klein was no longer Harrison's manager. The judge determined that the damage amount requested, $1,599,987, was fair.

Judge Owen ordered that the money be held in a trust, and he determined that Harrison should pay $587,000 plus interest. The decision was upheld on appeal in 1983. The case continued for eight more years, as the two sides argued over other legal questions, including the legal significance, if any, of Klein's past connection with Harrison and whether or not a lawsuit brought in England should figure into the settlement in the U.S. court case. In 1991, the case was back in appellate court and then returned to Judge Owen for further litigation. Two years later all parties agreed to resolve at least part of the issue—the disbursement of some disputed funds.

IMPACT

Commentaries on the plagiarism case against Harrison make it clear that proving plagiarism in music is extremely difficult. In a written work, an author who uses three or more words from another source must put those words in quotation marks and cite the source to avoid plagiarism. In music, the standard is more difficult. Composers often begin their creations by humming melodies, unaware of their sources. This was the case in the Harrison suit. Even a trained musician could find it difficult to conclude that a piece of borrowed music was so close to the original that it constituted plagiarism or whether the addition of new notes, chords, or harmonies would distinguish the piece so that it could stand alone.

Avoiding plagiarism in music composition is complex. Many universities now include courses on how to avoid music plagiarism, and in a move that seems to sound a warning, Columbia University School of Law compiled a list of hundreds of music copyright-infringement cases filed since the 1840's.

—*Julia Meyers*

FURTHER READING

Frith, Simon, and Lee Marshall, eds. *Music and Copyright*. 2d ed. Edinburgh, Scotland: Edinburgh University Press, 2004. A comprehensive examination of issues of copyright and plagiarism in the making and distribution of music. Contains brief discussion of the Harrison-Bright Tunes Music case.

Harrison, George. *I, Me, Mine*. San Francisco, Calif.: Chronicle Books, 2002. Harrison discusses his youth, early days as a musician, pilgrimages to India and reverence for Hindu mysticism, and even his love of gardening. Lyrics to more than eighty songs, many in his own hand and with commentary. Fifty archival photographs of Harrison with the Beatles and solo.

Leng, Simon. *While My Guitar Gently Weeps: The Music of George Harrison*. Milwaukee, Wis.: Hal Leonard, 2006. Contains interviews with many of Harrison's music collaborators. This book was originally planned to celebrate Harrison's music and is now a memorial and tribute.

Turner, Steve. *A Hard Day's Write: The Stories Behind Every Beatle's Song*. New York: Harper,

1999. Arranged by album, this book examines incidents in the lives of each Beatle and how those experiences influenced their music. Turner interviewed many people to find out the stories behind the songs. Contains more than two hundred photographs.

SEE ALSO: July, 1925: *Nosferatu* Is Found to Have Violated *Dracula* Copyright; Feb. 8, 1960: U.S. Congress Investigates Payola in Pop Music Industry; 1978: *Roots* Author Alex Haley Is Sued for Plagiarism; Nov. 19, 1990: Lip-Synching Duo Milli Vanilli Lose Grammy Award.

September, 1976
JIMMY CARTER ADMITS COMMITTING ADULTERY IN HIS HEART

In an interview with Playboy *magazine, U.S. presidential candidate Jimmy Carter admitted that he had looked on women with lust and committed adultery "in his heart." He also used the words "screw" and "shacking up" in the interview. The remarks received a great deal of media attention but did not keep him from being elected president of the United States.*

LOCALE: United States
CATEGORIES: Publishing and journalism; sex; politics; public morals; government

KEY FIGURES
Jimmy Carter (b. 1924), president of the United States, 1977-1981
Robert Scheer (b. 1936), freelance journalist

SUMMARY OF EVENT
While campaigning for the presidency of the United States in 1976, Jimmy Carter agreed to an interview with veteran journalist Robert Scheer, who was writing an article for *Playboy* magazine. The interview, conducted in September, 1976, ended with a lengthy soliloquy by Carter in which he admitted to having "looked on a lot of women with lust" and committing adultery "in his heart." This impromptu revelation combined references to the New Testament and Christian theology with colloquial references to "screwing" and "shacking up" with women outside marriage.

The interview was scheduled to appear in *Playboy* in November, 1976, but editors disclosed excerpts from it to the press two months earlier, releasing an onslaught of criticism and ridicule in the news media just weeks before election day. In a campaign that focused on presidential character and personal integrity, press coverage of the interview with Carter, whose bluntness provoked scandal, demolished Carter's substantial lead over Gerald R. Ford in the opinion polls but, in the end, it did not keep him from winning the election.

Though the interview covered a wide range of topics on political goals, foreign policy, economics, and civil rights, its emphasis on Carter's religious beliefs reflected a general preoccupation with his personal character. Carter had emerged from national obscurity as the former governor of Georgia to a decisive victory in the Democratic primaries. He campaigned as an outsider, untainted by government corruption and committed to restoring moral integrity to the presidency. This strategy appealed strongly to voters who were disillusioned by the 1972-1974 Watergate scandal involving President Richard Nixon and suspicious of the Washington, D.C., establishment.

In response to declining support among liberal democrats, Carter's campaign staff arranged the interview with *Playboy* to appeal to voters who might be wary of his religious commitments as an outspoken born-again Christian. Scheer accompanied Carter throughout the spring campaign, eventually

Jimmy Carter. (Library of Congress)

accumulating five hours of interview material. Scheer had a reputation for relentless persistence, and he pressed Carter repeatedly on the relationship between the candidate's moral certainty and his politics. Carter was candid about his religious beliefs, telling Scheer that he was not afraid of death (in response to a question about assassination) because he was assured of eternal life. He even admitted some ambivalence about legal restrictions on sexual behavior he personally believed to be sinful, such as adultery and homosexuality.

As Scheer was preparing to leave at the end of the final interview session, he casually asked Carter if he thought the interview would successfully reassure people who worried that his self-righteousness would make him a stubborn, inflexible president. Carter responded with a deeply personal monologue on his upbringing and his beliefs on religion and sin, fully aware that Scheer was still taping their conversation. Carter claimed that humility was central to Christ's teachings. Salvation by grace en-

tailed the recognition that no one was entitled to claim moral superiority over anyone else. Carter did not consider himself an exception: He, too, had looked upon women with lust, committing adultery in his heart, and he had done so many times. He could not condemn other people for having sex out of marriage, even if God had forgiven him for his own sexual sins. The dramatic intensity of this speech was heightened by his blunt sexual slang, intermingled with references to the Bible and the writings of theologian Paul Tillich.

Carter's juxtaposition of religiosity and coarse language shocked, amused, and offended many people. The vulgarity clashed with the wholesome image he strived to maintain, while the biblical references to lust in the heart made the incongruity all the more salient. References to the interview became ubiquitous in the election coverage. Surveys of public opinion and political commentaries reported that readers were repelled by the personal nature of the remarks as much as they were by the abrasive language. Those who were familiar with the context of the remarks typically approved of Carter's views on pride, but any discussion of his personal sexuality seemed beneath the dignity of a candidate for president. Democratic U.S. senators Robert Byrd and Ernest Hollings characterized the incident as a foolish political move. Byrd wondered why Carter would want to be featured in *Playboy*, while Hollings expressed the hope that, once Carter was president, he would stop talking about adultery.

Jokes at Carter's expense played on the absurdity of his confession. A cartoon in the *Los Angeles Times* depicted him fantasizing about a disrobed Statue of Liberty. Reporters asked Joan Mondale, wife of Carter's running mate, Walter Mondale, if she, too, suspected her husband of committing adultery in his heart. She shrugged and responded that he probably had. Before the *Playboy* story broke in mid-September, election coverage had consistently portrayed Carter as the preferred candidate. By the first presidential debate on September 24, Carter and Republican opponent Ford were nearly even in the polls.

Ford surpassed Carter for the first time after the first presidential debate, a development that some attributed in part to the *Playboy* interview. It took a more serious political gaffe by Ford during the second presidential debate for the Republican candidate to lose his momentum. (He had said that Eastern Europe was not dominated by the Soviet Union.) The emphasis on political issues during the debates, a topic that had garnered relatively little public interest earlier in the campaign, shifted attention from Carter's blunder in *Playboy*, but he was unable to recover from the initial blow to his public image before the election.

In November the election results were so close that Carter was not declared the winner until 3 A.M.; he had 51 percent of the popular vote. One member of Carter's campaign staff later claimed that the *Playboy* interview had robbed Carter of the decisive victory he needed to begin his presidency with strong popular support.

IMPACT

The media attention surrounding Carter's admission of adultery eventually came to represent his confusing image as an impassioned reformer with an unclear political agenda. The memory of the Watergate scandal and Ford's pardon of Nixon fostered a unique political climate that allowed Carter to run for president based on his lack of experience in federal government and the absence of any ties to Washington, D.C. While political correspondents tried to discern Carter's specific policy agendas, Carter's campaign emphasized more abstract themes of honesty, integrity, and the renewal of Americans' faith in government. He presented himself as a foil to Lyndon B. Johnson, Nixon, and Ford, who had become associated with political corruption and the Vietnam War.

Carter compensated for his unconventional mix of conservative and liberal views by framing the presidential campaign in terms of what kind of person the president should be. His discussion of religion and sexuality, delivered with an uncomfortable degree of personal disclosure, suggested that he had less in common with his constituency than voters might have assumed. It was Carter's first high-profile blunder, a moment when he looked less like a president than did his opponent.

During a campaign in which general interest in the candidates' activities had been conspicuously low, the surge in attention over Carter's embarrassing statements soured his relationship in the press and forced him to defend his own judgment as a leader. From the beginning of his campaign, journalists had accused Carter of being vague, inconsistent, and naïve, a criticism that his confusing portrayal in the *Playboy* interview appeared to confirm and one that persisted through his presidency, which ended in January, 1981.

—*Shaun Horton*

FURTHER READING

Anderson, Patrick. *Electing Jimmy Carter: The Campaign of 1976*. Baton Rouge: Louisiana State University Press, 1994. Provides an inside view of Carter's election campaign from the perspective of his speech writer.

Apostolidis, Paul, and Juliet A. Williams, eds. *Public Affairs: Politics in the Age of Sex Scandals*. Durham, N.C.: Duke University Press, 2004. A study of politics and political culture in the context of sex scandals.

Brinkley, Douglas. *The Unfinished Presidency: Jimmy Carter's Journey Beyond the White House*. New York: Penguin Putnam, 1998. Chronicles Carter's active involvement in national and global politics after his term as president.

Richardson, Don, ed. *Conversations with Carter*. Boulder, Colo.: Lynne Rienner, 1998. A selection of Carter's most revealing and well-known interviews from 1975 to 1997, with some commentary from the editor. Includes the full text of the *Playboy* interview.

Strong, Robert. *Working in the World: Jimmy Carter and the Making of U.S. Foreign Policy*. Baton Rouge: Louisiana State University Press, 2000. Describes obstacles and strategies involved in formation of Carter's approach to global politics.

SEE ALSO: May 19, 1962: Marilyn Monroe Sings "Happy Birthday, Mr. President"; July 18, 1969: Senator Edward Kennedy's Driving Accident

Kills Mary Jo Kopechne; Oct. 7, 1974: Congressman Wilbur D. Mills's Stripper Affair Leads to His Downfall; May 23, 1976: *Washington Post* Exposes Congressman Wayne L. Hays's Affair; Jan. 26, 1979: Former Vice President Nelson Rockefeller Dies Mysteriously; Late July, 1980: President's Brother, Billy Carter,

Registers as a Paid Agent for Libya; Dec. 7, 1980: Rita Jenrette's "Diary of a Mad Congresswife" Scandalizes Washington; July 20, 1982: Conservative Politician John G. Schmitz Is Found to Have Children Out of Wedlock; July 20, 1983: Congress Members Censured in House-Page Sex Scandal.

October 4, 1976
AGRICULTURE SECRETARY EARL BUTZ RESIGNS AFTER MAKING OBSCENE JOKE

Earl L. Butz, an otherwise popular and successful U.S. secretary of agriculture, was forced to resign after an obscenity-laced, racist, and sexist joke is attributed to him in the national press. He left office in disgrace and later served time in prison for tax evasion.

LOCALE: Washington, D.C.
CATEGORIES: Racism; government; politics; social issues and reform; law and the courts

KEY FIGURES
Earl L. Butz (1909-2008), U.S. secretary of agriculture, 1971-1976
John W. Dean (b. 1938), *Rolling Stone* reporter and former White House counsel
Pat Boone (b. 1934), Christian conservative commentator and singer
Gerald R. Ford (1913-2006), president of the United States, 1974-1977

SUMMARY OF EVENT
Earl L. Butz was born on an Indiana farm and became devoted to a life of farming. His passion extended into his professional life, as he served on many agriculture-related boards and with many interest groups, and he served as the dean of the School of Agriculture at his alma mater, Purdue University. He also was a racist and sexist who brought farm humor to the table. While Butz's so-

called earthy style was normal for the old boys' network of Washington, D.C., vulgarities and racist remarks would no longer be tolerated in the post-civil-rights era. It was this earthy style—the jokes—that led to his demise.

In 1974, Butz was forced to apologize for a public indiscretion that smacked of racism but was overlooked. At the World Food Conference in Rome, Butz mocked Roman Catholic pope Paul VI's position on abortion with the words "He no play-a the game, he no make-a the rules," delivered with a mock, Italian-like accent. The fact that he was mocking a culture and the celibacy of a religious leader did not sit well with many, but he was merely forced to make a public apology. Life went on and he would produce even bigger gaffes.

Butz was not actually a newcomer to Washington, D.C., having first been appointed to the Department of Agriculture by President Dwight D. Eisenhower in 1954. Butz was successful because he knew Washington, knew the players, and was very comfortable being himself. This comfort would be his undoing.

Butz was a proponent of changing the ways of agriculture in the United States. He argued that rather than paying farmers not to produce, which kept prices artificially high, agriculture should embrace a free market approach with less government interference. He believed that farmers should grow crops—lots of them. His general theme was to push farmers to grow "fence row to fence row." This would serve the Butz plan in two ways. First, it would mean lower prices for domestic food, and second, it would lead to surplus crops, which could be sold internationally.

Lower food costs and open foreign markets for export (most notably wheat sales to the Soviet Union during the Cold War) were two signature marks of the Butz policy, and both seem to have been successful. Food prices lowered, making food relatively inexpensive. In turn, many believe that cheap food led to a rise in obesity rates in the United States. As for opening markets and making money for farmers, the five years under Butz saw farm income increase almost twofold over the previous decade—largely through exports that nearly tripled during his short tenure. Butz was so successful that he received the American Farm Bureau Federation Award for Distinguished Service—an award rarely bestowed upon agricultural secretaries.

The great Butz scandal began while on an airplane leaving from the Republican National Convention in 1976. Butz settled back with a small group that included politically conservative singer Pat Boone and former Richard Nixon staffer John W. Dean. After a few drinks, Butz began telling racist and sexist jokes. He was famous for his one-liners and relished the role of entertainer. At one point he was asked by Boone why African Americans were not associated in large numbers with the Republican Party. Butz's response was not a surprise. He casually responded that blacks were interested only in shoes, sex, and a place to go to the toilet (his words were actually more descriptive and vulgar). Dean, a former Butz associate, was a reporter for *Rolling Stone* magazine at the convention. Butz's comments, attributed to a certain "shirt-sleeved cabinet member," hit the next issue of *Rolling Stone*. It did not take a tremendous amount of investigative work to figure out that Butz was the source of the disparaging remarks, given the limited passenger manifest from the airline, which was checked by the media, and his reputation for using such language.

The story was then carried by all of the major news sources and triggered a firestorm, especially among African Americans. Many in the Washington establishment wanted Butz's head, and he was now clearly a campaign liability. At a time when President Gerald R. Ford was trying to break from the shadow of Nixon, and Jimmy Carter was doing his best to make a campaign out of moral integrity, Butz provided Carter with ammunition and reminded everyone that the Nixon-Ford administration was largely the same because Ford opted to retain most of Nixon's cabinet appointees, including Butz. Ford summoned Butz to the White House and immediately chastised and reprimanded him for language that was personally offensive and inexcusable from any member of his cabinet. Butz offered to issue a public apology. This was not enough for many of Ford's advisers, who suggested that he fire Butz immediately. That was not Ford's style— he had a certain sense of loyalty to all of his people and did not want to react too quickly. Ultimately,

Earl Butz, right. (AP/Wide World Photos)

the pressure from advisers, political groups, and his own wife, Betty, would prove to be too much. Butz's comments were not only racially offensive but also were sexist, which Ford would not tolerate.

Eventually, Ford asked Butz to resign, and Butz did so tearfully on October 4, 1976. Ironically, as Butz was cleaning out his office, he reportedly said that he had told the same basic joke hundreds of times and nobody had ever complained. He still did not understand that times had changed or that he had done anything wrong.

In 1981, Butz was convicted of federal tax evasion and served twenty-five days in jail after being sentenced to five years—all but thirty days were suspended. He pleaded guilty to a charge that he underreported his 1978 income.

IMPACT

The Butz scandal came at a time of change in the way the public tolerated the indiscretions of elected officials. Indeed, the way people interact with one another had changed as well. Butz had believed he was in safe company on the airplane coming back from the Republican National Convention, but there was no longer a "safe" zone for racist and sexist banter. In addition, the scandal showed how political and public pressure in the face of racism and sexism can effectively remove a racist or sexist person from office.

Since the Butz scandal, a number of high-profile celebrities and politicians have fallen from grace because they were insensitive to others and used language that led to their demise. Furthermore, after the scandal, workers began to report inexcusable workplace behavior. This behavior was condemned during the mid-1970's with the passage of new workplace laws on sexual harassment.

—*Jeffrey S. Ashley*

FURTHER READING

Ashley, Jeffrey S. *Betty Ford: A Symbol of Strength.* New York: Nova History, 2004. While the text centers primarily on former first lady Betty Ford, it also includes discussion of the Butz scandal, how it damaged reelection hopes for Gerald Ford, and how Betty Ford took a stand in having Earl Butz fired. A common theme in the book is the Ford's relationship and partnership.

Carlson, Michael. "Earl Butz: U.S. Politician Brought Down by Racist Remark." *The Guardian*, February 4, 2008. Butz's obituary in a leading British newspaper of record. Includes the uncensored text of Butz's racist and sexist remark that led to his resignation in 1976.

Ford, Gerald R. *A Time to Heal.* New York: Harper & Row, 1979. While somewhat dated, this work is unique in that it comes from the source. Ford discusses many of the painful decisions he had to make during his presidency—including the firing of Earl Butz. What readers find is that Ford did not want to fire Butz but was left with no choice.

Greene, John Robert. *The Presidency of Gerald Ford.* Lawrence: University Press of Kansas, 1995. A comprehensive examination of the Ford presidency. Included in the text is a brief look at the Butz scandal. Of particular interest is that Ford appears to be much angrier at John Dean for reporting the incident than with Butz for his racism and sexism.

SEE ALSO: June 25, 1956: President Truman's Appointments Secretary Is Convicted of Tax Conspiracy; May 9, 1969: Supreme Court Justice Abe Fortas Is Accused of Bribery; Oct. 7, 1974: Congressman Wilbur D. Mills's Stripper Affair Leads to His Downfall; Dec. 16, 1982: Congress Cites Environmental Protection Agency Chief for Contempt; June 26, 1992: U.S. Navy Secretary Resigns in the Wake of Tailhook Sexual Assault Scandal; Sept. 24, 1992: British Cabinet Member David Mellor Resigns over Romantic Affair; June 1, 1994: Congressman Dan Rostenkowski Is Indicted in House Post Office Scandal; Aug. 5, 1994: Kenneth Starr Is Appointed to the Whitewater Investigation; Aug. 21, 1994: Sex Scandal Forces Dismissal of NAACP Chief Benjamin Chavis; Dec. 11, 1997: HUD Secretary Henry Cisneros Is Indicted for Lying to Federal Agents; Apr. 11, 2007: Shock Jock Don Imus Loses His Radio Show Over Sexist and Racist Remarks.

November 9, 1976
GERMAN GENERALS MUST RETIRE FOR SUPPORTING A NEO-NAZI PILOT

Two leading West German air force generals were forced to retire after inviting to a military reunion the unrepentant neo-Nazi extremist Hans-Ulrich Rudel. The generals suggested that Rudel, a decorated World War II bomber pilot, deserved the same chance at forgiveness the former communist Herbert Wehner had received when he became a Social Democratic leader in the German parliament.

LOCALE: Bonn, West Germany (now in Germany)

CATEGORIES: Military; politics; government

KEY FIGURES

Hans-Ulrich Rudel (1916-1982), former German World War II combat pilot

Walter Krupinski (1920-2000), lieutenant general, commander of the West German air force

Karl Heinz Franke (b. 1923), major general, West German air force, and Walter Krupinski's deputy

Georg Leber (b. 1920), West German defense minister, 1972-1978

Hermann Schmidt (1917-1983), parliamentary secretary for the West German ministry of defense, 1975-1976

Manfred Wörner (1934-1994), West German defense minister, 1982-1988

Herbert Wehner (1906-1990), chairman of the Social Democratic delegation in the West German parliament, 1969-1983

SUMMARY OF EVENT

The Bundeswehr (the West German armed forces) was created only a decade after the complete defeat of Nazi Germany in 1945, and most of the initial volunteer officers and noncommissioned officers had served in Adolf Hitler's Wehrmacht (armed forces). The new democratic West German government and its military advisers, however, wanted to insulate the Bundeswehr from Nazi traditions and

to ensure that it, unlike several previous German military forces, was completely compliant with the democratic civilian government established in 1949.

Both of these goals were challenged by the presence of the highly decorated, right-wing, World War II Stuka bomber pilot Hans-Ulrich Rudel at an air force squadron's unit-tradition meeting in October, 1976. Rudel's participation at the meeting was defended by two air force generals who suggested that Rudel should be forgiven for his neo-Nazi political past just as Herbert Wehner, a major Social Democratic leader in the Bundestag, was forgiven for his communist past.

In 1965, the defense ministry issued a directive on the issue of tradition in the Bundeswehr. The directive allowed air, naval, and land forces to name some units and bases after prominent Wehrmacht officers as long as those persons were not involved in Nazi crimes. However, the army chose not to adopt old unit designations from pre-1945 German military units. The air force, however, with the permission of its chief of staff, did allow links to German squadrons of that war. One of the Bundeswehr's reconnaissance squadrons was named Immelmann for the World War I German fighter pilot Max Immelmann. In 1935, the new German air force under Hitler had selected that name as well for one of its units.

The major problem that an air unit faced in planning any tradition meeting with members of the World War II Immelmann squadron was that its former leader was Rudel, who served as commander of the Immelmann dive-bomber squadron during World War II. He was the most highly decorated German fighter, credited with destroying over five hundred enemy tanks, but he did not detach himself from the Nazis. His postwar career included support of former Nazis who had fled to Latin America, and after his return to Germany he campaigned for neo-Nazi political parties. Not surprisingly, until

1976, defense ministers banned Rudel from West German military bases.

In 1975, the commander of the Bundeswehr's Immelmann reconnaissance squadron 51 asked his superiors to allow a tradition meeting with survivors of the World War II Stuka Immelmann squadron. The state secretary for the defense ministry, Hermann Schmidt, refused to permit the meeting, fearing what might happen if Rudel were allowed to appear at an air force base. Manfred Wörner, a member of the Christian Democratic defense committee in parliament and a reserve officer, joined the debate after being notified of Schmidt's decision. He wrote Schmidt a letter that praised Rudel's military accomplishments in World War II and claimed ignorance of his political views.

Three months after receiving this letter, Schmidt informed Wörner that the issue had been resolved. Schmidt allegedly had approved of the meeting if held outside the air force base. The tradition meeting also received the enthusiastic support of General Walter Krupinski, the commander of West Germany's combat air force. Krupinski, a recipient of the Knight's Cross with Oak Leaves award during World War II, had flown cover for Rudel's unit on the eastern front. Krupinski informed the Immelmann squadron that the meeting could take place on the base.

The Immelmann tradition meeting was held on October 23 at the Bremgarten air base near Freiburg in southwestern West Germany. Rudel participated in the weekend festivities, which included a review of German jet flights, and he signed autographs for enthusiastic pilots. German press accounts noted Rudel's visit but initially did not predict major consequences. What produced the crisis was the off-the-record statement to the press by General Karl Heinz Franke, Krupinski's deputy.

After the meeting, Franke defended Rudel's appearance by suggesting that the decorated pilot had changed his political views, as had former "left-wing extremists." He specifically named Bundestag member Wehner as an example; General Krupinski supported Franke. Although Wehner had joined the Communist Party in 1927, after the war he became a member of the West German Social

Democratic Party and, unlike Rudel, fully accepted the new democratic state established in 1949. Rudel told the German magazine *Der Spiegel* after the tradition meeting that he was a proud ultraconservative.

The West German defense minister, Georg Leber, a World War II air force veteran who had a reputation for being too promilitary, had to react to this attack on a leading Social Democratic politician. Moreover, forty Social Democratic members of the Bundestag demanded action from Leber and cautioned that political control of the army had declined. Indeed, one general had accepted a free vacation from the government of apartheid South Africa, and another general took part in a victory parade in Madrid commemorating Spanish general Francisco Franco's triumph in 1939 over the republican government in Spain.

In an interview with *Der Spiegel*, Leber declared that he fired the two generals on November 1 because of their comments to the press about a member of the Bundestag. The two resigned on November 9. For the first time in the twenty-five-year history of the Bundeswehr, two generals were dismissed summarily to send a message that the Bundeswehr must rely on its own tradition for dealing with internal crises and, just as important, not meddle in parliamentary affairs.

IMPACT

The immediate consequences of the Rudel affair were the resignation of State Secretary Schmidt and Leber's announcement that the general who had accepted a trip to South Africa had asked to be relieved and that no general would again participate in a Franco victory parade. Parliamentary control over the military leadership was clearly demonstrated by this time.

More important for the long run was an attack on the tradition guidelines of 1965, beginning with Chancellor Helmut Schmidt's announcement on West German television on November 12 that the guidelines would have to be reexamined. Leber also asked his military advisers for a position paper on that topic, but he could not complete that project because he resigned in 1978 in the wake of a military

504

counterintelligence scandal. Still, the Social Democrats and the left wing in general launched a massive attack on traditions that linked the Bundeswehr to the Wehrmacht, an attack that was supported by the new Social Democratic defense minister. Subsequent research by scholars, which revealed the Wehrmacht's complicity in Nazi atrocities, provided even more support for a revision of the 1965 guidelines.

On September 20, 1982, those new guidelines became a reality, making it clear that the Third Reich and Wehrmacht had no place in the tradition of the Bundeswehr. One paragraph in particular rejected the defenders of Rudel, who had stressed his military deeds by declaring that military accomplishments must be rooted in "a state grounded in the law." Another paragraph allowed tradition meetings but only by individuals who supported the Basic Law, West Germany's constitution. Although the new Christian Democratic government after 1982 modified some of the clauses of the new guidelines, the guidelines remained basically unchanged.

Increasingly, the German defense ministry and the Bundestag removed traces of the Wehrmacht's tradition. In 1995, a base named for General Eduard Dietl in Füssen was renamed for its location, Allgäu, and pilot Werner Mölder's name was removed from an air force base in 2005. Moreover, the German government and press continued to monitor extreme right-wing activities in the Bundeswehr.

—*Johnpeter Horst Grill*

FURTHER READING

Abenheim, Donald. *Reforging the Iron Cross: The Search for Tradition in the West German Armed Forces.* Princeton, N.J.: Princeton University Press, 1988. An excellent work on the attempts to establish democratic symbols and references for the Bundeswehr. Includes an informative chapter on changes in the military after the Rudel scandal. Solid bibliography.

Brust, Klaus-Markus. *Culture and the Transformation of the Bundeswehr.* Berlin: Hartmann Miles, 2007. Focuses on the impact of European identity on *innere führung* (inner leadership) in the Bundeswehr.

Just, Günther. *Stuka-Pilot Hans-Ulrich Rudel: His Life Story in Words and Photographs.* Translated by David Johnston. West Chester, Pa.: Schiffer, 1990. Complimentary treatment of Rudel's military career, which reflects his views. Unfortunately ignores his persistent postwar Nazi sympathies.

Large, David Clay. *Germans to the Front: West German Rearmament in the Adenauer Era.* Chapel Hill: University of North Carolina Press, 1996. Scholarly examination of the establishment of the Bundeswehr. Includes sections on veterans' organizations.

Shpiro, Shlomo. "Barking or Biting? Media and Parliamentary Investigation of Right-Wing Extremism in the Bundeswehr." *German Politics* 9, no. 2 (August, 2000): 217-240. Revealing account of the problem of contacts between right-wing extremists and the Bundeswehr, particularly in 1997-1998.

Thompson, Wayne C. *Political Odyssey of Herbert Wehner.* Boulder, Colo.: Westview Press, 1993. Based on sources that reveal Wehner's questionable collaboration with the Soviet secret police during his exile in Moscow.

SEE ALSO: Apr. 22, 1942: French Prime Minister Pierre Laval Wants Germany to Win World War II; Aug. 14, 1945: French War Hero Pétain Is Convicted of Nazi Collaboration; Oct. 26, 1962: West German Police Raid *Der Spiegel* Magazine Offices; Apr. 25, 1983: German Magazine Publishes Faked Hitler Diaries; Aug. 19, 1985: West German Counterintelligence Chief Defects to East Germany; Mar. 3, 1986: Former U.N. Secretary-General Kurt Waldheim's Nazi Past Is Revealed; Aug. 12, 2006: Novelist Günter Grass Admits to Youthful Nazi Ties.

January, 1977
SINGER ANITA BRYANT CAMPAIGNS AGAINST LESBIAN AND GAY RIGHTS

Conservative Christian entertainer Anita Bryant started a campaign to overturn a human rights ordinance in Florida's Dade County that prohibited discrimination against lesbians and gays. Buoyed by her initial success with the ordinance's repeal, she transformed her campaign into a national Christian political movement but also unleashed a newly determined gay rights movement.

LOCALE: Dade County, Florida

CATEGORIES: Human rights; music and performing arts; politics; religion; sex; social issues and reform

KEY FIGURES

Anita Bryant (b. 1940), American singer and entertainer

Jerry Falwell (1933-2007), American conservative evangelist and commentator

SUMMARY OF EVENT

During the 1970's, a fledgling lesbian and gay rights movement was taking shape in certain regions of the United States, fueled especially by the 1969 Stonewall Rebellion in New York City. In addition to encouraging pride parades and rallies, the movement had begun to win legal cases and helped institute local ordinances against discrimination at the city and county levels. On January 18, 1977, in Florida, the Dade County Commission passed one of the first human rights ordinances in the United States that also prohibited discrimination based on a person's sexual orientation.

The American Psychiatric Association, the American Psychological Association, and the American Medical Association had dropped homosexuality from their lists of mental disorders. Given these swift and powerful social changes, the Southern Baptist community responded with calls against lesbian and gay rights and for the repeal of the new antidiscrimination laws. Christian psychologists, including Charles W. Socarides, promoted the idea that homosexuality not only was a disorder but also was curable. Many Christians believe that this cure is possible through faith in Jesus Christ.

Anita Bryant, a Christian singer and entertainer, began her singing career at the age of six, performing at local fairgrounds near her hometown of Barnsdall, Oklahoma. At the age of sixteen she persuaded her Southern Baptist father to allow her to attend a local audition for Arthur Godfrey's talent show. This exposure encouraged her to enter other talent and beauty pageants. At the age of eighteen she won Miss Oklahoma and became second runner-up in the 1959 Miss America contest. After this victory, Bryant was dedicated to a career in Christian music, where she accumulated a modicum of success. At the height of her career, during the late 1960's, she became the national spokesperson for the Florida Citrus Commission and appeared in many of its television commercials. It was in this role that she became almost a household name.

Armed with strongly held religious beliefs and aware of her celebrity, Bryant spearheaded an attempt to repeal the human rights measure passed by voters in Dade County, a county that includes the cosmopolitan and relatively progressive city of Miami. Soon after the ordinance was passed, she founded a campaign called Save Our Children and became its lead spokesperson and crusader. She gathered fellow social conservatives to develop a strong political machine centered on "Christian beliefs regarding the sinfulness of homosexuality" and the "proclivity" of gays and lesbians to recruit children into their "lifestyle."

"As a mother," Bryant argued, "I know that homosexuals cannot biologically reproduce children; therefore, they must recruit our children." She continued,"If gays are granted rights, next we'll have to give rights to prostitutes and to people who sleep with St. Bernards and to nail biters." This message, coupled with a still-fledgling gay and lesbian rights movement without a visible and vocal leadership, led to public fears of pedophilia and child abuse. Bryant's campaign was successful, and the Dade County ordinance was repealed by 69 percent of the county's voters.

Bryant moved her campaign to the national stage. *Newsweek* magazine featured her on its cover on June 6, 1977. Through this media exposure she began to inspire many national leaders to join her campaign. The campaign coalesced into what is now known as the Religious Right, or Christian Right. Among those figures who joined her was Baptist preacher Jerry Falwell. Falwell, in 1979, formed the powerful Moral Majority and broadened the political scope of his conservative Christian organization.

In 1978, California state senator John V. Briggs attempted to use Bryant's techniques to pass an antigay initiative (called the Briggs Initiative) that would have kept gay and lesbian teachers from working in California schools. Gay and lesbian rights advocates, led by San Francisco councilman Harvey Milk (who was assassinated in 1978), countered these arguments. They gathered support from an unlikely coalition of politicians, liberals as well as conservatives, and defeated the initiative.

The rise in social conservatism, along with an atmosphere of fear, prompted many reversals of antidiscrimination laws. Political candidates with antigay campaign platforms were swept into office throughout the country. In Florida, a law was passed outlawing adoption by gays and lesbians. Lesbian and gay activists soon mobilized and challenged the Religious Right. A well-organized boycott against the Florida Citrus Commission secured a number of celebrity endorsements, including those of entertainers Bette Midler and Barbra Streisand.

Bryant was not prepared for the fierce resistance to her campaign. Her contract with the Florida Citrus Commission was not renewed, leading to the boycott's cancellation. At a televised press conference in Des Moines, Iowa, she was publicly humiliated when someone threw a pie in her face. Her marriage ended in divorce in 1980, disappointing her Christian fan base and harming her Christian music career. She remarried and attempted to revive her career as a singer. During the 1990's, she filed for bankruptcy in two states.

In 1998, Dade County officially repudiated Bryant's successful campaign of twenty years earlier and reauthorized, after a 7-6 vote, an antidiscrimination ordinance protecting people from discrimination based on sexual orientation. In 2002, a Florida ballot initiative, Amendment 14, which attempted to repeal the 1998 antidiscrimination law, failed at election time, with 56 percent of the voters in favor of keeping the 1998 law in place. In 2004, a

1970's

Anita Bryant was famously "pied" in the face at a televised news conference in 1977. "Well, at least it's a fruit pie" was her first response. With her is her husband, Bob Green. (AP/Wide World Photos)

federal appellate court upheld Florida's antigay adoption law against a constitutional challenge.

IMPACT

Bryant's Save Our Children campaign prompted a national dialogue on gay and lesbian rights. A line was drawn, however, between the views of the Religious Right and those of the gay rights movement. The AIDS epidemic that began during the early 1980's gave new life to the Religious Right and its antigay politics, and moral-values voters remained a powerful faction of the electorate into the first decade of the twenty-first century.

In turn, the movement for gay and lesbian rights also was given new life. Beginning during the late 1980's with the radical politics of groups such as the AIDS Coalition to Unleash Power (ACT UP) and Queer Nation, gay rights advocates began to frame the argument as a civil rights issue. In *Lawrence v. Texas* (2003), the U.S. Supreme Court found state sodomy laws unconstitutional, a ruling that re-energized the gay rights movement. Same-gender relationships in the form of marriages, civil unions, and domestic partnerships became legal in several states; in May, 2008, California's Supreme Court ruled that gays and lesbians could legally marry.

The trend toward supporting lesbians and gays continues, long after Bryant's very public and successful campaign of 1977. A noticeable change has occurred in television, film, and literature, as gay and lesbian characters and story lines are now featured more prominently. Celebrities and other public figures have been coming out of the so-called closet, especially since the early 1990's, and continue to do so. Even many religious leaders have embraced gays and lesbians. The United Methodist Church, the Episcopal Church, and the United Church of Christ, in particular, have made positive strides toward acceptance, and many of those churches that retain a position against homosexuality have tempered their criticism.

—*Daniel-Raymond Nadon*

FURTHER READING

Bryant, Anita. *The Anita Bryant Story: The Survival of Our Nation's Families and the Threat of Militant Homosexuality*. Old Tappan, N.J.: Revell, 1977. Bryant's autobiography, focused on her war against "militant" homosexuality and its alleged destruction of the family.

Faderman, Lillian, et al., eds. *Great Events from History: Gay, Lesbian, Bisexual, Transgender Events, 1848-2006*. 2 vols. Pasadena, Calif.: Salem Press, 2007. This two-volume set, which includes an article on Anita Bryant and her Save Our Children campaign, highlights significant events and people in the history of lesbian and gay culture around the world.

Howard, John. *Men Like That: A Southern Queer History*. Chicago: University of Chicago Press, 1999. Explores the history of gay culture in the southern United States, an area often neglected in histories of lesbians and gays, which normally focus on urban life.

Lane, Frederick S. *The Decency Wars: The Campaign to Cleanse American Culture*. Amherst, N.Y.: Prometheus Books, 2006. A study of the conservative campaign against First Amendment rights in the United States. Includes the chapter "'A Soldier in God's Army': Anita Bryant, Jerry Falwell, and the Rise of Evangelical Politics."

Miller, Neil. *Out of the Past: Gay and Lesbian History from 1869 to the Present*. Rev. ed. New York: Alyson Books, 2006. First published in 1995, this comprehensive work by an award-winning author is a classic reference in lesbian and gay history. A good starting point that includes many primary source materials.

SEE ALSO: Oct. 7, 1964: President Lyndon B. Johnson's Aide Is Arrested in Gay-Sex Sting; 1970: Study of Anonymous Gay Sex Leads to Ethics Scandal; Oct. 25, 1974: Evangelist Billy James Hargis Resigns College Presidency During Gay-Sex Scandal; Sept., 1976: Jimmy Carter Admits Committing Adultery in His Heart; Aug. 4, 1978: British Politician Jeremy Thorpe Is Charged with Attempted Murder; Sept. 3, 1980: Congressman Bauman Is Arrested for Liaison with Teenage Boy; July 20, 1982: Conservative Politician John G. Schmitz Is Found to Have

Children Out of Wedlock; Mar. 19, 1987: Jim Bakker Resigns as Head of PTL Television Network; Feb. 21, 1988: Evangelist Jimmy Swaggart Tearfully Confesses His Adultery; Sept. 19, 2000: Ex-gay Leader John Paulk Is Photo-

graphed Leaving a Gay Bar; Aug. 19, 2004: Blog "Outs" Antigay Congressman Edward Schrock; Nov. 2, 2006: Male Escort Reveals Sexual Liaisons with Evangelist Ted Haggard.

February 25, 1977
FILM PRODUCER DAVID BEGELMAN IS FOUND TO HAVE FORGED CHECKS

David Begelman, the studio president of Columbia Pictures since 1973, wrote checks to others that he cashed himself. The forgeries came to light when actor Cliff Robertson received an IRS Form 1099 from Columbia for income he never received. Investigators found that Begelman had written a check to Robertson, forged the actor's name, and cashed the check himself. Years after the scandal, Begelman was found dead in an apparent suicide.

ALSO KNOWN AS: Begelman affair; Robertson affair; Begelgate; Hollywoodgate
LOCALES: Los Angeles, California; New York, New York
CATEGORIES: Forgery; hoaxes, frauds, and charlatanism; corruption; banking and finance; business; law and the courts; Hollywood

KEY FIGURES
David Begelman (1921-1995), studio president of Columbia Pictures
Cliff Robertson (b. 1925), Academy Award-winning actor
Alan Hirschfield (b. 1936), president and chief executive officer of Columbia
Herbert Allen, Jr. (1940), member of the board of directors of Columbia
Ray Stark (1915-2004), film producer
Robert Todd Lang (b. 1924), Columbia's chief legal counsel
Joyce Silvey (1943-1982), detective, Beverly Hills Police Department
Peter Gruenberger (b. 1937), attorney

SUMMARY OF EVENT
On February 25, 1977, actor Cliff Robertson, who earlier had been represented by Hollywood agent and later studio executive David Begelman, received Internal Revenue Service Form 1099 (for miscellaneous income) from Columbia Pictures, indicating he had received $10,000 from the company in 1976. However, Robertson never received the money. Furthermore, he soon discovered that his endorsement on the check in question had been forged. The handwriting clearly was not his, and the check was signed incorrectly as, simply, "Cliff Robertson." The real Cliff Robertson signed his full name, "Clifford T. Robertson," on all legal documents, including checks. The actor then reported the forgery to police.

The Los Angeles and Beverly Hills Police departments, led by detective Joyce Silvey, and the Federal Bureau of Investigation verified that the $10,000 check was indeed a forgery and interviewed the manager of the Beverly Hills branch of the Wells Fargo Bank where the check was cashed. The manager informed the investigators that Begelman, now head of Columbia's motion picture division, had exchanged the check, made out to Robertson, for traveler's checks, also for Robertson. However, in retrospect, what was odd about the transaction was that the two had parted ways before Begelman cashed the check. Their business relationship had ended acrimoniously: Begelman (as a Hollywood agent) had been fired by Robertson (his client at the time) for siding with a film company in a dispute with the actor.

509

Columbia allowed Begelman to take a leave of absence in July, 1977, and began its own investigation, led by attorney Peter Gruenberger, a partner in Columbia's primary law firm of Weil, Gotshal, and Manges. Gruenberger had previous experience with sensitive inquiries and was considered ideal for the job. His team consisted of associates from the law firm and members of the accounting firm Price Waterhouse. Team members interviewed Begelman for two days and Begelman's psychiatrist for two hours. They also examined about twenty thousand checks and discovered that Begelman had embezzled an additional $65,000 through forgery. In addition, they found that he had abused his expense accounts and used company cars for personal business.

Upon presenting his report to the board, Gruenberger found to his surprise that some of the Columbia board members were openly hostile to him and questioned his objectivity. However, Alan Hirschfield, Columbia's president and chief executive officer, accepted Gruenberger's findings and decided to fire Begelman. Columbia's chief counsel, Robert Todd Lang, concurred with Hirschfield in private, but his legal opinion on the issue was neutral. This opinion gave the board of directors the option to retain Begelman. The board, led by Herbert Allen, Jr., chose to retain Begelman and disputed Hirschfield's decision.

Begelman also had the support of Ray Stark, who was the most important independent producer working with the studio at the time. Stark persuaded a majority of board members that Begelman, not Hirschfield, was primarily responsible for Columbia's success during the 1970's, especially with the hit film *Close Encounters of the Third Kind* (1977), and that he was indispensable. Hirschfield backed down, and Begelman was reinstated in December.

Still angry with Begelman, Robertson gave an interview to *The Washington Post*. Other mainstream newspapers and magazines began their own investigations. *New West Magazine* resurrected an old accusation against Begelman, also involving theft. Rumors existed that Begelman, as actor-singer Judy Garland's agent, embezzled some of her money as well. A writer for *New West Magazine*

also discovered that Begelman's claim to be a graduate of Yale Law School was false, and that his time on the Yale campus consisted only of a short stint with a U.S. Air Force training school during World War II.

On January 12, 1978, syndicated columnist Liz Smith devoted a column to the story and later interviewed Robertson herself. On February 28, the U.S. Securities and Exchange Commission (SEC) launched an investigation of its own. The SEC did not find violations of federal law, but its investigation ended much more quietly than it began. Allen and the rest of the Columbia board came to realize that Begelman could no longer work effectively for the company, and he was allowed to resign to become an independent producer. Having lost the confidence of the Columbia board, Hirschfield, too, was fired in July.

Begelman pleaded no contest to the forgery and embezzlement charges and was sentenced to community service. Through this service he produced the documentary *Angel Dust* (1979), a film about the dangers of the drug PCP. By the mid-1990's, Begelman was broke and he declared bankruptcy. In 1995, he was found dead, shot in an apparent suicide in a Los Angeles hotel room.

IMPACT

As a result of the scandal, the Los Angeles District Attorney's Office established an Entertainment Industry Task Force to investigate wrongdoing in the industry. A special hotline was developed for anonymous tips. After two years, the task force received more than six hundred tips about possible wrongdoing at nearly every major film studio in the region.

Begelman's career did not suffer in the immediate aftermath of the scandal. In 1979, he was hired as chief executive officer of Metro-Goldwyn-Mayer (MGM). He was unable to repeat his success at Columbia, so he left MGM in 1982. He had some success as an independent producer with *Mannequin* (1987) and *Weekend at Bernie's* (1989). Hirschfield became chief executive officer of Twentieth Century Fox in 1981. Robertson believed he was blacklisted for his role in exposing the scandal. Ironically, Robertson's first film role after the scandal broke was *Brainstorm* (1983), a film produced at MGM during Begelman's tenure there.

It remains a mystery why Begelman took the money, which he did not need. Begelman's psychiatrist believed that his client felt guilty about his success and had a neurotic need to self-destruct.

—*Thomas R. Feller*

FURTHER READING

Clarke, Gerald. *Get Happy: The Life of Judy Garland.* New York: Random House, 2000. The author supports the allegation that studio executive David Begelman embezzled money from his onetime client, actor-singer Judy Garland.

Fink, Steven. *Crisis Management: Planning for the Inevitable.* New York: American Management Association, 1986. One chapter in this work on managing particular crises at work analyzes the Begelman forgery and embezzlement scandal as an example of how not to handle a crisis at the corporate level.

Harpole, Charles, et al. *Lost Illusions: American Cinema in the Shadow of Viet Nam and Watergate, 1970-1979.* New York: Simon & Schuster, 2000. This work on American cinema during the 1970's examines the David Begelman-Alan Hirschfield administration at Columbia Pictures.

McClintick, David. *Indecent Exposure: A True Story of Hollywood and Wall Street.* New York: William Morrow, 1982. A comprehensive account of the Begelman forgery and embezzlement scandal by a reporter for *The Wall Street Journal.*

SEE ALSO: Feb. 1, 1922: Director Taylor's Murder Ruins Mabel Normand's Acting Career; Jan. 18, 1923: Actor Wallace Reid's Death in Drug Rehab Shakes Film Industry; Sept. 4, 1932: Film Star Jean Harlow's Husband Is an Apparent Suicide; May, 1955: Scandal Magazine Reveals Actor Rory Calhoun's Criminal Past; Feb. 3, 1975: Honduras's "Bananagate" Bribery Scandal Leads to Executive's Suicide; July 28, 2006: Actor Mel Gibson Is Caught Making Anti-Semitic Remarks.

1970'S

September 21, 1977
CARTER CABINET MEMBER RESIGNS OVER ETHICS VIOLATIONS

Bert Lance was forced to resign as head of the U.S. Office of Management and Budget during the first year of U.S. president Jimmy Carter's administration because of allegations of illegal banking by Lance while chairman of the National Bank of Georgia and due to his overly familiar business dealings with the Carter family.

LOCALE: Washington, D.C.
CATEGORIES: Corruption; government; banking and finance; politics

KEY FIGURES

Bert Lance (b. 1931), head of the U.S. Office of Management and Budget, 1977, and former chairman of the National Bank of Georgia

Jimmy Carter (b. 1924), president of the United States, 1977-1981

Abraham A. Ribicoff (1910-1998), U.S. senator from Connecticut, 1963-1981, and chairman of the Senate Government Affairs Committee

John G. Heimann (b. 1929), comptroller of the U.S. Treasury, 1977-1981

Donald Tarleton (fl. 1970's), regional director, U.S. Office of Comptroller of the Currency, Atlanta

SUMMARY OF EVENT

Jimmy Carter, inaugurated as president of the United States on January 20, 1977, appointed Bert Lance, one of his closest friends, to head the U.S. Office of Management and Budget (OMB). Over

511

the years, Carter's association with Lance had grown into an enduring friendship. The Carters, including First Lady Rosalyn Carter, even considered Lance a surrogate family member.

Lance, a small-town banker in Calhoun, Georgia, ran unsuccessfully for the governorship of Georgia in 1974 and, in doing so, incurred debts that he never fully repaid. Following his failed gubernatorial campaign, he left Calhoun to become president of the National Bank of Georgia (NBG), based in Atlanta. Shortly afterward, Lance and some business associates, using a complicated network of loans involving millions of dollars, bought a controlling interest in the bank of which Lance had become president. Lance owned more than 200,000 shares of stock in NBG and derived a substantial portion of his income from the dividends his shares paid.

To avoid being accused of conflicts of interests, persons appointed to high public office usually divest themselves of assets that might raise questions about their impartiality. In Lance's case, President Carter knew that Lance's major holding in NBG could prove embarrassing, if not unethical. He also realized that this holding constituted a major portion of Lance's net worth and that it had declined in a deteriorating stock market, making it a bad time for Lance to be forced to liquidate his stock.

On July 10, 1977, Carter wrote to Senator Abraham A. Ribicoff, chairman of the Senate Government Affairs Committee, requesting a modification in an earlier agreement that forced Lance to dispose of his stock by the end of 1977. Carter explained to Ribicoff that if Lance were forced to dispose of his stock, he would be placed under considerable financial pressure. Requests of this sort were frequently viewed as routine.

As early as 1975, however, the U.S. Office of Comptroller of the Currency had been investigating some irregularities involving Lance at the Calhoun First National Bank (CFNB), where he still served as chairman of the board of directors. This investigation revealed that during a four-year period, Lance and members of his family had run up as much as $450,000 in overdrafts at CFNB.

Other unsettling facts began to emerge, including information that NBG, to attract Lance as its president, had agreed to provide him with an airplane that ultimately was bought from Lancelot & Company, a partnership owned by Lance and his wife, LaBelle Lance, for $120,000. Lancelot & Company had a year earlier paid $80,000 for that aircraft. It also was revealed that Lance's bank earlier had lent money to the peanut company owned by President Carter and his brother, Billy Carter. Although such a loan was legitimate, it raised discomfiting questions about the Carter-Lance relationship.

An agent with the Federal Bureau of Investigation looking into an embezzlement case that focused on a CFNB official stumbled upon irregularities that involved the Lances. The agent attempted to subpoena bank records but was rebuffed by the bank's president. Lance apparently did not apprise President Carter of this ongoing investigation or of the bank's refusal to cooperate fully.

Lance met with Carter following the November election to discuss being appointed head of the OMB. Lance then approached Donald Tarleton, director of the comptroller's regional office in Atlanta and, telling him of Carter's wish to appoint him to the OMB post, suggested that he ease up on the investigation of CFNB. Tarleton did so immediately after his meeting with Lance.

Senior officials in the comptroller's Washington, D.C., office, including its acting director, Robert Bloom, were outraged by Tarleton's actions. Bloom, however, wanted to cooperate with the Carter administration in the hope of being appointed comptroller. Bloom did what he could to help Lance, even writing a press release that Lance could use to cover up details relating to CFNB's difficulties.

Lance's problems might have ended at this point had it not been for Carter's appointment of John G. Heimann to the comptroller's post. On December 1, 1976, Sidney Smith, Lance's attorney, asked U.S. attorney John Stokes about the status of the Lance case. Stokes removed the prosecutor from the case the same day and, on the following day, said the case was closed. Carter then announced Lance's appointment as head of the OMB. Carter, who had campaigned on a platform of restoring integrity to the government, was placed in an awkward position, although he and the First Lady supported Lance as fully as they could for the nine months he served the administration.

It was also revealed that the day before his appointment, Lance had sought a loan of some $3.4 million, which he finally obtained from the First National Bank of Chicago. When he took office, he was more than $5 million in debt. Senators Ribicoff and Charles H. Percy led an investigation that unearthed many irregularities in Lance's business dealings. Following Lance's forced resignation, however, he was found innocent of intentional criminal wrongdoing.

Meanwhile, Jody Powell, Carter's press secretary, surreptitiously circulated press stories accusing Percy of unethical practices, a tactic that eventually came to light and evoked memories of the attempted Watergate cover-up that brought down the administration of U.S. president Richard Nixon. Investigative reporters latched onto the attempted cover-up, which led to further investigations by the Senate's Government Affairs Committee.

On September 19, Lance had a forty-five minute White House conference with Carter, and on September 21, he resigned as head of the OMB. Carter, in an emotional press conference the following day, announced Lance's resignation.

IMPACT

The scandal of Lance's bank dealings and his resignation as head of the OMB was unfortunate for the president and the United States as a whole. The status of the new Carter administration, devoted to upholding ethics in government, was badly damaged in the eyes of the public. The government comptroller and the Senate committee appointed to investigate the matter discovered an increasingly complex muddle of questionable actions, more oversights than intentional crimes, on Lance's part.

The closeness of Lance to the president and his family increased substantially the impact of these revelations. Actions by both the president and Lance led people to believe the two were participating in a cover-up, which, in the context of govern-

mental affairs, could bring down an entire administration. If any lesson was learned from the Lance debacle, it was that transparency in government affairs is inevitably the best policy. Deception and duplicity eventually come to light, especially in countries in which a free press scrutinizes the government and civil servants.

—R. Baird Shuman

FURTHER READING

Dumbrell, John. *The Carter Presidency: A Reevaluation.* New York: Manchester University Press, 1993. Dumbrell offers fleeting references to the Bert Lance affair. Valuable for placing this scandal within the broader context of Jimmy Carter's presidency.

Fink, Gary M., and Hugh Davis Graham, eds. *The Carter Presidency: Policy Choices in the Post-New Deal Era.* Lawrence: University Press of Kansas, 1998. Melvyn Dubofsky's chapter, "Jimmy Carter and the End of the Politics of Productivity," contains cogent insights into the Carter-Lance matter.

Johnson, Haynes. *In the Absence of Power: Governing America.* New York: Viking Press, 1980. Although dated, this account of the Lance scandal is detailed, accurate, well written, and easily accessible.

Lance, Bert, with Bill Gibson. *The Truth of the Matter: My Life In and Out of Politics.* New York: Summit Books, 1991. In this book, Lance tries to vindicate himself, largely by emphasizing the differences between banking practices in the rural South and those of the great financial centers of the United States.

Lance, LaBelle. *This, Too, Shall Pass.* New York: Bantam Books, 1978. A heartfelt account of the problems of LaBelle Lance's husband during the Carter administration, published a year after his forced resignation. Although not wholly objective, provides many useful details.

Roberts, Robert North. *Ethics in U.S. Government: An Encyclopedia of Investigations, Scandals, Reforms, and Legislation.* Westport, Conn.: Greenwood Press, 2001. A comprehensive encyclopedia documenting American political scandals, ethical controversies, and investigations from 1775 to 2000.

SEE ALSO: Mar. 2, 1923: U.S. Senate Investigates Veterans Bureau Chief for Fraud; May 30, 1923: U.S. Attorney General Harry M. Daugherty's Aide Commits Suicide; Oct. 22, 1923: U.S. Senate Begins Hearings on Teapot Dome Oil Leases; Nov. 16, 1951: Federal Tax Official Resigns After Accepting Bribes; Sept. 22, 1958: President Eisenhower's Chief of Staff Resigns for Influence Selling; 1976-1977: U.S. Congress Members Are Implicated in Koreagate Scandal; Sept., 1976: Jimmy Carter Admits Committing Adultery in His Heart; Oct. 11, 1979: Senate Denounces Herman E. Talmadge for Money Laundering; May 7, 1985: Banker Jake Butcher Pleads Guilty to Fraud; Dec. 11, 1997: HUD Secretary Henry Cisneros Is Indicted for Lying to Federal Agents; Mar. 4, 2004: Former United Way Charity Chief Pleads Guilty to Embezzlement.

September 23, 1977
HORSE-SWAPPING FRAUD UPSETS BELMONT PARK RACEWAY

Belmont Raceway veterinarian Mark Gerard collected a large payoff when he wagered on the horse Lebón, a long-shot entry who finished first in a claiming race. It was later revealed that the winning horse was not actually Lebón but a faster horse imported from Uruguay. The Gerard affair led to improved identification standards for thoroughbreds in horse racing.

LOCALE: Hempstead, New York
CATEGORIES: Hoaxes, frauds, and charlatanism; sports; corruption; organized crime and racketeering; business

KEY FIGURES
Mark Gerard (b. 1934), Belmont Raceway veterinarian and horse importer
Jack Morgan (fl. 1970's), former assistant to Mark Gerard and owner of racehorse Lebón
William Berry (fl. 1970's), chief of the New York Racing and Wagering board
Ogden Mills Phipps (b. 1940), chairman of the New York Racing Association

SUMMARY OF EVENT
Mark Gerard was a well-respected track veterinarian at Belmont Park Raceway in New York. He had cared for the famous racehorse Secretariat, winner of the Triple Crown in 1973, and for many other outstanding thoroughbreds. Gerard had a successful practice and was able to hire other veterinarians and assistants to work with him.

Although his veterinary practice returned a substantial income, Gerard hoped to increase his wealth by purchasing horses in South America and then importing and reselling them in the United States. He bought the horses at bargain prices and then resold them for many times the price he paid. As a veterinarian practicing at a thoroughbred racetrack, he could not own and race the horses himself. Such activity was considered a conflict of interest. However, importing horses for resale was legal, and it was an acceptable way for him to profit financially.

Early in June of 1977, Gerard imported three horses from Uruguay for resale. One of the horses was a raced-out claiming horse named Lebón, who was bought for six hundred dollars a few weeks before Gerard purchased him, for sixteen hundred dollars. The trio of horses also included Boots Colonero and the 1976 Horse of the Year in Uruguay, Cinzano. Lebón and Cinzano looked alike. Each had a white marking on his forehead.

The horses were transported to Gerard's farm in Muttontown, New York. According to Gerard, a barn accident led to severe head injuries to Cinzano, but details of the accident remained unclear. Gerard stated only that the injuries to Cinzano were so severe that the horse had to be destroyed. Gerard was reimbursed for his losses by his insurance company.

Gerard then sold Lebón to his former assistant, Jack Morgan, who was active in racing as an owner and a trainer. Morgan paid ten thousand dollars for Lebón. He began racing the horse, but Lebón finished last in his final start before what turned out to be a significant race on September 23. This event was a claiming race run on the inner-turf track at Belmont. The field included twelve horses, neither of which was a particular standout. The odds on Lebón were 57-1, making him a long shot to win. Because of the poor odds, Lebón normally would not have attracted a large amount of bets. Lebón led the entire race and won, finishing four lengths ahead of the field. At the betting windows, he returned $116 for every $2 bet.

A bettor appeared at one of the cashiers' windows with $1,300 in win tickets and $600 in show tickets on Lebón. The total owed to the bettor was $80,440, a sum the cashier did not have at his window. The cashier had a courier obtain the money from the track's main safe. Upon returning, the courier, who also worked as a stable hand at the track, recognized the bettor and addressed him as Doc. As it turned out, Doc was Gerard. Approximately three weeks after the race, a Uruguayan newspaper reporter called a Belmont employee and told him that the horse in the winner's circle photograph, taken after the race on September 23, was Cinzano, not Lebón, as identified.

Growing suspicion among owners and trainers at Belmont targeted Gerard as engaging in some sort of illegal activity at the track. Several owners refused to let him treat their horses, and some owners even refused him entry into their barns. In addition, Gerard's receipt of insurance money for Cinzano's mysterious death brought the Federal Bureau of Investigations (FBI) into the case, arousing even more suspicion. Adding to suspicion was the large amount of money bet by one individual (later found to be Gerard) on Lebón, despite the horse's last-place finish in his previous race.

Lebón raced again on October 12 in New Jersey. Although officials could not identify the horse as Cinzano, they were certain the horse was not Lebón. New York Racing Association chairman Ogden Mills Phipps insisted on a firm handling of the issue and suspended Gerard and Morgan from racing. On October 31, another horse, which Gerard also had imported, was put under police guard because racing officials believed this horse might also be a "ringer" in a racetrack and insurance fraud. Officials began to suspect similar switches of horses at tracks in New Jersey and Florida.

New York Racing and Wagering Board chief William Berry added to the investigation with computerized screenings of all the owners, trainers, and jockeys who were licensed to participate in racing at the state's fifteen tracks. Because the horse in question had been sold by Gerard to a former assistant who owned and trained horses, it seemed possible that other individuals involved in racing might also have links to Gerard. He was now assumed to have owned several horses racing under other people's documented ownership.

The investigation concluded that the horse entered in the claiming race as Lebón was not Lebón but another horse with similar markings. Although it could not be proved absolutely that this horse was Cinzano and that Gerard had committed fraud, several other facts led to his arrest and conviction nonetheless: the unexplained, mysterious death that claimed the life of Cinzano at Gerard's farm; the fact that the horse that was being raced was capable of distancing a field of claimers; Gerard collecting insurance money for Cinzano's alleged death; and the racehorse's wager that led to extremely large winnings.

IMPACT

The horse-swapping scandal perpetrated by Gerard, which was the first such case in thirty years at Belmont Park, changed the methods used for identifying horses in the thoroughbred racing industry. Gerard's scheme using Lebón and Cinzano worked simply through switching the papers of the two horses before they left Uruguay. He easily replaced Cinzano's papers with those of Lebón and Lebón's papers with those Cinzano. Having papers on a horse no longer suffices in the thoroughbred racing industry.

Horses in the United States are required to be tattooed once they arrive for a race. Traditionally, checking a horse's identity involved simply looking at its lip tattoo as it enters the saddling paddock. Tattoos have limitations, however: They are created when a horse arrives at a racetrack, tend to fade with age, and can be altered.

As a result of the Belmont Park horse-swapping scandal, the state of New York implemented a more thorough identification process, which begins two days before a race. Horses being registered for a race must now have foal papers, a registered blood type, and accompanying photographs. The various markings on a horses's head, legs, and body, including chestnuts (horny growths inside their legs, which are also called night eyes), must be documented as well. Like the human fingerprint, chestnuts are unique to each horse. A horse cannot race if its identity is unverifiable, untraceable, or otherwise questionable.

—Shawncey Webb

FURTHER READING

Ashforth, David. *Ringers and Rascals: The True Story of Racing's Greatest Con Artists*. Lexington, Ky.: Eclipse Press, 2004. Includes an account of the Gerard fraud. Also links Gerard to other horse-racing scams.

Brenner, Reuven, Gabrielle A. Brenner, and Aaron Brown. *A World of Chance: Betting on Religion, Games, Wall Street*. New York: Cambridge University Press, 2008. In this wide-ranging academic study of betting in human society, the authors contend that with widespread gambling in sports, corruption becomes inevitable.

Davidowitz, Steve. *The Best and Worst of Thoroughbred Racing*. New York: DRF Press, 2006. Good overview of all aspects of thoroughbred racing, including breeding, training, racing, handicapping, and betting.

Sullivan, George. *Great Sports Hoaxes*. Pittsburgh, Pa.: Scholastic Press, 1983. Recounts Gerard's horse-swapping scandal and other similar cons in a variety of sports.

SEE ALSO: Dec. 26, 1926: Ty Cobb and Tris Speaker Are Accused of Fixing Baseball Games; Spring, 1947: Baseball Manager Leo Durocher Is Suspended for Gambling Ties; Jan. 17, 1951: College Basketball Players Begin Shaving Points for Money; Nov. 2, 1959: Charles Van Doren Admits Being Given Answers on Television Quiz Show; Fall, 1969-Winter, 1971: Japanese Baseball Players Are Implicated in Game Fixing; Nov. 29, 1979, and Jan. 31, 1983: Baseball Commissioner Suspends Mickey Mantle and Willie Mays for Casino Ties; Aug. 24, 1989: Pete Rose Is Banned from Baseball for Betting on Games; July 26, 2006: Tour de France Is Hit with a Doping Scandal; Aug. 20, 2007: Football Star Michael Vick Pleads Guilty to Financing a Dogfighting Ring; July 29, 2008: NBA Referee Tim Donaghy Is Sentenced to Prison for Betting on Games.

1978

ACTOR JOAN CRAWFORD'S DAUGHTER PUBLISHES DAMNING MEMOIR, *MOMMIE DEAREST*

One year after the death of star Joan Crawford, her adopted daughter, Christina Crawford, published Mommie Dearest, *a controversial memoir that claimed the film star was cruel and abusive outside the limelight. The book was made into a much-criticized film of the same name in 1981 and is now a classic for its campiness, overacting, and sensationalism.*

LOCALE: New York, New York

CATEGORIES: Families and children; publishing and journalism; film; popular culture; Hollywood

KEY FIGURES

Joan Crawford (1905-1977), American film star
Christina Crawford (b. 1939), American author and actor

SUMMARY OF EVENT

Joan Crawford first found fame on a significant scale in the 1928 film *Our Dancing Daughters*, which paved the way for her to become one of Metro-Goldwyn-Mayer's leading stars. She stayed with the studio for eighteen years and, during the Depression era, played a series of roles as a working-class woman, including an empowering role in *The Woman* (1939). After switching to Warner Bros. in 1943, Crawford filmed *Mildred Pierce*, which was released two years later and won for the ascending star an Oscar for Best Actress in a Leading Role. Her career's most pivotal role came in 1962, when she starred with Bette Davis in *What Ever Happened to Baby Jane?* Crawford's performance led to a wave of publicity.

Crawford was incredibly well liked by the public, who not only adored her work (the American Film Institute named her tenth among the greatest female stars of all time) but also found her personal life to be a subject of fascination. Her personal life

became public fodder with the publication of Christina Crawford's *Mommie Dearest* in 1978. Rather than recounting her mother's vibrant career, Crawford made several shocking allegations of child abuse and neglect by her famous mother. She suggests in the book that her mother adopted her and her four siblings as a public relations move rather than out of true love and concern. *Mommie Dearest* also details the film star's incredibly meticulous personal habits, such as her obsession with cleanliness and order within their luxurious household.

Even before *Mommie Dearest* was published, Joan began falling out of favor with her fans and co-workers. She was drunk when she appeared on *The Secret Storm* soap opera in 1968 (she had been filling in for her daughter, Christina, during the latter's illness). Two years later, Joan starred in the horror picture *Trog*, a critical and commercial failure that became her last film; she died in 1977 (from pancreatic cancer). While the film industry and faithful fans mourned her loss, her legacy was quickly tarnished with the tell-all exposé, published the year after she died.

While quirky personal details could be overlooked, the press and public at large could not ignore Christina's more severe allegations of abuse. Several headline-grabbing stories included the claim that Joan mentally, emotionally, and physically harmed Christina. Incidents included a simple shouting match between the child and her mother after competing in a swimming race, and also an incident in which Joan had Christina's hair cut off as punishment for putting on makeup.

Mommie Dearest includes episodes in which Joan furiously chops down the household's rose garden in a fit of rage, and several sagas that are referred to as night raids (Joan's late-evening outbursts against Christina). One particularly famous episode in the book is a recounting of Joan's discovery that Christina had a wire hanger in her closest.

517

Joan Crawford and her daughter, Christina, in 1944. (Hulton Archive/ Getty Images)

the interview allegedly included Joan slapping Christina several times and choking her (Christina had apparently claimed that Joan was battling alcoholism). Several years of amicable contact passed between mother and daughter after these encounters, as Christina entered adulthood. However, Christina (and her brother, Christopher) would receive nothing from their mother upon her death, "for reasons that are well known to them."

Joan's estate was certainly substantial, so skeptics found *Mommie Dearest* to simply be a cash-conscious, knee-jerk reaction by Christina to being denied an inheritance. Those attempting to add credence to that claim suggested Christina could have published the book when her mother was alive but chose not to because Joan could have responded with her own side of the story. Joan's two other children, Cindy and Cathy, went on record to say they never saw any of the episodes described by Christina in the book, while Joan's first husband, Douglas Fairbanks, Jr., and several celebrity friends stepped forward with similar support for Joan. They also said that Christina often misbehaved and was subsequently punished in proper, though far-from-cruel, contexts.

Christina sold the rights to her story to Paramount Pictures, which turned *Mommie Dearest* into a full-length film of the same name starring Faye Dunaway as Joan Crawford. However, the 1981 film cut out many of the book's darker details, combined multiple incidents into a single scene, and sensationalized the entire affair. Christina was upset at the changes, and the public actually laughed at the melodramatic (and at times seemingly overacted) violence. Critics rejected the script as a whole.

The film, originally intended to be a drama, soon became a comedic camp classic, particularly

Joan clears the entire clothing rack and eventually whips Christina with the wire hanger. Another episode is the now-notorious nighttime bathroom incident, in which Joan dumps soaps and detergents on the floor and insists Christina clean up the mess on command.

Though Christina focuses heavily on incidents from her childhood, she details additional episodes into her teens and young adulthood. After being caught with a boy at a Roman Catholic boarding school in a situation that was not intimate, an inconsolable Joan sends her home and later enrolls her in an even stricter Catholic institution. In another instance, a reporter visits the house to write a "day in the life" article on the Crawford family, but among gays and in drag circles (in which stage actors regularly impersonate Joan's most glamorous film scenes and the intense moments of *Mommie Dearest*). Paramount rereleased the film on digital video disc (DVD) in 2006 as *Mommie Dearest: Hollywood Royalty Edition*, suggesting that even with the scandal attached to her name and legacy, Joan remains a Hollywood icon. Dedicated fans continue to support the star, leading to a reduction in the original shock value of *Mommie Dearest* and to overlooked claims of abuse in favor of the actor's larger-than-life personality.

IMPACT

Christina's book *Mommie Dearest* was a first-of-its-kind work. Previously, celebrity biographies rarely were negative, let alone revealing of a star's reputedly scandalous home life. Celebrity tell-all books are now commonplace, but during the late 1970's, when *Mommie Dearest* was published, the concept was unheard of and unexpected (especially given the subject's celebrity status).

Furthermore, the book made an impact as a platform for discussions of child abuse. Though Christina's claims (and their varying degrees of severity) remain subjects of contention for skeptics, her claims were among the first such revelations to go into vivid detail on a taboo topic: The topic of child abuse entered the mainstream. The Crawford family saga (as fact or fiction) continues to impact readers, moviegoers, and even victims of abuse, while simultaneously serving as Christina's platform for vindication.

—*Andy Argyrakis*

FURTHER READING

Chandler, Charlotte. *Not the Girl Next Door: Joan Crawford, a Personal Biography*. New York: Simon & Schuster, 2008. A biography of Joan Crawford that argues that Christina Crawford's claims of abuse contradict the portrait of Joan provided by her daughter, Cathy Crawford. Chandler makes this claim after Cathy relates a wholly different story of her mother.

Crawford, Christina. *Mommie Dearest*. Tensed, Idaho: Seven Springs Press, 1997. An expanded and more detailed twentieth anniversary edition that builds upon Christina Crawford's original tell-all tale of her mother's abuse and rage.

Newquist, Roy. *Conversations with Joan Crawford*. Secaucus, N.J.: Citadel Press, 1980. A compilation of more than twenty personal interviews with Joan Crawford conducted by Newquist between 1962 and 1977.

Quirk, Lawrence J., and William Schoell. *Joan Crawford: The Essential Biography*. Lexington: University Press of Kentucky, 2002. A generally favorable look at Joan Crawford's life, dedicating significant attention to her films and much less to Christina Crawford's claims.

Walker, Alexander. *Joan Crawford: The Ultimate Star*. New York: Harper & Row, 1983. Assessment of Joan Crawford's numerous films and shades of her personal life. Fully authorized by film studio Metro-Goldwyn-Mayer.

SEE ALSO: Summer, 1936: Film Star Mary Astor's Diary Becomes a Public Sensation; Jan. 14, 1943: Film Star Frances Farmer Is Jailed and Institutionalized; Aug. 31, 1948: Film Star Robert Mitchum Is Arrested for Drug Possession; May 27, 1949: Actor Rita Hayworth Marries Aly Khan After Adulterous Affair; Feb. 7, 1950: Swedish Film Star Ingrid Bergman Has a Child Out of Wedlock; 1980: Biographer Claims Actor Errol Flynn Was a Nazi Spy; July 28, 1980: Magazine Reveals Baseball Star Steve Garvey's Marital Problems; July 23, 1984: Vanessa Williams Is the First Miss America to Resign; Jan. 13, 1992: Woody Allen Has Affair with Lover Mia Farrow's Adopted Daughter; Nov. 20, 2006: News Corp Abandons Plan to Publish O. J. Simpson's Book.

1970's

1978
ROOTS AUTHOR ALEX HALEY IS SUED FOR PLAGIARISM

Alex Haley's quasi-autobiographical and semifictional book Roots, *marketed as nonfiction by its publisher, earned him a Pulitzer Prize and raised his status as a writer and model of the value of genealogical research. In 1978, writer Harold Courlander sued Haley for plagiarizing parts of his 1967 novel* The African. *In later years, Haley faced other charges of falsification of his research. The importance of his landmark work survived, however, and its lasting significance has overshadowed the controversy.*

LOCALE: United States
CATEGORIES: Law and the courts; literature; plagiarism; public morals

KEY FIGURES
Alex Haley (1921-1992), American writer
Harold Courlander (1908-1996), American
　　novelist and anthropologist

SUMMARY OF EVENT
The publication of Alex Haley's *Roots: The Saga of an American Family* in the U.S. bicentennial year of 1976 was a landmark event. The book's publisher, Doubleday, planned what was, for an African American author, an unprecedented initial print run of 200,000 copies, but that printing quickly sold out. In its first year, *Roots* would sell more than one million copies, leading to Haley's receipt of a special Pulitzer Prize. Twenty-five years later, the book had sold more than eight million copies in twenty-eight countries and had been translated into thirty-three languages.

Haley called *Roots* "faction," or a mix of fact and fiction, and later referred to the work as symbolic history, but Doubleday had marketed the book as straight nonfiction, which only worsened the controversy. In 1978, novelist and anthropologist Harold Courlander sued Haley for having plagiarized passages from his novel *The African* (1967). After a five-week trial, Haley and Courlander settled out of

court, with Haley publicly acknowledging his debt to Courlander (claiming research assistants had given him material from the novel without fully citing its source) and paying him $650,000. The incredible success of *Roots*, first as a book and then, in January, 1977, a twelve-hour television miniseries, seems to have eased the scorn of the plagiarism scandal. Haley's fabrications seem forgotten in the light of the longevity and popularity of *Roots*.

Roots the miniseries had been a broadcasting sensation, breaking viewership records as it was watched closely by more than 130 million people over eight successive nights (January 23-30). The story clearly had touched a chord in the American consciousness, not only among African Americans but also among Americans of every ethnicity and race. The story dramatized the violence against one group of Americans by another, and it had viewers learning about an ethnic history not known by many. For the book, Haley claimed that he had traced seven generations of his family, from the coast of Gambia in West Africa—where his distant ancestor, Kunta Kinte, was captured by slave traders in 1767—to the plantation in Tennessee where he first worked and started the family that would lead, two centuries and five generations later, to Haley's re-creations of his family history. The last three chapters of the book recount this search for Haley's roots.

This case was only the first of a series of revelations about the questionable research methods used to write *Roots*. In 1988, novelist Margaret Walker sued Haley, claiming he had plagiarized material from her novel *Jubilee* (1966). That case was dismissed, but in 1984, noted historians Gary Mills and Elizabeth Shown Mills challenged Haley's research, showing that his genealogy was flawed in a number of ways. In 1993, writer Philip Nobile published in the weekly newspaper *Village Voice* an exhaustive investigation into the Haley papers (deposited after Haley's death in 1992 at the University of Tennessee). In the report, "Uncovering *Roots*,"

Nobile details how Haley fabricated much of his family's story.

The charges against Haley, however, had less effect than critics expected. The book had become a staple in college courses during the late 1970's, and although fewer courses after the controversy listed *Roots* as required reading, this dip was mostly likely due to the publication of other related works— books that were sparked in part by *Roots*. Before the arrival of *Roots*—the book and the television mini-series—most Americans knew African history only through such caricatures as the Tarzan films and knew of slave life through works such as Harriet Beecher Stowe's melodramatic novel *Uncle Tom's Cabin* (1852) or Margaret Mitchell's romantic novel *Gone with the Wind* (1936) and the 1939 film of the same name.

Following *Roots*, black history became an even greater focus of study in colleges and universities nationwide, leading to the further creation of a stream of ethnic history and literature that would flow from writers of all races and ethnicities into the twenty-first century. Related narratives included Toni Morrison's Pulitzer Prize-winning novel *Beloved* (1987), which tells the story of a fugitive Kentucky slave in 1851 who kills her baby rather than return it to a life of slavery; the National Book Award-winning novel *Middle Passage* (1990) by Charles Johnson, which is a fictionalized account of the journey that captured African slaves were forced to take from their homeland to the Americas; and the National Book Award-winning *Slaves in the Family* (1998) by Edward Ball, about his family's slaveholding past and his attempts to connect to those African Americans his family had owned as slaves.

Some scholars have dismissed Haley's work as something other than historical research; Henry Louis Gates, Jr., questions whether Haley actually found the Gambian village of Kunta Kinte. Other scholars have challenged the account of the griot, or oral historian, relating to Haley the story of his ancestors. Despite all the criticisms and charges, however, most scholars understand the imaginative power of Haley's work and its lasting symbolic effect. Like Haley's other best-known work, *The Autobiography of Malcolm X* (1965), which is based

on interviews with the black Muslim leader, *Roots* remains a key chapter in the American narrative. The book dramatizes the cruelties of slavery—the economic and sexual exploitation and the separation of families.

IMPACT

The effect of the charges against Haley was less severe than experts predicted. Most critics have come to realize that the scandal was caused, in part, by the publisher's marketing of *Roots* as a nonfiction work. Readers naturally expected that "nonfiction" meant "not fictionalized," as are works of history. In retrospect, it is clear that *Roots* is closer to being a novel, or an autobiographical novel, because so much of its narrative was reconstructed from oral cultures. Had Doubleday advertised *Roots* as a work of fiction, the controversy would have been negligible. Likewise, if *Roots* had been marketed more strictly as a memoir, it might have been granted greater latitude as well. In the end, *Roots*, and even Haley's reputation, has outlasted the 1978 scandal. The book is a work of imaginative power that filled a crucial gap in U.S. history when it was published. Whether a novel, "faction," memoir, historical fiction, or straight nonfiction, it tells a necessary story that continues to intrigue.

—*David Peck*

FURTHER READING

Bundles, A'Lelia. "Looking Back at the *Roots* Phenomenon." *Black Issues Book Review* 3 (July/August, 2001): 12-15. Pays tribute to Haley for his contributions to African American literature and oral history, and compares other works on African history.

Courlander, Harold. *The African.* New York: Crown Books, 1967. Courlander, who sued Haley for plagiarism, prefigures the story of Kunta Kinte in his novel about a twelve-year-old boy's capture and horrific sea voyage to the United States and his attempts to hold onto or recreate his African background in the New World.

Mills, Gary B., and Elizabeth Shown. "The Genealogist's Assessment of Alex Haley's *Roots.*" *National Genealogical Society Quarterly* 72

1970's

(March, 1984): 35-49. The authors, who visited archives in Virginia, North Carolina, and Maryland, reveal evidence to challenge both the chronology and the character identification of *Roots*.

Nobile, Philip. "Uncovering *Roots*." *Village Voice*, February 23, 1993. Nobile followed the court cases, studied the manuscripts of *Roots*, and interviewed a number of people connected with the book to conclude it was a fabrication.

Osagie, Iyunolu. "Routed Passages: Narrative Memory and Identity in Alex Haley's *Roots*." *CLA Journal* 47 (June, 2004): 391-408. Examines the themes of the book, including collective memory and identity formation.

Rasmussen, R. Kent. "'*Roots*': A Growing Thicket of Controversy." *Los Angeles Times*, April 24, 1977, p. V1. Op-ed article by a historian of Africa challenging Haley's research methods, particularly his alleged reliance on the evidence of a Gambian griot.

Taylor, Helen. "'The Griot from Tennessee': The Saga of Alex Haley's *Roots*." *Critical Quarterly* 37 (June, 1995): 46-62. Comprehensive schol-arly coverage of the controversy, plus a balanced assessment of the lasting impact of *Roots*.

SEE ALSO: 1928-1929: Actor Is Suspected of Falsely Claiming to Be an American Indian; June 5, 1944: Australian Poets Claim Responsibility for a Literary Hoax; Jan. 28, 1972: Clifford Irving Admits Faking Howard Hughes Memoirs; Sept. 1, 1976: Former Beatle George Harrison Loses Plagiarism Lawsuit; Dec. 3, 1989: Martin Luther King, Jr.'s, Doctoral-Thesis Plagiarism Is Revealed; Mar. 12, 1997: Prize-Winning Aborigine Novelist Revealed as a Fraud; Apr., 1998: Scottish Historian Is Charged with Plagiarism; June 18, 2001: Historian Joseph J. Ellis Is Accused of Lying; Jan. 4, 2002: Historian Stephen E. Ambrose Is Accused of Plagiarism; Jan. 18, 2002: Historian Doris Kearns Goodwin Is Accused of Plagiarism; Oct. 25, 2002: Historian Michael A. Bellesiles Resigns After Academic Fraud Accusations; July 24, 2007: University of Colorado Fires Professor for Plagiarism and Research Falsification.

February 1, 1978
ROMAN POLANSKI FLEES THE UNITED STATES TO AVOID RAPE TRIAL

Roman Polanski, the director of the hit films Rosemary's Baby *and* The Pianist, *among others, became a central figure in real-life Hollywood drama. First, his pregnant wife, actor Sharon Tate, was murdered by followers of cult figure Charles Manson. Several years later, Polanski was charged with raping a thirteen-year-old girl. After pleading guilty to unlawful sexual intercourse with a minor, he fled to France before he could be tried in court, fearing a long prison sentence.*

LOCALES: Los Angeles, California; Paris, France
CATEGORIES: Drugs; families and children; Hollywood; law and the courts; public morals; sex crimes

KEY FIGURES
Roman Polanski (b. 1933), French filmmaker
Samantha Gailey (b. 1964), American teen model
Sharon Tate (1943-1969), American film actor

SUMMARY OF EVENT
Roman Polanski, director of films such as *Rosemary's Baby* (1968), *Macbeth* (1971), *Chinatown* (1974), and *The Pianist* (2002), was notorious for his interest in young women and older girls. His first wife, Barbara Lass, was eighteen years old when they met, and his second wife, actor Sharon Tate, was still a teenager when she met Polanski. He was more than thirty years older than his third wife, Emmanuelle Seigner. None of this mattered to most

Roman Polanski is escorted by deputies with the Los Angeles County Sheriff's Department outside a Santa Monica courtroom in August, 1977. (AP/Wide World Photos)

people in the permissive cultures of Hollywood and filmmaking. What did matter was Polanski's flight from the United States to avoid trial and likely imprisonment for statutory rape on February 1, 1978.

Polanski was no stranger to Hollywood scandal. Almost a decade before being charged with statutory rape in 1977, Polanski's pregnant wife, Tate, was murdered, along with several others, on August 9, 1969, in a Hollywood Hills home by Manson-family cult members. Polanski was not in the United States at the time of the murders but returned immediately to mourn the loss of his wife and their unborn child.

Eight years later, in March, 1977, Polanski allegedly drugged and sexually assaulted a thirteen-year-old girl, Samantha Gailey (later Samantha Gelmer), whom he had met at a photo shoot for the French edition of *Vogue* magazine. Before this ini-

tial photo shoot, Gailey and her mother had agreed to a second modeling opportunity, an encounter that ended with charges against Polanski for rape. Polanski and Gailey had been alone at this second photo session, which took place at the home of actor Jack Nicholson (who was not home at the time), on March 10. Polanski allegedly provided alcohol and drugs to Gailey, and then reportedly raped her. (Police officers who were searching the home after Polanski was accused of the crime arrested Nicholson's then-girl-friend, actor Angelica Huston, for cocaine possession.)

Polanski was arrested on March 11 at the Beverly Wilshire Hotel and originally charged with six counts, including sodomy, lewd and lascivious acts involving a minor, drug use, and statutory rape. On March 25, he was indicted by a grand jury on six felonious counts but was released on two thousand dollars bail. On August 8, after a plea bargain with prosecutors, he entered a guilty plea to one count of committing an unlawful sexual act with a minor, a less serious charge than rape; the other charges were dropped. He appeared in court on September 19. The court ordered him to undergo ninety days of psychiatric testing and therapy in a federal penitentiary in Chino, California, but he was allowed to delay the start date until December 19 so that he could finish a film.

Lawyers for Polanski first believed that ninety days in the federal penitentiary would mark the end of his sentence. They thought that California Superior Court judge Laurence J. Rittenband would not sentence their client to prison time. However, despite the plea bargain during the initial court appearance and a reduction in charges, and fearing a sentence of up to fifty years, Polanski, a French citizen, fled to London on February 1, 1978, and then to Paris a day later. He remained a fugitive there after leaving the United States, insulated from the risk of extradition because France did not have an extradition agreement with the United States (the French would not extradite one of its own citizens). A return to the United States would lead to his arrest, further charges, and sentencing.

IMPACT

Polanski continued to make films in the years following his flight from the United States. However, very few of them were critically supported. He regained a good deal of renown, though, with his film *The Pianist*. Not surprisingly, the film emerged under a shroud of scandal and suspicion because of Polanski's continued notoriety. The film, based on the true story of Polish pianist Władysław Szpilman, is set during World War II and touches close to home for Polanski, who survived the Kraków ghettoes during the Holocaust years. The film received overwhelming acclaim and received several Academy Award nominations, including Best Picture and Best Director, which he won. The film also received Oscars for Best Actor and best writing (adapted story). Polanski did not return to California to receive his Oscar; actor Harrison Ford accepted on his behalf.

In a July, 2002, article in *Vanity Fair*, writer A. E. Hotchner discussed Polanski's mood in the days following the sensational 1969 murder of Tate. Hotchner quotes writer Lewis Lapham as remarking that "the only time I ever saw people gasp" was when Polanski approached a Swedish model, attempted to seduce her, and told her "I will make another Sharon Tate out of you." Polanski denied the encounter and sued for libel. He argued that the accusatory account tarnished not only his character but also his memory of Tate. Because of his fugitive status in the United States, and because of Great Britain's cooperation with U.S. extradition law (the case originated in London), Polanski acquired permission to appear via satellite from Paris for the duration of the court proceedings. The British court ruled 3-2 in favor of Polanski.

—*Meredith A. Holladay*

FURTHER READING

Cronin, Paul, ed. *Roman Polanski: Interviews.* Jackson: University Press of Mississippi, 2005. This book presumes Polanski had a career of dark and brutal films that reflect the filmmaker's troubled life. Contains interviews that cover forty years of his career. Most of the interviews come from foreign film journals, but also included are American television interviews with Dick Cavett and Charlie Rose.

Hotchner, A. E. "Queen of the Night." *Vanity Fair*, July, 2002. The article that was the subject of Polanski's libel and slander charge against the Conde Nast publication. Polanski sued the publication in a British court in November, 2003.

Morrison, James. *Roman Polanski.* Urbana: University of Illinois Press, 2007. Focuses on Polanski's film career. Begins with his earliest films, which were made in Eastern Europe. Includes thorough commentaries on Polanski's films that give a great deal of attention to the greater social, economic, political, and moral contexts of the mid- to late twentieth century.

Polanski, Roman. *Roman.* New York: William Morrow, 1984. Polanski's autobiography. A candid look inside the life, mind, and work of the notorious filmmaker. Offers a rare glimpse into his upbringing, relationships, and approach to his filmmaking, in addition to addressing the events of 1977 that led to his self-imposed exile.

SEE ALSO: Jan. 20, 1933: Hedy Lamarr Appears Nude in the Czech Film *Exstase*; Summer, 1936: Film Star Mary Astor's Diary Becomes a Public Sensation; Jan. 14, 1943: Film Star Frances Farmer Is Jailed and Institutionalized; May 27, 1949: Actor Rita Hayworth Marries Aly Khan After Adulterous Affair; Feb. 7, 1950: Swedish Film Star Ingrid Bergman Has a Child Out of Wedlock; May, 1955: Scandal Magazine Reveals Actor Rory Calhoun's Criminal Past; Dec. 12, 1957: Rock Star Jerry Lee Lewis Marries Thirteen-Year-Old Cousin; 1978: Actor Joan Crawford's Daughter Publishes Damning Memoir, *Mommie Dearest*; Mar. 30, 1991: William Kennedy Smith Is Accused of Rape; Jan. 13, 1992: Woody Allen Has Affair with Lover Mia Farrow's Adopted Daughter; Feb. 26, 1997: Teacher Mary Kay Letourneau Is Arrested for Statutory Rape; Dec. 18, 2003: Pop Star Michael Jackson Is Charged with Child Molestation.

June 27, 1978
EVANGELIST HERBERT W. ARMSTRONG EXCOMMUNICATES HIS OWN SON

Herbert W. Armstrong, founder of the Worldwide Church of God, excommunicated his son, Garner Ted Armstrong, a famous television evangelist and church leader as well, for personal misconduct. Ted, accused by his father several years earlier of being in the "bonds of Satan," later founded his own church and faced a sexual assault charge in 1995.

LOCALE: Pasadena, California
CATEGORIES: Religion; communications and media; radio and television; families and children

KEY FIGURES
Garner Ted Armstrong (1930-2003), televangelist, Worldwide Church of God leader, and later founder of the Church of God International
Herbert W. Armstrong (1892-1986), founder of the Worldwide Church of God
Stanley Rader (1930-2002), attorney and minister, Worldwide Church of God
Bobby Fischer (1943-2008), chess champion

SUMMARY OF EVENT
In June, 1978, Herbert W. Armstrong publicly excommunicated his son, Garner Ted Armstrong, from the Worldwide Church of God (WCG), which Herbert had founded in 1933. Although long in coming, Ted's removal was a shocking development to the adherents of the church and millions who followed Ted through the media. The event made national news. At the time, Ted was heir apparent to his father. He also was vice president of the church, vice chancellor of the church's Ambassador College, and the telegenic face of the sect, watched by millions of people worldwide.

Herbert founded the WCG with unique doctrines that included the following: God consisted of a family of members to which his followers could aspire,

the use of triple tithing, the observance of the Old Testament Sabbath, feasts and regulations, the prohibition of medical assistance, a racially segregated Heaven, and the identification of the British with the ten lost tribes of Israel. The chief engine of the church's remarkable growth was Herbert's *Plain Truth* magazine and radio and television programs, in which he would describe current events as prophetically ushering in "the world tomorrow," when God would establish His kingdom on Earth after a violent apocalypse.

The programs provided a natural platform for Herbert's youngest son, Ted. Born in 1930, Ted began his career as his father's office manager in 1952. In 1953, Ted married Shirley Hammer, with whom he would have three sons. In 1955, he was ordained to his father's ministry. Soon appearing on the *World Tomorrow* broadcasts, Ted's smooth manner and silver voice attracted a wide audience. Like his father, Ted employed the tools of modern advertising to promote his show. By 1957, Ted had taken over *World Tomorrow* and was the lead voice and face of the ministry, eventually appearing on about 400 radio stations and 165 television stations with an audience of about twenty million people. In 1962, Ted gained for the WCG its best-known enthusiast, chess champion Bobby Fischer, who joined the church after hearing Ted's radio broadcast.

Ted's popularity even led to appearances on the popular television comedy show *Hee-Haw*. His progress was not slowed, even after his yearly prophecies of imminent doom did not materialize. In 1968, Ted was made executive vice president of the church and vice chancellor of the church's flagship Ambassador College. However, allegations of gambling, drinking, and adultery soon surfaced. They were ignored by Herbert until Ted began a long-term affair with a flight attendant and threatened to leave his wife, despite the church's strict teachings against divorce. In 1971, Ted was relieved of his duties and placed on leave of absence.

525

In 1972, Herbert removed Ted's ministerial authority, claiming Ted was in the "bonds of Satan." On May 15, 1972, *Time* magazine published an exposé of Ted's scandalous behavior. Fischer was disturbed by the revelations and eventually spoke out against the WCG.

Missing broadcasts by Ted, the listening audience declined and church income plummeted. After six months, Herbert felt obliged to reinstate Ted, yet, seemingly incorrigible, Ted was again suspended by his father in 1974. Within months, Herbert once more reinstated Ted to his position as heir apparent, announcing that his son was his divinely appointed successor—Solomon to Herbert's King David. By 1978, however, Herbert felt compelled to act. Ted had been participating in a so-called systematic theology project designated to reexamine some of his father's doctrines in the light of mainstream theology and to gain secular accreditation for Ambassador College. There also were reports

that Ted was engaged in a power struggle with WCG attorney Stanley Rader for influence over his father.

Time magazine reported in a June 19, 1978, article that Herbert admonished Ted in an open letter to the faithful that stated

> I derived my authority from the living Christ. You derived what you had from me, and then used it totally CONTRARY to THE WAY Christ has led me.

Finally, on June 27, Herbert excommunicated Ted for conspiring to seize control of the WCG and Ambassador College. The next day, Herbert wrote to his congregation, saying his letter to them was "the most difficult letter I have ever been compelled to write." He continued, "I would rather have cut off my right arm than having to do this." In this lengthy letter, he revealed a lifetime of difficulties with Ted, leading to his dramatic expulsion from the WCG.

Garner Ted Armstrong at Ambassador College in Pasadena, California, in 1972. (AP/Wide World Photos)

This excommunication represented an irrevocable breach between father and son with dramatic consequences. Without the facile Ted, the success of the *World Tomorrow* broadcast was imperiled, Herbert was left without a successor, and his public anointing of his miracle son had come to naught.

Ted moved to Tyler, Texas, and formed, with several other former church ministers, the Church of God International, affiliated with his Garner Ted Armstrong Evangelistic Association. Ted launched his own magazine, *Twentieth Century Watch*, and television broadcasts. He also accused his father of committing financial improprieties, one of the factors that prompted the California attorney general to launch an investigation of the church in early January, 1979, for misappropriation of funds. The attorney general also requested that the California courts place the WCG in receivership for one year.

Although Ted's media charm kept his denomination alive, his scandalous behavior did not die. In 1995, a masseuse, who had secretly videotaped Ted's offensive sexual advances, brought a sexual assault suit against Ted. Ted was soon removed from the Church of God International but launched a new church, the Intercontinental Church of God. Despite several overtures, Herbert and Ted never reconciled, and Herbert died in 1986 at the age of ninety-three. On September 15, 2003, at the age of seventy-three, Ted died of pneumonia.

IMPACT

Herbert's excommunication of his son, Ted, was the most traumatic event in the history of the WCG. In its first forty years, the denomination had experienced explosive growth. Although its membership would reach 150,000, its worldwide reach through its magazine, *The Plain Truth*, and its radio and television program, *The World Tomorrow*, reached tens of millions of people. Ted was the star evangelist of this religious empire, Herbert's second-in-command, and his heir apparent. That Ted's transgressions finally compelled his father to excommunicate and disown him damaged the credibility of the church. Only four years earlier, Herbert had claimed that God appointed Ted his successor.

Moreover, Ted's excommunication deprived the church of its most charismatic presence. He began his own splinter denomination, which, in turn, split into the Biblical Church of God (1979), Philadelphia Church of God (1989), Global Church of God (1992), and United Church of God (1995). By 1993, membership in the WCG had begun to drop sharply, and many of Herbert's doctrines were rejected. Within a couple of years, *The World Tomorrow* program was canceled and Ambassador College closed. In 1997, WCG became a member of the mainstream National Association of Evangelicals, a final rejection of Herbert's teachings.

Herbert and Ted Armstrong were significant figures in the development of Christian evangelism on radio and television. They pioneered religious broadcasting's use of certain advertising techniques—saturation programming, free giveaways, appearances with world figures, and Madison Avenue hyperbole—now staples in televangelism. Ted brought the glib manner of a television anchor to his broadcast delivery. Most of all, he perfected the sales pitch during the show, which accounted for much of the church's revenue.

Ted also was farsighted in urging more tolerance of other denominations, a more scholarly Ambassador College, and the easing of some of the denomination's most onerous restrictions. However, his good deeds were overshadowed by accusations that he used his religious message and appeal to accumulate personal riches and have extramarital affairs. Ted would tell his liaisons that his indiscretions mattered little in the light of the important prophetic messages he was bringing to the world. The troubles he brought to the Worldwide Church of God, and televangelism in general, would seem to say otherwise.

—*Howard Bromberg*

FURTHER READING

Armstrong, Garner Ted. *The Real Jesus*. New ed. Tyler, Tex.: Emerald, 1984. In this book, often insightful but at times banal and bizarre, Ted Armstrong revises traditional teachings about Jesus, rejecting, for example, the holidays of Christmas and Easter and claiming that Jesus was the senior partner in a construction business.

Flurry, Stephen. *Raising the Ruins: The Fight to Revive the Legacy of Herbert W. Armstrong.* Edmond, Okla.: Philadelphia Church of God, 2006. A Herbert Armstrong loyalist argues that Ted Armstrong attempted a coup against his father and the church in 1978.

Gufeld, Eduard. *Bobby Fischer: From Chess Genius to Legend.* Davenport, Iowa: Thinkers' Press, 2001. Recounts the chess genius's involvement and disaffection with Herbert and Ted Armstrong and their church.

Oliver, Myrna. "Garner Ted Armstrong." *Los Angeles Times*, September 16, 2003. An obituary of Ted Armstrong that discusses his life, evangelistic career, and his troubles.

Tkach, Joseph. *Transformed by Truth.* Sisters, Oreg.: Multnomah, 1997. An account by Herbert Armstrong's eventual successor about the movement of WCG into the evangelical mainstream. Includes information on Ted's failed predic-

tions, his 1972 removal for "moral and doctrinal" failures, and his 1978 excommunication for "liberalism" and "modernizing" tendencies.

SEE ALSO: May-June, 1926: Evangelist Aimee Semple McPherson Claims She Was Kidnapped; Oct. 25, 1974: Evangelist Billy James Hargis Resigns College Presidency During Gay-Sex Scandal; Sept. 10, 1981: *Chicago Sun-Times* Reports That Cardinal Cody Diverted Church Funds; Oct. 23, 1985: Guru Bhagwan Shree Rajneesh Is Indicted for Immigration Fraud; Apr. 22, 1986: Faith Healer Peter Popoff Is Exposed as a Fraud; Mar. 19, 1987: Jim Bakker Resigns as Head of PTL Television Network; Feb. 21, 1988: Evangelist Jimmy Swaggart Tearfully Confesses His Adultery; Nov. 2, 2006: Evangelist Kent Hovind Is Convicted of Federal Tax Violations; Nov. 2, 2006: Male Escort Reveals Sexual Liaisons with Evangelist Ted Haggard.

July 23, 1978
UTAH MILLIONAIRE IS MURDERED BY HIS GRANDSON

Franklin James Bradshaw became a millionaire by building a chain of auto-parts stores and acquiring federal and state oil and gas leases over several decades. Frances Schreuder, his daughter, was a New York socialite who spent her days recklessly spending or installing herself in boardrooms. When her father tired of her lavish lifestyle and threatened to cut her out of his will, Schreuder coerced her own son to murder the Utah magnate.

LOCALE: Salt Lake City, Utah
CATEGORIES: Murder and suicide; families and children; business

KEY FIGURES
Franklin James Bradshaw (1902-1978), Salt Lake City businessman

Berenice Jewett Bradshaw (1902-1996), Franklin Bradshaw's wife
Frances Schreuder (1939-2004), New York socialite and a daughter of the Bradshaws
Marc Schreuder (b. 1961), son of Frances Schreuder and grandson of the Bradshaws

SUMMARY OF EVENT
During the mid-1970's, Frances Schreuder was living the high life in an apartment in the upper East Side of Manhattan in New York and was determined to climb the social ladder. She was aggressively working to make herself an important fixture in such high-profile groups as the New York City Ballet's board by courting administrator Lincoln Kirstein and principal choreographer George Balanchine. To keep up the appearance of having an elite social position and lifestyle, Schreuder also

was spending recklessly—reportedly paying out as much as $40,000 at one time for one item, a pair of earrings from Tiffany's.

Evidence points to Schreuder having a greedy side even as a teenager. For example, she was a student at the prestigious Bryn Mawr College but was suspended in 1958 for check theft and forgery. Reports also suggest Schreuder, a mother of three, was less maternal than monstrous: She was described as manipulative and domineering, and she abused her children, Larry and Marc (children by her first marriage to Vittorio Gentile) and Lavinia (daughter of her second marriage with Frederik Schreuder). She would, it turned out, combine her greed and her abusive ways to concoct one of the most sensational murders of the decade.

Schreuder was living to extremes her father, Franklin James Bradshaw, would never indulge in himself. A self-made millionaire who made his fortune with a chain of auto-parts stores and by acquiring federal and state oil and gas leases, Bradshaw nevertheless lived frugally and carefully, even eccentrically, some would say. Despite being worth approximately $10 million, his primary transportation vehicle was a rusty old pickup truck, he wore clothes from thrift stores, and his briefcase was an emptied beer box. In contrast, his daughter's wasteful lifestyle appalled him, and he threatened that if she did not curb the lavish spending, he would cut her from his will.

Incensed and fearful that her father would keep his word, Schreuder began plotting. In the summer of 1977, her sons, Larry and Marc, were working at their grandfather's Utah auto-parts warehouse. Schreuder directed the boys to steal money from the business. Marc later testified that she gave her sons poison and instructed them to put it in her father's oatmeal. Marc claimed he refused to poison his grandfather, but with Larry, he did follow through with the theft: The two teens stole about $200,000 in checks, stock certificates, and cash and handed over a sizable portion of the stash to their mother.

Still not satisfied, Schreuder paid a hit man, Myles Manning, $5,000 to murder her father. Manning took the money but never followed through

with the hit. Schreuder became more adamant that Marc do the job. When he resisted, she threatened to kick him out of the house if he did not comply with her wishes. Marc later testified that his mother cajoled with the words "Look Marc, it is not really killing. It is the right thing to do for us." Marc gave in: On July 23, 1978, he entered his seventy-six-year-old grandfather's Salt Lake City auto-parts warehouse and, at point-blank range with a .357 Magnum handgun, shot and killed Bradshaw.

Uninvolved family members believed a robber killed Bradshaw, but Schreuder's sister, Marilyn Bradshaw Reagan, was reportedly less than convinced. Reagan offered a $10,000 reward for information regarding the murder of her father. Despite Marc's petitions for his mother to get rid of the evidence by destroying or dumping the murder weapon, Schreuder had turned the .357 over to a friend to whom she allegedly owed $3,000, offering the firearm as repayment. The less-than-thrilled friend went to Reagan for the reward money instead. When Reagan delivered the weapon to authorities, fingerprints traced back to Marc and Frances Schreuder.

Arrested in 1981, Marc Schreuder went on trial in 1982—represented by Paul Van Dam, the lawyer who later became Utah's attorney general. Implicated as the mastermind, Frances Schreuder went on trial in 1983. Berenice Jewett Bradshaw, Schreuder's mother, reportedly spent up to $2 million to provide legal support for her daughter and grandson. According to Van Dam and others, including biographer Jonathan Coleman, Marc was a tense and guarded young man who was reticent to testify against his controlling mother. Marc, Van Dam said, was "the most psychologically abused kid" he had ever seen. Marc did not decide to testify until the evening before the trial began.

Marc's agreeing to testify was no doubt linked to the work of sympathetic detectives and prosecution, and to Marc's realization that his mother was more than willing to see him take the full blame while she took the majority of her mother's financing of their defense. According to Coleman, Marc knew that he needed to distance himself from his mother's hold, and it is more likely that he decided to testify because he wanted to protect his younger sister, Lavinia, from their mother.

Frances Schreuder consistently denied culpability, but despite her claims to having no involvement in the murder of her father, and despite her fight against extradition to Salt Lake City from New York, she was brought to trial in Salt Lake City, convicted of first-degree murder, and sentenced to life in prison. At Utah State Prison, until her parole in 1996, Schreuder behaved as a model inmate, earning two psychology degrees from Utah State University by way of the inmate-education program sponsored by her own mother.

Marc Schreuder, who at his mother's trial testified he had begged and pleaded with his mother not to force him to kill his grandfather but who acquiesced when she threatened to disown him, was convicted of second-degree murder and sentenced to five to ten years in prison. He actually served thirteen years, earning a degree in construction from Salt Lake Community College while incarcerated at Utah State Prison. He was paroled in 1995 and moved to Provo, Utah, where he began work for a nutritional and personal-care products company.

In 1996, at the age of ninety-four, Berenice Bradshaw died, leaving her daughter $1 million in a trust fund to be dispersed annually. Marc and Frances attended Berenice's funeral, but they did not speak to one another. On April 7, 2004, the sixty-five-year-old Frances Schreuder died of chronic obstructive pulmonary disease at a San Diego, California, hospice house. Lavinia, living in San Diego, and Larry, living in Los Angeles, attended their mother's funeral. Marc Schreuder, who had reconciled with his mother the year before, attended as well. Interviewed that morning, he merely told reporters his mother should be left to rest in peace.

IMPACT

The crime and trial caused a national sensation. The picture of Frances Schreuder's arrest depicted her not as a socialite dripping with the thousands of dollars worth of jewels she was said to indulge in but as a dark and disturbed person—eyes glowering at the camera with a sinister stare. The media offered extended coverage, two journalists published best-selling books, and television hosted two miniseries and a Court TV (now truTV) documentary on the scandal.

The scandal impacted Frances Schreuder's sons as well—particularly Marc, who, after suffering the mental abuse and manipulation by his mother for years, was sentenced to prison for the crime she convinced him to commit. Marc had, he told reporters, done everything he could to please his Svengali-like mother.

—*Roxanne McDonald*

FURTHER READING

Alexander, Shana. *Nutcracker: Money, Madness, Murder—A Family Album*. New York: Doubleday, 1985. A veteran journalist offers a narrative of the scandalous murder of Bradshaw with telling detail.

Coleman, Jonathan. *At Mother's Request: A True Story of Money, Murder, and Betrayal*. New York: Atheneum, 1985. Former editor Coleman brings a massive amount of research to this true-crime retelling of the Bradshaw-Schreuder murder scandal.

Davis, Carol Ann. *Couples Who Kill*. London: Allison & Busby, 2007. Among the eighteen entries providing a thorough examination of partners in crime is "Mother Knows Best," the study of Frances and Marc Schreuder and the psychodynamics of their collaborative murder.

SEE ALSO: July 27, 1917: Millionaire Socialite Dies Under Suspicious Circumstances; Sept. 5, 1967: Socialite Nancy Wakeman Shoots Her Politician-Husband; Apr. 15, 1974: Kidnapped Heir Patty Hearst Helps Rob a Bank; Mar. 21, 1976: Actor Claudine Longet Kills Ski Champion Vladimir Sabich; Mar. 10, 1980: Scarsdale Diet Doctor Is Killed by His Lover; Mar., 1990: Menendez Brothers Are Arrested for Murdering Their Parents; Aug. 16, 1996: Belgian Media Reveal How Police Bungled Serial Murder Case.

August 4, 1978

BRITISH POLITICIAN JEREMY THORPE IS CHARGED WITH ATTEMPTED MURDER

British Liberal Party leader Jeremy Thorpe was accused of hiring an assassin to kill Norman Scott, Thorpe's alleged former lover. Scott later said that Thorpe threatened to kill him if he revealed the affair. After his release from prison, the gunman said he had been hired to kill Scott. Thorpe and three codefendants were acquitted, but the incident ended Thorpe's political career.

ALSO KNOWN AS: Rinkagate

LOCALES: Exmoor National Park and London, England

CATEGORIES: Murder and suicide; government; politics; law and the courts

KEY FIGURES

Jeremy Thorpe (b. 1929), British member of Parliament, 1959-1979, and leader of the Liberal Party, 1967-1976

Norman Scott (fl. 1970's), former British model

Andrew Newton (fl. 1970's), former British airline pilot

David Holmes (fl. 1970's), British deputy treasurer of the Liberal Party

George Deakin (fl. 1970's), British nightclub owner

John Le Mesurier (fl. 1970's), British businessman

SUMMARY OF EVENT

Flashy and opinionated, Jeremy Thorpe was elected to Parliament from Britain's North Devon District in 1959. He became Liberal Party leader in 1967 and remained popular enough to retain his seat when the Conservative Party drove the Liberals from the majority in 1970. However, in 1971, the start of a scandal would affect the rest of Thorpe's political career.

In 1971, former model Norman Scott alleged that he and Thorpe had been lovers between 1961 and 1963. His claim was a shock to the public. Male homosexuality had been decriminalized in England only in 1967. Though the Liberal Party's subsequent investigation cleared Thorpe, Scott maintained the truth of his allegations.

The situation remained at a standstill until 1975, the year Scott began to feel unsafe. He would later claim Thorpe had threatened to kill him for revealing the affair. In one incident, Scott had been walking a friend's dog, a Great Dane named Rinka, in Exmoor National Park (in the south of England) in October. During the walk he encountered former pilot Andrew Newton. Newton shot the dog dead but his gun misfired when he turned it on Scott.

At Newton's trial in 1976, Scott again claimed to have been Thorpe's lover during the 1960's, adding that Thorpe had threatened to kill him if he brought the relationship to light. Scott also sold the press personal letters, allegedly written by Thorpe to Scott, calling Scott by a pet name and discussing a planned trip. This time, Thorpe's political position was threatened, and he resigned his Liberal Party leadership in May of that year. Newton was convicted of the attempted murder and spent one year in prison. Thorpe's name was never mentioned in conjunction with Newton at this time.

However, when Newton was released from prison in 1977, he stirred the scandal back to life, insisting that he had, in fact, been hired to kill Scott. After Thorpe's name was associated with the case, the scandal became known as Rinkagate. Thorpe, who always maintained that his friendship with the former model had been platonic, repeatedly denied the accusations. By this time, Thorpe was married to his second wife, Marion. His first wife had died in a car accident in 1970, before the initial allegations were made. Thorpe firmly insisted on his innocence, refusing to resign his seat in Parliament.

Over a year later, on August 4, 1978, Thorpe and three codefendants, David Holmes, George Deakin,

Jeremy Thorpe outside a courtroom in London in June, 1979. (Hulton Archive/Getty Images)

and John Le Mesurier, were formally charged with plotting to murder Scott and dispose of his body. Only Thorpe was accused of hiring Newton to commit the murder. The prosecution listed as a motive the continuing damage Scott's allegations had been having on Thorpe's political career. Thorpe allegedly told fellow liberal Peter Bessell at a meeting of Parliament that Scott had to disappear. Thorpe also allegedly tried to get Liberal Party treasurer Holmes to murder Scott, but when that idea had fallen through, he had begun to plot against his alleged former lover with nightclub owner Deakin and carpet-company tycoon Le Mesurier. Finally, Thorpe was accused of having hired Newton to commit the crime and of paying Newton's £5,000 assassination fee from Liberal Party funds.

It was nearly a year before the case came before a British jury. At that time, the trial drew enormous public attention, focusing as it did on a government official's alleged sexual peccadilloes and outrageous behavior. Indeed, the case destroyed Thorpe politically. In the election, which preceded the trial by only a week, he lost his seat to a Conservative opponent, as voters had little patience with homosexual love affairs, scandals, and murder plots; furthermore, Thorpe's guilt generally was assumed. In an interesting addendum, the British Broadcasting Corporation (BBC) turned up surprising hints that Scott may not have been the only source of accusations against Thorpe.

During the 1979 trial, which lasted just over a month, Thorpe admitted he had discussed the possibility of trying to scare Scott into silence, but he categorically denied the murder-for-hire charges. In fact, he and his codefendants were completely cleared by the jury on June 29.

Over the course of Thorpe's political career, England's prime ministry changed hands several times. Twice, Labour Party candidate Harold Wilson held the seat (1964-1970, 1974-1976). Wilson was something of a character himself, insisting that the Security Service, or MI5 (Britain's equivalent of the U.S. Central Intelligence Agency), plotted to drive him from office during the late 1970's. In 2002, the BBC reported that Wilson had supposedly had a minor clerk, Jack Straw, examine evidence in Scott's social security file to determine the truth of Scott's allegations against Thorpe. Straw, who became much more prominent in British politics, acknowledged reading the file on order of his superiors, but he did not believe he violated anyone's privacy. However, parts of Scott's file disappeared, bringing suspicion that it had been examined to incriminate Thorpe. If so, the motive would have been a purely political effort by Wilson to prevent an anti-Labour Party alliance between Thorpe's Liberals and the Conservative Tory Party. The media made much of the mystery when it came to light in 2002, but no political action was taken.

IMPACT

The impact of Thorpe's trial needs to be considered in the proper context. The gay and lesbian rights movement was fully under way in Britain by the time the scandal broke, but gay and lesbian public figures were unheard of. Thus, news of Thorpe's alleged homosexual trysts came as an enormous shock to the public. His actions were considered to be criminal behavior, even though they came to light several years after male homosexuality was decriminalized in the United Kingdom. Furthermore, the public refused to believe that a political figure such as Thorpe could be involved in something as sordid as a murder-for-hire scheme.

Thus, the popular press covered the event exhaustively, and most people considered Thorpe guilty, even though the jury exonerated him. The event remains part of contemporary popular history

in Britain; indeed, the BBC's investigation into the case in 2002 proves its staying power. The scandal was enough to end Thorpe's political career, even as it left several questions unanswered, including, Why did Newton confront Scott if not to murder him?

—Jessie Bishop Powell

FURTHER READING

Freeman, Simon, and Barrie Penrose. *Rinkagate: The Rise and Fall of Jeremy Thorpe*. London: Bloomsbury, 1996. Comprehensive rehearsal of the scandal, including its political significance and analysis of Thorpe's career.

Purton, Peter. *Sodom, Gomorrah, and the New Jerusalem: Labour and Lesbian and Gay Rights, from Edward Carpenter to Today*. London: Labour Campaign for Lesbian and Gay Rights, 2006. Discusses the historical relationship between gay and lesbian rights and politics in Britain, placing the Thorpe scandal in context.

Thorpe, Jeremy. *In My Own Time: Reminiscences of a Liberal Leader*. London: Politico's, 1999. Thorpe provides perspective on his trial and acquittal but focuses more in this work on his years in office.

Waugh, Auberon. *The Last Word: An Eyewitness Account of the Trial of Jeremy Thorpe*. Boston: Little, Brown, 1980. Journalist Waugh delivers his own judgments on the Thorpe trial, contesting the judge's claim to the last word. Discussions of the British justice system are interspersed with trial reporting.

SEE ALSO: Dec. 8, 1906: Former U.S. Senator Arthur Brown Is Murdered by Lover; Sept. 4, 1932: Film Star Jean Harlow's Husband Is an Apparent Suicide; July 10, 1934: Sex Scandal Forces Resignation of Alberta Premier Brownlee; Oct. 7, 1964: President Lyndon B. Johnson's Aide Is Arrested in Gay-Sex Sting; Oct. 25, 1974: Evangelist Billy James Hargis Resigns College Presidency During Gay-Sex Scandal; Sept. 3, 1980: Congressman Bauman Is Arrested for Liaison with Teenage Boy; Oct. 14, 1983: British Cabinet Secretary Parkinson Resigns After His

Secretary Becomes Pregnant; Jan. 22, 1987: Pennsylvania Politician Kills Himself at Televised Press Conference; Aug. 19, 2004: Blog "Outs" Antigay Congressman Edward Schrock;

Jan. 21, 2006: British Politician Resigns After Gay-Sex Orgy; Nov. 2, 2006: Male Escort Reveals Sexual Liaisons with Evangelist Ted Haggard.

October 20, 1978
FIRESTONE RECALLS MILLIONS OF DEFECTIVE CAR TIRES

Consumer groups and the federal government received hundreds of complaints about Firestone 500 radial tires being defective. The tires also were directly linked to more than forty deaths and countless vehicle accidents. In the fall of 1978, under pressure from the National Highway Traffic Safety Administration and companies that bought the tire for resale, Firestone recalled the line, leading to one of the largest and most expensive consumer product recalls in American business history.

LOCALE: Washington, D.C.
CATEGORIES: Business; ethics; government

KEY FIGURES
Thomas A. Robertson (fl. 1970's), director of development for Firestone
Mario A. DiFederico (1921-2007), president of Firestone

SUMMARY OF EVENT
The 500 line of radial tires manufactured by Firestone had an increased probability of tread separation from a wheel's steel frame. Documents indicate that Firestone management, including the president of Firestone, Mario A. DiFederico, was aware of the tire's defect. Apparently, Firestone could not adequately test the problem in its manufacturing plants because the tread separation occurred as the tires aged.

Firestone opted to not disclose the defect to consumers, an estimated forty-one of whom died and hundreds of whom were in traffic accidents caused

by blowouts. After being less than cooperative with the U.S. National Highway Traffic Safety Administration (NHTSA), Firestone nevertheless decided to recall the tires in 1978, marking one of the largest and most expensive product recalls in the history of American business.

To compete with the radial tire that had been manufactured in Europe for several decades, the tire companies Goodrich and Michelin introduced radial tires to the United States during the late 1960's. Although more expensive and requiring greater technical skill to produce, radial tires were widely regarded to be superior to previous types of tires in the areas of fuel efficiency and longevity.

The Firestone Tire and Rubber Company, founded in 1900, trailed only Goodyear in its control of the domestic tire market at the beginning of the 1970's. Firestone began manufacturing its first radial tires, the 500 steel-belt line, in January, 1972. To deliver the product to the market as quickly as possible so that it could capitalize on the high demand for radial tires, Firestone converted machinery that was originally used to produce other types of tires, such as the biased-ply model. The biased-ply model was the most widely used tire in the United States prior to the introduction of the radial tire.

Firestone's radial tires initially received positive reviews by consumer magazines. The 500 steel belt became one of the most popular tires on the market. Over the course of the 500 line, Firestone produced and sold approximately twenty-four million tires at an estimated cost of about fifty dollars per tire. However, as Firestone soon realized, the tire had a defect. Firestone employees alerted upper management that the tire had a problem involving tread separation. The 500 radial tire was prone to tread separation because moisture seeped into the tire and caused corrosion of the steel frame of the tire. Consequently, the tire was susceptible to blowouts, particularly at high speeds.

As early as 1973, just months after Firestone began selling the tires, dissatisfied customers were returning the product to dealers. Firestone's own director of development, Thomas A. Robertson, wrote in a September, 1973, internal company memorandum to top management expressing concern about the 500 radial. In the memo he wrote, "We are making an inferior quality radial tire which will subject us to belt-edge separation at high mileage." Firestone received negative feedback from other sources. Major tire buyers, such as General Motors, Ford, Atlas Tire, Montgomery Ward, and Shell, threatened to terminate their contracts with Firestone. In 1973, Atlas wrote to Firestone: "In the eyes of Atlas, it appears Firestone is coming apart at the seams and drastic action is required." The safety issue was not disclosed to company stockholders or the public; instead, Firestone tried to correct the problem while still manufacturing the tire with its known defect.

In 1976, the Center for Auto Safety, a lobbying group for consumers founded in 1970, informed the NHTSA of the disproportionate amount of complaints filed about the Firestone 500 radial tire: more than fourteen thousand. The following year, the NHTSA surveyed about ninety thousand tire owners regarding their satisfaction with different types and brands of tires, including the Firestone 500. Survey results revealed consistent dissatisfaction with the Firestone 500, more so than any other tire. Furthermore, the NHTSA presented data that indicated that the 500 radial tire was more than twice as likely to be returned to dealers than other tires.

In May, 1978, bolstered by the research findings, the NHTSA issued a recommendation to Firestone that the company recall all steel-belted radial tire models in the line. Millions of tires would be subject to recall, at an estimated cost of $275 million. The annual net income of the company in 1977 was $110 million; clearly, the recall would be a serious financial burden to Firestone.

Firestone opted to not abide by the recommendations made by the NHTSA. Instead, the company asserted that it had conducted its own testing and then denied any problem with the 500 radial tire. Firestone blamed problems with the tires on consumer misuse, such as speeding, overinflation or underinflation of tires, improper maintenance, and rough use.

Firestone management also appeared before a U.S. House of Representatives subcommittee and initiated a lawsuit against the NHTSA. At the same time, Firestone was listed as the defendant in a substantial number of civil lawsuits stemming from the injuries, fatalities, and damages caused by the faulty performance of the tire. In one case, the company settled for $1.4 million.

U.S. transportation secretary Brock Adams, left, and National Highway Traffic Safety Administration head Joan Claybrook announce the Firestone tire recall. (AP/Wide World Photos)

On October 20, 1978, after Firestone was left with no other options, it voluntarily recalled 500-model tires produced in 1975 and 1976. The recalled tires were replaced with a newer model, the 721 line of radials, which received favorable safety reviews. Firestone also offered a discount to customers who were trading in tires that had been manufactured prior to 1975. The recall led to the replacement of an estimated ten million tires. The cost to Firestone, estimated at $150 million, nearly bankrupted the company.

IMPACT

Firestone was fined $500,000, one of the biggest fines levied against an American company up to that time, for its failure to disclose the safety issue to the public. While other tire makers experienced problems with the manufacturing of radial tires, these problems were not as large or as costly as those of Firestone.

Also in 1978, Firestone ceased production of the 500 steel-belt line; however, this was not the end of radial tires. Instead, radial tires are now the most commonly used tires in the industry. In 1979, Firestone president DiFederico resigned and was replaced by John Nevin, former chief executive officer of Zenith. Forced to make difficult decisions to save the floundering company, Nevin closed plants and laid off workers, eventually cutting the number of Firestone employees to half its total workforce. Firestone headquarters were relocated from Akron, Ohio, to Chicago, Illinois. In 1988, Nevin negotiated a buyout of Firestone by Bridgestone, a Japanese-owned company.

In 2000, after another NHTSA investigation and testimony before the U.S. Congress, a voluntary recall of approximately six million Firestone/Bridgestone tires was implemented. Several similarities exist between the 1978 and 2000 recalls. Tread separation was the defect and impetus behind both. As during the 1970's, Firestone/Bridgestone reportedly had been aware of the defect in 2000 as well. As was the case during the 1970's, Firestone initially denied any tire defect and reiterated that tire failure was caused by consumer misuse. However, whereas the 1978 recall largely centered on

passenger vehicles, the foci of the 2000 recall were the sport utility vehicle, especially the Ford Explorer, and lightweight trucks. Defective tires led to rollovers, especially, and caused between sixty-two and two hundred or more deaths. The cost of the 2000 recall was estimated to be $350 million.

—*Margaret E. Leigey*

FURTHER READING

Healey, James R., and Chris Wayward. "Tire Concerns Go Back 1 1/2 Years Before Recall: Ford Documents from January '99 Refer to Problems." *USA Today*, September 11, 2000. Provides a summary of events that led to the 2000 tire recall by Firestone/Bridgestone.

Love, Steve, and David Giffels. *Wheels of Fortune: The Story of Rubber in Akron*. Akron, Ohio: University of Akron Press, 1999. This book provides a comprehensive history of the tire industry and includes discussion of Firestone.

McDonald, Kevin M. *Shifting Out of Park: Moving Auto Safety from Recalls to Reason*. Tucson, Ariz.: Lawyers & Judges Publishing, 2004. A comparative study of the auto recall process that includes discussion of regulations, the courts and litigation, federal investigations, and consumer awareness.

Stanley, Guy D. D. *Managing External Issues: Theory and Practice*. Greenwich, Conn.: JAI Press, 1985. One case study in management this text examines the Firestone 500 tire scandal from the perspectives of Firestone and government safety experts.

SEE ALSO: 1930: Liberia Is Accused of Selling Its Own Citizens into Slavery; Sept.-Oct., 1937: Prescription Elixir Causes More than One Hundred Deaths; Sept. 17, 1985: Media Allege Canadian Officials Allowed Sale of Rancid Tuna; Feb. 4, 1996: Whistle-Blower Reveals Tobacco Industry Corruption; Nov. 17, 2005: Liberian Workers Sue Bridgestone Firestone over Slave Labor; Summer, 2006-Mar. 16, 2007: Manufacturer Recalls Pet Food That Killed Thousands of American Pets.

January 26, 1979

FORMER VICE PRESIDENT NELSON ROCKEFELLER DIES MYSTERIOUSLY

Nelson A. Rockefeller, former U.S. vice president and four-term New York State governor, was found dead in his townhouse suite of an apparent heart attack. Present with Rockefeller when emergency medical personnel arrived was Rockefeller's twenty-six-year-old assistant, Megan Marshak, furthering speculation of a romantic affair between the two. The reason for Rockefeller's death remains a mystery.

LOCALE: New York, New York
CATEGORIES: Sex; politics; publishing and
journalism

KEY FIGURES

Nelson A. Rockefeller (1908-1979), vice president
of the United States, 1974-1977, and governor
of New York, 1959-1973
Megan Marshak (b. 1952), Rockefeller's aide and
alleged lover
Ponchitta Pierce (b. 1942), television journalist
and Marshak's friend

SUMMARY OF EVENT

By the mid-twentieth century, Nelson A. Rockefeller was one of the towering figures in U.S. politics and public life. Born in 1908, he was the grandson of John D. Rockefeller, founder of the vast Standard Oil fortune, and Nelson Aldrich, an influential Republican senator from Rhode Island. These twin heritages of wealth and politics, along with patronage of the arts, were lifelong keynotes of Rockefeller's life. His foremost interest was politics.

When Vice President Gerald R. Ford became the thirty-eighth president of the United States in the wake of Richard Nixon's resignation in 1974, he nominated Rockefeller to be vice president. Ford was focused on healing the country after the Watergate scandal. As a centrist, Rockefeller seemed an obvious choice, but he first had to be confirmed by

both the House of Representatives and the Senate. The process took an unexpectedly long four months, with hearings that probed Rockefeller's financial holdings. He was sworn in on December 19, 1974.

Rockefeller had served, in some capacity, every U.S. president from Franklin D. Roosevelt to Gerald R. Ford, except one, and had been an accomplished four-term governor of New York. More than most politicians, however, his ultimate ambitions were focused on the presidency. In addition to his wealth and having a panel of knowledgeable advisers, he was energetic and charismatic and had many contacts on the international scene. From all

Nelson A. Rockefeller in 1964. (AP/Wide World Photos)

Megan Marshak, alleged lover of former vice president Nelson A. Rockefeller. (AP/Wide World Photos)

accounts, he felt he was a "natural" for the office, yet in his three serious tries for the presidency—in 1960, 1964, and 1968—he was unable to win his party's nomination.

After becoming vice president, Rockefeller found the office's round of ceremonial duties boring. His protégé, Henry Kissinger, was largely steering foreign policy, and Rockefeller expected to have a similarly large voice in shaping domestic policy. President Ford had his own ideas to the contrary, and so did his chief of staff, an ambitious forty-two-year-old, Donald Rumsfeld. During Rockefeller's last year as vice president, he added a young journalist, Megan Marshak, to his staff. Marshak was in her early twenties; Rockefeller was sixty-eight years old. After she was on staff, Marshak was promoted rapidly and was often at Rockefeller's side.

When Rockefeller left office at the end of Ford's

term in January, 1977, Marshak was one of the few staff members who continued to work for him in private life. Upon leaving politics, Rockefeller announced that his political ambitions were over. He planned to devote his energies to two projects related to his vast collection of original art: marketing good reproductions of his collection and writing a book about the holdings. Marshak worked closely with him on these projects and seemed genuinely interested in the art collection. In public she had a respectful demeanor, but it was inevitable that rumors would arise about a romantic or sexual relationship between her and Rockefeller.

Rockefeller had a private town house apartment on Fifty-fourth Street in Manhattan. It was connected to a suite of offices next door. On the evening of Friday, January 26, 1979, emergency medical technicians were summoned to the town house. Present when they arrived were Rockefeller, unconscious and probably dead from a heart attack, and Marshak. Rockefeller was rushed to Lenox Hill Hospital. His wife, Happy, and his brother, Laurence, were called in. Also called were his physician, Ernest Esakof, and a Rockefeller family spokesperson, Hugh Morrow. Esakof announced Rockefeller's death at 12:20 A.M. Marshak accompanied Rockefeller in the ambulance and held his oxygen bottle. She, too, was at the hospital but soon got out of the family's way.

Soon, the press arrived. Morrow issued several different versions of what had happened. First, he had announced that Rockefeller died at his desk, alone except for a bodyguard. This story was soon dismissed after the press found out that Marshak was with Rockefeller when he died. Reports leaked out that she had been wearing a black caftan and Rockefeller had been wearing a suit and tie. The time factors, too, failed to add up. The time of the heart attack was placed at 10:15 P.M., but the emergency call was not made until one hour later. It was later discovered that Marshak did not make the 911 call. By her own account, the call was made by Marshak's friend and neighbor, journalist Ponchitta Pierce, whom Marshak called to help when Rockefeller collapsed. Pierce made the phone call then left the apartment.

The Rockefeller family abhorred scandal and, after the flurry of conflicting reports by Morrow, said nothing further about the circumstances of Rockefeller's death. No autopsy was performed; thus, it remains unclear what caused his death. It remains unknown as well whether he died while having sex with Marshak, although this scenario, to many, seems likely. Marshak has never spoken publicly about the death of her boss.

The scanty facts available only added to the salacious speculation surrounding Rockefeller's death. Besides the common assumption that he and Marshak were having an affair, others claim that Marshak's presence was a cover for a liaison Rockefeller was conducting with someone else, possibly Pierce.

IMPACT

Rockefeller's death came at the cusp of a sea change in the press's coverage of prominent politicians' sexual behavior. Until this point, unless a public figure did something outrageous in public—such as the 1974 scandal involving Congressman Wilbur D. Mills and a stripper—journalists kept silent. The facts in the death of the former vice president were scanty, but the circumstances could not be ignored, and the press covered them accordingly. Within a decade, the press was relentless in its coverage of political sex scandals.

—*Emily Alward*

FURTHER READING

Apostolidis, Paul, and Juliet A. Williams, eds. *Public Affairs: Politics in the Age of Sex Scandals*. Durham, N.C.: Duke University Press, 2004. A study of politics and political culture in the context of sex scandals.

Persico, Joseph E. *The Imperial Rockefeller: A Biography of Nelson A. Rockefeller*. New York: Simon & Schuster, 1982. A highly readable biography of Rockefeller that is generally sympathetic but not uncritical. Persico's study remains a reliable and relevant source.

Reich, Cary. *The Life of Nelson A. Rockefeller*. New York: Doubleday, 1996. An excellent biography of Rockefeller. Based on solid research, Reich's interpretation is comprehensive and laudatory but still critical.

Roberts, Sam. "Serving as Ford's No. 2, Rockefeller Never Took His Eye Off Top Job." *The New York Times*, December 31, 2006. Insights, in the light of later events, into Rockefeller's frustrations as vice president.

Rockefeller, David. *David Rockefeller's Memoirs*. New York: Random House, 2002. A comprehensive memoir by Nelson Rockefeller's brother, David. Includes valuable insights on Nelson's early years and his impact as governor of New York and vice president of the United States.

SEE ALSO: Mar. 2-Sept. 25, 1963: John Profumo Affair Rocks British Government; July 18, 1969: Senator Edward Kennedy's Driving Accident Kills Mary Jo Kopechne; Oct. 7, 1974: Congressman Wilbur D. Mills's Stripper Affair Leads to His Downfall; May 23, 1976: *Washington Post* Exposes Congressman Wayne L. Hays's Affair; Sept., 1976: Jimmy Carter Admits Committing Adultery in His Heart; Dec. 7, 1980: Rita Jenrette's "Diary of a Mad Congresswife" Scandalizes Washington; Aug. 10, 1989: Japanese Prime Minister Sosuke Resigns After Affair with a Geisha; Sept. 24, 1992: British Cabinet Member David Mellor Resigns over Romantic Affair; Jan. 17, 1998: President Bill Clinton Denies Sexual Affair with a White House Intern; May 2, 2000: New York Mayor Rudy Giuliani's Extramarital Affair Is Revealed.

1970's

April 18, 1979
ACTOR LEE MARVIN IS ORDERED TO PAY PALIMONY TO FORMER LOVER

The term "palimony" was coined during the trial of Michelle Triola against her former lover, actor Lee Marvin. After their breakup, Triola sued Marvin for a property settlement, claiming that she had given up a promising career to live with and care for him. The California Supreme Court ruled that unmarried couples could sue for property settlements even if no express contract exists, as long as some sort of legal agreement was made between partners.

ALSO KNOWN AS: *Marvin v. Marvin*
LOCALE: Malibu, California
CATEGORIES: Law and the courts; civil rights and liberties; women's issues; social issues and reform; Hollywood

KEY FIGURES

Lee Marvin (1924-1987), American film star
Michelle Triola (b. 1933), American actor, dancer, and singer
Marvin Mitchelson (1928-2004), Triola's divorce attorney

SUMMARY OF EVENT

Michelle Triola had lived with actor Lee Marvin for seven years beginning in 1964. He was married at the time. She would claim in her lawsuit against him that she had been his cook, housekeeper, and companion, and had taken care of him after he had been drinking, devoting herself to his welfare. She also claimed that he told her, "What I have is yours and what you have is mine," and that they agreed to appear as husband and wife in public. During the time of their cohabitation, Triola used the name Michelle Triola Marvin. The court would later rule that because Triola took Marvin's last name, Marvin is presumed to have implicitly agreed to support her as her husband.

At the time of the lawsuit, California law required that married couples equally divide the assets of their marriages (assets were called community property). Although the couple was not formally married, Triola believed that she was entitled to compensation from Marvin because she fulfilled her obligations under their informal agreement and gave up her career as an entertainer to care for him. He disagreed with her contentions, and the dispute went to court. Celebrity divorce lawyer Marvin Mitchelson insisted that Triola receive her claim of Marvin's earnings of more than one million dollars. The so-called palimony (from "pal" and "alimony") suit led to a media scandal.

Even in the first decade of the twenty-first century, cohabitation by unmarried couples was a crime in several states, and adultery was a crime in about half of the states. Such criminal statutes, however, were rarely enforced. As used in criminal statutes, cohabitation includes nonmarital relationships that had been called "meretricious," or sexual. Illicit relationships were once considered void in the realm of public policy. If an agreement between the partners is supported by a quid pro quo or what the law calls "consideration," however, courts have become more and more liberal in upholding these agreements. In a nonspousal agreement that one partner will provide services in the home and the other will support the household, for example, the value of the services constitutes the consideration that validates the agreement.

An express agreement is one in which the parties state their understanding either orally or in writing. An implied agreement is inferred from behavior or conduct in which the parties act in such a way that it is reasonable to conclude that they must have reached an understanding. Unjust enrichment is the doctrine holding that one person should not profit inequitably at another's expense. If one party has received something of value at another's expense, or benefited unjustly, the nonenriched party may seek the remedy of restitution or reimbursement. To prevent unjust enrichment of one partner at the other's expense, a partner who provides services may recover in *quantum meruit* or the reasonable value of the services rendered. The reasonable value of the services must exceed the reasonable value of the support received if it can be shown that the services were rendered with the expectation of monetary reward. That may be difficult to demonstrate. Another possible remedy involves a constructive trust, inferred from the behavior of the parties. It is imposed by the courts to do justice and to prevent the unjust enrichment of one party at the other's expense.

Triola's 1976 lawsuit relied, in part, on the legal doctrine of quasi-contract, or an implied-in-law contract imposed by the courts to prevent injustice. It is a special form of contract that lacks all the trappings of a formal written document such as mutual assent of the parties, but it is imposed on the parties by the courts to avoid unjust enrichment. Under this doctrine, courts may infer a legally enforceable agreement from the circumstances surrounding the dealings of the parties, even though the parties have not entered into any formal written agreement. Triola asserted that similar logic should be applied to her relationship with Marvin, and that their conduct should be viewed as an "implied agreement" granting her many of the same rights given by law to a spouse. The court, however, declined to treat unmarried cohabitants like married persons. In her suit, Triola argued that, aside from a marriage license, she and Marvin were essentially married from 1964 until 1970. As such, Triola contended that she was entitled to half of what he had earned during their relationship, or $1.8 million including $100,000 for loss of her own potential earnings. Her attorney, Mitchelson, demanded palimony and had to prove that Marvin breached an oral or implied contract to share his assets.

Initially, Triola lost her 1976 case on legal grounds. On appeal, the California

Supreme Court decided that her case should be heard again in the lower courts, sparking a number of similar cases in other states. On rehearing, the superior court ruled, on April 18, 1979, that Triola had failed to prove her alleged agreement, that there was no express or implied contract, and that there was no unjust enrichment. Judge Arthur K. Marshall denied her community property claim for half of the $3.6 million that Marvin had earned during their seven years of cohabitation. However, Marshall did order Marvin to pay Triola $104,000 for "rehabilitation purposes," that is, job training.

Marvin appealed, and on August 11, 1981, the California Court of Appeal reversed Marshall's decision, declaring that Triola was entitled to no money, including the $104,000 she was awarded in 1979. The appeals court, although upholding the

Lee Marvin and Michelle Triola in 1966. (Hulton Archive/Getty Images)

concept of palimony, ruled that a cohabitant (Triola) in a nonspousal relationship has no community property claim. Instead, a cohabitant has a contract claim. Without evidence that there had been a contract between Marvin and Triola stipulating that Marvin would support her should their relationship end, Triola could not recover any money.

IMPACT

Although Triola lost her 1976 palimony case on technical grounds, *Marvin v. Marvin* nonetheless created new law when the court decided to address the issue of "property rights of a nonmarital partner in the absence of an express contract." The court's ruling, in effect, said that a nonmarital partner can attempt to establish an implied contract in the absence of an express contract. Furthermore, it ruled that the law cannot *assume* that an unmarried couple intends to keep their properties and earnings separate and, thus, the law must take into account all possible arrangements between an unmarried plaintiff and defendant. The court stated,

> [W]e conclude that the mere fact that a couple have not participated in a valid marriage ceremony cannot serve as a basis for a court's inference that the couple intend to keep their earnings and property separate and independent; the parties' intention can only be ascertained by a more searching inquiry into the nature of their relationship.

In *Marvin v. Marvin*, the court also spoke of the growth of nonmarital partnerships in contemporary society. The court recognized the diversity among cohabitants and gave the trial courts an opportunity to tailor their remedies to the particular circumstances of the parties. Without specific guidelines for application of quasi-contractual remedies in nonspousal agreements, however, *Marvin* left uncertain the circumstances and limitations for each type of recovery. The court's rationale also has been applied to same-gender couples.

The 1979 appeals court ruling, in which Marvin was ordered to pay for Triola more than $104,000, was unique because it determined that Triola's case had at least some merit. It therefore extended the 1976 ruling that the "nature of" a couple's relationship should be probed in deciding the contractual intentions, if any, of both the plaintiff and the defendant.

—Marcia J. Weiss

FURTHER READING

Booth, Alan, and Ann C. Crouter, eds. *Just Living Together: Implications of Cohabitation on Families, Children, and Social Policy*. Mahwah, N.J.: Erlbaum, 2002. A collection of articles exploring the social significance of cohabitation. Articles look at legal policy, child development, and the culture of cohabitation.

Kay, Herma Hill, and Carol Amyx. "*Marvin vs. Marvin*: Preserving the Options." *California Law Review* 65, no. 5 (September, 1977): 937-977. A scholarly guide to statutory and case law prior to the *Marvin* case.

Moller, Mark K. "Almost Like Being Married." *Legal Times*, April 5, 2004. An informally written account of the *Marvin* case.

Weitzman, Lenore J. *The Marriage Contract: Spouses, Lovers, and the Law*. New York: Free Press, 1981. A thorough and insightful guide to the law surrounding marriage and the family.

Zec, Donald. *Marvin: The Story of Lee Marvin*. New York: St. Martin's Press, 1980. An illustrated biography of Lee Marvin written by a syndicated entertainment columnist. Contains detailed accounts of Marvin as a drunken rebel and overnight successful actor and discusses incidents that occurred during the trial.

SEE ALSO: June 4, 1943: Actor Charles Chaplin Is Sued for Paternity; Mar. 21, 1976: Actor Claudine Longet Kills Ski Champion Vladimir Sabich; Jan. 26, 1979: Former Vice President Nelson Rockefeller Dies Mysteriously; Mar. 10, 1980: Scarsdale Diet Doctor Is Killed by His Lover; July 28, 1980: Magazine Reveals Baseball Star Steve Garvey's Marital Problems; Apr. 28, 1981: Tennis Star Billie Jean King Is Sued for Palimony; June 12, 1994: Double Murder Leads to Sensational O. J. Simpson Trial.

June 4, 1979
SOUTH AFRICAN PRESIDENT B. J. VORSTER RESIGNS IN MULDERGATE SCANDAL

South African president B. J. Vorster was found to have used government funds to finance a propaganda war to sway local and international opinion in favor of apartheid. Vorster's Afrikaner National Party established The Citizen, *an English-language newspaper that supported apartheid. Vorster, along with other government ministers, resigned in disgrace.*

ALSO KNOWN AS: Muldergate; Rhoodiegate; Infogate
LOCALE: South Africa
CATEGORIES: Corruption; government; politics; publishing and journalism; social issues and reform; colonialism and imperialism

KEY FIGURES
B. J. Vorster (1915-1983), president, 1978-1979, and prime minister, 1966-1978, of South Africa
Connie Mulder (1925-1988), minister of information for South Africa
Eschel Rhoodie (1933-1993), secretary to the Department of Information

SUMMARY OF EVENT
With increased international television access, media manipulation is one of the more common types of government corruption. The information scandal in South Africa, nicknamed Muldergate by local newspapers, involved such media manipulation. Coconspirators included officials Connie Mulder, Eschel Rhoodie, and President B. J. Vorster. A significant amount of money had been funneled through the Department of Information and placed into outside accounts. The funds were used to finance a government-furnished newspaper to fight a propaganda war in favor of the Afrikaner National Party (NP) and apartheid, or government-sanctioned racial segregation. The secret operation was soon discovered, and investigations unfolded the story before the public eye.

As early as the mid-seventeenth century, English and Dutch colonizers settled in South Africa for the fertile lands, eventually establishing communities and laws that ensured white influence throughout the country. Apartheid laws were enacted in 1948, legalizing racial segregation. This represented an effort by the NP to take control of economic and social systems in South Africa. A strict set of laws was put into place as a means of separation, categorizing citizens based on appearance and acceptance within society. Regulations were placed on employment positions, voting, and marriage. Blacks were forced to carry identity documents—pass books—before they were permitted travel around the region. Land was divided into homelands, which further segregated communities by family origin. Mass disagreement with such policies eventually led to guerrilla warfare tactics from some citizens, with the government refusing to nullify apartheid laws. A civil war was beginning to seem like a possibility.

While South Africans fought for their rights, government officials did what they could to affirm legislation. At this time, Vorster was a supporter of the apartheid government, a member of the NP, and an official in Parliament. In 1966, he was elected prime minister, succeeding Hendrick Frensch Verwoerd, an active supporter of apartheid rule as well.

While an advocate and enforcer of apartheid, Vorster recognized that the white minority would not be able to stay in power indefinitely. He knew that campaigners for the African National Congress (ANC) were fighting to have their voices heard, demanding reform in South African society. It was feared by Vorster and the NP that as the struggle persisted, foreign political opinion could be swayed toward the plight of the people. Determined to get the support of English-speaking whites and black African states, Vorster needed a new platform. Specifically, the government needed a new English-speaking newspaper to counter the *Rand Daily Mail*, an English-speaking newspaper that reported

1970's

B. J. Vorster. (Hulton Archive/Getty Images)

on racial issues and was against apartheid. The NP believed the *Rand Daily Mail* was part of what the apartheid government called a "hate South Africa crusade."

Rhoodie was the secretary of information working under Vorster. Before working at the Department of Information (DOI), Rhoodie helped establish *To the Point,* a secret government-funded magazine formed to counter foreign-news headlines unfavorable to the pro-apartheid government of South Africa. The newest secret project to create NP propaganda under the direction of Vorster would be called Operation Annemarie (named for Rhoodie's teenage daughter). Rhoodie worked closely with the bureau of state security to ensure this illegal operation was kept secret. In addition, he brought in relatives to hold key positions so that secrets would not be leaked. Rhoodie, Vorster, and Mulder, the minister of information, met at Cape Town in early 1974 to plan the covert operation. They agreed that typical campaign methods such as

films and flyers were no longer effective in the political world. It was then agreed that they would create *The Citizen,* an English-speaking newspaper that would attempt to sway public and foreign opinion toward the ideas of the NP.

To finance *The Citizen*, the DOI used budgeted money from the Department of Defense. It also involved millionaire Louis Luyt to handle the business end of the budget transaction. Luyt acted as the newspaper's owner, and the NP government created ghost organizations to make the transfer of funds look less suspicious. The first issue of the paper came out in September, 1976.

Problems within the framework of the operation existed from the beginning, however, and one significant part of the plan was called into question in 1978. The conspirators were under the impression that the money was coming from the DOI, but the money had never been allocated to the department. In essence, there should have been no money available, and by the time it was realized, the funds, which were stolen, had already been spent.

Rumors of missing funds and a government-furnished newspaper soon reached other government officials, who immediately ordered an audit of the DOI. Mulder was brought before Parliament and claimed innocence in the matter. Supreme court justice Anton Mostert presented details of the information scandal and divulged intentions and identities in his report of November, 1978. Mulder's claim of innocence was disproved in the report, and all other participants were implicated. Known as the Muldergate scandal, the secret project was labeled as a government-furnished campaign plot. Mostert's report also exposed illegal activities such as bribes of international news agencies and the use of taxpayer monies to fund personal activities.

Ironically, the first paper to report Operation Annemarie was the *Rand Daily Mail*, which painted a colorful picture of the information scandal. Media coverage brought Vorster, Mulder, and Rhoodie into the spotlight. Vorster resigned on June 4, 1979, and Mulder soon resigned as well. Taking the place of Vorster was his longtime competitor, P. W. Botha. Botha's first official action as prime minister was to create a commission, led by Judge Roelof

Erasmus, to look into the corruption. Anonymous sources began coming forward with additional information on financial discrepancies and other fraudulent activities, making it impossible to argue the innocence of those involved. The final report of the Erasmus Commission was issued in June, 1979.

IMPACT

While Mulder and Vorster were forced out of office, Rhoodie did not admit to the accusations against him. Instead, he fled South Africa and moved first to Ecuador, then Great Britain, where he tried to attain political asylum. The attempt failed and Rhoodie fled once more, this time to France, where he was finally caught and incarcerated. He was soon extradited back to South Africa and tried. Rhoodie was acquitted on all charges and eventually wrote *The Real Information Scandal* (1983), which detailed his covert projects.

Muldergate caused great disappointment within the NP, which was depending on Vorster and Mulder to continue white domination in South Africa. The party knew that apartheid law would be at serious risk under Botha's leadership and that the future of racial segregation was in jeopardy. The ANC, led by Nelson Mandela, continued advocating against apartheid and eventually influenced the leadership of South African society. Nelson was president of South Africa from 1994 to 1999.

—Lauren Riggi and Brion Sever

FURTHER READING

Barber, James P. *South Africa in the Twentieth Century: A Political History—In Search of a Nation State*. Malden, Mass.: Blackwell, 1999. The author traces the history of the politics, international relations, and key trends that help define South Africa's place in the twentieth century.

Guelke, Adrian. *Rethinking the Rise and Fall of Apartheid: South Africa and World Politics.* New York: Palgrave Macmillan, 2005. A history of apartheid in South Africa and its influence on global politics. Includes the chapter "From Vorster to Botha: New Departure or Militarized Cul de Sac?," which asks whether Muldergate was a strong anomaly or a political diversion from the movement against apartheid.

O'Meara, Patrick. *South Africa's Watergate: The Muldergate Scandals.* Hanover, N.H.: American Universities Field Staff, 1979. The author details the events surrounding B. J. Vorster's scandal, as it occurred.

Rees, Mervyn, and Chris Day. *Muldergate: The Story of the Info Scandal.* Johannesburg: Macmillan South Africa, 1980. This book focuses on the scandal's unfolding and examines its possible causes.

SEE ALSO: Nov. 15, 1908: Belgium Confiscates Congo Free State from King Leopold II; 1930: Liberia Is Accused of Selling Its Own Citizens into Slavery; Mar. 31, 1933: *New York Times* Reporter Denies Reports of a Soviet Famine; Late 1955: British Atrocities in Kenya's Mau Mau Rebellion Are Revealed; Nov. 17, 2005: Liberian Workers Sue Bridgestone Firestone over Slave Labor.

1970'S

September 26, 1979
LOVE CANAL RESIDENTS SUE CHEMICAL COMPANY

During the 1940's and 1950's, Hooker Chemical buried approximately twenty-two thousand tons of toxic waste at its landfill in Love Canal, a neighborhood in Niagara Falls, New York. By the late 1970's, residents of Love Canal began noticing serious health problems in the neighborhood, including large numbers of miscarriages and birth disorders. In 1983, Hooker Chemical's parent company agreed to an out-of-court settlement with more than one thousand residents who had sued. The dumping scandal led to the creation of the multibillion-dollar federal Superfund program for cleaning up of toxic-waste sites around the United States.

LOCALE: Niagara Falls, New York
CATEGORIES: Law and the courts; environmental issues; business; medicine and health care; families and children

KEY FIGURES
Lois Gibbs (b. 1951), president of the Love Canal Homeowners Association
Robert P. Whalen (b. 1930), New York State health commissioner, 1975-1978
Hugh Leo Carey (b. 1919), governor of New York, 1975-1982
Jimmy Carter (b. 1924), president of the United States, 1977-1981

SUMMARY OF EVENT
In 1892, businessman William T. Love purchased the land that separated the upper and lower parts of the Niagara River, situated near the City of Niagara Falls, to dig a canal that would connect the two river branches. What came to be called Love Canal was never completed, however, and during the 1920's, the City of Niagara Falls purchased the property to use as a landfill. In 1942, Hooker Chemical (HC) in turn bought the sixteen-acre parcel for private use as a chemical disposal site. Be-

tween 1947 and 1952, the company buried approximately twenty-two thousand tons of hazardous waste at Love Canal. After the area was completely filled, the company backfilled the site and then encased it with four feet of clay to contain the toxic waste.

In 1953, HC sold the land to the Niagara Falls School District for one dollar. The property deed included a warning about the chemicals buried on the site and also released HC from any future legal responsibilities. Shortly thereafter, the school district built the Ninety-ninth Street Elementary School on the site of the former landfill and, as expected, residential homes began to be built near the school. By the 1970's, the Love Canal neighborhood had about

A sign warns against entering a fenced-off area of the Love Canal neighborhood. (AP/Wide World Photos)

1,800 single-family homes and 240 apartments for low-income residents.

Beginning during the late 1950's, Love Canal residents frequently complained to the city about burns suffered by their children and pets, strange odors, oozing sludge, and the existence of unknown substances on their properties. In cooperation with Niagara County, the city hired Calspan Corporation to investigate the complaints. The company reported that it had found toxic chemicals in the Love Canal area and provided the city with a list of corrective procedures. In response, the city did nothing.

During the mid-1970's, years of abnormally heavy rains caused chemicals to surface. Ominous pools of multicolored liquid appeared following storms. Burns and mysterious rashes became increasingly common, a section of the schoolyard collapsed, gardens and backyard trees died, and strange substances seeped through basement walls. The *Niagara Gazette* began investigating these problems in October, 1976.

In April, 1978, the *Niagara Gazette* published several newspaper articles about the buried toxic waste. The articles revived the residents' fight for the chemical cleanup of their neighborhood and also focused national attention on Love Canal. On August 2, Love Canal was declared unsafe by the commissioner of the New York State Department of Health (DOH), Robert P. Whalen. Citing high rates of miscarriages and birth defects, Whalen ordered the school closed and recommended that pregnant women and infants leave Love Canal immediately. However, residents were outraged at his suggestion. They believed the area was unsafe for all residents That same year, the U.S. Environmental Protection Agency (EPA) completed its own investigation and determined that serious health risks indeed were endangering the community.

The community began to be more actively involved in the crisis. One community leader was Lois Gibbs, who started a petition to close the Ninety-ninth Street school. She believed her son's

"CHEMICALS LINGER IN THE SOIL"

American biologist Rachel Carson stunned the public when she condemned the widespread use of chemicals, namely pesticides, for causing the slow death of the environment—and the slow death of humans. Her warnings in Silent Spring *(1962) presaged the toxic waste disaster at Love Canal.*

For the first time in the history of the world, every human being is now subjected to contact with dangerous chemicals, from the moment of conception until death. In the less than two decades of their use, the synthetic pesticides have been so thoroughly distributed throughout the animate and inanimate world that they occur virtually everywhere. They have been recovered from most of the major river systems and even from streams of groundwater flowing unseen through the earth. Residues of these chemicals linger in the soil to which they may have been applied a dozen years before. They have entered and lodged in the bodies of fish, birds, reptiles, and domestic and wild animals so universally that scientists carrying on animal experiments find it almost impossible to locate subjects free from such contamination. They have been found in fish in remote mountain lakes, in earthworms burrowing in soil, in the eggs of birds—and in man himself. For these chemicals are now stored in the bodies of the vast majority of human beings, regardless of age. They occur in the mother's milk, and probably in the tissues of the unborn child.

All this has come about because of the sudden rise and prodigious growth of an industry for the production of man-made or synthetic chemicals with insecticidal properties. This industry is the child of the Second World War.

health problems were directly linked to the school being located on top of the toxic landfill. While going door to door obtaining signatures, she found that many residents also were suffering from similar health problems. In July, 1978, New York governor Hugh Leo Carey granted emergency powers to the DOH to handle the growing crisis at Love Canal, allocating $500,000 for health studies on the residents of the area. On August 2, the DOH declared a medical state of emergency at Love Canal and ordered the temporary evacuation of all pregnant women and children under the age of two. The agency also closed the Ninety-ninth Street school.

CHEMICALS DISPOSED OF IN LOVE CANAL BY HOOKER CHEMICAL, 1942-1953

Type of Waste	Physical State	Total Est. Quantity—Tons	Container
Misc. acid chlorides other than benzoyl— includes acetyl, caprylyl, butyryl, nitro benzoyls	liquid and solid	400	drum
Thionyl chloride and misc. sulfur/chlorine compounds	liquid and solid	500	drum
Misc. chlorination—includes waxes, oils, naphthenes, aniline	liquid and solid	1,000	drum
Dodecyl (Lauryl, Lorol) mercaptans (DDM), chlorides and misc. organic sulfur compounds	liquid and solid	2,400	drum
Trichlorophenol (TCP)	liquid and solid	200	drum
Benzoyl chlorides and benzo-trichlorides	liquid and solid	800	drum
Metal chlorides	solid	400	drum
Liquid disulfides (LDS/LDSN/BDS) and chlorotoluenes	liquid	700	drum
Hexachlorocyclohexane (Lindane/BHC)	solid	6,900	drum and nonmetallic containers
Chlorobenzenes	liquid and solid	2,000	drum and nonmetallic containers
Benzylchlorides—includes benzyl chloride, benzyl alcohol, benzyl thiocyanate	solid	2,400	drum
Sodium sulfide/sulfhydrates	solid	2,000	drum
Misc. 10% of above		2,000	

Source: Interagency Task Force on Hazardous Wastes, New York State Department of Health, *Draft Report on Hazardous Waste Disposal in Erie and Niagara Counties*, New York, March, 1979.

On August 4, Gibbs and her neighbors organized the Love Canal Homeowners Association (LCHA) and began an aggressive campaign to prove that the toxic chemicals buried in Love Canal were directly linked to the unusually high number of health problems in the area. These health problems included epilepsy, asthma, cancers, urinary tract infections, miscarriages, and birth disorders. On August 7, U.S. president Jimmy Carter declared a federal state of emergency at Love Canal and ordered the relocation of all the families living on the first two blocks closest to the landfill. In September, the U.S. House of Representatives allocated four million dollars toward the cleanup of the site. In November, more than two hundred chemicals, including benzene and dioxin, were found buried at Love Canal.

Throughout 1979, while state and federal agencies continued testing for chemical contamination and cleaning up the area, the LCHA continued its fight to have all remaining families relocated from Love Canal. On September 26, the first residents' lawsuits were filed, holding HC liable for the environmental disaster. By October 31, more than eight hundred suits were filed against HC, the city, the county, and the board of education. Combined, these lawsuits sought approximately $800 billion in damages. On December 20, the U.S. Department of Justice, on behalf of the EPA, also filed a $124 million suit against HC's parent company, Occidental Chemical, a subsidiary of Occidental Petroleum.

Several months later, in May, 1980, the EPA announced that after extensive medical examinations of Love Canal residents, the agency found thirty-six individuals with chromosome damage. On May 19, LCHA president Gibbs and other LCHA members held two EPA employees hostage at the association's office and demanded that President Carter do something to help the residents of Love Canal. Two days later, Carter declared another health emergency that temporarily relocated the remaining families. On October 1, Carter signed a bill that made the relocations permanent.

Three years later (October, 1983), a lawsuit filed by 1,328 former residents of Love Canal against Occidental Petroleum was settled out of court for approximately $20 million. In June, 1994, the company agreed to reimburse the state of New York a total of $98 million for Love Canal cleanup expenses, and in December, 1995, the company agreed to pay $129 million in damages to the federal government for costs associated with cleaning the site.

IMPACT

The Love Canal toxic-dumping scandal had far-reaching consequences not only for the residents of Love Canal but also for the country, its industry, and its government. Through hard work and perseverance, Gibbs and the homeowners' association fought to convince local, state, and federal authorities that the toxic chemicals buried underneath their homes were causing serious health problems. They demanded relocation and corporate accountability. As a result of their efforts, the public gained a new understanding of the hidden dangers of chemical exposure and the importance of proper chemical disposal.

Most significantly, the toxic-dumping scandal led to the creation of the Comprehensive Environmental Response, Compensation, and Liability Act

(CERCLA) that was passed on December 11, 1980. Commonly known as the Superfund Act, it oversees the cleanup of abandoned hazardous-waste sites in the United States. Love Canal was the first Superfund site. The total cost of the cleanup was approximately $400 million and took twenty-one years to complete.

—Bernadette Zbicki Heiney

FURTHER READING

Collin, Robert W. *The Environmental Protection Agency: Cleaning Up America's Act.* Westport, Conn.: Greenwood Press, 2006. This book documents the history of the Environmental Protection Agency and reviews some of its most notable cases, including Love Canal.

Fletcher, Thomas H. *From Love Canal to Environmental Justice: The Politics of Hazardous Waste on the Canada-U.S. Border.* Orchard Park, N.Y.: Broadview Press, 2003. Beginning with the tragedy at Love Canal, the author traces the history of environmental disasters and the government policies and procedures that have been created to handle them, both in the United States and in Canada.

Freudenberg, Nicholas. *Not in Our Backyards! Community Action for Health and the Environment.* New York: Monthly Review Press, 1984. Excellent source of information on community action in response to environmental problems. Chapters begin with case studies and then focus on a particular issue such as government regulation, public education, public protest, or legal and legislative action. References, index, and helpful lists of relevant books, manuals for environmental activists, and environmental organizations.

Gibbs, Lois Marie, with Murray Levine. *Love Canal: The Story Continues.* Stony Creek, Conn.: New Society, 1998. An autobiographical account, first published in 1982, by Gibbs about her struggles as the president of the Love Canal Homeowners Association and getting help for the residents of Love Canal.

Levine, Adeline Gordon. *Love Canal: Science, Politics, and People.* Lexington, Mass.: D. C. Heath,

1982. The author chronicles the events at Love Canal, focusing primarily on the community's reactions and responses to the chemical disaster and their fight with the U.S. government for help.

SEE ALSO: 1956-1962: Prescription Thalidomide Causes Widespread Birth Disorders; May 29, 1981: Court Finds That Ford Ignored Pinto's Safety Problems; Dec. 16, 1982: Congress Cites

Environmental Protection Agency Chief for Contempt; Feb. 4, 1996: Whistle-Blower Reveals Tobacco Industry Corruption; Feb. 17, 2002: Rotting Human Bodies Are Found at Georgia Crematory; July, 2002: Journalist Alleges Release of Genetically Modified Corn Seeds in New Zealand; Beginning Aug. 29, 2005: Government Incompetence Mars Hurricane Katrina Relief Efforts.

October 10, 1979
FRENCH PRESIDENT GISCARD D'ESTAING IS ACCUSED OF TAKING A BRIBE

The investigative, satirical newspaper Le Canard enchaîné *reported that French president Valéry Giscard d'Estaing had accepted a bribe in diamonds from the African military ruler Jean-Bédel Bokassa in 1973 while serving as minister of economy and finance of the French government. The scandal led to Giscard d'Estaing's downfall.*

LOCALES: Paris, France; Bangui, Central African Republic
CATEGORIES: Corruption; forgery; publishing and journalism; government; international relations

KEY FIGURES
Valéry Giscard d'Estaing (b. 1926), president of France, 1974-1981
Jean-Bédel Bokassa (1921-1996), military ruler of the Central African Republic, 1966-1976, and emperor of the Central African Empire, 1976-1979
Roger Delpey (1926-2007), French writer and journalist
Claude Angeli (b. 1931), French journalist

SUMMARY OF EVENT
On October 10, 1979, the respected French satirical newspaper *Le Canard enchaîné* published an

article accusing President Valéry Giscard d'Estaing of having improperly received diamonds from Jean-Bédel Bokassa, the military ruler of the Central African Republic (CAR), in 1973. To understand the significance of the scandal that developed (rivaling the impact of the Watergate scandal in the United States), one must first understand the relationships then existing between France and the CAR.

The CAR is a former French colony that gained its independence on August 13, 1960. Located north of the Republic of the Congo-Brazzaville and the Democratic Republic of the Congo, east of Cameroon, south of Chad, and west of Sudan, this 240,324-square-mile country is slightly smaller than the state of Texas. From its independence to the first democratic elections of 1993, the country was ruled by a series of presidents who took power by force, often with the support of France. The first was David Dacko, who governed the country until his cousin, Bokassa, overthrew him on December 31, 1965. For the first few years of his rule, Bokassa was supported by many Western countries, particularly the United States, Switzerland, Spain, Belgium, and France, all of which sought access to the CAR's rich natural resources of gold, diamonds, uranium, copper, iron, manganese, cobalt, and nickel. The nation's immense mineral wealth, combined with Bokassa's imperial style of governing, created an environment in which corruption and bribery could flourish.

Giscard d'Estaing's involvement in the scandal began when, as minister of economy and finance under President Georges Pompidou, he discovered the potential of the CAR as a vacation spot. In December, 1970, Giscard d'Estaing, an avid hunter, was invited to spend some time in the northern part of the CAR by his wife's cousin, Henry de la Tour d'Auvergne, who owned a large estate there. Entranced by the experience, he returned in 1971 and again in 1973, when Bokassa invited him to visit him in the capital, Bangui. As he had done for many political guests, including U.S. diplomat Henry Kissinger, Bokassa presented Giscard d'Estaing with two stars made of diamonds. Like most Western nations, France at the time had strict rules concerning gifts made to its public officials. The diamond stars that were given to him should have been registered with the French government, then sold for charity or sent to a museum. Unfortunately, Giscard d'Estaing failed to register the gift, later offering the unsatisfying, though possible, explanation that he had simply put them in a drawer and forgotten them.

The friendly relationship between the two politicians continued through the 1970's. Giscard d'Estaing met with Bokassa in France, again receiving gifts of ivory and diamonds, and returned to vacation at the estate of his wife's cousin in the CAR in 1976 and 1978. Around this time, Bokassa was remaking himself as Bokassa I, grandiose emperor of the Central African Empire, but his increasingly bizarre behavior did not produce a break with Giscard d'Estaing.

Finally, in 1979, civil unrest in Bangui was savagely repressed in a bloodbath that included the murder of more than one hundred schoolchildren, some of whom were further victimized when Bokassa reportedly consumed their flesh in a cannibal feast. Only after these outrages did Giscard d'Estaing's government move to oust the dictator, organizing a September coup that took advantage of Bokassa's absence on a trip to Libya to replace him with Dacko, the cousin whom Bokassa had overthrown in 1965.

About a month after the coup, on October 10, 1979, the French newspaper *Le Canard enchaîné* published the story "Pourquoi Giscard a organisé la casse des archives de Bokassa" (why Giscard organized the destruction of Bokassa's archives), written by chief editor Claude Angeli. The article purported to show a copy of an order signed by Bokassa in 1973, directing the Comptoir National du Diamant (the organization producing diamonds in the CAR) to provide him with multiple diamonds for the stars to be presented to Giscard d'Estaing. If these diamonds were of jewelry quality, the two stars would have been worth millions of French francs—certainly enough to buy loyalty and too much to forget in a drawer. Of course, if the diamonds were of lower—industrial—grade, their value would have been far less.

The possibility of a major bribe led to a national media frenzy of speculation on the honesty of the French president. While the newspaper *Le Monde* virtually accused the president of dishonesty, the newspaper *Le Point* took a more moderate view, speculating that the value of the diamonds was low and that the signature on the order was forged.

Unfortunately, Giscard d'Estaing fed the fires of speculation and rumor by refusing to answer any questions about the diamonds, later asserting that he saw no point in defending his honor and claiming that anyone who knew him would never believe him capable of behaving in a dishonorable way. It was a gentleman's response to a slur on his character, and it was, of course, totally ineffective in the real world of French politics. Finally, on November 27, 1979, he addressed the issue in a televised interview. Openly contemptuous of those who accused him, he claimed that Bokassa's signature on the document was forged.

Following the president's pronouncement, the Direction de la Surveillance du Territoire (the French equivalent of the Federal Bureau of Investigation) investigated the source of the information published by *Le Canard enchaîné*. When it was determined that Roger Delpey, a journalist and writer, brought Bokassa's order to the newspaper, Delpey was promptly incarcerated as a dealer in forged documents. However, the president's actions did not convince everyone of his innocence in the matter. He was voted out of office in 1981 and replaced by François Mitterrand.

IMPACT

At the end of his presidency, Giscard d'Estaing had the gifts he had received during his tenure in office examined by experts prior to their legal disposition. Among the items evaluated were the two stars given to the president by Bokassa. The stars were judged to be of inferior quality and sold for a little more than 100,000 French francs. However, were they really Bokassa's stars? Critics of the president believed that they had been altered, with the original high-quality diamonds replaced with lesser stones. His supporters continued to proclaim that the scandal was manufactured by Giscard d'Estaing's political enemies, who forged the document to damage the president's prospects for re-election.

History will probably never know whether or not Giscard d'Estaing used the diamonds for his own profit. However, his experience clearly delineated the emerging nature of modern politics, in which personal honesty and honor are no longer taken for granted and must be forever bolstered by meticulous record keeping and a scrupulous regard for appearances.

—*Denyse Lemaire and David Kasserman*

FURTHER READING

Abadie, Frederic. *Valéry Giscard d'Estaing*. Paris: Editions Balland, 1997. This is an excellent resource that traces the life and political career of the French president. In French.

Bell, David S. *Presidential Power in Fifth Republic France*. New York: Berg, 2000. Highlights the tenures of French presidents between 1958 and 2000, with a particular focus on the presidency of Giscard d'Estaing.

Loughlin, John. *Subnational Government: The French Experience*. New York: Palgrave Macmillan, 2007. This book offers an extensive history of the manner in which the French government functions. It gives an overview of the machinations of subnational government in France.

Titley, Brian. *Dark Age: The Political Odyssey of Emperor Bokassa*. Montreal: McGill-Queen's University Press, 1997. An excellent political biography of Bokassa that details the government of the dictatorial leader of the Central African Republic and, later, Central African Empire.

SEE ALSO: Nov. 15, 1908: Belgium Confiscates Congo Free State from King Leopold II; Nov., 1929: Banque Oustric et Cie Failure Prompts French Inquiry; Jan. 8, 1934-Jan. 17, 1936: Stavisky's Fraudulent Schemes Rock French Government; Dec. 23, 1998: Prominent Belgians Are Sentenced in Agusta-Dassault Corruption Scandal.

October 11, 1979
SENATE DENOUNCES HERMAN E. TALMADGE FOR MONEY LAUNDERING

U.S. senator Herman E. Talmadge was denounced by the Senate for his participation in a scheme to launder public money and campaign funds through a secret bank account and then convert the money for personal use. His censure in the form of a denouncement led to his political downfall and made him one of only nine senators to have been censured since 1789.

LOCALE: Washington, D.C.
CATEGORIES: Corruption; government; politics; banking and finance

KEY FIGURES
Herman E. Talmadge (1913-2002), governor of Georgia, 1948-1955, and U.S. senator, 1957-1981
Betty Talmadge (1923-2005), Herman Talmadge's former wife
Daniel Minchew (fl. 1970's), Herman Talmadge's aide
Robert S. Talmadge (1948-1975), Herman and Betty Talmadge's son

SUMMARY OF EVENT
On October 11, 1979, a six-month investigation of U.S. senator Herman E. Talmadge ended when the full U.S. Senate voted to censure, or denounce, him for his "reprehensible" conduct while in office. By a vote of 81-15, the full Senate chamber supported a punishment that was less than the more severe punishment of expulsion. During the investigation, dozens of witnesses, including Talmadge, his former wife Betty Talmadge, and many of his former and current aides testified not only about the senator's honesty but also about his unusual habits involving money.

The Talmadge investigation was one of the first following congressional reforms passed after the Watergate scandal of 1972-1974. The new ethics rules created the Senate Ethics Committee, which

was assigned the duty of investigating violations by senators. With scandal having dominated Washington politics through much of the 1970's, Talmadge became the first example of the U.S. Congress sweeping clean its own house after having forced a president to resign.

In one of the first investigations by the newly created Ethics Committee, six senators heard testimony about a complicated money laundering scheme initiated by Talmadge to hide his misuse of funds. Talmadge, a twenty-two-year veteran of the Senate, was charged with five violations of Senate ethics rules, including filing false expense reports and pocketing excess monies for personal use. The amounts ranged from twenty-eight to thirty-seven thousand dollars, with several thousand more dollars disappearing without a trace.

Talmadge, a conservative Democrat, also was charged with two campaign violations, including filing false disclosure forms in a case in which he failed to list all donations and campaign spending, and laundering campaign money for personal use. Finally, the senator was accused of not reporting gifts given him by supporters, as required by Senate rules, and for filing false tax returns for other gifts, a charge that led to an Internal Revenue Service investigation of his tax returns.

Senator Talmadge's legal troubles came at the tail end of a stormy political career. Son of former Georgia governor Eugene Talmadge, Herman Talmadge grew up in a segregated society with a father who earned political fame by threatening force to maintain segregation. The young Talmadge would follow in his father's racist footsteps during the 1940's, threatening to use a baseball bat against any African American who tried to integrate the state.

Talmadge attempted to seize power after the 1946 election, which his father won (his father died before taking office). The young Talmadge's grab for the governorship provoked a state constitutional crisis involving the lieutenant governor, the state

553

legislature, the Georgia Supreme Court, and the Georgia National Guard, which tried to seat Talmadge with force. Denied power through an attempted political coup, he engineered an electoral coup instead and won the governor's seat in 1948. His move to the U.S. Senate proved easier, as he challenged incumbent Walter George in the 1956 Democratic primary. The ailing George, intimidated by Talmadge's outrageous tactics and reputation, dropped out of the race, opening the way for Talmadge's easy victory. He would win three more elections before his censure in 1979.

Even with all the turmoil in Talmadge's political past, the Senate investigation would be the most difficult test of his career. Talmadge testified before the Ethics Committee and rejected the charges against him. He sought to undermine the credibility of those testifying against him, then provided a series of explanations for his behavior. During the investigation, he admitted to having a drinking problem, delaying the committee hearings as he attended a month-long alcohol treatment program. After leaving the program, Talmadge went before the committee and asked the senators to end the investigation, but they refused to do so. When asked about the large sums of cash he had in his possession, Talmadge explained that the money came from small donations, five to ten dollars, from his Georgia supporters. Talmadge said that he had lived on these small donations for more than five years, not having to rely on his Senate salary to pay for housing and food.

Talmadge's next defense was his hard work on the Senate Agriculture Committee, his past service, and his close relationship with colleagues. The senators on the Ethics Committee were not swayed by his arguments, noting that it was his past conduct that they were investigating. For Talmadge, it would be his personal rather than his professional past that would haunt him throughout the hearings. The bitter divorce from his wife of thirty-seven years included her claim of considerable compensation for their years of married life. The terms of the settlement alerted the media to the senator's financial misdeeds and eventually to the Senate investigation. Betty Talmadge would also strike another blow at her former husband's defense when she testified before the committee.

Although Betty was not expected to have personal knowledge of her husband's money laundering scheme, she was expected to reveal details of his spending and unusual money-collection techniques. Married to the senator for more than three decades, she had little interest in hiding his dirty dealings and described in detail how he kept large sums of money throughout the house.

According to Betty, her husband kept rolls of hundred-dollar bills in his pockets and distributed those bills to her and others. Talmadge also stored envelopes full of money in his dresser drawers, in amounts totaling more than fifteen thousand dollars. According to Betty, her husband transported large sums of cash from Washington, D.C., to his Georgia home, then left the money in his coat pockets. She had seen and used the money, taking several thousand dollars out on one occasion for her personal expenses. Betty then gave the committee more than seven thousand dollars in one-hundred-dollar bills she said she had taken from her husband's coat, providing an element of proof to her accusations.

The most damaging witness, other than his wife, against the senator was one of his top aides, Daniel Minchew, who served in Talmadge's Senate office and his reelection campaign. Minchew had created a secret bank account at the behest of Talmadge, who used the account as a slush fund. Because the account was not in the senator's name, it allowed him to deny knowledge of it or how the money reached the account, denials that came the moment the account was discovered.

According to Minchew, the secret account included monies from false reimbursements and excess campaign funds that the senator then used for personal expenses. Minchew claimed that he had given large sums to Robert S. Talmadge, the senator's son (Robert drowned in 1975). Minchew admitted to withdrawing money from the account for expenses.

Talmadge had his defenders, including several of his then-current and former aides. They disputed Minchew's claims about Talmadge's knowledge of excessive expenditures. These aides claimed that because the senator signed expense reports without reading them, his staff had overcharged without Talmadge being aware. However, another aide testified he had witnessed Talmadge transferring eighty thousand dollars from an office bank account to the senator's personal account, supporting Minchew's testimony that Talmadge was mixing personal and government money.

IMPACT

Given the conflicting testimony, the Ethics Committee, composed of three Democrats and three Republicans, recommended that the full Senate censure Talmadge through denouncement rather than expel him from Congress. His Senate colleagues recognized that he violated ethics rules by improperly signing expense reports.

While it appeared Talmadge had escaped any long-term consequences that normally would have followed expulsion, the Senate vote undermined his influence among his colleagues, forcing him from his chairship of the Senate Agriculture Committee and weakening his hold over the Georgia electorate. In the 1980 general election, Talmadge faced the head of Georgia's Republican Party, Mack Mattingly, who made the senator's legal troubles one of the core issues in the campaign. Mattingly barely defeated Talmadge, winning by a few thousand votes, and became the first Republican senator from Georgia since the 1870's.

—*Douglas Clouatre*

FURTHER READING

Bernstein, Adam. "Georgia Sen. Herman Talmadge, Integration Opponent, Dies at 88." *The Washington Post*, March 22, 2002. A Talmadge obituary that examines his early career in state politics and his move into the national limelight at the time of segregation. Also addresses, briefly, his censure by the U.S. Senate.

Cook, James F. *The Governors of Georgia, 1754-2004.* 3d ed. Macon, Ga.: Mercer University Press, 2005. An encyclopedia covering Georgia governors since the time of the British colonies through 2004. Includes an entry on Herman Talmadge that explores his brief career as governor and his subsequent career in the U.S. Senate.

Long, Kim. *The Almanac of Political Corruption, Scandals, and Dirty Politics.* New York: Delacorte Press, 2007. A wide-ranging book detailing the various scandals and corrupt practices that have plagued U.S. politics. Includes discussion of the Talmadge hearing and the criminal acts he was accused of perpetrating.

Roberts, Robert North. *Ethics in U.S. Government: An Encyclopedia of Investigations, Scandals, Reforms, and Legislation.* Westport, Conn.: Greenwood Press, 2001. A comprehensive encyclopedia documenting American political scandals, ethical controversies, and investigations from 1775 to 2000.

SEE ALSO: Jan. 23, 1904: Senator Joseph R. Burton Is Convicted of Bribery; Nov. 16, 1951: Federal Tax Official Resigns After Accepting Bribes; June 25, 1956: President Truman's Appointments Secretary Is Convicted of Tax Conspiracy; Mar. 1, 1967: Adam Clayton Powell, Jr., Is Excluded from Congress; June 23, 1967: Senator Thomas J. Dodd Is Censured for Misappropriating Funds; May 9, 1969: Supreme Court Justice Abe Fortas Is Accused of Bribery; June 17, 1972-Aug. 9, 1974: Watergate Break-in Leads to President Nixon's Resignation; July 31, 1972: Thomas F. Eagleton Withdraws from Vice Presidential Race; Oct. 10, 1973: Spiro T. Agnew Resigns Vice Presidency in Disgrace; Oct. 7, 1974: Congressman Wilbur D. Mills's Stripper Affair Leads to His Downfall; Sept. 21, 1977: Carter Cabinet Member Resigns over Ethics Violations; Feb. 2, 1980: Media Uncover FBI Sting Implicating Dozens of Lawmakers; Sept. 23, 1987: Plagiarism Charges End Joe Biden's Presidential Campaign.

November 29, 1979, and January 31, 1983
BASEBALL COMMISSIONER SUSPENDS MICKEY MANTLE AND WILLIE MAYS FOR CASINO TIES

Motivated by a desire to distance Major League Baseball from any trace of gambling, Commissioner Bowie Kuhn banned retired superstars Willie Mays and Mickey Mantle from working for both major league clubs and gambling casinos at the same time. Mays, in 1979, and Mantle, in 1983, had accepted lucrative public relations positions for Atlantic City, New Jersey, casinos. The sanctions were lifted by Peter Ueberroth, who succeeded Kuhn as commissioner in 1985.

LOCALES: New York, New York; Atlantic City, New Jersey

CATEGORIES: Corruption; gambling; sports

KEY FIGURES

Willie Mays (b. 1931), retired Hall of Fame baseball player

Mickey Mantle (1931-1995), retired Hall of Fame baseball player

Bowie Kuhn (1926-2007), commissioner of Major League Baseball

Peter Ueberroth (b. 1937), commissioner of Major League Baseball

SUMMARY OF EVENT

In 1979, former San Francisco Giants and New York Mets star player Willie Mays accepted a lucrative job offer from the newly opened Bally's Park Place Hotel Casino Resort in Atlantic City, New Jersey. In reaction, baseball commissioner Bowie Kuhn banned Mays from being employed by any baseball club while he worked for a gambling enterprise. Four years later, former New York Yankees star Mickey Mantle took a similar position with Claridge Casino Hotel, also in Atlantic City. He, too, was banned from baseball. In taking these actions to separate baseball and gambling, Kuhn followed in the footsteps of baseball's first commissioner, Kenesaw Mountain Landis, a staunch opponent of corruption in baseball. Kuhn's sanctions provoked controversy because Mays and Mantle were two of the greatest players in baseball history. To remove them from working for baseball in their retirement years seemed to many an overreaction.

Despite their historic accomplishments on the baseball field, both Mantle and Mays entered retirement after the 1968 and 1973 seasons, respectively, with few marketable skills. Both served as goodwill ambassadors for Major League Baseball. Also, Mays was a special instructor for the New York Mets and Mantle for the New York Yankees. Mantle also had a brief and undistinguished career as a sports announcer. Both had done promotional work for various businesses.

Mays was earning $100,000 for a two-year contract with the Mets when Bally's representatives approached him with an offer: one million dollars over ten years for Mays to do public relations and entertain the casino's big spenders. The position did not ask Mays to promote gambling directly, and New Jersey state law forbid him from gambling. It is believed that the casino required about 120 days of work per year from Mays.

From the moment Commissioner Kuhn learned of Bally's interest in Mays, he expressed his deep concern to Bally and the Mets. The office of baseball commissioner had been created after the notorious Black Sox scandal of 1919. Eight members of the Chicago White Sox had been accused of taking money from gamblers to throw the World Series. When the judicial system failed to produce convictions, the new commissioner, Landis, banned the eight players from any connection with baseball. Using his power to protect "the best interests of baseball," Landis restored confidence in the integrity of the sport.

After Landis's death in 1944, gambling was considered not a major problem. Kuhn, however, warned Mays that he could not remain a special hitting instructor for the Mets and work for a casino.

Mays argued that he had been doing public relations work already, that gambling was legal in New Jersey, and that as part-time coach he could not possibly corrupt the outcomes of games. For Kuhn, the mere appearance of a gambling-baseball link was unacceptable, and he encouraged Mays to stay with baseball. Proclaiming the need to provide for his family, Mays began his public relations work for Bally's on November 29, 1979.

When Mantle accepted a similar offer from Claridge on January 31, 1983, Kuhn reminded him of the consequences. Mantle was earning only $20,000 from the Yankees as a spring-training batting instructor in addition to doing public relations work for a Dallas insurance company. Claridge offered Mantle $100,000 per year to attend a wide variety of public and charitable functions and to play golf with good customers. Nevertheless, Kuhn forbid Mantle from working in baseball.

Mantle and Mays put public pressure on Kuhn by avoiding all baseball functions, including Old Timers' games and the yearly Hall of Fame ceremonies. An exasperated Kuhn explained that his decision did not prohibit all association with baseball. The two stars, however, repeatedly referred to being "banned" and "kicked out of baseball." Mantle, Mays, and sympathetic sportswriters accused Kuhn of hypocrisy because team owners in the past had invested in casinos, and George Steinbrenner of the Yankees and John Galbreath of the Pittsburgh Pirates participated in the horse-racing business. Kuhn defended himself by citing his policy of forcing owners to divest of all interests in casinos, and he had recognized that gambling on horses also was unseemly. To that end he had frustrated an attempt by Edward DeBartolo to purchase the Chicago White Sox in 1981 because of his ownership of racetracks.

The ostracizing of Mantle and Mays did not help Kuhn's increas-ingly rocky tenure as commissioner, as he also faced labor strife and the advent of free agency. The owners did not reelect Kuhn to a third term and instead chose Peter Ueberroth as his successor. Ueberroth had been recognized as the genius behind the profitable 1984 Los Angeles Summer Olympics. He took over from an embattled Kuhn in October, 1984. On March 18, 1985, Ueberroth welcomed Mantle and Mays back into baseball. The new commissioner asserted he was not soft on gambling but that there was a need for new rules. A grateful Mantle noted that "no one likes to be banned."

Impact

Mantle and Mays earned their Hall of Fame credentials during the 1950's and 1960's when players' salaries were shockingly low. Soon after they retired they witnessed far-less-able players earn enormous sums of money because of the introduction of free agency rules. The two stars' acceptance of the casino offers was perfectly understandable. Mays later admitted another benefit of the casino job: It exposed him to the workings of the business world and, thus, compelled him to be better disciplined to survive in that setting.

Mickey Mantle, left, and Willie Mays in 1962. (Hulton Archive/Getty Images)

Kuhn's puritanical stance on gambling connections and other related issues led to his demise as commissioner, but his fierce resolve is understandable. Gambling has been an ever-present threat to the reputation of baseball. In 1989, allegations surfaced that Pete Rose, the manager of the Cincinnati Reds and baseball's all-time hits leader as a player, had placed bets on baseball games, including those involving his own team. In an age when baseball was wracked by labor disruptions and faced increasing competition for the public's entertainment dollars, it could not afford the Rose scandal, nor any other.

Commissioners and club owners desperately sought to maintain the profitability of the multibillion-dollar business. At the same time, Kuhn and his successors wrestled with how to preserve baseball's almost mythological status in the United States and the devotion of its fans to its heroes, including Mays and Mantle.

—*M. Philip Lucas*

FURTHER READING

Burk, Robert E. *Much More than a Game: Players, Owners, and American Baseball Since 1921.* Chapel Hill: University of North Carolina Press, 2001. Solid and concise history of baseball as a business that provides an overview of the commissioner's and baseball's role in curtailing gambling.

Castro, Tony. *Mickey Mantle: America's Prodigal Son.* Washington, D.C.: Brassey's, 2002. Contains a solid account of Mantle's difficult retirement years.

Fimrite, Ron. "Mantle and Mays." *Sports Illustrated*, March 25, 1985. Celebrates the return of both Mantle and Mays to baseball after they were reinstated by Ueberroth, with a focus on the star players' retirement activities.

Ginsberg, Daniel E. *The Fix Is In: A History of Baseball Gambling and Game Fixing Scandals.* New York: McFarland, 2004. A valuable overview of a neglected aspect of baseball history.

Kuhn, Bowie. *Hardball: The Education of a Baseball Commissioner.* New York: Times Books, 1987. Commissioner Kuhn's perspective on the casino controversy with Mays and Mantle.

Mantle, Mickey. *The Mick.* New York: Doubleday, 1985. A straightforward narrative of Mantle's life that includes discussion of his dealings with Kuhn.

Mays, Willie. *Say Hey: The Autobiography of Willie Mays.* New York: Simon & Schuster, 1988. Contains Mays's version of his "banishment" from baseball.

SEE ALSO: Apr. 2, 1915: Players Fix Liverpool-Manchester United Soccer Match; Sept. 21, 1919: White Sox Players Conspire to Lose World Series in "Black Sox" Scandal; Dec. 26, 1926: Ty Cobb and Tris Speaker Are Accused of Fixing Baseball Games; Spring, 1947: Baseball Manager Leo Durocher Is Suspended for Gambling Ties; May 3, 1950: U.S. Senate Committee Begins Investigating Organized Crime; Fall, 1969-Winter, 1971: Japanese Baseball Players Are Implicated in Game Fixing; Sept. 23, 1977: Horse-Swapping Fraud Staggers Belmont Park Raceway; Feb. 28, 1986: Baseball Commissioner Peter Ueberroth Suspends Players for Cocaine Use; Aug. 24, 1989: Pete Rose Is Banned from Baseball for Betting on Games; Mar. 17, 2005: Former Baseball Star Mark McGwire Evades Congressional Questions on Steroid Use.

1980
BIOGRAPHER CLAIMS ACTOR ERROL FLYNN WAS A NAZI SPY

While a number of biographies have discredited as untrue writer Charles Higham's claims of film star Errol Flynn's pro-Nazi loyalties, Flynn nevertheless has acquired a posthumous reputation as having been a Nazi spy. Later biographers counter that Flynn supported leftist causes, including the Cuban Revolution, indicating that Flynn was a political leftist and not a fascist.

LOCALE: United States
CATEGORIES: Espionage; publishing and journalism; public morals; military

KEY FIGURES
Errol Flynn (1909-1959), Tasmanian-born film star
Charles Higham (b. 1931), English-born biographer, writer, and poet
Hermann F. Erben (Gerrit H. Koets; 1897-1985), Austrian-born medical doctor and photographer

SUMMARY OF EVENT
It is plausible to suggest that British writer Charles Higham's book *Errol Flynn: The Untold Story* (1980) is not so much a biography as it is an exposé. Whereas biographies, at least in the truest sense, seek to offer an account of the events of a person's life written by someone other than the figure in question, an exposé often aims to uncover revelatory, surprising, or shocking information about a particular person. That Higham's *Errol Flynn* presents more like an exposé than a biography is substantiated to some degree by Higham himself. He claims in his prologue that the revelation of Tasmanian-born film star Errol Flynn's apparently traitorous activities motivated his own personal sense of grief and shock, as well as his objective to "blow Flynn's cover."

Higham reportedly based his scandalous claims of Flynn's activities as a spy on evidence he ob-

tained under the U.S. Freedom of Information Act of 1966. Higham claims he found evidence of Flynn's political espionage and Fifth Column activities at the National Archives in Washington, D.C., as well as documentation supporting the same from both the U.S. State Department and the Federal Bureau of Investigation (FBI). Higham's book also includes a list of declassified FBI documents that Higham argues either directly or indirectly implicates Flynn in espionage activities during World War II. Additionally, Higham claims that Hermann F. Erben admitted to him that he indoctrinated Flynn into Nazism, a claim Higham does not substantiate.

While subsequent biographers—perhaps most notably Tony Thomas in *Errol Flynn: The Spy Who Never Was* (1990)—have since denounced as fabrications Higham's allegations of Nazi collaboration against Flynn, Flynn's political affiliations continue to fascinate biographers and fans alike. In fact, a growing body of evidence supports the claim that Flynn maintained expressly leftist political leanings. Such claims include assertions that Flynn was a supporter of the Spanish Republic during the Spanish Civil War (1936-1939) and of the Cuban Revolution during the late 1950's.

Just as Higham's exposé undoubtedly sustained Flynn's posthumous, though apparently erroneous, reputation as a Nazi collaborator and spy during World War II, the enduring interest in debunking Higham's allegations continues to prolong that reputation. Most of the post-1980 biographical accounts of Flynn's life recapitulate Higham's assertion of Flynn's double life as a Nazi conspirator, accounts that, in turn, contribute to the endurance of this allegation within contemporary popular culture.

The special appendix of Buster Wiles's 1988 autobiography *My Days with Errol Flynn*, "The Flynn Controversy," written by William Donati, accuses Higham of having falsified his primary-source material to prove his own thesis: that Flynn admired

1980's

559

Adolf Hitler, was both Nazi sympathizer and agent, and was bisexual, anti-Semitic, and a murderer. Moreover, Donati, like Tony Thomas in *Errol Flynn: The Spy Who Never Was*, argues that the true source of the Flynn controversy was never really Flynn at all but rather his association with photographer Erben. Flynn reportedly met Erben for the first time in Salamaua, New Guinea, on April 14, 1933.

That Flynn narrated and appeared in a documentary produced by Victor Pahlen called *The Truth About Fidel Castro* [sic] *Revolution* (1959) is accepted, in part, as evidence of his outward support of the Cuban Revolution against the regime of General Fulgencio Batista y Zaldívar. Flynn and Pahlen reportedly owned a movie theater in Havana when revolutionary Fidel Castro arrived in the city on January 8, 1959, to spearhead plans to install a revolutionary government. Castro himself appears in the film.

Moreover, Flynn himself appears to have substantiated claims that he supported the Cuban Revolution. In *My Wicked, Wicked Ways* (1959), for instance, he writes that he considered Castro a friend. Furthermore, Flynn also traveled to Cuba to experience the revolution at first hand. Indeed, he scooped the world press by securing the first interview with Castro following the revolution. Other public declarations that seem to indicate Flynn's leftist leanings include his appearance on a Canadian television program called *Front Page Challenge*, which aired on January 13, 1959. During the program, Flynn stated, among other things, that Castro will rank in history with some of the greatest leaders of all time.

IMPACT

Most post-1980 biographical narratives about Flynn, whether in book form or on film, include the scandal motivated by Higham's biography in their accounts dedicated to the events of Flynn's life. As such, it is possible to argue that such accounts continue to sustain and strengthen the controversy itself because the question of Flynn's anti-British and anti-U.S. political affiliations did not surface publicly during Flynn's life but rather some twenty-one years after his death.

In 2006, director Simon Nasht released the film *Tasmanian Devil: The Fast and Furious Life of Errol Flynn*. Written by Robert de Young and produced by Sharyn Prentice, the film highlights the lesser known aspects of Flynn's personal life and professional career, including his documentary filmmaking enterprises with Castro (*The Truth About Fidel Caestro Revolution*). The project received script development funding from Film Victoria (Australia) and ABC TV (Australia). In fact, publicity for the project claimed television presales were brokered with ABC TV (Australia), the British Broadcasting Corporation (BBC; Britain), ZDF/Arte (Germany/France), AVRO (the Netherlands), YLE (Finland), DR TV (Denmark), and TV Ontario (Canada). That these projects persist shows a real and continuing international fascination with the private and public life of Flynn.

—*Nicole Anae*

FURTHER READING

Flynn, Errol. *My Wicked, Wicked Ways*. New ed. London: Aurum, 2005. Flynn's telling autobiography, first published in 1959, was cowritten by Earl Conrad, author of *Errol Flynn: A Memoir*. Flynn writes tellingly of his association with and support of Fidel Castro, even considering him a friend.

Higham, Charles. *Errol Flynn: The Untold Story*. New York: Doubleday, 1980. In this scandalous biography, Higham alleges that Flynn was a fascist sympathizer and Nazi spy during World War II.

McNulty, Thomas. *Errol Flynn: The Life and Career*. Jefferson, N.C.: McFarland, 2004. McNulty's documentary analysis of Flynn's life and career includes rare and some previously unpublished photographs.

Thomas, Tony. *Errol Flynn: The Spy Who Never Was*. New York: Citadel Press, 1990. This account denounces as fabrications Charles Higham's allegations that Flynn was a fascist sympathizer and Nazi spy.

Wiles, Buster. *My Days with Errol Flynn: The Autobiography of a Stuntman*. Santa Monica, Calif.: Roundtable, 1988. The appendix written by William Donati, "The Flynn Controversy," accuses Higham of falsifying his primary-source material to prove his own thesis: that Flynn was both a Nazi sympathizer and an agent for the Nazis.

SEE ALSO: Summer, 1936: Film Star Mary Astor's Diary Becomes a Public Sensation; Feb. 6, 1942: Film Star Errol Flynn Is Acquitted of Rape; Mar. 3, 1986: Former U.N. Secretary-General Kurt Waldheim's Nazi Past Is Revealed; Dec. 1, 1987: Yale Scholar's Wartime Anti-Semitic Writings Are Revealed; July 28, 2006: Actor Mel Gibson Is Caught Making Anti-Semitic Remarks; Aug. 12, 2006: Novelist Günter Grass Admits to Youthful Nazi Ties.

February 2, 1980
MEDIA UNCOVER FBI STING IMPLICATING DOZENS OF LAWMAKERS

In 1978, the Federal Bureau of Investigation began a sting operation to investigate organized crime and the trafficking of stolen property. The agency set up a fictitious company, Abdul Enterprises Ltd., as a cover and staffed it with federal agents posing as wealthy Arab businessmen. In 1979, the focus of the operation shifted to the investigation of corrupt U.S. politicians taking money for political favors. A number of legislators were caught in the sting, but the scandal led to accusations against the FBI for its investigative techniques and for possible entrapment. The media also were criticized for reporting on the operation before anyone had been criminally indicted.

ALSO KNOWN AS: Abscam
LOCALE: Washington, D.C.
CATEGORIES: Corruption; government; law and the courts; organized crime and racketeering

KEY FIGURES
Melvin Weinberg (b. 1925), convicted con artist employed by the FBI
Angelo Errichetti (b. 1928), New Jersey state senator, 1976-1981, and mayor of Camden, 1973-1981
Harrison A. Williams (1919-2001), U.S. senator from New Jersey, 1959-1982

John W. Jenrette, Jr. (b. 1936), U.S. representative from South Carolina, 1975-1980
Richard Kelly (1924-2005), U.S. representative from Florida, 1975-1981
Raymond Lederer (b. 1938), U.S. representative from Pennsylvania, 1977-1981
Michael Myers (b. 1943), U.S. representative from Pennsylvania, 1976-1980
Frank Thompson (1918-1989), U.S. representative from New Jersey, 1955-1980

SUMMARY OF EVENT
In 1978, the U.S. Department of Justice (DOJ) authorized a request by the Federal Bureau of Investigation (FBI) to set up a sting operation, code-named Abscam (for Abdul scam), to investigate organized crime and the trafficking of stolen property. The FBI hired Melvin Weinberg, a convicted con artist, to manage the operation from the FBI office in Hauppauge, Long Island. In return for his services, the FBI purportedly paid him $150,000 and voided his three-year prison sentence.

The FBI then set the stage for the sting by setting up a fictitious company, Abdul Enterprises Ltd., as a cover. The business was staffed by undercover agents posing as wealthy Arab businessmen. In the spring of 1979, the focus of the operation shifted to the investigation of government corruption on local, state, and federal levels. This decision was based on a promise made by New Jersey state senator and Camden mayor Angelo Errichetti that he could provide undercover agents with a list of politicians who were willing to provide the services of the federal government in return for cash. These services included granting asylum in the United States, money laundering, obtaining gambling licenses, and investment schemes.

As part of the operation, an undercover agent called Sheikh Kambir Abdul Rahman arranged meetings with thirty-one politicians named by Errichetti. The meetings, which were secretly videotaped by the FBI, took place in several different locations, including a property in Washington, D.C., a yacht in Florida, and hotel rooms in Pennsylvania and New Jersey.

On Saturday, February 2, 1980, the National Broadcasting Company (NBC) broke the story of the FBI's Abscam investigation during its evening news segment. *The New York Times* and other media outlets reported on the operation the following day. Within a day, the FBI investigation into political corruption turned into a major scandal. In total, six federal lawmakers, three city-level officials, one federal employee, and one state senator-city mayor were convicted on felony bribery and conspiracy charges for their role in the illegal activities. On October 30, the DOJ indicted U.S. senator Harrison A. Williams for bribery and conspiracy. He was convicted on May 1, 1981, received a three-year prison sentence, and finally resigned from the Senate on March 11, 1982. He was the only U.S. senator implicated and was the first senator to be imprisoned in almost eighty years.

Five U.S. representatives also were convicted for bribery and conspiracy in connection with the sting operation. These Congress members included John W. Jenrette, Jr., who was tape-recorded telling a colleague that he had been given fifty thousand dollars in exchange for special favors. He received a two-year prison sentence and resigned on December 10, 1980. Richard Kelly accepted a bribe of twenty-five thousand dollars from federal agents during the sting operation. He was convicted for bribery and served thirteen months in prison. Raymond Lederer was convicted for bribery and sentenced to three years in prison. Michael Myers was videotaped accepting a fifty-thousand-dollar bribe by undercover agents on August 2, 1979. He was convicted for bribery and sentenced to three years in prison. On October 2, 1980, he was expelled from the House, making him the first Congress member to be expelled since 1861. Frank Thompson also was convicted for bribery and conspiracy. He received a three-year prison sentence and resigned from the House on December 29, 1980.

A videotape from a television screen showing Representative Michael Myers, second from left, holding an envelope containing $50,000, which he just accepted from an undercover FBI agent in the Abscam sting operation. (AP/Wide World Photos)

Five other government officials were convicted of bribery and conspiracy. These included Errichetti, three Philadelphia City Council members, and a U.S. Immigration and Naturalization Service inspector. It is important to note that on appeal, all of the aforementioned convictions were upheld.

Other notable politicians associated with Abscam include U.S. senator Larry Pressler from South Dakota and Representative John Murtha of Pennsylvania. When approached by undercover agents, Pressler simply refused to take the bribe and then reported the incident to the FBI. Murtha, on the other hand, expressed an interest in the fifty-thousand-dollar bribe because he wanted to use the money to improve the local economy in his congressional district. Because of these extenuating circumstances, Murtha was never indicted on bribery charges.

IMPACT

The Abscam scandal had far-reaching consequences, mostly negative. The operation was much maligned by government critics who accused the FBI of entrapping those thought to be involved in the affair. Entrapment is a significant accusation, given that criminal defendants could win acquittal if they can prove that they had no previous disposition to violate the law but were pressured into such violations by the urging of law enforcement officers. However, in the case of Abscam, various appeals courts ruled repeatedly that the operation did not constitute entrapment. Critics also questioned the hiring of a convicted felon to manage the investigation.

In response to these accusations, on January 5, 1981, Attorney General Benjamin R. Civiletti issued specific guidelines, the *Attorney General Guidelines on FBI Undercover Operations*, a complete set of guiding standards to direct the FBI in the best way to conduct undercover investigations. Es-

---

PUBLIC RESPONSE TO ABSCAM

Public opinion regarding the FBI's Abscam investigation ranged from support for the agency's successful probe to scorn for the agency's undercover tactics to catch Congress members taking bribes. In the following letter addressed to President Ronald Reagan, dated March 11, 1983, and made available through the Freedom of Information Act, an anonymous citizen questions the legality of the FBI's tactics:

Dear Mr. Reagan:

I am interested in finding out the methods used by the F.B.I. during their ABSCAM investigations. I am specifically interested in knowing the answers to these questions.

What kind of law allows the F.B.I. to bribe people?

Why was the F.B.I. not indicted for attempted bribery?

Why is this type of procedure not considered entrapment?

Can any other agency in the Justice Department use this type of procedure to catch potential criminals?

I would appreciate you answering these questions. I would also like you to send me any other information concerning this topic. Thank you for your time.

---

tablished to protect civil liberties, the guidelines, the first of their kind in U.S. law enforcement, are updated periodically in response to changing types of crime and evolving approaches to law enforcement.

The Senate also held its own probe into the operation and the FBI's investigative techniques. In December, 1982, the Senate's final report supported the FBI but also cautioned the public that the kind of techniques it used in the Abscam affair might infringe on a person's right to privacy.

For Americans who were already disenchanted with government because of the Watergate scandal and U.S. president Richard Nixon's resignation, Abscam led to further disappointment and disgust. Although criminals were brought to justice because of the operation, the case had the ultimate effect of making Americans even more distrustful of their elected officials. Voters began to critically question the integrity of their representatives. Conversely, and more positively, the scandal also exemplified how well the U.S. system of government worked. The politicians who broke the law were charged, convicted, sentenced, imprisoned, removed from office, and publicly shamed, thus showing that no person, even a government official or one elected, is above the law.

—*Bernadette Zbicki Heiney*

FURTHER READING

Caplan, Gerald M., ed. *ABSCAM Ethics: Moral Issues and Deception in Law Enforcement.* Cambridge, Mass.: Ballinger, 1983. A compilation of seven essays that examine the moral issues that surround undercover operations by law enforcement agencies. Uses the Abscam affair as a starting point for discussion.

Greene, Robert W. *The Sting Man: Inside Abscam.* New York: E. P. Dutton, 1981. Based on more than two hundred interviews with Melvin Weinberg, this book provides readers with the inside story of the Abscam sting operation through Weinberg's eyes.

Roberts, Robert North. *Ethics in U.S. Government: An Encyclopedia of Investigations, Scandals, Reforms, and Legislation.* Westport, Conn.: Greenwood Press, 2001. A comprehensive encyclopedia documenting political scandals, ethical controversies, and investigations in the United States between 1775 and 2000. Includes discussion of Abscam.

Tolchin, Susan J., and Martin Tolchin. *Glass Houses: Congressional Ethics and the Politics of Venom.* Boulder, Colo.: Westview Press, 2001. This book examines the ethical pressures routinely confronted by politicians and how politicians handle those pressures. Several case studies are reviewed, including Abscam.

U.S. Congress. Senate. *Final Report of the Select Committee to Study Law Enforcement Undercover Activities of Components of the Department of Justice to the U.S. Senate.* 97th Congress, 2d session. Senate Report 97-682. Washington, D.C.: Government Printing Office, 1981. Contains analysis of ethical issues raised by the Abscam prosecutions. A basic, but important, compendium of primary sources.

SEE ALSO: Jan. 23, 1904: Senator Joseph R. Burton Is Convicted of Bribery; May, 1930: Postmaster's Division of Airmail Routes Creates a Scandal; Mar. 17, 1937: Atherton Report Exposes San Francisco Police Corruption; May 3, 1950: U.S. Senate Committee Begins Investigating Organized Crime; Nov. 16, 1951: Federal Tax Official Resigns After Accepting Bribes; Oct. 7, 1963: Vice President Lyndon B. Johnson Aide Resigns over Crime Connections; May 14, 1974: *Washington Post* Reveals That the Nixons Received Jewelry Gifts; 1976-1977: U.S. Congress Members Are Implicated in Koreagate Scandal; Oct. 11, 1979: Senate Denounces Herman E. Talmadge for Money Laundering; Oct. 19, 1982: Car Manufacturer John De Lorean Is Arrested in a Drug Sting; June, 1988-June, 1989: Insider-Trading Scandal Rocks Japanese Government; June 1, 1994: Congressman Dan Rostenkowski Is Indicted in House Post Office Scandal; Dec. 23, 1998: Prominent Belgians Are Sentenced in Agusta-Dassault Corruption Scandal; July 1, 2005: Federal Agents Raid Congressman Randall Cunningham's Home.

March 10, 1980
SCARSDALE DIET DOCTOR IS KILLED BY HIS LOVER

Herman Tarnower, the creator of the famous Scarsdale diet, was shot and killed by his lover, Jean Harris, the head of an exclusive Virginia girls' school. Harris became jealous over Tarnower's relationship with a younger woman. The well-publicized trial included scandalous testimony on the doctor's sex life and his fourteen-year relationship with Harris.

LOCALE: Purchase, New York
CATEGORIES: Murder and suicide; law and the courts; sex

KEY FIGURES
Herman Tarnower (1910-1980), cardiologist who created the popular Scarsdale diet
Jean Harris (b. 1923), head of a girls' school in Virginia
Lynne Tryforos (fl. 1980's), Tarnower's secretary

SUMMARY OF EVENT
Herman Tarnower, a cardiologist, practiced medicine in Scarsdale, New York, where he developed his famous diet and best-selling book, *The Complete Scarsdale Medical Diet* (1979), cowritten with Samm Sinclair Baker. Tarnower did not specialize in weight-reduction programs but believed in good nutrition. His diet derived from concern for his patients' health and from numerous requests for copies of his weight-loss plans.

Jean Harris, an educator and head of the Madeira School for Girls in McLean, Virginia, suspected that Tarnower, her lover of fourteen years, was leaving her for a younger woman. A confrontation between Tarnower and Harris ended with Tarnower being shot and killed. Harris claimed she had intended to commit suicide but instead accidentally shot Tarnower when he attempted to take the gun away from her.

Harris's early career was marked by intense devotion to her work and very little social life. That changed at a party in December, 1966, when a

friend introduced her to Tarnower. Harris, divorced and with two children, was attracted to the gregarious doctor and began dating him in March, 1967. The couple continued to see each other for the next fourteen years. Although they considered marrying each other, Harris ultimately rejected the idea because Tarnower clearly enjoyed being unmarried. Also, Harris wanted to remain independent. Tarnower, who was not possessive, encouraged Harris to see other men while he began to date other women. Harris, however, would not date others, creating an imbalance in the relationship. She initially did not seem to mind Tarnower's interest in other women, and he certainly did not attempt to conceal his other sexual affairs. Harris knew as well that Tarnower was seeing his secretary, Lynne Tryforos.

Harris said that she began receiving disturbing phone messages from an anonymous caller around the time Tarnower was beginning to date Tryforos. Harris was told by the caller that she was getting old and needed instruction in sex, messages that were demeaning and humiliating and made her feel powerless and pathetic. Curiously, Harris did not suspect that Tryforos made the calls; she could not even identify the caller's gender. Harris and Tryforos, though, did engage in several angry phone calls at other times.

In 1979, *The Complete Scarsdale Medical Diet* became a best seller, making Tarnower a millionaire. Harris had provided significant help during the production of the book, and Tarnower thanked her in his acknowledgments. For Harris, however, the acknowledgments meant little at this time: Tarnower had decided to take Tryforos instead of Harris with him on his book tour, leaving her feeling excluded from her lover's life. Depressed and exhausted, she despaired of competing with Tryforos for his attention. She also hated the idea of him choosing a woman who was so poorly educated and who seemed to lack sophistication. Others, however, said Tryforos made a good impression as a modest and impeccably groomed professional woman.

Harris had found her career as head of a girls' school stressful, especially at Madeira, where she spent a good deal of time restoring the school's fading reputation. At such moments, she relied on Tarnower for reassurance, but he seemed unconcerned about her worries, even as she feared she might be fired after receiving a poor performance review in May, 1979.

The following year, on March 10, 1980, Harris's suicidal thoughts intensified after she had run out of the antidepressant medication that Tarnower had prescribed for her. Suffering emotionally, she wanted to take her own life, and to do so at Tarnower's residence in Purchase, New York.

Harris said that she found Tarnower sleeping upon her arrival at his house. When she woke him, he advised her to get some sleep. She then went into

Jean Harris en route to sentencing at the Westchester County Courthouse, 1981. (AP/Wide World Photos)

his bathroom and noticed hair curlers that were not hers. She threw them at a dresser and broke its mirror. Tarnower, now awake, hit her on the face and told her to leave. She pulled out the gun in her purse, put it to her head, and, as she fired, Tarnower deflected the shot, which hit his hand. The two continued to struggle, leading to a shot to the doctor's torso. Harris admitted to the police who were first on the scene that she shot Tarnower. He died later that night, and Harris was arrested for his murder. She was released on bail and then entered a psychiatric treatment facility. She repeatedly denied that she intended to murder Tarnower and insisted on testifying on her own behalf at her trial, which began on November 21, 1980. She pleaded not guilty by reason of temporary insanity and claimed Tarnower's death was accidental. In the meantime, sales of *The Complete Scarsdale Medical Diet* soared during public discussion of the case.

While it could not be proven that Harris planned to murder her lover, a jury found her explanation of Tarnower's death unconvincing. Expert testimony for the prosecution suggested that the doctor had been shot in bed and that his wounds were inconsistent with the story of a struggle for the gun. Although an expert for the defense challenged the prosecution's expert, the defense expert admitted he was not completely certain of his analysis of Tarnower's death. The prosecution's experts, however, said they had no doubts about their analyses.

After eight days of deliberation, the jury found Harris guilty of second-degree murder. She was sentenced to fifteen years to life in Bedford Hills Correctional Facility, a maximum-security women's prison in New York. Harris appealed her verdict three times to no avail, and her requests for clemency were denied until December 29, 1992, when New York governor Mario Cuomo commuted her sentence. She had suffered two heart attacks in prison.

IMPACT

The Harris-Tarnower murder case received enormous press attention. Harris, a high-achieving professional woman, seemed nevertheless in thrall to the arrogant but charismatic Tarnower. Her conflicted nature made her an appealing figure with a complex psychology. Reporters wrote about Tarnower's success with women, a success that seemed built upon his candor. Women had to take him as he was: a man who did not promise fidelity but who nevertheless created a charm that attracted women such as Harris, who sought relationships with powerful men.

Although Harris did not believe she could survive prison, she managed to do so, and she even wrote three books: *Stranger in Two Worlds* (1986), her autobiography; *They Always Call Us Ladies: Stories from Prison* (1988), which looks at an inhumane prison system in which guards and administrators abuse their authority; and *Marking Time* (1991), a collection of letters written to her biographer, also a friend.

A model prisoner, Harris worked with incarcerated mothers and presented parenting and sex-education classes. She founded the prison's Children's Center. Following her release from prison, she lectured and worked to raise funds for educating the children of incarcerated women.

—*Carl Rollyson*

FURTHER READING

Alexander, Shana. *Very Much a Lady: The Untold Story of Jean Harris and Dr. Herman Tarnower.* New York: Simon & Schuster, 2006. Originally published in 1983, this work is more of a biographical study than the book by Diana Trilling. Alexander, who became Harris's friend, provides a revealing and intimate look at Harris's life.

David, Jay. *The Scarsdale Murder: The Slaying of Dr. Herman Tarnower of "The Complete Scarsdale Medical Diet."* New York: Leisure Books, 1980. One of the first books written about the Harris case; this is now chiefly valuable for its use of news items and magazine profiles.

Harris, Jean. *Marking Time: Letters from Jean Harris to Shana Alexander.* New York: Maxwell Macmillan International, 1991. The story of how Harris's biographer became a friend of her subject.

_____. *Stranger in Two Worlds.* New York: Macmillan, 1986. Harris's autobiography, including her early life, career, the killing of Tarnower, and her life in prison.

Hendin, Josephine G. *Heartbreakers: Women and Violence in Contemporary Culture and Literature.* New York: Palgrave Macmillan, 2004. A literary study of cultural representations of women convicted of violent crimes. Brief but pointed discussion of Diana Trilling's book on Jean Harris. Argues that violent women not only challenge ideas of femininity but also present new forms of behavior and self-identity.

Spencer, Duncan. *Love Gone Wrong: The Jean Harris-Scarsdale Murder Case.* New York: New American Library, 1981. Like Jay David's book, this is chiefly valuable as a collection of contemporary writings about Harris and Tarnower in periodicals.

Trilling, Diana. *Mrs. Harris: The Death of the Scarsdale Diet Doctor.* New York: Harcourt Brace Jovanovich, 1981. One of the best books on Harris and Tarnower by a distinguished literary and cultural critic.

SEE ALSO: Apr. 4, 1958: Actor Lana Turner's Daughter Kills Turner's Gangster Lover; Sept. 5, 1967: Socialite Nancy Wakeman Shoots Her Politician-Husband; Mar. 21, 1976: Actor Claudine Longet Kills Ski Champion Vladimir Sabich; July 23, 1978: Utah Millionaire Is Murdered by His Grandson; Jan. 26, 1979: Former Vice President Nelson Rockefeller Dies Mysteriously; Apr. 18, 1979: Actor Lee Marvin Is Ordered to Pay Palimony to Former Lover; Apr. 28, 1981: Tennis Star Billie Jean King Is Sued for Palimony; Mar., 1990: Menendez Brothers Are Arrested for Murdering Their Parents; June 23, 1993: Lorena Bobbitt Severs Her Husband's Penis; June 12, 1994: Double Murder Leads to Sensational O. J. Simpson Trial.

1980's

April 27, 1980
MOBSTER'S ARREST REVEALS POINT SHAVING BY BOSTON COLLEGE BASKETBALL PLAYERS

Several Boston College basketball players conspired with gamblers and mobsters to engage in an illegal gambling scheme known as point shaving, that is, conspiring to avoid winning by a certain spread, or margin, predicted by gamblers. After the arrest of mobster Henry Hill revealed the shocking conspiracy, Boston center Rick Kuhn was sentenced to ten years imprisonment, reportedly the heaviest penalty ever given to an athlete for point shaving.

LOCALES: Mineola, New York; Boston, Massachusetts

CATEGORIES: Corruption; drugs; gambling; law and the courts; organized crime and racketeering; sports

KEY FIGURES

Henry Hill (b. 1943), member of the Lucchese crime family and an FBI informant

Rick Kuhn (b. 1955), Boston College basketball player

James Burke (1931-1996), member of the Lucchese crime family

Paul Mazzei (b. 1944), gambler, convicted drug dealer, and friend of Henry Hill

Anthony Perla (fl. 1980's), gambler, brother of Rocco Perla

Rocco Perla (fl. 1980's), gambler, brother of Anthony Perla, and a friend of Rick Kuhn

James Sweeney (fl. 1980's), Boston College basketball player and a friend of Rick Kuhn

Ernie Cobb (fl. 1980's), Boston College basketball player

SUMMARY OF EVENT

The arrest of mobster Henry Hill in 1980 led to the discovery of point shaving at Boston College during the 1978-1979 basketball season. Several gamblers and mobsters were involved in the scheme with three Boston basketball players. The athletes would win or lose games within a certain point margin to increase gambling profits. The unearthing of the scandal shocked the sports world and impacted the regulation and enforcement of illegal gambling in athletics.

The point-shaving scheme, devised in the summer of 1978, involved an intricate web of individuals, ranging from low-end gamblers and drug dealers to powerful criminal figures. Hill, a member of New York's Lucchese crime family, became acquainted with gambler and cocaine dealer Paul Mazzei in 1972 while both were incarcerated in Pennsylvania's Lewisburg federal prison for extortion. Hill and Mazzei designed the point-shaving scam while they were in prison.

After being released from prison in July, 1978, Hill met with Mazzei in Pittsburgh, Pennsylvania, to further plan the gambling scheme. It was at this time that Hill was introduced to Mazzei's drug affiliates, Anthony Perla and his brother, Rocco Perla. Anthony informed Hill and Mazzei that Boston College would be the ideal venue for implementing the point-shaving plot because of Rocco's friendship with Boston College center Rick Kuhn. After Kuhn agreed to participate in the scheme, he coaxed his friend and fellow player James Sweeney to help carry out the plan.

Mazzei and the Perla brothers wanted Hill to involve his Lucchese crime family bosses James Burke and Paul Vario in the scheme as financial backers. Their involvement would help increase profits and, because of their wide influence, ensure control over bookies and nonpaying debtors. After receiving the consent and support of Burke and Vario, Hill further developed the details of the scheme: The Lucchese family would finance the gambling plot, and Mazzei would transfer the funds to the Perlas to pay the Boston College players involved.

Kuhn was given the responsibility of deciding which games to fix and of ensuring that the games' scores would result in the desired point spreads necessary for payout. Common methods that were used for controlling the point spread in basketball games included fouling other players and missing free throws. The scheme was finalized shortly after Hill and the Lucchese crime family conducted a heist of $5.8 million from a vault at New York's John F. Kennedy International Airport.

The point-shaving plan was first put into action during the game between Boston College and Providence College on December 6, 1978. The game ended unfavorably for the gamblers when Boston won outside the wagered point margin. The gamblers considered the Providence game a failure because of their lack of control over players scoring on the court. The gamblers were convinced that more Boston players had to be involved for the scheme to work. Boston's top scorer, Ernie Cobb, and several bookies were coerced into the scam.

Before the start of the next fixed game, the scheming Boston players were threatened by Hill and Burke to adhere to the plan. Kuhn, Sweeney, and Cobb began to realize the growing risks of working with the mob, including violent repercussions, but the players also feared legal authorities and being sanctioned by the National Collegiate Athletic Association.

The Boston players continued to shave points and produce a substantial profit for the gamblers between December, 1978, and the following March, and were instrumental in fixing a total of nine games after the failed game against Providence. To counter any growing suspicions of their point shaving, the gamblers rigged several games to break even in their payouts. A significant upset in gambling profits occurred during a game with Holy Cross, in which a basket by Cobb placed Boston beyond the wagered point margin at the end of the game; this error led to Burke's withdrawal from the scam. Boston ended its season with a 22-9 record, and the gamblers profited from six of the nine games that were fixed. Hill allegedly made close to $100,000, and his associates made up to $250,000. Each Boston player reportedly earned an average of $10,000. The players and gamblers parted ways at the end of the season, but only for a short time.

The point-shaving scandal would bring the players and gamblers together once again during the early 1980's. Hill was arrested on April 27, 1980, in Mineola, New York, for six drug-related felonies and was later charged in connection with the heist at the airport in 1978. Hill agreed to cooperate with authorities for two big reasons: First, the evidence against him was overwhelming, and second, Lucchese family members and others involved in the airport heist were murdered to keep them from revealing details of the crime should they be arrested.

Fearing for his safety, Hill entered the witness protection program and became an informant for the Federal Bureau of Investigation (FBI), providing critical information on the Lucchese family's criminal activities. Under the terms of the contract with the FBI, Hill was required to provide a full and honest account of all his crimes to avoid conviction and imprisonment. He revealed the Boston College point-shaving scandal to shocked authorities.

IMPACT

The scam remained undetected until Hill's testimony to the FBI and became known publicly only after Hill agreed to sell his story to *Time* magazine for $10,000. After the article was published in *Time*, the Lucchese family issued a $100,000 hit on Hill. The FBI was forced to increase security measures to protect its informant.

On October 27, 1981, the federal trial began in a Brooklyn court. Burke, Mazzei, Anthony and Rocco Perla, and Kuhn were charged with conspiracy, bribery, and racketeering. Hill's testimony in the case helped the prosecution seal convictions against four of his former associates. In 1982, Burke received a prison sentence of twenty years and Mazzei was sentenced to ten years. Anthony Perla was sentenced to ten years (later reduced to six years), Rocco Perla received a four-year prison term and was fined, and Kuhn was sentenced to ten years, the longest prison term ever given to a college player for point shaving. Kuhn's prison term was later reduced to four years; he was released in 1986. Cobb was not indicted until 1983 and was found not guilty in 1984. Vario also was acquitted of all charges. Sweeney avoided being charged in the scandal because he cooperated with authorities and testified against the others in court.

Although the scandal stunned the sports world and damaged the reputation of Boston College, point shaving continues unabated in college sports. Players still risk being expelled from their respective colleges or universities and face indictment and imprisonment, yet the schemes continue.

One positive outcome of the scandal was the development of several deterrence and detection techniques. These new techniques include monitoring the amount and frequency of wagers and comparing team odds with expected point margins, all in the hope of catching perpetrators in their acts of crime.

—*Sheena Garitta*

FURTHER READING

Hill, Henry, with Douglas Looney. "Anatomy of a Scandal: The Mastermind's Inside Story of the Boston College Point-Shaving Scheme." *Sports Illustrated*, February 16, 1981. Offers a detailed firsthand account of the scandal by gangster turned FBI informant Henry Hill.

McCarthy, Michael. "Point-Shaving Remains a Concern in College Athletics." *USA Today*, May 9, 2007. Discusses the common problem of point shaving and illegal gambling practices in college sports, and details the methods used to prevent and detect such activities.

Porter, David. *Fixed: How Goodfellas Bought Boston College Basketball.* Dallas, Tex.: Taylor Trade, 2000. Provides a chronological narrative of the people and events involved in the point-shaving scandal. Includes news references, interviews, and details of the investigation and trial.

Staurowsky, Ellen J. "Piercing the Veil of Amateurism: Commercialization, Corruption, and U.S. College Sports." In *The Commercialization of Sport*, edited by Trevor Slack. New York: Routledge, 2004. Staurowsky discusses how amateur athletics in the United States has moved to commercialized and corrupt spectacle.

Thelin, John R. *Games Colleges Play: Scandal and Reform in Intercollegiate Athletics.* Baltimore: Johns Hopkins University Press, 1994. Provides a chronicle of college sports from 1910 to 1990. Discusses specific scandalous events and examines how college sports are an integral part of university, and American, life.

SEE ALSO: Apr. 2, 1915: Players Fix Liverpool-Manchester United Soccer Match; May 3, 1950: U.S. Senate Committee Begins Investigating Organized Crime; Jan. 17, 1951: College Basketball Players Begin Shaving Points for Money; Fall, 1969-Winter, 1971: Japanese Baseball Players Are Implicated in Game Fixing; Feb. 25, 1987: NCAA Imposes "Death Penalty" on Southern Methodist University Football; Mar. 27, 2002: Georgia Basketball Coach Jim Harrick, Sr., Resigns over Fraud Allegations; July 14, 2006: *New York Times* Exposes Grading Scandal at Auburn University; July 29, 2008: NBA Referee Tim Donaghy Is Sentenced to Prison for Betting on Games.

Late July, 1980
PRESIDENT'S BROTHER, BILLY CARTER, REGISTERS AS A PAID AGENT FOR LIBYA

Billy Carter, the brother of U.S. president Jimmy Carter, reportedly received $220,000 in loans from the government of Libya between 1978 and 1980. The U.S. Justice Department agreed not to indict the president's brother but required him to register as a Libyan agent. Given that Libya was a suspected terrorist state, Billy's association with the Libyan government damaged his brother's 1980 campaign for reelection.

LOCALE: Washington, D.C.

CATEGORIES: Corruption; international relations; politics; government; law and the courts

KEY FIGURES

Billy Carter (1937-1988), brother of U.S. president Jimmy Carter

Jimmy Carter (b. 1924), president of the United States, 1977-1981

Bert Lance (b. 1931), director, U.S. Office of Management and Budget

Benjamin Civiletti (b. 1935), U.S. attorney general, 1979-1981

SUMMARY OF EVENT

Billy Carter, the younger brother of U.S. president Jimmy Carter, was notorious throughout his brother's presidency for his involvement in a variety of scandals. The most serious was his association with Libya, deemed by the United States to be a state sponsor of terrorism.

Billy achieved notoriety immediately after his brother became president. He attracted the media and tourists to his service station in the Carter family's hometown of Plains, Georgia. There, he regaled his audiences with his colorful language, beer drinking, and outrageous commentary. He became a popular entertainer, making up to $500,000 a year appearing on television talk shows and at sports events around the country while his popularity

lasted. However, Billy soon became an embarrassment to the president because of his perceived corruption.

A congressional investigation involving Bert Lance, President Carter's director of the Office of Management and Budget (OMB), uncovered evidence of corrupt financial practices during Jimmy Carter's 1976 presidential campaign. Lance, as president of the National Bank of Georgia, had approved loans and a line of credit in the amount of $3.65 million to Billy and Jimmy Carter and the Carter Peanut Warehouse, which Billy managed. On September 23, 1976, Lance increased the line of credit for the Carter Warehouse to $9 million. Despite Lance's resignation as OMB director on September 21, 1977, both he and Billy remained under investigation.

In November, 1978, Billy was called to testify and produce records showing how the loan money was spent. Carter Warehouse records showed much less money spent for the warehouse business than was received in loans approved by Lance. The investigators questioned Billy as to whether the loan money was transferred illegally into his brother's 1976 campaign fund. Five times during his testimony, Billy asserted his Fifth Amendment rights and refused to answer questions on grounds of possible self-incrimination. Lance was acquitted. He then returned to Calhoun, Georgia, and again became chairman of the National Bank of Georgia. He acquired new partners and investors, four of whom were influential Arab businessmen.

Questions about Billy's financial dealings drew more attention when he made several visits to Libya between 1978 and 1980. Billy's first visit in 1978 was an all-expenses-paid trip with Georgia legislators and businessmen seeking investments and business deals with Libya. In addition to his travel expenses, Billy received several gifts valued at about $3,000. In 1978, Libya was providing only 10

Billy Carter just prior to his appearance before a session of the special Senate Judiciary subcommittee regarding his dealings with Libya. (AP/Wide World Photos)

percent of United States oil imports, and it wanted to increase that percentage. The U.S. National Security Council briefed Billy and cautioned him against saying or doing anything that would disturb the delicate peace negotiations that were under way in the Middle East. An investigation by the U.S. Justice Department in 1980 revealed that Billy had accepted the Libyans' offer of a commission for using his influence to arrange the sale of additional oil to the United States. The Libyans promised him loans up to $500,000 in advance of any earned commissions. Billy later admitted that he had received $220,000 in loans from Libya.

Following his 1978 visit to Libya, Billy arranged a reception for Libyan delegates visiting Georgia and organized the Libyan-Arab-Georgia-Friendship Society to promote further business relations.

At that time, Libya was trying to purchase C-130 transport planes from the United States, but President Carter had blocked the sale because of Libyan terrorist activities. Libya wanted Billy to influence his brother to cancel that embargo.

In January, 1979, Congress was pressuring the Justice Department to investigate President Carter's possible involvement with his brother's Libyan dealings. The U.S. attorney general privately tried to persuade Billy to register as an agent for Libya under the Foreign Agents Registration Act, which allows citizens to lobby for the interests of a foreign government. Billy refused, saying that the Libyans were his friends and that he was not a foreign agent.

In March, under increasing pressure from the U.S. Congress, the Justice Department began a formal investigation to determine whether Billy was violating the law in his dealings with Libya and whether the president was participating in the Libyan deals. President Carter denied any knowledge of his brother's financial dealings with Libya.

In August, Billy spent an entire month in Libya, celebrating the tenth anniversary of Muammar al-Qaddafi's successful revolution and takeover of the Libyan government. By June, 1980, the Justice Department was certain that Billy's loans from Libya were compensation for using his influence upon the president to further Libya's interests. By July, daily media reports featured what came to be called "Billygate" and began to compare President Carter's alleged cover-up of his Libyan dealings to President Richard Nixon's Watergate scandal.

On July 22, both the U.S. Senate and the U.S. House of Representatives called for a full investigation and pressed Carter to disclose everything he knew of his brother's Libyan activities. Carter admitted that he had asked Billy to use his influence with his Libyan friends to help arrange the release of American hostages held in Iran. Later, the president released secret cables from Libya concerning oil dealings and the purchase of C-130 transport planes. Carter also acknowledged that Billy had been given access to those cables and other U.S. State Department documents. The Senate investigation further revealed that Billy's connection with Libya may have been linked with Robert Vesco, a fugitive financier who was fighting extradition back to the United States. Vesco told Senate investigators that he had helped arrange the initial contacts between Billy and the Libyans.

The Senate investigation committee, growing impatient with U.S. attorney general Benjamin Civiletti's so-called foot-dragging on the Billy Carter investigation, called for Civiletti's resignation. In late July, Civiletti brought Billy in for questioning. After Billy admitted that he had received $220,000 from Libya, the attorney general informed him that he was facing criminal charges for influence peddling on behalf of Libya. Civiletti recommended again that Billy register as a Libyan agent. Billy then contacted White House counsel Lloyd Cutler, who referred him to two Washington,

D.C., attorneys. Billy's attorneys met with Justice Department lawyers and worked out an agreement whereby he would register as a Libyan agent and thus avoid criminal prosecution. Under threat of criminal prosecution, Billy finally registered as an agent for the Libyan government.

IMPACT

The Billygate scandal was highly publicized in 1980, the year of President Carter's reelection campaign for the presidency. Comparison of Billygate to Watergate was inevitable because Jimmy Carter had run his 1976 campaign on promises of a corruption-free, honest, and open government that would be completely different from Nixon's. Billygate had a broad impact because Billy's activities brought the president's own integrity into question.

President Carter admitted that he could not control his brother's activities. Billy had no official position from which he could be fired or asked to resign, as had Lance and others in the Carter administration. President Carter's competence was already in question because of his administration's failures to alleviate problems in the economy, such as high interest rates and a high unemployment rate, as well as address the oil and gas crisis, and Carter seemed unable to resolve the Iranian hostage situation. Billygate made the president's integrity as well as his competency an important issue in the 1980 campaign. Consequently, Carter lost his bid for reelection and Republican Ronald Reagan became president.

—*Marguerite R. Plummer*

FURTHER READING

Brinkley, Douglas G. *The Unfinished Presidency: Jimmy Carter's Quest for Global Peace.* New York: Viking Press, 1998. Details Jimmy Carter's postpresidency activities, including his intrusions into foreign affairs during succeeding presidencies.
Carter, Jimmy. *Keeping Faith: Memoirs of a President.* 1982. New ed. New York: Bantam Books, 1995. A collection of memories by Carter that includes commentary on the scandals of his administration.

1980's

Carter, William. *Billy Carter: A Journey Through the Shadows*. Atlanta: Longstreet Press, 1999. A narrative of Billy Carter's life, including the scandals, from his son's point of view.

Jordan, Hamilton. *Crisis: The Last Year of the Carter Presidency*. New York: G. P. Putnam's Sons, 1982. Carter's chief of staff discusses multiple crises that affected Carter's reelection campaign, including Billygate.

Lasky, Victor. *Jimmy Carter: The Man and the Myth*. New York: Richard Marek, 1979. Provides details of the numerous Carter administration scandals that were never fully investigated, in contrast to the unrelenting pursuit of Nixon in the Watergate scandal.

Mollenhoff, Clark R. *The President Who Failed: Carter Out of Control*. New York: Macmillan, 1980. An investigative journalist discusses the Carter administration's incompetence and corruption and questions why the national media seemed reluctant to expose the Carter scandals.

Strong, Robert. *Working in the World: Jimmy Carter and the Making of U.S. Foreign Policy*. Baton Rouge: Louisiana State University Press, 2000. Describes obstacles and strategies involved in the formation of Carter's approach to global politics.

SEE ALSO: May 14, 1974: *Washington Post* Reveals That the Nixons Received Jewelry Gifts; 1976-1977: U.S. Congress Members Are Implicated in Koreagate Scandal; Sept., 1976: Jimmy Carter Admits Committing Adultery in His Heart; Sept. 21, 1977: Carter Cabinet Member Resigns over Ethics Violations; Dec. 7, 1980: Rita Jenrette's "Diary of a Mad Congresswife" Scandalizes Washington; May 7, 1985: Banker Jake Butcher Pleads Guilty to Fraud.

July 28, 1980
MAGAZINE REVEALS BASEBALL STAR STEVE GARVEY'S MARITAL PROBLEMS

Steve and Cyndy Garvey were known as a clean-living, conservative couple whose perfect family life mirrored their perfect looks. Freelance journalist Pat Jordan's article about them in Inside Sports *magazine includes Cyndy discussing her dissatisfaction with the marriage and wishes for an affair. The Garveys sued the magazine and Jordan for libel, invasion of privacy, and breach of contract but settled out of court. The article was the beginning of the end of the Garveys' marriage and perfect image.*

LOCALE: Los Angeles, California

CATEGORIES: Publishing and journalism; popular culture; families and children; women's issues

KEY FIGURES

Steve Garvey (b. 1948), professional baseball player

Cyndy Garvey (b. 1949), television talk-show cohost

Pat Jordan (b. 1941), freelance writer

SUMMARY OF EVENT

Steve and Cyndy Garvey were media darlings during the late 1970's, appearing in various magazine spreads with their two young daughters. The pair, married since 1971, frequently appeared on television together talking about their perfect family and their devotion to one another. Steve, who was a star baseball player with the Los Angeles Dodgers, had political aspirations and was considered the perfect family man, and Cyndy was starting make a name for herself as the cohost, with Regis Philbin, of the Los Angeles morning television show *AM Los Angeles*.

In the spring of 1980, freelance writer Pat Jordan was contracted by *Inside Sports* magazine to write a story about the couple, popularly known as Ken and Barbie, a reference to the popular toy dolls with seemingly perfect physiques and lives. The unflattering article, "Trouble in Paradise," which appeared on newsstands on July 28, 1980, in *Inside Sports*, was based primarily on taped conversations with Cyndy. Jordan depicted the couple as drifting apart, and Cyndy was portrayed as an angry, somewhat empty woman who felt trapped by her image. Cyndy also appeared as a neglected "baseball wife" considering an affair. In her 1989 memoir *The Secret Life of Cyndy Garvey*, she reveals that she already had an affair before the interview with Jordan in 1980.

Cyndy also claims in her memoir that Jordan told her that his article would be about the struggles of baseball families, so she assumed that other baseball wives would be interviewed for the piece as well. This would not be the case. She also claims that the conversation between herself and Jordan was so relaxed that she did not even realize that he had begun to tape-record their discussion.

The article breaks down the couple's story into sections such as "The House," "The Wife," "The Job," and "The Husband." It notes that they have money, but not taste. Cyndy is quoted as saying, for example, "I'll only go with my husband to talk shows if I have a vehicle of my own. I can sing you know. I can dance, I can talk. I can chew gum." She also shares her feelings of frustration about her husband being withdrawn, even distant, when he is not on the road with the Dodgers, and she shares her anger about having been alone when their first child, a girl, was born; Steve was playing for the Dodgers in the World Series at the time of their daughter's birth. She also is cynical about her husband's political ambitions, noting that in a decade she would be a "senator's wife."

Jordan portrayed Steve more sympathetically, however, casting him as a calculating person, but a person who also loves his wife and who cannot understand why she is upset. Jordan wrote, "Steve Garvey is infatuated with his wife. He has loved her

Steve and Cyndy Garvey with their daughters, Whitney and Krisha, in 1978. (Hulton Archive/Getty Images)

in the same way for 10 years, and now that that is no longer enough for her, he is confused."

Cyndy took most of the blame for the revelations in the damaging article. Many readers felt sympathy for Steve. Cyndy recalls in her memoir a time when she was listening to a radio call-in show on her way home from work. Callers said she was an "ingrate" and a "bimbo." In a letter to the editor in the November 30, 1980, issue of *Inside Sports*, Dani Torre, married at the time to New York Mets manager Joe Torre, wrote that "Cyndy needs help" and "Bravo to the real good boys who play ball, and their women, who plan babies for the off-season."

The Garveys sued Jordan and Newsweek, Inc. (owners of *Inside Sports* magazine) for libel, invasion of privacy, and breach of contract, arguing that Jordan broke an oral agreement that his feature would be "favorable" to the couple and would focus on the "special challenges" they faced in their marriage. Cyndy later wrote that she was the one who had insisted on suing, while Steve had been concerned that the suit would interfere with his attempt to maintain his streak of consecutive games played. The *Los Angeles Herald-Examiner*, also named in the lawsuit, wanted to reprint the *Inside Sports* article but was blocked from doing so, temporarily. The Garveys sought the court's help in preventing the newspaper from publishing the piece. Attorneys for Newsweek and the *Herald-Examiner* appealed, and the paper was cleared to publish the story. (The *Los Angeles Times* reprinted the story first, though, the day after the *Herald-Examiner* was given permission to do so by the court.)

In July of 1981, the Garveys announced they had settled the suit out of court. The couple's lawyer stated publicly that the suit was settled for "a lot of money," which was not the case. Lawyers for Newsweek struck back. They noted that the Garveys' attorney violated a written confidentiality agreement between parties in the lawsuit. The Garveys, Newsweek attorneys added, "dropped this $11.2 million suit for about 1 cent on the dollar." In September of that same year, the Garveys separated; they divorced in 1985.

IMPACT

Steve continued playing baseball until May, 1987, ending his career with the San Diego Padres. Cyndy wrote her memoir. She tells her readers in the book that she had been physically abused by her father and was emotionally abused by Steve, whom she referred to as "a sociopath who doesn't take responsibility for his actions." She added, "If Ted Bundy [a serial murderer] is a 10, then Steve's a 7." Her memoir brought much-needed attention to domestic violence. Cyndy also claims that Steve did not provide child support (a claim he denied). That same year, two women sued Steve, claiming he was the father of their children. He later

admitted that he had fathered children with two other women.

The paternity cases, coupled with Cyndy's comments about him in the *Inside Sports* article, made Steve into a national joke of sorts. A popular bumper sticker of the time read, "Honk if you're carrying Steve Garvey's baby." Later that year, Cyndy was sentenced to 130 days in jail for violating a court order that allowed Steve to visit the children. Steve did not run for public office, but he started his own company, Garvey Communications, in 1988 and also works as a motivational speaker.

It was no secret during the height of Garvey's baseball career that he hoped to enter politics after retiring from baseball. Cyndy says in the article that she had been hoping for a more rewarding broadcasting career. "Trouble in Paradise" was the first crack in the Garveys' image of perfection, leading to the picture-perfect couple's separation within a year.

Neither Steve nor Cyndy recovered professionally from the bad press that began to appear after *Inside Sports* revealed the true couple behind the image. The divorce and the paternity suits ended Steve's political ambitions, and Cyndy's television career went nowhere. She had moved to New York in 1983 to host *The Morning Show* and was joined by Philbin, but she left the show in 1984. Steve and Cyndy's marriage, seemingly untouchable, became the stuff of tabloids, talk-show television, and one-line jokes.

—Julie Elliott

FURTHER READING

Fleming, Anne Taylor. "Garvey vs. Garvey: The Latest Chapter." *The New York Times*, August 2, 1989. Discusses Cyndy Garvey's thoughts about her former husband and her memoir, and examines Steve Garvey's comments on the paternity suits against him.

Garvey, Cynthia, with Andy Meisler. *The Secret Life of Cyndy Garvey*. New York: St. Martin's Press, 1989. Cyndy Garvey's memoir details the abuse she suffered at the hands of her father, as well as problems in her marriage to Garvey, who

Congressman Bauman Is Arrested for Liaison with Teenager

she claimed was emotionally abusive and having affairs for much of their marriage.

Garvey, Steve. *My Bat Boy Days: Lessons I Learned from the Boys of Summer.* New York: Scribner, 2008. Steve Garvey reminisces about his early years in baseball.

"Going to Bat for a Marriage." *Time*, August 25, 1980. Discusses the immediate aftermath of the *Inside Sports* article as well as the lawsuit against Jordan and attempts to stop the story from being reprinted.

Jordan, Pat. "Trouble in Paradise." *Inside Sports*, August 31, 1980. The article revealed that Cyndy's frustrations with being a baseball wife and with being lonely and needing affection. This article was the first to hint of anything negative in the Garvey marriage.

Reilly, Rick. "America's Sweetheart." *Sports Illustrated*, November 27, 1989. Discusses the messy divorce between the Garveys as well as Steve's numerous affairs and the paternity cases against him.

SEE ALSO: Nov. 23, 1946: Tennis Star Bill Tilden Is Arrested for Lewd Behavior with a Minor; Dec. 7, 1980: Rita Jenrette's "Diary of a Mad Congresswife" Scandalizes Washington; Apr. 28, 1981: Tennis Star Billie Jean King Is Sued for Palimony; Dec., 1982: Julie Andrews and Blake Edwards Deny Being Gay; Sept. 22, 1997: Sportscaster Marv Albert Is Tried for Sexual Assault; July 1, 2003: Basketball Star Kobe Bryant Is Accused of Rape.

September 3, 1980
CONGRESSMAN BAUMAN IS ARRESTED FOR LIAISON WITH TEENAGE BOY

Republican representative Robert E. Bauman, a board member of the American Conservative Union and an outspoken advocate of traditional values, was arrested and charged for soliciting sex with a sixteen-year-old male prostitute. His arrest shocked his constituents and colleagues and led to the end of his career in politics.

LOCALE: Washington, D.C.
CATEGORIES: Law and the courts; prostitution; sex crimes; public morals; government; politics

KEY FIGURE
Robert E. Bauman (b. 1937), U.S. representative from Maryland, 1973-1981

SUMMARY OF EVENT
In the fall of 1980, the conservative Christian backlash against the gay and lesbian rights movement was in full swing in the United States. November

would see Ronald Reagan, backed by the Religious Right, elected president by a landslide. On Capitol Hill, being antigay was the accepted de facto political position, and prominence in conservative groups was a stepping-stone to political advancement.

Robert E. Bauman was riding the tide. A seven-year veteran of the U.S. House of Representatives, Bauman's political history was staunchly conservative and Christian. He was a founding member of the American Conservative Union in 1964 and was director of the conservative lobbying group Young Americans for Freedom. He and his wife worked together for numerous conservative political causes, and they outwardly presented an ideal picture to conservative voters. Bauman, a Roman Catholic, served in the Maryland state senate from 1971 to 1973 and was elected to the U.S. Congress in 1972, beginning his term in 1973. He was up for reelection in 1980 when scandal derailed his career and life.

577

The gay and lesbian rights movement was well established in Washington, D.C., by 1980, and it showed no signs of leaving town just because a conservative Republican was about to win election to the White House. One of the most popular gay bars in the city was Chesapeake House, operated by John Rock. When Rock opened the bar, he initially featured female and male strippers, but by 1980 he focused on entertainment for gay men.

Bauman allegedly frequented the bar and picked up lovers there. Around six months before the scandal broke, his wife found his gay porn magazines and confronted him. He began counseling with a priest and believed he was on the road to "recovering" from his sexual orientation. However, the Federal Bureau of Investigation (FBI) had been following him. On September 3, 1980, he was arrested for oral sodomy with a sixteen-year-old male prostitute he had picked up in the District of Columbia. In his autobiography *Gentleman from Maryland: The Conscience of a Gay Conservative* (1986), Bauman points out that the FBI had been investigating several members of Congress at this time, and that only he was charged. He believes his behavior came under attack for political reasons, even though he admits that his arrest was justified. Bauman was formally charged on October 3.

In his autobiography, Bauman discusses his trysts. He explains that his conservative background caused him to try to repress his homosexuality. Married and with four children, he also drank heavily, then went to confession to purify himself for church. He hoped that if he could control his political career, his personal life would not matter. He marketed himself as pro-family, which meant antigay, but eventually his behavior caught up with him.

Conservatives were shocked by Bauman's arrest. Known as the House watchdog for his ability to stall Democratic measures, he had been a conservative his entire life, starting down his chosen path in military school, where he had vowed to himself that he was not gay. He continued to deny his homosexuality into adulthood and throughout his political career. As a member of the House, he voted for three bills containing antigay legislation, and he cosponsored the Family Protection Act (1977), anti-

gay employment legislation. The few constituent letters he received in support of gay and lesbian rights were answered with a Roman Catholic, antigay response: condemnation of homosexual acts though not the individuals practicing them ("love the sinner, not the sin").

Bauman pleaded no contest to charges of solicitation of a minor and was convicted of a misdemeanor. He made a statement to the press that he was fighting the demons of homosexuality and alcoholism, and he spent the next three years undergoing psychiatric treatment. He remained in the 1980 political race, ultimately losing by only 2 percentage points, one of only four Republican representatives to lose their seats that year. Because the loss was so close, he attempted to return to Congress with a run in the 1981-1982 Republican primary but withdrew from the race after realizing he would always face attacks for his criminal past and his homosexuality. His wife eventually requested an annulment, and it was only after the annulment was granted that Bauman started to admit his homosexuality to himself. That was in 1982.

IMPACT

Bauman was clear about his not choosing to be gay. In fact, he fought against his sexuality for much of his life and came to terms with his sexual orientation only after years of psychotherapy. His case is an argument for those who insist sexual orientation is a matter of biology, rather than choice. He agreed that he was forced out of the closet and hoped his case would draw attention to the roughly 10 percent of the U.S. population that is gay or lesbian and that gays and lesbians can be conservative as well as liberal. In 1985, he attempted to found a gay Republican congressional group that would have been a predecessor to Log Cabin Republicans, but his efforts failed because most gay Republicans at the time were too afraid of exposure to join such a group.

Bauman's critics believe that his being "forced out" of the closet takes away from the value of his candor in his autobiography, in which he recounts his journey through alcoholism and into accepting his homosexuality. Bauman, however, did not use his arrest and subsequent outing in the media to transform into a liberal or abandon his Catholicism. Some say his autobiography outed liberal gay representative Barney Frank, but Frank had been out to his friends and close associates for some time and came out publicly without losing stature once Bauman's book broadcast the information.

Indeed, in his book, Bauman addresses his own situation uniquely. He began to speak out for gay rights, having experienced some of the prejudice that comes with being gay. His positions were not popular with fellow conservatives, but in spite of this, he refused to change his politics. He could no longer claim to be a traditionalist conservative who supports a hands-off government in most respects except "enforcing" public morality. However, he remained basically conservative, especially in financial issues. After the scandal, he began to write books on financial issues and to work for the group Sovereign Society, which is dedicated to conservative money issues. He remained Catholic as well, in spite of Catholicism's staunch antigay position.

—*Jessie Bishop Powell*

FURTHER READING

Bauman, Robert. *The Gentleman from Maryland: The Conscience of a Gay Conservative*. New York: Arbor House, 1986. Bauman discusses his homosexuality and addresses the conflict between his expressed antigay views and his later coming out, and his change in perspective on gay and lesbian rights.

Danforth, John C. *Faith and Politics: How the "Moral Values" Debate Divides America, and How to Move Forward Together*. New York: Viking Press, 2006. Argues the Republican Party must move away from fringe issues to unite. Contrasts with the views of the Religious Right-dominated party that brought Bauman into office.

Gunderson, Steve, and Rob Morris, with Bruce Bawer. *House and Home*. New York: Dutton, 1996. Discusses the outing of Republican representative Gunderson of Wisconsin. Examines his political positions and his political career. Shows that scandal does not necessary follow revelations of homosexuality.

Marcus, Eric. *Making Gay History*. New York: HarperCollins, 2002. Includes a three-part interview with Bauman, discussing the scandal and his life as a conservative Republican since coming out of the closet.

Tafel, Richard. *Party Crasher: A Gay Republican Challenges Politics as Usual*. New York: Simon & Schuster, 1999. Argues that gays and lesbians do not have to be Democrats to remain loyal to both their politics and their sexuality.

SEE ALSO: 1970: Study of Anonymous Gay Sex Leads to Ethics Scandal; Oct. 25, 1974: Evangelist Billy James Hargis Resigns College Presidency During Gay-Sex Scandal; Jan., 1977: Singer Anita Bryant Campaigns Against Lesbian and Gay Rights; July 20, 1982: Conservative Politician John G. Schmitz Is Found to Have Children Out of Wedlock; July 20, 1983: Congress Members Censured in House-Page Sex Scandal; Sept. 19, 2000: Ex-gay Leader John Paulk Is Photographed Leaving a Gay Bar; Aug. 19, 2004: Blog "Outs" Antigay Congressman Edward Schrock; Dec. 6, 2005: Spokane, Washington, Mayor Recalled in Gay-Sex Scandal; Sept. 29, 2006: Congressman Mark Foley Resigns in Sex Scandal Involving a Teenage Page; Nov. 2, 2006: Male Escort Reveals Sexual Liaisons with Evangelist Ted Haggard; July 11, 2007: Florida Politician Is Arrested for Soliciting an Undercover Male Police Officer.

1980's

October 9, 1980
BENDIX EXECUTIVE RESIGNS AMID RUMORS OF AN AFFAIR

Mary Cunningham was an executive at Bendix Corporation who advanced from executive assistant to vice president for strategic planning in only fifteen months. She resigned after a series of well-publicized rumors claimed that her rise in the company was a direct result of her romantic relationship with Bendix chairman William Agee. Cunningham and Agee married in 1982.

LOCALE: Southfield, Michigan
CATEGORIES: Business; sex; women's issues

KEY FIGURES

Mary Cunningham (b. 1951), vice president of strategic planning at Bendix Corporation
William Agee (b. 1938), chairman of Bendix Corporation
William Panny (b. 1930), president of Bendix Corporation

SUMMARY OF EVENT

Mary Cunningham had more than two dozen job offers from major financial corporations after she received her master's degree in business administration from the prestigious Harvard Business School in 1979. Cunningham rejected all the offers and instead opted to take what some corporate recruiters and Harvard Business School classmates might consider a less important position within corporate America. In June, 1979, she accepted a position as an executive assistant to William Agee, chairman of Bendix Corporation, a *Fortune* 500 aerospace manufacturer in Southfield, Michigan.

Cunningham, who had striking good looks and was described by several independent sources as beautiful, brilliant, and ambitious, worked closely with Agee on a series of corporate initiative projects. Agee soon became her mentor at the company. One year later, in June, 1980, Agee promoted Cunningham to vice president of corporate and public affairs. Her corporate responsibilities increased, and her relationship with Agee grew stron-

ger. Some Bendix executives became envious of their relationship, and they considered her an obstacle to their access to Agee (she seemed to consume a good deal of his valuable time, often at their expense). In addition, some managers criticized her work. In particular, they were critical of a report she wrote on work at one of the company's automobile plants. Her detractors believed that her report did little to improve conditions in the plant. Despite their criticisms and concerns, Cunningham's reputation continued to soar with Agee.

Agee increased Cunningham's corporate responsibilities at Bendix. Many people within the organization believed that she had done very little there to deserve the vast amount of power that Agee had given her. She rose too rapidly, they said, through the organization in too short a time period.

The corporate grapevine can be deadly. Quiet rumors began to swirl around the company that Cunningham and Agee were having a relationship outside the workplace. Some executives registered their disapproval with William Panny, the president of Bendix, who reported directly to Agee. Allegedly, Panny was getting ready to inform the board of directors about the relationship, now a scandal, and its organizational impact. In early September, 1980, before Panny was able to talk to the board, he was fired by Agee. In what might appear to be an expression of sympathy over Panny's firing, Jerome Jacobson, the vice president of strategic planning, left Bendix as well. Unsigned letters were sent to Bendix board members about the Agee-Cunningham affair. Agee vehemently denied any romantic link with Cunningham in his conversations with corporate executives and board members.

On September 24, Agee held a meeting with about six hundred Bendix employees. One item on the agenda was his internal reorganization plan to replace Jacobson. Agee announced that he had appointed Cunningham as Jacobson's replacement, an executive decision that would bring their relationship into the limelight. Soon, the story of their personal relationship and news of her executive-level promotions attracted national media attention.

Cunningham quickly began to stem the tide of public opinion against her. She initially entertained the idea of resigning from the company. For her, a leave of absence would be the perfect solution. It would give her some political and public leverage by allowing her to resign if the board wanted to dismiss her. Moreover, a board would be hard-pressed to reverse itself so soon after it voted to promote her earlier in the week. Ever the strategist, Cunningham sent a letter to the board of directors on September 28, asking that board members grant her a leave of absence. A small subcommittee of the board declared it had "full confidence" in her, but the majority of the board determined that her continued employment at Bendix would compromise the company.

Mary Cunningham. (Hulton Archive/Getty Images)

On October 9, some fifteen months after being hired at Bendix, Cunningham resigned as a corporate officer. In her resignation letter, she stated that an "unusual convergence of events" prevented her from carrying out the duties of her position and, therefore, she was severing her employment with Bendix in the best interest of all parties.

IMPACT

Despite her resignation, Cunningham had no problem finding another job in the corporate world. In March, 1981, she was hired as vice president of strategic planning for Seagram and Sons. She continued her friendship with Agee, and about fifteen months later, in June, 1982, she and Agee were married.

In September, Agee led Bendix to a $1.5 billion hostile takeover bid of Martin Marietta, another aerospace manufacturer. However, Bendix failed in its attempt for two reasons: Agee seriously miscalculated the situation, which resulted in golden parachutes (for Bendix employees), and Martin Marietta was rescued by United Technologies Corporation by means of the infamous Pac Man defense (a strategy in which a company being bought mounts a defense to purchase the takeover company). Cunningham, now a former Bendix employee, was at Agee's side during the negotiations. Her presence sent the wrong signal to people in high-level corporate circles and, according to some familiar with the case, even helped break the deal between Bendix and Martin Marietta. In fact, a Martin Marietta board member reportedly stated, "We'll burn this company to the ground before we let that (woman) have it." That board member was speaking of Cunningham. In the end, Bendix was sold to Allied Technology, and Agee lost his job at Bendix in February, 1983.

—*Joseph C. Santora*

FURTHER READING

Cunningham, Mary, with Fran Schumer. *Power-play: What Really Happened at Bendix.* New York: Linden Press/Simon & Schuster, 1984. Cunningham gives her side of the story and details her relationship with William Agee.

"Mary Agee." *U.S. News & World Report*, February 28, 2005. A brief follow-up article on Mary Cunningham (now Agee), twenty-five years after the Bendix scandal.

"Mary Cunningham Redux." *Time*, March 9, 1981. A newsmagazine article on the scandalous affair, published six months after Cunningham's resignation from Bendix.

Pfeffer, Jeffrey. *Managing with Power: Politics and Influence in Organizations*. Boston: Harvard Business School Press, 1992. This book is a classic on power in organizations. It devotes a brief section to the conflict between Agee and Cunningham and Bendix president William Panny, and it assesses Agee's ability to gain advantage by "striking first."

Sloan, Allan. *Three Plus One Equals Billions: The Bendix-Martin Marietta War*. New York: Arbor House, 1983. This book discusses Bendix Corporation's attempt to take over Martin Marietta. Also considers Agee and Cunningham's affair and their conflict with William Panny.

SEE ALSO: Mar. 29, 1962: Billie Sol Estes Is Arrested for Corporate Fraud; Feb. 4, 1976: Lockheed Is Implicated in Bribing Foreign Officials; Apr. 15, 1992: Hotel Tycoon Leona Helmsley Enters Prison for Tax Evasion; Mar. 5, 2004: Martha Stewart Is Convicted in Insider-Trading Scandal; Sept. 18, 2006: *Newsweek* Reveals That Hewlett-Packard Spied on Its Own Board.

December 7, 1980
RITA JENRETTE'S "DIARY OF A MAD CONGRESSWIFE" SCANDALIZES WASHINGTON

Shortly after her husband, a three-term Democratic representative from South Carolina, resigned his House seat after being convicted as part of the Abscam sting operation, Rita Jenrette provoked a scandal with her account of her time as a "Congresswife" in Washington, D.C. The magazine excerpt and subsequent book, My Capitol Secrets, *tell the tale of profligate behavior, alcohol abuse, influence peddling, rampant promiscuity, and wild sex.*

LOCALE: Washington, D.C.
CATEGORIES: Publishing and journalism; sex; politics; corruption

KEY FIGURES
Rita Jenrette (Rita Carpenter; b. 1949), former Republican Party operative from Texas
John W. Jenrette, Jr. (b. 1936), U.S. representative from South Carolina, 1975-1980

SUMMARY OF EVENT
After graduating from the University of Texas in 1971, Rita Jenrette made an immediate impact in the Texas Republican Party with her savvy knack for political strategy. She was a lecturer in political science at Trinity University and, by 1975, she headed the Republican National Committee's Opposition Research branch, a division of the party that, in the wake of the post-Watergate turmoil and the downfall of the Richard Nixon White House, investigated Democratic nominees for problematic pasts and designed often incendiary attacks ads to promote Republican nominees for office.

In 1976, the strikingly beautiful Jenrette (she was a regional beauty queen and briefly toyed with a singing career) surprised many by marrying not a Republican but a left-leaning Democrat, John W. Jenrette, Jr., a U.S. representative from the well-to-do environs of Myrtle Beach, South Carolina. John had ridden to election in 1974 on the wave of anti-Nixon sentiment and the public's distrust of the Republican Party and was, by 1976, one of the rising stars of the Jimmy Carter-era Dixiecrats. Engaging, savvy, youthful, and vigorous, John advanced quickly within the party power structure and was elected the majority whip of the U.S. House of Representatives by 1978. For a time, the Jenrettes were among the most sought-after power couples in Washington, D.C., as Rita maintained her credentials as a Washington insider working for the Food for Peace Program and other agencies. However, everything would soon change dramatically.

In 1978, the Federal Bureau of Investigation (FBI), reeling from public outrage over revelations of corruption in the Nixon administration that brought down a presidency, initiated a sting operation targeting powerful and influential state and national politicians. The sting had federal agents pose as Middle Eastern business operatives representing a fictitious sheik trying to bribe these corrupt politicians into securing special considerations. The considerations included political asylum and money laundering for a dummy sheik (the operation was code-named Abscam, from the words "Abdul scam"). In hotel rooms under videotaped surveillance, public officials, including state governors, U.S. representatives, and U.S. senators, were offered huge sums of money in return for such assistance. In 1980, John Jenrette was among the more than thirty politicians indicted in connection with the FBI sting. He claimed the operation was entrapment. Nevertheless, he was convicted for accepting $50,000 in bribe money and was sentenced to thirteen months in federal prison. He was defeated for reelection later in the year and resigned from Congress on December 10, just ahead of his term's expiration.

It was during the subsequent public outcry that Rita Jenrette first gained national attention. At the televised congressional hearings, the charismatic Jenrette, long comfortable in front of cameras, electrified the proceedings by testifying how she had found $25,000 in one of her husband's shoes. Later, capitalizing on her newfound celebrity, she ap-

Representative John W. Jenrette, Jr., and Rita Jenrette outside the capitol in Washington, D.C., in 1976. (AP/Wide World Photos)

peared on *The Phil Donahue Show*, a popular television talk show of the time. Her husband called in to the show from jail (the format of Donahue's live show involved such audience participation). The subsequent conversation, charged with emotion, made riveting television.

Far more scandalous and damaging was Jenrette's decision to publish her memoir. On December 7, 1980, *The Washington Post Magazine* ran an excerpt of her as-yet-unpublished manuscript. The excerpt, "Diary of a Mad Congresswife," was a lengthy exposé about her time in Washington; its publication created a sensation. It revealed the private lives of Beltway insiders, including her own husband's numerous affairs, in unflinching and uncensored detail. Perhaps most famously, the article offered an account of the time she and her husband made love on the steps of the Capitol Building behind a pillar during a break of a particularly long all-night House session. It was a story that, much later, she said she invented. However, the story of lovemaking on the Capitol steps secured her instant notoriety and made her husband the target of comedians and political pundits. Indeed, the satiric comedy troupe The Capitol Steps used the alleged incident as the inspiration for its name, seeing in the couple's dalliance a metaphor for reprehensible public behavior among politicians so eccentric that it bordered on the absurdly comic. Far more disturbing than Jenrette's sexual revelations, however, were her reports of how politicians abused alcohol, even during sessions of Congress, and willingly dealt influence using sex. The Jenrettes divorced in 1981.

"Diary of a Mad Congresswife" secured for Jenrette a book deal, and within one year her memoir, *My Capitol Secrets*, was published. She became an instant celebrity. She posed for *Playboy* magazine in April, 1981, and *Playboy* also ran expanded versions of *The Washington Post Magazine* excerpt. Not surprisingly, the book became an immediate best seller. It depicted politicians as quasi-rock stars who attracted a bevy of groupies, specifically women—among them lobbyists, reporters, and staffers—attracted by the aphrodisiac of power and willing to use sex as a strategy for access to these men. Jenrette spoke of rented apartments, clandestine affairs carried out in rented houses and limousines, quickies, and "nooners." Her book was cited by the emerging conservative political movement during the early Ronald Reagan years as evidence of the sorry moral condition of the Washington, D.C., establishment, meaning the entrenched interests of the liberal wing of the Democratic Party.

Jenrette tried to parlay her notoriety into an acting career—appearing in several low-budget films during the 1980's (with titles like *Zombie Island Massacre*, 1984, and *The Malibu Bikini Shop*, 1986). In May, 1984, she appeared again in *Playboy*, this time on the cover in a racy pictorial with her lover at the time, hunky actor-model Phillip Anderson. Given that she was often dismissed as trying to cash in on her husband's political crimes, she was seldom given much critical respect, although her

appearance in Los Angeles in a 1982 revival of the drawing room comedy *The Philadelphia Story* garnered her plaudits and several regional acting awards. She appeared briefly (in 1989) as a field reporter for the entertainment news show *A Current Affair*, but by the end of the decade her celebrity appeared to have been exhausted.

IMPACT

Most obviously, Jenrette exemplifies the fifteen-minutes-of-fame principle. Indeed, there is much to suggest that she manipulated the media to secure her celebrity and to cash in on what was one of the more disturbing political scandals of the Carter years. Her turn to nude modeling and then to a string of lamentable B movies did not add much luster to her reputation. Because her tell-all book did not name specific political figures, it was more sensational than legitimate exposé.

Jenrette's notoriety includes being one of the few women at the center of a political scandal to put together a second career, notably, a professional career in business. During the early 1990's, with her broadcasting career at a dead end, Jenrette was still only in her forties. Determined to succeed and to use her considerable education in business and marketing, she completed a rigorous three-year program at the Harvard Business School. By 1994, she began a lucrative career in real estate in the Manhattan area, overseeing more than a decade of high-powered negotiations in excess of a billion dollars in transactions and involving some of New York's best-known business figures. Secure in her position as one of Manhattan's most influential real estate brokers, Jenrette has said her life in Washington represented a different person, and that her strategy of cashing in on her notoriety and playing to the media as a sex object represented poor judgment. She understands she can never entirely erase her past poor judgment, but it is one that she is content to live with.

—*Joseph Dewey*

FURTHER READING

Jenrette, Rita. *My Capitol Secrets*. New York: Bantam Books, 1981. Vivid and fascinating account of Jenrette's years in Washington, D.C. Creates a disturbing picture of Washington political opportunism and amorality.

Katzmann, Gary S. *Understanding the Criminal Process: The Abscam Case*. New York: Pergamon Press, 1985. Clear and lucid detailed look into the scandal that brought Jenrette into the national spotlight. Looks into the impact of Jenrette's testimony without the distractions of her later celebrity and treats Jenrette as a Washington insider who essentially acted as a whistleblower.

Thompson, Hunter S. *Generation of Swine: Tales of Shame and Degradation in the '80's*. New York: Simon & Schuster, 2003. Classic appraisal of the decade by a distinguished cultural critic and "gonzo" journalist. Provides significant context for understanding politicians' rise and precipi-

tous fall into obscurity by providing a scathing indictment of the political sex scandals of the era.

SEE ALSO: 1927: President Warren G. Harding's Lover Publishes Tell-All Memoir; Sept. 5, 1967: Socialite Nancy Wakeman Shoots Her Politician-Husband; May 23, 1976: *Washington Post* Exposes Congressman Wayne L. Hays's Affair; Sept., 1976: Jimmy Carter Admits Committing Adultery in His Heart; Feb. 2, 1980: Media Uncover FBI Sting Implicating Dozens of Lawmakers; Late July, 1980: President's Brother, Billy Carter, Registers as a Paid Agent for Libya; Dec., 1982: Julie Andrews and Blake Edwards Deny Being Gay; July 19, 1985: Mayflower Madam Pleads Guilty to Promoting Prostitution; July 9, 2007: Senator David Vitter's Name Is Found in D.C. Madam's Address Book.

1980's

April 15, 1981
JANET COOKE ADMITS FABRICATING HER PULITZER PRIZE-WINNING FEATURE

Journalist Janet Cooke's article "Jimmy's World," the story of an eight-year-old heroin addict, earned for her a Pulitzer Prize in 1981. Inconsistencies in her credentials led colleagues to question the veracity of her prize-winning story, which she confessed to having fabricated. The journalistic fraud, one of the first such scandals in the United States, tainted the credibility of journalists but also led to updated truth-in-reporting standards for news media.

LOCALE: Washington, D.C.
CATEGORIES: Communications and media; drugs; hoaxes, frauds, and charlatanism; publishing and journalism

KEY FIGURE
Janet Cooke (b. 1954), reporter for *The Washington Post*

SUMMARY OF EVENT
In August and September of 1980, *The Washington Post* published eight articles about the scourge of heroin use. The last article in the series, "Jimmy's World," was written by journalist Janet Cooke and published in the September 28 edition of the newspaper.

"Jimmy's World" focuses on the life of an eight-year-old heroin addict named Jimmy by Cooke. Cooke describes Jimmy's life as one "of hard drugs, fast money and the good life he believes both can bring." Jimmy, Cooke writes, is motivated by the pursuit of material wealth—through illegitimate methods. His only interest in school is to learn enough mathematics so he can buy and sell drugs in his neighborhood.

In 1969, U.S. president Richard Nixon had described drugs as "public enemy number one in the United States." By 1971 he had officially declared a so-called war on drugs. However, the drug war be-

585

came stagnant after Nixon's resignation following the Watergate scandal. By the presidential election of 1980, drug use, which never subsided, was back on the national agenda.

In the article, Cooke tells readers that Jimmy became a heroin addict at the age of five. He had asked his mother's live-in boyfriend when he would be allowed to "get off." According to the article, his mother's boyfriend "let him snort a little" and was surprised when "the little dude" Jimmy "really did get off." The article asserts that Jimmy was hooked within six months. The article also suggests that Jimmy's mother knew of her son's addiction. Cooke, who is African American, claims that his mother viewed his drug use as an inevitable aspect of the life of a black child growing up in the city.

The article also thoroughly describes specific circumstances in the life of Jimmy's mother that affected her life and the life of her son. According to Cooke, Jimmy's mother never knew her father. She had been sexually abused by her mother's live-in boyfriends (Jimmy was the son of one of these men), and she turned to drugs for escape. Eventually, she turned to prostitution and property crime to support her drug addiction. Cooke ends her article by writing that at the end of a long day in which

Jimmy answered her questions about his life, his behavior and demeanor began to change; he became "jittery" and "ill-behaved," clearly suffering withdrawal symptoms. Cooke describes how the mother's live-in boyfriend calls Jimmy over to him and injects him with his next drug fix.

Citizens and community leaders in the Washington, D.C., area were outraged by the living conditions and drug abuse Cooke featured in her article. District of Columbia mayor Marion Barry and Police Chief Burtell Jefferson ordered a districtwide search for a child who fit Jimmy's description. Social service agencies and schools were told to instruct their employees to look for children with needle marks on their bodies and for children exhibiting behaviors that resembled withdrawal from drugs.

The managing editors of *The Washington Post* were asked to produce information about where Jimmy could be found, but they refused on the grounds that it would violate the confidentiality of the sources used in the feature. As a goodwill gesture, *The Washington Post* established a team of eleven reporters who were given the task of finding other children who suffered like Jimmy, reasoning that if there was one Jimmy there had to be others.

Given the reality of the case, it is not surprising, then, that city officials and journalists could not locate Jimmy or any other child like him.

An assistant managing editor at *The Washington Post*, Bob Woodward, himself a Pulitzer winner for helping to break the Watergate affair, nominated Cooke's article for a Pulitzer Prize. He deflected mounting criticism of Cooke and maintained the story was true. On April 13, 1981, Cooke won a Pulitzer for her story. Upon hearing about her receipt of the prestigious award, editors at the newspaper *Toledo Blade* (Cooke's former employer) noticed inconsistencies in the biography of her that accom-

Janet Cooke reacts to news that she won a Pulitzer Prize. (AP/Wide World Photos)

panied the prize-winning article. They contacted *Washington Post* editors and told them of the errors. Cooke admitted to her editors that she had indeed falsified information on her résumé.

The veracity of "Jimmy's World" was now in question. Initially, Cooke was adamant that the story was accurate. However, she soon admitted that she had fabricated the story. She resigned from *The Washington Post* on April 15, and her prize was rescinded by the Pulitzer committee. In a statement made upon resigning, Cooke conceded, "The [article] was a serious misrepresentation which I deeply regret. I apologize to my newspaper, my profession, the Pulitzer board and all seekers of the truth."

IMPACT

In the aftermath of the discovery that Cooke had fabricated her prize-winning story, *The Washington Post* conducted a full-scale investigation of the debacle. Its findings and analysis suggested that Cooke's ambition to succeed and advance at the newspaper had blinded her to her ethical and moral obligations to the newspaper and its readers. The findings of the investigation also suggested that the paper's editorial staff was partially responsible in that they had become so entrenched in wanting stories that were contextually relevant to the evolving social and political agenda concerning drug use that they, too, had allowed their editorial judgment to be compromised.

Sociologists Craig Reinarman and Ceres Duskin, however, offered another explanation as to how one of the country's most powerful newspapers published a fake story. In a 1998 journal article, Reinarman and Duskin maintained that a major aspect of the problem was journalistic beliefs and preconceptions about drugs and the nature of drug use. The authors wrote that in covering drug-related stories, the mass media had erred on the side of sensationalism by "rhetorically re-crafting worse cases into typical cases, and profoundly distorting the nature of drug problems in the interest of dramatic stories."

Reinarman and Duskin supported their position by showing that there were certain key aspects of

the case that should have led the editors of the paper to question the validity of the story. The sociologists argued that questions were not raised largely because the specific elements of the story fit rather nicely with dominant social assumptions about drug use and addiction. For instance, they noted that it should have been questionable that a five-year-old child would ask to have a needle stuck into his arms daily for the weeks that it would take the child to become addicted to heroin.

Reinarman and Duskin also stressed that it is unlikely that a journalist would have unlimited access to drug users and sellers and even more unlikely that an addict would allow a journalist to watch him or her shoot heroin into the arm of a young child. It would be unlikely as well that the typical mother, even the typical mother on heroin, would allow someone to shoot heroin into the arm of her child.

On a positive note, the affair led media outlets to revisit their standards for reporters and editors. It also intensified discussion of the rights of reporters to conceal facts about their sources.

—*Kevin Buckler*

FURTHER READING

Cooke, Janet. "Jimmy's World." *The Washington Post*, September 28, 1980. Cooke's award-winning, but faked, feature story about Jimmy, an eight-year-old heroin addict living in Washington, D.C.

Iggers, Jeremy. *Good News, Bad News: Journalism Ethics and the Public Interest*. Boulder, Colo.: Westview Press, 1998. A study of journalistic ethics that also fully examines the Janet Cooke case and its significance for journalism.

Maraniss, David A. "*Post* Reporter's Pulitzer Prize Is Withdrawn." *The Washington Post*, April 16, 1981. The newspaper article announcing that Cooke's Pulitzer for best feature story had been withdrawn by the Pulitzer Prize Committee.

Nemeth, Neil. *News Ombudsmen in North America: Assessing an Experiment in Social Responsibility*. Westport, Conn.: Praeger, 2003. Looks at the role of news ombudsmen in monitoring and checking the veracity of news stories. Examines the Janet Cooke case and who was responsible for the story.

Reinarman, Craig, and Ceres Duskin. "Dominant Ideology and Drugs in the Media." *International Journal of Drug Policy* 2, no. 1 (1992): 6-15. Provides a different explanation of how a fabricated story could be published by *The Washington Post*. Argues that preconceptions about drugs and drug users held by the news editors were factors that contributed to the decision to publish the story.

Seitz, Don Carlos. *Joseph Pulitzer: His Life and Letters*. Whitefish, Mont.: Kessinger, 2004. Examines Joseph Pulitzer's efforts to raise the standards of journalism, and his establishment of the Pulitzer Prize. Also looks at his beliefs about journalism and journalists' responsibilities.

SEE ALSO: June 5, 1944: Australian Poets Claim Responsibility for a Literary Hoax; Jan. 28, 1972: Clifford Irving Admits Faking Howard Hughes Memoirs; Jan. 22, 1987: Pennsylvania Politician Kills Himself at Televised Press Conference; Jan. 18, 1990: Washington, D.C., Mayor Marion Barry Is Arrested for Drug Use; Spring, 1996: Physicist Publishes a Deliberately Fraudulent Article; May 11, 1998: Journalist Stephen Glass Is Exposed as a Fraud; June 18, 2001: Historian Joseph J. Ellis Is Accused of Lying; Jan. 18, 2002: Historian Doris Kearns Goodwin Is Accused of Plagiarism; Apr. 29, 2003: *New York Times* Reporter Jayson Blair Is Exposed as a Fraud; Feb. 18, 2007: *Washington Post* Exposes Decline of Walter Reed Army Hospital.

April 28, 1981
TENNIS STAR BILLIE JEAN KING IS SUED FOR PALIMONY

Tennis champion Billie Jean King was sued by her former lover Marilyn Barnett, who was seeking financial support from King under California's landmark palimony decision in Marvin v. Marvin *(1976). King first denied that she and Barnett had been lovers but admitted a few days later to their relationship. King also said that she never promised to support Barnett financially.*

LOCALE: Los Angeles, California

CATEGORIES: Law and the courts; sex; social issues and reform

KEY FIGURES

Billie Jean King (b. 1943), former professional tennis player

Marilyn Barnett (fl. 1980's), secretary and lover of Billie Jean King

Larry King (fl. 1980's), Billie Jean King's husband

SUMMARY OF EVENT

By the time Billie Jean King's tennis career was winding down during the mid-1970s because of her increasing physical problems, she was involved in a romantic relationship with her secretary, former hair stylist Marilyn Barnett. The affair reportedly lasted about two years, and at the end of that time King discontinued Barnett's formal employment. The two remained friends, and Barnett continued to reside in King's Malibu house, which Barnett rented.

Larry King, a lawyer and King's husband since 1965, presumably did not know about the relationship with Barnett. In addition to staying at the Malibu house, Barnett had been using the Kings' credit cards to pay many of her expenses. When the Kings tried to evict her from the Malibu home in 1981, Barnett revealed the love affair and sued Billie Jean King for spousal support, in this case, palimony.

Barnett's suit, filed April 28, was the first major lawsuit involving a same-gender application of the palimony doctrine. This doctrine was reaffirmed by the California Supreme Court in a 1976 decision involving actor Lee Marvin and his former live-in lover, Michelle Triola. Barnett claimed in her own suit that she had been promised lifetime financial support, even though King had already offered to settle with her financially.

Long before the palimony suit, King had transformed tennis by campaigning tirelessly for equal treatment for women players. She had the clout of her championship credentials to back up her crusade. By the age of seventeen in 1961, she had won her first Wimbledon doubles tournament and five years later triumphed to win the first of twelve Grand Slam singles titles. These were great accomplishments for a woman who as a young player had been described as "short, fat, and aggressive" by a tennis coach.

Billie Jean King with her husband, Larry King, speaks to reporters about Marilyn Barnett's palimony lawsuit. (AP/Wide World Photos)

Among the disparities King sought to address was a financial one. Male players earned far more in prize money than female players. To inspire change, King threatened to boycott the U.S. Open in 1973, and in 1974 the open became the first tournament to provide equal prize money to men and women. King's other accomplishments include being the first female tennis player to win more than $100,000 in prize money in a single year (1971), organizing the Women's Tennis Association, and founding the magazine *womenSports* (later *Women's Sports and Fitness*). She also coauthored several books on how to play tennis. She also faced considerable negative publicity, however, for her longtime advocacy of cigarette-company sponsorship of women's tennis, namely the Virginia Slims Tour, which she cofounded.

In 1973, former Wimbledon men's champion Bobby Riggs had challenged King to a match, hoping to demonstrate that male players of any age were superior to women in the sport. At the age of fifty-five, he was some twenty-five years older than King and had already defeated a former women's champion, Margaret Court. The media dubbed the match the battle of the sexes, and the game was watched by an estimated forty million people on television. King decisively defeated Riggs in three straight sets.

In a 1981 press conference, King first denied the romantic affair with Barnett, then she publicly admitted to being bisexual, thus making her one of the first major athletes to acknowledge any kind of gay or lesbian relationship. Prior to the press conference, however, King and her husband had been discrediting Barnett, at one time suggesting that she had been "in and out of institutions" and had attempted to kill herself. One particular accident from October, 1980, was interpreted by some people as a suicide attempt by Barnett. She had been found lying on the sand below the balcony of her Malibu home. She had a broken back, and the incident left her paralyzed below the waist. She began to use a wheelchair for mobility but could not work to support herself.

Marilyn Barnett in court in December, 1981, after being sued by the Kings to vacate their home. (AP/Wide World Photos)

Barnett ultimately lost her palimony lawsuit when it was dismissed on November 19, 1982. The suit failed, in part, because she and King were not cohabitants in the sense outlined in *Marvin*. The court found no evidence that King and Barnett joined their finances. A related case, *Jones v. Daly*, was in the courts in 1981. In that case, a California appeals court ruled against gay palimony or, as it came to be known, galimony.

It was not until many years later that King finally admitted that she was lesbian. Many lesbians and gays had been disappointed and angered when she termed her affair with Barnett a "mistake." They thought she was trying to avoid the question of her sexuality. She then added that the mistake was being unfaithful to her husband, not having an affair with another woman.

IMPACT

Citing high attorney's fees to defend against the lawsuit, King, who was almost forty years old by this time, returned to the tennis tour. She remained active in the sport as a coach and in other capacities, and she regained the reputation she had prior to the scandal. However, by admitting her bisexuality in 1981, King lost millions of dollars in potential earnings as a product spokesperson and sportscaster, a job at which she already had been working. She estimated that the fallout from the scandal cost her about $1.5 million.

Barnett's palimony suit initially forced the legal system to address several same-gender palimony cases, but many of the cases were not resolved successfully because no precedent existed for such cases. On a personal and social level, the palimony suit did not harm King's future impact on lesbian and gay activism. King became something of an icon for many in the gay community, and she supported causes such as the Human Rights Campaign and the fight against AIDS. In 2001 she received an award from the influential media watchdog group GLAAD (Gay and Lesbian Alliance Against Defamation) for "furthering the visibility and inclusion of the [gay] community in her work."

King has been quoted as saying that one reason she refrained from telling the truth earlier was that her parents were homophobic. Also, she feared disclosure would mean the end of her participation in women's tennis. Her eventual openness about her own sexuality eased the way for other professional tennis players to come out as lesbian, notably Martina Navratilova and Amélie Mauresmo.

King and her husband divorced in 1987. He had publicly supported her, but their marriage was irretrievably broken by the revelation of her affair. The marriage apparently had been shaky since the early 1970's.

—*Roy Liebman*

FURTHER READING

King, Billie Jean, and Frank Deford. *Billie Jean.* New York: Viking, 1982. A candid autobiography that helped to reestablish King's reputation following the palimony scandal.

Lipsyte, Robert. "Prophets: Avery Brundage, Muhammad Ali, Billie Jean King." In *The Gospel According to ESPN: Saints, Saviors, and Sinners*, edited by Jay Lovinger. New York: Hyperion Books, 2002. With an introduction by Hunter S. Thompson, this collection of essays looks at the revered status of sports stars, including Billie Jean King. Lipsyte's chapter examines how King brought gender equity to the sport of tennis.

Schwabacher, Martin. *Superstars of Women's Tennis*. Philadelphia: Chelsea House, 1997. A work that explores the world of women's tennis, with a chapter on King's career and her tennis legacy. Part of Chelsea House's Female Sports Stars series.

SEE ALSO: Jan., 1977: Singer Anita Bryant Campaigns Against Lesbian and Gay Rights; Apr. 18, 1979: Actor Lee Marvin Is Ordered to Pay Palimony to Former Lover; Mar. 10, 1980: Scarsdale Diet Doctor Is Killed by His Lover; July 28, 1980: Magazine Reveals Baseball Star Steve Garvey's Marital Problems.

May 23, 1981
ITALIAN JUSTICE MINISTER RESIGNS BECAUSE OF CRIME CONNECTION

Propaganda Due, a secret Masonic lodge reportedly involved in criminal activities, was found to have nearly one thousand of Italy's political and economic elite as members. The resulting scandal became one of the biggest in Italy and shook the coalition government of Prime Minister Arnaldo Forlani when it became known that Justice Minister Adolfo Sarti had applied for membership.

LOCALE: Italy
CATEGORIES: Organized crime and racketeering; corruption; government; politics

KEY FIGURES
Arnaldo Forlani (b. 1925), prime minister of Italy, 1980-1981
Licio Gelli (b. 1919), businessman and head of Propaganda Due Masonic lodge
Adolfo Sarti (1928-1992), Italian justice minister, 1980-1981
Roberto Calvi (1920-1982), chairman of the Banco Ambrosiano of Milan and Vatican banker
Michele Sindona (1920-1986), Vatican and Mafia banker

Silvio Berlusconi (b. 1936), prime minister of Italy, 1994-1995, 2001-2006, 2008-

SUMMARY OF EVENT
On March 17, 1981, the Italian financial police (one of the four branches of the national police force) raided Licio Gelli's villa in the Tuscan countryside. Ostensibly a mattress manufacturer and owner of a furniture store in the city of Arezzo, the seemingly reformed Gelli, also a fascist, turned out to be the head of a right-wing Masonic lodge known as Propaganda Due, or P-2. Lodge members were intent on preventing a feared takeover of the Italian government by Il Partito Comunista Italiana, or PCI (the Italian Communist Party), the largest communist party outside the Soviet Union.

The financial police had been directed to search Gelli's villa by the Bank of Italy. Investigators had fortuitously come across Gelli's name in connection with Mafia financial dealings with Michele Sindona, a banker. In the course of the raid, the police came upon a list of 964 members of a previously unknown and, as later determined, influential and rogue Masonic lodge. The list was a who's who of right-wing politicians and civic officials and clergy members, including figures from industry, journalism, law, and all branches of the police forces and military.

Gelli had been a convinced and active fascist and remained a supporter of Italian fascist dictator Benito Mussolini. After World War II, Gelli was put on a list of fascists to be kept under observation. He remained there well into the 1950's. After becoming a businessman and giving no cause for alarm, he was removed from the list. As events would prove, however, he was a right-wing organizer who was dedicated, as were virtually all members of P-2, to preventing PCI from coming to power in Italy's government.

In 1965, Gelli decided to join the Grand Lodge of Masons in Rome in 1965. In contrast to the United States, where Masons reveal their membership by wearing rings and insignia, Italian Masons have always taken the greatest care not to reveal their membership in the order. By 1969, the suave and urbane Gelli succeeded in forming the breakaway sublodge P-2. Gelli held court in a five-star hotel in Rome. Through his Banco Ambrosiano and with the consent of Roman Catholic archbishop Paul Marcinkus, Roberto Calvi was bankrolling Gelli's lifestyle and activities. It was estimated at the time of Banco Ambrosiano's collapse during the early 1980's, Gelli and P-2 owed the bank close to $300 million.

Gelli's lodge exercised significant influence over the various sectors of Italian high society, of which P-2 members were a part. In addition, P-2 had editorial control of Italy's leading newspaper, the Milanese *Corriere della Sera*, after controlling interest in the newspaper had been purchased by Calvi's Banco Ambrosiano.

By 1970, Gelli had developed membership in P-2 to the point where he could organize an attempted coup d'etat of PCI, the decadent, weak government he perceived ripe for a takeover by the major party in Italy. Scholars of P-2 are convinced that Gelli was employed by the U.S. Central Intelligence Agency (CIA), which ordered a stop to the coup just after it had begun and just short of the president of the republic becoming a prisoner. After the aborted coup, P-2 went deeper underground.

Throughout the 1970's, Italy was racked by the political violence of the Red Brigades. However, it was P-2 that likely planned and financed the worst act of violence in Italy's postwar history: the 1980 bombing at the Bologna railway station. The widespread outcry forced government agencies to act vigorously against domestic terrorism. Identification of Gelli in conjunction with the investigation into the Sindona and Calvi banking scandals ultimately generated the search of Gelli's villa and the discovery of the P-2 membership list. P-2 was officially declared a criminal organization.

In 1981, a coalition Italian government was cobbled together and headed by the nondescript Christian Democrat prime minister, Arnaldo Forlani. Forlani appointed a likewise unprepossessing party stalwart, Adolfo Sarti, who was a former minister of public education, of defense, and of justice. The seized P-2 membership list had been turned over to Forlani. Despite his attempts to keep the membership from becoming public, word about the raid leaked and the media's response to Forlani's stonewalling was ear splitting.

One journalist, Mino Pecorelli, who clearly had damning insider information and was producing one compromising article after another in 1981, was murdered in Rome in broad daylight. The murder was considered a threat and warning to journalists in general. A high-ranking Mafia figure, arrested well after the fact and revealing inside secrets in exchange for reduction of his sentence, stated that P-2 had commissioned Pecorelli's murder, which was executed by the Mafia.

A primary aim of P-2 was to control the judiciary as well as law enforcement so that P-2 members could count on escaping trial or, failing that, receive lighter than normal sentences. P-2 came close to achieving that particular aim when it was discovered among papers confiscated in the raid on Gelli's villa that Sarti, the recently appointed minister of justice in the short-lived Christian Democratic-coalition government, was an applicant for P-2 membership. When his application became known, demonstrating the high reach of P-2, Sarti was forced to resign from the cabinet.

Gelli was in Argentina at the time of the police raid on his villa. He was likely serving as a mule, that is, delivering money laundered in one or more of Calvi's many off-shore banks in Roman Catholic countries in Central and South America. For this work, Gelli took commissions and siphoned P-2 funds for his own secret Swiss bank account. Now indicted and wanted by the Italian police, Gelli remained incognito and outside Italy until he needed money. He returned to Europe and was arrested by Swiss police while entering Switzerland with a fake passport in an attempt to withdraw three million dollars from his account.

Gelli succeeded in bribing his way out of a Swiss jail and fled to prevent his extradition. He was eventually arrested and extradited to Italy, where he was tried. Although the major charges against him could not be proven and he was not sentenced to prison, Gelli was placed under house arrest for lesser P-2-related charges. He lived under house arrest until 2007 when, because of his age and ill health, was permitted freedom of movement within Italy.

IMPACT

As a consequence of the P-2 scandal, the days of governmental control by the center-right Christian Democratic Party, which had ruled Italy since 1948, became numbered. Following the collapse of the Forlani government in 1981, the reverse of P-2's aims became reality: Sandro Pertini, a Socialist, was elected president of Italy. Given the crisis conditions, Pertini appointed as prime minister the first non-Christian Democrat, Giuseppe Spooling of the Republican Party. When that coalition failed, Pertini appointed as prime minister fellow Socialist Bettino Craxi, in 1983. Craxi's party, it turned out, was financed by Calvi, his fellow Milanese and a P-2 member.

Following the next big scandal, P-2 member and politician Silvio Berlusconi, accused of bribery, formed the Forza Italia Party and was appointed prime minister for the first time in 1994 and then again in 2001 and 2008. Berlusconi's center-right coalition lasted the entire election period and enabled him to enter Italian history as the longest-serving prime minister in postwar Italy.

—*Robert B. Youngblood*

FURTHER READING

Raw, Charles. *The Moneychangers: How the Vatican Bank Enabled Roberto Calvi to Steal Two Hundred Fifty Million for the Heads of the P2 Masonic Lodge*. London: Harvill, 1992. A comprehensive study of the Ambrosiano-Calvi scandal that details virtually every known transaction in the case.

Willan, Philip. *The Last Supper: The Mafia, the Masons, and the Killing of Roberto Calvi*. London: Robinson, 2007. Argues that P-2 was a remnant of Cold War politics, with its dueling fears of democracy and communism and the hunger for power and wealth.

Williams, Paul L. *The Vatican Exposed: Money, Murder, and the Mafia*. Amherst, N.Y.: Prometheus Books, 2003. An excellent first source for understanding the connections among players in the P-2 and related scandals.

SEE ALSO: Sept. 10, 1981: *Chicago Sun-Times* Reports That Cardinal Cody Diverted Church Funds; Aug. 6, 1982: Banco Ambrosiano Collapses Amid Criminal Accusations; Nov. 3, 1996: Car Crash Reveals Depth of Government Corruption in Turkey; Oct. 22, 2006: Chilean Politicians Use Community Funds for Personal Campaigns.

1980's

May 29, 1981
COURT FINDS THAT FORD IGNORED PINTO'S SAFETY PROBLEMS

The California Courts of Appeal determined that Ford Motor Company was responsible for the death and injuries sustained in an accident involving a Ford Pinto that was rear-ended and caught on fire. The court determined that Ford was aware of the potential fire hazard because of design flaws built into the Pinto but that the company failed to address the safety issue and repair the problem. Critics of the legal case argue that the Pinto was no more prone to catch fire upon a rear-end impact than other similar cars of the time.

ALSO KNOWN AS: *Grimshaw v. Ford Motor Co.*
LOCALE: San Diego, California
CATEGORIES: Business; law and the courts; trade and commerce

KEY FIGURES
Lily Gray (d. 1972), driver of the stalled Ford Pinto
Richard Grimshaw (b. c. 1959), plaintiff, who was a passenger in the Ford Pinto
Harley Copp (fl. 1980's), head of Ford's crash-testing program

SUMMARY OF EVENT
On May 28, 1972, a Ford Pinto driven by Lily Gray stalled on a Southern California freeway near San Bernardino. Gray's Pinto hatchback was rear-ended by another car on the freeway and immediately caught fire. Testimony at trial indicated that when the car was struck from behind, the gas tank ruptured. Gray died several days later of complications from her burn injuries. Thirteen-year-old Richard Grimshaw, the sole passenger in Gray's Pinto and Gray's neighbor, sustained serious burns to 90 percent of his body, including his face. His nose, an ear, and several fingers were incinerated, and he was permanently disfigured.

Grimshaw as well as Gray's heirs—her husband and two daughters—sued Ford Motor Company in civil court, alleging that the company manufactured the Pinto even though it knew the car was unsafe. In February, 1978, after a six-month trial, a jury awarded Grimshaw more than $2.5 million in compensatory damages and $125 million in punitive damages. The Grays received $559,680 in compensatory damages. Gray's family was statutorily prohibited from seeking punitive damages. Determining that the amount awarded to Grimshaw was excessive, trial judge Leonard Goldstein reduced Grimshaw's punitive damage award to $3.5 million, at the time the largest such award in U.S. legal history. Ford appealed the decision, particularly the punitive damages, and claimed legal mistakes were made during the trial.

On May 29, 1981, the California Courts of Appeal in San Diego affirmed the lower court's decision, including the punitive damages award. Writing for the court was Judge P. J. Tamura. His opinion included a review of the history of the Pinto. The car was initially conceived in 1968 by Lee Iacocca, vice president at Ford, and was sold beginning in September, 1970. The Pinto was hurried into production to rival imported subcompact automobiles. As such, it was designed to weigh less than two tons and was priced at less than $2,000. Because of the haste in readying the car for retail, the product development time frame was shortened. Styling determinations were made prior to engineering decisions, which ultimately meant that the engineering design would need to accommodate the already determined styling design.

Designers had placed the gas tank behind the rear axle instead of above the rear axle, a more common location for gas tanks at the time. Also, the Pinto had an insubstantial bumper, and the area between the bumper and the axle was narrower than in other cars. The structure of the car lacked reinforcement,

594

and several bolts in the differential housing were left exposed. When combined, these design elements increased the likelihood that the Pinto would catch fire in a rear-end collision. The back of the vehicle would crumble and lead to a punctured gas tank and fuel leak.

The appellate judges agreed that Ford was responsible for Grimshaw's injuries and Gray's death. The court noted that Ford's upper management knew that the Pinto performed poorly in crash tests yet approved its manufacture. The automobile was unable to withstand a rear-end impact from a car traveling 20 miles per hour without rupturing its gas tank. Harley Copp, the former head of Ford's crash-testing program, testified in court that Ford executives, including Iacocca, were aware of the Pinto crash-test results but advanced the car's manufacture regardless. Copp said that executives knew of inexpensive modifications that could fix the gas leakage problem. These modifications included reinforcing the car's structure to reduce collapse at impact, adding more space between the axle and bumper, and better protecting the gas tank from puncture. Even though Ford's costs would have been less than $20 per car, no changes were made.

Other damaging evidence suggested that Ford used a cost-benefit analysis to decide whether to correct the gas-leakage concern. A 1973 report indicated that Ford determined it would be less expensive to pay for any lawsuits associated with injuries and deaths in accidents than to correct the design flaws. Ford used estimates provided by the National Highway Traffic Safety Administration, which showed that the monetary value of a burn death was $200,000 and the value of a severe burn injury was $67,000. Ford calculated the expense of potential lawsuits involving 180 burn deaths and 180 burn injuries: approximately $50 million. Ford also found that the cost to correct flaws in

11 million cars and 1.5 million trucks would be about $11 per vehicle, for a total of about $137 million, far more than the estimated $50 million in potential lawsuit awards. As such, Ford decided that the costs of making repairs outweighed the benefit of protecting car occupants from potential injuries or death.

An appellate court found that Ford acted in callous disregard of public safety, yet it upheld the reduced punitive damages award, ruling that the amount was reasonable in relation to Ford's net worth of approximately $8 billion. The court also ruled that the ratio between punitive damages and compensatory damages was fair, and ruled that the amount of the award would deter similar unethical and reckless business practices by Ford or any other automobile manufacturer.

The court also rejected the appeals of Grimshaw and Gray's heirs. It determined that the judge in the lower court did not abuse his authority by reducing the punitive damages to $3.5 million. The court also rejected the claim by the Grays that they, too, should be entitled to seek punitive damages against Ford.

1980's

A 1977 model Ford Pinto. (AP/Wide World Photos)

IMPACT

The Ford Pinto has a legacy of being one of the most dangerous cars ever made, but it is a legacy that remains questionable and, some argue, even unfair. At the time the Pinto was first produced, no government safety standards existed to ensure against fuel leakage in rear-end collisions. Also, early estimates of the number of deaths from rear-end collisions in Pintos—estimates that ranged from five hundred to nine hundred—were likely exaggerated. A 1991 law journal article claims that the number of deaths is much lower—even as low as twenty-seven—and that the car was no more prone to fire after an accident than other similar subcompact vehicles of the time.

—*Margaret E. Leigey and Madeleine Stelzmiller*

FURTHER READING

Banham, Russ. *The Ford Century: Ford Motor Company and the Innovations That Shaped the World*. New York: Artisan, 2002. A comprehensive and lavishly illustrated corporate history of the Ford Motor Company.

Birsch, Douglas, and John H. Fielder, eds. *The Ford Pinto Case*. Albany: State University of New York Press, 1994. Compilation of newspaper articles, safety reports, and commentary on the ethics and decision making related to the Ford Pinto.

Dowie, Mark. "Pinto Madness." *Mother Jones*, September-October, 1977. Published during the *Grimshaw* trial, this often-cited and Pulitzer Prize-winning exposé claims Ford executives were aware of the potential fire hazard in the Pinto but failed to correct the problem.

Lee, Matthew T., and M. David Ermann. "Pinto 'Madness' as a Flawed Landmark Narrative: An Organizational and Network Analysis." *Social Problems* 46, no. 1 (1999): 30-47. Presents evidence alleging that traditional journalistic accounts of the Ford Pinto are not accurate. For example, the authors claim that the Pinto was about as safe as similar cars produced during the same time.

SEE ALSO: Sept.-Oct., 1937: Prescription Elixir Causes More than One Hundred Deaths; Summer, 1974: Dalkon Shield Contraceptive Is Removed from the Market; Sept. 26, 1979: Love Canal Residents Sue Chemical Company; Oct. 19, 1982: Car Manufacturer John De Lorean Is Arrested in a Drug Sting; 1985-1986: Westland Affair Shakes Prime Minister Thatcher's Government; Feb. 4, 1996: Whistle-Blower Reveals Tobacco Industry Corruption; Summer, 2006-Mar. 16, 2007: Manufacturer Recalls Pet Food That Killed Thousands of American Pets.

September 10, 1981
CHICAGO SUN-TIMES REPORTS THAT CARDINAL CODY DIVERTED CHURCH FUNDS

After almost two turmoil-ridden decades as archbishop of one of the largest Roman Catholic dioceses in the United States, John Patrick Cody was accused in a series of articles in the Chicago Sun-Times *of having diverted tax-exempt church funds to the benefit of two family members. U.S. attorneys had been investigating the cardinal since late 1980.*

LOCALE: Chicago, Illinois
CATEGORIES: Publishing and journalism; corruption; law and the courts; religion

KEY FIGURES

John Patrick Cody (1907-1982), Roman Catholic archbishop of Chicago
Andrew M. Greeley (b. 1928), Catholic priest, sociologist, novelist, and public critic of Cody
Carlton Sherwood (b. 1946), investigative journalist
Helen Dolan Wilson (b. 1908?), Cody's stepcousin by marriage
David Wilson (fl. 1980's), Helen Dolan Wilson's son
Joseph Louis Bernardin (1928-1996), Catholic archbishop of Cincinnati

SUMMARY OF EVENT

John Patrick Cody was a difficult person. Particularly after the Second Vatican Council decreed that the governance of the Catholic Church should become more democratic, his authoritarian style of leadership had become increasingly out of step with the times. Rumors existed that the priests of the Archdiocese of New Orleans sang a *Te Deum* (a Catholic hymn of praise) in delight at being rid of him when he was transferred to Chicago. Cody himself regarded this change as key to his ambitions because Chicago was a cardinalatial see, that is, an archdiocese whose incumbent was traditionally made a cardinal by the pope. Some priests even

claimed Cody saw Chicago as a stepping-stone to becoming the first pope from the United States.

By 1981, Cody had become an embattled ruler surrounded by angry subjects. His own priests had accused him of deception and dishonesty, and the laity was writing letters of complaint to the Vatican about his high-handed policies. The endless conflicts had made major inroads into Cody's health, and his once rosy cheeks had grown sallow and hollow with the ravages of congestive heart failure. However, he refused to even consider allowing a younger bishop to take over any of his duties and did all he could to conceal his worsening health from both his archdiocese and the Holy See. A stint working in the Vatican as a young priest had taught him the ins and outs of court intrigue, and he had plenty of information that could be used against the Vatican if the congregation of bishops were to attempt to move against him. He even had threatened to reveal some choice secrets in 1979 when Cardinal Sebastiano Baggio, cardinal-prefect of the congregation of bishops, had tried to compel him to resign shortly before the death of Pope Paul VI.

Only the aging Pope Paul's death, followed by the successive elections of the two John Pauls, saved Cody from being replaced, or at least forced to accept a coadjutor (a situation in which Cody would have become a figurehead and his nominal subordinate would have exercised the actual authority of the archdiocese). John Paul I reigned for a mere thirty-three days, not enough time to consolidate his power and move against Cody, and John Paul II did not wish scandal in one of the most important dioceses in the free world to distract from his moral efforts against the Soviet bloc. Thus, any further opposition to Cody would have to come not from the Vatican hierarchy but from the grass roots within his own archdiocese.

How the information about Cody's questionable financial dealings reached the *Chicago Sun-Times*, one of the city's two leading daily newspapers, is uncertain, but Father Andrew M. Greeley remains suspect. Almost from the beginning of Cody's tenure as archbishop, Greeley had been an outspoken critic of the cardinal's methods of administration. Greeley's novel *The Cardinal Sins*, which was published in 1981, featured a villain who was a thinly disguised version of Cody and came to an ignominious (shameful) end. Greeley was accused of plotting to "get" Cody on the basis of some private papers he had entrusted to the archives of Notre Dame University in South Bend, Indiana. However, he later claimed the papers were no more than musings about possibilities, not a plan for action.

Carlton Sherwood, an investigative journalist, wrote a series of articles about Cody, and his first consultation was with Greeley. The first of these articles, published by the *Chicago Sun-Times* on September 10, 1981, announced that a federal grand jury investigation was already under way into Cody's administration of church finances. The U.S. Attorney's Office had been investigating Cody's administration of the archdiocese's treasury since the fall of 1980, one year before the *Chicago Sun-Times* series appeared.

The federal investigation centered on Cody's relationship with Helen Dolan Wilson, an elderly woman whom he called a cousin but in fact was the stepdaughter of his aunt. They had been raised together, and after Helen had been divorced by her husband, he had seen after her and her young children. When her son, David Wilson, had become older and entered the insurance business, Cody had given him diocesan insurance contracts for the successive dioceses he headed. By the time Cody was transferred to Chicago, David had left the insurance business, and the two entered a real estate partnership that involved selling archdiocesan properties for secular use.

Although there was some effort to portray Helen as Cody's mistress, both of them insisted that their relationship was in the manner of brother and sister. Of far greater interest was the financial nature of their relationship. Although Helen had never held any position more responsible than that of church secretary, and her former husband had left her nothing, she enjoyed a condominium in one of Chi-

cago's Gold Coast high-rises and a vacation home in a tony area of Florida, as well as numerous furs, jewels, and other expensive possessions. Cody's extreme secretiveness about his administration of the archdiocese's finances, combined with his closing of several archdiocesan facilities on the basis of supposed lack of money, lent credence to the conclusion that he had diverted it to Helen and her family.

The question was of interest to the U.S. attorney because of the tax-free status of religious institutions and funds. If Cody had transferred church money to private use, he would have violated U.S. tax code. The newspaper series claimed that up to one million dollars had been diverted by Cody.

Cody's response to the accusations only escalated the situation. He regarded any call for accountability as an affront to his authority as archbishop. Rather than document his handling of the archdiocese's finances, he accused the *Chicago Sun-Times* of anti-Catholicism. Many Chicago Catholics, even some who had previously been unhappy with Cody's administration, felt obligated to come to the defense of the archbishop against supposed attacks on the Church as a whole. Cody also made himself so inaccessible that a federal marshal could deliver a subpoena to court only by cornering the cardinal in a church sacristy as he was vesting for an important Mass.

Cody's position was saved only by revelations that Greeley had been involved in pointing Sherwood toward the cardinal's financial dealings. Cody's supporters were able to spin it as a supposed plot, and they suggested that Archbishop Bernardin of Cincinnati, a widely popular prelate whose name had been put forth as a possible successor to the see of Chicago, had been a coconspirator with Greeley. By shifting attention to Bernardin, Cody was able to gain just enough of a reprieve that his worsening health would forestall any further investigation.

IMPACT

In the end, Cody never was formally indicted of any crime. He spent the first several months of 1982 convalescing in the archbishop's residence when he was not actually in the hospital. On April 25, he died in his sleep of a heart attack, and many in the archdiocese breathed a collective sigh of relief. Pope John Paul II appointed Bernardin as Cody's successor and subsequently created Bernardin a cardinal at the next consistory. Bernardin made it plain on his first public appearance as archbishop of Chicago that he regarded his mission as that of a conciliator, and he invited all who held grudges against Cody to set their burdens down.

To lay to rest questions of fiscal wrongdoing, Bernardin hired the accounting firm of Arthur Anderson (implicated in the Enron scandal of 2001) to examine the archdiocese's books. It found that while Cody had occasionally mingled funds in ways that were not in accordance with generally accepted accounting principles, there was no evidence of actual fraud or diversion of funds. However, Bernardin would spend the rest of his tenure in Chicago dealing with the long-term damage to relationships within the local church, and the stress may have contributed to his death by pancreatic cancer.

—*Leigh Husband Kimmel*

FURTHER READING

Greeley, Andrew M. *Confessions of a Parish Priest: An Autobiography*. New York: Pocket Books, 1987. Written while some of the principals of the scandal were still living, this book by Greeley reads as somewhat evasive because individuals cannot be named.

————. *Furthermore! Memories of a Parish Priest*. New York: Forge, 1999. A second volume in the memoirs of Cody's chief public critic in the archdiocese. Names Helen Dolan Wilson in the scandal.

Kennedy, Eugene. *My Brother Joseph: The Spirit of a Cardinal and the Story of a Friendship*. New York: St. Martin's Press, 1997. Includes material on Cody's last years and Bernardin's arrival in Chicago.

Larsen, Roy. "In the 1980's, a Chicago Newspaper Investigated Cardinal Cody." *Nieman Reports* 57, no. 1 (Spring, 2003): 66-68. A look back at the investigation by U.S. attorneys of the diversion of church funds by Cody, with a focus on the scandal's financial aspects.

Thomas, Gordon, and Max Morgan-Witts. *Pontiff.* Garden City, N.Y.: Doubleday, 1983. History of the elections of the two John Pauls that also touches on the Cody scandal.

Yallop, David A. *In God's Name: An Investigation into the Murder of Pope John Paul I*. New York: Bantam Books, 1984. Claims that Cody knew of the circumstances that led to the death of John Paul I.

SEE ALSO: May-June, 1926: Evangelist Aimee Semple McPherson Claims She Was Kidnapped; Feb. 23, 1963: Play Accuses Pope Pius XII of Complicity in the Holocaust; May 20, 1974: French Cardinal Daniélou Dies in a Prostitute's House; June 27, 1978: Evangelist Herbert W. Armstrong Excommunicates His Own Son; May 23, 1981: Italian Justice Minister Resigns Because of Crime Connection; Aug. 6, 1982: Banco Ambrosiano Collapses Amid Criminal Accusations; Apr. 22, 1986: Faith Healer Peter Popoff Is Exposed as a Fraud; Feb. 21, 1988: Evangelist Jimmy Swaggart Tearfully Confesses His Adultery; May 6, 1992: Irish Bishop Eamonn Casey's Romantic Affair Leads to His Resignation; Jan. 6, 2002: *Boston Globe* Reports on Child Sexual Abuse by Roman Catholic Priests.

1980's

May 11, 1982
PHILIPPINE PRESIDENT MARCOS FORCES THE ENTIRE SUPREME COURT TO RESIGN

In the Philippines, the bar examination score needed to practice law was determined by the national supreme court. After allegations that the passing score of a supreme court justice's son had been fixed, President Ferdinand Marcos obtained the resignations of all fourteen members of the court. Although the charges of juridical corruption may have been valid, Marcos's action also helped him further consolidate his dictatorial power in the country.

LOCALE: Manila, Philippines
CATEGORIES: Law and the courts; corruption; hoaxes, frauds, and charlatanism; politics; government; cultural and intellectual history

KEY FIGURES

Ferdinand Marcos (1917-1989), president of the Philippines, 1965-1986
Enrique Fernando (1915-2004), justice of the supreme court of the Philippines, 1967-1985, and chief justice, 1979-1985
Vicente Ericta (b. 1915), associate justice of the supreme court of the Philippines, 1981-1982
Ameurfina Melencio Herrera (b. 1922), associate justice of the supreme court of the Philippines, 1979-1992

SUMMARY OF EVENT

By 1982, Ferdinand Marcos had been dictatorial president of the Philippines for a decade, having declared martial law on September 22, 1972. Although martial law was lifted in 1981, the wily Marcos consolidated his power and firmly controlled the institutions of government, media, and society. Nevertheless, criticism of his authoritarian regime had increased steadily, on both international and domestic fronts. The Philippine supreme court scandal of 1982 allowed Marcos to further strengthen his grip over the judiciary, while provid-

ing his critics with another reason to attack the corruption of his regime.

The Philippine bar examination is of great importance and prestige in Philippine society. It has been continually administered since 1901, the same year the supreme court of the Philippines was established, as a mark of determination to turn the Philippines into a modern and meritocratic nation. The bar is the licensing exam to become a lawyer and enter the highest professional and economic echelons of Philippine society. It is a mark of the prestige and rigor of the exam that it is administered by the fifteen-member supreme court, a unique professional distinction in the Philippines.

The exam is a comprehensive, rigorous test of a law student's knowledge. Passage rates are adjusted annually; a high score on the exam brings great prestige and the promise of success in the legal and political communities. In a manner similar to the civil service exams of imperial China, the Philippine bar exam is considered the highest standard for aspiring professionals. The supreme court traditionally released a list of highest scores on the nationally administered exam; those obtaining the highest scores were known as bar topnotchers.

Bar topnotchers have played a storied role in Philippine society. Manuel Roxas, who placed first in the 1913 bar exam, would become the first president of the Philippines. Sergio Osmeña and Manuel Quezon, who finished second and fourth in the 1903 bar exams, respectively, would also become Philippine presidents. Other Philippine presidents who first came to prominence as bar topnotchers include Jose Laurel (1915), Carlos Garcia (1923), Arturo Tolentino (1934), Diosdado Macapagal (1936), and Emmanuel Pelaez (1938). Marcos himself launched his political career on the basis of his brilliant first-place result on the 1939 exam. Likewise, numerous supreme court justices and senators proudly boasted as their first, and perhaps most important, success a top score on the national exam.

Marcos Forces Entire Philippine Supreme Court to Resign

Although there had been previous scandals regarding the exam, the most sensational occurred in 1982. At the time, there were fourteen justices on the court, with one seat vacant. The scandal surfaced in April when Justice Ameurfina Melencio Herrera wrote a confidential letter to the court in which she alleged a serious impropriety. Herrera claimed that the exam score of Gustavo Ericta, the son of Justice Vicente Ericta, had been altered to obtain a passing grade. As a result, Herrera resigned from the bar committee and returned her honorarium fee. The letter was leaked to the press, creating an outcry.

Upon investigation it was revealed that Justice Ramon Fernandez told Justice Ericta that his son failed the exam. Justice Ericta then suggested that his son's grade be changed, which was permitted by Chief Justice Enrique Fernando. Ericta's grade on the commercial law portion of the test was revised from 56 to 58 percent, which resulted in a total score of 73 percent, just above the passing grade of 72.5 percent. Controversy swirled for weeks, with justices blaming each other for the impropriety. In a press conference, Chief Justice Fernando took responsibility for allowing the altering of Ericta's exam results and broke into tears. After a few weeks of intense publicity, all fourteen justices offered their resignations. On May 7, twelve justices resigned, and a few days later the other two justices, who had been outside the country, followed.

The year 1982 was already proving to be crucial for Marcos. With the 1980 election of U.S. president Ronald Reagan, Marcos was assured of friendship with his most important ally, the United States. In fact, in 1982, Marcos made his first state visit to the United States in sixteen years, entailing two expensive weeks and much pomp and publicity. Feeling emboldened, Marcos was cracking down on his increas-

ingly vocal critics in the Philippines. He repressed church progressives who denounced his government, even insulting Cardinal Jaime Sin, the archbishop of Manila. Marcos arrested two prominent labor leaders and kept close watch on domestic political opponents such as Assemblyman Salvador Laurel and those in exile, most notably Benigno Aquino, Jr.

Marcos was eager to make use of this scandal for political advantage. By acting firmly against the supreme court, he could appear as an opponent of corruption and strengthen his hold over the judiciary. Marcos asked the justices to appear before him on May 8. On May 11, Marcos accepted all fourteen resignations and announced that he would search for a new supreme court. He consulted with retired chief justices Roberto Concepcion, Querube Makalintol, and Cesar Bengzon. Then, on May 15, he reinstated all the resigned justices of the court with the exception of Ericta and Fernandez, who were most directly implicated in the scandal. Two justices were appointed to fill their places, and a third justice was appointed to fill a previously vacant fifteenth spot. Fernando publicly expressed gratitude for his reappointment.

Ferdinand Marcos. (Library of Congress)

601

IMPACT

This scandal illustrates the adroit and calculating nature of the Marcos regime. By demanding the resignation of all fourteen justices, all of whom he had appointed, Marcos made it appear he was cracking down on personal corruption in his government, even while he was enriching himself through illicit means. Also, reinstating the justices made it appear he was being lenient, even though he was repressing political opponents and dissenters. Moreover, by reappointing the justices, he could claim even greater authority over a supreme court that was already considered subservient to him.

Ironically, Marcos's calculation may have backfired, in at least one respect. In August of 1983, Marcos's chief political opponent, exiled senator Benigno Aquino, Jr., was assassinated upon returning to the Philippines. Marcos's government was widely believed to be behind the murder. To absolve his regime, Marcos appointed a special commission headed by former justice Fernando to investigate the assassination. Many assumed that the compliant Fernando would exonerate Marcos. However, Fernando's own credibility had been shaken to a good degree by the Ericta scandal, and the Fernando-led commission retired after only a few weeks, claiming a lack of credibility. It was to be replaced by the Agrava Fact-Finding Commission, which dismissed the government's version of the killing and blamed a conspiracy of Marcos's military officers for the death of Aquino. In a little more than two years, Marcos would be chased out of power by an outraged populace in the People's Revolution.

—*Howard Bromberg*

FURTHER READING

Burton, Sandra. *Impossible Dream: The Marcoses, the Aquinos, and the Unfinished Revolution.* New York: Warner Books, 1984. An account of the assassination of Aquino, the Fernando and Agrava Commissions, and the People's Revolution.

Celoza, Albert F. *Ferdinand Marcos and the Philippines: The Political Economy of Authoritarianism.* Westport, Conn.: Praeger, 1997. Examines the period between 1972 and 1986, the year in which Marcos was ousted from the Philippines.

Cruz, Isagani, and Cynthia Cruz Datu. *Res Gestae: A Brief History of the Supreme Court from Arellano to Narvasa.* Manila: Rex Book Store, 2000. A history of the supreme court of the Philippines that includes an account of the Ericta scandal.

Paras, Corazon, and Ramon Ricardo Rogue. *The Chief Justices of the Supreme Court of the Philippines.* Pasig City, Philippines: Anvil, 2000. Short biographies of Philippine chief justices, with information as well on some associate justices of the supreme court.

Sevilla, Victor. *Justices of the Supreme Court of the Philippines: Their Lives and Outstanding Decisions.* 3 vols. Quezon City, Philippines: New Day, 1985. Much material on the prestigious chief justices of the supreme court, including Enrique Fernando.

SEE ALSO: Jan. 13, 1913: Federal Judge Is Impeached for Profiting from His Office; May 9, 1969: Supreme Court Justice Abe Fortas Is Accused of Bribery; Aug. 21, 1983: Filipino Opposition Leader Aquino Is Assassinated on Return Home.

July 20, 1982
CONSERVATIVE POLITICIAN JOHN G. SCHMITZ IS FOUND TO HAVE CHILDREN OUT OF WEDLOCK

News media reported that ultraconservative California politician John G. Schmitz had fathered two children outside his marriage. His lover, Carla Stuckle, revealed his paternity after she was charged with child neglect. The revelation led to Schmitz's downfall in politics.

LOCALE: Orange County, California
CATEGORIES: Public morals; families and children; government; politics; sex

KEY FIGURES
John G. Schmitz (1930-2001), California state senator, 1964-1970 and 1978-1982, and U.S. representative, 1970-1973
Carla Stuckle (d. 1994), Republican campaign volunteer

SUMMARY OF EVENT
John G. Schmitz was a college instructor, California state senator, U.S. representative, and 1972 Republican presidential candidate who had outspoken views on family values, abortion, immigration, welfare, desegregation, homosexuality, and other controversial topics, branding him an ultraconservative politician. Consequently, the discovery in 1982 of his lengthy extramarital affair with former student and longtime Republican campaign volunteer Carla Stuckle, with whom he had two children, exposed Schmitz as a hypocrite and effectively ended his political career. Stuckle shocked the nation by naming Schmitz as the father of both children. His paternity became headline news on July 20. What ensued was a media frenzy and a political spiral downward for Schmitz.

A devout Roman Catholic of German descent, Schmitz was born in Milwaukee, Wisconsin, and graduated from Marquette University in 1952. He became a second lieutenant and pilot in the U.S. Marine Corps and eventually was stationed in El Toro, California. Schmitz became a local celebrity when he interrupted an assault on a woman with his stern voice and not a weapon. Schmitz's political career was set in motion after his heroics became front-page news.

Schmitz left the Marine Corps in 1960 and settled in Orange County, California—known for its relative wealth and conservative views—with his wife, Mary Suehr Schmitz. The couple raised a family of seven children and emphasized traditional family values. Schmitz joined the Marine Reserves and became a colonel. He also taught philosophy and political science at Santa Ana College, where he met Stuckle, a student who had emigrated from Germany. Eventually, Schmitz and Stuckle would have a secret nine-year affair and two children.

In the meantime, Schmitz became known for his outspoken and fiercely conservative views. While many Orange County residents found his anti-feminist, anti-Semitic, antigay, segregationist overtones offensive, he earned favor with a few wealthy Republicans, who supported his election to the California state senate in 1963 (he served from 1964 to 1970). After receiving several awards as Legislator of the Year from the Republican Assembly, he was elected by his district to replace U.S. Representative James Utt, who died suddenly, close to the end of his term in 1970. A few months later, Schmitz was elected to a full term in the U.S. Congress, where he continued with his critical—and often witty—comments. No one was spared, including the seated Republican president, Richard Nixon, who also was from Orange County. Schmitz accused Nixon of being too liberal. After Nixon left for what would be a monumental trip to communist China, Schmitz quipped, "I have no objection to President Nixon going to China. I just object to his coming back." Subsequently, Schmitz was abandoned by many of his constituents, and he lost his bid for reelection to Congress in the 1972 Republican primary.

Schmitz immediately bounced back by securing

the 1972 presidential candidacy of the American Independent Party, the party to which he switched. An extremely conservative group, its first presidential choice was George Wallace, Alabama's former governor who vehemently opposed desegregation and was shot just weeks before the nominating convention. Schmitz lost the election, returned to California, and resumed teaching at Santa Ana College. Schmitz also had introduced the Human Life Amendment months before the landmark *Roe v. Wade* (1973) decision by the U.S. Supreme Court, wrote the book *Stranger in the Arena: The Anatomy of an Amoral Decade, 1964-1974* (1974), and was a popular speaker at conservative events. Just weeks before his presidential nomination, Schmitz spoke at a God, Family, and Country rally for the Fourth of July. He regained his California senate seat in 1978, where he remained until his sex scandal became front-page news.

In July, 1982, Stuckle took her thirteen-month-old son, John George, to Children's Hospital of Orange County, complaining of an injury to his genitals. Doctors discovered a hair strand so tightly wrapped around the boy's penis that it was nearly severed. Surgery was required to remove the hair. Suspecting abuse, child protective services would not allow Stuckle to take the boy home. Investigators visiting Stuckle later discovered Eugenie, Stuckle's three-week-old infant girl. The boy was placed in protective custody on July 19, despite appeals by Schmitz in court, and Stuckle was arrested and spent one night in jail on felony child-neglect charges. Schmitz had told the court a few days earlier that he was the father of the children.

Although out-of-wedlock births and extramarital affairs were not uncommon during the 1980's, the revelation that Schmitz had two children out of wedlock reached scandalous proportions because of his reputation as a crusader for traditional family values. He was on the national council of the John Birch Society, an ultraconservative political group whose membership at one point included white supremacist Tom Metzer. Schmitz's sharp tongue was too extreme even for this group, and he was relieved of his national council seat in 1982. His expulsion followed an abortion-rights debate in the

state senate, after which an aide to Schmitz issued a press release that said Gloria Allred, a feminist attorney, was a "slick butch lawyeress." The press release, titled "Attack of the Bull Dykes," also described Allred's supporters as "a sea of hard, Jewish and (arguably) female faces." Schmitz did not deny his aide's claim that the release was approved by Schmitz himself. Allred sued Schmitz for libel and won.

Following the discovery of this second family, the Schmitz family went into hiding and Schmitz did not reappear until the senate reconvened on August 2 after its summer recess. He refused to comment on his paternity or extramarital affair. However, during the court proceedings against Stuckle for child neglect, Schmitz—through his attorney—confirmed he fathered Stuckle's two children. The charges against Stuckle were dismissed for insufficient evidence on August 24. On the same day as the dismissal, the state senate passed a resolution honoring Schmitz—as he was retiring from the senate and such ceremony was customary. Even so, some senators signed a letter of protest.

In September, Stuckle declared personal bankruptcy, and one month later her attorney confirmed that Schmitz agreed to pay child support. A year later, in a *Los Angeles Times* interview (October 9, 1983), Stuckle said she still loved Schmitz and had no regrets regarding their relationship, even though the scandal ended their affair. She also indicated Schmitz had limited contact with the children. When she died in 1994 from complications related to diabetes, psychic Jeanne Dixon, a close friend of Mary Schmitz, took custody of the children. Unfortunately, Dixon died three years later, and the children were placed in a group home.

IMPACT

Given his increasingly offensive comments, as well as Orange County redistricting, Schmitz's political future was already questionable in 1982. However, it was the sex scandal that effectively ended his political career. Attempting a revival in 1984, Schmitz ran for reelection to Congress but decisively lost in the primary. Moreover, the repercussions did not stop there. His wife, Mary, was a conservative commentator on the political talk show *Speak Out*. Not long after she defended family values on air, her husband's indiscretions were revealed, and she left the show. The couple remained married until Schmitz's death in 2001.

After Schmitz left the political arena, he continued to teach at Santa Ana College until he retired in 1990. In 1995, he moved to Virginia and became a vineyard owner. His oldest daughter, Mary Kay Letourneau, was found guilty in 1997 of statutory rape of a thirteen-year-old boy. At the time the sexual relationship began with sixth grader Vili Fualaau, Letourneau was married, had young children, and was a schoolteacher in Washington State. Even though she went to prison, Letourneau and Fualaau eventually had two children of their own and married after she was divorced from her first husband. The media and public quickly compared Letourneau's behavior to that of her father: an extramarital sexual relationship with her student who was an immigrant mirrored her father's earlier behavior. As in his own case, Schmitz refused to comment on his daughter's sex scandal.

Another family scandal occurred in September, 2005, when Schmitz's conservative son, Joseph E. Schmitz, resigned his position as George W. Bush's Defense Department inspector general and accepted a job with Blackwater, a defense contractor with a major security role in Iraq. However, Joseph's departure occurred during accusations of unethical behavior related to his role as inspector general, including expense-account irregularities and interference with investigations of senior Bush officials. While Joseph denied any wrongdoing, the public—once again—compared the "sins of the father" to those of the children.

Response to the Schmitz family scandals suggests the public expects private morals to be consistent with the publicly stated values and behavior of certain public figures, especially politicians but also, as in the case of Letourneau, teachers. As holders of the public trust, credibility and integrity remain paramount values. The public's message seems clear: Do as I say—not as I do—is unacceptable.

—*Felicia Friendly Thomas*

FURTHER READING

Haldane, D., and J. Pasco. "Fiery O.C. Ultraconservative Schmitz Dies." *Los Angeles Times*, January 11, 2001. This obituary of Schmitz is a good summary of his political career and the scandals that rocked his family. Includes infamous quotations by Schmitz.

Koplinski, Brad. *Hats in the Ring: Conversations with Presidential Candidates—John Schmitz*. North Bethesda, Md.: Presidential Publishing, 2000. Verbatim question-and-answer interview. Schmitz discusses his presidential candidacy and his career. Includes comments about Nixon, Ronald Reagan, Wallace, and the Supreme Court case *Roe v. Wade*.

Schmitz, John G. *Stranger in the Arena: The Anatomy of an Amoral Decade, 1964-1974*. Santa Ana, Calif.: Rayline, 1974. Schmitz candidly discusses his political views, especially on the issue of the right to life, or antiabortion.

Steinbacher, J. *John Schmitz and the American Party*. Fullerton, Calif.: Educator's, 1972. Outlines the history of the American Independent Party and Schmitz's involvement during the height of his political career.

SEE ALSO: Oct. 7, 1974: Congressman Wilbur D. Mills's Stripper Affair Leads to His Downfall; Oct. 25, 1974: Evangelist Billy James Hargis Resigns College Presidency During Gay-Sex Scandal; Sept., 1976: Jimmy Carter Admits Committing Adultery in His Heart; Sept. 3, 1980: Congressman Bauman Is Arrested for Liaison with Teenage Boy; July 20, 1983: Congress Members Censured in House-Page Sex Scandal; Feb. 21, 1988: Evangelist Jimmy Swaggart Tearfully Confesses His Adultery; Feb. 26, 1997: Teacher Mary Kay Letourneau Is Arrested for Statutory Rape; Apr. 30, 2001: Washington Intern Chandra Levy Disappears; Oct. 2, 2003: Newspaper Claims That Arnold Schwarzenegger Groped Women; Dec. 17, 2003: Senator Strom Thurmond's Biracial Daughter Is Revealed; Dec. 6, 2005: Spokane, Washington, Mayor Recalled in Gay-Sex Scandal; July 9, 2007: Senator David Vitter's Name Is Found in D.C. Madam's Address Book.

1980's

August 6, 1982
BANCO AMBROSIANO COLLAPSES AMID CRIMINAL ACCUSATIONS

The collapse of Banco Ambrosiano was the first large bank failure since World War II. The collapse sent shock waves through world finance and led to a series of international bank crises and collapses. The criminal activities of bank officials, the shootings and suicides of persons involved in the crimes, and the large sums of Vatican and Mafia funds involved in the bank's dealings have kept the scandal alive into the twenty-first century.

LOCALES: Milan and Vatican City, Italy

CATEGORIES: Banking and finance; corruption; business; organized crime and racketeering; law and the courts; murder and suicide

KEY FIGURES

Roberto Calvi (1920-1982), Milanese banker, chairman of Banco Ambrosiano

Paul Marcinkus (1922-2006), American Roman Catholic archbishop, president of the Vatican Bank, 1971-1989

Michele Sindona (1920-1986), Sicilian banker for the Vatican and the Mafia

John Paul II (Karol Jozef Wojtyla; 1920-2005), Roman Catholic pope, 1978-2005

Paul VI (Giovanni Battista Montini; 1897-1978), Roman Catholic pope, 1963-1978

John Paul I (Albino Luciani; 1912-1978), Roman Catholic pope, August 26-September 28, 1978

SUMMARY OF EVENT

Pope Paul VI appointed Archbishop Paul Marcinkus, an American, to head the Vatican Bank in 1971—a strange appointment, given Marcinkus's lack of banking experience. Marcinkus had served as a translator in the last months of Pope John XXIII's pontificate and then as translator and de facto bodyguard outside the Vatican for Paul VI. Possibly failing mentally, it seems that Paul VI appointed the tall and imposing archbishop for preventing an assassi-

nation attempt on the pope's life during a visit to the Philippines.

Marcinkus accepted Roberto Calvi as the Vatican's Italian banker on the recommendation of Sicilian banker Michele Sindona, who had been a successful moneymaker for the Vatican but was now moving his criminal operations to the United States for financial dealings with the Mafia. Because of Sindona's successful work for Marcinkus, Calvi was appointed chairman of the private Banco Ambrosiano.

Milan remains the financial capital of not only Italy but also Europe. Sindona was a fast, loose, and inventive banker. Partly owing to his knowledge of English and the profiteering he engaged in with American goods and Mafia collusion after the allied invasion of Sicily, he had been able to move his operations north to Milan. It was there that Sindona and Calvi entered into a banking relationship and, over time, found that they were of similar mind about transactions that skirted the edge of legitimacy or were illegal.

Sindona had already established an offshore bank in Panama that laundered Mafia narcotics-trafficking money. On the basis of Sindona's Panama model, Calvi opened at least one dozen of his own overseas banks in the Caribbean and Central and South America. These banks served as postbox banks for the conversion of Italian lira into U.S. dollars. Italian millionaires deposited lira in the Banco Ambrosiano. Calvi, in turn, deposited those funds into the Vatican Bank. From this bank, the Italian currency would be exported to Calvi's offshore banks. Calvi could export the money because the Vatican, as a sovereign state, is not subject to Italian laws that restricted—then outlawed—the export of Italian capital.

After commission payments for the laundering and conversion, the offshore banks would forward the proceeds to haven banks in Luxembourg, Lichtenstein, and Switzerland to finance political and other operations requiring payment in hard currency. Some of these operations included the following: On order of Pope John Paul II, the sole head of the Vatican Bank, millions of lira were funneled into Poland to support that country's anticommunist solidarity movement. Also, Calvi leveraged takeovers of northern Italian private banks by spreading deposits of large amounts coming into Italy and thereby hindering detection of those takeovers. These banks included the legitimate Catholic bank in the Veneto, managed by Cardinal Albino Luciani, patriarch of Venice. Calvi's actions so outraged the cardinal that, after becoming Pope John Paul I, he made no secret that he would discharge Marcinkus—as head of the Vatican Bank—for complicity in Calvi's hostile takeover of "his" bank, among other Calvi sins.

Further operations included Calvi's purchase of 40 percent of the large Rizzoli publishing concern that also owned *Corriere della Sera*, the Italian equivalent of *The New York Times*. *Corriere della Sera* became an organ of propaganda for the secret Masonic lodge Propaganda Due, or P-2. The lodge was eventually unmasked and found to be a virtual state within a state, whose members included Vatican officials, politicians, government officials, military and intelligence officers, and Mafia figures who allegedly had been plotting a right-wing coup d'etat to prevent a feared shift of Italian government to the left. Calvi was found to be a P-2 member as well.

Given that Calvi was dispensing enormous sums of money, the director of the Bank of Italy ordered an investigation into his personal and bank activities. Calvi's problems were exacerbated by shootings (by the Mafia, as informers later revealed) of a journalist who continued to expose the Ambrosiano story, of a former Ambrosiano officer who knew secrets, and of a current Ambrosiano officer who had been pressuring Calvi to account for his actions. Calvi's secretary died either after jumping or being pushed—likely by a mafioso—from the top floor of the Ambrosiano bank building.

Calvi was arrested, charged, tried, and sentenced to four-and-one-half years in prison, where he made a feeble attempt at suicide. Provisionally released to appeal his sentence, Calvi vowed that he would never return to prison. Against the conditions of his release (which included turning over his passport and remaining in Italy), Calvi was flown out of Italy by a Mafia consigliere (adviser) on a private jet to a private airport in England. Imprudently, Calvi revealed that he was carrying documents that would incriminate many of his high-standing clients. He was taken to a prearranged London residential hotel. The next day, June 18, 1982, he was found hanging from London's Blackfriars Bridge. Calvi's wife left Milan for Nassau in the Bahamas with her

Banco Ambrosiano chair Roberto Calvi, right, is escorted into a courtroom in Milan, Italy, at the start of his trial for banking-related crimes in May, 1981. (Hulton Archive/Getty Images)

daughter and son. The three remained there for some time as permanent residents, likely living on funds earmarked for them. Calvi's son became a banker in Montreal, Canada.

In the immediate aftermath of Calvi's murder, Banco Ambrosiano collapsed, unable to raise the money to cover the indebtedness Calvi had created. On August 6, the bank was declared insolvent and it went into receivership. More than $1 billion in losses were never accounted for. The Vatican, to repair its deeply damaged image, pledged to repay the millions lost by Ambrosiano's individual stockholders but did so without admitting culpability in the scandal.

One decade after Calvi's murder and after two exhumations, his death was ruled a homicide. It is believed that a mafioso, specialized in strangulation, murdered him before hanging him from Blackfriars Bridge.

IMPACT

In 1989, after the collapse of the Soviet Union, John Paul II removed Marcinkus, who was under subpoena by the Italian police, as director of the Vatican Bank. The directorship was assigned to a committee of two ecclesiastical and two secular members. Marcinkus spent his years waiting to return to the United States within Vatican City. He had been granted Vatican citizenship and thereby avoided arrest. Until his death—having failed to attain the cardinalship he so ardently wanted— Marcinkus served as a country-club priest in Sun City, near Phoenix, Arizona. Banco Ambrosiano, with the help of the Bank of Italy and the Vatican, was reformed and resumed the banking business.

In the wake of Ambrosiano's collapse, which led to the collapse of Franklin National Trust of New York, the Bank of Italy mandated several new rules, including that Italian banks maintain, regularly disclose, and prove the availability of a minimum percentage of capital, based on their respective size. At the international level, the collapse of Ambrosiano moved a number of banks to examine their practices as well and to develop stringent rules of operation.

—*Robert B. Youngblood*

FURTHER READING

Cornwell, Rupert. *God's Banker: The Life and Death of Roberto Calvi*. London: Unwin, 1984. This work remains an excellent, detailed account of the Banco Ambrosiano-Calvi scandal.

Hammer, Richard. *The Vatican Connection*. New York: Holt, Rinehart & Winston, 1982. Forensic investigation of the Sindona years as Mafia and Vatican banker to the collapse of Banco Ambrosiano. Valuable background information.

Jones, Tobias. *The Dark Heart of Italy*. New York: North Point Press, 2004. The Ambrosiano-Calvi scandal is discussed in a chapter on Catholicism among individuals and the Vatican's mandates on practicing Catholicism.

Raw, Charles. *The Moneychangers: How the Vatican Bank Enabled Roberto Calvi to Steal Two Hundred Fifty Million for the Heads of the P2 Masonic Lodge*. London: Harvill, 1992. A comprehensive study of the Ambrosiano-Calvi scandal that details virtually every known transaction in the case.

Willan, Philip. *The Last Supper: The Mafia, the Masons, and the Killing of Roberto Calvi*. London: Robinson, 2007. Argues that Calvi's murder and the Banco Ambrosiano scandal were played out on the stage of the Cold War, with its dueling fears of democracy and communism, and in the context of a hunger for power and wealth.

Williams, Paul L. *The Vatican Exposed: Money, Murder, and the Mafia*. Amherst, N.Y.: Prometheus Books, 2003. Historical account of the formation of the Vatican Bank, Calvi's selection as its banker, and the resulting scandal.

Youngblood, Robert B. "Roberto Calvi." In *Great Lives from History: Notorious Lives*, edited by Carl L. Bankston III. Vol. 1. Pasadena, Calif.: Salem Press, 2007. An introductory article on Calvi's life and death.

tion; Sept. 10, 1981: *Chicago Sun-Times* Reports That Cardinal Cody Diverted Church Funds; Nov. 3, 1996: Car Crash Reveals Depth of Government Corruption in Turkey; June 25, 1997: Swiss Banks Admit to Holding Accounts of Holocaust Victims; 2001: Clearstream Financial Clearinghouse Is Accused of Fraud and Money Laundering; Dec. 2, 2001: Enron Bankruptcy Reveals Massive Financial Fraud; Sept. 20, 2008: American Financial Markets Begin to Collapse.

October 19, 1982
CAR MANUFACTURER JOHN DE LOREAN IS ARRESTED IN A DRUG STING

Automobile manufacturer and engineer John De Lorean attempted to save his failing company by conspiring to sell drugs. He was arrested by the FBI in a case that generated widespread publicity and scandal. He was later acquitted on grounds of entrapment but his name is now synonymous with white-collar crime.

LOCALE: Los Angeles, California
CATEGORIES: Law and the courts; business; drugs; organized crime and racketeering

KEY FIGURES
John De Lorean (1925-2005), American automotive engineer and founder of De Lorean Motor Company
James Hoffman (fl. 1980's), former neighbor of De Lorean and FBI informant
Benedict Tisa (fl. 1980's), FBI agent

SUMMARY OF EVENT
Charismatic and well-known automotive manufacturer and engineer John De Lorean was arrested by the Federal Bureau of Investigation (FBI) for conspiracy to distribute cocaine on October 19, 1982. His arrest made international headlines, as the timing coincided with the closing of the Northern Ireland plant for De Lorean Motor Cars Ltd., whose parent company was De Lorean Motor Company (DMC), based in Detroit, Michigan.

Founded in Detroit in 1975, DMC had gained in-

ternational publicity with the introduction of the DMC-12 sports car, which was manufactured in Northern Ireland, in 1981. However, delays in building the cars, as well as flaws in design and manufacturing, led to sales well below the projections needed to make a profit. The DMC-12 ended its production run in late 1982, with about nine thousand sold. By the time DMC had entered into receivership and bankruptcy, De Lorean was seeking ways to recapitalize his business so that he could continue production and develop more cars.

The story of how and why De Lorean, who also gained fame as the creator of the Pontiac GTO "muscle car" during the early 1960's, became involved in the drug-dealing conspiracy remains a two-version tale. The FBI claimed that De Lorean played an active role in the conspiracy to bring 220 pounds of cocaine (worth tens of millions of U.S. dollars) into the United States. FBI tape transcripts indicate that De Lorean did indeed participate in several meetings, in which he demonstrated a willingness to pay a $1.8 million commission for a transaction.

De Lorean, however, claimed that he never intended to participate in an illicit drug deal. Instead, he was looking for investors in his struggling car company. His willingness to seek creative and unconventional financing methods was a product of his inability to gain more bank financing. After being contacted by James Hoffman, the father of one of his son's friends in Pauma Valley, California, De

1980's

John De Lorean and his wife, Cristina Ferrare, outside court in November, 1982. (AP/Wide World Photos)

Lorean listened to a deal that would possibly recapitalize his company.

In reality, Hoffman was a federal law-enforcement informant with a history of drug-trafficking convictions. On July 11, 1982, De Lorean met Hoffman at the Marriot Hotel in Newport Beach, California. Hoffman described a plan in which De Lorean would pay Hoffman a $1.5 million brokerage fee plus $300,000 in expenses to provide financing for De Lorean's company. Soon after the meeting, however, De Lorean realized that his money would be used for the purchase of cocaine and that the proceeds from the sale would be laundered through a bank account that De Lorean was to set up through Eureka Federal Savings and Loan in San Carlos, California. Little evidence indicates that De Lorean came up with the complex plan to buy the drugs and launder the money, but numerous federal law-enforcement tapes indicate that he willingly took part in the discussions to participate in the plan.

Discussions about the deal continued, though De Lorean would later claim that he participated in these later discussions because Hoffman had threatened the lives of his children and not, as was alleged by federal authorities, to commit a crime. Regardless, he had flown to Washington, D.C., on September 4 to meet with Hoffman at the L'Enfant Plaza Hotel.

Through various meetings and contacts, De Lorean was introduced to banker James Benedict, the person who would see that the financing on the deal was handled appropriately. (Benedict was undercover FBI agent Benedict Tisa.) Around this time as well, De Lorean was reacquainted with William Morgan Hetrick, a pilot and aviation company owner with a history of drug-running who also was being set up in the FBI sting. On September 20, De Lorean, Hetrick, and Benedict met at the Bel Air Sands Hotel in Los Angeles. FBI tapes yielded incriminating statements made by De Lorean and Hetrick, showing they clearly knew they were involved in a illegal drug transaction. However, De Lorean could not get the $1.8 million in cash needed to complete the deal.

As his company continued to face significant losses and could not pay creditors and suppliers, De Lorean decided that his only contribution to the deal would be DMC stock. This option was made clear by De Lorean at a September 28 meeting, also in Los Angeles, with drug dealer John Vicenza (undercover Drug Enforcement Agency agent John Valestra). De Lorean later noted in a postarrest interview that the stock he offered was worthless.

De Lorean claimed after his arrest that his participation in the deal continued only through the threats of harm to his family and the constant pushing of Benedict. The sting operation was so complex that a real banker volunteered to play a role in affirming the legitimacy of Benedict as a banker with whom De Lorean should deal.

On October 19, De Lorean entered room 501 of the Sheraton Plaza Hotel near Los Angeles International Airport. He saw the cocaine, said it looked "good as gold," and was arrested by Benedict and Vicenza. The two, along with Hoffman, were with De Lorean in the hotel room.

After putting up as collateral his New York apartment, New Jersey estate, and Pauma Valley home, De Lorean was released on $250,000 bail. His trial, long and complex, began on April 18, 1984. The cross-examination of two witnesses for the prosecution, Benedict and Hoffman, greatly harmed the case against De Lorean, leading to his acquittal on all eight charges on August 16. Benedict testified that he continued with the deal even though he had known at the time that De Lorean did not have the $1.8 million to complete the transaction. This testimony led to charges by the defense that government agents had to put up the money to make De Lorean continue with the deal. Hoffman's admission during trial that he had demanded a share of the money seized in the deal led to suspicion about the truthfulness of his testimony. In the end, the jury determined that De Lorean had been entrapped by federal law enforcement, and he was freed.

IMPACT

De Lorean's arrest bridged high-profile crime such as drug dealing with the "lesser" acts of falsifying reports and bad-faith negotiations for the development of a car company. Although acquitted of criminal charges, he spent years defending himself from numerous lawsuits related to his failed company. He also faced numerous charges of tax evasion and fraud related to his operation of DMC.

De Lorean's name has been immortalized by the DMC-12 sports car that captivated the attention of automobile enthusiasts during the early 1980's. Still, even with the car's continuing legacy, the fact remains that the British government and investors, including celebrities Johnny Carson and Sammy Davis, Jr., lost approximately $250 million when the company failed. The British government had invested in DMC to help with high unemployment in Northern Ireland. Although these monetary losses mostly came from failed attempts to further develop DMC, De Lorean's arrest and trial affected the company as well. De Lorean would ask, even after his acquittal, "Would you buy a used car from me?"

The novelty of the DMC-12 and the public-relations campaign of his daring venture to build a car that challenged the powers of automobile manufacturers in Detroit made him a hero to many. Analysis of the drug deal indicates, however, that he simply wanted to single-handedly save his dream.

—*John C. Kilburn, Jr.*

FURTHER READING

Fallon, Ivan, and James Srodes. *Dream Maker: The Rise and Fall of John Z. De Lorean*. New York: G. P. Putnam's Sons, 1983. A detailed biography of De Lorean's rise as an automotive executive after founding De Lorean Motor Company. This book, published before De Lorean's criminal trial, contains few details about the cocaine-trafficking case.

Haddad, William. *Hard Driving: My Years with John De Lorean*. New York: Random House, 1985. Haddad spent fifteen years with De Lorean as a business associate and executive with the De Lorean Motor Company. Displays both admiration and contempt for the complex De Lorean.

Hakim, Danny. "John Z. De Lorean, Father of Glamour Car, Dies at 80." *The New York Times*, March 21, 2005. De Lorean's obituary. A brief account of his life and career, including some discussion of the scandal.

Latham, Aaron. "Anatomy of a Sting: John De Lorean Tells His Story." *Rolling Stone*, March 17, 1983. After his arrest but before his trial, De Lorean tells his version of the story in this magazine piece.

Levin, Hillel. *Grand Delusions: The Cosmic Career of John De Lorean*. New York: Viking Press, 1983. This biography chronicles De Lorean's early life, rapid rise in Detroit's automotive industry, and the development of De Lorean Motor Company. De Lorean is characterized as both brilliant and vain, with a keen sense for public relations and a willingness to do anything to succeed.

SEE ALSO: Mar. 29, 1962: Billie Sol Estes Is Arrested for Corporate Fraud; Feb. 4, 1976: Lockheed Is Implicated in Bribing Foreign Officials; Feb. 2, 1980: Media Uncover FBI Sting Implicating Dozens of Lawmakers; May 29,

1980's

1981: Court Finds That Ford Ignored Pinto's Safety Problems; May 2, 1984: E. F. Hutton Executives Plead Guilty to Fraud; Jan. 15, 1988: *ZZZZ* Best Founder Is Indicted on Federal Fraud Charges; Mar. 29, 1989: Financier Michael

Milken Is Indicted for Racketeering and Fraud; Apr. 15, 1992: Hotel Tycoon Leona Helmsley Enters Prison for Tax Evasion; Dec. 23, 1998: Prominent Belgians Are Sentenced in Agusta-Dassault Corruption Scandal.

December, 1982
JULIE ANDREWS AND BLAKE EDWARDS DENY BEING GAY

Singer-actor Julie Andrews, along with her husband, Blake Edwards, denied claims that she was lesbian and that he was gay in an interview with Playboy *magazine. Edwards, a filmmaker, was long rumored to be gay or bisexual.*

LOCALE: Beverly Hills, California
CATEGORIES: Publishing and journalism; sex

KEY FIGURES
Julie Andrews (b. 1935), British singer and film star
Blake Edwards (b. 1922), American screenwriter and film director and producer
Lawrence Linderman (fl. 1980's), journalist

SUMMARY OF EVENT
Julie Andrews and Blake Edwards married in 1969, when both were well known in the entertainment world. Andrews was best known for her sweet, classic governess roles in films such as *Mary Poppins* (1964) and *The Sound of Music* (1965), as well as the spectacular vocal talents that made her a child star in England during the 1940's and a Broadway smash during the 1950's and 1960's. She skyrocketed to fame when she appeared on stage in such shows as *My Fair Lady* (1956), *Camelot* (1960), and *The Boy Friend* (1954), for which she earned critical acclaim.

Edwards was best known for writing and directing *The Pink Panther* (1963), starring Peter Sellers, and its sequels. Edwards also wrote and directed *A Shot in the Dark* (1964), *This Happy Feeling* (1958), and *10* (1979). He directed *Operation Petti-*

coat (1959), starring Cary Grant, and *Breakfast at Tiffany's* (1961), starring Audrey Hepburn, and created two popular private-eye series for television.

From the mid- to late 1960's, following this period of immense achievement, both Andrews and Edwards experienced a series of professional failures, including their mutual film project *Darling Lili* (1969). Around the same time, both were having marital troubles. They began to see each other after their marriages ended. The couple's individual successes had made them celebrities in their own right, but together, Andrews and Edwards were subjected to closer scrutiny. They continued doing film projects together, but projects that were very different from those for which they were known.

In particular, Andrews broke out of her wholesome governess image by baring her breasts in the film *S.O.B.* (1981) and portraying a cross-dresser in *Victor/Victoria* (1982). The couple's enthusiasm for these projects, which had homosexuality as themes, renewed rumors about their own sexuality. Edwards, long assumed to be gay (and not out about his sexuality), had recently directed several other films with gay themes or subtexts, in addition to the more explicitly gay *Victor/Victoria*. Andrews, as a Broadway and film star and vocal diva, was already well on her way to becoming an icon of gays and lesbians. The existing rumors about Edwards grew to include Andrews as well.

In 1982, journalist Lawrence Linderman sat down with Andrews and Edwards in Beverly Hills, California, on assignment for *Playboy* magazine. (Each issue of the magazine includes an interview with a celebrity or a celebrity group or couple.)

Linderman met with the couple several times to prepare for the interview, which was recorded on tape. Linderman began the interview by asking about events surrounding the couple's first meeting. They discussed their mutual film projects and analyzed the challenges of creating an image for Andrews that would go beyond her classic, memorable roles in *Mary Poppins* and *The Sound of Music*.

During the interview, the conversation came to Edwards's later films and how the public reacted to their gay-related themes. Linderman asked Edwards to discuss *Victor/Victoria* and whether Edwards was dealing with his own sexuality through the film's message. Edwards acknowledged both the theme and the idea of dealing with his own sexuality, saying he believed that everyone must go through such examinations. Edwards spoke of dealing with his fears about being gay for his own peace of mind. Linderman then asked Edwards if he thought people who watched the film would assume Edwards was implying that he was gay. Edwards accepted that audiences might make that assumption, adding that he had begun exploring sexuality in more subtle ways in other films, such as *10* and *S.O.B.*, and that part of his goal was to get people to react to the issue.

Andrews suggested that Edwards's style of dealing with serious and complicated issues such as the social acceptance of homosexuality was to use humor and lighthearted moments to capture truth. Linderman pressed the point by asking if Edwards was worried about the rumors that these films meant he was coming out of the closet. Edwards answered that it would not bother him if people thought he was coming out as gay. He talked about undergoing psychoanalysis, which had helped him deal with his sexuality, and about his concerns about being gay. However, he then said he was relieved to learn, through analysis, that he was heterosexual, despite having had homosexual fantasies and engaging in some childhood experimentation with other boys.

Andrews, too, spoke of being relieved after going through a similar process of analysis, asserting that most people have homoerotic feelings and that having them is a normal part of life, even for heterosexuals. She supported Edwards in his desire to use his films to talk about homosexuality and suggested that he wanted to address other social issues as well, such as race. Edwards added that it was important that he champion gay rights and be supportive of gay friends who struggled to come out of the closet. Seemingly satisfied with the couple's explicit responses to the rumors of homosexuality, Linderman redirected the conversation. For the remainder of the interview, topics focused on other projects in which the two were working.

IMPACT

The manner in which Andrews and Edwards denied their homosexuality did more to fan the flames of public rumors than it did to squelch them. Though it was common for celebrities to publicly deny rumors of homosexuality, it was rare for such a denial to include mention of past homosexual experiences,

Blake Edwards and Julie Andrews in 1979. (Hulton Archive/Getty Images)

fantasies, and exploration, or to have acknowledged having questioned their own sexuality. The controversy of a straight Hollywood couple speaking so openly about having had homosexual desires and experiences shocked readers of the interview. *Playboy*'s target audience is traditionally heterosexual and male, a demographic that—particularly during the early 1980's, the early days of the HIV-AIDS crisis—tends to openly shun homosexuality.

Andrews and Edwards openly supported homosexuality and made clear their belief that people should confront their feelings about sexuality. This perspective injected some new life into the public debate. Their support, however, did little to prove to skeptics that they were truly heterosexual, fueling further claims that their attempt to justify homosexual affinity was more of a denial than an acceptance. Despite the ensuing controversy, the Andrews and Edwards interview was a success.

—*Kekla Magoon*

FURTHER READING

Andrews, Julie. *Home: A Memoir of My Early Years*. New York: Hyperion Books, 2008. An autobiography in which Andrews discusses intimate life details and memories from the time before she was a star.

Lehman, Peter, and William Luhr. "What Business Does a Critic Have Asking if Blake Edwards Is Gay? Rumor, Scandal, Biography, and Textual Analysis." In *Headline Hollywood: A Century of Film Scandal*, edited by Adrienne L. McLean and David A. Cook. New Brunswick, N.J.: Rutgers University Press, 2001. Part of the Communications, Media, and Culture series, Lehman and Luhr analyze the intersection of controversial reportage and biography.

Linderman, Lawrence. "Playboy Interview: Julie Andrews and Blake Edwards." *Playboy*, December, 1982. The candid interview in which Julie Andrews and Blake Edwards discuss their career, films, and marriage, and publicly deny rumors of their homosexuality.

Stirling, Richard. *Julie Andrews: An Intimate Biography*. New York: St. Martin's Press, 2008. A biography of Andrews exploring both the well-known and untold aspects of her public and private life. Includes some discussion of sex and sexuality.

Wolf, Stacy. *A Problem Like Maria: Gender and Sexuality in the American Musical*. Ann Arbor: University of Michigan Press, 2002. A unique look at musical theater in the United States and the women, including Andrews, who reinterpreted gender roles and sexuality in their performances. Explores, for example, the "delicious queerness" of Andrews's role as a "troublesome" nun in *The Sound of Music*.

SEE ALSO: 1927: Mae West's Play About Gays Is Banned on Broadway; Dec. 1, 1952: George Jorgensen Becomes Christine Jorgensen; Oct. 7, 1964: President Lyndon B. Johnson's Aide Is Arrested in Gay-Sex Sting; 1970: Study of Anonymous Gay Sex Leads to Ethics Scandal; Jan., 1977: Singer Anita Bryant Campaigns Against Lesbian and Gay Rights; July 28, 1980: Magazine Reveals Baseball Star Steve Garvey's Marital Problems; Sept. 3, 1980: Congressman Bauman Is Arrested for Liaison with Teenage Boy; Dec. 7, 1980: Rita Jenrette's "Diary of a Mad Congresswife" Scandalizes Washington; July 23, 1984: Vanessa Williams Is the First Miss America to Resign; Apr. 7, 1998: Pop Singer George Michael Is Arrested for Lewd Conduct; Sept. 19, 2000: Ex-gay Leader John Paulk Is Photographed Leaving a Gay Bar; Sept. 17, 2006: New Zealand Prime Minister's Husband Is "Outed" as Gay; Nov. 2, 2006: Male Escort Reveals Sexual Liaisons with Evangelist Ted Haggard.

December 16, 1982
CONGRESS CITES ENVIRONMENTAL PROTECTION AGENCY CHIEF FOR CONTEMPT

Anne Gorsuch, director of the Environmental Protection Agency, was cited for contempt of Congress after refusing to release documents for an inquiry into the Superfund, the federal toxic-waste cleanup program. She and twenty top aides, including Rita Lavelle, assistant EPA administrator, were either fired or forced to resign from the EPA.

LOCALE: Washington, D.C.
CATEGORIES: Government; corruption; environmental issues; business; politics

KEY FIGURES

Anne Gorsuch (1942-2004), director of the Environmental Protection Agency, 1981-1982
Rita Lavelle (b. 1947), assistant administrator of the EPA
John Dingell (b. 1926), U.S. representative from Michigan, 1955-
William Ruckelshaus (b. 1932), interim director of the EPA, 1983-1985

SUMMARY OF EVENT

Ann Gorsuch was appointed on May 20, 1981, to the position of administrator of the U.S. Environmental Protection Agency (EPA), the first woman to head the agency. She had served in the Colorado legislature for two terms and was a district attorney in Denver, but she had no experience managing large organizations nor any background in environmental work. In the legislature, she had been a member of a group that advocated states' rights and opposed federal environmental and energy policies.

Gorsuch was appointed the head of the EPA by President Ronald Reagan, who directed the new appointee to weaken the EPA's ability to oversee industry. The EPA had been created during the 1970's to consolidate government offices responsible for protecting public health and safeguarding the envi-

ronment. Many members of the U.S. Congress opposed the agenda set by Gorsuch, and she was soon dogged with charges that she was planning to cut the agency's budget by 40 percent. When she suspended a regulatory ban on the disposal of toxic waste in containers in landfills, Congress members considered the suspension a gross miscalculation. Gorsuch enacted a new ban after eighteen days of strong media scrutiny and discussion. Similarly, she devoted time to trying to phase out federal clean-air regulations, an effort thwarted by Congress.

An advocate of budgetary cuts and regulatory reform, Gorsuch did manage to drop the EPA's budget by $200 million and cut its staff by 23 percent, firing over one thousand people. She scattered the staff responsible for enforcement of EPA regulations among other programs, removing the EPA's ability to keep pollution in check.

While Gorsuch treated other EPA officials with aloofness, industry representatives found her door always open to them. When a proposal surfaced to phase out lead as an additive to gasoline, scientists and representatives from Ethyl Corporation, a company that manufactures fuel additives, met with her to express concerns that requiring a drop in lead levels would result in the closing of refineries and increased wear on automobile engines while not doing much to improve public health. Gorsuch finished the hearing by allegedly winking when asked if she had any plans to actually enforce the regulations.

This type of behavior by Gorsuch, signaling her complicity with industry, led to questions about her use of agency funds. In the summer of 1982, Representative John Dingell, a Democrat from Michigan, began an inquiry into reports that the EPA was being run through "political manipulation . . . interwoven with absurd incompetence." Dingell's inquiry was focused primarily on Rita Lavelle, a political appointee and EPA associate administrator in charge of the program formed by the Comprehensive Environmental Response Compensation and Liability Act of 1980 (better known as Superfund).

Superfund was formed to address chemical poisons in the environment. It was based on an EPA survey that had identified more than 250 hazardous-waste sites involving damages or significant threat of damages, and it was the only EPA program whose budget was untouched by Gorsuch. Under her leadership, the EPA announced national guidelines for cleaning up abandoned hazardous-waste sites and set up a $1.6 billion trust fund over five years, financed by taxes on the manufacture of some toxic chemicals and general revenues appropriated by Congress. The EPA also passed a rule requiring that schools test for asbestos in their buildings.

Lavelle had numerous corporate ties to chemical and aerospace companies. She had failed to cooperate with Dingell's investigation, which was looking into the misuse of Superfund monies for political purposes and irregularities at a major perchlorate toxic waste site, the Stringfellow Acid Pits in Riverside, California. (Perchlorate, an oxidizer used in rocket fuel, affects the human thyroid gland.) Dingell's investigation also uncovered secret meetings with the Monsanto Company and other corporations that dealt with regulatory matters. Monsanto, a leading manufacturer of herbicides and other chemicals, had actively worked to mask the dangers of polychlorinated biphenyls, or PCBs, by funding nonexistent public-interest groups to defend its interests and publicizing statements such as that made by a Monsanto toxicologist. He had declared that "There has never been a single documented case in this country where PCBs have been shown to cause cancer or any other serious human health problems." He went on to compare PCBs to ordinary table salt.

In September, Dingell requested EPA documents on Superfund sites but the agency withheld the documents on the advice of the Justice Department. Dingell then subpoenaed Gorsuch to appear before investigators with the requested documents; she refused. After a second attempt to subpoena her,

President Reagan intervened on November 30 and told her not to comply with the request. On December 16, the U.S. House of Representatives voted 259-105 in favor of a contempt of Congress citation against Gorsuch, but the Justice Department, also led by Reagan appointees, refused to prosecute.

In early 1983, the House voted 413-0 in favor of a contempt of Congress citation against Lavelle for refusing to appear before a House investigatory committee. She was fired by Reagan, was later acquitted of the contempt charge, and was convicted of perjury in a separate trial on December 1. She served three months of a six-month sentence.

On March 9, 1983, Gorsuch resigned as EPA director, adding in her announcement that congressional investigators now had ready access to the documents they had been seeking since the summer of 1982. She later would claim that her time with the EPA had been hampered by the agency's lack of management skills and outdated priorities. At the same time, her colleagues charged that she had in turn delayed energy development decisions by demanding direct control over all decision making processes rather than leaving them to be made at the state and regional level. They went on to say that Gorsuch had made herself inaccessible to the EPA's regular staff and had barricaded herself with a wall of assistants with connections to Secretary of the Interior James Watt, the Adolph Coors Company, and the Reagan campaign, all with limited to no experience with environmental issues.

Lavelle was involved in later criminal investigations and convicted in 2004 of one count of wire fraud and two counts of making misleading statements to FBI investigators. She served time in prison for this conviction as well. Gorsuch was appointed by Reagan to head the National Advisory Committee on Oceans and the Atmosphere, but she turned down the appointment. She wrote *Are You Tough Enough?* (1986) and then returned to law practice. In 2004, she died from cancer.

IMPACT

Gorsuch was replaced by William Ruckelshaus, who had served as the EPA's first director. The National Resources Defense Council sued the EPA in

1983 for violations related to secret meetings and collusion with industry leaders. The EPA agreed to end the practice of secret negotiations and private deal-making. The new regulations forbid the EPA from allowing industry negotiations to affect its decisions whenever it evaluates or registers high-risk pesticides.

Ruckelshaus, as interim director, established the EPA's so-called fishbowl policy, providing public participation in policy-making activities, and created a recusal policy to avoid conflicts of interest caused by his association with the timber company Weyerhaeuser and with Monsanto, among others. His appointment calendar was made public each week, as were those of other key EPA officials.

In an interview with the EPA History Office, Ruckelshaus observed that the Reagan administration's

> avowed purpose of lessening the impact of regulation on society really had the opposite effect, at least with respect to the environment. To the extent it acted at all, Congress increased the degree of regulation, imposing new restrictions on flexibility and on the administration of the states.

In the years after Gorsuch's tenure with the EPA, Congress passed prescriptive environmental legislation, believing that loosely worded amendments would be abused by administrations for whom the environment was not a priority. The acts included an amendment to the Hazardous and Solid Waste Act (1984), amendments to the Safe Drinking Water Act (1986), amendments and reauthorization of the Superfund Act (1986), and the Water Quality Act (1987).

—*Catherine Rambo*

Further Reading

Collin, Robert W. *The Environmental Protection Agency: Cleaning Up America's Act.* Westport, Conn.: Greenwood Press, 2006. This book documents the history of the Environmental Protection Agency and reviews some of its most notable cases. Includes a detailed biography of Gorsuch and her brief tenure at the EPA.

Davis, Devra Lee. *When Smoke Ran Like Water: Tales of Environmental Deception and the Battle Against Pollution.* New York: Basic Books, 2004. Includes discussion of Gorsuch's tenure with the EPA and the Reagan administration's approach to pollution in historical context.

Johnson, Haynes. *Sleepwalking Through History: America in the Reagan Years.* New York: W. W. Norton, 1991. Coverage of the multiple scandals that arose during the Reagan administration. Gorsuch is mentioned in passing.

Nakamura, Robert T., and Thomas W. Church. *Taming Regulation: Superfund and the Challenge of Regulatory Reform.* Washington, D.C.: Brookings Institution Press, 2003. Discusses administrative reform in the Superfund program and deals primarily with the aftermath of the scandal involving Rita Lavelle.

See also: Oct. 4, 1976: Agriculture Secretary Earl Butz Resigns After Making Obscene Joke; Sept. 26, 1979: Love Canal Residents Sue Chemical Company; Dec. 11, 1997: HUD Secretary Henry Cisneros Is Indicted for Lying to Federal Agents; July, 2002: Journalist Alleges Release of Genetically Modified Corn Seeds in New Zealand; Beginning Aug. 29, 2005: Government Incompetence Mars Hurricane Katrina Relief Efforts.

1980's

April 25, 1983
GERMAN MAGAZINE PUBLISHES FAKED HITLER DIARIES

The German weekly magazine Stern *published excerpts of a manuscript believed to be the diaries of Adolf Hitler. The diaries were found to be forged, however, leading to one of the most notorious publishing and forgery scandals of the twentieth century.*

LOCALE: Hamburg, Germany

CATEGORIES: Forgery; hoaxes, frauds, and charlatanism; publishing and journalism

KEY FIGURES

Konrad Kujau (Konrad Fischer; 1938-2000), German collector

Gerd Heidemann (b. 1931), German journalist

Peter Koch (fl. 1980's), editor in chief of *Stern* magazine

Hugh Trevor-Roper (1914-2003), English historian

SUMMARY OF EVENT

Konrad Kujau, a German collector of memorabilia, claimed to be in possession of sixty-two volumes of the secret "diaries" of Adolf Hitler. The diaries included details from Hitler's life between 1932 and days before his suicide on April 30, 1945. Kujau said he found the diaries in Börnersdorf, near Dresden, in the possession of farmers who discovered them in the wreckage of a Nazi SS plane that had crashed on April 21, 1945.

Kujau, who used the name Konrad Fischer, was an accomplished forger and antiquarian dealer. In addition to selling genuine items from his large memorabilia collection, he sold some of his forgeries with great success, making him a criminal as well. He even sold paintings allegedly created by Hitler. Kujau also forged handwritten copies of Hitler's infamous two-volume book *Mein Kampf* (1925-1926; *My Struggle*, 1939, complete translation). He fabricated inscriptions and additions and sold them to unsuspecting collectors. Any authority on the period, however, would know that the original manuscript of *Mein Kampf* had been typewritten, not handwritten.

In 1979, Gerd Heidemann, a reporter for the popular German weekly magazine *Stern* (star), obtained some of the diaries (Kujau's forgeries) but would not disclose where he got them. Before making contact with Kujau, he had learned of the 1945 crash of the SS plane and the existence of a mysterious box that contained almost thirty volumes of the diaries; the box, as it turned out, was in Kujau's possession. (Heidemann, who had been in the *Hitler-jugend*—the Hitler Youth movement—as a boy, was fascinated with the Nazi period and even knew a number of prominent former Nazis.)

Heidemann urged Kujau to sell the diaries to *Stern*, but Kujau initially was reluctant to sell for fear of being found out as a fraud. The offer, however, was too tempting. Kujau agreed to the sale but requested that his name be left out of the arrangements. He then forged more of the diaries in preparation for their transfer to *Stern*. He delivered the first "volumes" to Heidemann in January, 1981. *Stern* editors accepted them without questioning their authenticity. Kujau provided more diaries, and *Stern* greeted each one with enthusiasm, paying Kujau and Heidemann premiums.

Stern began to offer the diaries to other publications, including the Sunday *Times of London* for serialization, but for a fee. The *Sunday Times*, owned by media mogul Rupert Murdoch, purchased the diaries for $400,000, of which it paid half, before the forgery became known.

The editors of *Stern*, who debated whether to publish the diary excerpts before checking for authenticity, sent several photocopied pages from the diaries to the German Federal Archives (GFA). They also sent page copies to the noted British historian Hugh Trevor-Roper, who had worked as a military historian for the British armed services during World War II and had written several books and articles on Hitler, including the popular and well-received book *The Last Days of Hitler*. It should be noted, however, that despite his work on the war period and Nazi Germany, Trevor-Roper's main area of expertise was seventeenth century England. After his examination of the handwriting samples, Trevor-Roper assured the editors the diaries were real, stating, "I would stake my reputation" on their authenticity.

Within days, the publishers became skeptical. *Stern* asked Heidemann to look at the charges more closely. Heidemann, whose own interests depended on the dairies' authenticity, merely asked Kujau if the diaries were real. Naturally, Kujau assured Heidemann they were authentic. *Stern* held a dramatic press conference, led by editor in chief Peter Koch, on April 22, 1983, to announce its possession of the priceless diaries. Two days later, the *Sunday Times* announced its own acquisition of copies of the diaries in the news article, "Hitler's Secret Diaries to be Published." The following day, April 25, *Stern* published excerpts from the diaries, boldly announcing on its cover, "Hitlers Tagebücher entdeckt" (Hitler's diaries discovered).

By not allowing experts to examine the diaries directly before publication, *Stern* fell into a serious situation. Any reputable Hitler expert could have easily discovered the fraud. Upon publication of the diary excerpts, some experts were taken by their enthusiasm for such a find, but others were skeptical and saw clear inconsistencies. Kujau claimed that the diaries were in Hitler's own hand. Historians of the period argued that this was doubtful because Hitler suffered serious injuries in the attempt on his life in 1944 by a group of army officers, and he could not write legibly because of the injuries. Furthermore, those persons close to Hitler said that he had little time to write and would not do so if he could. In addition, the entries in the diaries were inane. They

showed little new information and much of what they did show contradicted other documents and archives. For example, the diaries indicated that Hitler was not personally involved with much of the actions against the Jews and the Holocaust.

David Irving, a well-known and respected scholar on Hitler, first proclaimed that the handwriting and language were not those of Hitler. He would later say the diaries were real. The uproar caused by the skeptics prompted *Stern* to seek further authentication. However, the effort backfired. A group of experts, including chemists, showed that ink used in the diaries and the bindings on the volumes were of postwar composition and that the diaries could not have been written before 1945. On May 6, the GFA in Koblenz proclaimed the diaries to be a fraud.

The publisher and editors of *Stern*, embarrassed and shocked by the revelation, fired Heidemann and others responsible for the fraud. The police also sought Kujau, who initially claimed that he had bought the diaries from someone in East Germany,

Journalist Gerd Heidemann holds up the alleged diaries of Adolf Hitler at a Stern *magazine news conference in Hamburg, Germany, on April 25, 1983. The diaries later proved to be forgeries.* (AP/Wide World Photos)

but his story was filled with inconsistencies. Finally, Kujau admitted his guilt and implicated Heidemann in the plot because the reporter did not give him a full share of money he received from *Stern*. On May 11, *Stern* announced that it would release the forgeries to prosecutors. The magazine had initially refused to do so.

IMPACT

In August, 1984, Kujau and Heidemann, along with Kujau's wife, Edith Leibling, were tried. Kurt Groenewald, Kujau's attorney, tried to lessen Kujau's guilt by shifting the blame to *Stern* publishers, claiming that they had the responsibility of checking the authenticity of the diaries before not only publishing them but also buying them. He argued that *Stern* neglected to check against forgery because it was eager to improve Hitler's public image and maximize its profits. Heidemann's lawyers claimed that Kujau alone was the forger, that their client was not involved in the plot. They argued he kept none of the money paid for the diaries and also blamed *Stern* for the scandal. Leibling's lawyers simply claimed she was not involved.

During trial, *Stern* witnesses were inconsistent in their testimony, leading Judge Hans-Ulrich Schroe-

der to conclude that they deserved much of the blame for the scandal. He said in his sentencing that the magazine "acted with such naivete and negligence that it was virtually an accomplice in the fraud." The judges found all three of the defendants guilty. Kujau and Heidemann were sentenced to four and a half years (about half the maximum allowable) in prison, and Leibling received eight months probation.

Kujau was released from prison in 1988 because he was suffering from stomach cancer. He continued a life of petty crime until his death in 2000. For *Stern*, its reputation was severely damaged. Editor Koch resigned, as did other top editors. Many regard the publication of the fake diary excerpts as one of the lowest points in twentieth century journalism and magazine publishing, not only in Germany but also the world.

—*Frederick B. Chary*

FURTHER READING

Hamilton, Charles. *The Hitler Diaries: Fakes That Fooled the World.* Lexington: University Press of Kentucky, 1991. A somewhat superficial narrative of the hoax, written by a handwriting expert. Lacks the detail of Robert Harris's account.

Harris, Robert. *Selling Hitler.* London: Arrow Books, 2000. Relates the story of the scandal in detail. Includes an account of David Irving's role in exposing the hoax.

Magnuson, Ed. "Hitler's Forged Diaries." *Time*, May 16, 1983. A comprehensive account of the hoax written in an accessible style. An excellent example of reportage from the time of the scandal. Also available online through *Time* magazine's Web site.

Rendell, Kenneth. *Forging History: The Detection of Fake Letters and Documents.* Norman: University of Oklahoma Press, 1994. Discusses the methods for detecting forgeries through examination of handwriting, paper, and ink. Uses the case of the forged Hitler diaries as an example of detection methods at work.

Rentschler, Eric. "The Fascination of a Fake: The

Hitler Diaries." *New German Critique* 90 (Fall, 2003): 177-192. A scholarly study of the forgery that argues the hoax was part of the sociological phenomenon of popular curiosity and fascination with Hitler and the Third Reich.

See also: Oct. 25, 1924: Forged Communist Letter Brings Down British Government; June 5, 1944: Australian Poets Claim Responsibility for a Literary Hoax; Nov. 21, 1953: Piltdown Man Is Revealed to Be a Hoax; Oct. 26, 1962: West German Police Raid *Der Spiegel* Magazine Offices; Jan. 28, 1972: Clifford Irving Admits Faking Howard Hughes Memoirs; Nov. 9, 1976: German Generals Must Retire for Supporting a Neo-Nazi Pilot; Apr. 15, 1981: Janet Cooke Admits Fabricating Her Pulitzer Prize-Winning Feature; Spring, 1996: Physicist Publishes a Deliberately Fraudulent Article; Mar. 12, 1997: Prize-Winning Aborigine Novelist Revealed as a Fraud; June 18, 2001: Historian Joseph J. Ellis Is Accused of Lying.

July 20, 1983
Congress Members Censured in House-Page Sex Scandal

The House Ethics Committee began an investigation into accusations that certain members of the U.S. Congress were engaging in sexual relations with teenage House pages. Although the committee found no wrongdoing during the period in question, it did find that two representatives, Gerry Studds in 1973 and Daniel Crane in 1980, had consensual but inappropriate relationships with pages. Both members were censured by Congress.

Also known as: Congressional page sex scandal
Locale: Washington, D.C.
Categories: Sex crimes; sex; government; drugs; families and children; public morals

Key Figures

Gerry Studds (1937-2006), U.S. representative from Massachusetts, 1973-1997
Daniel Crane (b. 1936), U.S. representative from Illinois, 1979-1985
Tip O'Neill (1912-1994), U.S. representative from Massachusetts, 1953-1987, and Speaker of the House, 1977-1987
Louis Stokes (b. 1925), U.S. representative from Ohio, 1969-1999, and chairman of House Ethics Committee

Summary of Event

The House Page Program, for students in their junior year of high school, is an immersion program that introduces students to the day-to-day workings of the U.S. House of Representatives. Pages, who live in Washington, D.C., during their residency in the program, run errands for House members, assist with telephone calls in the cloakroom, and assist on the House floor as needed. In addition to working on Capitol Hill as paid employees of the House, pages also attend early-morning classes.

The program has been in place for more than two hundred years, though the House as an institution has changed. About seventy-two pages serve in a given year. The program is administered by the clerk of the House, and daily activities are overseen by staff of the residence hall and school and by work staff. At the program's inception, only males were allowed to serve as pages, but females earned a permanent place in the program in 1973.

Until the early 1980's, pages were responsible for finding their own lodging and were largely unsupervised after leaving work. In 1982, however, a page commission recommended creating a residence hall near Capitol Hill for all pages so they could be properly supervised. Concurrently, the commission also recommended the establishment

Gerry Studds in 1995. (AP/Wide World Photos)

The committee did find, however, that two representatives had been sexually involved with pages prior to the time in question. Neither politician broke the law, however, because sixteen years old is the age of consent in Washington, D.C. In 1973, Gerry Studds had been in a consensual relationship with a seventeen-year-old male page. The youth was invited to Studds's Georgetown apartment and traveled with him during a two-week vacation to Portugal. When confronted with the charges in 1982, Studds admitted to the affair, stating that he had made a "very serious error in judgment." He made a public statement, in which he came out as gay and stated that he should not have engaged in a sexual relationship with a subordinate.

Representative Daniel Crane also had an affair with a seventeen-year-old page, a girl, in 1980. She had visited his apartment multiple times and testified that she was "perhaps more responsible for the sexual relationship than he was." While the relationship was consensual, Crane tearfully apologized for his behavior but said he did not violate his oath of office. The Ethics Committee recommended on July 14, 1983, that the two Congress members be formally reprimanded, but the full House pushed for a more serious punishment: Studds and Crane were censured by the House on July 20.

Studds and Crane ran for reelection in 1984. Crane won the Republican primary for his district but ultimately lost his seat to Terry Bruce in the general election. Studds, the first openly gay member of Congress, won the 1984 Democratic primary and the general election and served in the House until 1997. Crane returned to dentistry after his defeat in 1984. Studds married his long-time partner in 2004, just one week after the state of Massachusetts legalized marriage between persons of the same gender.

of a page board composed of current members of the House, "to ensure that the Page program is conducted in a manner that is consistent with the efficient functioning of the House and welfare of the Pages."

In 1982, a former House page claimed he had sexual relationships with three members of Congress. Speculation soon arose that Congress members also were involved in drug deals with pages. The Federal Bureau of Investigation (FBI) launched an investigation into the accusations. Several pages who were interviewed said they had feared their jobs would be in jeopardy had they not consented to the relationships.

After learning of the FBI investigation, Speaker of the House Tip O'Neill and Representative Louis Stokes, chairman of the House Ethics Committee, launched a congressional investigation into the accusations. The committee found that the former page's accusations were ungrounded, and investigators found no inappropriate behavior between members and pages during the 1981-1982 page cycle, the time period on which the investigation centered. Also dismissed were accusations about drug use.

Studds died two years later from a pulmonary embolism.

Impact

The page scandal led Speaker O'Neill to form a page commission in 1982 to reevaluate the program. Many questioned why the program was still operating and whether it should be retired, and changes were suggested in an effort to protect the pages and better serve the House membership. Pages now live in a residence hall located several blocks from the Capitol Building (pages formerly resided at the Old Congressional Hotel). This provides better supervision of the minors when they are not at work. A page board also was instituted, consisting of two Congress members from the majority party, one member from the minority party, the clerk of the House, and the House sergeant-at-arms. An official Page Program code of conduct also was developed, allowing for the immediate dismissal of any page found in violation of program rules.

The allegations of inappropriate contact between members of Congress and House pages did not cease following the findings of the Ethics Committee in the case of Crane and Studds. In 2006, scandal rocked Capitol Hill as Representative Mark Foley resigned amid allegations of sending sexually explicit electronic communications (e-mail and instant messages) to former House pages. House leadership came under fire for the way it dealt with previous reports of questionable behavior by Foley, leading to the early retirement of Speaker J. Dennis Hastert in November, 2007. The page board had been expanded in early 2007 to address ongoing concerns with the program and attempt to prevent similar sex scandals.

In December, the House Page Program came under scrutiny again when two Republican members of the page board resigned. Both board members stated that the clerk of the House did not notify them immediately of inappropriate page conduct. In this case, four pages—two for shoplifting and two for inappropriate sexual activity—had been expelled from the program during the fall, 2007, semester. House leadership was criticized once again for not disclosing all evidence presented to the page board.

House Speaker Nancy Pelosi, like others before her, called for an investigation into the charges and for further evaluation of the program.

—*Tessa Li Powell*

Further Reading

Amer, Mildred. "Pages of the United States Congress: History, Background Information, and Proposals for Change." *CRS Report for Congress*, February 6, 2007. Describes the page program and highlights changes that have been made or proposed since the Mark Foley scandal in 2006.

"Capitol Scandal." *Time*, July 12, 1982. Documents the reaction of Congress to the FBI investigation into possible scandals involving House pages.

"Housecleaning." *Time*, July 5, 1983. Reports on the investigation by the House into allegations of inappropriate conduct between pages and House members. Includes apologies from Daniel Crane and Gerry Studds.

Long, Kim. *The Almanac of Political Corruption, Scandals, and Dirty Politics*. New York: Delacorte Press, 2007. A wide-ranging book detailing the various scandals and corrupt practices that have plagued U.S. politics.

Roberts, Robert North. *Ethics in U.S. Government: An Encyclopedia of Investigations, Scandals, Reforms, and Legislation*. Westport, Conn.: Greenwood Press, 2001. A comprehensive encyclopedia documenting political scandals, ethical controversies, and investigations in the U.S. government between 1775 and 2000.

Turley, Jonathan. "A Page Protection Act: The Path to Saving a Historic Program." *Roll Call*, October 5, 2006. Written by a page alum and legal professor. Addresses the problems with the current page board and steps that should be taken to maintain the program.

See also: June 23, 1967: Senator Thomas J. Dodd Is Censured for Misappropriating Funds; Oct. 7, 1974: Congressman Wilbur D. Mills's Stripper Affair Leads to His Downfall; Oct. 25, 1974: Evangelist Billy James Hargis Resigns College Presidency During Gay-Sex Scandal; Sept., 1976:

1980's

Jimmy Carter Admits Committing Adultery in His Heart; Sept. 3, 1980: Congressman Bauman Is Arrested for Liaison with Teenage Boy; July 20, 1982: Conservative Politician John G. Schmitz Is Found to Have Children Out of Wedlock; Aug. 5, 1994: Kenneth Starr Is Appointed to the Whitewater Investigation; Jan. 17, 1998: President Bill Clinton Denies Sexual Affair with

a White House Intern; Sept. 19, 2000: Ex-gay Leader John Paulk Is Photographed Leaving a Gay Bar; Apr. 30, 2001: Washington Intern Chandra Levy Disappears; Dec. 6, 2005: Spokane, Washington, Mayor Recalled in Gay-Sex Scandal; Sept. 29, 2006: Congressman Mark Foley Resigns in Sex Scandal Involving a Teenage Page.

August 12, 1983-July 27, 1990
MCMARTIN PRESCHOOL IS EMBROILED IN CHILD-ABUSE CASE

The McMartin Preschool was at the center of one of the costliest and longest criminal trials in American history after its owners and several teachers were accused of sexually abusing the children in their care. The case, which initiated public hysteria over child sex-abuse, ended with no convictions but altered public views of child-abuse cases and pressured the justice system to modify how it handles such cases.

ALSO KNOWN AS: McMartin Preschool trial
LOCALE: Manhattan Beach, California
CATEGORIES: Law and the courts; hoaxes, frauds, and charlatanism; families and children; education; sex crimes

KEY FIGURES

Judy Johnson (1944-1986), parent of a student at McMartin Preschool
Virginia McMartin (c. 1907-1995), McMartin Preschool founder and owner
Raymond Buckey (b. 1955), preschool teacher
Peggy McMartin Buckey (1926-2001), preschool teacher
Peggy Ann Buckey (b. 1956), preschool teacher
Kee MacFarlane (fl. 1980's), social worker-psychologist

SUMMARY OF EVENT

The child-abuse allegations that emerged against McMartin Preschool owners and teachers in 1983 led to one of the longest and costliest trials in American history and initiated public hysteria over child sex-abuse in schools. Located in Manhattan Beach, near Los Angeles, California, the family-owned and operated preschool was a popular and acclaimed school with a long waiting list. The preschool's strong reputation contributed to the magnitude of the shock and outrage felt by the Manhattan Beach community—and all of Southern California—when the scandal surfaced.

The investigation began on August 12, 1983, when Judy Johnson, the mother of a two-year-old boy who attended the school, filed a complaint with police. Johnson reported that she had taken her son to a pediatrician after he complained of rectal discomfort and pain. She claimed that her son had been sexually abused and sodomized by the preschool's only male teacher, Raymond Buckey, during satanic rituals at the school.

Buckey was arrested on September 7 but soon released because of a lack of evidence. The following day, the Manhattan Beach Police Department issued a letter to two hundred parents whose children had attended the preschool, explaining its investigation into the allegations. The letter informed parents that Buckey was under investigation and that parents should speak with their children to learn whether or not their child had been victimized, had witnessed a classmate being abused, or had any other information about Buckey's activities at the preschool.

Knowledge of the McMartin investigation quickly spread throughout the community, caused mass panic, and led to death threats against the McMartin Preschool owners and teachers. It also led to the collective withdrawal of children by their parents from McMartin and neighboring preschools. The number of abuse reports soared after parents began to interrogate their children.

In October, 1983, McMartin parents were instructed to take their children to the Child Sexual Abuse Center at Children's Institute International (CII) for further evaluation. The review was headed by CII investigator and center director Kee Mac-Farlane. CII therapists videotaped their interviews with the children and used dolls to help the children articulate the alleged sex acts. Most of the children first denied being abused, but many later recanted and began to tell stories of sex abuse. The children's descriptions gradually transformed into incredible stories of satanic rituals, blood drinking, animal mutilation and sacrifice, corpse desecration, naked games, child pornography, hidden underground tunnels and rooms, and flying witches. From a lineup of photographs, the children named the preschool owners and teachers as their abusers, but they also selected from the photos community leaders, celebrities, and other public figures, such as actor Chuck Norris, as abusers.

The children also were evaluated by medical doctors for physical signs of sex abuse. By November, CII investigators determined that more than three hundred sixty of the four hundred children they interviewed had been sexually abused, a claim that intensified public hysteria and incited violence, including vandalism against the preschool building. The findings also led to a rise in child sex-abuse re-

ports from other preschools. After nearly thirty years in the preschool business, the McMartins closed the school on January 13, 1984, as the scandal began to dominate national headlines.

On March 22, McMartin owners and teachers were arrested and initially charged with one hundred fifteen counts of child molestation, despite weak evidence. The accused included the McMartin family—founder Virginia McMartin, Peggy McMartin Buckey, Raymond Buckey, Peggy Ann Buckey—and three of the preschool's teachers—Betty Raidor, Babette Spitler, and Mary Ann Jackson. By April, the scandal prompted other states to investigate their own growing reports of child sex-abuse. In May, the charges against the McMartin defendants included more than two hundred counts of child molestation and one count of conspiracy involving more than forty children.

During the pretrial from August, 1984, to January, 1986, the court examined the testimony of CII interviewers, doctors, child psychologists, child sex-abuse experts, and child witnesses. The case weakened as witness testimonies conflicted and McMartin parents kept their children from partici-

1980's

FALSE ALLEGATIONS OF SEXUAL ABUSE

Approximately 60 percent of all sexual abuse allegations receive dispositions of "unsubstantiated." A significant portion of these cases are false allegations, not harmless errors made by well-meaning persons. While one of the main purposes of the Child Abuse Prevention and Treatment Act of 1974 was to make reporting of suspected abuse easier, it has had the unintended consequence of creating a climate that encourages false allegations. The act provides immunity from prosecution for persons who report alleged abuse, thereby shielding even those who choose to make false allegations to harm another person's reputation (this is often the case in many divorces).

Once a child is in contact with the legal system and seen as a victim, the system tends to seek confirmation for that victim status. Social workers and those in law enforcement are well meaning but often untrained in interview techniques that are appropriate for alleged child victims of abuse. The investigators often ask leading questions, unintentionally encouraging children to give responses that are consistent with being victimized.

POLICE LETTER TO PARENTS OF McMARTIN STUDENTS

September 8, 1983

Dear Parent:

This Department is conducting a criminal investigation involving child molestation (288 P.C.). Ray Buckey, an employee of Virginia McMartin's Pre-School, was arrested September 7, 1983 by this Department.

The following procedure is obviously an unpleasant one, but to protect the rights of your children as well as the rights of the accused, this inquiry is necessary for a complete investigation.

Records indicate that your child has been or is currently a student at the pre-school. We are asking your assistance in this continuing investigation. Please question your child to see if he or she has been a witness to any crime or if he or she has been a victim. Our investigation indicates that possible criminal acts include: oral sex, fondling of genitals, buttock or chest area, and sodomy, possibly committed under the pretense of "taking the child's temperature." Also photos may have been taken of children without their clothing. Any information from your child regarding having ever observed Ray Buckey to leave a classroom alone with a child during any nap period, or if they have ever observed Ray Buckey tie up a child, is important.

Please complete the enclosed information form and return it to this Department in the enclosed stamped return envelope as soon as possible. We will contact you if circumstances dictate same.

We ask you to please keep this investigation strictly confidential because of the nature of the charges and the highly emotional effect it could have on our community. Please do not discuss this investigation with anyone outside your immediate family. Do not contact or discuss the investigation with Raymond Buckey, any member of the accused defendant's family, or employees connected with the McMartin Pre-School.

[Note: The following paragraph was in all capital letters in original] There is no evidence to indicated [sic] that the management of Virginia McMartin's pre-school had any knowledge of this situation and no detrimental information concerning the operation of the school has been discovered during this investigation. Also, no other employee in the school is under investigation for any criminal act.

Your prompt attention to this matter and reply no late than September 16, 1983 will be appreciated.

Harry L. Kuhlmeyer, Jr.
Chief of Police

John Wehner
Captain

pating in the court's interrogations. In March of 1985, enraged parents protested the court's actions by attempting to uncover, as a group, the tunnel at the preschool that had been described by their children. A private archaeological firm contracted by the Los Angeles District Attorney's Office on March 20 continued the excavation, but workers found no evidence of a tunnel or entryway.

On January 17, the court dropped charges against five of the seven defendants because of insufficient evidence. In preparation for the trial, prosecutors charged Raymond and Peggy Buckey with more than one hundred counts of child molestation. The exoneration of the other five defendants drew public protests, as crowds displaying signs in support of the McMartin children gathered outside the courthouse. On December 19, Judy Johnson, the mother who first alleged the child abuse at McMartin, died of liver disease; she had been an alcoholic. Prior to her death, she also had been diagnosed with paranoid schizophrenia, and although her condition may have been a factor in the abuse allegations, the McMartin trial continued in full force nevertheless.

On July 14, 1987, four years after the investigations began, the trial commenced with opening statements. Witness testimony and videotapes of the children's interviews were once again reviewed, but the evidence against the two defendants—Raymond and Peggy Buckey—remained weak and unclear. The Buckeys continued to proclaim their innocence throughout the trial.

Peggy Buckey was acquitted on January 18, 1990. She had spent two years in jail during the investigation and trial. All but thirteen charges against Raymond Buckey were dropped. Jurors cited the weak evidence and the suggestive and coercive manner in which evaluators obtained child testimonies as reasons for their deadlocking. Following her acquittal, Peggy Buckey filed a defamation lawsuit and Raymond Buckey prepared for his second trial (on the remaining thirteen charges), scheduled for May. For the second trial, the prosecution made a thorough excavation of the preschool grounds. Several collapsed tunnels were found underneath the preschool. However, research into when the tunnels had been built remained inconclusive. On July 27 the jury again deadlocked on the charges against Raymond Buckey, forcing the judge to declare a mistrial. District Attorney Ira Reiner decided not to pursue a third trial.

Raymond Buckey had served five years in jail during the investigation and trial. The McMartin case lasted for seven years, cost taxpayers sixteen million dollars, and ended without a single conviction. In 1991, the preschool was demolished.

IMPACT

The McMartin Preschool scandal—along with its hysteria, panic, and media coverage—convinced the public that child sex-abuse was a significant social problem. Although the case was referred to as a contemporary witch hunt that destroyed the lives of many people and saw death threats, vandalism, and physical attacks, the McMartin trial also inspired changes in the justice system. The courts, first of all, gained a new perspective on child-abuse allegations. The testimonies of children are now viewed with more caution and skepticism. The guidelines for conducting child interviews and utilizing child testimony during trials have been revised to reduce the harmful psychological and emotional effects the process may have upon children. Finally, defendant liberties have been reduced to avoid long trials.

—*Sheena Garitta*

FURTHER READING

Butler, Edgar, et al. *Anatomy of the McMartin Child Molestation Case*. Lanham, Md.: University Press of America, 2001. A comprehensive overview of the case, from the initial criminal charges

to pretrial publicity to the juries to the rights of alleged victims and perpetrators.

Carlson, Margaret. "Six Years Trial by Torture." *Time*, January 29, 1990. A brief overview of the McMartin case. Argues that the children were victimized by the criminal justice system.

Eberle, Paul, and Shirley Eberle. *The Abuse of Innocence: The McMartin Preschool Trial*. Buffalo, N.Y.: Prometheus Books, 2003. Provides a scandal time line and presents excerpts from the pretrial investigations and trial testimony.

Reinhold, Robert. "How Lawyers and the Media Turned the McMartin Case into a Tragic Circus." *The New York Times*, January 25, 1990. Discusses several mistakes made by prosecutors that led to the exoneration of all seven defendants and how the media shaped the public's views toward child abuse.

Talbot, Margaret. "The Devil in the Nursery." *The New York Times Magazine*, January 7, 2001. Offers a brief analysis of the effects of mass panic and hysteria on legal proceedings, using the McMartin case as an example of that panic.

Vieth, Victor I., Bette L. Bottoms, and Alison Perona, eds. *Ending Child Abuse: New Efforts in Prevention, Investigation, and Training*. Binghamton, N.Y.: Haworth Press, 2006. Social scientists and legal scholars examine concepts in the field of child abuse prevention as well as training methods, prosecution strategies, and other issues.

SEE ALSO: Mar. 2, 1906: Psychoanalyst Ernest Jones Is Accused of Molesting Mentally Disabled Children; Mar. 30, 1931: "Scottsboro Boys" Are Railroaded Through Rape Trials; Mar., 1990: Menendez Brothers Are Arrested for Murdering Their Parents; Aug. 16, 1996: Belgian Media Reveal How Police Bungled Serial Murder Case; Jan. 30, 2001: Liverpool Children's Hospital Collects Body Parts Without Authorization; June 30, 2001: Korean Religious Teacher Jung Myung Seok Is Charged with Rape; Jan. 6, 2002: *Boston Globe* Reports on Child Sexual Abuse by Roman Catholic Priests; Dec. 18, 2003: Pop Star Michael Jackson Is Charged with Child Molestation.

1980's

August 21, 1983
FILIPINO OPPOSITION LEADER AQUINO IS ASSASSINATED ON RETURN HOME

Benigno Aquino, Jr., became a focus of the opposition to President Ferdinand Marcos. After years of imprisonment in the Philippines and three years of exile in the United States, he returned to the Philippines only to face the bullets of assassins at Manila airport. His scandalous murder provoked public outrage and led to the overthrow of the dictatorial Marcos, the election of Corazón Aquino as president in 1985, and to his martyrdom.

LOCALE: Manila, Philippines
CATEGORIES: Murder and suicide; government; politics; violence

KEY FIGURES

Benigno Aquino, Jr. (1932-1983), Filipino senator, 1967-1972, and opponent of Ferdinand Marcos
Ferdinand Marcos (1917-1989), president of the Philippines, 1965-1986
Rolando Galman (1950-1983), Filipino gangster and alleged assassin
Fabian Ver (1920-1998), Filipino general and chief of the armed forces
Corazón Aquino (b. 1933), president of the Philippines, 1986-1992
Imelda Marcos (b. 1929), wife of Ferdinand Marcos

SUMMARY OF EVENT

The rivalry between Filipino president Ferdinand Marcos and his chief political opponent, Benigno Aquino, Jr., came to a violent end on August 21, 1983, when Aquino, who had also become a voice for democratic change, was assassinated at Manila International Airport after leaving the airplane that brought him back to the Philippines. He had just returned to his homeland from the United States, where he had been in exile for three years.

Marcos had been elected president of the Philippines in 1965. Limited by the constitution to two terms in office, he was mandated to leave the presidency in 1973. Aquino, a popular senator, was the most likely victor in the forthcoming presidential election. Instead of leaving office, Marcos declared martial law in 1972, assumed dictatorial powers, and imprisoned Aquino for seven years before exiling him to seek medical care in the United States.

Aquino resided in Newton, Massachusetts, and taught at Wellesley College, the Massachusetts Institute of Technology, and Harvard University. Aquino also kept in touch with the opposition to the Marcos regime. In August, 1983, Aquino decided to return to his homeland. Marcos had been in ill health, his dictatorship was increasingly unpopular, and Aquino hoped that the opposition would coalesce upon his return. However, both Marcos's flamboyant and powerful wife, Imelda Marcos, and Marcos's loyal supporter, the chief of the armed forces, General Fabian Ver, had publicly warned Aquino against returning to the Philippines.

Because the Filipino government was monitoring Aquino's travels, Aquino began his trip with evasive maneuvers, traveling with a fake Philippines passport under the name Marcial Bonifacio. On August 13, he flew from Boston to Los Angeles. He then flew to Singapore, Malaysia, and Hong Kong, and finally landed in Taipei, Taiwan. Aquino had determined to fly to Manila from Taipei, in part because Taiwan did not have diplomatic relations with the Philippines and, thus, was somewhat immune from Marcos's pressure.

On the morning of August 21, Aquino telephoned his family from the Grand Hotel in Taipei. He spoke with each of his children and listened to his religiously devout wife, Corazón Aquino, read a passage from the Bible. At 11:15 A.M., he left for Manila on China Airlines flight 811, accompanied by his brother-in-law and American Broadcasting

Company (ABC) news reporter Ken Kashiwahara, friend Noy Brizuela, about ten other journalists, and two Japanese television crews. Although Aquino believed the presence of the media afforded him some protection, he was also wearing a bulletproof vest.

Aquino's plane landed at 1:03 P.M. The plane was detained on the runway and several soldiers boarded the plane. While the other passengers were ordered to stay in their seats, the soldiers led Aquino out of the plane and onto the tarmac. Passengers on the plane reported hearing a jumble of voices, with shouts of "Shoot him! Shoot him!"

A single gunshot rang out moments later, at 1:15 P.M. Within seconds there was a barrage of shots. Two men lay dead on the tarmac: One was Aquino and the other was an unknown shooter later identified as petty gangster Rolando Galman. Aquino had sustained a fatal gunshot wound to the back of the head. The Marcos government claimed that Aquino had been killed by Galman, who in turn had been killed by an avalanche of bullets from the soldiers. This claim was met by widespread skepticism, if for no other reason than that Galman would have had to penetrate the one-thousand-person security force with which the Filipino army had surrounded the plane to get off his perfect shot. In contrast to the reaction of the Marcos government, Corazón Aquino would gain widespread sympathy for the dignified manner in which she returned to the Philippines for the funeral of her murdered husband.

Suspicion for the assassination fell on Ferdinand and Imelda Marcos and on General Ver. To deflect these suspicions, President Marcos appointed a commission headed by Chief Justice Enrique Fernando to investigate the facts of the assassination. After its hearings were frustrated, the commission was replaced in October 22 by a fact-finding board chaired by Justice Corazón Agrava. After an exhaus-

tive yearlong investigation, the Agrava board dismissed the army's version of the assassination and blamed a conspiracy of military officers for arranging the murder. Particularly incriminating was the autopsy evidence, which indicated that Aquino had been shot from an elevated position behind him, and eyewitness testimony that he was shot by the soldiers leading him down the stairs from the plane. Marcos was compelled to suspend Ver and ordered a trial of several military men before a special court, which acquitted the soldiers. The result outraged Filipinos and alarmed the United States, the most important ally of the Marcos regime.

In November, 1985, Marcos ordered a snap presidential election, convinced he would win. To his surprise Corazón Aquino announced that she would run for president. With the urging of Manila's Roman Catholic cardinal Jaime Sin, the powerful opposition leader Salvador Laurel threw his support behind Aquino as her vice presidential candidate. The election was marred by massive fraud, and no clear winner emerged. Millions of Filipinos took to the streets in protest, with the support of Minister of Defense Juan Ponce Enrile and General Fidel V. Ramos, who broke with Marcos. On February 25,

Philippine presidential candidate Corazón Aquino visiting, in December, 1985, the grave site of her late husband Benigno Aquino, Jr., who was assassinated in 1983. (Hulton Archive/Getty Images)

1986, Aquino and Laurel were sworn into office. The Marcos family and key supporters, including General Ver and his family, fled to Hawaii.

Aquino would serve as president until 1992. During her administration, fourteen soldiers were tried, convicted, and imprisoned for the murder of her husband, Benigno Aquino, Jr.

IMPACT

World-renowned figures have fallen to assassin's bullets, many of those killed during the twentieth century. Aquino's assassination ranks high on the scale of national and international impact. His murder at the Manila airport on August 21, 1983, was the catalyst for the People's Revolution in the Philippines, which, within two years, overthrew one of the world's richest and most entrenched dictators and brought about a revolution of hope.

The assassination of Aquino was of course a personal tragedy. His death left grieving family, friends, and supporters throughout the world. One can only imagine the pain felt by the intermediaries who assisted his surreptitious return to the Philippines only to learn that he was killed within minutes of his arrival. Although their efforts had tragic consequences, in the long run they must know that they played a precipitating role in bringing democracy to the Philippines.

Although the Marcos regime was able to avoid legal blame for the killing, its efforts proved to be in vain. The quiet dignity of Corazón Aquino, the support of Cardinal Jaime Sin, the last-minute alliance with Laurel, Ramos, and Enrile brought the Philippines its long overdue democracy. Aquino in his death became a national hero. The airport where he was gunned down was named for him, and August 21, the day of his death, was declared a national holiday.

—Howard Bromberg

FURTHER READING

Burton, Sandra. *Impossible Dream: The Marcoses, the Aquinos, and the Unfinished Revolution.* New York: Warner Books, 1989. An account of the assassination, investigation, and revolution by an American journalist who interviewed and accompanied Aquino on the flight to Manila. Burton also explains the basis of the adulation of the Aquinos and the hatred of the Marcoses.

Hill, Gerald N., and Kathleen Thompson Hill. *Aquino Assassination: The True Story and Analysis of the Assassination of Philippine Senator Benigno S. Aquino, Jr.* Sonoma, Calif.: Hilltop, 1983. Account of the assassination by an American lawyer and human rights advocate, with a commentary by the director of the Ninoy Aquino Movement for Freedom, Peace, and Democracy, who places responsibility for the murder directly on Ferdinand Marcos. Includes a time line and photographs of the assassination.

Reid, Robert H., and Eileen Guerrero. *Corazón Aquino and the Brushfire Revolution.* Baton Rouge: Louisiana State University Press, 1995. A fairly dense scholarly history of Corazón Aquino's rise to power from her husband's assassination through her election to the Philippine presidency and her ineffectual revolution.

Simons, Lewis M. *Worth Dying For.* New York: William Morrow, 1987. Straightforward account of the assassination and the revolution it sparked. Based on hundreds of interviews and the findings of the Agrava commission.

Umali, Ramoncito F. *Who Killed Senator Aquino: The Unsolved Assassination.* New York: iUniverse, 2005. A personalized account by the janitorial manager responsible for cleaning the scene of Aquino's assassination on the airport tarmac.

SEE ALSO: Aug. 14, 1963: Madame Nhu Derides Self-Immolation of Vietnamese Buddhists; Oct. 29, 1965: Moroccan Politician Mehdi Ben Barka Disappears in Paris; May 11, 1982: Philippine President Marcos Forces the Entire Supreme Court to Resign; Feb. 28, 1995: Former Mexican President Carlos Salinas's Brother Is Arrested for Murder.

October 14, 1983
British Cabinet Secretary Parkinson Resigns After His Secretary Becomes Pregnant

Cecil Parkinson was secretary of state for trade and industry in the Conservative government of Prime Minister Margaret Thatcher. It was revealed that his former secretary, Sara Keays, was pregnant, and he was the father. Parkinson met with public disapproval for his lack of contact with his child in the years after her birth.

Locale: London, England
Categories: Politics; sex; government; public morals; families and children; women's issues

Key Figures
Cecil Parkinson (b. 1931), chairman of the Conservative Party and cabinet member under Margaret Thatcher
Sara Keays (b. 1948), Parkinson's parliamentary secretary and mistress
Margaret Thatcher (b. 1925), British prime minister, 1979-1990

Summary of Event
Cecil Parkinson was a high-flying member of British prime minister Margaret Thatcher's Conservative government from its election in 1979 until the revelation of his affair with his former parliamentary secretary, Sara Keays, in 1983. He resigned his cabinet post on October 14. After four years in relative obscurity in Parliament, he was again promoted to cabinet rank by Thatcher. When she resigned as party leader in 1990, Parkinson resigned with her, bringing an end to his political career.

Parkinson came from humble origins, being the son of a railway worker in Carnforth, Lancashire. In 1942, the young Parkinson won a scholarship to nearby Lancaster Grammar School, a prestigious high school for academically gifted boys. He did well academically and at track and field events. At one point he was thinking of being ordained into the Church of England, and he was offered a place at Emmanuel College, Cambridge University, to read theology. He accepted the offer but then changed his mind and started to read English instead. He majored in law.

After graduation in 1955, Parkinson found employment as a trainee graduate with the Metal Box Company in London. While studying accountancy there he met Ann Jarvis, whom he married in 1957. They had three daughters, the first born in 1959. Politically, Parkinson had been brought up as a Labour Party supporter, a loyalty he maintained throughout his student years. However, after a period of political neutrality, he joined the Conservative Party in 1959 and was soon active as a public speaker.

In 1961, Parkinson began his own business, then bought up a number of small failing engineering firms between 1967 and 1979 to form a small business empire worth several million pounds. He was asked to stand in the 1970 general election for Northampton, but was unsuccessful. At a by-election in north London few months later, he was elected. He was then reelected for a slightly different constituency in Hertfordshire in 1974, and then again in 1979, the year that Thatcher became the new prime minister. Thatcher had led the Conservatives to power over Labour.

Keays, the daughter of an army colonel, became Parkinson's parliamentary secretary in 1971. They soon were lovers. Over the next few years, Parkinson promised Keays marriage on at least two occasions, and she claimed later to have continued the affair with the expectation of eventually marrying him. She left her job as his secretary in 1979, moved for a year to Brussels, Belgium, then returned to Westminster to take a job as secretary to another member of Parliament. The affair with Parkinson continued uninterrupted, however.

Meanwhile, Parkinson had attracted the favor of Thatcher and was being promoted within the government ranks. In 1981, he was made party chairman and was then included in the cabinet in 1982 as chancellor of the duchy of Lancaster. At the 1983 election, held in the summer, Thatcher was again very successful. She wanted to promote Parkinson to one of the top cabinet jobs, but Keays had already told Parkinson that she was pregnant. She later denied allegations that she allowed the pregnancy to go forward to force Parkinson to marry her.

Parkinson had to tell Thatcher what he believed was bad news. She decided to offer him a lower-level post in the cabinet and pressured him to break off the affair. In June, he became the secretary of state for trade and industry, a new department formed out of two previous departments. In the meantime, Parkinson told his wife of the affair and pregnancy. She and his two older daughters decided the marriage should continue and promised to support Parkinson.

On October 5, attorneys for Parkinson and Keays met and issued a statement in which Parkinson admitted the affair, his desire to marry her, his subsequent decision not to, and an expression of regret at the pain he had caused. The attorneys also announced that no questions would be answered from the press. However, one week later, Keays issued her own statement. She claimed the previous statement by her attorney had not been full enough and that she had been placed in an impossible situation.

A tremendous furor emerged in the press. At the time the scandal erupted, the annual Conservative Party conference was being held. Parkinson attended only to make a speech, which was greeted with great enthusiasm. However, it became obvious that a planned trip to the United States by Parkinson to promote British interests would be seriously compromised, and he offered his resignation to Thatcher. She had defended him all the while but accepted his resignation on October 14. Although he remained a backbench member of Parliament, he claimed that he still received thousands of letters of support.

IMPACT

Parkinson's resignation was the fourth one from a Thatcher cabinet, but it did little harm to her government. Norman Tebbit, a hard-hitting politician, took over Parkinson's job as secretary of state for trade and industry. At a personal level, Parkinson's

political career was on hold, and he became a regular object of satire as Thatcher's government gradually lost its popularity. However, after four years on the backbenches, he reemerged into front line politics, being appointed secretary of state for energy in 1987. He retained his popularity in the Conservative Party throughout the period.

Parkinson also made sure that a far-reaching gag order was issued against the press to protect his daughter, Flora, who was born to Keays in December, 1983. Flora had been born with some birth disorders and suffered from epilepsy and mental disabilities. The gag order was so strict that even school photographs of Flora were prohibited, and the order was in place until she was eighteen years old.

After their daughter's birth, Keays appeared at party conferences, apparently to embarrass Parkinson. She also wrote the book *Question of Judgement* (1985) to reveal her side of the affair. Her novel, *The Black Book*, a thinly disguised account of government corruption, followed in 1987.

The long-term repercussions of the Parkinson-Keays affair did not emerge until the media gag order was lifted in 2001. By this time, Parkinson had left active politics and been made a peer (Lord Parkinson of Carnforth). The affair became a press sensation once more, but this time the media was considerably more sympathetic to Keays. Keays claimed that in those eighteen years in which the gag order was in place, Parkinson never visited his daughter nor did he ever send a birthday card. However, he had made arrangements to pay for her living expenses and education. Keays sued one newspaper for libel, but lost the case and incurred heavy legal costs. She also sold her story several times. Flora appeared on national television in January, 2002, saying she would like to meet her father.

—*David Barratt*

FURTHER READING

Clark, Alan. *Diaries: In Power*. London: Weidenfeld & Nicholson, 2003. Clark's diaries recount the Thatcher and Major years of government and give intimate details into the affairs and indiscretions of a number of ministers.

Keays, Sara. *Question of Judgement.* London: Quintessential Press, 1985. Sara Keays's version of her affair with Parkinson and its subsequent development. A considerably more robust account than that of Parkinson.

Parkinson, Cecil. *Right at the Centre: An Autobiography.* London: Weidenfeld & Nicolson, 1992. Parkinson's autobiography, which covers his life through his retirement from active politics in 1990. Contains remarkably little discussion of the affair with Keays but explores his attempt to keep it a secret.

Thatcher, Margaret. *The Downing Street Years.* New York: HarperCollins, 1995. Thatcher's account of her years as British prime minister and her dealings with one of her favorites, Parkinson.

SEE ALSO: Mar. 2-Sept. 25, 1963: John Profumo Affair Rocks British Government; Aug. 4, 1978: British Politician Jeremy Thorpe Is Charged with Attempted Murder; July 25, 1987: Novelist-Politician Jeffrey Archer Wins Libel Trial Against the *Daily Star*; Sept. 24, 1992: British Cabinet Member David Mellor Resigns over Romantic Affair; Jan. 5, 1994: British Cabinet Member Resigns After Fathering a Child Out of Wedlock; May, 1999: Civil Rights Leader Jesse Jackson Fathers a Child Out of Wedlock; Sept. 28, 2002: British Politician Reveals Her Affair with Prime Minister John Major; Jan. 21, 2006: British Politician Resigns After Gay-Sex Orgy; Apr. 26, 2006: Britain's Deputy Prime Minister Admits Affair with Secretary.

January 25, 1984
JESSE JACKSON CALLS NEW YORK CITY "HYMIETOWN"

Civil rights leader Jesse Jackson called Jews "Hymie" and New York City "Hymietown" in a casual conversation with a reporter during his campaign for president of the United States. His words were printed in The Washington Post *and created a firestorm among Jewish protesters, Black Muslim supporters of Jackson, and much of the press in the United States. The slur did not surprise many, however, because of Jackson's history of making anti-Semitic comments.*

LOCALE: Washington, D.C.
CATEGORIES: Racism; social issues and reform; publishing and journalism; politics; civil rights and liberties

KEY FIGURES
Jesse Jackson (b. 1941), African American civil rights leader and Baptist minister
Milton Coleman (fl. 1980's), reporter for *The Washington Post*
Rick Atkinson (b. 1952), reporter for *The Washington Post*

Louis Farrakhan (b. 1933), leader of the Nation of Islam

SUMMARY OF EVENT
In early 1984, the Reverend Jesse Jackson, a political radical in the Civil Rights movement and a longtime civil rights leader, was campaigning to win the Democratic Party's nomination for the U.S. presidency. He was considered the first credible African American contender for candidacy, given his strong support among blacks. White voters did not seem to support him en masse. He spurred a large black voter turnout in the primaries and was picking up enough delegates to enable him to make the party concede some of his political demands at the Democratic National Convention. However, in a casual conversation with a black reporter on January 25, in a talk he assumed was off the record, he referred to Jews as "hymie" and to New York City as "hymietown."

Jackson had been waiting for a flight from National Airport in Washington, D.C., when Milton Coleman, an African American reporter for *The*

Jesse Jackson. (Library of Congress)

Washington Post, engaged him in a conversation. Jackson warmed up to the chitchat and said they should "talk black talk," that is, speak in confidence because both were black. The two talked about Jackson's campaign and its racial ramifications. Coleman also took note of Jackson's use, in what must have been an unguarded moment, of the terms "hymie" and "hymietown." Not until later, however, did Coleman decide the utterance was too significant to be kept private. Such comments constituted racial slurs, and he perhaps believed that the electorate should know that a person running for president of the United States had uttered anti-Semitic words to denigrate an entire group of people. Prejudice of any kind in a possible president was too important to keep secret from the voters.

Jackson's record on racial issues had been controversial and provocative for some time. Jackson

had a history of anti-Jewish comments, that is, about Jews in general and Israel in particular. In 1979, he suggested Jews were responsible for the ouster of Andrew Young, an African American, as ambassador to the United Nations. He suggested Jews orchestrated the removal because Young had a private meeting with a Palestine Liberation Organization (PLO) agent at the United Nations. (The PLO was the coordinating council for Palestine refugee groups, founded in 1964, which viewed Israel as an illegal country and was committed to establishing a Palestinian state.) On other occasions, Jackson said that Jews had a persecution complex that caused them to overreact to their own suffering. He said he was tired of hearing about the Holocaust, which, he said, was no worse than the suffering of blacks during the period of American slavery. He said that when Richard Nixon was U.S. president, several of his top advisers were German Jews who were more concerned about European and Asian affairs than with the poor and disadvantaged in the United States. He said Jews were false friends to blacks, and he disregarded the many instances in American history when Jews and blacks struggled side by side for civil, political, and human rights.

Jackson's trip to Israel in 1979 included his figurative embrace of PLO chairman Yasser Arafat as a personal friend and "the friend of justice and humanity." Jackson attributed negative media coverage of his trip to Jewish reporters' lack of objectivity about Arab affairs. He reacted to his critics by accusing Jews in the media of perpetuating negative stories about him.

Given this well-known background, especially to reporters covering the first African American to run seriously for presidential nomination by a major American political party, Coleman likely did not have much heart-wrenching deliberation about whether to pass along Jackson's "Hymietown" remarks to a white colleague. That reporter, Rick Atkinson, revealed Jackson's comments in a February 13 article in *The Washington Post* about the candidate's proposed foreign policy. However, the slurs were buried in the article's thirty-seventh paragraph.

Not unexpectedly, protests erupted in Jewish and

other communities. Liberal publications condemned Jackson and argued that his campaign could adversely affect interracial politics and scare voters away from the Democratic Party. With a white backlash fueled by white racism against blacks, critics argued, the United States could see the reelection of Republican president Ronald Reagan.

Attempting to distance himself from the controversy, Jackson initially claimed no recollection of making the remarks and then denied making them. What spurred his memory, however, were the coming primaries and curious voters. He went to Manchester, New Hampshire, two days before the New Hampshire primary, made an emotional speech at a synagogue, admitted his offense, and apologized for the slurs.

The controversy might have receded at this time except for an inflammatory radio sermon by Louis Farrakhan, the leader of the Black Muslim group Nation of Islam. In his sermon, he said that reporter Coleman should be punished for the pain he caused Jackson, whom Farrakhan supported. Farrakhan went on to warn Jews that if they harmed Jackson, it would be the last "black brother" they would harm. Jackson was expected to denounce Farrakhan for the comment and threats, but even though he noted that Farrakhan's remarks were counterproductive and even wrong, he did not disavow him. Reagan, Jackson countered, had not rejected the endorsement he received from the Ku Klux Klan. Jackson's failure to denounce Farrakhan weakened the salutary effect of his apology to the Jewish people.

IMPACT

Jackson's run for the presidency had been considered a long shot by politicians and others, but his campaign was effective for bringing unprecedented numbers of black voters to the polls. In turn, he accumulated enough delegates so that he would have considerable clout in pushing for political concessions at the Democratic convention. However, when the story broke about his racial slurs, his reputation was forever tarnished. Democratic Party leaders feared his comments would adversely affect the party's platform, which embraces racial and ethnic diversity. To what extent white racism would

emerge to influence the election was another concern. Jackson almost single-handedly caused even more white voters to vote Republican in the election and reelect Reagan.

Black leaders were dismayed by Jackson's strained relationship with Jews because many African Americans welcomed their generally supportive relationship with American Jews. That Jackson had offended Jews meant that domestic relations between the two groups would be endangered. Jewish leaders, in turn, were even more convinced that Jackson, who had so publicly embraced Arab and Palestinian issues, was anti-Semitic. The long-established affinity between African Americans and Jews became tenuous, and the long-standing suspicions many Jews had about Jackson remained as a result of the 1984 presidential campaign scandal.

—*Jane L. Ball*

FURTHER READING

Bruns, Roger. *Jesse Jackson: A Biography.* Westport, Conn.: Greenwood Press, 2005. Examines Jackson's life from his early years through his civil rights work, his leadership roles, and his work in international diplomacy. Mostly complimentary but includes some critical views. Photographs.

Landess, Thomas H., and Richard M. Quinn. *Jesse Jackson and the Politics of Race.* Cheshunt, England: Jameson Books, 1985. A look at Jackson's political life. Less than approving of his career. Also discusses falsehoods attributed to him about his childhood and other aspects of his life.

Timmerman, Ken. *Shakedown: Exposing the Real Jesse Jackson.* Washington, D.C.: Regnery, 2002. Critical, candid revelations by so-called inner-circle Jacksonites about Jackson operations and how he manipulates American race relations for personal gain. Presents Jackson as a fraud. An entire chapter covers his association with Yasir Arafat and sheds light on Jackson's attitude toward Jews.

SEE ALSO: July 2, 1963: Muslim Leader Elijah Muhammad Is Sued for Paternity; Sept. 23, 1987: Plagiarism Charges End Joe Biden's Presidential

Campaign; Dec. 1, 1987: Yale Scholar's War-time Anti-Semitic Writings Are Revealed; Oct. 11-13, 1991: Justice Clarence Thomas's Confirmation Hearings Create a Scandal; May, 1999: Civil Rights Leader Jesse Jackson Fathers a Child Out of Wedlock; Dec. 5, 2002: Senator

Trent Lott Praises Strom Thurmond's 1948 Presidential Campaign; Dec. 17, 2003: Senator Strom Thurmond's Biracial Daughter Is Revealed; July 28, 2006: Actor Mel Gibson Is Caught Making Anti-Semitic Remarks.

May 2, 1984
E. F. HUTTON EXECUTIVES PLEAD GUILTY TO FRAUD

One of the oldest, largest, and best-known brokerage firms on Wall Street, E. F. Hutton ran a major check-kiting scheme that allowed it to acquire interest-free loans, which in turn generated millions of dollars of income. Hutton eventually pleaded guilty to mail and wire fraud, the first criminal conviction for a Wall Street investment firm in U.S. history.

LOCALE: New York, New York
CATEGORIES: Law and the courts; banking and finance; business; corruption; hoaxes, frauds, and charlatanism

KEY FIGURES
Robert M. Fomon (d. 2000), E. F. Hutton chief operating officer, 1970-1986, and chairman, 1977-1987
Thomas Morley (fl. 1980's), E. F. Hutton senior vice president
Tom Curnin (fl. 1980's), E. F. Hutton defense attorney
Griffin Bell (1918-2009), former U.S. attorney general, 1977-1979, headed investigation of E. F. Hutton
George L. Ball (fl. 1980's), president of E. F. Hutton, 1977-1982

SUMMARY OF EVENT
On May 2, 1984, the E. F. Hutton Company, the fifth largest investment firm in the United States, pleaded guilty to two thousand counts of wire and mail fraud. Beginning around 1980, Hutton had im-

plemented and executed an elaborate, illegal, check-kiting scheme that would earn the company millions of dollars from interest-free loans. Hutton floated checks that were still in the clearing process, allowing the firm to earn interest during the time banks processed the checks and deposits. This approach worked for Hutton because of the slow rate in which checks cleared the banks, all in the days before electronic banking.

Hutton provided a vast array of services to its clients, including, primarily, stock trading and underwriting bond issues. A major benefit to Hutton was the speed at which it could offer communications and services. It had an aggressive management staff and numerous brokers (more than six thousand) who had direct wire access to the New York Stock Exchange. This success, especially during the 1970's and early 1980's, may arguably have been the starting point of the near collapse of the thriving company, which was founded in 1904 by Edwin Francis Hutton, a New York financier, along with his brother, Franklin Hutton, and Gerald Loeb. Hutton was unique when compared to other firms because it offered services to its customers from coast to coast. Hutton also was the first company to gain access from the West Coast directly to New York. The company eventually opened seasonal branch offices in Florida, California, and New York, allowing it to market to a wide range of customers across the country.

Another technique Hutton used to make money was chaining. Hutton branch employees would simply write checks for amounts that exceeded available funds, and Hutton covered those checks with other checks drawn from company branches (checks written by Hutton to Hutton), mainly among rural bank accounts. This made it appear that the company had funds available in more than one account until all checks cleared. The banks used for the scheme were, primarily, United Penn Bank in Wilkes-Barre, Pennsylvania; American Bank and Trust Company in Reading, Pennsylvania; and Genesee County Bank in Batavia, New York. A number of overdrafts of these local bank accounts triggered the start of the investigations against Hutton. These investigations would be headed by former U.S. attorney general Griffin Bell.

Thomas Morley, a senior vice president who had been hired to better manage the company's cash flow, later reported in a company memo that chaining checks allowed the company to profit as much as thirty thousand dollars per month, per branch, in extra income. George Ball, Hutton's president, was pleased with this report and encouraged these practices throughout the company. Essentially, Hutton was provided the equivalent of interest-free loans. Reports showed that on some days Hutton "earned" $250 million in interest-free loans. Hutton executives were committing white collar crimes, a phrase coined in 1939 by Edwin Sutherland, considered the founder of the study of occupational crime. Sutherland referred to white collar crimes as those committed by individuals (white collar criminals) of higher socioeconomic status, usually within the workplace.

For nearly three years, Hutton continued with the scheme, but the firm's downfall came when officials at the Genesee County Bank questioned the large deposits that were being made by Hutton. The bank in Batavia was a small branch with four employees, and the deposits seemed far too large for the office. Hutton soon came under question by New York examiners, and it retained Thomas F. Curnin for legal services. Even with Curnin helping, company chairman Robert M. Fomon openly defended all senior executives against criminal charges.

In addition to the guilty plea, the company agreed to pay a $2 million fine, $750,000 for the expenses of the investigation, and restitution in the amount of $8 million. This is the estimated amount the company received in illegal income. The plea bargain and guilty plea freed individual executives from culpability, but the company was barred from practicing within the securities industry. Only the company as a whole would face any repercussions for the criminal offenses. Some critics have argued that Hutton received a lenient sentence because of the plea bargain.

IMPACT

The Hutton scandal led many customers to pull their accounts, led star employees within the company to take jobs with other firms, and kept public agencies from conducting business with the firm. Hutton also was harshly scrutinized by the media, and it was given the sort of attention the company would rather not have. Instead, media reports brought irreparable damage to the company's reputation.

On December 3, 1987, Hutton, the first Wall Street investment company to be convicted of a crime, was auctioned off to Shearson Lehman Brothers for $1 billion and was renamed Shearson Lehman Hutton. Hutton later came under the ownership of Citigroup. The investment firm, even with its new owner and name, would never again have the respected reputation it held prior to the scandal.

—*Lisa M. Carter*

FURTHER READING

Brancato, Carolyn Kay, and Christian A. Plath. *Corporate Governance Best Practices: A Blueprint for the Post-Enron Era.* New York: Conference Board, 2003. A study that examines corporate leadership, ethics, and responsibility at a time of increased public awareness of corporate fraud and mismanagement.

Carpenter, Donna S., and John Feloni. *The Fall of the House of Hutton.* New York: Henry Holt, 1989. Corporate biography that includes the history and background of the company, the investigation, and court proceedings surrounding the scandal.

Ermann, M. D., and R. L. Lundman, eds. *Corporate*

and Governmental Deviance: Problems of Organizational Behavior in Contemporary Society. New York: Oxford University Press, 2002. An overview of governmental and corporate deviance, written from the perspective of organizational behavior and practice.

Green, G. S. *Occupational Crime.* Chicago: Nelson-Hall, 1990. Focuses on occupational crime and deviance. One chapter discusses the early beginnings of white collar crime as an area of study in the fields of criminology and criminal justice.

MacDonald, Scott B., and Jane E. Hughes. *Separating Fools from Their Money: A History of American Financial Scandals.* New Brunswick, N.J.: Rutgers University Press, 2007. This book provides readers with a detailed history of American financial scandals. Useful for its analysis of corporate fraud.

SEE ALSO: 1932: Insull Utilities Trusts Collapse Prompts New Federal Regulation; Mar. 29, 1962: Billie Sol Estes Is Arrested for Corporate Fraud; Nov. 28, 1967: Investor Louis Wolfson Is Convicted of Selling Stock Illegally; May 7, 1985: Banker Jake Butcher Pleads Guilty to Fraud; Jan. 15, 1988: ZZZZ Best Founder Is Indicted on Federal Fraud Charges; Mar. 29, 1989: Financier Michael Milken Is Indicted for Racketeering and Fraud; 2001: Clearstream Financial Clearinghouse Is Accused of Fraud and Money Laundering; Dec. 2, 2001: Enron Bankruptcy Reveals Massive Financial Fraud; June 25, 2002: Internal Corruption Forces Adelphia Communications to Declare Bankruptcy; Sept. 3, 2003: Mutual Fund Companies Are Implicated in Shady Trading Practices; Oct. 14, 2004: Insurance Brokerage Marsh & McLennan Is Charged with Fraud; Sept. 12, 2005: Westar Energy Executives Are Found Guilty of Looting Their Company; Sept. 18, 2006: *Newsweek* Reveals That Hewlett-Packard Spied on Its Own Board.

July 23, 1984
VANESSA WILLIAMS IS THE FIRST MISS AMERICA TO RESIGN

Vanessa Williams, the first African American to be crowned Miss America, resigned her title after Penthouse *magazine announced that it would publish nude photographs of her. A photographer sold the photos to the magazine without her consent. The scandal combined issues of race, sexuality, gender, the ideal of feminine beauty, and the right to privacy.*

LOCALE: New York, New York

CATEGORIES: Publishing and journalism; social issues and reform; sex; women's issues; racism

KEY FIGURES

Vanessa Williams (b. 1963), Miss America 1984
Bob Guccione (b. 1930), founder and publisher of *Penthouse* magazine
Albert A. Marks (1913-1989), executive director of Miss America Organization
Tom Chiapel (b. 1950), photographer
Helene Freeman (fl. 1980's), Williams's attorney
Suzette Charles (b. 1963), Miss America 1984
Ramon Hervey II (b. 1950), publicist and film producer

SUMMARY OF EVENT

Vanessa Williams gained much media exposure as the first African American woman to be crowned Miss America on September 17, 1983. The following summer, Bob Guccione, owner and publisher of the adult magazine *Penthouse*, announced he would publish photographs of Williams nude. Pageant officials pressured Williams to resign, which she did. The risqué issue of *Penthouse*, which hit news-

Vanessa Williams announces her resignation as Miss America. (AP/Wide World Photos)

1980's

stands the weekend before she resigned, sold out within one week and went through a second printing of tens of thousands of copies. Williams subsequently filed a lawsuit against Guccione and the photographer involved but later dropped the charges. To deal with the negative publicity, she hired a publicist, and with his guidance she successfully revived her career, winning awards as a singer and as a stage, film, and television actor.

In 1982, Williams was a student at Syracuse University majoring in theater arts. She spent the summer as a receptionist for modeling photographer Tom Chiapel at his agency in Mount Kisco, New York. He convinced her to pose for some nude photo shoots; on at least one occasion the photo shoots included another woman. Williams later claimed that she was convinced by Chiapel that the shots would be artistic, adding that she did the shoot

because she was curious and that she had never agreed to any later duplication or distribution of the images.

The next year, after winning Miss Greater Syracuse and then Miss New York, Williams went on to Atlantic City to represent her state in the annual Miss America pageant. She won the preliminary talent and swimsuit competitions and was crowned Miss America. She did a good job of performing her titular functions during her reign as Miss America 1984, though she received hate mail and castigation from two extremes: racist reactionaries who were opposed in principle to any nonwhite woman winning the pageant and Afrocentric radicals who were disappointed that the first black Miss America had light skin.

The media highlighted Williams's breaking of the race barrier in the most revered beauty pageant in the United States, and more than once she was compared to Jackie Robinson, who had broken the color line in professional baseball in 1947. Photographer Chiapel saw an opportunity for profit in Williams's new celebrity. Without consulting Williams, he approached Hugh Hefner, founder and publisher of the adult magazine *Playboy*, and offered to sell him the photos of Williams nude. Hefner turned him down, later stating on *The Today Show* that he saw the release of the photos as an inappropriate invasion of the current Miss America's privacy. His publishing rival, Guccione, had no such qualms, however.

Guccione bought the rights to the now-infamous photographs. The September, 1984, issue of *Penthouse* included several photos of Williams, some depicting simulated lesbian sex. Sales of the magazine increased by more than two million copies over the average issue distribution of 3.4 million. *Penthouse* published a follow-up photo feature, accompanied by an interview with the photographer, in its November, 1984, issue. Guccione made millions of dollars from the first Miss America exposé alone.

Albert A. Marks, the executive director of Miss America Organization, saw the photographs of Williams before publication and insisted that Williams resign. She did so at a news conference in New York City on July 23; the September issue of

639

Penthouse appeared on newsstands just days before her resignation. Williams said she relinquished her title because she did not want harm to come to the pageant. She was allowed to keep her scholarship money but did lose endorsement deals. She also lost a deal for her autobiography.

The pageant weathered the scandal. Miss New Jersey, Suzette Charles, had been one of three other African American women, the highest number to make it so far in the history of the pageant, competing for Miss America in Atlantic City in 1983. Charles was first runner-up in the overall competition, so she took over as Miss America following Williams's resignation. Her reign was for a short two months. That Charles was a woman of color might have mollified some of the theories circulating that the publication of the nude photos of Williams was racially motivated.

Williams's lawyer, Helene Freeman, filed a $500 million lawsuit against Chiapel and Guccione in early September, 1984, claiming that the development and distribution of the photos had never been authorized or approved. Guccione had answered such assertions earlier by responding that he had in his possession a model release form that Williams herself had signed. He said that two different, respected handwriting-analysis experts had verified the signature as that of Williams. While Williams maintained throughout the controversy that she was a naïve young woman who had been misled by the photographer, she eventually dropped the charges.

Williams's career was salvaged, in no small part, because of the help of her publicist, Ramon Hervey II, who had been hired to do spin control. Hervey was an effective publicist and, later, he became her manager. Hervey helped transform her 1984 notoriety, which started scandalously, into an impressive, award-winning career in music, theater, film, and television. Williams and Hervey married in 1987.

IMPACT

It is clear that the September, 1984, issue of *Penthouse* was controversial. It also was incredibly lucrative financially for Guccione. Its cultural impact, however, was less clear at the time the scandal broke. The nude-photo feature would soon set the tone for an increasing emphasis on salacious articles and images of celebrities in American popular culture in the closing decades of the twentieth century.

At the time of the controversy, feminist leaders such as Gloria Steinem and influential African American leaders such as Jesse Jackson rallied in defense of Williams, creating enough of a support base to indicate that the risque photos, which, in the past, surely would have destroyed a young Miss America's future, did not—and should not—negate Williams's overall accomplishments as a person.

The scandal also led to discussions about how African American celebrities are held to a different standard of public acceptability than are white celebrities. It also brought to light the different standards of acceptability and beauty among African Americans, standards based on the lightness or darkness of one's skin. The scandal also raised feminist questions about the significance and purpose of how women are treated and represented in both beauty-pageant culture and men's pornography, and ways in which the two categories might intersect. Furthermore, the scandal led to more open and frank discussions about fantasies of lesbian sex.

Subsequent beauty pageant scandals would have less dramatic impact, and the general public would be more willing to forgive beauty queens some tarnish on their crowns, particularly if the women involved publicly apologized and asked for forgiveness. Williams's comeback after the scandal made her a powerhouse star, ultimately suggesting that the notoriety of such a scandal, when handled adroitly by a good publicist, could indeed be used to further one's career.

—*Scot M. Guenter*

FURTHER READING

Banet-Weiser, Sarah. *The Most Beautiful Girl in the World: Beauty Pageants and National Identity.* Berkeley: University of California Press, 1999. A cultural history of the Miss America pageant that considers how the pageant process shapes and influences female identity at both the personal and social levels.

Elmer, Jonathan. "The Exciting Conflict: The Rhetoric of Pornography and Anti-Pornography." *Cultural Critique* no. 8 (Winter, 1987): 45-77. A scholarly evaluation of the Williams scandal in the context of cultural debate over defining the boundaries of pornography.

Jones, Trina. "Shades of Brown: The Law of Skin Color." *Duke Law Journal* 49, no. 6 (2000): 1487-1557. Historical legal review of "colorism," the issue of varying acceptances and perceptions of light skin versus dark skin, within the larger construct of dealing with African American racism.

Shalit, Willa. *Becoming Myself: Reflections on Growing Up Female.* New York: Hyperion Books, 2006. Williams and sixty-six other inspiring women celebrities and writers share short, personal essays on significant events in their journeys to becoming women.

Watson, Elwood, and Darcy Martin, eds. *"There She Is, Miss America."* New York: Palgrave, 2004. Interdisciplinary anthology that explores the intersections of race, gender, ethnicity, and consumerism in the Miss America pageant.

SEE ALSO: Jan. 20, 1933: Hedy Lamarr Appears Nude in the Czech Film *Exstase*; Summer, 1936: Film Star Mary Astor's Diary Becomes a Public Sensation; Dec. 1, 1952: George Jorgensen Becomes Christine Jorgensen; 1978: Actor Joan Crawford's Daughter Publishes Damning Memoir, *Mommie Dearest*; July 28, 1980: Magazine Reveals Baseball Star Steve Garvey's Marital Problems; Dec. 7, 1980: Rita Jenrette's "Diary of a Mad Congresswife" Scandalizes Washington; Dec., 1982: Julie Andrews and Blake Edwards Deny Being Gay; July 18, 1988: Actor Rob Lowe Videotapes Sexual Tryst with a Minor; June 24, 1994: *Time* Magazine Cover Uses Altered O. J. Simpson Photo; Early Nov., 2003: Paris Hilton Sex-Tape Appears on the Web.

1980's

December 22, 1984
SUBWAY VIGILANTE BERNHARD GOETZ SHOOTS FOUR BLACK YOUTHS

Bernhard Goetz's shooting of four black teenagers on a New York City subway train launched a heated public debate about vigilantism, self-defense, urban crime, and racism. After prolonged criminal and civil trials, Goetz, an electrician, was sentenced to jail for unlicensed gun possession and found liable for paralyzing one of the assailants.

LOCALE: New York, New York
CATEGORIES: Violence; law and the courts; racism; social issues and reform

KEY FIGURES
Bernhard Goetz (b. 1947), self-employed electrician
Darrell Cabey (b. 1965), New York City resident
Barry Slotnick (fl. 1980's), Goetz's attorney
Robert M. Morgenthau (b. 1919), New York district attorney
Stephen G. Crane (b. 1940), New York State judge

SUMMARY OF EVENT

On December 22, 1984, Bernhard Goetz shot four young African American men on a subway car in New York City. This violent incident, lasting no more than six seconds, would have local and national repercussions, as it touched on issues that are central to urban life in the United States.

Goetz seemed an unlikely person to have sparked this public debate. A bespectacled, slender, eccentric, Caucasian, thirty-seven-year-old loner, he operated his own electronics repair business out

Bernhard Goetz, left. (AP/Wide World Photos)

of his Manhattan apartment. However, he had been traumatized by a violent mugging on the subway in 1981 and by the subsequent denial of his request for a gun permit.

On Saturday, December 22, at 1 P.M., Goetz boarded a downtown subway car carrying in a waistband holder a .38 caliber Smith & Wesson handgun. He had purchased the gun legally in 1970 but did not have a New York license to carry the weapon. Four black youths—Troy Canty, Barry Allen, James Ramseur, and Darrell Cabey—already on the subway train, had been acting raucously before Goetz boarded. The four young men all were between eighteen and nineteen years old and all had criminal records. Two of them had screwdrivers in their pockets. Their behavior led passengers to move to the other end of the subway car. Two of the

youths, Canty and Allen, approached Goetz after he boarded and demanded five dollars from him. A third youth, Ramseur, gestured toward a bulge in his pocket, suggesting that he had a weapon. Goetz pulled out his handgun and fired four shots.

Canty apparently was shot first; the bullet penetrated through his body. Allen was shot in the back; Ramseur was shot through his arm and chest; and another shot missed. Goetz then walked over to Cabey and fired into his side with his fifth and final shot, severing Cabey's spinal cord. After telling a conductor that the youths had tried to rob him, Goetz leaped off the train onto the platform and disappeared into downtown Manhattan. He then rented a car and drove to Vermont, where he disposed of his gun.

Meanwhile, New York City was riveted by news of the shooting. Newspapers acclaimed the shooter as the "subway vigilante." He was likened to actor Charles Bronson's character, Paul Kersey, in the 1974 film *Death Wish*, in which Kersey avenged terrorized citizens of New York against hoodlums. Goetz, who surrendered to police in Concord, New Hampshire, on December 31, reinforced his vigilante image in his videotaped confessions to New Hampshire and New York police. In language freighted with images of Old West gunfights, Goetz recounted the incident. He talked of quick-draw holsters and laying down a "pattern of fire." He explained that his violent reaction was triggered when he saw that Canty's "eyes were shiny" and he "had a big smile on his face."

Unlike the media, police and government officials were outraged that Goetz took the law into his own hands. U.S. president Ronald Reagan denounced vigilantism, and New York City mayor Edward I. Koch described the shooting as "animal behavior." The National Association for the Advancement of Colored People likened Goetz to a Ku Klux Klan lyncher. New York district attorney Robert M. Morgenthau launched a criminal investigation. Cabey, paralyzed from the waist down from Goetz's shot, was represented by famous civil rights lawyer William Kunstler. Cabey sued Goetz for fifty million dollars. (The other youths recovered from their wounds.)

On January 25, 1985, a grand jury indicted Goetz only on a charge of illegal gun possession. Morgenthau, criticized for the grand jury's tame indictment, convened a second grand jury, appointing his leading assistant district attorney, Gregory Waples, to present the case and granting immunity to Canty and Ramseur for their testimony. On March 27, the second grand jury indicted Goetz on ten counts that included assault and attempted murder.

One year later, on January 21, 1986, Judge Stephen G. Crane dismissed nine of the counts on technical grounds relating to self-defense, dismissals that would assume great importance in the case. Waples had instructed the grand jury that Goetz would have been justified in acting in self-defense only if a reasonable person would have believed such actions necessary—a so-called objective standard. However, New York courts had evolved a "subjective belief" standard over the previous few years; that is, the defendant would be justified in using force if he or she believed such force necessary for his or her self-defense. Morgenthau appealed Crane's self-defense ruling to New York's appellate division, which affirmed Crane's decision on April 17. The district attorney then appealed this decision to the New York Court of Appeals, the state's highest court. In a July 8 ruling, the appeals court reinstated all the counts against Goetz on the grounds that the decision to use self-defense must be objectively reasonable, although the court emphasized that a determination of reasonableness can be based on the defendant's characteristics and circumstances, including any prior experience. The case of *People v. Goetz* was sent back to Crane for trial.

Goetz's trial before Judge Crane began on December 12 under intense media scrutiny. Although Goetz asserted his Fifth Amendment right not to testify, his attorney, Barry Slotnick, argued that Goetz shot the youths out of fear that they were about to assault him. Following the guidance from the court of appeals, Crane instructed the jury that Goetz was justified in defending himself if his experiences, including that he had been injured in a 1981 mugging, indicated to him that his actions were necessary. On June 16, 1987, the jury returned a verdict of not guilty on all the charges except criminal possession of a weapon in the third degree. On November 22, 1988, Goetz's appeal of his conviction was denied and he was sentenced to one year in jail as well as community service and was fined $5,075. Goetz served eight months of his sentence.

The civil trial against Goetz had a different outcome. On April 23, 1996, a jury, which had been instructed to assess Goetz's convictions on an objective standard, found that he acted recklessly and without justification when he shot Cabey. The jury awarded Cabey forty-three million dollars for his physical injuries and emotional distress. Goetz filed for bankruptcy soon after the case was decided.

IMPACT

The impact of the case of *People v. Goetz* was twofold, affecting both the theoretical interpretation of self-defense law and the day-to-day perceptions and lives of New York City residents. As to legal affairs, the microscopic attention paid to New York's justification law during the lengthy litigation process against Goetz represented an elaborate explanation of what it means to employ violence in self-defense. The result was a hybrid standard combining objective and subjective factors. The New York courts ruled that the objective reasonableness of a defendant's actions must be evaluated according to his or her background and subjective life experiences. This was a new and widely commented on standard in the centuries-old law of criminal self-defense.

As to life in the city, *Goetz* was one of the most important cases in the urban history of New York. Goetz injured four young men, paralyzing one of them. The case laid bare the racial divisions in the city and the legal system, which would only be exacerbated in the years that followed the shooting. The case also exposed the fear of crime that was overtaking cities in the United States and the desperation of urban residents for remedies—even violent ones—that would frustrate urban hoodlums.

Perhaps the greatest impact of the Goetz case was that it brought to light the petty lawlessness that public authorities had allowed to fester and grow in New York. At the time of the shooting, New York City had reached the highest crime rate in its history and was notorious throughout the country for muggings and other urban dangers. Over the next decades, city officials made a determined effort to crack down on petty offenses. It was perhaps no coincidence that crime rates would soon decline dramatically.

—*Howard Bromberg*

FURTHER READING

Fletcher, George P. *A Crime of Self-Defense: Bernhard Goetz and the Law on Trial*. Chicago: University of Chicago Press, 1990. A Columbia Law School professor focuses on legal questions of justification and self-defense raised during the Goetz trials and appeals.

Gladwell, Malcolm. *The Tipping Point: How Little Things Can Make a Big Difference*. Boston: Little, Brown, 2000. Chapter four explains the Goetz shooting as the result of a decline in living standards and the rise of offenses that affected the quality of life in New York City.

Kennedy, Randall. *Race, Crime, and the Law*. New York: Pantheon Books, 1997. A Harvard Law School professor briefly analyzes the Goetz prosecution in terms of racial relations.

Lesly, Mark, with Charles Shuttleworth. *Subway Gunman: A Juror's Account of the Bernhard Goetz Trial*. Latham, N.Y.: British American, 1988. A juror's perspective on the trial that also features trial documents, including the indictment, the prosecution's opening and closing statements, and notes from juror deliberations.

Markovitz, Jonathan. "Bernhard Goetz and the Politics of Fear." In *Violence and the Body: Race, Gender, and the State*, edited by Arturo J. Aldama. Bloomington: Indiana University Press, 2003. This chapter on the Goetz shooting is part of a collection that examines the significance of "body politics" in a culture that fears violence. The Goetz case is considered in light of white panic and white rage, politicized responses that justify vigilantism.

Rubin, Lillian B. *Quiet Rage: Bernie Goetz in a Time of Madness*. New York: Farrar, Straus & Giroux, 1986. An account of the shooting that probes the psychological states of those involved in the incident, especially Goetz. Claims Goetz was emotionally unstable at the time of the shooting.

SEE ALSO: Mar. 30, 1931: "Scottsboro Boys" Are Railroaded Through Rape Trials; Nov. 28, 1987: Black Teenager Claims to Have Been Gang-Raped by Police Officers; Mar., 1990: Menendez Brothers Are Arrested for Murdering Their Parents; May 19, 1992: Amy Fisher Shoots Mary Jo Buttafuoco; June 23, 1993: Lorena Bobbitt Severs Her Husband's Penis; June 12, 1994: Double Murder Leads to Sensational O. J. Simpson Trial.

1985-1986
Westland Affair Shakes Prime Minister Thatcher's Government

The Westland affair was a bitter disagreement within Margaret Thatcher's cabinet over how to support Great Britain's ailing Westland helicopter company. Thatcher and Leon Brittan, minister for trade and industry, wanted to see a takeover by the American company Sikorsky, while Defence Minister Michael Heseltine wanted to pursue a European option. In the tussle, cabinet disunity led to a leak of the conflict, Heseltine's and Brittan's resignations, and an enquiry in which the government had to defend its integrity.

Locale: London, England
Categories: Government; politics; space and aviation; business; trade and commerce

Key Figures
Margaret Thatcher (b. 1925), British prime minister, 1979-1990
Michael Heseltine (b. 1933), minister of defence, 1983-1986
Leon Brittan (b. 1939), minister for the Department of Trade and Industry, 1985-1986
Robert Armstrong (b. 1927), cabinet secretary, 1979-1987

Summary of Event
Westland Aircraft Limited, a helicopter company located in Yeovil, Somerset, England, was a mid-size British manufacturer, with a turnover of some $600 million annually during the 1980's. Unlike the rest of the British aircraft industry, Westland had not been nationalized by a previous Labour government and remained Britain's only maker of helicopters. During the mid-1980's, Westland began to encounter financial difficulties following a lack of orders from the British military. So the company turned to the British government for help in April, 1985, when financier Alan Bristow put in a bid for the manufacturer. He wanted a write-off of govern-

ment aid due for repayment and assurance of orders, if not from Britain, then from India with British aid.

At the time, the issue was not a major one, commercially or politically. The government of Margaret Thatcher, on the whole, took a hard line on ailing industries, but defense needs suggested the wisdom of keeping a British-based company running. In the end, the bid was unsuccessful but a new board of directors was installed under the chairship of Sir John Cuckney. On October 4, the newly appointed minister for the Department of Trade and Industry, Leon Brittan, reported the need for a new minority shareholder to inject more capital into the company. The American helicopter giant, Sikorsky, was willing to become the minority shareholder, and the Westland board agreed. Sikorsky already had been allowing Westland to build some of its patents.

At this stage, Michael Heseltine, the ambitious and energetic minister of defence, began to make his views known that a European future, rather than an American one, was necessary for Westland. From 1978 there had been an agreement among some European countries that, where possible, helicopter purchases should be kept to European manufacturers. Heseltine gathered the national armament directors of Germany, France, and Italy to get them to say that if Westland moved into American hands, it would not be possible to deal with the company in the future. At the same time, Heseltine was actively trying to put together a rescue package among European companies for Westland. By this time, Westland directors were actively proposing a takeover by Sikorsky.

By December, 1985, the differences between Brittan and Heseltine entered into serious departmental rivalry, and Prime Minister Thatcher had to intervene. She called a series of three meetings, the first two fairly informal, the third, held December 9, a fuller meeting of involved ministers. It was decided to keep the European option open until Friday, December 13. A firm decision would have to be taken at this meeting to maintain confidence in the company because Westland's annual accounts were to be published two days before the ministers met.

Accounts of this last meeting differed between Heseltine and Thatcher. Heseltine was expecting one further meeting; Thatcher was not and did not call one. The deadline passed without an agreed rescue bid from the Europeans. However, Heseltine continued to act as though everything was still negotiable. Thatcher wrote to Cuckney to say that the government would continue to see Westland as a British company and do its best to protect the company.

Though Heseltine seemed to be flouting the rules of collective cabinet decision-making, nothing was done to stop him. It could be that Thatcher feared his wide popularity within the Conservative Party. It was decided in early 1986 to ask one of the leading government lawyers, the solicitor-general Christopher Mayhew, to give a legal opinion as to Heseltine's contention that Westland would lose all European business. Mayhew's carefully worded letter suggested that there were "material inaccura-

cies" in Heseltine's statements. The letter was almost immediately leaked by Brittan's department, probably with the connivance of the prime minister's office. The national press seized on the scandal, accusing Heseltine of lying.

At the cabinet meeting of January 9, the prime minister told members that great damage was being done to the government by the leak of the letter, and that in the future all communications about Westland must be cleared through her office before being circulated. By now, it seems Heseltine had had enough; he promptly resigned and walked out, issuing a long and carefully worded statement a few hours later.

The matter did not stop there, however. Mayhew's senior in government, Attorney General Michael Havers, demanded an enquiry into the leak, which had the confidentiality of a legal document as well as being a leak of one minister against another. The enquiry was conducted by Robert Armstrong, the senior civil servant in the cabinet office. He concluded that Brittan had indeed authorized the leak. In the parliamentary debates that followed, Thatcher had to defend Brittan and herself. While seeing off the threat to her own position by claiming ignorance on the one hand, and making some apologies on the other, the Conservative backbenchers saw the need for Brittan to resign. Thatcher "reluctantly" accepted his resignation.

IMPACT

The Westland company was taken over by Sikorsky and managed to do well. However, Thatcher lost her reputation for straight and honest dealing as prime minister, and grave fault lines in her cabinet came to light. Her cabinet style also was scrutinized. A further review by the all-party Parliamentary Defence Committee grilled Armstrong, and the integrity of the civil service also come

Former British defence secretary Michael Heseltine in London in January, 1986. (Hulton Archive/Getty Images)

under suspicion. However, it was felt that the Labour opposition had lost a major opportunity in the parliamentary debate, when its leader, Neil Kinnock, made a blustering and ineffective attack on Thatcher, which did no more than reveal the insignificance of the Westland decision. Brittan, though, was unable to return to the cabinet and eventually ended his political career as a commissioner in Brussels, Belgium, for the European Union.

In the long term, Thatcher created an independent and vocal critic of her policies. Heseltine's politics were more akin to Thatcher's predecessor, Edward Heath, in its desire for government intervention. In the end he became a rival for her post. During the 1990 contest for leadership of the party, it was Heseltine who emerged as her chief rival at first, and his support in the first round of voting was the main cause of her resignation as party leader. In fact, Heseltine was unable to increase his support and John Major became the new leader. However, Heseltine did become deputy prime minster during the later stages of the Major ministry.

—*David Barratt*

FURTHER READING

Her Majesty's Stationery Office. *Fourth Report from the Defence Committee, 23 July, 1986.* London: Author, 1986. A full account of one of the most revealing enquiries into misconduct produced by an all-party select committee.

Heseltine, Michael. *Life in the Jungle: An Autobiography*, London: Hodder & Stoughton, 2000. Contains Heseltine's account of the affair in considerable detail.

Linklater, Magnus, and David Leigh. *Not with Honour.* London: Sphere, 1986. A thorough account of the affair produced shortly after the scandal subsided. Shows some signs of haste.

Thatcher, Margaret. *The Downing Street Years, 1979*-1990. New York: HarperCollins, 1993. Thatcher's account of the affair, which, of course, does no favors to Michael Heseltine.

Uttley, Matthew R. H. *Westland and the British Helicopter Industry, 1945-1960: Licensed Production Versus Indigenous Innovation.* Portland, Oreg.: Frank Cass, 2001. Argues that Westland succeeded in the postwar years because it focused on the licensed production of helicopter technology developed in the United States, such as that by Sikorsky.

Young, Hugo. *The Iron Lady: A Biography of Margaret Thatcher.* New York: Farrar, Straus & Giroux, 1989. Of all the biographies and autobiographies, this perhaps gives the most balanced account of the affair, taken from personal interviews with those involved.

SEE ALSO: Jan., 1913: British Prime Minister's Staff Is Investigated for Insider Trading; May, 1915: British Government Falls Because of Munitions Shortages and Military Setbacks; June 22, 1922: British Prime Minister David Lloyd George Is Accused of Selling Honors; May, 1930: Postmaster's Division of Airmail Routes Creates a Scandal; May 20, 1936: British Cabinet Member Resigns After Budget Information Leak; Mar. 2-Sept. 25, 1963: John Profumo Affair Rocks British Government; June 22, 1972: Police Arrest Architect John Poulson for Bribery and Fraud; Nov. 20, 1974: British Politician John Stonehouse Fakes His Suicide; May 29, 1981: Court Finds That Ford Ignored Pinto's Safety Problems; July 25, 1987: Novelist-Politician Jeffrey Archer Wins Libel Trial Against the *Daily Star*; Sept. 24, 1992: British Cabinet Member David Mellor Resigns over Romantic Affair; Nov. 18, 1995: Former Canadian Premier Brian Mulroney Is Exposed in Airbus Scandal; Dec. 23, 1998: Prominent Belgians Are Sentenced in Agusta-Dassault Corruption Scandal.

1980's

May 7, 1985
BANKER JAKE BUTCHER PLEADS GUILTY TO FRAUD

After building a large banking empire, twice running for governor of Tennessee, and working as the chief planner and backer of a world's fair in Knoxville, Jake Butcher witnessed the collapse of his banking empire in a scandal involving fraudulent loans and other financial crimes that sent him to federal prison. The collapse of his United American Bank in 1983 marked one of the largest bank failures in U.S. history.

LOCALE: Knoxville, Tennessee
CATEGORIES: Banking and finance; business; corruption; forgery; law and the courts

KEY FIGURES
Jake Butcher (b. 1936), Tennessee banker
Cecil H. Butcher, Jr. (1939-2002), Tennessee banker

SUMMARY OF EVENT
On November 1, 1982, the banks of the Butcher brothers, Jake and C. H., Jr., were raided by the Federal Deposit Insurance Corporation (FDIC). To prevent transfers of loans and assets between banks, almost two hundred federal investigators descended on the banks simultaneously. Investigators soon discovered that the twenty-nine banks and branches ran a network of forged documents, illegal and unsecured loans, and other forms of bank fraud. The revelations shocked the banking world and investors.

Jake Butcher was born in Union County, Tennessee, in 1936. His father, Cecil H. Butcher, Sr., owned a general store and was the founding partner in 1929 of the Southern Industrial Banking Corporation, which made loans to farmers. Jake's father also organized and presided over Union County Bank in Maynardville during the 1950's. Jake's career in banking began by sweeping bank floors and counting pennies for his father. After some college (he never graduated) and time in the U.S. Marine Corps, Jake founded an Amoco Oil distributorship.

He and his younger brother, C. H. Butcher, Jr., entered the banking industry in 1968 by aggressively borrowing large sums of money to buy stock in a number of banks. Eight Tennessee banks and other business properties were under their control by 1974.

Also in 1974, Jake began his career in politics by running for the Democratic nomination for governor of Tennessee. Although he lost this first nomination bid, he won it in 1978. He was defeated in the general election by Republican Lamar Alexander.

By 1976, the name of Jake Butcher was circulating in the business world. He lent Calhoun, Georgia, banker Bert Lance $443,000 to finance some of Lance's financial endeavors. Lance soon became the director of the U.S. Office of Management and Budget under newly elected president Jimmy Carter, who had already met Jake. Lance was soon accused of mismanaging his Calhoun bank, was forced to resign his position in the Carter administration, and was tried but acquitted of corruption charges. President Carter had actively campaigned for Jake during his 1978 bid for Tennessee governor.

The year 1978 remained a pivotal one for Jake. The family banking empire by the late 1970's included fourteen banks in Tennessee and Kentucky, still supported by heavy borrowing, and Jake claimed assets of more than $8 million. From the Carter administration, he received a $12.5 million grant for his next big project, the 1982 World's Fair in Knoxville. At its peak, the Butcher empire included twenty-seven banks.

The world's fair, which opened on May 1, brought about eleven million visitors to Knoxville in its six-month run. However, the celebration for Jake and his investors would be hampered later that year. Rumors began to circulate about Jake's banking practices, including the use of round-robin loans, in which loans are transferred to affiliate banks prior to auditor visits. One such loan was drafted in 1980, when Milton A. Turner signed a guarantee for a $2 million loan from Jake's United

American Bank (UAB), the cornerstone of his banking empire. After the bank collapsed in 1983, the loan defaulted, leading the Federal Deposit Insurance Corporation (FDIC) to sue Turner for collection. Turner was shocked to find that the name of the loan guarantor had been changed—with correction fluid—from United American to City and County Bank of Knoxville, which was controlled by Jake's brother. In 1989, a federal appeals court ruled that Turner had been defrauded by Jake and UAB, so he was not required to repay the loan.

The collapse of UAB on February 14, 1983, marked the fourth largest bank failure in U.S. history. Other Butcher-controlled banks soon collapsed as well. The collapse of C. H. Butcher's SIBC, an uninsured thrift bank, caused many people to lose their life savings. C. H. pleaded guilty to bank fraud and other charges, served six years in prison, and was paroled in 1993. Other family members and friends of the brothers went to prison for their part in various illegal transactions.

In August, Jake was declared bankrupt with assets of $11.9 million and liabilities of $32.5 million. During bankruptcy proceedings, Jake used his Fifth Amendment right against self-incrimination so that he would not have to produce potentially damaging real estate documents. The U.S. Court of Appeals, Sixth Circuit, ruled in Jake's favor, partially, in its decision of January 11, 1985.

Because Jake's United American Financial Services Company, a separate entity, had filed for reorganization under bankruptcy laws, his asset auction was in full force during bankruptcy proceedings. His assets included a forty-room mansion with thirteen bathrooms in Knoxville, two condominiums in Lexington, Kentucky, a 1983 Lincoln Mark IV sedan, a private jet, a helicopter, and dozens of houseboats. The houseboats had been equipped as floating motels during the world's fair.

In November, 1984, the Securities and Exchange Commission (SEC) had charged Jake with violating the antifraud provisions of federal securities laws. The SEC claimed that after the initial raid of Butcher banks, Jake deceived purchasers of UAB's securities prior to its own collapse. On May 7, 1985, Jake pleaded guilty to federal bank fraud and was

sentenced to twenty years in prison. In 1992, after serving almost seven years, he was paroled. He moved to a quiet suburb of Atlanta, Georgia.

The Butchers were related in one way or another with several court cases. Jake was named an unindicted coconspirator in the 1987 case against U.S. representative Harold E. Ford, Sr., of Memphis, Tennessee. Butcher banks had made unsecured loans to Ford and his family's funeral-home business several years earlier. Brother C. H., too, was charged in the Ford case but had already pleaded guilty in an agreement involving other cases. Ford was acquitted of all charges in 1993.

Perhaps the most significant court case in which Jake had ties was that involving Karl A. Schledwitz, a Memphis attorney. The Eastern District Court of Tennessee indicted Schledwitz in January, 1992, on eight counts of mail fraud. Schledwitz took out loans from Butcher-controlled banks during the early 1980's, at a time when Schledwitz did not have the income to justify the loans. Some of the loans, which totaled more than $1.5 million, were used to buy UAB stock, a stock purchase that, in turn, would raise the selling price of the bank. Some of the loan proceeds were given to the Butcher brothers for their personal use. In return, Schledwitz received referrals to his law firm. Although Schledwitz owed more than $2 million when the Butcher banks failed, he settled with the government for $120,000. He was convicted on some of the charges and his motions for a new trial were denied by the U.S. Court of Appeals in 1995.

Impact

The FDIC led the investigation of the Butcher banks and ultimately inherited most of the empire's debts. The FDIC also received a share of the blame for those enormous debts. In early 1984, the FDIC estimated that its losses in the Butcher bank failures would be about $400 million. By September of that year, that estimate was raised to $1.1 billion.

In November, 1983, the U.S. House Committee on Government Operations had issued a report that criticized the FDIC for not taking stronger action against the Butcher empire prior to 1982. With a 1987 lawsuit, the FDIC passed the blame to the accounting firm of Ernst & Whinney for being lax in its audits of four Butcher banks in 1981.

If the Butcher banking scandal had any positive impact, it was a procedural change within the FDIC. After the Butcher crisis, the federal banking agency strengthened its regulatory capacities, making it more difficult for similar crises to develop among American banks.

—*Glenn L. Swygart*

FURTHER READING

Adams, James Ring. *The Big Fix: Inside the S & L Scandal—How an Unholy Alliance of Politics and Money Destroyed America's Banking System.* New York: John Wiley & Sons, 1990. Examines the Butchers' use of round-robin loans, the practice of transferring loans to an affiliate bank just prior to an auditor's visit.

Lea, Sandra. *Whirlwind: The Butcher Banking Scandal.* Brookline, Mass.: Whirlwind, 2000. Discusses the setting for the Butcher brothers when they moved to Knoxville, Tennessee, and began their rise to power in the banking industry. Includes glimpses of most major figures in the scandal.

Ruble, Drew. "Vestige of Empire." *Business Tennessee*, July, 2006. Summarizes the life and influence of Jake Butcher, including his activities after prison. Analyzes the impact he had on the community of Knoxville, Tennessee.

"Tapped Out." *Time*, February 28, 1983. One of the first national stories about the collapse of the Butcher banking empire. Published one week after the failure of UAB.

Walker, John A., Jr. "Whirlwind: The Butcher Banking Scandal." *Tennessee Bar Journal* 37, no. 5 (May, 2001). A critical review of the 2000 book by Sandra Lea. Recognizes some value in the book but details the work's weaknesses in research and style.

Wheeler, William Bruce. *Knoxville, Tennessee: A Mountain City in the New South.* 2d ed. Knoxville: University of Tennessee Press, 2005. Extensive coverage of the Butcher family. Discusses the economic impact of the Knoxville world's fair championed by Butcher as well as the collapse of the Butcher banking empire.

SEE ALSO: 1919-1920: Ponzi Schemes Are Revealed as Investment Frauds; Nov., 1929: Banque Oustric et Cie Failure Prompts French Inquiry; Mar. 29, 1962: Billie Sol Estes Is Arrested for Corporate Fraud; Sept. 21, 1977: Carter Cabinet Member Resigns over Ethics Violations; May 2, 1984: E. F. Hutton Executives Plead Guilty to Fraud; Mar. 29, 1989: Financier Michael Milken Is Indicted for Racketeering and Fraud; Jan., 1997: Pyramid Investment Schemes Cause Albanian Government to Fall; 2001: Clearstream Financial Clearinghouse Is Accused of Fraud and Money Laundering; Dec. 2, 2001: Enron Bankruptcy Reveals Massive Financial Fraud; Sept. 3, 2003: Mutual Fund Companies Are Implicated in Shady Trading Practices; Early 2007: Subprime Mortgage Industry Begins to Collapse; Sept. 20, 2008: American Financial Markets Begin to Collapse.

July 10, 1985
FRENCH SECRET SERVICE SINKS THE GREENPEACE SHIP *RAINBOW WARRIOR*

As part of its summer Pacific Peace Voyage, the Greenpeace ship Rainbow Warrior *was scheduled to take part in a protest against French nuclear bomb tests on an island in the Pacific. While the ship was docked in Auckland, New Zealand, two bombs were attached to its hull by French secret service agents. The bombs exploded, leading to the death of a Greenpeace photographer and the ship's sinking.*

LOCALE: Auckland, New Zealand

CATEGORIES: Violence; politics; environmental issues; government; murder and suicide

KEY FIGURES

Fernando Pereira (1950-1985), Portuguese-born Dutch photographer and *Rainbow Warrior* crew member

Steve Sawyer (b. 1956), American director of Greenpeace's Pacific Peace Tour

David McTaggart (1932-2001), Canadian chairman of Greenpeace International

Dominique Prieur (b. 1948), captain in the French secret service

Alain Mafart (b. 1949), major in the French secret service

Christine Huguette Cabon (b. 1951), French army lieutenant

SUMMARY OF EVENT

The environmental organization Greenpeace—which takes political action against whaling, seal hunting, environmental pollution, nuclear testing, and other ecological concerns—was founded by a group of Canadian antinuclear activists who were protesting nuclear testing by the U.S. government in 1969. The tests, conducted on earthquake-prone Amchitka Island in the Aleutian chain in the North Pacific off the coast of Alaska, prompted the group's slogan "Don't make a wave. It's your fault if our fault goes " because of fears that a bomb deto-

nation could trigger earthquakes and tsunamis. In 1971, in Vancouver, British Columbia, Canada, group members selected the name Greenpeace for their fledgling organization and for the ship with which they mounted a protest against another nuclear test at Amchitka. The word "green" reflects the group's concern with ecological problems and the word "peace" reflects the group's commitment to peaceful direct action.

Greenpeace's early strategy involved the Quaker practice of bearing witness. For Greenpeace, this meant being present at the scene of ecological abuse so that perpetrators would know they were being watched and monitored. The strategy was soon expanded to include peaceful interference such as driving small boats between harpooners and the whales they targeted for killing, and placing boats in the region of expected fallout from nuclear tests, thus preventing a bomb's detonation. The group continues to publish and to inform the news media—all in an effort to make public the dangers faced by the environment and, thus, the earth's human population.

Greenpeace groups initially appeared in many countries, with little international unity. However, as the network grew, it coalesced into an international organization during the 1980's. Even after their unification as Greenpeace International, the regional groups continued to operate independently.

Given that protests often involved marine contexts, the ownership and maintenance of ships, boats, and other watercraft have been important parts of Greenpeace history. One of the first seaworthy ships the organization owned was a former research vessel from the British ministry of agriculture, the *Sir William Hardy*. Greenpeace bought it, cleaned it up, repaired it, and christened it the *Rainbow Warrior*. It became a symbol of Greenpeace as the organization's flagship. The name was inspired by an American Indian legend that assures that after

The Greenpeace ship Rainbow Warrior *begins to sink in Auckland Harbor, New Zealand, after being damaged by two bombs attached to the ship's hull by French government agents.* (© Greenpeace)

itself was part of Greenpeace's Pacific Peace Voyage, which also involved moving the inhabitants of the Marshall Island atoll, Rongelap, to another island (Mejato) less contaminated with radioactivity. Rongelap had been contaminated with radioactive fallout from earlier atmospheric nuclear tests. After the Rongelap residents were transferred, the *Rainbow Warrior* continued its trip to Moruroa. On the way, on July 7, it stopped at Auckland harbor in New Zealand.

On July 10, while the ship was moored at Auckland, Jean-Michel Bartelo and another member of the team from the French secret service placed two bombs with timing devices on the ship's hull. The two bombs exploded in succession just before midnight. Damage was so extensive that the *Rainbow Warrior* sank. Only a few crew members were present at the time of the blasts. Steve Sawyer, the director of the Pacific protest effort in 1985, and most of the crew were celebrating Sawyer's birthday on board. All but one of the crew members on the ship escaped. Fernando Pereira, a Greenpeace photographer, drowned while attempting to retrieve his cameras. The Moruroa demonstration continued as planned, but without the *Rainbow Warrior*.

Greenpeace chairman David McTaggart's first thought was that the French government was involved in the blasts. Greenpeace and McTaggart had a long, contentious history with the French. He dismissed the idea, however, unable to believe that they would be so foolish. French government personnel who were at the harbor at the time of the explosions condemned the bombing and swore their innocence, but overwhelming evidence of their in-

civilization compromises the earth's ability to sustain life, the warriors of the rainbow would restore that ability to Earth.

During the 1980's, Greenpeace was active on several fronts. One goal for the organization was to bring an end to French nuclear-weapons testing on islands in the Pacific. One island, Moruroa, was used repeatedly by the French, and Greenpeace demonstrated at the island nearly as often. Another test was scheduled for Moruroa in the summer of 1985. Greenpeace commissioned the *Rainbow Warrior* to be part of the demonstration. The protest volvement in the violent action quickly came to light.

Near where the ship was moored and on the day of the bombing, witnesses had seen two men transfer a package from a small boat to a Toyota van, in which they drove away. The van's registration number was traced to a rental company and to French secret service agents Dominique Prieur and Alain Meaford, who had rented the van using aliases (Sophie Turenge and Alain Turenge, respectively). The agents had dumped, into harbor waters, the oxygen tanks and the outboard motor of the boat used to approach the *Rainbow Warrior*, and they beached the boat near the scene as well. All items were found, and all indicated a French connection.

One agent, French army lieutenant Christine Huguette Cabon, had volunteered at the Greenpeace Auckland office under the alias Frederique Bonlieu before the *Rainbow Warrior*'s stop, passing information about Greenpeace plans to other members of the sabotage team. Abundant evidence implicated the French, and even included accusations against President François Mitterrand.

Whereas most of the dozen or so perpetrators disappeared, Prieur and Mafart were arrested when they returned the van to the rental agency. Although they were not involved in placing the explosives, they were sentenced to ten years in prison for aiding the saboteurs. They served less than three years of their sentences, however, and continued their careers with the French military. Each wrote a book about the affair.

The *Rainbow Warrior* was too badly damaged to be repaired. It was moved to Matauri Bay off the Cavalli Islands near New Zealand's North Island. A Maori (native New Zealander) burial ceremony accompanied the ship's scuttling. The sunken ship transformed over the years into a reef, enhancing the structure of the marine environment in the bay.

IMPACT

The *Rainbow Warrior* burial site became a memorial, and has been visited frequently by divers. Four years after the ship was buried, the *Grampian Fame*, an old fishing ship, was refurbished by Greenpeace and renamed *Rainbow Warrior II*. It

carries the wheel and bell of the original *Rainbow Warrior* and has played a critical role in Greenpeace protests.

The French response to the first *Rainbow Warrior*'s attempt to demonstrate at Mururoa suggests that France feared the effects of the protest on their nuclear-testing program. The immediate impact of the bombing was profound. On one hand, Pereira's children lost their father and his wife lost her husband. Greenpeace lost a crew member and photographer, as well as a symbolic ship. On the other hand, membership in the organization increased rapidly, as did public sympathy for Greenpeace.

France was ordered to compensate Pereira's family, Greenpeace, and the government of New Zealand for their losses in the attack. At least one French official lost his position, and the affair was probably a factor in the Socialist Party's loss of positions in the 1986 legislative election. That election reduced Mitterrand's effectiveness for the rest of his first term because he had to deal with a strong opposition majority in Parliament. The bombing also likely played a role in Mitterrand's defeat in the election of 1995 and in the French abandoning their nuclear-testing program in 1996.

Furthermore, the bombing strained France's relationship with New Zealand for several years. It was the first terrorist attack in New Zealand's history and perhaps helped New Zealanders realize that their geographic isolation no longer protected them from such acts.

—*Carl W. Hoagstrom*

FURTHER READING

Bohlen, Jim. *Making Waves: The Origins and Future of Greenpeace*. Tonawanda, N.Y.: Black Rose Books, 2001. Memoir by one of Greenpeace's founding members describes the organization's earliest days and its evolution into a worldwide force for environmental activism. Includes an index.

Brown, Michael, and John May. *The Greenpeace Story: The Inside Story of the World's Most Dynamic Environmental Pressure Group*. New York: Dorling Kindersley, 1991. Gives the bombing context and perspective; two chapters cover the specifics of the *Rainbow Warrior* and the bombing. Illustrations, maps, index.

Dyson, John. *Sink the Rainbow! An Enquiry into the "Greenpeace Affair."* London: Gollancz, 1986. Analyzes the actions and motives of the primary participants. Includes illustrations and maps.

Robie, David. *Eyes of Fire: The Last Voyage of the Rainbow Warrior.* 4th ed. Philadelphia: New Society, 2005. Describes the use of the *Rainbow Warrior* to transfer the population of an island contaminated with radiation to an island with less contamination, as well as the bombing and its aftermath. Illustrations, maps, index, and further readings section.

Sheehan, Sean. *Greenpeace.* Chicago: Raintree, 2004. Written for young readers, this book briefly outlines the history of Greenpeace, including the role of the *Rainbow Warrior* and its destruction in that history. Illustrations, glossary, index.

Wallace-Bruce, Nii Lante. *The Settlement of International Disputes: The Contribution of Australia and New Zealand.* Boston: Martinus Nijhoff, 1998. Pages 189 to 197 explore the *Rainbow Warrior* incident as an example of an international dispute. Includes an index and a bibliography.

Weyler, Rex. *Greenpeace: How a Group of Ecologists, Journalists, and Visionaries Changed the World.* Emmaus, Pa.: Rodale Press, 2004. Comprehensive biographical account of the founders and evolution of the organization, its political divisions, and its campaigns. Includes photographs and an index.

SEE ALSO: Sept. 26, 1979: Love Canal Residents Sue Chemical Company; Dec. 16, 1982: Congress Cites Environmental Protection Agency Chief for Contempt; Feb. 4, 1996: Whistle-Blower Reveals Tobacco Industry Corruption; July, 2002: Journalist Alleges Release of Genetically Modified Corn Seeds in New Zealand.

July 19, 1985
MAYFLOWER MADAM PLEADS GUILTY TO PROMOTING PROSTITUTION

Sydney Barrows, a descendant of Mayflower *pilgrims, drew national attention when she was charged with running a prostitution service that catered to an exclusive clientele. She pleaded guilty to the lesser charge of promoting prostitution. While losing some status as a socialite, Barrows profited from the scandal through the sale of her 1986 book* Mayflower Madam *and through marketing her life story.*

LOCALE: New York, New York
CATEGORIES: Prostitution; law and the courts; sex crimes; sex; business; publishing and journalism

KEY FIGURE
Sydney Barrows (b. 1952), owner of Cachet, an escort service

SUMMARY OF EVENT
On the evening of October 11, 1984, police delivered a search warrant at 307 West Seventy-fourth Street on the upper West Side of New York City, the main office of Cachet, an exclusive escort service that opened for business in 1979. The owner of Cachet was Sydney Barrows, a thirty-two-year-old graduate of the Fashion Institute of Technology, who majored in fashion buying and merchandising.

Barrows, a socialite who could trace her ancestry to *Mayflower* pilgrim William Brewster, pleaded guilty on July 19, 1985, to promoting prostitution and paid a fine of five thousand dollars. Legal problems at Cachet had begun two years earlier with a seemingly benign conflict with the building's landlord in November of 1983. Wishing to raise the rent in the apartment-restricted Manhattan but hindered by a signed contract, the landlord attempted to evict Barrows for running a business in her apartment. Adding to the controversy with the landlord was Barrows's firing of a call girl, who later sought revenge by going to the police. Shortly thereafter, employees reported that Cachet was under police surveillance.

After arresting a Cachet escort, police obtained a warrant to search Cachet on October 11. They seized documents, business records, and business machines, including an overfilled paper shredder. The following day Barrows learned that police had a warrant for her arrest. With her legal advisers she surrendered to the district attorney. She later explained that she did not surrender to police because she believed the officer in charge was using the action on Cachet to ensure his own promotion. Barrows posted bail and was released from custody.

Media competition in New York is especially fierce. In the first few days after the police bust of Cachet, much of the reportage was speculative. By the third day of reporting, the media had discovered Barrows's identity (she had been using the name Sheila Devin at the time of her arrest). Media reports, which described Cachet as a million-dollar, exclusive escort service, were filled with inaccuracies, especially in conflating the terms "bordello," "escort service," and "brothel." Cachet was an escort service that hired out women to spend time with paying clients. It did not "sell" sex, at least not explicitly. Escorts included university students and professors, women working in semiprofessional jobs, and career women. Each woman was scheduled for three nights of escort work per week. Sex between client and escort was acceptable only if the sex was "straightforward"; that is, it had to be conventional.

Prosecutors pressed Barrows to plead guilty in exchange for a lighter sentence and fine. However, regardless of her plea, the fine would remain substantial—possibly fifty thousand dollars (which Barrows did not have)—and she would receive

Sydney Barrows, the Mayflower Madam, at a news conference with a television producer. (AP/Wide World Photos)

some jail time or probation. Her defense announced its intention to go to trial in an attempt to force the prosecution to liberalize its plea offer, which it did not do. The case went to the grand jury, which handed down its indictment just before Christmas, 1984, charging Barrows with promoting prostitution in the third degree.

Barrows's defense had five components: First, it exposed the double standard of a criminal justice system that prosecutes women who provide escorts for hire but seldom prosecutes the men (johns) who pay for the service. Defense attorneys in the Barrows case hinted to the prosecution that they would read the list of prominent men who purchased services from Cachet to the jury in open court. Second, the defense argued that selective prosecution also was applied to the charge of promoting prostitution.

Among those who run escort services and brothels, women tend to be prosecuted while men are seldom prosecuted.

Third, the defense illustrated the illogic of the expense of money, time, and labor devoted by authorities in closing Cachet—an expense that exceeded that of other crackdowns on escort services or bordellos. Even the authorities agreed that Cachet was not implicated in acts of violence or drug use and was not associated with organized crime or police corruption. Why, the defense asked, the expense for Cachet? Fourth, the defense argued that Barrows ran an escort service, which was not in the business of selling sex; rather, Cachet was paid by men for the young women's time.

Fifth, the defense challenged the validity of analyses of Barrows's handwriting. Prosecutors attempted to prove that her handwriting matched the writing on documents seized at Cachet. The defense would support handwriting analyses only if Barrows's handwriting could be picked from ten samples provided to the prosecution experts by the defense. As a result of this demand, the prosecution experts excused themselves from the case.

Fearing the defense would name Cachet's wealthy and powerful clients, the district attorney's office continued to press Barrows for a plea bargain so that the case would not go to trial. Barrows pleaded guilty to the lesser charge of prostitution in the third degree, for which she paid a fine of five thousand dollars.

After her legal troubles, Barrows published her autobiography *Mayflower Madam: The Secret Life of Sydney Biddle Barrows* (with William Novak), which detailed the organization and operation of Cachet, emphasizing the unique factors that made the escort service so successful. In the book's first few chapters, Barrows discusses her working-class background, childhood, education, and the ethics of running an escort service. The last few chapters explain Barrows's struggles with the criminal justice system and how her defense was successful in trivializing the prosecution's criminal case against her. The core of the book, however, is a detailed description of Barrows's management principles and staff training procedures.

IMPACT

No long-term negative impact came from Barrows's conviction. In fact, she profited from the scandal. *Mayflower Madam* is now used as a management training manual for commercial escort and sex services, and the value of the book has not been overlooked by trade journals and businesses and organizations selling sex-related products or services. Barrows's life story was featured as a television biography and was the focus of a 1987 film starring Candice Bergan.

The police crackdown on Cachet, if it had any immediate significance, was its potential for revealing the names of the escort service's clientele. Interestingly, Barrows's eight-inch-thick "black book" was lost or stolen in the chaos of the police raid of Cachet. The black book contained the names, descriptions, addresses, and professional affiliations of male clients, many of whom were corporate executives, religious officials, foreign representatives to the United Nations, sheiks, socialites, and celebrities. It is possible, maybe even probable, that the black book was used for the purposes of financial or political blackmail.

In a wave of police actions, other escort agencies, including those of Alex Adams and Heidi Fleiss, were raided shortly after Cachet was shut down. Many have argued that the policing of organized commercial sex establishments is intermittent, and that this policing is based on what Nebraska madam Josie Washburn argued, in 1909, political or professional aggrandizement. Because commercial prostitution is traditionally owned, supported, and served by the community elites (politicians, legal officials, business owners), it is the elites who determine when and if commercial prostitution will be policed.

—Edward J. Schauer

FURTHER READING

Adams, Alex, and William Stadiem. *Madam 90210: My Life as Madam to the Rich and Famous*. New York: Villard Books, 1993. A discussion of the experiences of Hollywood's foremost madam, Alex Adams, creator of the notorious madam to the stars, Heidi Fleiss.

Barrows, Sydney. *Getting a Little Work Done*. New York: HarperCollins, 2000. In this self-help-style book, Barrows offers advice on balancing sex and career.

Washburn, Josie. *The Underworld Sewer: A Prostitute Reflects on Life in the Trade, 1871-1909*. New ed. Lincoln: University of Nebraska Press, 1997. Provides historical insight into the life of late nineteenth and early twentieth century madam Josie Washburn. Provides contrast and comparison with modern commercialized sex agencies. Originally published in 1909.

Wiltz, Christine. *The Last Madam: A Life in the New Orleans Underworld*. New York: Faber & Faber, 2000. Examines how a commercialized sex agency can exist for decades with little police interference and, as Josie Washburn argued a century earlier, how the shutting down of these agencies is used as a successful political campaign tactic.

SEE ALSO: 1907: Elinor Glyn's Novel *Three Weeks* Shocks Readers; May 13, 1913: Boxer Jack Johnson Is Imprisoned for Abetting Prostitution; July 28, 1980: Magazine Reveals Baseball Star Steve Garvey's Marital Problems; Dec. 7, 1980: Rita Jenrette's "Diary of a Mad Congresswife" Scandalizes Washington; June 27, 1995: Film Star Hugh Grant Is Arrested for Lewd Conduct; Sept. 22, 1997: Sportscaster Marv Albert Is Tried for Sexual Assault; Nov. 2, 2006: Male Escort Reveals Sexual Liaisons with Evangelist Ted Haggard; July 9, 2007: Senator David Vitter's Name Is Found in D.C. Madam's Address Book; Mar. 12, 2008: New York Governor Eliot Spitzer Resigns in Prostitution Scandal.

1980's

August 19, 1985
WEST GERMAN COUNTERINTELLIGENCE CHIEF DEFECTS TO EAST GERMANY

After four years as head of West German counterintelligence, Hans-Joachim Tiedge defected to East Germany, beginning the most serious German spy scandal in more than a decade.

LOCALE: Bonn, West Germany (now Germany)
CATEGORIES: Espionage; corruption; international relations; government

KEY FIGURES
Hans-Joachim Tiedge (b. 1937), head of West German counterintelligence
Markus Wolf (1923-2006), head of East German foreign intelligence service
Heribert Hellenbroich (b. 1937), head of the West German Federal Intelligence Service

SUMMARY OF EVENT
Even with a serious drinking problem, a penchant for gambling, and the accumulation of almost a quarter million German marks in personal debt, Hans-Joachim Tiedge had worked sixteen years in West German intelligence without facing any of the background checks that were normally required every five years. He had become despondent over the recent loss of his wife and had even been the subject of a manslaughter investigation following her accidental death. All this notwithstanding, he had managed to hold onto his very sensitive job for four years as head of the Office for the Protection of the Constitution, West Germany's equivalent of the Federal Bureau of Investigation.

Feeling that his personal situation had become hopeless, on August 19, 1985, Tiedge approached East German guards at a crossing in the Magdeburg region and asked to speak with a representative of East German intelligence to arrange his defection to the East. Thus began the most serious spy scandal to rock West Germany in a decade.

Because of their common language and cultures,

657

East and West Germany were ideal places for their spies to work during the Cold War. Both countries' importance to the North Atlantic Treaty Organization (NATO) and the Warsaw Pact also provided motivation for a very aggressive espionage system between the two states. In the days leading up to Tiedge's defection, the East had definitely held the advantage, having arrested almost two hundred West German agents during Tiedge's tenure while during the same period, Tiedge and his West German agency had enjoyed very little success. In Tiedge's defense, it should be noted that security was very lax for anyone who wanted to come into West Germany from the East, and was very strict for those going in the other direction.

Heribert Hellenbroich, Tiedge's boss until four months prior to Tiedge's defection, was also his good friend. Given Tiedge's behavior since the death of his wife (even his neighbors had called Tiedge's office to complain of his drunkenness), it is perhaps not a surprise that the friendship was a major reason Tiedge continued in his job. Only four months before the defection, Hellenbroich had been promoted to head of the Federal Intelligence Service. The loss of Hellenbroich as his immediate superior probably contributed to Tiedge's despondence. In any case, Hellenbroich was forced to resign his post after the defection as a direct result of his relationship with Tiedge.

Tiedge's principal adversary during this period was Markus Wolf, the head of the General Reconnaissance Administration, East Germany's foreign intelligence service. The opposite of the overweight and alcoholic Tiedge, Wolf was a most effective spy. At the time of the defection, Wolf was suspected of recruiting Tiedge, but it was unclear whether Tiedge had already been working as a mole for Wolf before 1985. Wolf stated in his autobiography *Man Without a Face* (1997) that his first contact with Tiedge was on the day of his defection.

Whether Wolf was telling the truth or not, it is worth noting that in the weeks just before the Tiedge defection several longtime East German spies disappeared. One of them, Johanna Olbricht, had been living in West Germany under the false identity of Sonja Lüneburg for twenty years. She

had served as secretary to the then-leader of the Free Democratic Party, Martin Bangemann. She was last seen in West Germany three weeks before Tiedge's defection. One could speculate that Olbricht and the other fleeing spies might have been under Tiedge's protection and had been warned that he was leaving.

Regardless of whether he was a mole or simply a defector, Tiedge still was a great prize for the East Germans, and they took great care of him. After he was in the hands of the Stasi, the East German secret police, he was placed in a hospital to recover from his alcohol addiction. The overweight spy was also diabetic and was placed on a stringent diet. Wolf commented on Tiedge's appearance at the time of his defection by comparing him to a giant panda, bloated and pale with dark-rimmed eyes. Wolf also described him as very frank, noting that he did not try to justify his actions on idealistic grounds but instead described himself simply as a traitor.

When Tiedge was back on his feet, he was told to write a dissertation for a doctorate. The title would be "The Counterintelligence Task of the Office for the Protection of the Constitution of the Federal Republic of Germany." He would detail in two-hundred-plus pages all the methods employed by his office, including its electronic surveillance techniques. In addition to providing operational details, he also provided names of agents from the West. The East Germans boasted at one point that they had arrested 170 West German agents in an eighteen-month period thanks to information provided by Tiedge.

Tiedge stopped drinking and lost thirty pounds within a month. According to Wolf's autobiography, women who were loyal to the party were made available for Tiedge, and he eventually married one of them. The woman Tiedge married was a Stasi secretary.

In 1989, when the communist government in East Germany began to fall, Tiedge left for Moscow with his new wife and the equivalent of almost $100,000 in so-called severance pay. When interviewed by the magazine *Der Spiegel* in 1993, he was still in Moscow, living under the name Hans Ottowitsch, on a pension and living well. Asked if he was a traitor, he replied that of course he was. He showed no remorse, choosing to blame his superiors for failing to come to his aid when he was in such need of help. He said that defection and suicide were his only choices but that he did not have the courage for the latter. He reportedly remained in Moscow even after the statute of limitations for treason expired in 2005.

IMPACT

The most obvious and most immediate impact of Tiedge's defection was the complete disarray of West German intelligence. Its methods revealed and their agents compromised, they were faced with the task of reorganizing and restaffing their operations.

The initial bipartisanship among West German politicians in face of the scandal soon gave way to accusations, and there was much talk about how the scandal would or should affect relations between East and West Germany. Cooler heads prevailed, however, and there was little long-lasting or serious impact on the relations between the two countries. Negotiations continued for a cultural treaty, and an invitation for the leader of East Germany, Erich Honecker, to visit West Germany was not hampered by the scandal.

Strengthened by the scandal was NATO's feeling that, because of its cultural and historical ties to East Germany, West Germany was the weak sister in the alliance in terms of espionage. Undoubtedly, the scandal would give the Allies cause to consider even more carefully their intelligence and technological cooperation with the German Republic. Luckily, compartmentalization of intelligence operations for just such an occurrence prevented Tiedge from having very much useful information about NATO and its other members. The Allies had always understood that West Germany was exposed "in a special way" to attacks from East Germany.

The defection and the resulting confusion were not enough to stave off the collapse of the communist regime in East Germany. Within five years of the Tiedge scandal, the infamous Stasi and the East German communist state were matters of history, as the two German nations became one in 1990.

—Wayne Shirey

FURTHER READING

Koehler, John O. *Stasi: The Untold Story of the East German Secret Police*. Boulder, Colo.: Westview Press, 1999. An informative look at the East German Ministry for State Security, better known as Stasi. Includes details about Tiedge.

Minnick, Wendell L. *Spies and Provocateurs: A Worldwide Encyclopedia of Persons Conducting Espionage and Covert Action, 1946-1991*. Jefferson, N.C.: McFarland, 1992. An alphabetical who's who of spies from the Cold War era.

Wolf, Markus, with Anne McElvoy. *Man Without a Face: The Autobiography of Communism's Greatest Spymaster*. New York: Times Books/ Random House, 1997. An autobiography of the East German spy who recruited Tiedge.

1980's

SEE ALSO: July 12, 1906: French Court Declares Alfred Dreyfus Innocent of Treason; May 26, 1945: Norwegian Writer Knut Hamsun Is Arrested for Treason; Sept. 12, 1962: British Civil Servant Is Arrested for Spying; Oct. 26, 1962: West German Police Raid *Der Spiegel* Magazine Offices; Mar. 2-Sept. 25, 1963: John Profumo Affair Rocks British Government; Mar. 4, 1966: Munsinger Sex and Spy Scandal Rocks Canada; Nov. 9, 1976: German Generals Must Retire for Supporting a Neo-Nazi Pilot; 1980: Biographer Claims Actor Errol Flynn Was a Nazi Spy; Feb. 18, 2001: CIA Agent Robert Hanssen Is Arrested for Spying for the Russians; Mar. 2, 2003: U.S. National Security Agency Is Found to Have Spied on U.N. Officials.

September 17, 1985
MEDIA ALLEGE CANADIAN OFFICIALS ALLOWED SALE OF RANCID TUNA

The Canadian Broadcasting Corporation television newsmagazine The Fifth Estate *reported that large quantities of possibly rancid tuna had been distributed to Canadian consumers. The minister of fisheries and oceans, who approved of the distribution despite warnings, resigned. Prime Minister Brian Mulroney's role in the scandal was questioned as well.*

ALSO KNOWN AS: Tunagate
LOCALE: St. Andrews, New Brunswick, Canada
CATEGORIES: Corruption; government; medicine and health care; business; ethics

KEY FIGURES
John Fraser (b. 1931), Canadian minister of fisheries and oceans, 1984-1985
Brian Mulroney (b. 1939), Canadian prime minister, 1984-1993

SUMMARY OF EVENT
On September 17, 1985, the television newsmagazine *The Fifth Estate*, broadcast by the Canadian Broadcasting Corporation (CBC), reported that large quantities of rancid tuna fish had been distributed to Canadian consumers. Despite being aware that inspectors had rejected the tuna as being unfit for human consumption, John Fraser, who was appointed as the federal minister of fisheries and oceans in 1984, overruled the decision and approved the distribution of the tuna.

StarKist Canada, Inc., acquired in 1981 by the American company H. J. Heinz, had the only tuna canning plant in Canada and controlled approximately 40 percent of the Canadian canned-tuna market. The allegedly tainted tuna was manufactured at StarKist's plant in St. Andrews, New Brunswick.

Quality issues with the canned tuna manufactured at the St. Andrews plant began several years before the story broke in the media. Using sight, smell, and taste tests, Department of Fisheries and Oceans inspectors had declared that a total of approximately one million cans of tuna were not suitable for human consumption. The tuna, which was imported from other parts of the world, including Africa and Asia, and canned in Canada, was described as rancid and emitting a strong odor. It was later reported that a type of tuna frequently processed at the plant was of a smaller kind and that it had a greater fat content, which increased the likelihood of oxidation or rotting. Oxidation could have occurred during storage or through thawing of the fish.

The value of the amassed one million cans of rejected tuna was estimated to be between $600,000 and $800,000. As a result of the potential loss of revenue, StarKist was threatening to close the St. Andrews plant, one of the largest employers in the county. StarKist executives, along with the New Brunswick premier, Richard Hatfield, petitioned Fraser and sought his approval to distribute the tuna to consumers anyway. Fraser asked the New Brunswick Research and Productivity Council (RPC), an independent agency that traditionally used a more sophisticated chemical analysis of food than did the Department of Fisheries and Oceans, to examine the tuna. In contrast to the fisheries and oceans inspectors, the RPC found the tuna to be suitable for public consumption.

Conflicting reports exist as to whether Fraser waited for the results of the RPC tests prior to overruling the decision of the fisheries and oceans inspectors and approving the sale of the tuna. RPC representatives claimed that Fraser had approved the distribution of the tuna prior to the completion of testing. The tuna was distributed to supermarkets and other food stores throughout Canada and even purchased by the Department of National Defense. However, the food product was later returned because of its poor appearance and smell. The tuna also was rejected by an African famine-relief organization.

Fraser was interviewed for the broadcast of *The Fifth Estate* and was thus questioned by the Canadian House of Commons. He defended his decision to approve the otherwise rejected tuna. He claimed that the inspection techniques used by the fisheries and oceans department were subjective. He testified that he had consumed the tuna himself and had no problems for doing so. While some store owners had already voluntarily removed the tuna from store shelves, a formal recall was announced on September 19. In addition to the StarKist brand, the allegedly tainted tuna was sold under the different labels. Less than one week after the scandal was broadcast, Fraser resigned his position.

Fraser was not the only public official who faced increased scrutiny as a result of Tunagate, as the incident was dubbed by the press. While admitting that two staff members were aware of the situation involving the supposedly tainted tuna in July, 1985, Prime Minister Brian Mulroney claimed that he did not learn of the incident until the day the story broke on *The Fifth Estate*. Initially, Fraser and another public official testified that Mulroney had been aware of the release of the tuna prior to the news report. However, several days later, both recanted their stories and corroborated Mulroney's account. Mulroney defended his actions, claimed he acted appropriately, and then took credit for issuing the recall. He offered to resign as prime minister if it was proven that he was aware of the distribution before the CBC report.

StarKist never recovered from the scandal. The St. Andrews plant closed in October, leaving its four hundred workers unemployed. StarKist's share of the Canadian canned-tuna market was reduced from nearly 40 percent to zero. In 1987, the St. Andrews plant resumed packaging tuna. Two years later, StarKist tuna was reintroduced to Canadian grocery stores. Despite its marketing and advertising efforts, sales of the fish lagged. In 1990, StarKist ceased its operations in Canada.

In the recall, more than twenty million cans of tuna, valued at an estimated $17 million, were confiscated. Although cans of the tuna were later tested and deemed fit for human consumption, the government mandated that the entire lot was not suitable for humans but could be sold in Canada and abroad as pet food.

In 1992, the tainted tuna resurfaced when it was reportedly repackaged as tuna suitable for human consumption and sold in thirteen states in the United States. The tuna could be traced to the St. Andrews plant by a code printed on the can. A recall was subsequently issued in the United States. Not only was the tuna intended to be sold in the United States, but a plan to relabel the cat food as tuna suitable for humans and import it back into Canada from the United States was uncovered when the cans were inspected at the U.S.-Canadian border.

IMPACT

Tunagate was covered heavily by a press that critics contended was biased against the Conservative government. The scandal, despite its widespread press attention, led to nothing but fear. No official reports surfaced of persons becoming ill from eating the fish, and no one died from consuming the questionable tuna. Later reports indicated that although the tuna smelled and looked inedible, it was consumable and had posed no health threats to those who did chose to eat the product. Furthermore, the cans that held the tuna had been sterilized at the plant during manufacturing, thus reducing any threat of food-related illness. Nonetheless, the incident incited widespread fear. It also became a popular source of jokes, even spawning a card game called "Tunagate," in which the cards were packaged in a round tin container.

The scandal weakened the public's faith in the government agencies that approved food for human consumption. Food inspection in Canada was later centralized under the administration of one agency. This centralization limited the conflicting goals of departments in promoting and regulating industries and products.

After resigning from the Department of Fisheries and Oceans, Fraser restarted his career and was elected speaker of the Commons in 1986 and re-elected in 1988. Mulroney, despite questions raised about his knowledge of Tunagate, was reelected prime minister in 1988 and served until 1993.

—Margaret E. Leigey

1980's

FURTHER READING

Harris, Michael. "PM Is Caught by New Snag in Tuna Affair." *Globe & Mail*, September 25, 1985. Reviews public statements that contradict Mulroney's statements about his knowledge of the distribution of the rejected tuna to Canadian consumers.

Savoie, Donald J. *Breaking the Bargain: Public Servants, Ministers, and Parliament.* Toronto, Ont.: University of Toronto Press, 2003. Argues that "Canada's machinery of government is out of joint." Discusses the challenges facing the tradition of deal-making between elected officials and career officials. A good introduction to the workings (and problems) of the Canadian system of government.

"Tuna Casualties Mostly Political." *Financial Post* (Toronto), September 28, 1985. Provides a thorough summary of the scandal, including details of the resignation of John Fraser.

"Two Hundred Fifty Workers to Lose Jobs as N.B. Tuna Plant Closes." *Globe & Mail*, May 18, 1990. Reports on the closing of the StarKist Canada tuna canning plant in St. Andrews, New Brunswick.

SEE ALSO: 1956-1962: Prescription Thalidomide Causes Widespread Birth Disorders; Feb. 4, 1996: Whistle-Blower Reveals Tobacco Industry Corruption; Nov. 26, 1997: Canadian Health Commissioner Releases Report on Tainted Blood; May 7, 1999-Mar. 2, 2001: Ethics Counselor Exonerates Canadian Prime Minister Jean Chrétien; Summer, 2006-Mar. 16, 2007: Manufacturer Recalls Pet Food That Killed Thousands of American Pets.

October 23, 1985

GURU BHAGWAN SHREE RAJNEESH IS INDICTED FOR IMMIGRATION FRAUD

In 1981, followers of Indian guru Bhagwan Shree Rajneesh founded an ambitious religious community on a desert ranch in eastern Oregon. Plagued from the outset by local hostility and conflicts with land-use laws, the community, Rajneeshpuram, collapsed in 1985 when its leader was arrested for immigration fraud and several key figures faced criminal charges and convictions.

LOCALE: Portland, Oregon

CATEGORIES: Law and the courts; organized crime and racketeering; government; religion; social issues and reform; civil rights and liberties

KEY FIGURES

Bhagwan Shree Rajneesh (1931-1990), Indian guru and cult leader

Ma Anand Sheela (b. 1950), Rajneesh's personal secretary

David Frohnmayer (b. 1940), Oregon attorney general, 1981-1991

SUMMARY OF EVENT

On October 28, 1985, federal agents in Charlottesville, North Carolina, detained Indian guru Bhagwan Shree Rajneesh when his private airplane stopped for refueling. Alleging that he was attempting to flee the United States, they arrested him and several followers and returned them to Portland, Oregon, to face charges of racketeering and immigration fraud. The charges stemmed from attempts to form a spiritual community eighteen miles from Antelope, Oregon. Rajneesh and some of his followers had been indicted on October 23 by a federal grand jury, just days before his arrest.

The arrests marked the end of a controversial utopian experiment, though not the end of the movement. Rajneeshism, sometimes ironically dubbed the "rich man's path to enlightenment," draws upon Hinduism and other Eastern traditions. The spiritual writings of the founder, together with veneration of his person, form the core of a movement emphasizing meditation, personal spiritual fulfillment, a relaxed and fun-filled attitude toward life, and for some devotees, investment in a communal lifestyle. During the 1970's, the movement established a large study and residential center near Pune (Poona) in India and a network of study centers in the West, mainly in Europe.

In contrast to other cults spawned by the unrest of the 1960's, the Rajneesh movement attracted an older, well-educated population that brought with them considerable skills and capital. Adherents shunned high-pressure proselytizing, relying on more conventional marketing to spread the message. By 1980, Rajneeshism could claim thirty thousand adherents, most of them concentrated in Europe.

The movement outgrew the center in Pune. Other Indian sects mistrusted an ostensibly religious movement that sanctioned extramarital sex and seemed to cater to the needs and appetites of affluent foreigners. There were tax issues as well. In the light of these pressures, Ma Anand Sheela, Rajneesh's personal secretary and effectively the administrative head of the cult, decided in 1981 to purchase land and begin building a utopian community that would serve as a permanent residence for Rajneesh and a core of dedicated followers, termed "sannyasins," and a place of study and pilgrimage for the movement as a whole. To this end they bought a 64,000-acre cattle ranch near the desert town of Antelope (population less than 50).

From the outset, the project met with open hostility at local and state levels. Longtime residents of Wasco County, who were conservative and mainly fundamentalist Christian, strongly opposed any development that would shift the population balance and voter base in favor of outsiders with alien philosophies and lifestyles. People in sleepy eastern Oregon towns reacted, sometimes violently, after their streets were inundated with hundreds of enthusiastic young people wearing the red and orange garb of Rajneeshism and a portrait of the charismatic leader dangling from a string of prayer beads.

Support from the more liberal and populated western half of Oregon was minimal. After the 1978 mass suicide of hundreds of members of a religious cult in Jonestown, Guyana, South America, the public was extra-suspicious of cults in general. Although the Rajneeshism development incorporated many innovations designed to reduce environmental impact, its size triggered objections that were capitalized upon by the political action group 1000 Friends of Oregon.

Attempts to incorporate the new town of Rajneeshpuram were challenged by Oregon's attorney general, David Frohnmayer, on the grounds that a town government and infrastructure tied to a specific religious sect violated the United States Constitution's strictures on separation of church and state. The Rajneeshis challenged this claim in court. Unable to incorporate, the new town could not comply with state land-use laws. Attempts to purchase property and swing elections in Antelope itself backfired. At one point the cult began soliciting homeless people, busing them to Oregon, and registering them to vote in an effort to replace the county commissioners of Wasco County with a more favorable board.

During the years 1981 to 1985, against a background of growing hostility, outside investment and the labor of the inhabitants turned Rajneeshpuram into a thriving community, though increasingly resembling an armed camp. Rajneesh was silent, interacting with his adoring followers by touring the town in one of his many Rolls-Royce cars and leaving the governing to Sheela and a tight circle of mostly female devotees. Members of the town's security forces paraded around with assault rifles, giving rise to rumors that weapons were being stockpiled in anticipation of a military assault on the citizens of Oregon. In July of 1985, Rajneesh resumed communicating directly with his community and began taking steps to regain control from Sheela.

In September, Sheela and her close associates abruptly left for Germany. Rajneesh, aware of being investigated for immigration fraud, attempted through lawyers to surrender at a remote location rather than provoke an assault by armed federal agents on Rajneeshpuram. The immigration fraud charges were based on Rajneesh having arranged sham marriages between U.S. citizens and foreign sannyasins. He was charged by federal prosecutors in Portland on October 28 with criminal conspiracy and making false statements to officials of the U.S. Immigration and Naturalization Service. He accepted a plea bargain, pleaded guilty to two counts of immigration fraud, and paid a $400,000 fine. He also paid $4 million in investigative costs to the state of Oregon, $5 million to the state's victims' fund, and $500,000 to the restaurants involved in a salmonella outbreak. He also agreed to leave the United States for ten years.

Investigations following Rajneesh's arrest, and Sheela's flight to Germany, had uncovered a web of illegal activity instigated by Sheela, including wiretapping and surveillance, misappropriation of funds, and cultivating pathogens for possible biological terrorism. Sheela was subsequently convicted of causing a salmonella outbreak in The Dalles, Oregon, by ordering deliberate contamination of salad bars frequented by Wasco County commissioners, and of attempting to murder Rajneesh's personal physician by jabbing him with a hypodermic needle containing an unidentified toxin. She served three years in a federal penitentiary before being deported.

Rajneeshpuram closed and was subsequently sold to pay off the judgments against Rajneesh, Sheela, and others. Rajneesh returned to the community outside Pune in India, after failing to gain entry into several other countries around the world. He changed his name to Osho, founded a new movement, and kept a very low profile. He died of natural causes in 1990.

IMPACT

At its height, the Rajneesh movement attracted roughly 200,000 members worldwide, of whom a maximum of 7,000 lived at Rajneeshpuram in Oregon and perhaps 20,000 visited the ranch for festivals and retreats. For most, the movement represented an interlude, disappointing in that it failed to deliver the hoped-for spiritual utopia but not entirely without value. Few thought that they had been brainwashed or traumatized. Since the commune attracted mainly single adults and discouraged starting families, none of the accusations of child abuse and corruption of minors that plagued so many alternative communities accompanied this movement.

On July 13, 1986, a monument was dedicated outside the Wasco County Court House. Beneath the statue of a stately antelope read the inscription "Dedicated to all who steadfastly and unwaveringly opposed the attempts of the Rajneesh followers to take political control of Wasco County: 1981-1985." The ranch, having fallen into disrepair, soon housed a Christian youth

Bhagwan Shree Rajneesh is escorted by federal officers in North Carolina after he fled Oregon. He had been indicted one week earlier for immigration fraud and racketeering. (AP/Wide World Photos)

camp. The local sense of having heroically staved off the "red tide" of alien cultists, strong during the 1980's, faded with time.

The episode helped channel mainstream liberal opinion in Oregon into an emphatically secular direction. Opposition to an intentional religious community, originally fueled by Christian fundamentalism and xenophobia, became transformed into a civil rights issue. State attorney general Frohnmayer became president of the University of Oregon system, seeming assurance that the prevailing intellectual view will consider the judicial destruction of Rajneeshpuram and seizure of its assets by the state of Oregon to be a triumph for American freedom of religion.

Voices of dissent spoke as well. Apologists for the sect, which still has a worldwide following, maintain that they consistently tried to work within the law, that the objectionable acts were the responsibility of a small group of people surrounding Sheela, and that the federal government was trying to provoke an armed confrontation such as occurred at the Branch Davidian compound in Waco, Texas, several years later, in 1993.

The various claims and counterclaims concerning incorporation of Rajneeshpuram leave unresolved the question of whether a nonmainstream religious sect with a nontraditional life philosophy can even operate in the United States. Some people argued that if a religiously mandated lifestyle violates existing community zoning ordinances, and the U.S. Constitution prohibits incorporating communities based on a religious beliefs and practices, religious freedom is seriously compromised.

—*Martha A. Sherwood*

FURTHER READING

Braun, Kirk. *Rajneeshpuram, the Unwelcome Society: Cultures Collide in a Quest for Utopia.* West Linn, Oreg.: Scout Creek Press, 1984. A countercultural view of the land-use battles between Rajneeshpuram representatives and the locals of Antelope, Oregon.

Davisson, Sven. "The Rise and Fall of Rajneeshpuram." *Ashe Journal* 2, no. 2 (2003): 1-21. Explores repressive state actions and treats Sheela's offenses as a reaction to outside pressure. From an alternative spirituality publication.

Goldman, Marion. *Passionate Journeys: Why Successful Women Joined a Cult.* Ann Arbor: University of Michigan Press, 1999. Tells the story of the Rajneeshpuram commune through composite portraits. Places emphasis on the motives of sannyasins.

Richardson, James T. *Regulating Religion: Case Studies from Around the Globe.* New York: Kluwer Academic/Plenum, 2004. This general study includes analysis of court challenges to Rajneeshpuram.

Strelley, Kate, with Robert D. San Souci. *The Ultimate Game: The Rise and Fall of Bhagwan Shree Rajneesh.* San Francisco, Calif.: Harper & Row, 1987. Personal story of an English woman who was a follower of Rajneesh in Pune and Oregon.

SEE ALSO: May-June, 1926: Evangelist Aimee Semple McPherson Claims She Was Kidnapped; Oct. 31, 1975: Buddhist Teacher Orders His Students to Remove Their Clothes; June 27, 1978: Evangelist Herbert W. Armstrong Excommunicates His Own Son; Apr. 22, 1986: Faith Healer Peter Popoff Is Exposed as a Fraud; June 30, 2001: Korean Religious Teacher Jung Myung Seok Is Charged with Rape; Nov. 2, 2006: Evangelist Kent Hovind Is Convicted of Federal Tax Violations.

1980's

February 28, 1986
BASEBALL COMMISSIONER PETER UEBERROTH SUSPENDS PLAYERS FOR COCAINE USE

Major League Baseball commissioner Peter Ueberroth suspended several players with the Pittsburgh Pirates, including the team's mascot, and other players from around the league in a drug scandal that marked the first major dark cloud for baseball since the 1919 Black Sox game-fixing scandal. Baseball then faced the Pete Rose gambling affair, labor-union strikes, game cancellations, declining ticket sales, and the steroids scandal.

ALSO KNOWN AS: Baseball drug trials
LOCALES: Pittsburgh and Philadelphia, Pennsylvania
CATEGORIES: Sports; corruption; drugs; law and the courts; medicine and health care; organized crime and racketeering; popular culture; social issues and reform

KEY FIGURES

Peter Ueberroth (b. 1937), baseball commissioner
Dave Parker (b. 1951), Pittsburgh Pirates outfielder
Dale Berra (b. 1956), Pittsburgh Pirates infielder
Keith Hernandez (b. 1953), New York Mets infielder
Lonnie Smith (b. 1955), Philadelphia Phillies outfielder
Kevin Koch (b. 1953), Pittsburgh Pirates mascot

SUMMARY OF EVENT

Following a successful decade during the 1970's that brought six divisional championships and one World Series victory to the city of Pittsburgh, Pirates fans were caught off guard during the 1980's. Following the firing of general manager Pete Peterson and clubhouse manager Chuck Tanner, as well as dwindling attendance, talks of dismantling the team, and potential buyouts, the 1986 season brought the baseball drug trials. In February of

1986, in the first major drug scandal for Major League Baseball, baseball commissioner Peter Ueberroth, harsh but fair in his punishments of players of all skills, was forced to suspend several players with the Pittsburgh Pirates, including star Dave Parker, and other players for using cocaine in their respective clubhouses.

The testimony of dozens of players resulted in the arrest and conviction of seven Philadelphia and Pittsburgh area drug dealers, including Curtis Strong, who was convicted on eleven counts of selling cocaine. Pittsburgh area dealer Shelby Greer pleaded guilty to seven counts associated with drug dealing, and five other men would serve time for the largest drug scandal in baseball history.

During the late 1970's and 1980's, cocaine became a regular fixture in Major League clubhouses. Players were purchasing drugs in stadium restrooms and locker rooms. Rumors began to circulate that players were playing games while high and were even carrying drugs in vials in their uniforms. In a May 14, 1985, memorandum to the Major and Minor League teams, Ueberroth outlined the league's updated drug policy.

In late 1985, a Philadelphia grand jury called Parker, along with Pirates teammates Lee Mazzilli, John Milner, Lee Lacy, Rod Scurry, and Dale Berra, son of New York Yankees great Yogi Berra, to testify. Other major leaguers called before the grand jury were Willie Aikens, Vida Blue, Jeffrey Leonard, Tim Raines, Enos Cabell, Keith Hernandez, and Lonnie Smith, who all testified to the rampant use of cocaine and amphetamines. Their testimony led many to believe that drug use affected as many as 40 percent of major league baseball players (a claim that is often challenged).

Prosecutors in the case stated that baseball was not on trial; drug use in society was the problem at hand, and the goal was to eradicate the drug pushers and dealers and to keep drugs from tarnishing the game of baseball. For their testimony, major league players were granted full immunity by law, meaning they would receive no jail or prison time. This immunity from prosecution allowed for open discussion of clubhouse secrets, including the secret of drug use. Testimony confirmed drug use during games and the existence of locker-room drug deals on game days.

Kevin Koch, the Pirates' Parrot mascot, was eventually implicated in the scandal for introducing players—both local and visiting—to area drug dealers. Seven local drug dealers, most notably Strong, were convicted and sentenced to prison. Strong's lawyer maintained that the baseball players were highly paid junkies, and not heroes. Player Milner admitted to buying cocaine during a game in which he participated. Hernandez, a future All-Star with the New York Mets, admitted to using drugs for more than three years while playing. Although the players who testified in return for immunity avoided jail or prison sentences, the organization of professional baseball, which had been harshly criticized by judicial officials throughout the trials for ignoring the drug problem for decades, would have free rein to punish the guilty.

Major League Baseball meted out punishments to twenty-one players on February 28, 1986. In his press conference announcing the sanctions, Ueberroth said that ten players who were mentioned during the drug trials were forced to submit to random drug testing for the remainder of their respective careers. Eleven players were given stricter punishments. Of the eleven, the four who admitted to using cocaine—Al Holland, Lee Lacy, Larry Sorensen, and Claudell Washington—received sixty-day suspensions and monetary fines of up to 5 percent of their salaries. They also were mandated to perform drug-education-related community service in their communities and had to submit to drug

tests. Holland's career ended only one year after the league sanctions. Lacy also ended his career in 1987 as a member of the Baltimore Orioles. Sorensen continued to battle his substance abuse, ended his career in 1988 with the San Francisco Giants, and served time for multiple driving-under-the-influence offenses after his playing days. Washington was traded many times and finished his career in 1990 with the Yankees.

The remaining seven players—Berra, Smith, Parker, Hernandez, Cabell, Leonard, and Joaquin Andujar—received even harsher penalties. One-year suspensions would be waived in return for 10 percent of the player's salary, two years of community service, and mandatory drug testing for the life of their careers. Berra, a top prospect in 1977, never had a productive season, and following the drug trials he played in 1987 for the Houston Astros, where he ended his career. Leonard received the 1987 National League Championship Series MVP award for his play for the Giants and ended his career in 1990 with the Seattle Mariners. Andujar, a former All-Star pitcher, was traded many times following the drug trials and sustained several injuries; his career ended in 1988. Cabell played one more season

Peter Ueberroth announces Major League Baseball's drug-testing plan at a news conference in New York. (AP/Wide World Photos)

1980's

MAINTAINING BASEBALL'S INTEGRITY

In his Memorandum from Commissioner Peter V. Ueberroth to All Clubs Re: Baseball's Drug Education & Prevention Program (May 14, 1986), the baseball commissioner outlined the long-term effect of drugs and drug use on the sport of baseball.

Our other principal concern is the maintenance of the integrity of the game. It is most important that all of us in Baseball and our fans have the fullest confidence in our game. Drug involvement or the suspicion of drug involvement is inconsistent with maintaining that essential goal.

following the drug trials with the Los Angeles Dodgers. Smith won the MLB Comeback Player of the Year Award in 1989 and had a productive career following the scandal. He is most remembered, however, for his base-running error during the 1991 World Series, in which his team, the Atlanta Braves, lost the game. He finished his career in 1994.

Parker, a favorite in Pittsburgh, was traded around the league during the 1980's and found his niche as a designated hitter in the American League. He was an All-Star in 1986 and 1990. He finished his career with the Toronto Blue Jays in 1991. Hernandez, probably the most famous player of the drug scandals, was best known for his defensive skills with the Mets at first base and for the team's 1986 World Series victory over the Boston Red Sox. Hernandez won more Gold Glove Awards in 1986, 1987, and 1988 (he won eleven in his career) and was an All-Star in 1986 and 1987. He finished his career in 1990 with the Cleveland Indians and was inducted into the Mets Hall of Fame in 1987.

IMPACT

Ueberroth was chastised by the players' union for unfairly levying penalties against the players involved in the drug scandal, but his sanctions would hold. His belief in mandatory drug testing as a collective bargaining issue may have been his most famous attempt at making baseball a legitimate organization. He was a strong proponent of removing drugs, especially stimulants such as cocaine, from

the game in an effort to minimize inflated performance statistics.

Ueberroth is considered a visionary by some, as the mid-1990's saw the beginnings of the steroid-use scandal, brought about, in part, by the league's failure to instill mandatory drug testing. As the legal community once again criticized Major League officials for ignoring drug use in the sport, many began to wonder if Ueberroth also should have been ignored.

The baseball drug trials of 1985-1986 cleaned the game of illegal street drugs such as cocaine, but the trials did very little to quell the coming storm of synthetic drugs, such as steroids, and their abuse by some of the biggest names in professional baseball. Synthetic drugs, the new drug of choice for many players, poisoned the game and the record books during the 1990's and into the twenty-first century.

—*Keith J. Bell*

FURTHER READING

Bryant, Howard. *Juicing the Game: Drugs, Power, and the Fight for the Soul of Major League Baseball*. Monrovia, Md.: Paw Prints, 2008. Examines the effect of drugs on professional baseball and discusses what the Major League has done to address the problem. A questioning work about the iconic status of baseball in the United States.

Conner, Floyd, and John Snyder. *Baseball's Most Wanted*. 3 vols. Dulles, Va.: Brassey's, 2004. A discussion of the "national pastime's outrageous offenders, lucky bounces, and other oddities." Brings into one boxed set past volumes that explored the top scandals in professional baseball.

Mottram, David R., ed. *Drugs in Sport*. 4th ed. New York: Routledge, 2005. A comprehensive reference work on the use and abuse of drugs by athletes in sports around the world. Also includes detailed analyses of cocaine use.

Rader, Benjamin G. *Baseball: A History of America's Game*. 3d ed. Urbana: University of Illinois Press, 2008. A detailed history of baseball in the United States that also examines the scandals that have affected the game.

March 3, 1986

FORMER U.N. SECRETARY-GENERAL KURT WALDHEIM'S NAZI PAST IS REVEALED

Kurt Waldheim faced accusations during his campaign for the Austrian presidency that he had concealed his membership in Nazi organizations and a substantial portion of his service in the Wehrmacht during World War II. The scandal raised questions about guilt for crimes committed during the war and about how much was known of his past before he was elected United Nations secretary-general.

ALSO KNOWN AS: Waldheim affair
LOCALE: Vienna, Austria
CATEGORIES: Publishing and journalism; atrocities and war crimes; international relations; government; politics; military

KEY FIGURES
Kurt Waldheim (1918-2007), United Nations secretary-general, 1972-1981, and president of Austria, 1986-1992
Simon Wiesenthal (1908-2005), Nazi hunter
Edwin Meese III (b. 1931), U.S. attorney general, 1985-1988

SUMMARY OF EVENT
The Waldheim affair broke when the Austrian magazine *Profil* and the World Jewish Congress (WJC) and *The New York Times* alleged in early March of 1986 that Waldheim's 1985 autobiography, *In the Eye of the Storm*, concealed several key facts. These omissions included his membership in a Nazi student organization, the National Socialist German Students League; membership in a Sturm Abteilung, or storm trooper, mounted regiment; and that units to which he was attached committed atrocities in the Balkans in World War II.

The Balkan atrocities included General Friedrich Stahl's massacre of civilians at Kozara, West Bosnia, in Yugoslavia (June-August, 1942), operations against partisans in Yugoslavia (May-June, 1943) known as Operation Black, and transportation of 42,000 Jews from Salonika, Greece, to concentration camps by German general Alexander Löhr's Army Group E (May-August, 1943). Löhr was subsequently executed in 1947 by Yugoslavia for war crimes. Waldheim had served as a Wehrmacht intelligence officer under Stahl and Löhr, and the implication was that Waldheim would have at least been aware of these incidents.

After these charges were raised, it came to light that questions about Waldheim's past already had been asked in 1979. An inquiry by the Israeli government led to questions for so-called Nazi hunter Simon Wiesenthal. He was asked whether Wald-

Kurt Waldheim, center, is shown in this 1943 photograph with other German Nazi officers in Yugoslavia. (AP/Wide World Photos)

zations but offered that he did serve in the Balkans in World War II as an interpreter. His supporters condemned the allegations as unfounded and claimed that they were merely an attempt to discredit Waldheim.

On March 22, 1986, the WJC released a bombshell document listing Waldheim in the Central Registry of War Criminals and Security Suspects, developed by the U.S. Army, which listed suspected war criminals. It also had been revealed that the Yugoslav government had prepared a file accusing Waldheim of murder and presented this to the United Nations War Crimes Commission in 1948. This formal accusation became the basis for Waldheim's name being added to the registry. Subsequent research by historians revealed that this 1948 file was prepared to attempt to derail Austria's position in diplomatic negotiations with Yugoslavia over financial and territorial issues because Waldheim was part of Austria's diplomatic delegation. This information was not used against Waldheim at that time, nor did Yugoslavia raise it in the future.

heim had served in the SS, the German Nazi police, or otherwise had been a Nazi. Wiesenthal answered no to both questions. In 1980, U.S. Congress member Stephen Solarz, a New York Democrat, wrote to Waldheim to ask him about his war record and his alleged membership in a Nazi student organization. Waldheim denied membership in the student organization and stated that he was incapacitated after being wounded on the Russian front in December, 1941. He said that he left the German army after his recovery and completed his law degree in 1944. The U.S. Central Intelligence Agency (CIA) backed Waldheim's assertions in a written statement to Solarz.

The timing of the allegations seemed suspect, given that the Austrian presidential elections were two months away. Waldheim, who was running for president, denied membership in any Nazi organi-

Waldheim had advanced through the Austrian foreign service and served as Austria's delegate to the United Nations in the postwar years. He ran unsuccessfully for president of Austria in 1971. If he had been elected, Waldheim would have served until 1977. Because he lost the election, Waldheim was able to stand for the position of U.N. secretary-general when U Thant did not seek another term. Waldheim served two terms from 1972 to 1982.

Throughout the spring and summer of 1986, the WJC, international media, and various researchers released additional documents pertaining to Waldheim's concealed past. Many Austrians believed that the charges were part of a Jewish conspiracy to embarrass Waldheim and Austria, and even Wiesenthal defended Waldheim, which surprised many Jews. The vote in Austria on May 4 for president resulted in a run-off because no candidate received a majority—Waldheim received 49.6 percent and Socialist challenger Kurt Steyrer received 43.7 percent; minor candidates split the remaining 6.7 percent. In the June 8 election, Waldheim triumphed with 53.9 percent of the vote.

At the time of the release of its initial allegations, the WJC had requested that the U.S. Justice Department add Waldheim's name to the U.S. Immigration and Naturalization Service's so-called watch list. The watch list bars certain persons from entering the United States, including suspected war criminals who persecuted people based on political, religious, racial, or national factors during the Nazi era. After more than one year of consideration, during which time Waldheim and his lawyers were given the opportunity to present written responses to material in the Justice Department's file, Attorney General Edwin Meese placed Waldheim's name on the watch list on April 27, 1987, which prevented the Austrian president and former U.N. secretary-general from entering the United States. There was shock in Austria, and although some Austrians urged Waldheim to resign the presidency, he did not. He called Meese's decision "grotesque."

Following the watch-list debacle, the Austrian government, under Waldheim's direction, prepared the report *Kurt Waldheim's Wartime Years: A Documentation*, also known as the White Book, to rebut the charges that led to Waldheim's placement on the watch list. A flawed document, the October, 1987, report it did not examine all relevant material and offered exculpatory explanations for Waldheim's actions. Earlier, however, at the behest of Waldheim himself in the spring of 1987, the Austrian government formed an international commission of military historians to investigate Waldheim's World War II service. The commission began its study in August and issued *The Waldheim Report* on February 8, 1988. The report stated that although Waldheim knew of war crimes committed in Yugoslavia and Greece, he did not participate in them and was not in a position to oppose them or protest against them. Some have questioned the report's

thoroughness. A June, 1988, television production by Thames Television/HBO called *Kurt Waldheim: A Case to Answer*, concluded that Waldheim's activities in the Balkans did not involve criminal behavior.

IMPACT

The Waldheim affair damaged Austria's international standing and curtailed his effectiveness as president. He was banned from the United States, and many other countries refused his entry for state visits. The United States never removed his name from its watch list. No major leaders visited Austria during his presidency, and his contacts were limited to the Middle East and some communist bloc nations. Critics have noted that Waldheim never explained why he had concealed the controversial portions of his past, but he did apologize for "mistakes" in a statement released after his death.

Questions subsequently arose concerning which governments knew of his concealed wartime activities when he was nominated as U.N. secretary-general and whether they had used such knowledge to gain favorable treatment during his United Nations tenure. Some have speculated that because Yugoslavia knew, it is likely that the Soviet Union knew as well, and that the Soviets took advantage of this knowledge to increase their espionage activities under United Nations cover. Another theory is that the United States knew of his activities and protected him because he was a source of intelligence. No evidence has been put forth to substantiate these claims.

The reactions of many Austrians and the media to the controversy raised the specter of lingering anti-Semitism in Austria. Waldheim's supporters claimed that the accusations against Waldheim were part of an attempt by Jews to smear his reputation.

—*Mark C. Herman*

FURTHER READING

Hazzard, Shirley. *Countenance of Truth: The United Nations and the Waldheim Case.* New York: Viking Press, 1990. A somewhat polemical treatment of the United Nations' role in the

Waldheim investigation by a former United Nations employee.

Herzstein, Robert Edwin. *Waldheim: The Missing Years*. New York: William Morrow, 1988. An objective treatment by the historian hired by the World Jewish Congress to investigate Waldheim's military career. The book is based on archival research and extensive interviews.

International Commission of Historians. *The Waldheim Report*. Copenhagen: University of Copenhagen and Museum Tusculanum Press, 1993. This report, submitted to the Austrian federal chancellor on February 8, 1988, came without a final answer to the question of Waldheim's wartime guilt.

Mitten, Richard. "Bitburg, Waldheim, and the Politics of Remembering and Forgetting." In *From World War to Waldheim: Culture and Politics in Austria and the United States*, edited by David F. Good and Ruth Wodak. New York: Berghahn, 1999. A concise summary of the basic facts of the controversy and an interpretation of its symbolic importance in public memory.

Rosenbaum, Eli, with William Hoffer. *Betrayal: The Untold Story of the Kurt Waldheim Investigation and Cover-up*. New York: St. Martin's Press, 1993. A detailed, passionate account by the general counsel of the World Jewish Congress, which helped launch the 1986 investigation of Waldheim.

Tittmann, Harold H., III. *The Waldheim Affair: Democracy Subverted*. Dunkirk, N.Y.: Olin Frederick, 2000. Weighs the evidence for allegations of Waldheim's participation in Nazi atrocities. Especially examines the role of the media in presenting the evidence. Finding the accusations groundless, he considers the affair as an example of how false perceptions can dupe a free society.

Waldheim, Kurt. *In the Eye of the Storm: A Memoir*. London: Weidenfeld & Nicholson, 1985. Waldheim attempts to explain his objectives and his actions in the course of the various conflicts he experienced during his ten years as secretary-general of the United Nations. The controversial work that neglects the facts of his military career.

SEE ALSO: July 12, 1906: French Court Declares Alfred Dreyfus Innocent of Treason; Apr. 22, 1942: French Prime Minister Pierre Laval Wants Germany to Win World War II; Dec. 5, 1942: Industrialist Charles Bedaux Is Arrested for Nazi Collaboration; May 9, 1945: Norwegian Politician Quisling Is Arrested for Nazi Collaboration; May 26, 1945: Norwegian Writer Knut Hamsun Is Arrested for Treason; Aug. 14, 1945: French War Hero Pétain Is Convicted of Nazi Collaboration; Dec. 14, 1945: Poet Ezra Pound Is Charged with Treason and Institutionalized; Oct. 26, 1962: West German Police Raid *Der Spiegel* Magazine Offices; Nov. 9, 1976: German Generals Must Retire for Supporting a Neo-Nazi Pilot; 1980: Biographer Claims Actor Errol Flynn Was a Nazi Spy; Dec. 1, 1987: Yale Scholar's Wartime Anti-Semitic Writings Are Revealed; Aug. 12, 2006: Novelist Günter Grass Admits to Youthful Nazi Ties.

April 22, 1986

FAITH HEALER PETER POPOFF IS EXPOSED AS A FRAUD

Pentecostal evangelist Peter Popoff built a financially successful empire from donations given by the desperate, sick, and elderly. He based his empire on his claim that God spoke to him. In 1986, professional skeptics James Randi and Steven Shaw investigated Popoff and discovered that the voice he heard came not from God but from a radio transmitter operated by his wife, Elizabeth Popoff. Randi exposed Popoff's fraud on The Tonight Show. *Within a year, Popoff was bankrupt, but he did return to televangelism.*

LOCALE: Burbank, California

CATEGORIES: Hoaxes, frauds, and charlatanism; religion; communications and media; radio and television; public morals; business

KEY FIGURES

Peter Popoff (b. 1946), Pentecostal faith healer and televangelist

Elizabeth Popoff (fl. 1980's), Popoff's wife and a major player in the scam

James Randi (b. 1928), professional skeptic

Steven Shaw (b. 1960), professional skeptic

SUMMARY OF EVENT

Pentecostal evangelist and faith healer Peter Popoff built a financially successful empire from donations given by the desperate, sick, and elderly after he conducted a strategically targeted direct-mail campaign offering the faithful items that included anointed healing oil. It was his televised healing ministries, however, in which he claimed to hear the voice of God "call out the sick" that brought him success and fortune.

In 1986, professional magician and skeptic James Randi and magician and mentalist Steven Shaw, better known as Banachek, began investigating the Reverend Popoff. It did not take long for Randi and his team to discover that the voice Popoff heard came not from God but from a radio transmit-

ter. Randi first turned to the authorities with his evidence of fraud, but when they showed little interest in pursuing Popoff, he took his evidence to national television. He exposed Popoff on one of the most popular network television shows of the day, *The Tonight Show*, hosted by Johnny Carson, on April 22, 1986. Within a year, Popoff was bankrupt. However, he returned to televangelism and sending miracle healing oil through the mail.

Popoff was born in 1946, reportedly behind the Iron Curtain in Berlin, East Germany. He stated that the Soviet Union's official antireligious stance forced him and his family to flee to the United States. In his new homeland, he began preaching from the age of nine. A Pentecostal evangelist, Popoff claims to have been granted the nine gifts of the Holy Spirit, which, as explained in 1 Corinthians 12:8-10, include knowledge and healing. This claim of being spiritually gifted lifted Popoff from the rank-and-file televangelists and made him a budding superstar.

Prior to 1985, Popoff's ministries in Upland, California, made its money from the evangelist's slick direct-mail ministry campaign and crusades. Radio and television ministries added to the coffers initially by adding names to Popoff's mailing lists. Popoff would send the faithful computer-generated letters that, at first glance, appeared to be personalized. The mailings would include novelties ranging from miracle-healing water to handkerchief swatches "soaked in Popoff's sweat." The letters also included a pathos-laden appeal for money to help Popoff's ministries overcome some purported crisis.

In September of 1985, Popoff's office ordered radio-broadcasting equipment from Audio Specialties in Los Angeles. Soon after this purchase, Popoff's use of the "gifts of the spirit" became much more pronounced during his crusades.

Popoff began displaying an incredible ability to use the gift of knowledge, meaning that God was speaking directly to him during his sermons, telling him who to heal. He would stand before assemblies and call out names, street addresses, names of physicians, and describe a selected person's illness. Then, in a flashy display, he would "heal" a chosen person before a camera through the "laying on of hands." The newly healed person would rise from his or her wheelchair, or let go of his or her aides, and walk from the stage, all the while shouting "hallelujah!" with Popoff and the other congregants in the assembly hall. These crusades made wonderful theater that played even better on television. Popoff's ministry was soon raking in millions of dollars. The spectacle caught the eye of Randi and Banachek, both of whom were specialists in investigating and exposing pseudoscientific and other frauds.

As a young man, Randi (born Randall James Hamilton Zwinge) was isolated, in many ways, by his startling intelligence. He read books on magic and fell in love with the craft after spending more than one year in a body cast from a bicycle accident, The constant practice required to master the art of sleight-of-hand and misdirection offered solace for the isolation that Randi felt in his youth. He recognized early that magicians are "honest charlatans" because audiences expect to be deceived. When Randi saw others utilizing the tricks and apparatus of magic to pose as spiritualists, psychics, mediums, healers, and the like, he felt that an important role that he was to play was to use his skills and knowledge to debunk these frauds.

Randi's stage career as a so-called escapologist began in 1946. His popularity grew as host of his own radio show, *The Amazing Randi Show*, during the 1960's, and a television show, *Wonderama*, during the 1970's. He also made frequent appearances on one of the most popular network television shows of the era, *The Tonight Show*. He appeared often enough to become Carson's friend and a household name across much of the United States. However, it was Israeli spoon-bender, Uri Geller, who made Randi world famous in 1972. Carson invited Geller to appear on *The Tonight Show* to display his ability to bend spoons using the power of his mind. However, Carson had Randi secretly set up tests for the show to make certain that Geller

could not bend the spoons using sleight-of-hand. Geller was unable to bend anything during the show. Carson later explained why, leading to Randi's new fame.

In 1986, Randi was awarded the MacArthur Foundation's genius award for educating the public about magic fraud and other forms of pseudoscience. He used this money to pursue the wave of televangelist faith healers who were incredibly popular during the late 1980's. The leader of this Pentecostal group was Popoff. Randi, Banachek, and their team began investigating Popoff by attending his revival meetings in Houston, Texas, and other U.S. cities.

The team soon uncovered the method to Popoff's fraud. His wife, Elizabeth Popoff, and other members of his team would meet with those who arrived at the revival early and would ask the audience members questions and give them prayer cards to fill out. The cards were then collected. How was the information getting to Popoff on stage?

From those cards, Elizabeth was able to transfer facts about certain audience members through radio transmission to an earphone used by her husband. One of Randi's confederates, Alec Jason, an expert in electronics, brought a sophisticated radio scanner, hooked up to a tape recorder, to the parking lot of the San Francisco Civic Auditorium, where Popoff was preparing for his next crusade. Just before showtime, Jason recorded the voice of God on 39.17 megahertz. Unfortunately for Popoff, God's voice was a feminine one; in fact, it was Elizabeth's voice. She was backstage feeding information from those same prayer cards to a tiny receiver in the evangelist's ear.

Randi's team was inside the auditorium videotaping the event as well. When the video- and audiotapes were paired, the evidence was damning. To effect their magic, the Popoffs collaborated as God and faith healer: Through radio transmission, Elizabeth told her husband certain facts (obtained from the prayer cards) about his audience. Claiming he was receiving messages from God, he then healed those whom God instructed him to heal. Randi and Banachek first tried to get legal authorities interested in pursuing Popoff based on this evidence, which was obtained over a period of six months in several cities around the United States. When the law showed no interest, Randi turned to his friend, Carson.

Popoff was exposed on *The Tonight Show*. Although it took some time for the news of the truth to reach the world of the faithful, donations to Popoff's ministries eventually fell to such a low level that he was forced to declare bankruptcy in 1987. Despite this fall from grace, by 2005, Popoff was once again leading a multimillion-dollar ministry, based in Upland, in no small part because of the ease of direct mail and the power and reach of infomercials.

IMPACT

Randi's and Banachek's public expose of Popoff's deception helped to dismantle what was an enormous upswing in Pentecostal televangelist faith healers during the late 1980's. The two investigators exposed other similar fraudulent healers as well and forced many of the faithful to take, for the first time, a skeptical look at practices they had always accepted on faith. The unveiling of the scam also led to a revival in skepticism. Randi's milliondollar "psychic challenge" brought all manner of fraud into the harsh light of skepticism and scientific analysis.

—*B. Keith Murphy*

FURTHER READING

Blackmore, Susan. *The Meme Machine*. New York: Oxford University Press, 1999. In this well-researched work on social psychology, sociobiology, and the evolution of human behavior, Blackmore explores, among other issues, how Peter Popoff's ministries used fake miracles to convert nonbelievers.

Huston, Peter. *More Scams from the Great Beyond! How to Make Even More Money Off Creationism, Evolution, Environmentalism, Fringe Politics, Weird Science, the Occult, and Other Strange Beliefs*. Boulder, Colo.: Paladin Press, 2002. An astonishing collection of scams based on strange religious and other fringe beliefs. Huston includes analysis of Randi's investigation and exposure of Popoff's fraudulent actions.

Randi, James. *The Faith Healers*. Rev. ed. Buffalo, N.Y.: Prometheus Books, 1989. Randi traces the history of faith healing, misplaced faith, and unquestioned trust. An indictment of televangelist fraud. The book, originally published in 1987, includes a chapter on his investigation and exposure of Popoff and his fraudulent "healings." Also includes a foreword by astronomer Carl Sagan.

SEE ALSO: May-June, 1926: Evangelist Aimee Semple McPherson Claims She Was Kidnapped; June 27, 1978: Evangelist Herbert W. Armstrong Excommunicates His Own Son; Sept. 10, 1981: *Chicago Sun-Times* Reports That Cardinal Cody Diverted Church Funds; Oct. 23, 1985: Guru Bhagwan Shree Rajneesh Is Indicted for Immigration Fraud; Mar. 19, 1987: Jim Bakker Resigns as Head of PTL Television Network; Feb. 21, 1988: Evangelist Jimmy Swaggart Tearfully Confesses His Adultery; June 30, 2001: Korean Religious Teacher Jung Myung Seok Is Charged with Rape; Nov. 2, 2006: Evangelist Kent Hovind Is Convicted of Federal Tax Violations; Nov. 2, 2006: Male Escort Reveals Sexual Liaisons with Evangelist Ted Haggard.

1980's

November 13, 1986-May 4, 1989
IRAN-CONTRA WEAPONS SCANDAL TAINTS REAGAN'S ADMINISTRATION

U.S. weapons were sold to Iran and funds from the sale were secretly provided to the Contras, the anticommunist rebels seeking to overthrow the government of Nicaragua. A series of federal investigations raised questions of balance of power between the executive and legislative branches of government in the United States. Several top government officials were implicated in the scandal and more faced indictments.

ALSO KNOWN AS: Iran-Contra affair
LOCALE: Washington, D.C.
CATEGORIES: Drugs; government; politics; military; corruption; international relations

KEY FIGURES

Oliver North (b. 1943), National Security Council military aide, 1981-1986, and former lieutenant colonel, U.S. Marine Corps
Richard V. Secord (b. 1932), retired U.S. Air Force general
Ronald Reagan (1911-2004), president of the United States, 1981-1989
Bud McFarlane (b. 1937), national security adviser, 1983-1985
John M. Poindexter (b. 1936), national security adviser, 1985-1986
William J. Casey (1913-1987), director of the Central Intelligence Agency, 1981-1987
Caspar Weinberger (1917-2006), U.S. secretary of defense, 1981-1987

SUMMARY OF EVENT

Two secret, interrelated U.S. government operations, both conducted by staff of the U.S. National Security Council (NSC) and both of which violated U.S. law and stated policy, were exposed in November, 1986. One operation encompassed the sale of arms to Iran to attempt to secure the release of U.S. hostages in the Middle East while the other operation used profits from the sale of these arms to fund the Contras, the anticommunist rebels in Nicaragua. The Iran-Contra affair, as the operations collectively came to be known, represented the most serious scandal involving a U.S. president since that of Watergate in 1972-1974.

During Ronald Reagan's first term as U.S. president, several events set the stage for the Iran-Contra affair. First, Iran and Iraq were engaged in a bitter civil war that began in 1980. Second, Hezbollah and other Middle East terrorist groups began taking more and more Western hostages, including U.S. citizens. Third, the Marxist Sandinistas, who took control of Nicaragua in 1979, were supporting leftist movements in other parts of Central America, particularly El Salvador. Reagan believed the Sandinistas were communists.

U.S. laws forbade trading arms with Iran following the events of 1979-1981, when Iranian students backed by their government seized and held American embassy staff hostage for 444 days. President Reagan had publicly pressured other nations to refrain from selling weapons to Iran. He reemphasized U.S. policy that mandated against negotiating with terrorists or making concessions to them.

At the same time, the Reagan administration, which took a hard line against communism around the world, also offered training and funds to anticommunist governments and movements through the Reagan Doctrine. In 1981, Reagan had approved covert support for the anti-Sandinista guerrilla groups that came to be known as the Contras, the anticommunist rebels in Nicaragua. However, in 1982, the U.S. Congress passed the Boland Amendments, which restricted U.S. Department of Defense and U.S. Central Intelligence Agency anticommunist military actions in Nicaragua. Reagan, seemingly emboldened by the attempt to curtail his support of the Contras, then instructed his national security adviser, Bud McFarlane, to keep the Contras together, "body and soul."

After Reagan's overwhelming reelection as president in 1984, certain representatives of the Iranian government contacted the United States about the possibility of buying weapons for its use against Iraq. U.S. policymakers debated the move. While Secretary of State George Shultz and Secretary of Defense Caspar Weinberger opposed the transaction, it was supported by CIA director William J. Casey and McFarlane. Casey and McFarlane reasoned that the sale not only would improve relations with Iran but also could hasten the release of American hostages held in Lebanon and other locations.

Reagan, who was adamant about freeing the hostages, one of whom was a CIA agent being brutally tortured, approved the sale of weapons on July 18, 1985. At first, the arms were funneled through Israel to Iran, with the United States promising to reimburse Israel with the same weapons. However, the resignation of McFarlane as national security adviser in December changed the nature of the operation. On the same day that John C. Poindexter replaced McFarlane, a military aide working at the NSC came up with two new ideas pertaining to the sale of missiles and other arms to Iran. That aide, U.S. Marine lieutenant colonel Oliver North, proposed selling weapons to Iran directly. In a move that brought the two operations together, North also suggested using the profits from the sale of arms to Iran to fund the Contras. Poindexter asked North to manage the operation, and North turned for assistance to retired U.S. Air Force general Richard V. Secord.

For the arms-sale ruse to work, the price of U.S. arms was inflated by as much as fifteen million dollars. Additionally, an Iranian arms broker who facilitated the transactions placed his own markup on the purchases. The overcharge for the weapons angered Iran and almost ruined the deal. However, by the time the sales and diversion were discovered, Iran had paid about thirty million dollars for

several shipments of TOW missiles and assorted spare parts for HAWK antiaircraft missiles. One shipment of eighteen HAWK missiles was rejected by Iran.

While the Iranian initiative unfolded, Poindexter struggled to carry out Reagan's directive to hold the Contras together. North, who handled operational details, brought Secord in to help in the Contra operation. North and Secord set up an organization they called the Enterprise to help carry out their activities. As Congress cut off funds for Contra military operations, North headed a campaign to raise money from private donors, and he secretly funneled millions of dollars from Saudi Arabia to the Contras through a network of nonprofit organizations and Swiss bank accounts. The Enterprise had aircraft, warehouses, arms and other supplies, ships, and boats, and even had a hidden runway located in Costa Rica. North, with McFarlane's and Poindexter's knowledge, had created a secret government organization operating outside the authority of Congress. In his search for funds, North intermingled the Iran and Contra operations. He diverted profits from Iranian arms sales to the

Marine lieutenant colonel Oliver North testifies in July, 1987, before a joint congressional committee investigating the Iran-Contra affair. (AP/Wide World Photos)

Contras. This diversion of funds became the focal point of the investigations that began when news of the operations surfaced in November, 1986.

Following the downing of an Enterprise cargo plane that was supplying the Contras in Nicaragua on October 6, 1986, the combined operations began to unravel. The lone survivor of the crash initially stated that the two persons killed in the plane crash were CIA agents. A book of telephone numbers found in the wreckage traced the plane to an airbase in Central America.

On November 3, a Lebanese newspaper, *Al-Shiraa*, broke the story of the weapons-for-hostages deal between Iran and the United States. On November 13, after ten days of White House denials over the story, Reagan admitted that there had been some sort of a deal, but he insisted that it was a deal to provide to Iran "small amounts of defensive weapons and spare parts for defensive systems" in an attempt to lessen the "animosity" between the United States and Iran. He added that about one thousand TOW missiles were involved and that the sale included only the United States and Iran as participants. Reagan misstated the facts, however.

Over the next few days, the Justice Department continued to investigate the matter, and on November 22 it found what would become a critical April, 1986, memo from North to the president that outlined how the "residual funds" from the arms sales would be diverted to aiding the Contras. Simultaneously, Attorney General Edward Meese III discovered that only twelve million of the thirty million dollars paid by Iran for the U.S. arms had been deposited in the U.S. treasury. Meese briefed Reagan about the diverted funds on November 24 and announced it publicly the next day before Congress and the full Reagan cabinet. They also announced that Poindexter resigned and North was removed from his job with the NSC and reassigned with the Marine Corps. It was later divulged that North had destroyed pertinent evidence about the operations over a five-day period in late November.

On December 1, Reagan appointed former Texas senator John Tower to chair a commission to investigate the matter. Not to be left out, the U.S. Senate and House of Representatives set up investigative committees in early January, 1987. The Tower Commission released its report on the scandal on February 26. A special prosecutor, independent counsel Lawrence E. Walsh, was appointed to investigate as well, and his report was released over a five-month period beginning on August 4, 1993.

The *Tower Commission Report* was the product of ten weeks of research that included the testimony of fifty-six witnesses. Though placing primary responsibility for the operations on the president's staff, the report chided Reagan for being out of touch and for failing to oversee the implementation of his own administration's policies. Televised congressional committee hearings into the scandal started on May 5 and lasted three months. They included 250 hours of testimony from twenty-eight witnesses, and they riveted television viewers. The congressional Iran-Contra committees issued their reports on November 18.

Congress largely agreed with the Tower Commission that Reagan's detached management style was to blame for the scandal, though it found that Reagan was unaware of the diversion of funds to the Contras. The congressional report identified several violations of law, including failure to notify Congress of covert U.S. operations, diversion of federal funds for purposes prohibited by Congress, tampering with and destroying official documents, and lying to or misleading Congress.

On March 16, 1988, North, Poindexter, Secord, and several others were indicted on conspiracy to defraud the United States, theft of government property, and wire fraud. North's charges included obstruction of congressional investigations, making false statements to a congressional committee and the attorney general, shredding and altering official documents, acceptance of an illegal gratuity from Secord in the form of a home-security system, conversion of traveler's checks, and tax-fraud conspiracy. Eleven persons were convicted. The convictions of Poindexter and North were overturned on appeal. Most of the public's attention to the Iran-Contra scandal diminished after May 4, 1989, with the end of North's trial.

On December 24, 1992, U.S. president George H. W. Bush—who had been vice president during

PRESIDENT REAGAN DENIES ARMS DEAL WITH IRAN

In a televised speech on November 13, 1986, U.S. president Ronald Reagan firmly denied that his administration was involved in any arms-for-hostages deal with Iran, a claim later proven false.

The charge has been made that the United States has shipped weapons to Iran as ransom payment for the release of American hostages in Lebanon, that the United States undercut its allies and secretly violated American policy against trafficking with terrorists. Those charges are utterly false. The United States has not made concessions to those who hold our people captive in Lebanon. And we will not. The United States has not swapped boatloads or planeloads of American weapons for the return of American hostages. And we will not. Other reports have surfaced alleging U.S. involvement: reports of a sealift to Iran using Danish ships to carry American arms; of vessels in Spanish ports being employed in secret U.S. arms shipments; of Italian ports being used; of the U.S. sending spare parts and weapons for combat aircraft. All these reports are quite exciting, but as far as we're concerned, not one of them is true.

During the course of our secret discussions, I authorized the transfer of small amounts of defensive weapons and spare parts for defensive systems to Iran. My purpose was to convince Tehran that our negotiators were acting with my authority, to send a signal that the United States was prepared to replace the animosity between us with a new relationship. These modest deliveries, taken together, could easily fit into a single cargo plane. They could not, taken together, affect the outcome of the 6-year war between Iran and Iraq nor could they affect in any way the military balance between the two countries. Those with whom we were in contact took considerable risks and needed a signal of our serious intent if they were to carry on and broaden the dialog. At the same time we undertook this initiative, we made clear that Iran must oppose all forms of international terrorism as a condition of progress in our relationship. The most significant step which Iran could take, we indicated, would be to use its influence in Lebanon to secure the release of all hostages held there....

To summarize: Our government has a firm policy not to capitulate to terrorist demands. That no concessions policy remains in force, in spite of the wildly speculative and false stories about arms for hostages and alleged ransom payments. We did not—repeat—did not trade weapons or anything else for hostages, nor will we. Those who think that we have gone soft on terrorism should take up the question with Colonel Qadhafi. We have not, nor will we, capitulate to terrorists. We will, however, get on with advancing the vital interests of our great nation—in spite of terrorists and radicals who seek to sabotage our efforts and immobilize the United States. Our goals have been, and remain, to restore a relationship with Iran; to bring an honorable end to the war in the Gulf; to bring a halt to state-supported terror in the Middle East; and finally, to effect the safe return of all hostages from Lebanon.

1980's

Reagan's presidency—pardoned six persons associated with the Iran-Contra scandal. The pardon of Weinberger kept him from being tried on charges of perjury and making false statements. The pardon of McFarlane occurred after he pleaded guilty and was sentenced to probation and community service. The seven-year investigation by the independent counsel cost $48.5 million, which accounted for almost one-fourth of total funds spent by twenty-two special prosecutors on unrelated cases from 1978 to 1999.

After the 1986 discovery of the Iran-Contra operations, several investigations by think tanks, congressional committees, and journalists focused on the question of whether the CIA had engaged in criminal activity by financing the purchase of arms with the proceeds from illegal drug sales. Though the results of previous probes were inconsistent, a 1998 report by the CIA inspector general confirmed that the Contras were involved in drug trafficking and that their activities had been protected from law enforcement by the Reagan administration. The report stated that North and the NSC were aware of drug transactions by the Contras.

IMPACT

The Iran-Contra scandal had consequences on several levels. First, President Reagan suffered a

679

twenty-one-point decline in his approval rating after the dual operations were discovered in November, 1986. This represented the largest drop of presidential popularity within a month's time ever recorded. The revelations put the Reagan White House on the defensive, where it remained for almost all of the ensuing year. In March, 1987, Reagan admitted in a press conference that his previous assertions that the United States had not traded arms for hostages were incorrect.

Throughout the summer months, the televised congressional hearings into the scandal kept the public's attention. The deep decline in the stock market in the fall of 1987 only compounded the image problem for the White House. However, time seemed to heal the public's view of the president's performance. By the end of 1988, Reagan's popularity rating was close to where it had been before the scandal broke.

A second result of the Iran-Contra scandal was increased acrimony between the executive and legislative branches of federal government. That Reagan was the first of four chief executives in succession to experience split or opposition party control of Congress meant that the Reagan administration would have challenges in dealing with the legislature. Still, the Reagan team had an extremely successful initial year in 1981, enjoyed a forty-nine-state victory in the 1984 presidential election, and even had some notable second-term achievements, such as tax reform. However, the discovery that the president and his staff carried out the Iran-Contra operations in secret and violated several laws did not sit well with Congress. In like fashion to the post-Watergate period, Congress sought to curtail unilateral executive authority to restore a balance of power. For example, the Senate rejected the nomination of Robert Bork for the U.S. Supreme Court in October, 1987, and Congress overrode three of President Reagan's vetoes after the Iran-Contra operations became public.

A third consequence of the Iran-Contra affair was the scandal's international ramifications. Unquestionably, the sale of arms to Iran adversely affected the U.S.-led campaign against international terrorism. Not only did the operation contradict the policy of no negotiations with terrorists, it also likewise gave enemies of the United States the impression that the United States was prepared to offer concessions to hostage-takers.

The immediate result of America's effort to gain release of its citizens held in Lebanon and elsewhere was nil: while three American hostages were released, others were subsequently taken and held for ransom. The expressed goal for the Iran operation—for the United States to improve relations with that nation—was similarly a failure. In 1987, the two nations traded attacks in the Persian Gulf after Iranian forces launched a missile at a tanker under U.S. escort. In 1988, a U.S. warship shot down an Iranian passenger jet after mistaking it for an F-14 fighter, killing all 290 persons aboard.

A final legacy of the Iran-Contra scandal involves its impact on the principal participants other than President Reagan. It was assumed that Vice President Bush was aware of the activities related to the Iran-Contra operations. However, he was not directly linked with the day-to-day running of the operations. The political damage suffered by Bush was minor. He was able to secure the 1988 Republican nomination and win the presidential election that year. Other participants in the operations went on to work in the administrations of Bush and, later, his son, George W. Bush.

Perhaps the person most responsible for the scandal, North, fared best. North retired from active military duty and became a television commentator, syndicated columnist, and speaker for various conservative causes.

—*Samuel B. Hoff*

FURTHER READING

Carter, John J. *Covert Action as a Tool of Presidential Foreign Policy: From the Bay of Pigs to Iran-Contra.* Lewiston, N.Y.: Edwin Mellen Press, 2006. Focuses on the ongoing tensions between an executive branch that tries to subordinate the intelligence community and that community's desire to play a major role in policymaking. Includes a chapter on Reagan and the Iran-Contra scandal.
DeGregorio, William. *The Complete Book of Amer-

ican Presidents. New York: Gramercy Books, 2001. Chapter on the Reagan presidency includes an extensive description of the Iran-Contra affair.

Draper, Theodore. *A Very Thin Line: The Iran-Contra Affairs.* New York: Hill and Wang, 1991. A definitive account of the Iran-Contra scandal from a source not associated with the U.S. government.

Kitts, Kenneth. "The Politics of Scandal: The Tower Commission and Iran-Contra." In *Presidential Commissions and National Security: The Politics of Damage Control.* Boulder, Colo.: Lynne Rienner, 2005. An account of "the highly political, behind-closed-doors world of blue-ribbon investigative commissions convened in the aftermath of national security crises," including the Iran-Contra affair.

Martin, Al. *The Conspirators: Secrets of an Iran-Contra Insider.* Pray, Mont.: National Liberty Press, 2002. Every scandal has its conspiracy theories. This book explores the idea of an untold Iran-Contra conspiracy.

Mayer, Jane, and Doyle McManus. *Landslide: The Unmaking of the President, 1984-1988.* Boston: Houghton Mifflin, 1989. A substantial part of this book about Ronald Reagan's second term as president is dedicated to the Iran-Contra scandal.

North, Oliver L., with William Novak. *Under Fire: An American Story.* New York: HarperCollins, 1991. North's own telling of the Iran-Contra story is controversial, as many of its key claims have been disputed by others.

Walsh, Lawrence E. *Firewall: The Iran-Contra Conspiracy and Cover-Up.* New York: W. W. Norton, 1997. Detailed account of events by the independent counsel for the Iran-Contra investigation from 1986 to 1993.

SEE ALSO: Oct. 22, 1923: U.S. Senate Begins Hearings on Teapot Dome Oil Leases; May 28, 1970: Irish Politicians Are Tried for Conspiring to Import Weapons; June 17, 1972-Aug. 9, 1974: Watergate Break-in Leads to President Nixon's Resignation; Oct. 10, 1973: Spiro T. Agnew Resigns Vice Presidency in Disgrace; Feb. 3, 1975: Honduras's "Bananagate" Bribery Scandal Leads to Executive's Suicide; 1976-1977: U.S. Congress Members Are Implicated in Koreagate Scandal; Apr. 5, 1991: George W. Bush Is Investigated for Insider Trading; Aug. 5, 1994: Kenneth Starr Is Appointed to the Whitewater Investigation; Jan. 17, 1998: President Bill Clinton Denies Sexual Affair with a White House Intern; Sept. 8, 2004: *60 Minutes II* Reports on George W. Bush's Evasion of Wartime Duty.

1980's

January 12 and May 11, 1987
MEDIA REPORTS SPARK INVESTIGATION OF AUSTRALIAN POLICE CORRUPTION

Investigative media reports prompted the formation of a royal inquiry into high-level police corruption in Australia. The Fitzgerald inquiry, which spanned two years, broadened to include a much larger investigation into all levels of government. The inquiry resulted in fundamental changes to Parliament, party politics, law, police work, and the practices of commissions of inquiry. Furthermore, many officials were forced to resign, including the premier of Queensland and the state's police commissioner.

ALSO KNOWN AS: Fitzgerald inquiry
LOCALE: Brisbane, Queensland, Australia
CATEGORIES: Corruption; government; radio and television; publishing and journalism; law and the courts; politics; social issues and reform

KEY FIGURES
Phil Dickie (fl. 1980's), investigative journalist
Christopher Masters (b. 1948), broadcast journalist
Tony Fitzgerald (b. 1941), chairman of the Fitzgerald inquiry

Sir Johannes Bjelke-Petersen (1911-2005), premier of Queensland, 1968-1987
Terence Lewis (b. 1928), Queensland police commissioner, 1978-1987

SUMMARY OF EVENT

The Australian media had hinted that there was a major problem in the state of Queensland, and especially in the city of Brisbane, with illegal gambling, drugs, prostitution and brothels, bribery of officials at all levels of government, and police corruption during the 1980's. Two reports proved to be the end for the corrupt politicians and other civil servants. Journalist Phil Dickie wrote an investigative report that was published in the *Courier-Mail* (Brisbane) on January 12, 1987, and a follow-up report was aired on the television program *Four Corners* by Christopher Masters. The revealing television episode, "Moonlight State," aired on May 11 and provided further substantial evidence of government corruption. Both Dickie and Masters are award-winning journalists.

Soon after the television show aired its report, government officials formed the Commission of Inquiry into Possible Illegal Activities and Associated Police Misconduct in Queensland, which came to be known as the Fitzgerald inquiry. The commission confirmed the existence of systematic government corruption, confirmation that ultimately led to the resignation of Queensland's premier, Sir Johannes Bjelke-Petersen, as well as the state's police commissioner, Terence Lewis, and many others.

Premier Bjelke-Petersen was out of the country when *Four Corners* aired its May 14 episode. *Four Corners*, which first appeared on television in 1961, continued as the longest-running investigative television program in Australia into the twenty-first century. The program, which focuses on a single current-affairs issue with each episode, has received many awards and was one of the first such programs to expose questionable actions by public officials.

After the *Four Corners* broadcast, Bjelke-Petersen's deputy, Bill Gunn, ordered the inquiry in the premier's absence. Justice Tony Fitzgerald was appointed to conduct the inquiry. Fitzgerald, who was well respected in government and known for his upstanding character, twice extended the probe from police activities to include higher levels of government. The inquiry continued for two years and led to the creation of an independent oversight entity named the Criminal Justice Commission (CRC), now the Crime and Misconduct Commission.

The Fitzgerald inquiry began on May 26 as an initial examination of police corruption and included allegations against specific persons. On June 24, the terms of reference were expanded and a number of handpicked Queensland Police Service (QPS) officers assisted with the investigation. On July 27, Commissioner Lewis was brought forth as the first witness. The inquiry's focus of reference expanded once again on August 25. Three days later, police detective Harry Burgess admitted to corrupt activities and resigned his position. He was followed in resignation by the assistant police commissioner, Graham Parker, who also admitted to corrupt activities. In the next few months, two retired inspectors admitted to corruption as well.

In August, Fitzgerald, for the first time in an inquiry, granted an indemnity, a legal exemption from penalties or liabilities, to Jack Herbert—who was alleged to be a bagman, or collector-distributor of illicit funds—to persuade him to testify. Herbert was the bagman for Lewis and collected his bribes. In April of 1989, Lewis was removed as the police commissioner.

The Fitzgerald Report was submitted to parliament July 3, nearly two years after the inquiry began. Without the extension of the terms of reference, the inquiry would not have had the same long-ranging effects. One motivation that Fitzgerald had for extending the inquiry was the desire to go beyond specific allegations against single persons and explore the system that allowed such corruption to develop and exist. As a result of the Fitzgerald inquiry, the thirty-year reign of the National Party government came to an end. The rule of law in Queensland was drastically changed and a new standard for commissions of inquiry had been put into place by the efforts and practices of the inquiry.

Many of the prosecutions that resulted from the inquiry, including that of Lewis and Bjelke-

Petersen, were heard by Douglas Drummond of the Office of the Special Prosecutor, which had been appointed in December, 1988. Lewis was convicted of corruption and subsequently stripped of his knighthood and confined. Bjelke-Petersen was charged with perjury but was found not guilty because he supplied evidence for investigators.

The corruption extended to many others across the political and nonpolitical spectrum. Also revealed as participants in corrupt practices were celebrities, judges, businesspeople, bankers, lawyers, and real estate agents.

IMPACT

The inquiry included 339 witnesses and 21,504 pages of testimony transcript, received 2,304 exhibits, and approved 10 indemnities (immunities) against prosecution. The Fitzgerald Report contained 630 pages and more than 100 recommendations that fell into three categories: the establishment of the Electoral and Administrative Review Commission (EARC), the establishment of the CRC, and the reform of the Queensland police force.

One of the most important reforms to result from the Fitzgerald inquiry was the establishment of the CRC, an independent oversight body that was given the power to investigate any public servant, including police officers, and the power to investigate any politician. Another important reform was the implementation of whistle-blower legislation, which increased sanctions attached to serious misconduct, including questionable recruitment and promotions. Also, the Fitzgerald inquiry was the first such inquiry in Australia to implement the use of indemnities in exchange for testimony.

—Judy L. Porter

FURTHER READING

Brereton, David, and Andrew Ede. "The Police Code of Silence in Queensland: The Impact of the Fitzgerald Inquiry Reforms." *Current Issues in Criminal Justice* 8, no. 2 (1996): 107-129. This article examines the impact of the Fitzgerald inquiry on the code of silence among Queensland police officers and their supervisors.

Dickie, Phil. "Fateful Trail Had Dramatic End." *Courier Mail* (Brisbane), May 15, 2007. Award-winning journalist Dickie, who broke the story of police corruption in Queensland in January, 1987, provides a brief, twenty-year retrospective on the exposé and the start of the Fitzgerald inquiry.

_____. *The Road to Fitzgerald*. St. Lucia: University of Queensland Press, 1988. Written as the story unfolded. Dickie discusses the events that led to the formation of the Fitzgerald inquiry, still in session when this book was published.

Finnane, Mark. "Police Corruption and Police Reform: The Fitzgerald Inquiry in Queensland, Australia." *Policing and Society* 1, no. 1 (1990): 159-171. Examines the Fitzgerald inquiry's findings and places it in the context of the history of Australian police organization.

Herbert, Jack, and Tom Gilling. *The Bagman: Final Confessions of Jack Herbert*. Sydney: ABC Books, 2004. Jack Herbert, the so-called bagman who collected bribes for the police commissioner, Terence Lewis.

Prasser, Scott, Rae Wear, and John Nethercote. *Corruption and Reform: The Fitzgerald Vision*. St. Lucia: University of Queensland Press, 1990. A collection of papers presented at a conference on the Fitzgerald inquiry that address police, government, and electoral system reform, among other topics.

Queensland, Australia, Criminal Justice Commission. *Integrity in the Queensland Police Service: Implementation and Impact of the Fitzgerald Inquiry Reforms*. Brisbane: Author, 1997. A detailed assessment of the efforts to address police integrity in Queensland after the release of the Fitzgerald Report in 1989.

SEE ALSO: Mar. 17, 1937: Atherton Report Exposes San Francisco Police Corruption; May 3, 1950: U.S. Senate Committee Begins Investigating Organized Crime; Aug. 16, 1996: Belgian Media Reveal How Police Bungled Serial Murder Case; May, 1998: Police Corruption Is Revealed in Los Angeles's Rampart Division; Dec. 23, 1998: Prominent Belgians Are Sentenced in Agusta-Dassault Corruption Scandal.

1980's

January 22, 1987
PENNSYLVANIA POLITICIAN KILLS HIMSELF AT TELEVISED PRESS CONFERENCE

Pennsylvania state treasurer Budd Dwyer was convicted of taking a bribe after he obtained a state contract for a computer company. On the day before his sentencing, he called a press conference to proclaim his innocence and criticize the media for the scandal. He then put a loaded gun in his mouth and pulled the trigger. Several news outlets aired the graphic footage of his death, leading to public outrage and debate about journalistic ethics, broadcast television, newsworthiness, and sensationalism.

LOCALE: Harrisburg, Pennsylvania

CATEGORIES: Murder and suicide; radio and television; communications and media; publishing and journalism; politics; corruption; government

KEY FIGURES

Budd Dwyer (1939-1987), Pennsylvania state treasurer, 1980-1987

Dick Thornburgh (b. 1932), governor of Pennsylvania, 1979-1987

Robert P. Casey (1932-2000), governor of Pennsylvania, 1987-1995

SUMMARY OF EVENT

During the early 1980's, Pennsylvania officials discovered that all public employees in the state had been overpaying their Federal Insurance Contributions Act taxes. By 1984, the Pennsylvania Treasury Department was looking to hire a technology firm to determine how much to reimburse each taxpayer. On May 14, Pennsylvania governor Dick Thornburgh received an anonymous memo, alerting him to bribes that had been paid to secure a no-bid, $4.6 million contract for Computer Technology Associates (CTA), a California-based company.

Thornburgh opened an investigation into the allegations. The investigation uncovered evidence that John Torquato, Jr., of CTA had approached several state officials with monetary offers to guarantee his company the contract. In particular, Torquato had allegedly promised to pay Pennsylvania state treasurer Budd Dwyer $300,000.

Dwyer was indicted two years later, on May 14, 1986, on charges of conspiracy to commit bribery, mail fraud, interstate transportation in aid of racketeering, and perjury. Acting U.S. attorney James West offered Dwyer a deal that would have reduced his maximum jail time from fifty-five to five years, but Dwyer refused to plead guilty to gain a lighter sentence. Torquato accepted a plea bargain and agreed to testify against Dwyer. Dwyer was convicted in the fall of 1986 and scheduled for sentencing in early 1987.

On January 22, 1987, one day before his sentencing, Dwyer convened a press conference at his office in Harrisburg, Pennsylvania. Given that upon sentencing he would lose his job, the public expected he was going to announce his resignation. Instead, Dwyer addressed the crowd of reporters, again declaring his innocence. He criticized the judge, the U.S. attorney, Governor Thornburgh, and even the media that had reported on his conviction for its part in painting him as a criminal. He compared himself to Job (the biblical character who faced many unjust hardships) and suggested that his imprisonment would be an act of political persecution. His rambling remarks lasted nearly half an hour, by which point the press was ready to leave. Dwyer urged the reporters to stay.

As he concluded his remarks, Dwyer handed envelopes to three of his staff members. He then pulled a .357 Magnum revolver from a fourth envelope. He then said that anyone who might be offended should leave the room. Members of the press began to urge Dwyer to lower the weapon. However, he ordered those who approached him to stand back, waving his arm and telling them that the gun could hurt someone. Dwyer then lifted the gun toward his face. He put the barrel into his mouth and pulled the trigger.

The fatal moment was captured on film. Several cameramen had kept their tapes rolling throughout the incident. They took the footage back to their news directors, who were faced with the sudden dilemma of whether or not to broadcast Dwyer's suicide on television. The event was certainly newsworthy, but the graphic nature of the film caused concern. Several local stations, including WPVI-TV in Philadelphia and WPXI-TV in Pittsburgh, chose to air at least part of the suicide tape.

Viewers in the region were shocked by the media's decision to air the footage. Further complicating matters, many children had stayed home from school due to snow cancellations and saw the suicide as it was aired midday by WPXI. When those stations rebroadcast the film later in the day, it was edited to end just before Dwyer pulled the trigger. WCAU-TV in Philadelphia showed similarly edited footage, stopping as Dwyer put the gun in his mouth. Other stations, such as KYW-TV in Philadelphia, chose not to air the shooting at all.

The report was broadcast nationally, but not in its graphic entirety. *NBC Nightly News* edited the footage, including Dwyer with the gun and Dwyer's fatally wounded body. ABC and CBS displayed still photos of Dwyer with their report of his death. The Associated Press also distributed still photos of Dwyer before and after the shooting, but included an alert about the graphic content.

The envelopes Dwyer handed to his aides turned out to contain various items. One envelope had a letter to his wife, Joanne; another envelope contained a letter to the new Pennsylvania governor, Robert P. Casey; and a third envelope had Dwyer's organ-donor card and other items. The letter to his wife contained his request for funeral arrangements. The letter to the governor complimented Casey, and stressed that Dwyer had not resigned his post but had been treasurer to the end. He likely emphasized this point so that his wife and children could continue to collect benefits from the state after his death. Dwyer took the additional step of suggesting his wife as his successor in the job, though she was not hired. It is possible the suicide was at least partly motivated by Dwyer's desire to protect his family financially.

IMPACT

The graphic television broadcasts of Dwyer's final moments shocked the public, and it soon turned into a media scandal. Dwyer's suicide would have been newsworthy even if conducted in private, but the public manner in which he chose to end his life was enough to shake the nation. People were disturbed by not only Dwyer's plan but also the media's handling of the incident, which seemingly magnified the act. Parents and teachers began to discuss and question the advisability of letting children watch

Budd Dwyer, moments before he shoots himself to death in front of colleagues and media. (AP/Wide World Photos)

live television broadcasts, whether in school or at home. Dwyer's death was not broadcast live, but it highlighted the potential unpredictability of live television. Overall, viewers were most disturbed by the decision to rebroadcast the taped footage, especially unedited or underedited.

In academic circles, Dwyer's suicide continues to fascinate as a case study in journalistic ethics. The question of whether such graphic footage should be broadcast requires journalists to weigh the responsibility of reporting incidents thoroughly and with accuracy against public pressure to keep news broadcast images acceptable for all viewers. It also sparks debate about the changing perceptions of what is acceptable for television broadcast.

Decades after Dwyer's death, the footage of his final press conference is readily available on the World Wide Web. It is no longer current news, but the video's continued presence speaks to a cultural fascination with violence and death. Pop culture references to the suicide include several tribute songs and appearances in film and advertising.

Dwyer's suicide led the Associated Press (AP) to change its film protocols. Prior to 1987, AP photographers carried black-and-white film for everyday use and switched to color film only in anticipation of special events. Thus, the photographers present at Dwyer's final press conference had cameras loaded with black-and-white film only. As the story broke nationwide, however, hungry news outlets requested color pictures. AP did not have color photos. From that point on, AP photographers shot with color film.

—*Kekla Magoon*

FURTHER READING

Associated Press. "Facing Prison, Dwyer Kills Himself." *Philadelphia Daily News*, January 22, 1987. A wire-service news report of Dwyer's public suicide.

Friedman, David. "TV's Dilemma: How Much to Show." *Philadelphia Daily News*, January 23, 1987. Discusses the behind-the-scenes controversy among media professionals, spotlighting news directors from three local stations who had to decide whether or not to show the taped footage of Dwyer's suicide.

Gould, Madelyn S. "Suicide and the Media." *Annals of the New York Academy of Sciences* 932 (April, 2001): 200-221. A focused scholarly article on the consequences of media reportage of suicides.

"Pictures Raise News Issue." *The New York Times*, January 24, 1987. Identifies the television stations that aired Dwyer's suicide and describes the footage shown by each station.

Stevens, William K. "Official Calls in Press and Kills Himself." *The New York Times*, January 23, 1987. Provides concise details about the whole Dwyer scandal from the time of the bribe to Dwyer's conviction to his suicide and its immediate aftermath.

SEE ALSO: May 30, 1923: U.S. Attorney General Harry M. Daugherty's Aide Commits Suicide; Nov. 20, 1974: British Politician John Stonehouse Fakes His Suicide; Feb. 3, 1975: Honduras's "Bananagate" Bribery Scandal Leads to Executive's Suicide; May 28, 2007: Japanese Politician Charged with Corruption Hangs Himself.

February 25, 1987

NCAA IMPOSES "DEATH PENALTY" ON SOUTHERN METHODIST UNIVERSITY FOOTBALL

For rules violations that included alumni payments to college football players, the Southern Methodist University (SMU) football team was suspended from competition during the 1987 season and then voluntarily remained out of the 1988 season because of NCAA restrictions. The NCAA sanction against competition is known as the death penalty for its severity and seriousness.

LOCALE: Dallas, Texas
CATEGORIES: Corruption; sports; education

KEY FIGURES

Bill Clements (b. 1917), two-term governor of
    Texas, chairman of SMU's board of governors
Ron Meyer (b. 1941), SMU football coach
David Stanley (b. 1965), high school football star
    paid to attend SMU

SUMMARY OF EVENT

During the early to mid-1980's, Southern Methodist University (SMU) fielded one of the best college football programs in the United States. According to author David Whitford, from 1980 to 1985 no major college football program won as many games as SMU, few went to as many postseason bowl games, and few were ranked among the nation's elite as regularly. SMU was also one of the most corrupt college football programs in the country. It already had been penalized six times by the National Collegiate Athletic Association (NCAA) prior to its receiving the so-called NCAA death penalty in 1987.

Southern Methodist is a private, liberal arts university in Dallas, Texas, with an enrollment averaging about eleven thousand students. Founded in 1911, it is affiliated with the United Methodist Church. The university is governed by a board of trustees, which until 1987 was led by an executive committee called the board of governors. The board of governors during the 1980's consisted of elite Dallas businessmen and politicians, including Bill Clements, a Dallas politician who would be elected to serve a second term as governor of Texas in 1986.

In 1987, the SMU Mustangs competed in the Southwest Conference (SWC), an intercollegiate conference consisting of five large state universities (Texas, Texas A&M, Arkansas, Texas Tech, and Houston), as well as four smaller private universities (SMU, Baylor, Rice, and Texas Christian). Although SMU had experienced some success during the 1930's and 1960's, its football team was not competitive during most of the 1970's. Between 1973 and 1975, SMU won just sixteen of thirty-three games.

In 1976, however, the university made an enhanced commitment to football, hiring a brash young coach named Ron Meyer who had previously built a successful football program at the University of Nevada, Las Vegas (UNLV). Whitford suggested that Meyer's success at UNLV came from bending, if not breaking, the rules governing intercollegiate athletics.

Whatever he did at UNLV, at SMU, Meyer reinvigorated the Mustang football program by creating a system of boosters and rich alumni who were able to get elite high school athletes to enroll at SMU; the alumni-boosters also paid the athletes monthly cash stipends to stay at SMU. More than twenty athletes (or their families) were given thousands of dollars in cash, cars, and other valuables. Meyer's program reeked of hypocrisy. In addition to SMU, other schools in the SWC bribed high school athletes; paying players was rationalized as a necessary evil for a small private school without a glowing athletics reputation.

Within a few years, SMU's football program was riding high. By 1981, its record was 10-1 and it earned a SWC championship and a postseason bowl game. Its record in 1982 was even better (11-0-1) and the program ranked second in the nation. However, with the victory came NCAA probation in 1982, 1985, and 1987.

During the 1970's and 1980's, most universities in the United States competed against each other under the auspices of the NCAA, which is a voluntary association of more than one thousand schools that sets rules for intercollegiate athletics. The most sacrosanct rules concern the amateur status of student athletes. Although student athletes are given a host of benefits—room and board, tuition, books, health care, and apparel—they cannot be given money to play. For example, athletes cannot use their "star" status to generate personal income, nor can they sell tickets allotted to them, be reimbursed for expenses, or borrow money from coaches. Also, parents of student athletes are prohibited from receiving complimentary tickets to a sporting event.

SMU demonstrated considerable contempt for the rules and was repeatedly penalized by the NCAA. In 1985, the program was placed on three years' probation for paying players, a virtual "slap on the wrist" for promises that it would stop making illicit payments and that boosters who had paid players would be banned from contact with the football program. Clements, the head of the board of governors, knew about the payments yet ordered the athletics director to continue making them. Clements made the order even though he promised to comply with NCAA sanctions and rules.

Clements believed that the university had to honor its promises to the athletes until they graduated. He hoped that by 1987 those athletes who had been receiving money would have graduated or otherwise left the school. Moreover, he feared that if SMU stopped paying, disgruntled athletes would document for the NCAA and for the media the extent of the corruption. That is exactly what happened. After his monthly stipend was ended, David Stanley, a former football player who had been unhappy at SMU and had gotten into trouble with cocaine, revealed he had been paid twenty-five thousand dollars to enroll at SMU and received seven hundred fifty dollars per month until he left school. The news led to a yearlong investigation by the NCAA. Expecting another slap on the wrist, SMU was stunned by the penalty it received.

On February 25, 1987, as a result of sustained, repeated violations, the NCAA imposed its so-called death penalty on SMU. The infractions committee meted out severe punishments, including a ban on televised games and on postseason bowl games, limitations on scholarships for four years, and a one-year ban on competition (which, subsequently, was extended to two years). In announcing the penalty, the NCAA observed that the severity was justified because of the program's brazenness in flouting the sanctions and rules, even in the face of multiple investigations.

IMPACT

New York Times reporter Peter Appleborne noted that 1986 was to be a year of celebration for SMU. It was the school's seventy-fifth anniversary and the university community had been looking forward to celebrating SMU's development into a major regional university with hope for national prominence. In contrast, the year was marked by disgrace. As Appleborne noted, "What hurt most was not that a bunch of football-mad alumni had put together a $400,000-a-year slush fund for athletes, but that the university's response for years had reflected skewed priorities and an absence of leadership."

In short, the athletics director and the board of governors were willing to continue a corrupt system because football wins led to enhanced prestige, increased donations, and a larger student enrollment. They were willing to bet the university's reputation that the depth of the corruption would never be exposed and that any NCAA penalties would be minor. Resignations included senior university trustees, the university president, the athletics director, and the football coach. Some even called for the impeachment of Texas governor Clements because of his complicity in the scandal as a university official.

In the wake of the scandal, the SMU board of trustees voted to replace the select board of governors and to make the board of trustees smaller, more inclusive, and with shorter terms in office. There also were sweeping changes made to the football program. As SMU athletics directors realized, fielding a competitive team, let alone rebuilding the program, would be impossible in the short term. The two-year hiatus gutted the program, and virtually every SMU football player on scholarship in 1986 was gone by 1989. Many had transferred to other schools; others had graduated. Scholarship limitations imposed by the NCAA made it more difficult to attract topnotch athletes to SMU. In retrospect, the NCAA death penalty did not keep other university programs from cheating. Ironically, the severity of the penalty has kept it from being used by the NCAA.

The impact of the scandal extended beyond SMU. During the mid-1980's, four of the nine football programs in the SWC were on probation, including SMU. The reputation of the conference plummeted, and by 1994 most of the major universities in the SWC joined other conferences. Two years later, the SWC disbanded.

—*Michael R. Meyers*

FURTHER READING

Appleborne, Peter. "Is There Life After Football?" *The New York Times*, October 4, 1987. Appleborne details the changes made at SMU in the year after the imposition of the NCAA death penalty on the school's football program.

Bowen, Ezra. "Revolt In a Football Palace." *Time*, December 22, 1986. Bowen explores the NCAA's investigation into the SMU football program and the result of that inquiry on the university community.

Eitzen, D. Stanley. *Fair and Foul: Beyond the Myths and Paradoxes of Sport*. Lanham, Md.: Rowman & Littlefield, 1999. Argues that college athletics, and athletics in general, is inherently corrupt and that it breeds hypocrisy.

Goodwin, Michael. "NCAA Bans Football at SMU for '87 Season." *The New York Times*, February 26, 1987. A major newspaper's breaking news story of the scandal at SMU.

Padilla, Arthur. "The Message in the Morass at SMU." *The New York Times*, March 8, 1987. Provides an overview of the NCAA penalties against SMU and why those penalties were imposed.

Staurowsky, Ellen J. "Piercing the Veil of Amateurism: Commercialization, Corruption, and U.S. College Sports." In *The Commercialization of Sport*, edited by Trevor Slack. New York: Routledge, 2004. Part of the Sport in Global Society series. Staurowsky discusses how amateur athletics in the United States has moved to commercialized and corrupt spectacle.

Whitford, David. *A Payroll to Meet: Greed, Scandal, and Football at Southern Methodist University*. New York: Macmillan, 1989. Presents a narrative overview of the scandal, with a focus on the actual funding of the SMU athletes as well as the NCAA death penalty.

SEE ALSO: Jan. 17, 1951: College Basketball Players Begin Shaving Points for Money; Fall, 1969-Winter, 1971: Japanese Baseball Players Are Implicated in Game Fixing; Apr. 27, 1980: Mobster's Arrest Reveals Point Shaving by Boston College Basketball Players; Aug. 24, 1989: Pete Rose Is Banned from Baseball for Betting on Games; Mar. 27, 2002: Georgia Basketball Coach Jim Harrick, Sr., Resigns over Fraud Allegations; May 3, 2003: University of Alabama Fires New Football Coach in Sex Scandal; July 14, 2006: *New York Times* Exposes Grading Scandal at Auburn University; Aug. 20, 2007: Football Star Michael Vick Pleads Guilty to Financing a Dogfighting Ring; Sept. 13, 2007: New England Patriots Football Team Is Fined for Spying on Other Teams.

1980's

March 19, 1987
JIM BAKKER RESIGNS AS HEAD OF PTL TELEVISION NETWORK

Jim and Tammy Faye Bakker, evangelists who ran an empire that centered around the PTL television network, were enmeshed in personal problems that led to their fall from grace. Tammy Faye admitted to an addiction to painkillers and Jim admitted to having an affair with a church secretary and paying for her silence. This latter incident led to Jim's resignation and eventually a financial investigation of the ministry. Jim was imprisoned and the couple divorced.

LOCALE: Charlotte, North Carolina

CATEGORIES: Public morals; religion; radio and television; sex; law and the courts

KEY FIGURES

Jim Bakker (b. 1940), American televangelist and author

Tammy Faye Bakker (1942-2007), American televangelist, author, singer, and actor

Jessica Hahn (b. 1959), American model, actor, and church secretary

Jerry Falwell (1933-2007), American pastor and televangelist

SUMMARY OF EVENT

Married evangelists Jim and Tammy Faye Bakker began their television career in 1966 when working with evangelist Pat Robertson at his Christian Broadcasting Network. The burgeoning ministers first found fame via *The 700 Club*, a variety show focused on various conservative Christian topics. After spearheading the program through 1973, the couple joined Christian broadcasters Paul and Jan Crouch and founded Trinity Broadcasting Systems (now Trinity Broadcasting Network, or TBN) in Costa Mesa, California, beginning their on-air ministry with the show *Praise the Lord* on a local television station with rented airtime.

Even though the partnership with TBN lasted only one year, the Bakkers' success would continue. They moved from Southern California to Charlotte, North Carolina, and after securing the rights to the acronym PTL, formed Praise the Lord Network (also known as the PTL Network) and began their flagship show *The PTL Club*. Between the pair's surging popularity and ability to reach nearly one hundred stations around the globe, the program, in a talk-show format, earned tremendous traction throughout the late 1970's into the 1980's.

In addition to television outreach (which welcomed a diversity of people from all denominations), the couple unveiled Heritage USA, a 2,300-acre theme park (complete with a resort atmosphere and residences) in Fort Mill, South Carolina, in 1978. The park drew more visitors than any other park in the United States except Disneyland and Disney World. Though all appeared well at face value and PTL finances were strong (backed by over one million dollars per week in viewer donations), the cracks started to surface during the mid-1980's. The media became particularly suspicious of what skeptics claimed was an excessive empire (including reports that Jim and Tammy Faye's home included an air-conditioned doghouse and gold-plated bathroom fixtures, which the couple later denied).

Additional fuel was added to the fire in 1987, a year that included Tammy Faye's public admission of being addicted to prescription painkillers (and subsequent treatment at the Betty Ford Center) and Jim's looming sex scandal. Jim had sexual relations with one-time church secretary Jessica Hahn, and his staff paid her a reported $279,000 to keep the secret hidden from the media. On March 19, Bakker personally broke the silence, tearfully admitting of the affair (which happened in 1980) but denying allegations of rape. With this admission, Jim also resigned from PTL and turned over the organization to fellow televangelist (and longtime rival) Jerry

Falwell in hopes of rebuilding trust within the religious community.

Initially, the plan was for Falwell to maintain the ministry until Jim could be restored to a position of leadership following a time steeped in personal prayer. However, Falwell quickly turned against the couple, calling Jim a hypocrite, accusing him of homosexual leanings (which were never substantiated), and scorned him for the shame surrounding the ministry's downfall. With the change in command at PTL, Falwell now had control of the station's satellite and Heritage USA, but the negative publicity surrounding the circumstances led to a sharp decline in viewership and park attendance. To make matters worse for the Bakker legacy and for Falwell's attempt to regenerate the brand name, the Internal Revenue Service revoked Heritage USA's tax-exempt status, leading to the organization's filing for bankruptcy protection.

Additional turmoil set in when *The Charlotte Observer* published reports of potential financial wrongdoings during the Bakker reign of PTL. The paper claimed that, most notably, the organization sold lifetime memberships that gave donors of one thousand dollars or more an extended weekend vacation at Heritage USA every year. Approximately 165,000 people contributed to the program, but at the time of Jim's descent, only one five-hundred-room hotel had been constructed to accommodate the tens of thousands of donors.

As a result of subsequent bookkeeping discrepancies, Jim was tried in a well-publicized case that continued as tabloid fodder into 1988. In December of that year, he was indicted for fraud and conspiracy to defraud, resulting in a conviction on twenty-four counts and a forty-five-year prison sentence. The Bakkers would never

return as a couple to television nor to Heritage USA, which officially closed its doors in 1989 (lifetime donors each received $6.54 in legal compensation).

The Bakkers continued to make headlines even during the prison term, as Jim appealed his case and was sentenced to eighteen years in 1991 (though he would serve only five). The next year, Tammy Faye filed for divorce and married Roe Messner, the builder of Heritage USA, in 1993. In prison, Jim wrote in his autobiography *I Was Wrong* (1996) about his theological and sexual mistakes, though he maintained his innocence when it came to issues of financial fraud. (An epilogue written after he finished the text reveals a 1996 federal jury ruling that Bakker was not selling securities through his partnership offers at Heritage USA.)

Though much less publicity was granted to the epilogue and Jim's subsequent career moves, he regained some exposure by marrying Lori Graham in 1998. The pair sought to recapture his original tele-

Jim Bakker is escorted from his lawyer's office by U.S. marshals on August 31, 1989, in Charlotte, North Carolina. Bakker was ordered to undergo psychiatric evaluation to determine if he was competent to continue standing trial. (AP/Wide World Photos)

A JIM BAKKER CONFESSION

In prison for fraud, televangelist Jim Bakker wrote his autobiography I Was Wrong, *published in 1996. In the following excerpt from the book, Bakker shows remorse for practicing a negative form of prosperity theology, that is, he admits to teaching a false theology of materialism and abundance and leading people astray in the process.*

I may not always have been so blatant about it, but I often preached a prosperity message at Heritage USA and on our PTL television programs. But when I began to study the Scriptures in depth while in prison, something I am embarrassed and ashamed to admit that I rarely took time to do during the hectic years of constant building and ministering at PTL, I was very distressed at what I discovered. I realized that for years I helped propagate an impostor, not a true gospel, but another gospel—a gospel that stated "God wants you to be rich!" Christians should have the best because we are children of God, "King's Kids," as I often put it. And shouldn't the King's kids have the best this world had to offer?

The more I studied the Bible, however, I had to admit that the prosperity message did not line up with the tenor of Scripture. My heart was crushed to think that I led so many people astray. I was appalled that I could have been so wrong, and I was deeply grateful that God had not struck me dead as a false prophet!

through their television shows and their amusement park (perhaps more than anyone else within the Christian ministry at the time). Even with throngs of supporters, however, a more secular-minded public considered their lifestyles lavish, their methods deceptive, and their intentions deceitful. The entire episode leaves many lingering questions, ranging from Falwell's motives in his takeover of PTL and Heritage USA to whether or not the media focus on Jim's trial affected the outcome of the case, to Jim's detriment. It is clear from the Bakkers-PTL scandal that the public holds religious figures of any affiliation to high moral standards.

Even though triumph was followed by a fall from grace, the Bakkers proved they still had faithful followers. Jim and Tammy Faye both returned separately to television—albeit with a fraction of their previous viewers—but nonetheless resumed their careers. For admitting to some past mistakes they were greeted with some forgiveness.

—Andy Argyrakis

vision audience in 2003 with the variety-styled *Jim Bakker Show* (also broadcast throughout various satellite networks). Tammy Faye turned to secular television in 1996 with *The Jim J. and Tammy Faye Show* (a talk show with costar Jim J. Bullock, a gay comic), followed by VH1's reality show *The Surreal Life* in 2004. Despite Jim and Tammy Faye's split, they remained friends until Tammy Faye's death from cancer in 2007.

IMPACT

Though televangelists were sometimes viewed with skepticism prior to this scandal (either because of sexual or financial indiscretions), Jim's resignation marked the pinnacle of poor publicity for the television genre. The consequences of the resignation were particularly heavy because of Jim's and Tammy Faye's larger than life personalities, plus the massive amount of fame they accumulated

FURTHER READING

Albert, James A. *Jim Bakker: Miscarriage of Justice?* Chicago: Open Court, 1998. A legal analyst presents all sides to the story, while suggesting Jim's financial trial could have been hindered by endless media sensationalism.

Bakker, Jay, with Linden Gross. *Son of a Preacher Man: My Search for Grace in the Shadows.* San Francisco, Calif.: HarperSanFrancisco, 2001. Jim and Tammy Faye's son, Jay, discusses his father in this telling memoir of living "in the shadows" of scandal and controversey.

Bakker, Jim, with Ken Abraham. *I Was Wrong: The Untold Story of the Shocking Journey from PTL Power to Prison and Beyond.* Nashville, Tenn.: Thomas Nelson, 1996. Jim's personal account of his rise to fame and his downfall. Includes candid details about his time in prison and his declaration of innocence regarding financial wrongdoings.

Messner, Tammy Faye. *Telling It My Way*. New York: Villard, 1996. Tammy Faye tells her side of the story and supports Jim's accounts of innocence in the case of financial improprieties.

Miller, Brett A. *Divine Apology: The Discourse of Religious Image Restoration*. Westport, Conn.: Praeger, 2002. Analyzes religious figures accused of sexual misconduct. Includes some discussion of Jim Bakker in the chapter on fundamentalist preacher Jimmy Swaggart, whose scandalous dalliance with a prostitute was covered closely by the national media.

Richardson, Michael. *The Edge of Disaster*. New York: St. Martin's Press, 1987. A book with a tabloid tone that exposes the couple's wrongdoings. Richardson was Jim's personal bodyguard during the televangelist's peak professional period.

Shepard, Charles E. *Forgiven: The Rise and Fall of Jim Bakker and the PTL Ministry*. New York: Atlantic Monthly Press, 1989. A reporter from *The Charlotte Observer* analyzes the ascent and collapse of Jim and Tammy Faye's empire.

SEE ALSO: Oct. 25, 1974: Evangelist Billy James Hargis Resigns College Presidency During Gay-Sex Scandal; Jan., 1977: Singer Anita Bryant Campaigns Against Lesbian and Gay Rights; June 27, 1978: Evangelist Herbert W. Armstrong Excommunicates His Own Son; Apr. 22, 1986: Faith Healer Peter Popoff Is Exposed as a Fraud; Feb. 21, 1988: Evangelist Jimmy Swaggart Tearfully Confesses His Adultery; May 6, 1992: Irish Bishop Eamonn Casey's Romantic Affair Leads to His Resignation; Nov. 2, 2006: Evangelist Kent Hovind Is Convicted of Federal Tax Violations; Nov. 2, 2006: Male Escort Reveals Sexual Liaisons with Evangelist Ted Haggard.

1980's

April 9, 1987

BESS MYERSON RESIGNS AS NEW YORK COMMISSIONER OF CULTURAL AFFAIRS

Bess Myerson, a former Miss America, television personality, columnist, and consumer advocate, was appointed New York City's commissioner of cultural affairs by Mayor Edward I. Koch. She was indicted, then acquitted on charges of bribery, conspiracy, and mail fraud in a case involving her lover, contractor Carl Capasso. Capasso had bribed the judge, Hortense W. Gabel, by helping her daughter get a job in Myerson's city department.

ALSO KNOWN AS: Bess mess

LOCALE: New York, New York

CATEGORIES: Corruption; government; politics; law and the courts

KEY FIGURES

Bess Myerson (b. 1924), New York City commissioner of cultural affairs, 1983-1987

Carl Capasso (1945-2001), business contractor

Hortense W. Gabel (1912-1990), New York State Supreme Court justice

Edward I. Koch (b. 1924), mayor of New York City, 1978-1989

SUMMARY OF EVENT

Born in the Bronx to Russian immigrant parents, Bess Myerson was the first Jewish woman to win the Miss America title. She entered the contest because she wanted a new piano for her graduate studies in music. In the following decades, she made numerous television appearances on shows such as *The Big Payoff*, *The Jackie Gleason Show*, *The Name's the Same*, and *I've Got a Secret*.

Myerson became an icon for civil rights during her beauty pageant days when she refused to change her name to the pseudonym Beth Merrick to make it sound less Jewish. In response, numerous sponsors, including the Ford Motor Company, and events associated with the pageant refused to deal with her. A country club denied her admission to its facilities. She traveled around the United States for the Anti-Defamation League, speaking against anti-Semitism. She became involved in New York politics during the 1960's and 1970's, serving as New York City's first commissioner of consumer affairs.

In 1977, Myerson was a frequent companion to Edward I. Koch during his campaign for mayor of New York City, dispelling rumors that Koch was gay. In 1980, Myerson ran for the Democratic nomination to the U.S. Senate and lost by a slim margin. Her presidential appointments included sitting on committees for Lyndon B. Johnson, Gerald R. Ford, and Jimmy Carter. In 1983, Koch appointed Myerson commissioner of New York City's Department of Cultural Affairs, after the position had been turned down by former first lady Jacqueline Kennedy Onassis and opera star Beverly Sills. The department's principal function is to care for the city's cultural institutions, such as its museums, theaters, art centers, and gardens, although it fulfills other functions, such as facilitating and funding free public performances and concerts as well as small arts groups.

Myerson's tenure was marred by political and personal scandal. In a 1983 divorce case, a Bronx sewer contractor, Carl Capasso, was accused of bribing New York State Supreme Court justice Hortense W. Gabel to cut his alimony payments by inducing Myerson to give the judge's daughter, Suhkreet Gabel, a job as a special assistant in her department in 1983. (Gabel, who resigned in 1987, was indicted, then acquitted in late 1988 for her role in the case against Capasso.) Capasso was Myerson's lover.

Myerson had been summoned before a federal grand jury investigating Capasso's alleged bribery, but she invoked her Fifth Amendment rights to not testify against him. She did this despite Mayor Koch's earlier assertion that he would consider a refusal to appear before a grand jury grounds for dismissing any high-ranking city employee, including Myerson. In a report commissioned by the mayor and written by Harold Tyler, a former federal judge,

there were numerous infractions and other ethical issues to be concerned about.

Further investigations, led by U.S. attorney Rudy Giuliani, revealed that Suhkreet Gabel had been unfit for the government position she was given by Myerson. Gabel's former employers included a massage parlor, and she had a history of mental instability. At the time she was hired, the mayor's assistant, Herbert Rickman, raised questions about her qualifications, but the mayor was reassured by Myerson that Gabel was the most qualified candidate. She failed to mention, however, that no other candidates had been interviewed. Rickman, who was not the most reliable witness, told federal investigators that he was in the early stages of Alzheimer's disease. It was later revealed that an assistant commissioner, Richard Bruno, helped create a false story to justify Gabel's hire. The post had been eliminated and then re-created specifically to make the hire possible.

In the meantime, during the last months of the grand jury investigations, Capasso was convicted in a separate criminal case for tax evasion. He was sentenced to four years in prison and fined $500,000. A federal grand jury then indicted Myerson, Capasso, and Judge Gabel for their roles in hiring Gabel's daughter in exchange for reducing Capasso's alimony payments.

The scandal proved stressful for Myerson. Just before her trial opened, she was arrested and fined for shoplifting forty-four dollars worth of merchandise from a shop in a small Pennsylvania town. Her spoils included six bottles of nail polish, five pairs of earrings, a pair of shoes, and flashlight batteries. She was in the area to visit Capasso at the Allenwood Federal Prison Camp. Other past indiscretions were uncovered by the media, including a London shoplifting charge from decades earlier as well as later police reports of dozens of anonymous phone calls and abusive letters to people involved in personal relationships that affected Myerson's romantic involvements. Myerson's Cultural Affairs Commission staff described her as effective but not personable. A former deputy commissioner went so far as to call her "the meanest manager I ever saw."

The trial exposed details of Myerson's unethical

behavior, including having city employees run personal errands for her—such as grocery shopping and picking up dry cleaning—and she failed to disclose lavish gifts such as jewelry and a Mercedes sedan from Capasso, who had been a city contractor. Other erratic behavior included attending a morning meeting in hair curlers and talking through the first act of an opera before leaving at intermission.

Midway through the trial, Judge Kevin Thomas Duffy withdrew after U.S. attorney Giuliani submitted a motion to disqualify him on the basis that he had failed to disclose the extent of his relationship with one of Gabel's lawyers as well as with Gabel herself. Duffy, who said he was withdrawing because he resented the prosecution's tactics so much that he could no longer remain impartial, charged that Giuliani's motion had been driven by the judge's strict orders regarding publicity. Duffy had rebuked Giuliani for leaks of grand jury information that the judge believed could only have come from him. Duffy had an established contentious relationship with prosecutors. He accused them of delaying their response to defense motions in order to delay the trial, although he did not specify their motivation in doing so.

Duffy was replaced by Judge John F. Keenan, who was selected at random from the pool of active judges in federal district court. Myerson was indicted, then resigned on April 9, 1987. She was ultimately acquitted, as were Capasso and Judge Gabel.

IMPACT

Myerson was not the only city official accused of corruption during the administration of Mayor Koch. Other officials whose actions were examined in court during the Koch years included transportation commissioner Anthony R. Ameruso and comptroller Alan G. Hevesi. Despite the scandals, Koch's work led to an overall improvement in city services and the lowest unemployment rate in twelve years. Nonetheless, the Myerson scandal led to the end of the Koch era.

Even Myerson's detractors admitted that, in general, the Department of Cultural Affairs had been

handled well during her tenure as its commissioner. She was a conscientious and thorough advocate for the department, whose budget doubled from $60 million to $123.5 million, making it second in the nation only to the federal National Endowment for the Arts in the amount of government funding it administered.

After her resignation, Myerson remained a frequent philanthropist. She helped found the Museum of Jewish Heritage, where she established the Bess Myerson Film and Video Collection, and she endowed the Bess Myerson Campus Journalism Awards given out by the Anti-Defamation League each year.

—*Catherine Rambo*

FURTHER READING

Alexander, Shana. *When She Was Bad*. New York: Random House, 1990. Focuses on the Myerson scandal and the circumstances behind Myerson's employment of Judge Gabel's daughter.

Mollenkopf, John H. *A Phoenix in the Ashes: The Rise and Fall of the Koch Coalition in New York*. Princeton, N.J.: Princeton University Press, 1994. Lays out and explicates the major events of the Koch administration, including the Myerson scandal, and discusses the relationship between Koch and Myerson.

Preston, Jennifer. *Queen Bess: The Unauthorized Biography of Bess Myerson*. New York: Contemporary Books, 1990. An unauthorized biography of Myerson that explores the scandal and its aftermath on her life.

Seidemann, Joel. *In the Interest of Justice: Great Opening and Closing Arguments of the Last One Hundred Years*. New York: HarperCollins, 2005. Includes arguments from the Myerson legal case from both the defense and the prosecution.

SEE ALSO: May 2, 2000: New York Mayor Rudy Giuliani's Extramarital Affair Is Revealed; Mar. 4, 2004: Former United Way Charity Chief Pleads Guilty to Embezzlement.

July 25, 1987
NOVELIST-POLITICIAN JEFFREY ARCHER WINS LIBEL TRIAL AGAINST THE *DAILY STAR*

Jeffrey Archer was a best-selling British novelist and rising Conservative Party politician in 1986 when London's Daily Star *revealed that he had paid for sex, an accusation that led Archer to sue the newspaper successfully for libel. After two former associates came forward in 1999 to say that Archer lied during his testimony and manufactured evidence in the libel case, he was arrested, convicted of perjury, and imprisoned.*

LOCALE: London, England

CATEGORIES: Law and the courts; publishing and journalism; government; politics; sex

KEY FIGURES
Jeffrey Archer (b. 1940), novelist and politician
Monica Coghlan (1951-2001), prostitute
Michael Stacpoole (b. 1938), friend and business associate of Archer
Ted Francis (b. 1934), friend of Archer and freelance television producer
Angela Peppiatt (b. 1945), personal assistant of Archer
Terence Baker (1939-1991), Archer's film and television agent
Adam Raphael (1937-1999), journalist

SUMMARY OF EVENT
Jeffrey Archer became the United Kingdom's fourth youngest member of Parliament in 1969 when he won a seat as a Conservative representing Louth, Lincolnshire. However, he had to step down in 1974 after he was victimized in a stock swindle and was close to bankruptcy. He then turned to writing to make a living. He based his first novel, *Not a Penny More, Not a Penny Less* (1976), on his experience with the swindler, and the book became a best seller. After writing more best sellers, including the *Kane and Abel* trilogy (1979, 1982, 1987), Archer reentered politics in 1985 when he was appointed deputy chairman of the Conservative Party

by Prime Minister Margaret Thatcher, who chose to ignore warnings about his character.

Unfortunately for the Conservatives, those warnings turned out to be accurate. Archer resigned his position in October, 1986, when the newspaper *The News of the World* ran a story alleging that Archer had paid Monica Coghlan, a prostitute, £2,000 to leave England. She was allegedly paid through a go-between, Michael Stacpoole, a friend and business associate of Archer. However, the newspaper stopped short of saying that Archer actually had sex with Coghlan. It was another newspaper, the *Daily Star*, that reported Archer paid £70 for sex with Coghlan at the Albion Hotel in the Mayfair district of London. Archer sued the *Daily Star* for libel.

The civil trial began in early July, 1987. Archer testified that he had never met Coghlan, but journalist Adam Raphael testified under subpoena that Archer told him that he had met Coghlan about six months before the events in dispute. Archer explained the payment as the act of a kindhearted person rather than that of a guilty party trying to buy silence, and his wife, Mary Archer, a scientist, testified on his behalf. The reporters for the *Daily Star* and *The News of the World* testified that they had recorded telephone conversations between Archer and Coghlan without Archer's knowledge, had paid Coghlan £6,000, and had arranged to have Coghlan wear a microphone for a meeting she had with Stacpoole at Victoria Station. Their conversation was recorded.

Some confusion arose, however, regarding the exact date of the alleged sexual encounter. In any case, Archer had alibis from friends Ted Francis and Terence Baker for both nights in question, and Baker ultimately testified on Archer's behalf. Archer also provided an appointment book for the period that challenged the chronology of the *Daily Star* article. Observers at the trial felt that the judge was biased in Archer's favor, especially when he strongly argued for the support of Mary Archer in his instructions to the jury. (Judges in Britain are given more leeway in expressing their opinions before the jury than are judges in the United States.) On July 25, Archer won his lawsuit against the *Daily Star*, which had to pay him £500,000 in damages.

Archer then resumed his career as an author, writing plays, short stories, and novels. In 1992, he became Baron Archer of Weston-super-Mare at the recommendation of Prime Minister John Major for his fund-raising efforts for displaced Iraqi Kurds. In 1999, he was selected by the Conservative Party as its candidate for the London mayoral election of 2000.

After Archer's nomination, Francis, by then a former friend who claimed Archer owed him money, along with Archer's former personal assistant, Angela Peppiatt, whom Archer had fired in a dispute over expense reports, asserted that he had made up an alibi for the 1987 trial. They claimed it was their civic duty to report the fabricated alibi. It was later revealed, however, that Francis had accepted £19,000 from *The News of the World*. Francis claimed that Archer had asked him to lie under oath by testifying that they had dinner together on the night mentioned in the original *Daily Star* article. The newspaper later changed the date of the encounter in its story, so Francis never actually testified.

Peppiatt claimed that Archer had ordered her to forge an appointment book to back up his alibi, but that she had secretly kept the original book, photocopies of the false entries, and Archer's written instructions. Journalists also found Stacpoole, the intermediary who had given the money to Coghlan, in Thailand, where he was managing a brothel. Stacpoole revealed that Archer had given him £40,000 to live in Paris until after the 1987 trial was finished. Reportedly, Stacpoole had knowledge about Archer's business and marital affairs that would have damaged Archer's case. Finally, two friends of Archer's agent Baker, who had died in 1991, revealed that he had told them that he lied under oath to provide Archer with an alibi in return for the television and film rights to Archer's books.

The *News of the World* printed its investigative story in November, 1999, and Archer promptly withdrew from the election. In February, 2000, he was banned from the Conservative Party for five years; he was arrested in April and, in September, was charged with perjury and perverting the course of justice during the 1987 trial. The new trial took place from May through July, 2001. Archer was found guilty of both charges and was sentenced to four years in prison, of which he served two.

Archer was initially sent to Belmarsh Prison, a maximum-security facility, then moved to Wayland Prison (medium security) in August and finally to North Sea Camp (minimum security) in October. Media reports allege that he had been abusing his privileges, so in September, 2002, he was transferred to Lincoln Prison, a medium-security facility, for one month. In July, 2003, he was released on parole.

IMPACT

Archer's receipt of £500,000 in damages from the *Daily Star* in 1987 marked the highest award ever given in a libel case in the United Kingdom. Lloyd Turner, the newspaper's editor, was fired six weeks after the trial. In October, 2002, Archer repaid the monies he had received in 1987, plus £1 million for the newspaper's legal expenses. However, vindication came too late for Turner, who died in 1996.

Shortly after his release, Archer announced that he would never again enter politics, although he eventually joined a local branch of the Conservative Party. Instead, he concentrated on his writing career. He wrote the nonfiction trilogy *A Prison Diary* (2002, 2003, 2004) while in prison. After prison, he wrote the novels *False Impression* (2006) and *The Gospel According to Judas* (2007; cowritten with Francis J. Moloney) and the short-story collection *Cat O'Nine Tales* (2006). Nine of the stories in *Cat O'Nine Tales* were based on stories told to Archer by other prisoners during his incarceration.

—*Thomas R. Feller*

FURTHER READING

Archer, Jeffrey. *A Prison Diary*. New York: St. Martin's Griffin, 2003. The first volume of three, written as a form of therapy while in prison. This volume covers Belmarsh Prison. Volume 2, *Purgatory* (2005), describes his incarceration at Wayland Prison and volume 3, *Heaven* (2005), describes his incarceration at North Sea Camp.

Crick, Michael. *Jeffrey Archer: Stranger than Fiction*. 4th ed. London: Hamish Hamilton, 2000. An updated biography of Archer that includes discussion of the charges of perjury that surfaced in 1999. Both editions devote several chapters to the 1987 trial.

Mantle, Jonathan. *In for a Penny: Unauthorized Biography of Jeffrey Archer*. London: Hamish Hamilton, 1988. This was the first book-length biography of Archer and was favorably reviewed at the time. Unfortunately, the author did not have the benefit of the information revealed in 1999 and 2001, the year of Archer's new trial.

SEE ALSO: July 10, 1934: Sex Scandal Forces Resignation of Alberta Premier Brownlee; Dec. 10, 1936: King Edward VIII Abdicates to Marry an American Divorcée; Mar. 2-Sept. 25, 1963: John Profumo Affair Rocks British Government; Oct. 14, 1983: British Cabinet Secretary Parkinson Resigns After His Secretary Becomes Pregnant; 1985-1986: Westland Affair Shakes Prime Minister Thatcher's Government; Aug. 10, 1989: Japanese Prime Minister Sosuke Resigns After Affair with a Geisha; Sept. 24, 1992: British Cabinet Member David Mellor Resigns over Romantic Affair; Jan. 5, 1994: British Cabinet Member Resigns After Fathering a Child Out of Wedlock; Sept. 28, 2002: British Politician Reveals Her Affair with Prime Minister John Major; Jan. 21, 2006: British Politician Resigns After Gay-Sex Orgy; Apr. 26, 2006: Britain's Deputy Prime Minister Admits Affair with Secretary.

September 23, 1987

PLAGIARISM CHARGES END JOE BIDEN'S PRESIDENTIAL CAMPAIGN

Joe Biden, a three-term U.S. senator from Delaware whose populist style marked him as a rising star in the Democratic Party, was forced to abandon his presidential campaign after he was accused of using the words of a British politician as his own in a campaign speech that was videotaped. The media also revealed his academic difficulties in law school. Biden's career in politics flourished, despite the accusations of plagiarism and misappropriation.

LOCALES: Iowa; Washington, D.C.

CATEGORIES: Politics; government; plagiarism; publishing and journalism

KEY FIGURES

Joe Biden (b. 1942), U.S. senator from Delaware, 1973-2009, and vice president, 2009-

Michael Dukakis (b. 1933), governor of Massachusetts, 1975-1979 and 1983-1991

Neil Kinnock (b. 1942), member of the British parliament, 1970-1995, and leader of the opposition Labour Party, 1983-1992

SUMMARY OF EVENT

In November, 1965, Joe Biden, a struggling first-year student at Syracuse University College of Law, plagiarized five pages from a May, 1965, *Fordham Law Review* article for a fifteen-page paper in a legal methodology seminar. When the plagiarism was detected, Biden, a graduate of the University of Delaware whose undergraduate record was itself undistinguished, claimed the borrowing was inadvertent and that he misunderstood the importance of source citation (he provided only one footnote in the paper). The law school, however, citing its code of integrity, maintained zero tolerance for material theft, and Biden was given a reprimand and a grade of F in the class.

Biden retook the class and earned a low B. He graduated three years later, seventy-sixth in a class of eighty-five. He returned to Delaware and moved from law into politics. Charismatic, good looking, and with a reputation for eloquence, Biden became the fifth youngest senator in U.S. history in 1972.

In 1987, Republican Ronald Reagan's presidency was coming to a close. Biden, by this time a popular three-term senator and chairman of the powerful Senate Judiciary Committee and considered a moderate liberal (important given the legacy of the conservative revolution over

Presidential hopeful Joe Biden denies charges of plagiarism in 1987. (AP/Wide World Photos)

which Reagan had presided), launched what appeared to be a promising presidential campaign. He quickly became one of the front-runners as he carried his campaign into Iowa, the first of the caucus states and, hence, critically important. The Democratic field was wide open and already quite contentious. Although the field of candidates included the Reverend Jesse Jackson, U.S. Representative Richard Gephardt, and U.S. Senator Al Gore, Biden's most significant challenge was Michael Dukakis, in his third term as governor of Massachusetts, whose reputation as a cool economics-driven technocrat and a reserved campaigner was juxtaposed against Biden's affable personality. Biden also was passionate and eloquent in his stump speeches and embraced a populist style that drew massive crowds and generated tremendous excitement despite his reputation for lengthy speeches.

In early September, Biden was delivering his stump speech at the Iowa state fairgrounds. As he closed the speech, he appeared to move off his prepared script and talk candidly and passionately about how, on his way to the fairgrounds, he had thought back over his own difficult childhood, about how his family had come from humble origins and had worked long hours in the forbidding conditions of the mines of northeastern Pennsylvania (he was born in Scranton). He spoke of how his family had never been able to attend college and yet managed to endure despite never having a voice in politics. He added that he was proud to now run as a candidate to be that voice. The closing surprised his staffers and was quite moving; indeed, it was vintage Biden.

Several days later a video, quietly (and anonymously) distributed to the media in Iowa, showed populist British Labour Party leader Neil Kinnock delivering virtually the same remarks weeks earlier at a rally in northern England. The video juxtaposed Biden and Kinnock in vivid split screen. Biden, however, had used the same words in speeches before the speech in Iowa and always acknowledged Kinnock as the source. On the one occasion that he failed to attribute the passage to Kinnock, Biden was videotaped. Reporters jumped on the story and quickly discovered that no relative in the Biden family had ever worked in the mines, that his father was in fact fairly successful in car sales, and that most of his mother's family had graduated from college.

The juxtaposition of Biden's apparent earnestness against his obvious pilfering of the sentiments of the British politician was particularly embarrassing because it raised questions of Biden's credibility and his sincerity. Accusations quickly surfaced that opposition campaigns had manipulated the media to create the controversy. Although responsibility was never established, it was held that the Dukakis campaign, then under the direction of veteran campaign coordinator John Sasso, had prepared the video. Dukakis, who maintained he knew nothing of the video, quickly acted to distance himself from what was considered a vicious attack campaign. He dismissed both Sasso and junior campaign political director Paul Tully, even as his staff repeatedly claimed the Kinnock video had been leaked to the Dukakis campaign by the staff of a struggling Gephardt eager to thwart Biden. Indeed, during the two weeks leading up to his withdrawal from the race, Biden dismissed the accusations of pilfering from Kinnock as ludicrous. Nevertheless, the damage to Biden's campaign was done.

In a series of investigative reports, *The New York Times* detailed Biden's problems in law school at Syracuse and, more damaging, found other instances in which Biden had used phrases and passages from other speeches earlier on the campaign trail in New Hampshire and New Jersey. The newspaper reported how he had used the words of others, including those of Democratic Party icon Robert F. Kennedy, to exaggerate his own public record, most notably his involvement in the Civil Rights movement of the 1960's.

The news coverage was devastating to the Biden campaign. In an emotional conference on September 18, he acknowledged that he had lifted the Kinnock passage and then admitted to his own mediocre academic record but attempted to defuse the implications of using Kinnock's words by insisting that politicians often echoed each other as a tribute and that the other occasions of borrowing reflected carelessness rather than deceit. He went on to describe himself as just an average Joe, hoping to draw on Reagan's winning legacy of charm. He vowed to stay in the presidential race.

Biden never recovered from the scandal, though, and he faced a continual barrage of questions about his intelligence and trustworthiness. Although the passages cited by reporters accounted for a small percentage of Biden's voluminous public record of speeches, and although the media acknowledged that plagiarism was hardly a criminal offense, questions persisted. Biden's consistently high ratings as a senator plummeted even as he continued to fend off questions of his integrity and ethics. Although dismissing the firestorm as politically motivated and trivial, Biden suspended his presidential run on September 23, only five days after he admitted to using Kinnock's words without attribution.

IMPACT

Biden certainly was not the first politician or student to plagiarize, and many supporters believe he was unfairly—or overly—targeted for an action that pales in comparison to the gravity of other offenses that ruin politicians with much thinner records of public service. Even so, once the revelations of his academic record came to light, and once the media found the pattern of misappropriation, Biden was considered a politician without core values or integrity. Because of this character assessment, his initial claims of innocence reaffirmed the belief by many that he was a moral relativist and an intellectual flyweight.

Furthermore, because Biden was a promising Democratic Party visionary and one of the party's most eloquent and articulate speakers, his downfall for plagiarism made him a point of reference for a generation of teachers and professors who, confronting the insidious opportunities for plagiarism brought by the Web, tirelessly remind students that academic and personal honesty matter.

Biden, however, survived the scandal politically. Several years after his 1987 campaign imploded, he jokingly presented Kinnock with a bound volume of his own speeches and invited the British politician to borrow what he wanted from that volume. Biden remained in the Senate and emerged in the post-September 11, 2001, era as a member of the Senate Foreign Relations Committee, working as one of the most passionate and articulate voices on international law and U.S. military deployment. When his presidential run in 2008 ended early, little notice was paid to the 1987 scandal, which indicated that his reputation and the perception of his integrity and intelligence had not been irrevocably defined by the scandal. Indeed, he was chosen as Barack Obama's vice presidential running mate during the presidential campaign of 2008, becoming vice president of the United States in January, 2009.

—Joseph Dewey

FURTHER READING

Biden, Joseph. *Promises to Keep: On Life and Politics*. New York: Random House, 2007. Provides important context for appreciating the magnitude of Biden's public record and his own frank assessment of the lessons learned from his failed presidential campaign.

Black, Christine, and Thomas Oliphant. *All by Myself: The Unmaking of a Presidential Campaign*. Guilford, Conn.: Globe/Pequot, 1989. Definitive account of the 1988 campaign that places the Biden collapse (and the staff chicanery behind its well-timed revelation) within the larger picture of how the scandal impacted the election. Valuable summary of the promise of Biden's presence and the precipitous nature of his collapse.

Mallon, Thomas. *Stolen Words: Forays Into the Origins and Ravages of Plagiarism*. 1989. New ed. San Diego, Calif.: Harvest Books, 2001. References the Biden controversy as well as other prominent cases of misappropriation of published work. Presents the definitive case for why plagiarism matters, and discusses its implications as a revelation of character, integrity, and work ethic.

Patterson, Thomas E. *Out of Order: An Incisive and Boldly Original Critique of the News Media's Domination of America's Political Process*. New York: Vintage Books, 1994. Written after the 1987 campaign, this work offers a clear assessment of how the media mishandled the Biden controversy and the disturbing implications of media influence in deciding presidential nominees, especially in the United States.

SEE ALSO: Mar. 1, 1967: Adam Clayton Powell, Jr., Is Excluded from Congress; June 23, 1967: Senator Thomas J. Dodd Is Censured for Misappropriating Funds; Oct. 11, 1979: Senate Denounces Herman E. Talmadge for Money Laundering; May 31, 1989: Speaker of the House Jim Wright Resigns in Ethics Scandal; June 1, 1994: Congressman Dan Rostenkowski Is Indicted in House Post Office Scandal; Jan. 17, 1998: President Bill Clinton Denies Sexual Affair with a White House Intern; Dec. 5, 2002: Senator Trent Lott Praises Strom Thurmond's 1948 Presidential Campaign.

1980's

November 28, 1987
BLACK TEENAGER CLAIMS TO HAVE BEEN GANG-RAPED BY POLICE OFFICERS

Tawana Brawley, an African American teenager living in upstate New York, alleged that she was abducted and gang-raped by several white men, including police officers. Her claim, which turned out to be a hoax, nevertheless focused public attention on racial inequalities within the U.S. legal system. Critics following the case accused local police of covering up the charges and the justice system of ignoring, or downplaying, crimes against African Americans.

LOCALE: Wappingers Falls, New York
CATEGORIES: Hoaxes, frauds, and charlatanism; racism; law and the courts; social issues and reform; women's issues; families and children

KEY FIGURES

Tawana Brawley (b. 1972), fifteen-year-old student who made a false claim of rape and abduction
Al Sharpton (b. 1954), Pentecostal minister and civil rights activist
C. Vernon Mason (b. 1946), politician, lawyer, and civil rights activist
Alton H. Maddox, Jr. (b. 1945), lawyer and civil rights activist
Steven Pagones (b. 1962), assistant district attorney, Dutchess County, New York

SUMMARY OF EVENT

Tawana Brawley, a fifteen-year-old African American girl living in Wappingers Falls, New York, failed to return home on November 24, 1987, prompting a neighborhood search by her parents, Glenda Brawley and Ralph King. Brawley was discovered by a neighbor several days later, on November 28, outside the Brawley family's previous residence, the Pavilion apartments complex.

A disheveled Brawley was found lying on the ground inside a garbage bag up to her neck, appear-ing weak and partially conscious. Her clothes were ripped, her hair was matted, and feces covered her arms, legs, chest, and hair. She was taken to St. Francis Hospital in Poughkeepsie, New York, where medical staff discovered burn marks in the crotch area of her pants, a grayish cottonlike mate-rial in her nose and ears, and several racial slurs written on her chest and stomach in a charcoal-like substance. Brawley exhibited no major injuries aside from a small bruise behind her ear, which sur-prised medical staff. The Federal Bureau of Investi-gation (FBI) joined the investigation because of the racial slurs on Brawley's body. The slurs would make the case a hate crime as well.

On November 29, Brawley remained silent dur-ing most of her first interview with a local white po-lice officer, but she began to disclose details about the alleged rape after a black police officer was as-signed to the interview upon her request. Brawley revealed that her assailants had been three white men, including police officers, and in a later inter-view she alleged that they had kidnapped, sodom-ized, and repeatedly raped her in the woods behind her old apartment building during the four days she was missing. Brawley did not name any of her at-tackers during the interviews, and many of the de-tails concerning her abduction and assault remained unclear. On January 13, 1988, Brawley and her mother, Glenda, were due to testify in front of a grand jury at the Dutchess County Courthouse in Poughkeepsie, but neither Brawley nor her mother appeared. By this time, Brawley was telling her friends that she was attacked by six white men in-stead of three. The media began to discuss the grisly details, and the mysteries, of the alleged abduction and sexual assault.

With growing public interest in the Brawley case, two black civil rights activists, lawyers Alton Maddox and C. Vernon Mason, began to rally be-hind Brawley and claim that local government officials were attempting to cover up the case to protect the white police officers who allegedly raped her. Support for this claim grew because of suspicious behavior and unexplained appointment changes in legal counsel in the criminal case. Three different prosecutors had been assigned to the case by New York governor Mario Cuomo; the first two prosecutors left after citing a conflict of interest in the case. Also, a local police officer committed suicide around this time, stirring further public distrust. In Maddox's and Mason's view, these events validated their accusations of a police cover-up. The Brawley media frenzy reached its height when Pentecostal minister and social activist the Reverend Al Sharpton began organizing rallies, holding conferences, and appearing on talk shows to demand that justice be served in the Brawley case.

Suspects in the Brawley case were left unnamed until March 13, 1988, when Brawley, Maddox, Mason, and Sharpton accused Steven Pagones, a white Dutchess County assistant district attorney, of being involved in the gang rape. Pagones, who had once lived near the Brawley family, received death threats, and the media and Brawley's supporters demanded his arrest. Protest marches that demanded racial equality and justice in the case became more widespread and drew the attention of celebrity supporters, including comedian Bill Cosby, boxing promoter Don King, and professional boxer Mike Tyson. Public donations for the Brawley family began to pour in as well.

By the end of June, the numerous discrepancies and a lack of concrete facts in the case led to increased public frustration and outrage. Most damning were the results of Brawley's medical examination, conducted the day she was found in the woods outside the apartment complex. The exam revealed that she had no bodily injuries consistent with sexual assault, and the only DNA found on her body was that of Brawley herself. Experts on rape testified that Brawley's story mimicked the testimony of those found to have falsely alleged rape.

Despite the burn marks on Brawley's pants, medical personnel found no sign of a burn to her body. Also, Brawley had been discovered outdoors during the cold month of November, but she showed no signs of exposure; indeed, the exam showed that she was well nourished, a finding that contradicted her claim that she had been abducted four days earlier. Prosecutors claimed that the cottonlike substance found in her nose and ears had been used to diminish the smell of feces that covered most of her body, except her face, and that the use of cotton was simply uncharacteristic of a hate crime. Prosecutors also claimed that the racial slurs found on her body were written by Brawley herself with burned wet cotton, identical to a substance found under her fingernails at the hospital.

The investigation also identified witnesses who said they saw Brawley at parties during the four-day-period she claimed she was abducted. The neighbor who first discovered Brawley on November 28 testified that she saw the girl climb into the

Tawana Brawley, left, with Al Sharpton at a rally protesting Brawley's mistreatment in her case alleging that she was raped. (AP/Wide World Photos)

garbage bag herself. Witness testimony also disclosed that Glenda Brawley's alibi the day her daughter was found was not concrete. The anomalies in the case pointed to a hoax.

Further details emerged as the case moved forward. Brawley had a history of running away from home, and her parents, particularly her stepfather, Ralph King, were known to be physically violent. The Brawleys also had financial problems at the time of the alleged rape, so they benefitted from the monies they received from sympathetic supporters.

The media began to report on the court testimony and the evidence that suggested Brawley's allegations were a farce. In response, her advisers scheduled a news conference so that she could counter the hoax claim. She never got the chance. On October 6, New York Supreme Court justice Angelo J. Ingrassia concluded from the grand jury's 170-page report that the gang-rape was fabricated, that Brawley's injuries had been self-inflicted, and that the accusations against Pagones were unfounded. Brawley never testified.

On May 21, 1990, attorney Maddox was disbarred from practicing law by the New York Supreme Court. In November, 1997, Pagones filed defamation lawsuits against Mason, Maddox, Sharpton, and Brawley, seeking $395 million in damages; he was awarded $345,000 from Brawley's advisers and $185,000 from Brawley on July 13, 1998.

In the meantime, Brawley maintained that she was raped. She also continued to receive support from Maddox and Mason, as well as from others who believed that justice was not served. Sharpton declined to pursue the case further. In November, 2007, Brawley's parents requested that their daughter's case be reopened and that Brawley receive not only justice but also monetary compensation.

IMPACT

Brawley's gang-rape allegations and their revelation as a hoax became a catalyst for intense discussion and debate about racism and racial inequalities in the United States. Despite suspicions that the Brawley family, as well as Maddox, Mason, and Sharpton, had used the case to further their own personal agendas, whether financial or political, the hoax focused attention on a broken legal system, a racist America, and a sensationalist media. Polls conducted during the investigations revealed a wide gap between blacks and whites on the question of whether Brawley was telling the truth.

The case also reveals the extent to which a person may go in seeking financial or political gain. The Brawleys concocted a hoax so real that it captured a legal system during months of grand-jury investigations, which included interviews of close to two hundred witnesses. In his opinion in Pagones's defamation suits in 1998, New York Supreme Court justice S. Barrett Hickman wrote,

> It is probable that in the history of this state [New York], never has a teenager turned the prosecutorial and judicial systems literally upside down with such false claims. The cost of the lengthy, thorough and complete grand jury investigation was reportedly estimated at one-half million dollars.

—Sheena Garitta

FURTHER READING

Chancer, Lynn S. *High-profile Crimes: When Legal Cases Become Social Causes*. Chicago: University of Chicago Press, 2005. An account of the "polarizing" criminal cases of the 1980's and 1990's, including the Brawley hoax.

Glaberson, William. "Plaintiff Is Awarded $345,000 in Brawley Defamation Suit." *The New York Times*, July 30, 1998. Details the defamation lawsuit filed by Steven Pagones following his exoneration in the Brawley gang-rape case.

McFadden, Robert D., et al. *Outrage: The Story Behind the Tawana Brawley Hoax*. New York: Bantam Books, 1990. Provides a narrative of the Brawley case from the point of view of several *New York Times* reporters.

Nadel, Adam. "Parents Want 'Hoax' Rape Reopened—Accusations in Brawley Case Ignited Racial Tensions Decades Ago." *Times Union* (Albany, New York), November 19, 2007. Gives a brief report of the continued support and pursuit of justice for Brawley by her family.

See also: Mar. 30, 1931: "Scottsboro Boys" Are Railroaded Through Rape Trials; Mar. 13, 1964: Kitty Genovese Dies as Her Cries for Help Are Ignored; Aug. 12, 1983-July 27, 1990: McMartin Preschool Is Embroiled in Child-Abuse Case; Dec. 22, 1984: Subway Vigilante Bernhard Goetz Shoots Four Black Youths; Jan. 22, 1987: Pennsylvania Politician Kills Himself at Tele-vised Press Conference; Mar. 30, 1991: William Kennedy Smith Is Accused of Rape; July 1, 2003: Basketball Star Kobe Bryant Is Accused of Rape; Mar. 14, 2006: Duke Lacrosse Players Are Accused of Gang Rape; Apr. 11, 2007: Shock Jock Don Imus Loses His Radio Show Over Sexist and Racist Remarks.

December 1, 1987
YALE SCHOLAR'S WARTIME ANTI-SEMITIC WRITINGS ARE REVEALED

The New York Times revealed that Paul de Man, noted for his work in deconstruction, had written a number of newspaper articles during World War II, at least one of which contained anti-Semitic views. Critics of deconstruction, a method of literary criticism, argued that this bigotry discredited deconstruction because it exposed its morally neutral inability to condemn bigotry. Among the most serious charges against de Man was his long-time silence about these early writings.

Locale: New York, New York
Categories: Racism; publishing and journalism; education

Key Figures
Paul de Man (1919-1983), Belgian-born American literary critic and philosopher
Ortwin de Graef (b. 1963), Belgian graduate student
Jacques Derrida (1930-2004), French philosopher and literary critic

Summary of Event
In August, 1987, a Belgian doctoral student, Ortwin de Graef, made a disturbing discovery while researching his dissertation on Belgian-born literary critic and philosopher Paul de Man. Early in World War II, when de Man was in his early twenties, he had over a three-year period written seventy articles as chief literary critic for the Belgian collaborationist newspaper *Le Soir*. Belgium was then under German occupation, which involved close Nazi editorial control of major newspapers such as *Le Soir*. Most of de Man's articles were standard reviews of books, music, and plays. However, a number of these articles had clear political implications. Some articles expressed both anti-Semitic and profascist opinions consonant with the Nazi Party line.

After the war, de Man had gone on to a very distinguished career as a literary critic and philosopher in the United States. His wartime journalism became public four years after his death in 1983. De Graef had sent photocopies of the most controversial articles to American scholars in de Man's field of deconstructionist criticism, most especially to scholars at Yale University, where he had held an endowed chair in the humanities.

The news from Belgium shocked de Man's colleagues and students. None could recall him expressing anti-Semitic or profascist sympathies. Nonetheless, the de Man scandal came to national and international attention when, on December 1, 1987, *The New York Times* published the article "Yale Scholar Wrote for Pro-Nazi Newspaper" on its front page. Accounts followed in other influential media, and an angry debate erupted among Western academics.

What exactly had the young de Man written between 1940 and 1942 that would provoke such heated disputes nearly fifty years later? On March 4, 1941, *Le Soir* had published a special edition devoted to "The Jews and Us." Among the articles was one by de Man. Next to his article, "The Jews in Contemporary Literature," was a caricature of two bearded, elderly Jews praying to God to "confound the gentiles." De Man's article appraised the quality of Jewish literature at the time and argued that it had "polluted" modern literature in unspecified ways. He thought it best for European society if Jews were isolated somewhere outside Europe.

By this time, Belgian legislation under Nazi guidance had excluded Jews from the professions of law, teaching, journalism, and government service. De Man later published a piece in *Le Soir* to counter the claim that the German occupiers of Belgium were barbarians. Their conduct, he wrote, had been impeccable and they were both disciplined and civilized. On other occasions de Man praised Italian dictator Benito Mussolini for his strong authoritarian rule as a possible model for Belgium. De Man also admired the place fascism gave to literature and art in society, and he praised the first generation of Italian poets under fascism.

After the war, in 1948, de Man emigrated to the United States and completed a doctorate in comparative literature at Harvard University. He taught at several American universities, until his appointment in 1970 as a humanities professor at Yale. Then he began to teach what was then a new mode of literary criticism: deconstruction. Deconstruction had not originated with de Man but with his close friend, French philosopher and literary critic Jacques Derrida. In 1967, Derrida published a book that elaborated a new strategy for analyzing philosophic and literary texts. For Derrida, there was no objective reality, no ultimate truth, and no absolutes. He insisted on the uncompromising questioning, or "deconstructing," of everything thinkable.

Deconstruction was a special kind of literary analysis that focused primarily on language and meaning in literature and in philosophy texts. The actual literary text conferred no meaning, as such, but only what each reader was able to "construct" from reading a given text and then creating a virtual

text for oneself. In this sense, no real world existed—only a construct of it existed in the minds of readers. For Derrida, nothing exists "outside the text." That is, meaning is derived from the mind's interaction with words to form a temporary virtual text.

Sharing Derrida's radical skepticism and interest in literary criticism, de Man published two books during the 1970's that brought him to the unchallenged leadership of the deconstructionist movement in the United States. Like Derrida, de Man made literary language his main focus. He insisted that language could never describe any objective reality because an author's words, and a reader's perception, were always shifting in meaning. For de Man, language was incapable of communicating what it intended because the author of a text had motives or "intentions" that could never be known in any permanent sense, even by the author. Basically, things are what one says they are. Truth cannot be defined. Every text, whether a novel, a history, a document of any kind, had to be deconstructed or "decoded" before it could be profitably approached.

The disclosure of de Man's articles in 1987 was greeted with vehement denunciations by academics and the general public. De Man's defenders were quick to accuse detractors of using the scandal to undermine deconstruction itself. What many critics found most objectionable and dangerous in deconstruction was its uncompromising relativism. For example, de Man's deconstructionist approach, they claimed, involved the rejection of any moral standards whatsoever, which rendered the approach incapable of confronting, for example, fascism and racial prejudice.

De Man's supporters and advocates of deconstruction countered that deconstruction was badly misunderstood by its critics. Deconstruction offered, rather, an exhilarating liberation from all stereotypes and stale certainties. Everything must be thought and experienced anew, always. Deconstruction was a subtle, complex, and ambivalent process that could not be generalized.

Most critics found inexcusable de Man's article of 1941. Supporters contend that the anti-Semitic article was a form of cultural anti-Semitism. It pertained only to the realms of literature and art, which distinguished it from the vulgar, or commonplace, racial and religious anti-Semitism so prevalent in occupied Belgium and the rest of Europe.

Among the most serious charges leveled against de Man, however, was that in his thirty-five years in the United States, he failed to mention publicly his early anti-Semitic, profascist writings. His great silence was considered a cowardly failure to come to terms with his secret. Defenders responded that his later writings showed a clear rejection of authoritarianism and, in other respects, could be seen as atonement for his questionable, though hidden, past.

IMPACT

Deconstruction reached its peak of influence and popularity during the 1970's and 1980's, especially at Yale, whose leading scholar was de Man. However, the deaths of the primary formulators of deconstruction (de Man in 1983 and Derrida in 2004) seemed, in retrospect, to be benchmark events in the diminishing profile of the movement. De Man's wartime articles clearly contributed to the waning popularity, but in ways difficult to measure.

Meanwhile, new varieties of literary criticism and philosophy appeared with other agendas. De Man's primary focus on literature was supplemented by a fresh emphasis on neglected issues of politics and ethics, and it came to include postcolonial, gender, and cultural studies. However, de Man's influence would remain, even though the Yale School of deconstruction lost prestige in the field of literary theory. Dozens of his students, and their students as well, would become professors at universities in the United States and Canada. Many testified to the vivid, inspirational quality of de Man's teaching.

As for the de Man scandal, many found his collaborationist conduct indefensible. Others were less condemning. Either way, it seemed essential to examine his later writings in the light of his early articles. De Man, it seemed, had carefully avoided racial and political topics, except for a firm rejection of authoritarian government. He also made occa-

sional oblique references to the burden of guilt and remorse carried by his generation after World War II.

De Man's reputation for integrity certainly suffered following the posthumous discovery of the *Le Soir* articles. For some, his subsequent public silence on the matter only compounded his moral offense. The question remained whether de Man would be remembered more as the dynamic and influential leader of deconstruction in literature or as the youthful wartime collaborator with Nazi politics. His legacy, overall, remains mixed.

—Donald Sullivan

FURTHER READING
Hamacher, Werner, Neil Hertz, and Thomas Kernan, eds. *Responses: On Paul de Man's Wartime Journalism.* Lincoln: University of Nebraska Press, 1989. Essays evaluating the charges of anti-Semitism against de Man and the impact of those claims on his scholarly reputation and character.

Julius, Anthony. *T. S. Elliot, Anti-Semitism, and Literary Fascism.* New York: Thames & Hudson, 2003. Makes a detailed case for convicting de Man of anti-Semitic and profascist sympathies as a young writer during World War II.

Kaplan, Alice. *French Lessons: A Memoir.* Chicago: University of Chicago Press, 1993. Kaplan, a literary scholar, discusses her work on French fascist intellectuals and reexamines her discovery that de Man, who had been one of her graduate-school professors at Yale, had written for the pro-Nazi Belgian press.

McQuillan, Martin. *Paul de Man.* New York: Routledge, 2001. Contains a sympathetic assessment of de Man's early articles. Concludes that de Man was not personally anti-Semitic and that his wartime writings should be considered in historical context. Includes a translation of de Man's controversial newspaper article of March 4, 1941.

SEE ALSO: July 12, 1906: French Court Declares Alfred Dreyfus Innocent of Treason; Apr. 22, 1942: French Prime Minister Pierre Laval Wants

707

Germany to Win World War II; Dec. 5, 1942: Industrialist Charles Bedaux Is Arrested for Nazi Collaboration; May 9, 1945: Norwegian Politician Quisling Is Arrested for Nazi Collaboration; May 26, 1945: Norwegian Writer Knut Hamsun Is Arrested for Treason; Aug. 14, 1945: French War Hero Pétain Is Convicted of Nazi Collaboration; Dec. 14, 1945: Poet Ezra Pound Is Charged with Treason and Institutionalized; Oct.

26, 1962: West German Police Raid *Der Spiegel* Magazine Offices; Feb. 23, 1963: Play Accuses Pope Pius XII of Complicity in the Holocaust; 1980: Biographer Claims Actor Errol Flynn Was a Nazi Spy; Mar. 3, 1986: Former U.N. Secretary-General Kurt Waldheim's Nazi Past Is Revealed; Aug. 12, 2006: Novelist Günter Grass Admits to Youthful Nazi Ties.

January 15, 1988
ZZZZ BEST FOUNDER IS INDICTED ON FEDERAL FRAUD CHARGES

ZZZZ Best, founded by Barry Minkow, was a carpet-cleaning and, later, insurance restoration company. It also had ties to organized crime and was essentially run as a Ponzi scheme. Auditors, investment bankers, attorneys, and federal investigators were badly fooled by Minkow and his associates, and stockholders lost more than $240 million when the fraud was uncovered.

LOCALE: Los Angeles, California
CATEGORIES: Law and the courts; hoaxes, frauds, and charlatanism; corruption; banking and finance; business; organized crime and racketeering

KEY FIGURES
Barry Minkow (b. 1967), founder and president of ZZZZ Best Company
Tom Padgett (b. 1950), insurance claims adjuster and coconspirator in the fraud scheme
Mark Morze (b. 1955), Minkow's financial consultant and coconspirator in the fraud scheme

SUMMARY OF EVENT
Barry Minkow started his own carpet-cleaning business, ZZZZ Best Company, when he was just sixteen years old, and within two years he was the president of his own corporate empire. However,

that empire, which expanded to include insurance restoration, was mostly nonexistent. Minkow had been perpetrating a gigantic fraud—one of the largest of the twentieth century. His real business was to create an attractive company that induced investors to hand over their money to ZZZZ Best.

Minkow's carpet-cleaning business never was profitable, so he had to borrow money to buy equipment and pay off debts. When it came time to repay his loans, Minkow began creating phony financial statements to fool the bankers. To make it look like he had more business than he really had, Minkow created the phony insurance restoration business, claiming to clean and remodel buildings that had suffered fire and other damage losses. Although this part of his business was fabricated, it nevertheless produced 90 percent of the company's revenues. Critical to Minkow's success was convincing the large international auditing firm of Ernst & Whinney (now Ernst & Young) that his restoration business was real.

The ultimate fraud would be to make ZZZZ Best a public company and thereby open the doors to investors around the United States. ZZZZ Best's chief financial officer, Mark Morze, had convinced Minkow that going public would enable the company to grow, and grow it did. Investors quickly pushed the company's market price up to eighteen dollars per share. Minkow's share of the company

(52 percent after the public offering) was worth well over $100 million, making him the so-called boy-wonder of Wall Street. He appeared on many television shows, including *Oprah*, and was the subject of numerous magazine articles.

Minkow used many tricks to convince auditors that his nonexistent clients really existed: One of those tricks was check kiting, that is, he wrote checks to his own company using an account without funds. His financial statements would show an account receivable, or payment, from a nonexistent customer. If an auditor tried to determine the validity of that receivable, Minkow would be able to show that the customer had indeed paid the account on the due date. However, it was Minkow himself who would pay the ZZZZ Best account with a check written on a ghost account—an account of a "customer."

In another instance, Minkow bribed a security guard to allow him to take auditors into a building in Sacramento, California, purportedly restored by Minkow's company after a fire. The auditors had no reason to doubt Minkow. Many critics would later argue that auditors failed to do their jobs, which made the scheme even more successful.

Minkow was aided in his fraud scheme by Morze and Tom Padgett, an insurance claims adjuster whom he had earlier befriended. Minkow, Padgett, and Morze, through their fictitious business Interstate Appraisal Services, prepared phony documents to support the scheme, so documentation was always available for auditors. The fraud involved the use of a copy machine for invoices and stationery for customers and suppliers—neither of which existed. Minkow, Padgett, and Morze worked hard to make the fraud look real, spending several million dollars to convince auditors that the company's restoration jobs were authentic.

Minkow's lifestyle also exuded success. He lived in a large mansion and drove one of the world's highest-priced cars, a Ferrari Testarossa. He lectured at business schools, and the mayor of Los Angeles even declared a Barry Minkow Day for the city. The glitz apparently blinded the auditors, lawyers, and underwriters. Minkow later stated that he tried to become friends with the auditors and their spouses so they would not be suspicious of him. He also manipulated the auditors by asking for their business advice; the result was that they spent their time as consultants rather than investigators. It would take the curiosity of a homemaker in Los Angeles to bring down Minkow's fraud scheme.

One of Minkow's minor schemes was overcharging customers who paid their carpet-cleaning bills with a credit card. If they complained about the overcharge, he would eventually refund their money. However, one woman whom he had cheated told her story to a reporter with the *Los Angeles Times*, which ran a damning story about ZZZZ Best and Minkow on May 22, 1987. At the time, Minkow also was trying to buy a rival carpet-cleaning company, KeyServe, for eighty million dollars. The price of ZZZZ Best stock dropped and subsequent investigations found that many of the ZZZZ Best customers did not exist. Another story alerted the Federal Bureau of Investigation that Minkow had done some work for the Genovese crime family. Essentially, a combination of media sources, initiated by one woman's anger at being overcharged for carpet cleaning, uncovered the full extent of the fraud.

Minkow and nine others associated with the fraud scheme were indicted on January 15, 1988, by a Los Angeles federal grand jury. Charges included racketeering, securities fraud, and tax fraud. Minkow was found guilty on December 15 and was sentenced to twenty-five years in prison but served just over seven years before being paroled in 1995. At the time of his indictment, he was twenty years old. While in prison, Minkow said that he found religion, and he also enrolled in a college program through Liberty University, founded by Christian conservative Jerry Falwell. In prison he earned a bachelor's degree, and he earned a master's degree in 1996.

Following his parole in 1995, Minkow became the associate pastor of a church near his hometown in the San Fernando Valley of Los Angeles, and in 1997 he became the pastor of Community Bible Church in San Diego. He speaks as an expert on corporate fraud and is associated with the Fraud Discovery Institute, which he cofounded, in San Diego. He also works undercover, on occasion, to expose fraud.

IMPACT

The bankruptcy of ZZZZ Best came at a time when other companies, including ESM Government Securities and a host of banks and savings and loan associations, were facing similar fraud charges. The ZZZZ Best fraud, which bilked $240 million from duped investors and others, led the U.S. Congress to begin its own investigation of the auditing industry. Partners from large accounting firms were called to testify to a congressional committee about how such blatant frauds were missed by auditors. An Ernst & Whinney partner said that the ZZZZ Best fraud, for example, was too complex for any single auditor. The committee members then asked why, then, did it take Los Angeles police a fraction of the time to solve the case against Minkow, Padgett, Morze, and others, once the scheme was brought to the attention of law enforcement. The auditor responded, "The police were tipped off."

Auditing and accounting firms would suffer the consequences of the scandal, mostly in the form of professional embarrassment. The American Institute of Certified Public Accountants soon changed the auditing standards of the accounting profession in the United States, leading auditors to be more proactive in combating fraud.

—*Dale L. Flesher*

FURTHER READING

Akst, Daniel. *Wonder Boy: Barry Minkow, the Kid Who Swindled Wall Street.* New York: Charles Scribner's Sons, 1990. The *Los Angeles Times* reporter who broke the story on Minkow describes the details behind the ZZZZ Best multimillion-dollar fraud.

Domanick, Joe. *Faking It in America: Barry Minkow and the Great ZZZZ Best Scam.* Chicago: Contemporary Books, 1989. An analysis of the fraud by an independent, somewhat cynical author. Domanick questions whether the auditors, lawyers, and underwriters really wanted to find anything wrong at ZZZZ Best. He claims they were all making too much money as consultants for the company.

Minkow, Barry. *Clean Sweep.* Nashville, Tenn.: Thomas Nelson, 1995. Minkow's autobiography, in which he discusses his leadership of one of the largest corporate frauds of the late twentieth century.

_____. *Cleaning Up: One Man's Redemptive Journey Through the Seductive World of Corporate Crime.* New York: Thomas Nelson, 2005. Minkow's come-back story. Discusses his work with the Fraud Discovery Institute. Analyzes fraud as a crime and the reasons why people commit fraud. Also discusses his relationships with principals in the fraud and fellow inmates in prison.

Podgor, Ellen S., and Jerold H. Israel. *White Collar Crime in a Nutshell.* 3d ed. St. Paul, Minn.: West, 2004. Chapters on white collar crime and corporate fraud, written in a concise and accessible format. Includes a breakdown of securities fraud, tax fraud, corporate criminal liability, conspiracy, and bribery.

SEE ALSO: 1919-1920: Ponzi Schemes Are Revealed as Investment Frauds; Mar. 29, 1962: Billie Sol Estes Is Arrested for Corporate Fraud; Nov. 28, 1967: Investor Louis Wolfson Is Convicted of Selling Stock Illegally; Oct. 19, 1982: Car Manufacturer John De Lorean Is Arrested in a Drug Sting; May 2, 1984: E. F. Hutton Executives Plead Guilty to Fraud; Mar. 29, 1989: Financier Michael Milken Is Indicted for Racketeering and Fraud; Aug. 27, 1990: Guinness Four Are Found Guilty of Share-Trading Fraud; Apr. 15, 1992: Hotel Tycoon Leona Helmsley Enters Prison for Tax Evasion; Jan. 28, 2000: John Spano Is Sentenced for Fraudulent Purchase of Ice Hockey Team; Sept. 3, 2003: Mutual Fund Companies Are Implicated in Shady Trading Practices; Sept. 12, 2005: Westar Energy Executives Are Found Guilty of Looting Their Company.

February 21, 1988
EVANGELIST JIMMY SWAGGART TEARFULLY CONFESSES HIS ADULTERY

Jimmy Swaggart was an internationally known Pentecostal preacher ordained through the Assemblies of God when church officials received photographs from a rival televangelist, Marvin Gorman, showing Swaggart entering and leaving a motel with a prostitute. After Swaggart made a vague confession to his congregation and begged forgiveness, the prostitute went public and described Swaggart's unconventional sexual tastes. Despite this and a later public debacle involving a prostitute, Swaggart continued to preach.

LOCALE: Baton Rouge, Louisiana
CATEGORIES: Prostitution; sex; religion; public morals; radio and television

KEY FIGURES
Jimmy Swaggart (b. 1935), American televangelist
Marvin Gorman (b. 1934), American televangelist
Debra Murphree (b. 1960), prostitute

SUMMARY OF EVENT
During the middle of the so-called holy wars between the multimillion dollar televangelists of the 1980's, Jimmy Swaggart seemed to the one, straight-shooting preacher who was above the fray. He was the one televangelist who was respected by the media, as he seemed to practice the strict Pentecostal dogma that he preached on *The Jimmy Swaggart Telecast*. Swaggart's blend of old-fashioned Pentecostal revival-meeting and rock-star pathos was netting his ministry millions of dollars in donations. Television made him a multimillionaire. The entire time, too, Swaggart was busy tearing down those televangelists whom he felt were not worthy of being anointed by God.

In 1986, Swaggart crushed up-and-coming rival televangelist Marvin Gorman by revealing that Gorman was having an extramarital affair with an-

other pastor's wife. In 1987, Swaggart turned on one of his main competitors, Jim Bakker, exposing Bakker's infidelities to the Assemblies of God's executive presbytery and then calling him a "cancer in the body of Christ" on CNN's *Larry King Live*. Swaggart's exposé of both Gorman and Bakker effectively destroyed their ministries. Gorman, not Bakker, would be the architect of Swaggart's downfall.

Gorman hired a private detective to follow Swaggart, tracking him and a local prostitute, Debra Murphree, to a seedy motel in Jefferson Parish, Louisiana. The private detective took photos of the couple entering and leaving the motel, providing Gorman with the proof he needed to crucify Swaggart. Gorman first attempted to blackmail Swaggart with the photos, but after he failed to do so, he took the photos to the leadership of the Assemblies of God. Swaggart was forced to apologize to his flock and family, and to God, after his tryst became known to church leadership.

Swaggart, first cousin to Jerry Lee Lewis and Mickey Gilley, was born to Pentecostal evangelists in Ferriday, Louisiana, in 1935. As a child, Swaggart brought attention to himself by uttering prophecy and speaking in tongues at a local Pentecostal church. In 1958, he began a successful traveling revival ministry, which he followed with a successful gospel music recording career and, by 1969, a syndicated radio program, *The Camp Meeting Hour*, which had made him a household name in much of the Bible Belt.

After receiving his ordination from the Assemblies of God Church, Swaggart made the move to televangelism. By 1980, *The Jimmy Swaggart Telecast* was a staple on two hundred stations and seen in two million homes. Jimmy Swaggart Ministries grew to a $100-million-per-year business and built its headquarters and a Bible college in Baton Rouge, Louisiana. Swaggart took a simple message: the average person is miserable and distracted by desire, and Swaggart could offer a means of escaping that misery. Naturally, that escape begins with a small monetary offering. Swaggart paired this with the dominant media of the day and became a media juggernaut. However, he was not content with the niche he had created; he took it upon himself to attack those whom he saw as rivals.

The Swaggart sex scandal erupted on February 18, 1988, three days before Swaggart made his public confession. He flew to the Assemblies of God international headquarters in Springfield, Missouri, to meet with the members of the executive presbytery, before whom he was supposed to confess his moral failures and receive his punishment. Instead, he was reportedly argumentative and said that he, rather than the church, spoke for God.

Three days later, on February 21, without providing details of the "sins" he had committed, Swaggart took the stage in front of about seven thousand of his flock at his Family Worship Center in Baton Rouge to deliver his sermon of apology. With tears streaming down his face, Swaggart apologized to his wife and family but still condemned

the Assemblies of God when he said, "Yes, the ministry will continue. . . . I step out of the pulpit at the moment for an indeterminate period of time and we will leave that in the hands of the Lord."

Following Swaggart's televised apology, the representative of the Louisiana district of the Assemblies of God explained that Swaggart showed true humility in blaming only himself for his actions after confessing to specific incidents of moral failure. The Louisiana district recommended that Swaggart be barred from the pulpit for a period of three months after this public confession and display of humility. It was somewhat of a surprise, however, when the executive presbytery accepted the sanctions suggested by the Louisiana regional leadership body that Swaggart not be allowed to preach for three months.

Just four days later, Murphree came forward on a New Orleans television news program and provided more details regarding Swaggart's unusual predilections. She said that while Swaggart was a regular customer, the two never had intercourse; rather, he paid her to pose in the nude.

Swaggart found he could not wait three months to preach again. After claiming that millions would go to Hell otherwise, he returned to the pulpit. On March 30, the executive presbytery defrocked Swaggart, banned him from the pulpit for a year, and demanded he seek two years of rehabilitation and counseling. Swaggart also was to be banned from distributing videotapes of his evangelical services, a practice that had enabled him to build both an enormous amount of wealth and an enormous worldwide audience. The church also removed Swaggart's ministerial license; yet, they consistently refused to make the details of Swaggart's confessions public.

In 1991, a highway patrol officer stopped Swaggart's car in Southern California. The preacher had yet another prostitute, Rosemary Garcia,

Jimmy Swaggart breaks down crying while confessing his sins to his congregation. (Hulton Archive/Getty Images)

SWAGGART'S APOLOGY

Jimmy Swaggart apologized for his "sin" in a sermon, excerpted here, delivered February 21, 1988, in Baton Rouge, Louisiana, but he did so without discussing his actual sin: adultery.

I do not plan in any way to whitewash my sin. I do not call it a mistake, a mendacity; I call it sin. I would much rather, if possible—and in my estimation it would not be possible—to make it worse than [instead of] less than it actually is. I have no one but myself to blame. I do not lay the fault or the blame of the charge at anyone else's feet. For no one is to blame but Jimmy Swaggart. I take the responsibility. I take the blame. I take the fault. . . .

Swaggart included in his apology a lengthy quotation from Psalm 51, "with the words of another man that lived 3,000 years ago."

Have mercy upon me, O God. According to thy lovingkindness; according unto the multitude of thy tender mercies, blot out my transgressions. Wash me thoroughly from mine iniquity, and cleanse me from my sin. For I acknowledge my transgressions; and my sin is ever before me. Against thee, thee only, have I sinned and done this evil in thy sight, that thou mightest be justified when thou speakest, and be clear when thou judgest. Behold, I was shapen in iniquity; and in sin did my mother conceive me. Behold, thou desireth truth in the inward parts; and in the hidden parts thou shalt make me to know wisdom. Purge me with hyssop, and I shall be clean; wash me, and I shall be whiter than snow.

Source: Quoted in Michael J. Giuliano, *Thrice Born: The Rhetorical Comeback of Jimmy Swaggart* (Macon, Ga.: Mercer University Press, 1999).

in his vehicle. In 2004, Swaggart said during a broadcast sermon on gay marriage, "if one [a gay man] ever looks at me like that I'm gonna kill him and tell God he died." Nevertheless, Swaggart continued to preach. By 1995, after the legal battles had ended, Jimmy Swaggart Ministries had been reduced to approximately 85 percent of its size before the scandal, when broadcasts brought in an estimated $140 million from viewer donations.

IMPACT

Swaggart's fall from grace marked the beginning of the end of the glory days of the so-called holy-roller television evangelists and their multimillion dollar crusades. Despite Swaggart, Bakker, Gorman, and the others returning to the pulpit following their well-publicized sins, Swaggart's fall seemed to be the one that broke the public's mass desire to send in their money to keep this message on the air.

At the time of the Swaggart scandal, Pat Robertson, another televangelist, ran an unsuccessful presidential campaign. After the Swaggart scandal, audience size and generosity shrank to the point that televangelist Oral Roberts could not convince his viewers to donate enough money to keep God from taking his life. This new skeptical view of televangelists reduced a major media market to a tiny trickle that struggled to purchase air time on a handful of local stations, turning instead mostly to late-night television, the World Wide Web, and direct mail to solicit donations.

Swaggart's defrocking also played a major role in the deflation of the political power of the Moral Majority and similar evangelical Christian political action groups. His actions tarred the credibility of all evangelical Christian leaders.

—*B. Keith Murphy*

FURTHER READING

Balmer, Randall. "Still Wrestling with the Devil: A Visit with Jimmy Swaggart Ten Years After His Fall." *Christianity Today*, March 2, 1998. A retrospective look at Swaggart's life, one decade after his tearful confession and downfall.

Lundy, Hunter. *Let Us Prey: The Public Trial of Jimmy Swaggart.* Columbus, Miss.: Genesis Press, 1999. Lundy, Gorman's attorney, recounts "Swaggart versus Gorman" from an insider's vantage point.

Miller, Brett A. *Divine Apology: The Discourse of Religious Image Restoration.* Westport, Conn.: Praeger, 2002. Analyzes religious figures accused of sexual misconduct. Includes a section on Swaggart, whose scandalous dalliance with prostitute Debra Murphree was covered closely by the national media.

1980's

713

"Reviewing the Fundamentals." *Christianity Today*, January, 2007. Focuses on the biblical teachings of the New Testament on sex and sexuality. Cites the book of James, which states that Christian leaders are placed under strict moral standards.

Seaman, Ann Rowe. *Swaggart: The Unauthorized Biography of an American Evangelist*. New York: Continuum, 2001. An excellent unauthorized biography of Swaggart that covers many details following his tearful fall from grace.

Swaggart, Jimmy, with Robert Paul Lamb. *To Cross A River*. Baton Rouge, La.: Jimmy Swaggart Ministries, 1984. Swaggart's authorized biography, which tells of, among other things, his "healing" an automobile. Also provides a unique look at Swaggart's self-perception.

SEE ALSO: May-June, 1926: Evangelist Aimee Semple McPherson Claims She Was Kidnapped; Oct. 25, 1974: Evangelist Billy James Hargis Resigns College Presidency During Gay-Sex Scandal; June 27, 1978: Evangelist Herbert W. Armstrong Excommunicates His Own Son; Sept. 10, 1981: *Chicago Sun-Times* Reports That Cardinal Cody Diverted Church Funds; Apr. 22, 1986: Faith Healer Peter Popoff Is Exposed as a Fraud; Mar. 19, 1987: Jim Bakker Resigns as Head of PTL Television Network; Nov. 2, 2006: Evangelist Kent Hovind Is Convicted of Federal Tax Violations; Nov. 2, 2006: Male Escort Reveals Sexual Liaisons with Evangelist Ted Haggard; July 9, 2007: Senator David Vitter's Name Is Found in D.C. Madam's Address Book.

June, 1988-June, 1989
INSIDER-TRADING SCANDAL ROCKS JAPANESE GOVERNMENT

Japan was scandalized when it learned that an upstart Tokyo company, Recruit, had offered, in exchange for political favors, inexpensive stock to seventeen members of parliament, civil servants, businessmen, a publisher, and two university professors. Because many beneficiaries were tied to the ruling Liberal Democratic Party, the scandal contributed to the party's temporary loss of power in 1993.

ALSO KNOWN AS: Recruit scandal
LOCALE: Tokyo, Japan
CATEGORIES: Corruption; business; government; politics; banking and finance

KEY FIGURES
Hiromasa Ezoe (b. 1936), chairman of the Recruit Company
Noboru Takeshita (1924-2000), prime minister of Japan, 1987-1989
Kiichi Miyazawa (1919-2007), finance minister of Japan, 1987-1989, and prime minister, 1991-1993
Hisashi Shinto (b. 1922), chairman of Nippon Telephone and Telegraph Company
Yusuke Yoshinaga (b. 1932), chief prosecutor, Tokyo district

SUMMARY OF EVENT
In postwar Japan, the relationship between politicians and business has been cozy, but the extent to which the Recruit Company tried to develop this relationship shocked the Japanese public. To most, it looked like Recruit's chairman, Hiromasa Ezoe, overstepped the boundaries of public decency.

In Japan, it is legal to make offers as gifts to select people, such as politicians, to buy shares before a company goes public. It is against the law, however, to give gifts in direct exchange for political favors. Thus, when the scandal broke, a big issue, apart from the moral outrage at a company making cleverly disguised gifts to public leaders, including

Hiromasa Ezoe. (Hulton Archive/Getty Images)

1980's

two university professors, was the question of whether the law had been broken—whether politicians and civil servants had been bribed.

Ezoe founded Recruit, a communications and publishing company, in 1960. His business idea was to help the government place college graduates in their first jobs. His annual *Recruit Book* listed employment opportunities and his *Recruit Shingaku Book* provided high school graduates with information about choosing the right college. As his company grew, Ezoe branched out into real estate and founded Recruit Cosmos Company in 1964. Later, he developed his own telecommunications business. During the mid-1980's, legal changes threatened Recruit's publishing business. At the same time, Recruit bought two American Cray supercomputers from Nippon Telephone and Telegraph Company (NTT) and profitably used them for high-speed computing.

The Recruit scandal broke in June, 1988. Later investigations revealed that, beginning in October, 1984, and culminating on September 30, 1986, Recruit had offered 159 influential Japanese politicians, civil servants, businessmen, newspaper publishers, and academics the opportunity to buy shares in its subsidiary, Recruit Cosmos. This offer was made before the company would go public on the stock exchange. The price per share was three thousand yen, about twenty dollars in 1986. In order for the beneficiaries to buy the shares, another subsidiary of Recruit, First Finance Company, gave them advantageous credit, financing with two billion yen (about thirteen million dollars) the purchase of about 666,666 shares. After Recruit Cosmos went public during the hot phase of Japan's bubble economy in late 1986, the value of the shares doubled. The scandal fully erupted in July, 1988, when seventy-six beneficiaries sold their shares.

In August and September, 1988, Recruit secretly offered five million yen ($32,500) to Yanosuke Narazaki, a member of the Diet, Japan's parliament, to stop his investigation of the scandal. Instead of accepting the bribe of Recruit's front man, Hiroshi Matsubara, Narazaki videotaped the bribery attempts. On September 8, Yusuke Yoshinaga, chief prosecutor of the Tokyo district, launched his investigation.

With a police investigation and a special committee of the Diet looking for culprits, the Recruit scandal made headlines in Japan in the fall of 1988. Ezoe resigned as chairman of Recruit and checked into a hospital in October. He was soon questioned by a Diet delegation.

Bowing to public pressure, and with the scandal at full force in November, Recruit provided to the Diet a list of all who had bought company shares early. The results shocked the public, because it was confirmed that seventeen members of the Diet as well had bought and sold Recruit shares. Even though five of them were members of opposition parties, the majority belonged to the ruling Liberal Democratic Party (LDP). Public pressure mounted, and the LDP government was faced with a crisis of public confidence.

Finance Minister Kiichi Miyazawa, a rising star

of the LDP, resigned when it was confirmed that he had bought ten thousand shares of Recruit Cosmos stock. The justice minister and his immediate replacement resigned as well. Also in December, Hisashi Shinto, chairman of NTT, resigned over the buying and selling to Recruit of two Cray supercomputers. Because the government held a stake in NTT, Shinto was considered a public servant. The Japanese found it especially distasteful that esteemed civil servants such as Shinto were part of the Recruit scandal.

As prosecutor Yoshinaga's investigation into Recruit continued, Ezoe, along with three Recruit executives, was arrested while still in the hospital on February 13, 1989. The four were put in a bleak jail to break their silence. In another stunning move, the public witnessed the scandalous spectacle of Yoshinaga's officers arresting a top businessman and civil servant, former NTT chairman Shinto, and his secretary, Kozo Murata, on March 6. The public was outraged by the time the scandal included Prime Minister Takeshita. In March, Takeshita admitted to gifts of 151 million yen ($1.4 million) from Recruit. Because he gave no special favors, Takeshita insisted, this acceptance of gifts was not criminal. However, on April 22, his office admitted that his secretary, Ihei Aoki, had received a loan of fifty million yen ($460,000) from Recruit that he later repaid in small installments, and that Aoki had been entrusted with twenty million yen from an unreported (which was illegal) thirty million yen fund-raiser for Takeshita. One day after Takeshita announced that he would resign, Aoki committed suicide.

On June 12, a few days after the resignation of Takeshita, prosecutor Yoshinaga issued his final report on the scandal. Ezoe and four other Recruit executives were indicted for bribery. Three officials were indicted for accepting bribes, and three executives of NTT, including former chairman Shinto, were charged with violating the NTT Public Corporation Law by accepting bribes. Two other high-level public servants were indicted for taking bribes in relation to their official duties. NTT's Murata was charged with violating the Securities Exchange Law. Three high-ranking secretaries of LDP politi-

cians were indicted for transgressing the Political Funds Control Law. The person who tried to bribe Diet member Narazaki, Hiroshi Matsubara, already had been sentenced for attempted bribery. Significantly, while all those indicted would be found guilty and given suspended jail sentences, all leading politicians escaped legal punishment.

Ezoe's trial began in December, 1989, required 322 sessions, and lasted fifteen years. On March 4, 2003, the Tokyo district court found Ezoe guilty of bribing politicians and civil servants, based on the sale of 53,000 Recruit Cosmos shares that could be traced to illegal actions. Ezoe received a sentence of three years, suspended for five years. At his sentencing, he apologized to the Japanese people for having caused moral outrage.

IMPACT

Immediately after the Recruit scandal reached its height with Prime Minister Takeshita's resignation, the LDP was punished by scandalized voters. In Niigata Prefecture in June, 1989, a Socialist housewife decidedly beat the LDP candidate for by-elections to the Upper House, and the LDP lost seats in the July 2 Tokyo municipal elections. On July 23, for the first time after World War II, the LDP lost its majority in the Upper House.

Despite these initial setbacks, however, the LDP maintained its crucial control of the Lower House of parliament, and pushed through the election of its prime ministers throughout the early 1990's. When Miyazawa, whom the Recruit scandal had forced out as finance minister, became prime minister on November 5, 1991, it looked as if the LDP had weathered the storm. However, the combined forces of the Recruit scandal, an unpopular new sales tax, Japan's economic crisis of 1990, and two further scandals tainting the LDP, finally caused the party to lose power in the 1993 elections. For the first time since it was founded in 1955, the stunned LDP did not rule Japan, punished by voters alienated by its scandalous affairs.

Intimations of political change proved premature. By 1994, the LDP joined the government again, and on January 11, 1996, Ryutaro Hashimoto became LDP prime minister. To some observers it looked like the Japanese electorate did not mind the connection of business and politics revealed by the Recruit scandal. After all, the system that made politicians and others accept Recruit shares also included a politician's customary requirement to make gifts for weddings and funerals of the constituents, and to push through public projects benefiting a home district. In the end, the LDP survived the scandal.

—*R. C. Lutz*

FURTHER READING

Bowen, Roger. *Japan's Dysfunctional Democracy.* Armonk, N.Y.: M. E. Sharpe, 2003. Argues that the postwar Japanese system is scandal-prone by Western standards because cash-strapped politicians need means to bestow favors on constituents. Also argues that the Recruit scandal did little to change the ruling party's power in the long run.

Christensen, Ray. *Ending the LDP Hegemony.* Honolulu: University of Hawaii Press, 2000. Chapter two credits the Recruit scandal with helping to make the ruling party lose power temporarily because of its unwillingness to enact real reform.

Herzog, Peter. *Japan's Pseudo-Democracy.* Sandgate, England: Japan Library, 1993. Detailed discussion of the Recruit scandal. Places event in the context of the dark side of Japanese postwar politics. Critical of Takeshita's government's ties to Recruit.

Taro, Yayama. "The Recruit Scandal: Learning from the Causes of Corruption." *Journal of Japanese Studies* 16, no. 1 (1990): 93-114. Surprisingly sympathetic account that blames the foundation of the Japanese political system rather than individuals caught up in the scandal. Warns that media hype and prosecutorial zeal may do more harm than good.

SEE ALSO: 1904: Theodore Roosevelt Is Accused of Accepting Corporate Funds; Jan. 23, 1904: Senator Joseph R. Burton Is Convicted of Bribery; Jan., 1913: British Prime Minister's Staff Is Investigated for Insider Trading; Feb. 4, 1976: Lockheed Is Implicated in Bribing Foreign Officials; Aug. 10, 1989: Japanese Prime Minister Sosuke Resigns After Affair with a Geisha; Aug. 27, 1990: Guinness Four Are Found Guilty of Share-Trading Fraud; Apr. 5, 1991: George W. Bush Is Investigated for Insider Trading; Mar. 5, 2004: Martha Stewart Is Convicted in Insider-Trading Scandal; May 28, 2007: Japanese Politician Charged with Corruption Hangs Himself.

1980's

July 18, 1988
ACTOR ROB LOWE VIDEOTAPES HIS SEXUAL ENCOUNTER WITH A MINOR

At the height of his career, actor Rob Lowe made a videotape of himself having sex with a teenage girl and a young woman he met at the Democratic National Convention in Atlanta. Lowe's career suffered, but only temporarily, after the tape was made public.

LOCALE: Atlanta, Georgia
CATEGORIES: Sex crimes; communications and media; drugs; public morals; popular culture; Hollywood

KEY FIGURES
Rob Lowe (b. 1964), American actor
Jan Parsons (b. 1972), hair salon employee
Tara Siebert (b. 1963), hair salon employee
Lewis Slaton (1922-2002), district attorney, Fulton County, Georgia

SUMMARY OF EVENT
On Saturday, July 16, 1988, Rob Lowe, a successful and popular motion-picture actor, arrived in Atlanta, Georgia, to attend the Democratic National

717

Convention. He was part of a delegation of three dozen people from the entertainment industry invited by California assemblyman Tom Hayden to help the Michael Dukakis presidential campaign. While most of the delegates were producers and directors, the most visible were actors Lowe, Judd Nelson, Alec Baldwin, Charlie Sheen, and Ally Sheedy.

Then at the height of his acting career, Lowe was a member of the so-called brat pack—a group of young actors including Emilio Estevez, Judd Nelson, and Demi Moore—who appeared together in films. He was best known for his roles in *St. Elmo's Fire*, *The Outsiders*, and *About Last Night*, among others. Off camera, Lowe also was involved with drugs, alcohol, and heavy partying.

On Sunday, July 17, Lowe went to Club Rio, a hip rock club that catered to a diverse crowd. Part of Atlanta's underground scene, the club brought well-

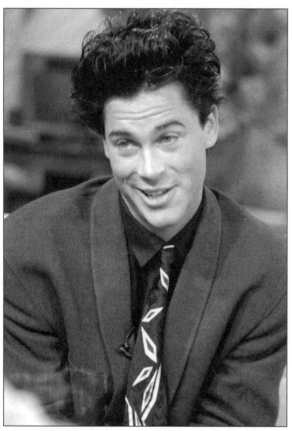

Rob Lowe in 1988. (AP/Wide World Photos)

known underground rock acts to its stage. Also in attendance that evening were sixteen-year-old Jan Parsons and twenty-five-year-old Tara Siebert, coworkers at SuperHair, a salon that catered to the cutting edge and the underground scene. In addition to being coworkers, the two were lovers. Even though Club Rio was a twenty-one-and-over club, Parsons nevertheless was admitted.

The club was packed that evening. Lowe was in attendance with friends, including actors Justine Bateman and Baldwin. Drinking and drugs were prevalent, not uncommon at Club Rio. The actors were congregated in the VIP room. Susan Sullivan, the club's publicity director, informed Parsons and Siebert that Lowe was among the celebrity guests partying in the VIP room. Parsons was excited to meet him, so Sullivan arranged for them to gain entry into the VIP room.

Parsons and Siebert were introduced to an intoxicated Lowe. They three left the club in a taxicab during the early morning hours of July 18 and went to Lowe's room at the Atlanta Hilton and Towers. It was in his hotel room that Lowe filmed himself having sex with the two young women. After Lowe passed out, Parsons and Siebert took two hundred dollars from his wallet, grabbed a bottle of pills, and then left with the videotape. In the days that followed they told their friends about the sexual encounter and played the videotape at private parties. Within a day, copies of the tape were circulated and its content was the subject of conversation at parties in the underground scene.

Consequently, Parsons's brother, Ashley Parsons, found a copy of the tape in his sister's bedroom, watched it, and promptly told their mother, Lena Parsons. News of the tape reached the media after Lena Parsons filed a personal-injury lawsuit against Lowe in August, 1989. In the lawsuit, Lena Parsons's alleged that she suffered emotional stress upon seeing Lowe seduce her daughter, a minor. A brief excerpt of the tape aired on WAGA-TV shortly after the lawsuit was made public. One day later, WAGA was offered ten thousand dollars for the tape by a nationally syndicated television show. The airing of the tape on WAGA brought print and broadcast media to Atlanta, and stories were carried in a wide range of publications. Lowe became the punch line for several late-night talk-show hosts. In Atlanta, reporters staked out Club Rio and Jan Parsons's home and school.

In no time the tryst became public. However, the taped scene with Parsons and Siebert was not included on some circulated copies. Instead, many of the copies had a scene recorded earlier in Paris, France, and was on Lowe's original tape. This scene showed Lowe and a male friend having sex with a woman. Many viewers had the impression that this scene was the one made in Atlanta with Parsons and Siebert. In truth, few people actually saw that portion of the tape.

In July, 1989, Judge G. Ernest Tidwell, dismissed portions of Lena Parsons's personal-injury civil lawsuit, claiming that under Georgia law, the plaintiff did not demonstrate that the defendant intentionally inflicted emotional distress on a minor. Lowe eventually arranged a plea deal with the Fulton County district attorney on the sexual misconduct charge and performed twenty hours of community service. He also made an out-of-court settlement with Lena Parsons. Shortly thereafter, he entered rehabilitation for alcohol, drug, and sex addiction in Phoenix, Arizona.

IMPACT

A twenty-minute segment of the first portion of the videotape that became commercially available (the scene filmed in Paris) transformed into the first so-called celebrity sex tape. Other actors and musicians have since been caught up in their own sex-tape controversies.

Lewis Slaton, Fulton County district attorney, investigated the circumstances of the making of the tape and indicated that if charges were filed against Lowe (for the sexual exploitation of a minor), the young actor could receive a maximum of twenty years in prison and a $100,000 fine. Lewis faced severe criticism when it was revealed he was given a copy of the videotape as early as August, 1988, but had taken no action. He had made several conflicting statements about the day his office received the tape and finally admitted that he indeed received the tape in August, 1988, but decided to hold it; he de-

clined to say why. Media reports alleged that Lewis, a Democrat, had a political reason for holding the tape: to prevent a criminal investigation into behavior by a Democratic National Convention delegate—Lowe—prior to the national election, which would have hurt the Dukakis campaign.

Lowe refused to be interviewed after the incident. His publicists worked hard to mend the damage, but his public image was tarnished, for a time. The actor continued to have problems with alcohol and drugs. While he continued to work as well, he was no longer an A-list star. He was dropped as a subject in several teenage film magazines, on whose covers he had regularly appeared. In 1991, he married makeup artist Sheryl Berkoff. The 1992 film *Wayne's World* is considered his comeback as an actor. In 1994 he landed a significant role in the Stephen King film *The Stand*. He also appeared in the film *Austin Powers: The Spy Who Shagged Me* and in the television series *The West Wing* and *Brothers and Sisters*. As part of his addiction recovery, and in an attempt to confront the scandal, he addressed his behaviors during two appearances on *Saturday Night Live*, where he mocked himself.

—*Jesus F. Gonzalez*

FURTHER READING

Carter, Bill. *Details*, May, 2004. A thorough, detailed biographical magazine article on Rob Lowe's life from childhood, to his early years of acting, to later accomplishments as an actor.

DePaulo, Lisa. "Lowe Down and Dirty." *George*, September, 1999. Magazine article about Rob Lowe. The sex-tape scandal is mentioned prominently.

Parish, James Robert. *Hollywood Bad Boys: Loud, Fast, and Out of Control*. Chicago: Contemporary Books, 2002. A revealing collection of biographies of Hollywood male celebrities, including Rob Lowe, who are known for extremes of behavior.

_____. *The Hollywood Book of Scandals: The Shocking, Often Disgraceful Deeds and Affairs of More than One Hundred American Movie and TV Idols*. New York: McGraw-Hill, 2004. Includes the chapter "Rob Lowe: Surviving His

1980's

Candid Camera Escapade," which explores the sex-tape scandal and the scandal's aftermath.

Sager, Mike. "Rob Lowe's Girl Trouble." *Rolling Stone*, August 24, 1989. A popular-magazine article that covers the sex-tape case. Gives background on Parsons and Siebert and provides an overview of the case as it was happening at the time.

SEE ALSO: Feb. 6, 1942: Film Star Errol Flynn Is Acquitted of Rape; Aug. 31, 1948: Film Star Robert Mitchum Is Arrested for Drug Possession; July 23, 1984: Vanessa Williams Is the First Miss America to Resign; Dec. 18, 1989: Prince Charles's Intimate Phone Conversation with Camilla Parker Bowles Is Taped; July 26, 1991: Comedian Pee-wee Herman Is Arrested for Public Indecency; June 27, 1995: Film Star Hugh Grant Is Arrested for Lewd Conduct; Sept. 22, 1997: Sportscaster Marv Albert Is Tried for Sexual Assault; Apr. 7, 1998: Pop Singer George Michael Is Arrested for Lewd Conduct; Early Nov., 2003: Paris Hilton Sex-Tape Appears on the Web; Dec. 18, 2003: Pop Star Michael Jackson Is Charged with Child Molestation; July 28, 2006: Actor Mel Gibson Is Caught Making Anti-Semitic Remarks; June 13, 2008: Singer R. Kelly Is Acquitted on Child Pornography Charges.

September 19, 1988
STEPHEN BREUNING PLEADS GUILTY TO MEDICAL RESEARCH FRAUD

Stephen Breuning, a University of Pittsburgh medical researcher, studied the long-term effects of tranquilizers on the mentally disabled, especially adolescents. His findings caught the eye of his long-term mentor, who became suspicious of Breuning's work and blew the whistle on him. After a federal investigation, Breuning was indicted and pleaded guilty to fraud. The case was particularly significant because it not only harmed vulnerable patients but also marked the first time an American scientist was prosecuted for falsifying research.

LOCALES: Pittsburgh, Pennsylvania; Coldwater, Michigan

CATEGORIES: Drugs; hoaxes, frauds, and charlatanism; medicine and health care; psychology and psychiatry; education; science and technology

KEY FIGURES
Stephen Breuning (b. 1952), University of Pittsburgh research psychologist
Robert Sprague (fl. 1980's), director of the Institute for Child Behavior and Development, University of Illinois
Breckenridge Wilcox (fl. 1980's), U.S. attorney

SUMMARY OF EVENT

On November 10, 1988, Stephen Breuning, one the nation's leading researchers on the use of psychoactive drugs for the treatment of the mentally disabled, became the first academic in American history to be sentenced to prison for scientific research fraud. In addition, it was later determined by both federal investigators and academic researchers in the field that most of Breuning's research starting from the mid-1970's through the late 1980's may have been fraudulent.

The major portion of Breuning's work concerned studies of drug-treatment therapies for mentally disabled persons who were institutionalized. In particular, most of his research participants suffered from extreme emotional, behavioral, and neurological disorders that were treated with various psychoactive drugs to control hyperactivity and violent behavior. In fact, it was quite common to see half of all residents at mental institutions throughout the United States prescribed certain types of drugs, mainly powerful tranquilizers to reduce any aggressive outbursts. The most commonly prescribed drugs for these patients had traditionally been antipsychotic drugs known as tranquilizers.

Breuning, along with a small group of his fellow clinicians, argued against the use of major tranquilizers for the mentally disabled, especially for adolescent patients. The main argument against the drug's use centered on the numerous and unpleasant side effects from using large doses over a long period of time. One major side effect was a neurological disorder known as tardive dyskinesia. This disorder causes abnormal and sometimes extreme, involuntary muscle movements of the body. Bruening and his colleagues believed that tranquilizers could be substituted with certain types of stimulant drugs, thus lowering the risk of disorders such as tardive dyskinesia.

After receiving his doctorate from the Illinois Institute of Technology in 1977, Breuning worked for one year as a research psychologist at the Oakdale Regional Center for Developmental Disabilities in Lapeer, Michigan. In 1978, he transferred to the Coldwater Regional Center for Developmental Disabilities (now the Coldwater Regional Mental Health Center), also in Michigan, and established himself as a researcher deeply dedicated to working with the mentally disabled. One year later, in 1979, Robert Sprague, director of the Institute for Child Behavior and Development at the University of Illinois, noticed the work of a team of young scholars at the Coldwater facility, especially the work of Breuning. Sprague had recently received a $200,000 grant from the National Institute of Mental Health (NIMH) and was looking to move his research laboratory to a place such as Coldwater, where he could enlist the services of hardworking researchers. He also wanted to continue his extremely valuable research on disorders such as tardive dyskinesia.

Sprague received approval from the Coldwater Center and invited Breuning to take the lead as one of the primary researchers. Over a two year period, Breuning wrote many manuscripts summarizing the work of his team at Coldwater. His findings not

only were astounding but also likely to revolutionize the way the medical world treated mentally disabled patients: if those findings were genuine. In January, 1981, Breuning was employed as an assistant professor of child psychiatry at the prestigious Western Psychiatric Institute at the University of Pittsburgh in Pennsylvania. During this time, he continued to collaborate with Sprague on various projects, including many funded by Sprague's original NIMH grant.

Sprague's suspicions of Breuning began in 1983. Breuning was a prolific author and coauthor, and his research produced near-perfect results. Indeed, his publications were making him a rising star in psychology. Between 1980 and 1984, he was part of nearly one-third of all the psycho-pharmaceutical, peer-reviewed studies regarding the effect of certain psychotropic drugs on the mentally disabled, especially adolescents. His findings had a considerable effect on the drug-treatment therapies used to manage these patients' behaviors in institutions throughout the United States, which makes his research fraud so significant.

In September, 1983, Sprague traveled to Pittsburgh to meet with Breuning to discuss research projects and the NIMH grant. It was during this trip that Sprague discovered that Breuning was obtaining far-fetched results in a study involving nurse ratings of patients with tardive dyskinesia. This realization led him to launch his own investigation of Breuning. In December, he confronted Breuning with his evidence, questioning him about his supposed follow-up study at Coldwater after taking the research position at Pittsburgh. Breuning claimed that he examined patients for two years after his departure. Sprague knew that Breuning had never returned to Coldwater, nor did he leave assistants to conduct the alleged examinations. Afer Breuning failed to produce evidence to counter the allegations, Sprague notified the NIMH in late December with a six-page letter. In January, 1984, the NIMH notified the University of Pittsburgh and then began its own independent investigation. In April, Breuning resigned from Pittsburgh to take a position at Polk Center, the largest state institution for the mentally disabled in Pennsylvania.

In 1985, the NIMH selected a council of five well-known scholars to investigate Breuning's work. After a lengthy investigation, the council concluded that on numerous occasions, while employed both at Coldwater and at Pittsburgh and while using federal grant monies, Breuning had committed "serious scientific misconduct." The council, which also questioned the veracity of Breuning's entire corpus of research, recommended that he be banned for ten years from receiving federal research grants. The council also recommended that the U.S. Department of Justice look into prosecuting Breuning because his research may have impacted the health and well-being of hundreds of people, many of whom were children at the time they were studied.

Breckenridge Wilcox, U.S. attorney for the state of Maryland, where Breuning's grant money originated, agreed with the NIMH council's recommendation and commenced a federal investigation. On April 16, 1988, a federal grand jury indicted Breuning on three criminal counts related to submitting fraudulent research results to a federal agency, marking the first time in American history that an independent research scientist was indicted for scientific fraud. On September 19, in a plea bargain with prosecutors, Breuning pleaded guilty and was convicted on two charges of filing false reports; the third, more serious, charge was dropped as part of the deal.

On November 10, Breuning was sentenced to five years probation and six days in a halfway house and was ordered to perform 250 hours of community service. He also was ordered to repay $11,352 to the NIMH and prohibited from conducting psychological research while on probation. The University of Pittsburgh was ordered to pay back about $163,000 in funds that Breuning had unlawfully used.

IMPACT

Breuning's empirical studies were outright deceptions. If not for the vigilance of his mentor, the deception likely would have continued and countless people with disabilities would have been further harmed. So wide-ranging was his fraudulent research that he became the first American academic to go to prison because of the untruthfulness of his work. His studies, fraudulent as they were, nevertheless had a major impact on the scientific disciplines of psychology and psychiatry and influenced health care policies for treating the mentally disabled. Some states even modified their health care guidelines for drug-treatment therapies for the mentally disabled based specifically on Breuning's research.

It should also be noted that the results of Breuning's fraudulent research during the 1980's played a primary role in increasing the rate of prescriptions for stimulant drugs such as Ritalin for treating children with hyperactivity disorders. Thousands of medical doctors throughout the United States still prescribe these stimulants at alarming rates for the treatment of conditions such as attention deficit hyperactivity disorder (ADHD) in children. The stimulants are still used for treatment even in the face of many clinical trials that debunked Breuning's research claims.

—*Paul M. Klenowski*

FURTHER READING

Shamoo, Adil, and David Resnik. *Responsible Conduct of Research*. New York: Oxford University Press, 2003. A comprehensive study of the various ethical issues in biomedical research. Includes a time line of Breuning's falsifications.

Sprague, Robert L. "Whistleblowing: A Very Unpleasant Avocation." *Ethics and Behavior* 3, no. 1 (March, 1993): 103-133. First-person account of the scandal by Breuning's mentor and former boss. Sprague writes that the article has a particular "focus on the great reluctance of universities and federal agencies to investigate vigorously an alleged case of scientific misconduct when it involves members of their own faculties or grant recipients."

Wible, James. *The Economics of Science: Methodology and Epistemology as if Economics Really Mattered*. New York: Routledge, 1998. This book offers a unique look at science from an economic perspective. In particular, it examines in detail various cases of scientific fraud.

March 23, 1989
SCIENTISTS' "COLD FUSION" CLAIMS CANNOT BE VERIFIED

1980's

While working at the University of Utah in 1989, electrochemists Martin Fleischmann and Stanley Pons announced their experimental achievement of cold fusion, a phenomenon believed to be unachievable. Although their announcement was initially received with some acclaim, the inability of other scientists to duplicate their results, standard practice in the sciences, led to the term "cold fusion" being associated with scientific scandal.

ALSO KNOWN AS: Fleischmann-Pons experiment
LOCALE: Salt Lake City, Utah
CATEGORIES: Cultural and intellectual history; education; science and technology

KEY FIGURES
Martin Fleischmann (b. 1927), British electrochemist
Stanley Pons (b. 1943), British electrochemist
Steven E. Jones (b. 1943), American physicist

SUMMARY OF EVENT
During the 1960's, electrochemical professor Martin Fleischmann and colleagues at the University of Southampton in England began investigating possible connections between chemical reactions and nuclear processes. In 1979, Stanley Pons earned his doctorate in chemistry at Southampton under the tutelage of Fleischmann. After Pons was appointed chairman of the Department of Chemistry at the University of Utah during the early 1980's, Fleischmann frequently visited Pons in Utah and collaborated with him about joint research ventures. The two were particularly interested in the possibility that nuclear fusion might occur at or near room temperature, a phenomenon known as cold fusion.

Between 1983 and 1988, Fleischmann and Pons invested more than $100,000 of their own money in cold-fusion experimentation. Their resulting experiment was quite simple. It consisted of an insulated glass jar containing a solution of lithium deuteroxide salts and 99.5 percent heavy water (deuterium oxide) into which two electrodes were immersed. One electrode was a coil of platinum wire and the other was a ten-centimeter-long rod of palladium. A small voltage between the electrodes decomposed the deuterium oxide into deuterium (an isotope of hydrogen) and oxygen. Some of the deuterium was absorbed into the palladium, a result that was previously discovered by Thomas Graham in the nineteenth century. Fleischmann and Pons reported that their experiment generated excessive amounts of heat energy.

In 1988, Fleischmann and Pons submitted a grant proposal to the U.S. Department of Energy for funding that was needed to support their cold-fusion research. The proposal was reviewed by Steven E. Jones, a physicist at Brigham Young University (BYU), who also was working on cold fusion. Jones and colleagues at BYU were doing experiments very similar to those being conducted by Fleischmann and Pons. In January, 1989, Jones reported some positive results from his team's cold-fusion research. They were seeing neutrons and a small amount of heat being generated from their electrolytic cell. Jones concluded that their experiment showed no potential as a possible commercial energy source, but that it had considerable scientific interest.

During the same period of time, Fleischmann, Pons, and their graduate student, Marvin Hawkins, identified excess heat energy from their experiment that could not be explained by only chemical reactions. They concluded that the energy must be generated by nuclear processes involving the fusion of tightly packed deuterium nuclei in the palladium. If their results were correct, their experimental device would have considerable commercial value. Evidently, Fleischmann and Pons met with Jones on March 6, 1989, to discuss the publication of their in-dividual results simultaneously in *Nature*. However, Fleischmann and Pons nixed that apparent agreement by submitting their paper for publication in the *Journal of Electroanalytical Chemistry* on March 11.

By mid-March, 1989, University of Utah president Chase N. Peterson believed it was best to release the results of Pons and Fleischmann's work due to the possible economic windfall from cold fusion as an inexhaustible source of energy. Peterson scheduled a press conference for March 23, breaking a promise of cooperation with Jones and BYU. At the press conference, Pons and Fleischmann reported that their room-temperature experiment was producing heat energy at a rate more than four times greater than the input power. The initial puzzle to their experiment was their report that neutrons and tritium (an isotope of hydrogen) were being released at rates that were a billion times slower than the fusion rate expected from the heat that was being generated. Pons and Fleischmann knew that their claims were theoretically problematic, but they were convinced that their experimental results were basically correct. As a result of the uncertainties, *The New York Times* initially refused to print the story. On the other hand, *Wall Street Journal* reporter Jerry Bishop presented the scientists' claims as a major breakthrough. Cold fusion soon became a major media event.

Several research groups immediately tried to duplicate Pons and Fleischmann's results. On April 10, researchers at Texas A&M University published results of excess heat from their experiment. The next day, a group from the Georgia Institute of Technology reported the production of neutrons. For a lack of concrete evidence, both groups withdrew their claims within a few days. On May 1, the American Physical Society (APS) conducted a session on cold fusion in

Stanley Pons and Martin Fleischmann testify about their cold fusion experiments before a House committee on April 1, 1989. (Hulton Archive/Getty Images)

which a number of failed experiments were reported. At a second APS session on the following day, eight of nine prominent speakers concluded that the claims of Pons and Fleischmann were irrelevant and should be dropped.

Over the next several weeks, many competing claims, counterclaims, and possible explanations for the cold-fusion experiment ran rampant. By not properly verifying their results prior to divulging them, Pons and Fleischmann had created their own scandal. They would now suffer the consequences. They broke all the rules of the scientific community with their premature announcement of having successfully achieved cold fusion in their laboratory. Instead of first seeking peer review by submitting their findings to a reputable journal, they chose to announce their results at a press conference. They also exaggerated some of their results. In addition, because of pending patent rights, they did not disclose the details of their experiment to other scientists. Amid accusations of fraud, incompetence, and deception, the euphoria about cold fusion eventually began to die down. Many journalists referred to cold fusion as a hoax that only generated "confusion."

As the fiasco played out, Pons and Fleischmann, humiliated by the scientific community, retreated to France to do further work on cold-fusion experiments in a lab in Provence. Although their reputations were ruined, their continued research was funded by multimillionaire Minoru Toyoda from 1992 until 1996. Because of conflict over the direction of the research and unproductive results, Fleischmann left in 1995 and returned to England. Pons left in 1996 to pursue other research opportunities in Europe.

IMPACT

The quick, widespread media dissemination of the claims of Pons and Fleischmann, the perceived simplicity of their cold-fusion experiment and the potential scientific, social, and economic significance of cold fusion, led to replication efforts being conducted in hundreds of laboratories worldwide. If the conclusions of Pons and Fleischmann proved to be correct, alterations would have to be made in the basic theoretical understanding of the physics of nuclear fusion. Since most laboratories could not replicate the reported cold-fusion results of Fleischmann and Pons, most scientists concluded that cold fusion was not possible. The few positive results that were reported were dismissed as experimental error or even manipulation of the data to show positive results. For the most part, cold-fusion research was ridiculed and denounced.

Despite the scandal and low level of acceptance by the scientific establishment, laboratories in several countries continued to pursue cold-fusion research. Some positive evidence for cold fusion continued to be reported, but most prominent academic journals did not publish those findings. Even though cold fusion may represent a colossal conspiracy of denial, millions of dollars continue to be spent on the concept because of the potential economic windfalls. Consequently, some researchers continue their hope of explaining and developing cold-fusion technology. As a result, some publications are devoted to publishing papers about cold fusion. A Web-based cold-fusion library has been established, and an international conference on cold fusion is held twice a year.

The cold-fusion debacle also led the scientific community to scrutinize reported scientific breakthroughs much more thoroughly and to make sure that proper protocol is followed prior to the release of any results. Experimental and theoretical work must be reviewed and replicated by peers and deemed publishable before it is released to the media. The bar for ethical standards associated with scientific research and the reporting of the results has been raised to a new level.

—Alvin K. Benson

FURTHER READING

Beaudette, Charles G. *Excess Heat: Cold Fusion Research Prevailed.* 2d ed. Brampton, Ont.: Oak Grove Press, 2002. Excellent review of the Pons-Fleischmann experiment, the cold-fusion controversy, and what has been done in cold-fusion research from 1989 until 2002. A good overview for general readers.

Kozima, Hideo. *The Science of Cold Fusion Phe-*

nomenon. Boston: Elsevier, 2006. Scientific examination of the possibility of cold fusion that investigates the work of Fleischmann, Pons, and Jones and proposes possible mechanisms for cold fusion and how it might be experimentally achieved.

Simon, Bart. *Undead Science: Science Studies and the Afterlife of Cold Fusion.* New Brunswick, N.J.: Rutgers University Press, 2002. Examines the Fleischmann-Pons debacle and traces some of the experimental and theoretical work involving cold fusion during the 1990's.

Taubes, Gary. *Bad Science: The Short Life and Weird Times of Cold Fusion.* New York: Random

House, 1993. Critical appraisal of the mishandling of science demonstrated by Fleischmann and Pons in prematurely announcing success with cold fusion.

SEE ALSO: Nov. 21, 1953: Piltdown Man Is Revealed to Be a Hoax; Spring, 1996: Physicist Publishes a Deliberately Fraudulent Article; Aug., 2002: Immunologist Resigns After Being Accused of Falsifying Research; Sept. 25, 2002: Inquiry Reveals That Physicist Jan Hendrik Schön Faked His Research; May 12, 2006: Scientist Is Indicted for Faking His Research on Creating Stem Cells.

March 29, 1989
FINANCIER MICHAEL MILKEN IS INDICTED FOR RACKETEERING AND FRAUD

Michael Milken, known as the junk-bond king of Wall Street during the 1980's, was indicted for insider trading and other illegal activities under the RICO Act, making him the first person not tied to organized crime to be charged under this act. He was sentenced to ten years in prison but served less than two years. He also paid $600 million in fines to the U.S. government and more than $1 billion to the Federal Deposit Insurance Corporation.

LOCALE: New York, New York
CATEGORIES: Corruption; organized crime and racketeering; banking and finance; law and the courts; business

KEY FIGURES
Michael Milken (b. 1946), Wall Street investment banker
Ivan Boesky (b. 1937), Wall Street arbitrageur
Rudy Giuliani (b. 1944), U.S. attorney for the Southern District of New York, 1983-1989, and mayor of New York, 1994-2001

SUMMARY OF EVENT
Michael Milken was born into a Jewish, middle-class family and was raised by his parents in the San Fernando Valley of Los Angeles. An exceptionally bright child, Milken discovered at an early age that he had both a photographic memory and an interest in mathematics and finances. In 1968, he graduated from the University of California, Berkeley, with a degree in business administration. That same year, he also married his high school sweetheart, Lori Hackel. They relocated to Philadelphia so that Milken could attend the Wharton School of Business at the University of Pennsylvania. After earning his master's degree in business administration, he was hired by the Drexel Corporation.

In 1973, Drexel had merged with Burnham and Company to become the Wall Street investment firm Drexel Burnham Lambert. Following the merger, Milken became the head of a bond-trading department. It was in this position that he began using his junk-bond theory, which he originally developed as an undergraduate student at Berkeley to make money.

Michael Milken. (AP/Wide World Photos)

In the financial world, a conventional bond was a certificate of debt that was usually sold by a government to a company that wanted to raise capital by borrowing money. Most often, these bonds were then repaid by the borrowing company with interest. Conventional bonds also were rated according to the value of the business minus its current liabilities. In contrast to these practices, Milken believed that junk bonds, which would be unrated, could be sold to small companies that lacked a credit history and were heavily in debt. By targeting these kinds of companies, he could potentially make a lot of money because junk bonds would be issued at a higher interest rate than conventional bonds. These higher interest rates would, in turn, earn higher profits for Milken. The junk-bond strategy was so successful that by 1976, Milken was earning more than five million dollars a year.

In 1977, Milken relocated his family and the company's noninvestment-grade bond-trading department to Los Angeles. By 1978, Drexel Burnham Lambert had issued approximately $439 million in junk bonds, and Milken was soon known as the junk-bond king of Wall Street. During the early 1980's, investors also began using junk bonds to finance leveraged buyouts (LBOs). By definition, a leveraged buyout was the purchase of a company using a significant amount of borrowed money, in the form of bonds and loans, to meet the cost of acquisition. By 1985, the junk-bond market on Wall Street was worth more than $100 billion.

Throughout the 1980's, the U.S. Securities and Exchange Commission (SEC) closely watched Milken's business dealings on Wall Street. In 1986, Ivan Boesky, a successful Wall Street arbitrageur, plea bargained with the SEC and implicated Milken and Drexel Burnham Lambert in several illegal financial transactions. These included insider trading, illegal takeovers, fraud, and stock manipulation. Milken also was charged with stock parking, a financial activity in which an investor conceals the real owner of a stock to bypass a tax liability or financial regulation. Simultaneously, Rudy Giuliani, the U.S. attorney for the Southern District of New York, began a criminal investigation of the embattled investor. Milken claimed his innocence on all charges.

In 1987, James B. Stewart, a reporter for *The Wall Street Journal*, began investigating that year's stock market crash and the scandal that implicated Milken and others in insider trading and other crimes. Stewart was awarded a Pulitzer Prize in 1988 for his investigative reporting, and his book, *Den of Thieves*, which details the crimes of Wall Street, was published in 1991. The book remains highly controversial and has been targeted by supporters of Milken.

On March 29, 1989, under the Racketeer Influenced and Corrupt Organizations (RICO) Act, Milken was indicted by a federal grand jury on ninety-eight counts of racketeering and fraud as well as insider trading, stock parking, and tax evasion. The indictment was especially significant because it was the first time in American legal history that the RICO Act was used against an individual with no connection to organized crime. In June, at the company's request, Milken resigned from Drexel Burnham Lambert and formed his own company, International Capital Access Group.

Milken had maintained his innocence throughout the affair, but on April 24, 1990, he pleaded guilty to six counts of violating federal securities and tax laws. The charges included insider trading, tax evasion, stock parking, filing false SEC reports, mail fraud, and the evasion of regulatory capital requirements. Interestingly, at his trial, Milken not only apologized for his crimes but also admitted to the court that he willingly conspired with Boesky to defraud financial clients. As part of his plea agreement, Milken was sentenced to a ten-year prison term by Judge Kimba Wood. He was fined $200 million, agreed to pay $400 million into a special fund set up by the SEC to reimburse his victims, and accepted a lifetime ban from the securities industry.

On January 2, 1993, Milken was released from a federal penitentiary in Pleasanton, California, after serving only twenty-two months of his ten-year sentence. He was relocated to a halfway house but was released from there on February 4. The court also required him to perform eighteen hundred hours of community service each year for three years. In addition, he settled a lawsuit with the Federal Deposit Insurance Corporation (FDIC) by agreeing to pay the agency more than $1 billion. Following his release from prison, Milken's net worth was estimated to be more than $125 million.

PROHIBITED ACTIVITIES UNDER THE RICO ACT

Michael Milken was indicted for various crimes under the Racketeer Influenced and Corrupt Organizations (RICO) Act of 1970. In part, "racketeering" is defined in the act as

Any act or threat involving murder, kidnapping, gambling, arson, robbery, bribery, extortion, dealing in obscene matter, or dealing in a controlled substance or listed chemical . . . which is chargeable under state law and punishable by imprisonment for more than one year.

RICO also includes a section, excerpted here, outlining prohibited criminal activities covered by the act.

It shall be unlawful for any person who has received any income derived, directly or indirectly, from a pattern of racketeering activity or through collection of an unlawful debt in which such person has participated as a principal within the meaning of section 2, title 18, United States Code, to use or invest, directly or indirectly, any part of such income, or the proceeds of such income, in acquisition of any interest in, or the establishment or operation of, any enterprise which is engaged in, or the activities of which affect, interstate or foreign commerce. A purchase of securities on the open market for purposes of investment, and without the intention of controlling or participating in the control of the issuer, or of assisting another to do so, shall not be unlawful under this subsection if the securities of the issuer held by the purchaser, the members of his immediate family, and his or their accomplices in any pattern or racketeering activity or the collection of an unlawful debt after such purchase do not amount in the aggregate to one percent of the outstanding securities of any one class, and do not confer, either in law or in fact, the power to elect one or more directors of the issuer.

IMPACT

Milken not only epitomized the Wall Street investor of the 1980's but also symbolized American capitalism and greed during the 1980's. The highly intelligent financier went to Wall Street as an outsider during the 1970's, and through diligence, hard work, and an obsession with making money, he redefined the stereotypical Ivy League image of the Wall Street careerist. Milken's reign on Wall Street, however, came to an abrupt end in 1989 when he was indicted, but in the end, his symbolic reign continues—as the junk-bond king who defined an era in American financial history.

—Bernadette Zbicki Heiney

FURTHER READING

Bailey, Fenton. *Fall from Grace: The Untold Story of Michael Milken.* Secaucus, N.J.: Carol, 1992. This book explores the power of the American media and its role in the downfall of Michael Milken.

Bruck, Connie. *The Predators' Ball: The Inside Story of Drexel Burnham and the Rise of the Junk Bond Raiders.* New York: Penguin Books, 1989. Bruck provides a detailed history of the junk-bond industry during the 1980's, with a look at Drexel Burnham Lambert and its hired junk-bond brokers.

Chancellor, Edward. *Devil Take the Hindmost: A History of Financial Speculation.* New York: Plume, 2000. A detailed history of financial speculation—the quest for money and assets—in the United States.

Grant, James. *Money of the Mind: Borrowing and Lending in America from the Civil War to Michael Milken.* New York: Farrar, Straus and Giroux, 1992. A history of the credit and lending systems in the United States and their profound effect on the American marketplace and consumerism.

MacDonald, Scott B., and Jane E. Hughes. *Separating Fools from Their Money: A History of American Financial Scandals.* New Brunswick, N.J.: Rutgers University Press, 2007. This book provides readers with an easy-to-read, detailed history of finance-related scandals in the United States, scandals that target those least able to afford it: ordinary consumers.

Sobel, Robert. *Dangerous Dreamers: The Financial Innovators from Charles Merrill to Michael Milken.* Washington, D.C.: Beardbooks, 2000. This book explores the history of America's most notable financiers and their impact on the American economy.

SEE ALSO: 1919-1920: Ponzi Schemes Are Revealed as Investment Frauds; Mar. 29, 1962: Billie Sol Estes Is Arrested for Corporate Fraud; Nov. 28, 1967: Investor Louis Wolfson Is Convicted of Selling Stock Illegally; May 2, 1984: E. F. Hutton Executives Plead Guilty to Fraud; May 7, 1985: Banker Jake Butcher Pleads Guilty to Fraud; Jan. 15, 1988: ZZZZ Best Founder Is Indicted on Federal Fraud Charges; Aug. 27, 1990: Guinness Four Are Found Guilty of Share-Trading Fraud; Dec. 2, 2001: Enron Bankruptcy Reveals Massive Financial Fraud; June 25, 2002: Internal Corruption Forces Adelphia Communications to Declare Bankruptcy; Sept. 3, 2003: Mutual Fund Companies Are Implicated in Shady Trading Practices; Mar. 5, 2004: Martha Stewart Is Convicted in Insider-Trading Scandal; Sept. 12, 2005: Westar Energy Executives Are Found Guilty of Looting Their Company; Sept. 18, 2006: *Newsweek* Reveals That Hewlett-Packard Spied on Its Own Board; Sept. 20, 2008: American Financial Markets Begin to Collapse.

1980's

May 31, 1989
SPEAKER OF THE HOUSE JIM WRIGHT RESIGNS IN ETHICS SCANDAL

Jim Wright served thirty-four years in the U.S. Congress before being forced to resign for ethical violations. A ten-month investigation into his finances showed that he violated his position of power dozens of times by securing various financial deals for himself, his immediate family members, and his friends, in violation of House ethics. His corrupt activities brought an immediate end to his congressional career but did not result in further legal action. Wright was the first Speaker of the House to resign from office because of a political scandal.

LOCALE: Washington, D.C.

CATEGORIES: Corruption; politics; ethics; government

KEY FIGURES

Jim Wright (b. 1922), U.S. representative from Texas, 1955-1989, and Speaker of the House, 1987-1989

Bill Mallick (fl. 1980's), Texas real-estate developer and friend of Jim Wright

Betty Wright (fl. 1980's), Jim Wright's wife

SUMMARY OF EVENT

Eleven years after becoming one of the most powerful Democrats in the U.S. Congress, Representative Jim Wright was at the center of an ethics scandal concerning his financial activities in 1988. Because of the severity of the allegations, the House of Representatives was forced to convene a bipartisan committee in early June of that year to conduct an official inquiry and, later, a full-fledged investigation of the numerous claims of financial misconduct.

Wright had been raised in the greater Dallas-Fort Worth area and attended Weatherford College from 1939 to 1940 and the University of Texas from 1940 to 1941. After the Japanese attack on Pearl Harbor in 1941, Wright joined the U.S. Army Air Force and was stationed in the South Pacific. During his World War II military service, he flew countless combat missions and was awarded the Distinguished Flying Cross. After the war, he returned home and entered politics in his home state of Texas.

In 1946, Wright was elected to the Texas house of representatives but was defeated after serving a single term. He then moved to Weatherford, Texas, home of his alma mater, and was elected mayor for a four-year term (1950-1954). In 1954, he ran unopposed for a seat in Congress, representing the Twelfth District, which included Forth Worth and Weatherford. He would be reelected to the House more than one dozen times. In 1977, Wright was named the new majority leader after Tip O'Neill was elected Speaker of the House. He served as majority leader from 1977 through 1987. After O'Neill retired from the speakership in 1987, Wright was elected to replace him. He served until his resignation on May 31, 1989.

At the center of the Wright investigation were four major areas of concern. First, real-estate developer George Mallick gave him the use of a luxury condominium in Fort Worth and, for his wife, Betty Wright, the use of a Cadillac and an annual salary of eighteen thousand dollars for a ghost job with her husband. Mallick's gifts, however, violated a congressional ban on members receiving gifts valued at more than one hundred dollars from any one person.

The committee also discovered that Mallick had a direct interest in legislation pertaining to savings and loan companies, especially in Texas, that were failing. Wright intervened with federal regulators on behalf of Mallick and two other Texas executives from a Fort Worth savings and loan and successfully lobbied on their behalf in their dealings with the Federal Home Loan Banks board. His efforts ultimately protected their financial interests.

The third concern was Mallick and Wright's questionable business relationship. In one case, Wright had secured $7.5 million for the restoration of Fort Worth's historic stockyards, and Mallick was given the contract to oversee the renovation. This relationship opened the door for Wright to receive financial kickbacks and gifts for securing the contract.

Finally, Wright's book *Reflections of a Public Man* (1984) was at the center of another ethics violation. The 117-page work was published by long-time friend Carlos Moore, whose printing firm had worked for Wright's campaigns for several years. Ethical concerns arose because of the money Wright made from sales of the book. He was earning 60 percent in royalties, far more than the common 10 to 15 percent in royalties for most authors. The book was purchased in bulk by various supporters of Wright, including business and labor groups. The money he earned from the sales allowed him to avoid the earnings limit placed on Congress members; with book sales, he was able to earn extra income while avoiding that limitation.

In May, 1988, the public citizens' action group Common Cause called upon Congress to inquire into the allegations against Wright. In a matter of days, leading House Republican Newt Gingrich sent a formal letter, cosigned by seventy-two of his Republican colleagues, to the House Committee on Standards of Official Conduct, the panel that oversees the ethical conduct of House members. The letter called for a complete investigation into Wright's conduct. On February 22, 1989, the chief investigator issued his preliminary 279-page report to the committee. The report alleged that on sixty-nine separate occasions, Wright had broken congressional rules of conduct.

At the conclusion of the full fifty-one-week investigation, the committee, comprising six Dem-ocrats and six Republicans, was ready to render its decision. In an 8-4 vote, the committee found that there was "reason to believe" that Wright violated House ethics rules. After dropping more than half of the original charges, the committee was ready to act on four issues of misconduct. Based on the insurmountable evidence, Wright was now set to face an ethics hearing with the power to exact three penalties: a letter of reproach, a formal reprimand, or censure.

Although Democrats dominated the House in numbers, Wright failed to gain his party's support to retain his position as House Speaker. Facing almost certain criminal indictment and conviction, Wright, now sixty-six years old, opted to resign as speaker on May 31. Less than one month later, on June 30, he resigned from the House altogether, ending a thirty-four-year congressional career.

IMPACT

Only the fourth House Speaker in U.S. history to step down from office, Wright was the first to leave office because of allegations of unethical conduct. During his resignation speech before members of Congress, he said that his stepping down from his

Jim Wright, right, one month before his resignation as Speaker of the House. (Hulton Archive/Getty Images)

position was a sacrifice for his country because he spared the House and its members further political hardship and negative publicity. He added that he was a victim of an ethical battle between warring political parties. In his final words, he urged both Democrats and Republicans to resolve their differences and hostilities so that they could refocus on more pressing and urgent matters for the American people.

At the same time Wright was leaving office, his own top aide was resigning amid a scandal related to an interview in *The Washington Post*. In the interview, a woman claimed she had been brutally assaulted by Wright's aide in the early 1970's. Another scandal erupted during the time of Wright's resignation when House Democratic whip Tony Coelho was forced from office because of his own alleged financial misconduct.

—*Paul M. Klenowski*

FURTHER READING

Barry, John. *The Ambition and the Power: Jim Wright and the Will of the House*. New York: Viking Press, 1989. A detailed look at the rise and fall of Representative and Speaker Wright, with specific attention to his misconduct and resignation.

Long, Kim. *The Almanac of Political Corruption, Scandals, and Dirty Politics*. New York: Delacorte Press, 2007. A wide-ranging book detailing the various scandals and corrupt practices that have plagued U.S. politics. A good general study of political scandals.

Thompson, Denis. *Ethics in Congress: From Individual to Institutional Corruption*. Washington, D.C.: Brookings Institute, 1995. This report chronicles corruption in the institution of Congress and by individual Congress members, including Wright.

U.S. Congress. House of Representatives. Committee on Standards of Official Conduct. *Report of the Special Outside Counsel in the Matter of Speaker James C. Wright, Jr.* Washington, D.C.: Government Printing Office, 1989. The official report of the findings against Wright, highlighting the numerous charges of unethical conduct found by the investigative congressional subcommittee.

SEE ALSO: Aug. 4, 1948: Columnist Drew Pearson Exposes Congressman's Corruption; June 23, 1967: Senator Thomas J. Dodd Is Censured for Misappropriating Funds; Dec. 7, 1980: Rita Jenrette's "Diary of a Mad Congresswife" Scandalizes Washington; Sept. 23, 1987: Plagiarism Charges End Joe Biden's Presidential Campaign; Dec. 5, 2002: Senator Trent Lott Praises Strom Thurmond's 1948 Presidential Campaign; July 1, 2005: Federal Agents Raid Congressman Randall Cunningham's Home; June 4, 2007: Congressman William J. Jefferson Is Indicted for Corruption.

August 10, 1989

JAPANESE PRIME MINISTER SOSUKE RESIGNS AFTER AFFAIR WITH A GEISHA

Following his appointment as Japan's prime minister in June, 1989, Sosuke Uno resigned his office after only sixty-nine days when the press revealed he had paid a geisha a monthly salary for sexual favors prior to being prime minister. The scandal inspired a newly active women's movement and led the media in Japan to rethink the significance of sex, gossip, and other scandal as relevant and newsworthy.

LOCALE: Tokyo, Japan

CATEGORIES: Government; politics; publishing and journalism; sex

KEY FIGURES

Sosuke Uno (1922-1998), prime minister of Japan, June 3-August 10, 1989
Noboru Takeshita (1924-2000), prime minister of Japan, 1987-1989

SUMMARY OF EVENT

In the summer of 1989, a woman describing herself as a geisha approached the *Mainichi Shinbun*, one of the largest newspapers in Japan, claiming that the married prime minister Sosuke Uno had paid her to have a sexual relationship in the months before he assumed office. The prestigious newspaper balked because the story was considered beneath its dignity, and she was referred to an affiliated magazine. That magazine, the *Sunday Mainichi*, broke the story, but it caused little stir among a public that expected sexual dalliance among its politicians. When, however, a socialist politician accused Uno in parliament of bringing shame to the nation, the public's interest deepened and Uno found himself at the center of a major scandal.

The son of a merchant family in western Japan, Uno had attended Kobe University of Commerce and served in the Japanese imperial army during World War II. During the war he spent two years as a prisoner of war in Siberia and later wrote a book

about that experience, one of several books he wrote over his career. He was elected to the Japanese diet, the legislative arm of the Japanese government, in 1960 and served without great distinction in various areas of government, including defense, the ministry of international trade and industry (MITI), and foreign affairs.

Uno's predecessor as prime minister, Noboru Takeshita, had been ruined by a corruption and bribery scandal. During Takeshita's term, it was revealed that at least thirty members of his Liberal Democratic Party, the LDP, had been receiving favors from Recruit, an upstart publishing and telecommunications company. In the face of this scandal, Takeshita was forced to resign his office on June 3, 1989. After a month-long search by the LDP, Uno was named as his successor.

The LDP, wanting Takeshita's replacement to be untouched by the Recruit corruption scandal, took its time to make a decision. The party settled on Uno only after Masayoshi Ito, its first choice, had demanded as a condition of his acceptance of the office that all LDP leaders who had received favors from Recruit resign from politics. Finding that demand unacceptable, the LDP settled on the bland Uno as the prudent choice. They were certainly unaware that for several months before his appointment, Uno had been paying a woman a salary for sexual favors.

The woman, whose name was never revealed, had lost patience with Uno because she received only a small amount of the payment she was due and because she did not receive a parting gift from him when the affair was terminated. She described Uno in her statement to the press as vain, rude, and self-centered. The article that broke the story, published by *Sunday Mainichi* magazine, on August 10, was sensationally titled "Accusation of an Office Lady: 'I Was Bought for 300,000 Yen per Month.'"

The scandal turned international after *The Washington Post* followed with its own story of the affair.

1980's

Despite Uno initially denying the story and later trying to mitigate the damage caused by it, the woman's accusation soon turned from being a subject of gossip and humor to one with serious political consequences for Uno's already troubled party.

In spite of a statement by the editor of *Sunday Mainichi* that the central part of the scandal was that Uno paid for a woman's companionship and that the moral standard for a prime minister was higher than the norm, to consider the Uno scandal simply a sex scandal would be a mistake. The Japanese public at that time would not have batted an eye at the disclosure of sexual infidelity of a married politician. That sort of behavior among powerful politicians was taken for granted. What seemed to bother many Japanese more than the moral issue was the payment. For some, particularly the women, the amount was far less than it should have been. For others it was taken as a sign of political incompetence that a man in his position did not deal quietly with the geisha and pay her the amount required to keep her quiet.

Uno's disrespect aroused the anger of Japanese women. Traditionally reticent, they campaigned vigorously to remove him from office. Over fifty women's groups joined in an effective anti-Uno movement. In fact, the campaign against Uno is considered by many the coming of age of women's activist politics in Japan and the first real flexing of women's political muscle.

The international coverage the scandal was receiving also irked the Japanese. As a member of an opposition party put it to Uno, the prime minister was making Japan look foolish in the eyes of the world. This was an unforgivable sin, especially for a Japanese prime minister.

On still another level, the breaking of the cherished geisha code of silence was another scandal in itself. Whatever is said to a geisha is privileged information, and a geisha is bound by honor never to reveal anything that passes between her and her client. The revelation of her affair with Uno was convincing evidence for geishas all over Japan that this woman was no true geisha.

The ill feeling caused by Uno's miserly dealings with the geisha was not the sole cause of the serious problems faced by Uno and his party in the polls. Also in the limelight at the time was the Recruit scandal. In addition, immediately upon assuming the job of prime minister, Uno had to implement an unpopular consumer tax.

For his part, Uno never admitted fault for his part in the affair and stubbornly refused to deal with it at all. He never apologized to the nation or to his wife or to the woman with whom he had the affair. In an odd twist, his wife apologized to the nation on his behalf during an interview in which she also stated that Uno had never talked with her about the matter. Uno resigned his office in disgrace on August 10, 1989, after sixty-nine days in as prime minister, one of the shortest terms of office on record in Japan. He died of cancer almost ten years later the age of seventy-five in the western Japanese city of Moriyama.

IMPACT

Uno's resignation was immediately preceded by the Japanese Socialist Party handing the LDP its worse defeat in over three decades. The sex scandal no doubt contributed to the party's defeat and Uno's resignation, but there were many other causes as well. Uno resigned not because of the scandal but because of his party's losses in the election, losses that ended the LDP's thirty-eight-year political rule within four years.

Also, the media coverage of the Uno scandal changed the way the Japanese press came to deal with such matters. After the Japanese public learned that the press knew about the Recruit and Uno scandals and did not report them until after the stories broke elsewhere, public confidence in the press fell drastically. No longer would even the "serious" newspapers consider sex and gossip irrelevant.

Furthermore, many consider that the Japanese women's movement came of age during the anti-Uno campaign of 1989. Before the scandal, women's political organizations were relegated to consumer and health matters. Their campaign to unseat Uno showed another, more public, side to their activism.

—*Wayne Shirey*

FURTHER READING

Downer, Lesley. *Geisha: The Secret History of a Vanishing World.* London: Headline, 2000. A good overview on the rich history of the geisha in Japan. Includes an eye-opening discussion of how geisha are both created and trained as "art persons" who do much more than act as companions to paying men.

Pharr, Susan J. *Media and Politics in Japan.* Honolulu: University of Hawaii Press, 1996. A scholarly look at the Japanese news media, including an examination of how it handled the Sosuke Uno sex scandal.

West, Mark D. *Secrets, Sex, and Spectacle: The Rules of Scandal in Japan and the United States.* Chicago: University of Chicago Press, 2006. A comparative study of how scandals come to be and are dealt with in Japan and the United

States. Includes discussion of the Sosuke Uno sex scandal.

SEE ALSO: Mar. 2-Sept. 25, 1963: John Profumo Affair Rocks British Government; Feb. 4, 1976: Lockheed Is Implicated in Bribing Foreign Officials; July 25, 1987: Novelist-Politician Jeffrey Archer Wins Libel Trial Against the *Daily Star*; June, 1988-June, 1989: Insider-Trading Scandal Rocks Japanese Government; Sept. 24, 1992: British Cabinet Member David Mellor Resigns over Romantic Affair; Jan. 17, 1998: President Bill Clinton Denies Sexual Affair with a White House Intern; Sept. 28, 2002: British Politician Reveals Her Affair with Prime Minister John Major; May 28, 2007: Japanese Politician Charged with Corruption Hangs Himself.

August 24, 1989
PETE ROSE IS BANNED FROM BASEBALL FOR BETTING ON GAMES

After a Major League Baseball investigation into star player Pete Rose's gambling habits, Commissioner A. Bartlett Giamatti banned Rose from baseball for life. Rose was accused of, and later admitted to, betting on baseball.

LOCALE: New York, New York
CATEGORIES: Corruption; gambling; law and the courts; sports

KEY FIGURES
Pete Rose (b. 1941), professional baseball player and manager
A. Bartlett Giamatti (1938-1989), commissioner of Major League Baseball
John M. Dowd (b. 1941), lawyer and lead investigator
Fay Vincent (b. 1938), assistant commissioner of Major League Baseball

Paul Janszen (fl. 1980's), Rose's long-time friend and owner of Gold's Gym in Cincinnati

SUMMARY OF EVENT
On August 24, 1989, Major League Baseball (MLB) commissioner A. Bartlett Giamatti announced Pete Rose's lifetime suspension from baseball. Rose, the subject of a six-month investigation led by Washington, D.C., attorney John M. Dowd, had been accused of gambling on baseball games, including those played by the Cincinnati Reds, for whom Rose served as a player-manager. Rose was not banned from the sport under the rule prohibiting gambling, which carries an automatic lifetime suspension. Instead, he was declared ineligible under a rule that governs other forms of misconduct. That rule carried a penalty decided at the commissioner's discretion, and Giamatti determined that a lifetime ban was appropriate.

Rose was one of baseball's biggest stars over the course of his twenty-four-year playing career. From 1963 to 1986, his awards included National League (NL) Rookie of the Year and NL Most Valuable Player, and he was a seventeen-time All Star. As a member of the Cincinnati Reds' teams commonly known as the Big Red Machine, and later as a player with the Philadelphia Phillies, Rose was known for his hard playing and competitive drive. Although he rarely hit for power, Rose consistently hit for a high average, winning three NL batting titles. He finished his career with 4,256 hits, a major league record. For the last two years of his playing career, Rose returned to the Reds as a player-manager. He continued to manage the club for three seasons after his retirement as a player in 1986.

Throughout much of his career, Rose was an avid gambler as well. Betting on horse races, football,

basketball, and other sports, he had begun to gamble uncontrollably by 1985. Through his gambling, he became involved with bookies and others engaged in criminal activities. In 1988, the Federal Bureau of Investigation (FBI) began a probe into the activities of cocaine dealers based out of a Gold's Gym in Cincinnati. Paul Janszen, one of the owners of the gym, had been a long-time friend of Rose and often placed bets for him at the horse track and with bookies. When the FBI interrogated Janszen, he offered extensive information about Rose's gambling. The FBI, investigating drug cases, showed little interest in pursuing Rose on gambling charges, and Janszen offered to sell his story to *Sports Illustrated*. Although the magazine refused the offer, rumors began to circulate about Rose's problem with gambling.

Near the end of his term as MLB commissioner,

Pete Rose is escorted outside federal court in Cincinnati, Ohio, in July, 1990, after he was sentenced to prison for tax evasion. (AP/Wide World Photos)

Peter Ueberroth had heard about Janszen's testimony and informed Giamatti. Ueberroth and Giamatti took the allegations against Rose very seriously. Major League Baseball had long considered gambling on the sport to be the most egregious offense a player or manager could commit. In 1919, members of the Chicago White Sox were paid by gamblers to throw the World Series in favor of the underdog Cincinnati Reds. When the plot was discovered the next year, major league owners, seeking to clean up the game, selected a federal judge, Kenesaw Mountain Landis, to become the first commissioner of MLB. Landis permanently banned all eight members of the Black Sox, as they came to be known, from baseball.

Since the time of the Black Sox scandal, MLB has had zero tolerance for gambling on baseball, and any player or manager who bets on the sport could receive a permanent expulsion. MLB's fear of gambling-related corruption runs so deep that even retired star players such as Mickey Mantle and Willie Mays were suspended for serving as greeters in casinos (Mantle and Mays later had their bans overturned). With such a history of opposition to gambling, MLB could not let the accusations against Rose go without inquiry.

Although Giamatti was not yet the commissioner, Ueberroth, as a lame duck, turned the Rose matter over to him. In office for only six months, Giamatti devoted his entire time as commissioner to investigating Rose's gambling. Following a private meeting with Rose and his attorneys, a meeting in which Rose proclaimed his innocence, Giamatti opened an investigation into allegations against the player. The commissioner appointed Dowd to head the investigation as special counsel to the commissioner. During the inquiry, Dowd interviewed Janszen and others through whom Rose had placed bets. Janszen, in particular, provided damaging testimony and damning evidence: Rose's betting slips from April, 1987, which listed bets on baseball games. A handwriting analyst confirmed that Rose had written the slips. At the end of the investigation, in August, 1989, Dowd reported that the evidence indicated that Rose had bet on baseball, including the Reds, from 1985 to 1987.

Giamatti, however, created difficulties for himself during the investigation. In June, 1989, after Giamatti revealed in an April letter that he had begun to think that Rose was guilty, Rose and his lawyers filed suit against the commissioner. Rose decried Giamatti as prejudiced against him and stated that the Dowd investigation was unfairly damaging his reputation. Rose asked that Giamatti be replaced by an unbiased party and requested that the Cincinnati Reds be forbidden from taking action against him for any information revealed in the investigation. For two months, the case bounced between state and federal courts, and no action had been taken when the investigation ended in August.

With his credibility tainted, Giamatti had Fay Vincent, deputy MLB commissioner, handle much of the negotiation between the MLB and Rose. On August 23 the two parties decided that Rose would accept a ban from baseball but would not admit to any wrongdoing, nor would he deny wrongdoing. It was understood that after one year, Rose could apply for reinstatement. The following morning, Giamatti revealed the findings of the Dowd Report and announced that Rose would be placed on baseball's ineligible list. Under the ban, Rose could not play or manage in the major or minor leagues and could not attend any official MLB function.

IMPACT

In September, 1989, Vincent became the new commissioner of baseball following Giamatti's death, leaving Rose to doubt that his appeal would be approved. Animosity separated him from Vincent because the two were in conflict during settlement negotiations before Rose's ban was official. However, another serious legal issue stood in the way: In 1990, an Internal Revenue Service investigation led to Rose's conviction for tax evasion, and he was sentenced to a brief prison term and a period of community service. Although Rose could have applied for reinstatement after one year on the ineligible list, he waited until 1997 to do so, after Vincent's term ended and upon Bud Selig's becoming the new MLB commissioner.

For more than a decade after being banned, Rose maintained his innocence. In 2002, however, Rose admitted to Selig in a private meeting that he had bet on baseball during the 1980's. Two years later, Rose confessed publicly in his autobiography, *My Prison Without Bars* (2004). Although Rose hoped to be reinstated by baseball after his confession, MLB did not act on his application. Selig stated that Rose did little to indicate that he has changed since Giamatti banned him.

Unlike the 1919 Black Sox scandal, Rose's banishment from baseball had little effect on the game of baseball itself. However, Rose became a lightning rod among baseball fans. In 1991, the board of the National Baseball Hall of Fame adopted a rule stating that any person on MLB's permanent ineligibility list could not be considered for election into the Hall of Fame. Despite having career statistics that warrant his induction, Rose remains ineligible. Like the case of Shoeless Joe Jackson, who was banned from baseball for his suspected role in fixing the 1919 World Series, Rose's banishment and his ineligibility for the Hall of Fame are topics of extensive debate among baseball fans and professionals.

—*Jacob F. Lee*

FURTHER READING

Jordan, David. *Pete Rose: A Biography*. Westport, Conn.: Greenwood Press, 2004. An updated biography of Rose, especially useful for its coverage of Rose's life after his suspension.

Reston, James, Jr. *Collision at Home Plate: The Lives of Pete Rose and Bart Giamatti*. New York: Edward Burlingame Books, 1991. Dual biography of Rose and Giamatti, focusing on Rose's gambling, Giamatti's time as MLB commissioner, and how the two figures clashed.

Rose, Pete, with Rick Hill. *My Prison Without Bars*. Emmaus, Pa.: Rodale Press, 2004. Autobiography in which Rose finally admits to having bet on baseball. Discusses his family life, early days in baseball, and why he gambled on the game.

Rose, Pete, with Roger Kahn. *Pete Rose: My Story*. New York: Macmillan, 1989. An early Rose autobiography, perhaps the best of his memoirs, published the year Rose was banned, which offers a defense against allegations of betting on baseball.

Sokolove, Michael Y. *Hustle: The Myth, Life, and Lies of Pete Rose*. New ed. New York: Simon & Schuster, 2005. Critical biography of Rose, first published in 1990 and updated here, detailing his gambling problems. Attempts to answer the question, who is Rose—the All-American overachiever or a symbol of corruption?

Vincent, Fay. *The Last Commissioner: A Baseball Valentine*. New York: Simon & Schuster, 2002. Autobiography by Vincent, the commissioner of MLB and Rose's postprofessional nemesis.

SEE ALSO: Sept. 21, 1919: White Sox Players Conspire to Lose World Series in "Black Sox" Scandal; Dec. 26, 1926: Ty Cobb and Tris Speaker Are Accused of Fixing Baseball Games; Spring, 1947: Baseball Manager Leo Durocher Is Suspended for Gambling Ties; Jan. 17, 1951: College Basketball Players Begin Shaving Points for Money; Fall, 1969-Winter, 1971: Japanese Baseball Players Are Implicated in Game Fixing; Nov. 29, 1979, and Jan. 31, 1983: Baseball Commissioner Suspends Mickey Mantle and Willie Mays for Casino Ties; Feb. 28, 1986: Baseball Commissioner Peter Ueberroth Suspends Players for Cocaine Use; Mar. 17, 2005: Former Baseball Star Mark McGwire Evades Congressional Questions on Steroid Use; Aug. 20, 2007: Football Star Michael Vick Pleads Guilty to Financing a Dogfighting Ring.

December 3, 1989

MARTIN LUTHER KING, JR.'S, DOCTORAL-THESIS PLAGIARISM IS REVEALED

In 1988, the editors of the Martin Luther King, Jr., papers made the unsettling discovery that King's doctoral dissertation as well as many of his academic papers had been substantially plagiarized. The editors were slow in reporting their discovery, but British journalist Frank Robert Johnson learned of it and broke the story in 1989.

LOCALE: London, England

CATEGORIES: Cultural and intellectual history; education; hoaxes, frauds, and charlatanism; plagiarism; publishing and journalism

KEY FIGURES

Martin Luther King, Jr. (1929-1968), Baptist minister and civil rights leader

Clayborne Carson (b. 1944), Stanford University historian and senior editor of the King papers

Frank Johnson (1943-2006), British political journalist

L. Harold DeWolf (1905-1986), King's dissertation adviser at Boston University

Coretta Scott King (1927-2006), civil rights activist, who was married to Reverend King

SUMMARY OF EVENT

Civil rights activist Coretta Scott King, the wife of slain civil rights leader Martin Luther King, Jr., initiated a project in 1984 to gather King's papers and publish them in a multivolume collection. She chose a prominent African American historian, Clayborne Carson, to direct the King Papers Project at Stanford University. In 1988, Carson and his assistants were shocked to discover instances of serious plagiarism in King's 1955 doctoral dissertation in theology for Boston University. The dissertation, "A Comparison of the Conception of God in the Thinking of Paul Tillich and Henry Nelson Wieman," included lengthy passages that were taken nearly word-for-word from various texts, es-

pecially from Boston University doctoral student Jack Boozer's thesis of 1952, without quotations, footnotes, or other attribution.

The King papers' editors soon discovered a pattern: King had placed extensive portions of other persons' writings in his graduate-school papers without documentation (citing one's sources is standard scholarly practice). Failing to check for accuracy, he replicated mistakes from those copied texts, errors that included footnotes with erroneous page numbers. Editors believed that disclosing the plagiarism would lead to public misunderstanding and do harm to the editorial project. Following discussions with the project's board of directors, the editors decided to first do exhaustive research to determine the extent of the plagiarism, after which Carson would announce the plagiarism in a scholarly article to appear just before publication of the first volume of King's papers.

Apparently the editors did not anticipate that putting off the announcement of their discovery would be interpreted as an attempt to conceal a scandal about a national hero. A few editors and board members, even after agreeing to not discuss the matter with outsiders, could not resist the temptation to inform friends and associates. American journalists began to hear rumors about problems with the project, but they apparently considered the matter too controversial to pursue, perhaps fearing their actions would be denounced as racist. However, when British journalist Frank Johnson heard the rumors, he telephoned Carson and assistant editor Ralph Luker to inquire about the matter. Although the two editors were noncommittal and vague, they did not entirely deny that King had probably engaged in plagiarism, at least to some extent. In a column appearing in the *Sunday Telegraph* (London) on December 3, 1989, Johnson reported his conversations. He wrote, in "Martin Luther King—Was He a Plagiarist?" that even if King were a plagiarist, "In my view this does not detract from his greatness, no more than did the revelations about his extramarital sex life."

Although other historians and journalists were aware of Johnson's scoop, they chose not to publicize the scandal further. Carson hoped to be the first to release the story more widely, and to do so in a scholarly article in the *Journal of American History*. Unexpectedly, his paper was rejected, reportedly because he had not taken a firm stand on the plagiarism issue. Meanwhile, while Carson was in the process of revising his paper (which was published in June, 1991), reporter Peter Waldman wrote a detailed story that appeared as "To Their Dismay, King Scholars Find a Troubling Pattern—Civil Rights Leader was Lax in Attributing Some Parts of His Academic Papers" on the front page of *The Wall Street Journal* on November 9, 1990. *Time* magazine presented a similar account ten days later. A large percentage of the reading public in the United States now knew about the scandal, and it was widely assumed, especially by conservatives, that the editors of the King papers were covering up the plagiarism.

The scandal occurred at a time when a revisionist portrait of King's human flaws was emerging from several books and academic articles. Several accounts, particularly Ralph Abernathy's autobiography, told of his philandering, claiming that King had spent time with three different women during the last night of his life. Scholars also discovered that Keith Miller, a professor of rhetoric at Arizona State University, had already published articles demonstrating that King had borrowed extensively from others. Some scholars tried to defend King's methods. Miller, for instance, argued that African American preachers looked upon concepts and words as resources to be shared for the benefit of the community, not private property to be selfishly guarded for individual advantage.

Other scholars, however, noted that King's academic writings showed that he understood the standard rules of documentation, and that at least one of his graduate courses covered the issue of academic honesty explicitly. In addition, King had been careful to copyright his speeches and published works, even bringing suit for the unauthorized use of his famous "I Have a Dream" speech in the case of *King v. Mister Maestro, Inc.* (1963).

Many scholars remain puzzled about King's plagiarism. He was an able writer, and the large original portions of his writings were competent, coherent, and clearly expressed. Carson suggested that King probably did not think he had done anything improper. As evidence, he showed that King did not destroy his papers but donated them to the Boston University archives. Perhaps King simply got in the habit of copying texts, and none of his teachers ever took the time and trouble to investigate. While writing his dissertation, he was working as pastor at the Dexter Avenue Baptist Church in Montgomery, Alabama. Perhaps his many duties caused him to be careless. It is also possible that he had instructed typists to paraphrase material and then neglected, or simply forgot, to check the final drafts.

It is particularly difficult to understand why King's thesis adviser, L. Harold DeWolf, was not more critical and vigilant in checking King's work. He was one of King's closest personal friends—a coworker who marched with him during the Civil Rights movement. In his funeral tribute to King in 1968, DeWolf declared that he had spent many hours reading King's papers. Because he also served as adviser for Boozer's thesis, much of which was appropriated by King, it appears strange that he failed to recognize the obvious similarities.

IMPACT

In 1991, authorities at Boston University appointed a panel of professors to investigate the allegations that King had plagiarized his doctoral thesis. The panel concluded that about one third of the thesis was clearly plagiarized. After considerable debate, nevertheless, university officials decided not to revoke the doctorate. While conceding that King had acted improperly, they announced that the thesis contained original ideas and made "an intelligent contribution to scholarship." Because he was no longer alive, moreover, the revoking of the degree would serve no valid purpose. Critics of the panel's decision argued that the officials were likely motivated by political correctness and the desire to maintain a connection between Boston University and King's great mystique.

Within a decade of the announcement, most had forgotten about the scandal. Those who did remember believed it to be a relatively minor flaw that did not significantly detract from the courage and high morality that King manifested in his long struggle on behalf of human rights and racial equality. Scholars commonly describe plagiarism as a form of academic dishonesty, even fraud. Students who are found guilty of such behavior are usually punished with a failing grade, sometimes even expulsion from a course or program. For academics who are familiar with the scandal, the use of the title of doctor as part of King's name will always sound inappropriate.

—*Thomas Tandy Lewis*

FURTHER READING

Carson, Clayborne, et al. "Martin Luther King, Jr., as Scholar: A Reexamination of His Theological Writings." *Journal of American History* 78 (June, 1991): 23-31. This journal issue contains several articles about King's work by David Levering Lewis, David Garrow, David Thelen, and John Highham.

_____, eds. *The Papers of Martin Luther King, Jr.* Vol. 2. Berkeley: University of California Press, 1994. This volume of King's collected papers includes an annotated edition of his doctoral thesis as well as other papers of the period.

Mawdsley, Ralph. *Academic Misconduct: Cheating and Plagiarism.* Topeka, Kans.: NOLPE, 1994. A useful guide for research into academic standards regarding plagiarism and the excessive borrowing of others' works.

Miller, Keith D. *Voice of Deliverance: The Language of Martin Luther King, Jr., and Its Sources.* Toronto, Ont.: Free Press, 1992. Denying that King was a plagiarist, Miller argues that he practiced "voice merging" and other longstanding rhetorical devices of African American ministers.

Pappas, Theodore. *Plagiarism and the Culture War: The Writings of Martin Luther King, Jr., and Other Prominent Americans.* Rev. ed. Tampa, Fla.: Hallberg, 1998. Thirteen early sources and essays about the scandal, including Johnson's *Sunday Telegraph* column of 1989 and Pappas's strong denunciation of King's plagiarism. Accuses King's apologists of ethical relativism and political correctness.

SEE ALSO: Jan. 28, 1972: Clifford Irving Admits Faking Howard Hughes Memoirs; 1978: *Roots* Author Alex Haley Is Sued for Plagiarism; Apr., 1998: Scottish Historian Is Charged with Plagiarism; June 18, 2001: Historian Joseph J. Ellis Is Accused of Lying; Jan. 4, 2002: Historian Stephen E. Ambrose Is Accused of Plagiarism; Jan. 18, 2002: Historian Doris Kearns Goodwin Is Accused of Plagiarism; Oct. 25, 2002: Historian Michael A. Bellesiles Resigns After Academic Fraud Accusations; July 24, 2007: University of Colorado Fires Professor for Plagiarism and Research Falsification.

1980's

December 15-25, 1989
HARASSMENT OF A CHRISTIAN MINISTER SPARKS THE ROMANIAN REVOLUTION

By late 1989, Romanian dictator Nicolae Ceauşescu was pressured by neighboring countries to change Romania's deplorable economic and social conditions. He responded by shifting the blame to the Communist Party and calling for improvements in living standards but not changes to the political system. A Protestant minister condemned the discrimination against Hungarians living in Romania, and authorities began harassing him and ordered his eviction from his church apartment. The minister was physically attacked, sparking protests that led to the downfall of Ceauşescu and his regime.

LOCALE: Timisoara, Romania

CATEGORIES: Atrocities and war crimes; social issues and reform; violence; politics; government; military

KEY FIGURES

Nicolae Ceauşescu (1918-1989), dictator of Romania, 1965-1989

Laszlo Tokes (b. 1952), pastor of the Hungarian Reformed Church in Timisoara, Romania

Vasile Milea (1927-1989), Romanian defense minister

Ion Iliescu (b. 1930), interim president, 1989-1990, and president of Romania, 1990-1992, 1992-1996, 2000-2004

SUMMARY OF EVENT

In December, 1989, Romanian leader Nicolae Ceauşescu's actions against Protestant minister Laszlo Tokes led to the dictator's own downfall and to the end of his repressive communist regime. Speaking out from his pulpit in Timisoara, Tokes had long criticized the Romanian government for its discriminatory practices, especially against his fellow Hungarians living in Romania. Ceauşescu's government, to silence the pastor, harassed him and ordered his eviction from his church apartment. On

November 2, armed attackers (some claim from the Romanian Securitate, or security police), had beat him in his home. Tokes's congregation and others from Timisoara assembled around his home and church for a vigil to protest his treatment and prevent his arrest, set for December 15. What followed was mass resistance, heretofore unheard of in Romania, which caught the imagination of Romanians in other towns, and protests began all over the country.

Romanian Protestant minister Laszlo Tokes speaks to his congregation in January, 1990, after being freed from house arrest. (Hulton Archive/Getty Images)

Romania, a small Central European country surrounded by Hungary, Serbia, Bulgaria, and the Black Sea, was ruled beginning in 1965 by Ceauşescu, the leader of the country's Communist Party. In his zeal to improve Romania's economy, Ceauşescu borrowed billions of dollars from Western countries to finance economic development programs. However, his programs backfired, and he started austerity programs to correct the situation. By the 1980's, Romania was exporting so much of its agricultural and industrial production that its own people were left without enough food and other basic resources. Ceauşescu instituted rationing and other programs, determined not to let the country's indebtedness reduce Romania to the condition of needing to rely on the largess of the West and the Soviet Union.

The shortages of food, fuel, and other basic necessities, along with the forced relocation of many rural residents, took their toll on the people. Many began to speak out against the government's insensitivity to their increasingly low standard of living and to inequitable treatment. The ruling class lived well, even luxuriously and decadently, while the general population lived in conditions similar to those during wartime, facing extreme rationing and shortages. Some reports claim the government's policies led to the death of fifteen thousand Romanians each year from starvation, cold, and various shortages of medical care and other necessities.

Minister Tokes, a young, handsome, ethnic Hungarian in Timisoara, a town in the Romanian region of Transylvania, preached a message about fairness and equality that appealed to many. His congregation started small but soon grew to more than four thousand members from all walks of life—the elderly, middle-age adults, and university students—all eager to hear his message of fairness for those not part of the ruling elite. His popularity soon caught the attention of the communist government's authorities.

Ceauşescu lived by the Marxist dictum that religion "is the opiate of the masses," and that Christians in general, and Tokes in particular, were not to be tolerated in a communist society. The dictator's initial reaction to Tokes's popularity was to have his

Romanian dictator Nicolae Ceauşescu around 1965, the year he took power in Romania. (Library of Congress)

security police harass and threaten the members of his congregation. When none of those actions deterred either Tokes or his congregants, Ceauşescu arranged to have Tokes suspended from his ministry and then denied him ration books that were needed to obtain food for himself and his family. Still resisting the efforts to be scared away from his mission, Tokes was attacked by masked men, who were rumored to be security police, and beaten and stabbed.

The townspeople of Timisoara began their protests after hearing of the brutal attack on Tokes. Crowds of unarmed men and women gathered about Tokes's church apartment on December 15, 1989, to prevent the authorities from taking the minister from his home. At this time Ceauşescu was out of the country on a state visit to Iran, but his security police, under the direction of his wife, Elena, tried to disperse the protesters, who quickly formed massive demonstrations. The police moved against the protesters with tanks and helicopter gun ships. A

743

state of emergency was declared after the Timisoara protests spread to several other Romanian cities: The population was fed up with life under Ceauşescu.

By December 22, with Romania in the middle of widespread revolt, Ceauşescu, who was back in the country, ordered his army to break up the protests and to fire on the protesters, most of whom were unarmed, if necessary. Defense Minister Vasile Milea, however, refused to order his soldiers to shoot civilians. Milea soon was found dead. His official cause of death was listed as a suicide. Another version of how he died claims that Milea had tried to incapacitate himself to relieve himself of having to follow orders with which he disagreed, and that he had botched the attempt and died accidentally. Most Romanians, though, believe that a security police officer had murdered him in retaliation for his refusal to lead the army against the protesters.

Fighting continued throughout the country, as demonstrators organized themselves into the Frontul Salvarii Nationale, or the National Salvation Front (NSF). Tokes was a part of the organization, as was the army chief of staff, Stefan Gusa. The army threw its support behind the protesters.

The Securitate remained loyal to Ceauşescu, and it used force and terrorism to try to quell the increasingly widespread insurrection. However, on December 25, the protesters and the army subdued the Securitate and took control of the government. The Ceauşescus tried to flee but were captured. They were tried in a secret trial on Christmas Day and summarily executed by a firing squad for crimes against the state and for genocide, the illegal gathering of wealth, and "undermining" the Romanian economy.

IMPACT

The NSF took power immediately and abolished the one-party system of the previous decades. However, the NSF also proclaimed that though Ceauşescu and the Communist Party brought disaster to the country, communism in and of itself was not to be abandoned. Some of the Communist Party members who held power during the Ceauşescu regime kept their leadership positions after his fall. The in-

terim president, Ion Iliescu, who had been mentored by Ceauşescu, became disaffected with the way his mentor was ruling the country, so Ceauşescu stripped him of all his party positions. During the elections of 1990, the NSF won a large majority in the legislature. Iliescu was reelected to the presidency in 1992.

Tokes eventually became a bishop of the Hungarian-speaking Reformed Church district of Oradea in Transylvania. In 2007, he was speaking out on issues relating to religion and ecumenical cooperation.

Though the economy lagged and civil unrest continued because of food shortages and price increases, Romania slowly pulled itself out of the depths of repression. By 2007, the constitution had been changed to protect the rights of ethnic minorities, and the country had joined the North Atlantic Treaty Organization and the European Union. Also, after having been deprived of the right by Ceauşescu beginning during the 1960's, Romanians could once again celebrate Christmas.

—*Jane L. Ball*

FURTHER READING

Campeanu, Pavel. *Ceauşescu: From the End to the Beginning*. New York: Columbia University Press, 2003. A prison cellmate and fellow communist, Campeanu bases his account of Ceauşescu's rise to power on previously unavailable documents and personal recollections.

Deletant, Dennis. *Ceauşescu and the Securitate: Coercion and Dissent in Romania, 1965-1989*. Armonk, N.Y.: M. E. Sharpe, 1996. An authoritative account of the Ceauşescu years, providing a history of the oppressors and the oppressed. It is the first major work to use the archives of the Romanian secret police.

Pacepa, Ion Mihai. *Red Horizons: The True Story of Nicolae and Elena Ceauşescu's Crimes, Lifestyle, and Corruption*. Washington, D.C.: Regnery Gateway, 1990. Pacepa was a high-ranking officer who defected from Romania. A first-person exposé of the Ceauşescu regime.

Siani-Davis, Peter. *The Romanian Revolution of December, 1989*. Ithaca, N.Y.: Cornell University Press, 2005. The causes of the revolution and way Ceaușescu was overthrown are discussed in a straightforward, journalistic style. A detailed account of how various leaders and ordinary people became involved in the chaos.

SEE ALSO: Oct. 25, 1924: Forged Communist Letter Brings Down British Government; Feb. 23, 1963: Play Accuses Pope Pius XII of Complicity in the Holocaust; Jan., 1997: Pyramid Investment Schemes Cause Albanian Government to Fall.

December 18, 1989
PRINCE CHARLES'S INTIMATE PHONE CONVERSATION WITH CAMILLA PARKER BOWLES IS TAPED

In 1993, an Australian magazine published a transcript of a private phone conversation in December, 1989, between lovers Prince Charles and Camilla Parker Bowles, leading to an international scandal. The scandal also led to the divorces of both parties and, for a time, threatened the stability of the House of Windsor. Also, the revelation of the tapes heightened fears that the British security service was monitoring the royal family—primarily Princess Diana— through bugging and wiretapping.

ALSO KNOWN AS: Camillagate
LOCALES: Chester and Wiltshire, England
CATEGORIES: Communications and media; politics; public morals; royalty; sex

KEY FIGURES

Charles, Prince of Wales (b. 1948), eldest son of Queen Elizabeth II and heir to the British throne
Camilla Parker Bowles (b. 1947), mistress and later wife of Prince Charles
Diana, Princess of Wales (1961-1997), first wife of Prince Charles
Andrew Parker Bowles (b. 1939), first husband of Camilla Parker Bowles

SUMMARY OF EVENT

Late in the evening of December 18, 1989, Prince Charles had a mobile-phone conversation with Camilla Parker Bowles, his friend of many years. The two had a long history together. Bowles often boasted that her great-grandmother had been the favorite mistress of King Edward VII, Charles's own ancestor. Charles had met Bowles when he was a young man. He was immediately attracted to her. While he was at sea with the Royal Navy, Bowles had married Andrew Parker Bowles. Eventually, they had two children.

Several years later, at the age of thirty-one and at the urging of his family, Charles was married as well. His bride, Diana Spencer, who had been approved by Bowles, had just turned twenty years old. Princess Diana would give birth to two sons, assuring the continuation of the House of Windsor. Later, according to Charles's report, after both their marriages had cooled, he and Bowles became lovers. Older friends of the prince observed that a mature Bowles resembled the most beloved nanny of his childhood. Whatever their deeper needs, the two were now committed lovers, meeting at the homes of friends and indulging themselves in long, ardent telephone conversations. To their misfortune, one was overheard and would eventually be reported to the entire world.

To the parties involved, the conversation was intimate and loving; to a prurient international audience, which later read transcripts of the call, the conversation was ludicrous and salacious. Charles and Bowles expressed their desire to be together and their feelings that Sunday nights were unbearable without each other. Yearning for another meeting before the family holiday festivities intervened, they arranged an assignation. An ambulance strike was keeping Bowles's husband away on official du-

1980's

745

ties, and the lovers expressed their hope that the strike would continue indefinitely. Surprisingly, to a world that regards princes as privileged, Charles revealed feelings of inferiority, speaking of his bad luck and his low estimate of himself. Bowles reassured him, confessing that she would willingly endure the world's "indignities, tortures, and calumnies" for him and asking for a copy of a speech he was preparing. He replied to her own expressions of inadequacy that her greatest achievement was her ability to love him. He told Bowles of his desire to be "all over you, and up and down you, and in and out." Near the end of their conversation they played with the word "tit," referring both to her anatomy and a button on the telephone.

Destined to be ruler of a land that has produced great bards, Charles attempted his own poetic conceits. Lovelorn English poets of the past have expressed the desire to be a glove upon their lady's hand, the falcon that lights upon her shoulder, or even a flea within her garments. However, Charles outdid them all, telling Bowles that he would like to live inside her trousers, but that it would be his luck to be reincarnated as a tampon to be flushed down her lavatory. They then agreed that to come back as an entire box of tampons would be a better fate for him.

The prince's slightly hesitant but well-enunciated speech was known throughout England, and the more voluptuous low register of Bowles's voice also was easily identified by a listening eavesdropper. Considerable mystery still surrounds the origin of the tape, which would later become a major embarrassment to the British monarchy. Amateur scanners during the decade of the 1980's found it relatively easy to listen in on personal conversations, and when the identity of these special parties became clear, one unseen listener realized his or her rare fortune. The tapes were later carefully analyzed by the journals that would publish the transcripts, and their authenticity was never denied even by the principals themselves.

The scandal, however, did not break until January 13, 1993, when *New Idea*, an Australian women's magazine, revealed the existence of the tapes. The scoop was soon picked up by avid media around the world, to the extreme embarrassment of

the lovers, their families, and the entire British government. Meanwhile, the general public savored the melodrama. Jokers started referring to the heir to the British throne as "the royal tampon," and London shop girls began asking their pharmacists for a "box of Prince Charlies."

Bowles already was an object of disdain to the millions of admirers of Princess Diana, who had earlier revealed her husband's adulterous relationship to journalists. Diana's designation of Bowles as "the Rottweiler" was repeated in the press, along with bewilderment that the prince would reject his beautiful wife, a beloved woman the world over, in favor of one they described as "plain and middle aged." Even Charles's father, Prince Phillip, is said to have told Diana that nobody in his right mind would prefer Bowles to her.

Bowles knew that loyalty to the prince had its price. She already had been deluged with hate mail, forced to change her telephone numbers, and been pelted with bread rolls when she attempted to do her grocery shopping. With the publication of the telephone conversation, matters came to a head. Andrew Parker Bowles, a tolerant husband who had his own long-time mistress, soon concluded it was time for a divorce. Princess Diana, whose personal life by this time was not above reproach and who had to endure the embarrassing revelation of some of her own telephone conversations with a lover, realized that her marriage was effectively over as well.

IMPACT

Celebrity journalism flourished in the last decades of the twentieth century. Accounts of the deeds and misdeeds of popular entertainers, royalty, and even U.S. presidents sold magazines and newspapers. Respect for privacy, previously enjoyed by royalty, disappeared. While Queen Elizabeth II had always behaved with decorum and dignity, the escapades of her children provided a national melodrama for the entire world. Servants were paid for inside stories, and royal vacations were plagued by paparazzi. Though divorce had been verboten in the established Church of England since the traumatic times of King Henry VIII, it was now deemed preferable to the continuing scandal.

After their divorces, Bowles and Charles started living openly at Highgrove House, one of Charles's favorite residences. Gradually the two started appearing together at social and charitable events, preparing the British people for eventual acceptance of their relationship. After the death of Queen Elizabeth, the Queen Mother, Clarence House became the prince's choice residence in London, and Bowles made herself at home there. Though she had never shown much interest in fashion, being more comfortable in a riding habit, she acquired a new polish and an expensive wardrobe of designer dresses.

The untimely death of Princess Diana in 1997 in a Paris car crash, one year after her divorce was final, sparked nationwide, indeed international, mourning. During this time, Bowles stayed out of public view. Charles was now free to remarry in the Church of England, though not to Bowles, who earlier had been divorced. This placed the prince, destined to be the head of the church upon assuming the throne, in an awkward position. With the help of his family and church dignitaries, a compromise was finally reached. On April 9, 2005, the couple were legally married in the town hall at Windsor, followed by a lavish blessing in Windsor Chapel conducted by the archbishop of Canterbury before families and friends. For romantics not still enthralled by the glamorous Princess Diana, this was a satisfying resolution for a man and woman who had been devoted to each other for thirty years, though separated in youth by status and circumstance.

Now designated the duchess of Cornwall, Bowles continued to support her husband in state visits and other royal engagements. She received his future subjects graciously, though never upstaging him as Diana had frequently done. It seemed only a matter of time before Bowles would be fully accepted as Charles's "proper" spouse and eventually, perhaps when they were both advanced in years, as queen of England on a throne by his side.

—*Allene Phy-Olsen*

FURTHER READING

Brown, Tina. *The Diana Chronicles*. New York: Doubleday, 2007. Even while focusing on Princess Diana, Brown provides unique information about the Parker Bowles family and the love triangle in Prince Charles's first marriage.

Graham, Caroline. *Camilla and Charles: The Love Story*. London: John Blake, 2006. A favorable portrait of Bowles, by her leading biographer. A gossipy read that seems to be well supported by facts.

Paxman, Jeremy. *On Royalty: A Very Polite Inquiry into Some Strangely Related Families*. New York: PublicAffairs, 2006. A serious exploration of the institution of royalty, with some insightful attention to the late twentieth century problems plaguing the House of Windsor.

Wilson, Christopher. *Charles, Camilla, and the Legacy of Diana*. New York: Citadel Press, 2002. Explores the coupling of Charles and Bowles through almost thirty years and the relationship's impact on the tragedy of Princess Diana's life and untimely death.

1980's

SEE ALSO: Dec. 10, 1936: King Edward VIII Abdicates to Marry an American Divorcée; Mar. 2-Sept. 25, 1963: John Profumo Affair Rocks British Government; Oct. 14, 1983: British Cabinet Secretary Parkinson Resigns After His Secretary Becomes Pregnant; July 25, 1987: Novelist-Politician Jeffrey Archer Wins Libel Trial Against the *Daily Star*; Aug. 23, 1992: Princess Diana's Phone Conversation with Her Lover Is Made Public; Sept. 24, 1992: British Cabinet Member David Mellor Resigns over Romantic Affair; Jan. 5, 1994: British Cabinet Member Resigns After Fathering a Child Out of Wedlock; Aug. 31, 1997: Princess Diana Dies in a Car Crash; Sept. 28, 2002: British Politician Reveals Her Affair with Prime Minister John Major; Jan. 21, 2006: British Politician Resigns After Gay-Sex Orgy; Apr. 26, 2006: Britain's Deputy Prime Minister Admits Affair with Secretary.

January 18, 1990

WASHINGTON, D.C., MAYOR MARION BARRY IS ARRESTED FOR DRUG USE

Marion Barry was a controversial Washington, D.C., mayor. During his first term, he was arrested in an FBI sting operation after he was captured on a surveillance camera smoking crack cocaine with a former girlfriend. After serving a six-month jail term, Barry was reelected to political office. The videotape of Barry smoking crack and yelling obscenities caused a sensation when it was repeatedly broadcast on television.

LOCALE: Washington, D.C.
CATEGORIES: Law and the courts; corruption; drugs; government; politics; public morals

KEY FIGURES
Marion Barry (b. 1936), mayor of Washington, D.C., 1979-1991, 1995-1999
Rasheeda Moore (fl. 1990's), Barry's former girlfriend
Wanda King (fl. 1990's), FBI special agent

SUMMARY OF EVENT

Marion Barry, the mayor of Washington, D.C., had been suspected of possessing and using drugs since the early 1980's. Previous efforts by law enforcement to indict him had failed, but his luck eventually ran out. On January 18, 1990, the mayor was caught smoking crack cocaine with former girlfriend Rasheeda Moore in a sting operation conducted by the Federal Bureau of Investigation (FBI). He was arrested, convicted of possession and use of narcotics, and sentenced to six months in federal prison. Upon his release from prison, he was elected to a second term as mayor in 1994.

On the day of the arrest, Moore had telephoned Barry's office several times between 6:00 and 6:25 P.M. His secretary picked up the phone on Moore's last attempt to reach him and informed her that the mayor had already left the office but had taken Moore's phone number with him. Soon after Moore's final call, Barry telephoned Moore, who

invited him to her room at the Vista International Hotel. She told Barry that she was in town visiting from Los Angeles with a friend and that they wanted to see him. That "friend" was FBI special agent Wanda King, undercover for this assignment as Wanda Moore.

Barry agreed to stop by the hotel after taking care of some city business (a drawing for a housing lottery program). He insisted on meeting Moore in the hotel lobby instead of in her room. This change of plans required quick thinking on the part of the agents running the sting operation. Three video cameras and microphones had been placed in room 727, where Moore was waiting for Barry. For the sting to work, Barry had to be coaxed to the room. Moore was instructed to ask Barry once again to meet her in her room and to tell him that she had ordered room service. Barry called Moore after he was finished with his mayoral duties. Although Barry first protested her request to meet in her room, he finally agreed to do so.

At 7:35, Barry entered room 727, greeted Moore's friend Wanda (Agent King) with a handshake, and then hugged Moore. Wanda left the room so that the former lovers could reconnect. Barry and Moore drank cognac, watched television, and talked. Barry then tried to talk Moore into having sex, and he groped her several times. She refused his advances and steered the conversation to drug use. They both agreed that they wanted some cocaine, but neither had the drug on hand. The banter about sex and drugs continued for some time, until Wanda telephoned to let them know she was returning to the room. Upon her return she pulled Moore into the bathroom, telling her she had drugs for them to buy. Barry offered to buy the drugs for $100 and Moore returned to the bathroom with the money, "bought" the cocaine, and returned to the bedroom with two $30 packets of crack cocaine. Barry told Moore that he no longer smoked crack and asked if Wanda had some powder cocaine.

Moore went back into the bathroom to discuss the situation with Wanda.

Believing the operation was now a failure, Wanda left the room, leaving Moore and Barry. Moore suggested to Barry that they leave the hotel. She, too, thought the setup had failed. Barry then asked what drugs Moore had purchased. When she indicated that she did not buy anything, Barry told her to "go get some." Moore found Wanda in the hallway and asked her if she could get some powder cocaine. Wanda said that she could, but that it would take about an hour to find some.

After Wanda left, Barry asked Moore for a crack pipe. Even though he had used crack before, he appeared to fumble with the pipe. He asked Moore to get it ready and then insisted she take the first hit, possibly to try to determine if she was setting him up. Moore refused, saying that crack made her nervous and hyperactive and that she was going to wait for the powder cocaine. In the meantime, Barry prepared the pipe and took two successive hits. He then drank the rest of his cognac and suggested they go downstairs to the lobby. In an attempt to stall their departure, Moore began cleaning up the evidence. Barry called his bodyguards, who had been notified (and quieted) by the FBI of the sting operation, to alert them that he was departing for the lobby. At that point, agents and officers from the FBI and Metropolitan Police Department of Washington, D.C., entered room 727 from an adjacent room and arrested Barry for possession and use of illegal drugs. Barry insisted that he did not have any drugs on his person and that he had not been using drugs. He began to verbalize his dismay about his decision to visit Moore in her hotel room, saying that he had been set up. "I'll be goddamn. Bitch set me up" is an oft-quoted line, attributed to Barry, from the sting operation transcript.

Barry was escorted from the hotel room discretely by service elevator, taken to FBI headquarters, fingerprinted, and photographed. As a courtesy, Mayor Barry was booked there instead of the central booking office in Washington, D.C. He also provided a urine sample (which later tested positive for marijuana, cocaine, and alcohol). Barry resigned as mayor and served six months in federal prison.

IMPACT

Barry's arrest and conviction were not as scandalous as his reelection to city office after serving time in prison. The sting operation leading to Barry's arrest interrupted but did not end his political career. He was elected to the Washington, D.C., city council in 1992 and elected to a second term as mayor in 1994. His success, after such public display of his shortcomings, may be due in part to where he served as mayor and councilman. Most residents of Washington, D.C. are African Americans. Barry, who is also African American, was well liked by those he represented.

As a councilman, Barry represented ward 8, an area that comprises mostly lower-income residents and is riddled with crime and violence. The residents of ward 8 perhaps felt connected to him because they believed he shared their struggles as racial minorities. Barry was well-educated (he had a

Washington, D.C., mayor Marion Barry in 1996. (AP/ Wide World Photos)

master's degree in organic chemistry from Fisk University), but he lived in the jurisdiction he represented, a working-class area whose residents were not well-educated. These factors gave him immense credibility and ultimately led to his ability to turn a scandalous situation, a career-ending situation in most cases, into a positive to further his political career.

—*Eileen M. Ahlin*

FURTHER READING

Agronsky, Jonathan I. Z. *Marion Barry: The Politics of Race*. Latham, N.Y.: British American, 1991. An overview of Marion Barry's life in the context of racial politics. Also examines the FBI sting and the minimal public scandal.

Barras, Jonetta Rose. *The Last of the Black Emperors: The Hollow Comeback of Marion Barry in the New Age of Black Leaders*. Baltimore: Bancroft Press, 1998. Journalist Barras examines Marion Barry's political comeback and his adoration by constituents and other supporters, and attempts to answer questions about his paradoxical life.

Gillette, Howard, Jr. "Protest of Power in Washington, D.C.: The Troubled Legacy of Marion Barry." In *African-American Mayors: Race, Politics, and the American City*, edited by David R. Colburn and Jeffrey S. Adler. Chicago: University of Illinois Press, 2001. Examines Marion Barry's political career. Provides an overview of various scandals occurring during his terms in office.

Kellerman, Barbara. *Bad Leadership: What It Is, How It Happens, Why It Matters*. Boston: Harvard Business School Press, 2004. A study of the scandals involving several leaders from throughout the world. Considers Marion Barry "intemperate" and lacking in self-control.

SEE ALSO: Dec., 1904: Boston Alderman Is Reelected While in Jail for Fraud; June 13, 1907: San Francisco Mayor Schmitz Is Found Guilty of Extortion; Apr. 15, 1981: Janet Cooke Admits Fabricating Her Pulitzer Prize-Winning Feature; Dec. 6, 2005: Spokane, Washington, Mayor Recalled in Gay-Sex Scandal.

March, 1990
MENENDEZ BROTHERS ARE ARRESTED FOR MURDERING THEIR PARENTS

Erik and Lyle Menendez murdered their parents with the blasts of two shotguns. The media went into a frenzy, first believing the murders were part of a mob hit, but after the brothers used battered child syndrome as their defense, the media could not be stopped in its incessant coverage. The transformation of a murder trial into media spectacle and entertainment raised questions about the impact of increasing media coverage on the justice system in the United States. The brothers were finally convicted in a second trial, but this time without cameras inside the courtroom.

LOCALE: Van Nuys, California

CATEGORIES: Communications and media; publishing and journalism; law and the courts; murder and suicide; public morals

KEY FIGURES

Lyle Menendez (b. 1968), son of Jose and Kitty Menendez

Erik Menendez (b. 1971), son of Jose and Kitty Menendez

Jose Menendez (1944-1989), father of Erik and Lyle Menendez

Kitty Menendez (Mary Louise Anderson; 1941-1989), mother of Erik and Lyle Menendez

SUMMARY OF EVENT

On the evening of August 20, 1989, Kitty and Jose Menendez were relaxing in their Beverly Hills home. Kitty was reviewing her son Erik's application to the University of California, Los Angeles, and Jose was having a snack while watching television. Later in the evening, Erik, age eighteen, and his brother Lyle, age twenty-one, each carrying a shotgun, entered the room where both parents were sitting and shot them to death. Before they called police to report the murders, the brothers concocted an elaborate cover-up. They told police that they had been out for the evening and found their parents' bodies when they got home.

Officials might never have discovered the truth if Lyle Menendez had not confessed the killings to his therapist, Jerome Oziel, in October, 1989. Oziel said that the brothers threatened to kill him and his family if he ever told of the confession. Out of fear, he taped their sessions. California law permits therapists to report to officials confidential material obtained from patients if that patient threatens violence against him- or herself or another person. Oziel felt justified in

Lyle Menendez, left, and brother Erik Menendez in a Santa Monica, California, court on August 6, 1990. (AP/Wide World Photos)

reporting the confession and providing the tapes to law enforcement. In March of 1990, the brothers were arrested and charged with the murders of their parents. Lyle was arrested close to his home on March 8 and Erik, arriving from a trip to Israel, was arrested at Los Angeles International Airport on March 11. They were indicted on December 8, 1992.

A Cuban refugee, Jose Menendez arrived in the United States at the age of sixteen and stayed with friends of his family until he married Kitty at the age of nineteen. After earning a degree in accounting from Queens College in Flushing, New York, he worked as an accountant in Manhattan and as a controller for a shipping company in Chicago before taking a position with Live Entertainment in Cali-

fornia. He was a driven person, a hard worker who expected excellence from himself and his family. The police, believing his murder could have been a mob hit, did not immediately consider the brothers as suspects, even though the two had gone on a spending spree after the death of their parents and did not exhibit normal signs of mourning.

Several circumstances, however, soon pointed to the brothers as suspects: Lyle and Erik were the sole beneficiaries of the family's fourteen-million-dollar estate and had been using the money after the deaths of their mother and father to buy expensive items. Also, Erik had written a screenplay with a plot that was similar to the murders, and a shotgun shell was found in a pocket of a jacket owned by Lyle. The brothers remained in jail for almost three years before their trial began, while the courts de-

751

bated, among other things, the admissibility of the testimony of the brothers' therapist and the therapist's taped sessions. The media covered every possible angle of the case to keep the trial in the public view, interviewing anyone even remotely involved with the Menendez family.

The trial itself was unusual. To save money for the state, the brothers were tried together but each had his own jury. Each time testimony or evidence was presented regarding one brother only, the jury of the brother not under discussion had to leave the courtroom. At trial, the Menendez brothers did not deny murdering their parents, but they alleged they shot them because they feared for their lives. The basis for their defense was battered child syndrome. Erik and Lyle told horror stories of emotional and sexual abuse that included forced oral sex, sodomy with a toothbrush, and even rape by both parents. Their parents were overly demanding, impossible to please, and forceful, even to the point that Lyle was ordered to wear a wig to hide his appearing baldness. The brothers said that they thought their parents had planned to kill them on the day before the murders, when the family had gone shark fishing.

IMPACT

The Menendez brothers' murder trials were two in a long line of high-profile cases that saw an increase in sensational media coverage, especially coverage using video cameras. What became scandalous in this case were not the murders but the behavior of the media and those working to transform the trials into entertainment.

The press obsessively followed the case from beginning to end, making it one of the most media-saturated trials in American history. Court TV, a new cable network series, covered the trial live. Attorneys and witnesses made dramatic statements outside the courtroom, knowing they would appear on national television. News reports and tabloid stories ranged from slightly factual to outright fantastical. Because of the widespread coverage, the court had to screen more than eleven hundred prospective jurors before the case opened. Most of the prospective jurors had heard at least something

about the murders, and some even admitted they had formed an opinion about the guilt or innocence of the brothers.

The scandalous behavior of the media included physical disagreements over the twelve seats in the courtroom allotted for the press. Fights broke out over who would be sitting in those seats. Outside the courtroom the media gathered in a circus-like atmosphere, focusing on everyone even remotely associated with the proceedings. Even vendors pitched their products outside the court building. Agents made book deals and spoke about possible films. As the trial progressed, media pundits discussed the case in the hope of making their own book deals.

The chaos continued through the trial, which ended with hung juries and a declared mistrial. The brothers were tried again beginning in October, 1995, but this time, with one jury and in a courtroom without cameras; they were found guilty of first-degree murder on March 20, 1996. Each was sentenced to two consecutive life terms without parole. Partly because of the Menendez case, the courts began to increasingly enforce a ban on cameras and limit the number of reporters authorized to cover cases from the courtroom.

—Elizabeth Gaydou-Miller

FURTHER READING

Clehane, Diane, and Nancy Grace. *Objection! How High-Priced Defense Attorneys, Celebrity Defendants, and a 24/7 Media Have Hijacked Our Criminal Justice System*. New York: Hyperion Books, 2005. Examines the effect of media sensationalism and instant celebrity—of defendants, attorneys, and others—on the American justice system.

Fox, Richard L., Robert W. van Sickel, and Thomas L. Steiger. *Tabloid Justice: Criminal Justice in an Age of Media Frenzy*. 2d ed. Boulder, Colo.: Lynne Rienner, 2007. Compares public opinion with several high-profile trials. Contains tables outlining changes in media coverage over time. Includes results of an extensive survey on media practices.

Runyon, William. "Bad Press." *Los Angeles Maga-*

zine, November, 1993. The author discusses the offensive and scandalous behavior of the media covering the Menendez brothers trials.

Scott, Gini Graham. "When Rich Kids Kill." In *Homicide by the Rich and Famous: A Century of Prominent Killers*. Westport, Conn.: Praeger, 2005. A look at acts of murder by the children of the rich and famous. Rich kids are an understudied demographic, especially in crime literature.

Thornton, Hazel. *Hung Jury. The Diary of a Menendez Juror*. Philadelphia: Temple University Press, 1995. A juror from the first trial discusses the case. Includes a time line. A unique look at the case from a person not affiliated with the media.

SEE ALSO: Mar. 21, 1976: Actor Claudine Longet Kills Ski Champion Vladimir Sabich; July 23, 1978: Utah Millionaire Is Murdered by His Grandson; Mar. 10, 1980: Scarsdale Diet Doctor Is Killed by His Lover; Dec. 22, 1984: Subway Vigilante Bernhard Goetz Shoots Four Black Youths; May 19, 1992: Amy Fisher Shoots Mary Jo Buttafuoco; June 12, 1994: Double Murder Leads to Sensational O. J. Simpson Trial; Aug. 16, 1996: Belgian Media Reveal How Police Bungled Serial Murder Case; Dec., 2000: Sexual Abuse of Children in France Leads to the Outreau Affair; Apr. 30, 2001: Washington Intern Chandra Levy Disappears.

August 27, 1990
GUINNESS FOUR ARE FOUND GUILTY OF SHARE-TRADING FRAUD

In 1990, the chief executive officer of Guinness and three other officials in the British brewery company were found guilty of accounting fraud and theft for inflating the price of company shares as part of a strategy to defeat a hostile takeover bid of Distillers Co., which Guinness wanted to obtain itself. The so-called Guinness Four supplied millions of pounds to buy Guinness stock, thus driving up the price of company shares and making Guinness appear as a more attractive bidder for Distillers.

LOCALE: London, England

CATEGORIES: Law and the courts; corruption; banking and finance; business, trade and commerce

KEY FIGURES

Ernest Saunders (b. 1935), British businessman and chief executive officer of Guinness

Jack Lyons (1916-2008), British financier, department-store owner, and philanthropist

Gerald Ronson (b. 1939), British businessman and real-estate developer

Anthony Parnes (fl. 1980's), British millionaire stock broker

Ivan Boesky (b. 1937), American stock trader

SUMMARY OF EVENT

The Guinness Four trading-fraud scheme was scandalous on two counts. One, three wealthy businessmen conspired with the chief executive officer of Guinness brewery to buy a large number of shares of Guinness stock and thus boost the value of all company stock. Two, government authorities gathered and presented evidence at the trial of the four men in a manner that was later condemned by a higher court. The authorities had made several legal and procedural mistakes even before bringing the four to trial.

The Guinness-Distillers takeover story broke in 1986 during the insider-trading trial of American stock trader Ivan Boesky in an unrelated case. Many in London financial circles considered the behavior to be noncriminal; even more believed it was not even scandalous. Share-price manipulation was a common practice in the mid-1980's in both London and Wall Street financial circles.

1990's

753

The scheme involved the hostile takeover bid of Distillers Co., of Edinburgh, Scotland, a company that Guinness had plans to acquire itself. To ensure that Guinness would be the company that acquired Distillers, Chief Executive Officer Ernest Saunders contacted Jack Lyons, Gerald Ronson, and Anthony Parnes, all self-made wealthy businessmen, and asked for their help. The four coconspirators supplied millions of pounds to buy Guinness stock, thus driving up the share price. This made Guinness appear as a more attractive bidder for Distillers. No evidence exists, however, to show that Saunders or the other three sought to benefit immediately by manipulating the share price of Guinness stock, but all four stood to make considerable profits at a later date if the multibillion-pound takeover came through. Guinness did manage to acquire Distillers, renamed United Distillers in 1987.

The Guinness Four, as they came to be called, included millionaire stock broker Parnes, who began his career in finance as an office boy. Lyons, a financier, department-store owner, and philanthropist, left school at the age of sixteen to work in his father's garment factory. Saunders's parents fled from the Nazis in Austria when Saunders was a baby and had to start life over again in England. Ronson, a real-estate developer, quit school at the age of fifteen to begin earning his own money. By dint of hard work, street smarts, and well-considered risk taking, the four independently acquired considerable personal wealth and social standing, both of which would increase if they could pull off the Guinness takeover of Distillers on their own terms.

Little, if any, evidence exists to suggest that Saunders and colleagues did anything out of the ordinary in the takeover. In the mid-1980's, stock ownership was still largely confined to institutions and wealthier individuals. The lifestyles of these individuals as well as their investment decisions were unfamiliar to ordinary people, many of whom envied the rich their successes and delighted more in their mistakes and downfalls.

Stock trading began to be computerized as well in the 1980's, but it was still quite possible to move around large amounts of money without leaving a trail of evidence or arousing suspicion. In the 1980's era of Reaganomics, under U.S. president Ronald Reagan and British prime minister Margaret Thatcher, making lots of money was celebrated, and no one closely examined the moneymaking process. Saunders, however, used company funds without the knowledge or permission of the Guinness board of directors, which caught the attention of company officials. It should be noted, though, that Guinness directors did not initiate the investigation into the actions of Saunders and his colleagues. Nor did the board call for charges to be brought against the four men.

Bringing the stock-trading scandal to the international stage, Saunders also had provided Boesky with millions of dollars to manipulate Guinness stock prices on the New York Stock Exchange. Boesky was the undisputed "king of greed" on Wall Street during the 1980's. He was the leader in insider trading, that is, using private information to make very lucrative, illegal investments. Like the Guinness Four, Boesky was not the only person on Wall Street using insider information for personal or client profit. He was, however, much more flamboyant and his trades much larger and more public than other traders. His obvious delight in flaunting stock-trading procedures attracted the attention of U.S. Securities and Exchange Commission (SEC) investigators.

The SEC began investigating Boesky on charges of stock fraud. Boesky told the investigators that Saunders had been a business associate. This information was turned over to inspectors with the British Department of Trade and Industry (DTI), who opened an informal investigation into Saunders's activities. The Guinness Four cooperated with the DTI investigation.

On August 27, 1990, the Guinness Four were found guilty of false accounting and theft (and, for Saunders, conspiracy), fined millions of pounds, and sentenced to prison for up to four years. The defendants did not dispute their actions, but they argued that what they did was business as usual in the world of hostile takeovers. Many in financial circles agreed. The Guinness Four argued that takeovers often involved share-price manipulation, but to DTI investigators, this "business-as-usual" argument was irrelevant.

Shortly after the Guinness Four were convicted, suggestions began to surface in the media that the authorities investigated and prosecuted the four because Boesky, Saunders, and Lyons were Jewish and were first-generation wealthy businessmen. The Guinness Four immediately appealed their respective convictions and prison sentences. Parnes's sentence was reduced to twenty-one months. Lyons was fined four million pounds in lieu of serving any prison time due to ill health. Ronson was fined five million pounds, but his sentence was reduced to six months. Saunders, the person in charge of the share-price manipulation, was originally sentenced to five years in prison, but his term was later reduced to thirty months and then to ten months. His attorney argued that Saunders suffered from dementia associated with Alzheimer's disease. Saunders later claimed to have recovered from the disease, which, if true, would have been a modern medical miracle.

British prime minister John Major also seemed to side with the Guinness Four. Only reluctantly did he strip Lyons of his knighthood, while assuring him that his services to the United Kingdom, including his many charitable activities, were still deeply appreciated. Many of those charitable organizations continued to proudly display Lyons's name as a major benefactor.

IMPACT

In 2001, the European Court of Human Rights (ECHR) ruled that the initial Guinness Four trial was unfair. The court found that information gathered in the course of the informal DTI investigation, in which defendants cooperated, should not have been used to bring criminal charges against the four. The four had essentially been forced to testify against themselves, a violation of the legal right to silence. The ECHR did not rule that the Guinness Four were innocent, only that their trial had been marked by legal and procedural mistakes.

The European parliament has since amended the law to make evidence obtained under any type of compulsion or in a civil investigation inadmissible in criminal proceedings. The Guinness Four were not acquitted, but the procedures for gathering evidence in possible stock-fraud cases changed. Despite repeated attempts, the convictions of the four were not formally overturned. Furthermore, the court refused their appeal for financial compensation on the grounds of procedural miscarriage of justice.

—Victoria Erhart

FURTHER READING

Coenen, Tracy. *Essentials of Corporate Fraud.* Hoboken, N.J.: John Wiley & Sons, 2008. An introductory guide to the white-collar crime of corporate fraud, written by a forensic, or investigative, accountant.

Davies, Peter. *Current Issues in Business Ethics.* New York: Routledge, 1997. Several case studies examine the relationship between individuals and businesses as well as the making of ethical and unethical decisions.

Podgor, Ellen S., and Jerold H. Israel. *White Collar Crime in a Nutshell.* 3d ed. St. Paul, Minn.: West, 2004. Chapters on white collar crime and corporate fraud, written in a concise and accessible format. Includes a breakdown of securities fraud, tax fraud, corporate criminal liability, conspiracy, and bribery.

Steger, Ulrich, and Wolfgang Amann. *Corporate Governance.* Hoboken, N.J.: Wiley, 2008. Using case studies, this text examines patterns of ethical and legal problems in corporate governance in both the United States and internationally. Governance concerns arise especially as companies try to boost the bottom line. Brief discussion of the Guinness Four share scandal.

SEE ALSO: Jan., 1913: British Prime Minister's Staff Is Investigated for Insider Trading; Nov. 28, 1967: Investor Louis Wolfson Is Convicted of Selling Stock Illegally; May 2, 1984: E. F. Hutton Executives Plead Guilty to Fraud; 1985-1986: Westland Affair Shakes Prime Minister Thatcher's Government; Jan. 15, 1988: ZZZZ Best Founder Is Indicted on Federal Fraud Charges; June, 1988-June, 1989: Insider-Trading Scandal Rocks Japanese Government;

1990's

Mar. 29, 1989: Financier Michael Milken Is Indicted for Racketeering and Fraud; Dec. 2, 2001: Enron Bankruptcy Reveals Massive Financial Fraud; Sept. 3, 2003: Mutual Fund Companies Are Implicated in Shady Trading Practices; Mar.

5, 2004: Martha Stewart Is Convicted in Insider-Trading Scandal; Sept. 12, 2005: Westar Energy Executives Are Found Guilty of Looting Their Company.

November 19, 1990
LIP-SYNCHING DUO MILLI VANILLI LOSE GRAMMY AWARD

One of the most promising pop-music acts of the late 1980's, Milli Vanilli blended pop, soul, and rap into a unique and successful hybrid. However, the duo, Fab Morvan and Rob Pilatus, did not actually sing, causing a widespread scandal in the recording industry. The revelation not only caused sales of their album to plummet but also led to the revocation of the group's coveted 1990 Grammy Award for Best New Artist. A series of consumer lawsuits emerged from the scandal as well. The name "Milli Vanilli" remains associated with lip-synching and fraud in the music industry.

LOCALE: Los Angeles, California

CATEGORIES: Hoaxes, frauds, and charlatanism; music and performing arts; popular culture; radio and television

KEY FIGURES

Fab Morvan (b. 1966), French African model, dancer, singer, and songwriter

Rob Pilatus (1965-1998), German African model, dancer, and singer

Frank Farian (b. 1941), German music producer, singer, and songwriter

SUMMARY OF EVENT

The origins of pop group Milli Vanilli date back to an early 1988 studio project in Germany under the helm of producer Frank Farian. The initial recordings were cut by a team of professional vocalists and studio musicians, including Charles Shaw, John Davis, Brad Howell, Jodie Rocco, and Linda

Rocco. In addition to lacking fame as singers, Farian's group lacked a marketable appeal, leading him to look for a pair of models capable of dancing and lip-synching to the songs on stage. After meeting Fab Morvan and Rob Pilatus at a Berlin dance club, he quickly handed them the keys to the musical project and christened the two Milli Vanilli.

During the middle of 1988, the group's debut disc *All or Nothing* (with Morvan and Pilatus on the cover) was released in Europe, inciting a craze on the dance circuit for the project's blending of pop, soul, and rap. The attention soon carried over into the United States, resulting in a deal with Arista Records and that album's new release in 1989 as *Girl You Know It's True*. The title track raced up the *Billboard* Hot 100 (to number 2) and was followed by singles "Baby Don't Forget My Number," "Girl I'm Gonna Miss You," and "Blame It on the Rain."

Despite the astounding sales figures (which eventually hit the seven-million sales mark in the United States), the group began to face growing skepticism. During a taping of an MTV special in the summer of 1989 in Connecticut, Morvan and Pilatus were "singing" the smash single "Girl You Know It's True" in concert when their backing track skipped repeatedly, much to the dismay of the performers. Critics picked apart the botched attempt at lip-synching. Another controversy came at the end of 1989, when Shaw claimed the pair did not actually sing on the album. He quickly retracted the claim after allegedly being bribed by Farian.

In either instance, fans did not seem to mind. They continued to purchase *Girl You Know It's True* (and all its corresponding singles releases) at a feverish pace, while voting in droves in polls for the American Music Awards (AMA). Milli Vanilli, in 1990, took home awards for Favorite Pop-Rock New Artist, Favorite Soul-R&B New Artist, and Favorite Pop-Rock Single (for "Girl You Know It's True"). The music industry also took notice of the escalating adoration of the group, giving the duo a Grammy Award in 1990 in the Best New Artist category (beating out the Indigo Girls, Tone-Loc, Soul II Soul, and Neneh Cherry).

Given all the additional attention and lightning-fast ride to international fame, Morvan and Pilatus began developing excessive behaviors, including inflated egos and a party-hard mentality, often associated with musicians and other celebrities. Pilatus in particular received scorn for suggesting in an interview with *Time* magazine that Milli Vanilli was in the same elite category of musical innovators as Elvis Presley and Bob Dylan. Also, the duo tried to convince Farian that they should sing lead vocals in the studio on the next Milli Vanilli album.

The entertainers' growing egos, coupled with media speculation, fueled Farian's increasing frustrations and led to his November 12, 1990, admission that Milli Vanilli consisted of an act of two models who did not sing on the hit album. As expected, reporters jumped on the fraud story and turned the disgraced pop group into international tabloid material. Milli Vanilli faced an even bigger disappointment one week later, on November 19, when the National Academy of Recording Arts and Sciences, which presents the annual Grammy Awards, revoked the duo's coveted Best New Artist Award, exposing all involved to even more public humiliation. Michael Greene, the academy's president, said that academy trustees, who voted to revoke the award, "were just livid about the situation."

Critics came out in full force to condemn the band with insults,

also suggesting the prefabrication and subsequent cover-up served as the ultimate mockery of the music industry. Fans also responded negatively to the revelation, immediately ceasing their radio station requests and sending the *Girl You Know It's True* album into a sales stall. Arista Records also acted adversely, voiding its recording contract with Milli Vanilli, deleting the CD from its catalog, and forcing the title to go out of production. The album then ranked as the top former-best-selling album to be taken from store shelves.

A flurry of lawsuits, more than two dozen, followed. One of the more famous lawsuits was a class-action suit representing more than one thousand people seeking refunds after purchasing Milli Vanilli albums and singles. The following year, a similar suit was filed in Chicago, followed by several others seeking compensation. On August 28, 1991 (after intense legal wrangling), a settlement allowed those who purchased a record or a concert ticket to be eligible for refunds, as long as claims were filed before March 8, 1992.

Even with the negative publicity, Farian attempted to redeem himself, releasing 1991's follow-up album *The Moment of Truth* (recorded before

Rob Pilatus, left, and Fab Morvan, best-known as the pop duo Milli Vanilli, show off their Grammy Awards in February, 1990. The awards were taken from them after it was revealed Pilatus and Morvan had lip-synched their work. (AP/Wide World Photos)

the scandal) by the newly minted The Real Milli Vanilli. Fans in the United States were still indignant at the previous deceit, so the album was released in Europe only. Morvan and Pilatus attempted to clean up their part of the scandal recording as Rob & Fab. They released an album in 1993, but it was a commercial and critical failure.

In early 1998, Morvan and Pilatus tried using the Milli Vanilli name one more time, recording *Back and in Attack*, but the pair never had the chance to prove itself. On April 2, Pilatus was found dead in a Frankfurt, Germany, hotel room after consuming pills and alcohol. Morvan pursued a solo career, released a solo album, *Love Revolution*, in 2003, and even had production talks with Universal Pictures for a film about the group's rocky history. *Milli Vanilli: Greatest Hits* was released in 2007.

IMPACT

The ultimate music industry disgrace is being stripped of a Grammy Award. Widely cited as one of the most shocking and embarrassing moments in music history is Milli Vanilli's loss of its Grammy for fraud. Also, the scandal has been analyzed as an instance of greed at the expense of originality and artistry, and is cited as an example of the significance of marketing to commercial success for a singer or band; some claim that marketability and appeal are more critical than actual musical talent.

Though lip-synching is not new to the music industry, the Milli Vanilli scandal marked the first time the deception was employed on such a massive scale. Lip-synching is generally accepted during televised performances, but the duo crossed an ethical line because "singers" Morvan and Pilatus were not simply lip-synching their own recorded vocals; rather, they claimed to be original singing artists—which they were not—who were lip-synching their own work.

—*Andy Argyrakis*

FURTHER READING

Brackett, Nathan, and Christian Hoar, eds. *The New Rolling Stone Album Guide*. New York: Simon & Schuster, 2004. Includes brief reviews and ratings of Milli Vanilli's music. Also includes a short biographical synopsis of the duo.

Romanowski, Patricia, and Holly George-Warren, eds. *The New Rolling Stone Encyclopedia of Rock & Roll*. New York: Fireside, 1995. A factual summary and critical assessment of the Milli Vanilli scandal, starting with the group's rise to fame to its demise.

Torassa, Ulysses. "Suit Seeks Refunds for Ohioans Who Bought Milli Vanilli Album." *Plain Dealer*, November 22, 1990. Reports on the initial class-action lawsuit by fans in Ohio who sought refunds for buying a fraudulent album.

SEE ALSO: Feb. 8, 1960: U.S. Congress Investigates Payola in Pop Music Industry; Sept. 1, 1976: Former Beatle George Harrison Loses Plagiarism Lawsuit; Apr. 22, 1986: Faith Healer Peter Popoff Is Exposed as a Fraud.

March 30, 1991
WILLIAM KENNEDY SMITH IS ACCUSED OF RAPE

A nephew of U.S. president John F. Kennedy and Senators Robert F. and Ted Kennedy, William Kennedy Smith was accused of raping a woman he had met at a bar in Palm Beach, Florida. After a sensational criminal trial, Smith was acquitted of the charge. The case led to debate over the anonymity given to Patricia Bowman by news stations televising the trial and whether that anonymity, in general, perpetuates the idea that being raped is shameful.

LOCALE: Palm Beach, Florida
CATEGORIES: Law and the courts; publishing and journalism; sex crimes; women's issues

KEY FIGURES
William Kennedy Smith (b. 1960), physician
Patricia Bowman (b. 1961), Smith's accuser
Michelle Cassone (b. 1964), Bowman's friend, and a waitress and bartender

SUMMARY OF EVENT

William Kennedy Smith, part of a prominent family in American politics, joined a long line of other Kennedy men involved in scandals including promiscuity, extramarital affairs, and even death by drowning. In March, 1991, Smith was accused of raping Patricia Bowman in Palm Beach, Florida, at the nearby Kennedy family compound. After a heavily publicized and sensational trial, he was acquitted of the charge.

Over Easter weekend, the thirty-year-old Smith was in Palm Beach with his uncle, U.S. senator Ted Kennedy, and his cousin, Patrick Kennedy (Ted's son). On the evening of March 30, the three went to the local bar, Au Bar, where Smith met twenty-nine year old Patricia Bowman, a single mother. Patrick began talking with another woman, Michelle Cassone. After consuming drinks, the two cousins and Bowman and Cassone left the bar for the nearby oceanfront beach house owned by the Kennedy family.

At the Kennedy property, Patrick and Cassone drank wine and talked while Smith and Bowman walked along the beach. Bowman later told authorities that Smith took off his clothes and ran into the water, upsetting Bowman, who headed back to the house. As she began walking, Smith got out of the water and returned to the beach. Bowman said that Smith tackled her to the sand, called her a "bitch," and raped her. Bowman insisted that she tried to fight off Smith's attack and that she screamed "no." She told police that despite her pleas, Smith raped her.

After the incident on the beach, Bowman placed a call from the Kennedy compound to a friend, Anne Mercer, whom she asked to pick her up. Bowman and Mercer then drove to the Palm Beach police station, where Bowman reported the rape. Bowman was then taken to Humana Hospital for treatment. Police later indicated that they were "99 percent" certain that the evidence obtained at the hospital that night supported Bowman's claim of rape. She had bruises on her midsection that were consistent with a forceful attack. Furthermore, Bowman passed two separate polygraph tests. Based on Bowman's claim, the hospital report, and polygraph results, Smith was charged with second-degree sexual battery and misdemeanor battery.

The criminal trial began later that year, and both Bowman and Smith testified before a jury of four women and two men. Testimony began on December 2, and the trial was nationally televised. Judge Mary E. Lupo heard the case. Bowman testified that she and Smith had been walking on the beach, that Smith had been forceful, and that he had called her "bitch" when she protested his sexual advances. She said that Smith then raped her, even though she clearly told him no and told him to stop. Bowman also testified that after she told him he had raped her, his response was that no one would believe she was raped while at the Kennedy home, let alone that she was at the home in the first place. Thinking ahead about the consequences of her accusations,

1990's

759

Bowman took a family urn and notepad from the mansion as evidence that she was at the Kennedy estate. The defense attorneys later tried to use this against Bowman, portraying her as a common criminal who could not be trusted.

Prosecutors tried to present testimony from three women who said they were assaulted by Smith—one was assaulted in 1983, a second in 1988, and a third in 1991, the same year Smith allegedly raped Bowman. These attacks, however, had not been reported to the police. Furthermore, Florida law prohibits revealing a defendant's criminal history in a sex-related case as evidence in another case if the modus operandi in that prior case differed from the

William Kennedy Smith leaves court after his arraignment on May 31, 1991. He pleaded not guilty to charges of sexual battery. (AP/Wide World Photos)

alleged crime in question. The defense, therefore, filed a motion to prevent the women's testimony. The court ruled that the prosecution in the Smith-Bowman trial failed to show how the previous three alleged attacks were relevant to the current case.

Smith recounted his version of the incident to the judge and jury, but it was a version very different from that of Bowman. The defense presented its case as consensual sex: Smith acknowledged that the couple engaged in sexual intercourse but he insisted that it was consensual. He testified that after they had sex, Bowman began to shake and cry. He did not dispute Bowman's testimony that she told Smith on the beach that he had just raped her. Smith said that during their rendezvous on the beach, he called Bowman by the wrong first name—Cathy, his former girlfriend's name. (Interestingly, during the trial, Bowman had mistakenly referred to Smith as Michael.) Smith said that his mistake infuriated Bowman. At this point, he said, she told him to get off of her and then slapped him. Smith contended that this slip of the tongue, calling Bowman by the name Cathy, led to Bowman's accusation of rape against Smith.

The jury agreed with the defense and believed Smith's version of what happened March 30. On December 23, after eighty minutes of deliberation, the jury returned a verdict of not guilty.

IMPACT

Had Smith's family not been famous, it is unlikely the media would have paid close attention to the case. However, it was the manner in which the trial was covered by the media that defines the scandal's impact and legacy. What led to heightened intrigue with this case was the anonymity given to Bowman by news stations. Bowman was never fully seen on television during the trial. The image of her face was concealed with a blurred, blue or grayish dot on the screen. The dot—and its effect on not only the case but also the issue of keeping alleged victims anonymous in rape cases—remains part of the trial's legacy.

Camera operators, photographers, and reporters gather outside the Palm Beach County courthouse during William Kennedy Smith's trial for sexual battery in December, 1991. (Hulton Archive/Getty Images)

Commentators questioned whether keeping Bowman anonymous to viewers really helped her in the public eye or made her into an object for sensational reportage. Some critics of media coverage of rape cases and trials argue that keeping rape victims—or alleged victims—anonymous adds a veil of shame to their victimization, that to keep that person's identity secret reinforces the idea that a raped woman (or man) is a shameful woman (or man). After the trial, however, Bowman appeared on ABC's *Prime Time Live* with Diane Sawyer so that she could speak about her experience without concealing her identity. She said she wanted to help other rape victims feel less afraid when confronting their attackers.

Rape cases are often difficult for prosecutors. An accuser's credibility and sexual history are often weighed more heavily than any material evidence presented at trial. Rape cases are difficult to prose-cute also because the case most often depends on differing versions of the same event. Even when solid rape-kit evidence points to an alleged perpetrator, the testimony of the alleged victim and the alleged rapist often overrides this evidence. This he said-she said aspect to rape cases clearly played a part in the outcome of Smith's trial: the jury believed Smith but not Bowman. Smith's resources and his family's notoriety may have influenced the jury's verdict as well.

—*Eileen M. Ahlin*

Further Reading

Chancer, Lynn S. *High-profile Crimes: When Legal Cases Become Social Causes*. Chicago: University of Chicago Press, 2005. An account of the "polarizing" criminal cases of the 1980's and 1990's, including the Kennedy Smith trial. Examines "how these cases became conflated with larger social causes on a collective level" as well as "how this phenomenon has affected the law, the media, and social movements."

Leamer, Laurence. *Sons of Camelot: The Fate of an American Dynasty*. New York: HarperCollins, 2004. Discusses the William Kennedy Smith rape trial, placing it in the context of numerous scandals and hardships faced by the Kennedy clan.

Matlock, Jann. "Scandals of Naming: The Blue Blob, Identity, and Gender in the William Kennedy Smith Case." In *Media Spectacles*, edited by Marjorie Garber, Jann Matlock, and Rebecca L. Walkowitz. New York: Routledge, 1993. Discusses the media portrayal of Patricia Bowman in William Kennedy Smith's criminal trial. Examines the effects of gender and class assumptions on the media's coverage of the trial. Focuses mainly on Bowman's anonymity.

Matoesian, Gregory M. *Law and the Language of Identity: Discourse in the William Kennedy*

Smith Rape Trial. New York: Oxford University Press, 2001. Examines the use of targeted language by the defense and prosecution in rape trials. Ties linguistics to law, gender, sexual identity, and power.

SEE ALSO: Early 1928: Joseph P. Kennedy Begins an Affair with Gloria Swanson; Feb. 7, 1960: President Kennedy's Romantic Affair Links Him to Organized Crime; May 19, 1962: Marilyn Monroe Sings "Happy Birthday, Mr. President"; July 18, 1969: Senator Edward Kennedy's Driving Accident Kills Mary Jo Kopechne; Oct. 7, 1974: Congressman Wilbur D. Mills's Stripper Affair Leads to His Downfall; Feb. 1, 1978: Roman Polanski Flees the United States to Avoid Rape Trial; Nov. 28, 1987: Black Teenager Claims to Have Been Gang-Raped by Police Officers; July 1, 2003: Basketball Star Kobe Bryant Is Accused of Rape; Mar. 14, 2006: Duke Lacrosse Players Are Accused of Gang Rape.

April 5, 1991
GEORGE W. BUSH IS INVESTIGATED FOR INSIDER TRADING

George W. Bush, elected U.S. president in 2000, sold more than 200,000 shares of Harken Energy two months before the company announced a huge loss. This led to claims of insider trading against Bush, but a U.S. Securities and Exchange Commission investigation, which began in April, 1991, cleared him of wrongdoing.

LOCALE: Dallas, Texas

CATEGORIES: Law and the courts; business; corruption; banking and finance; government

KEY FIGURE

George W. Bush (b. 1946), oil-industry businessman and later governor of Texas, 1995-2000, and president of the United States, 2001-2009

SUMMARY OF EVENT

The large sums of money George W. Bush collected from his involvement with Harken Energy Corporation was one of the more controversial aspects of his life before his election as Texas governor in 1994. In 1986, Bush was the forty-year-old son of U.S. vice president George H. W. Bush (later president) and had little success of his own. His ventures in the oil industry were struggling. He had lost the election for a Texas congressional seat in 1978. His luck seemed to change, however, when he became involved with Harken Energy Corporation.

Harken, based at the time in Dallas, Texas, engaged in exploratory drilling at sites throughout the world. Like many speculative resource companies, it seemed better at self-promotion than at finding oil. Its oil wells were dry, it was loaded with debt, and it lost money most years. Its accounting practices were byzantine, which made it difficult to correlate its assets with its stock price. However, in 1986, it added a famous name to its roster—the younger Bush. Harken purchased Bush's partly owned and failing Spectrum 7 oil company for $2.25 million. The buyout provided Bush with 212,000 Harken shares and additional stock options worth about $600,000, a position as a consultant to Harken paying between $80,000 to $120,000 a year from 1986 to 1993, and a membership on the Harken board of directors (with additional directors' fees).

In 1986 and 1988, Bush borrowed $180,000 from Harken to purchase an additional 105,000 shares at favorable terms available to directors. However, Harken's losses would continue. In 1989 the company lost over $12 million, and in 1990 it lost $40 million. Nevertheless, Harken was granted prime business opportunities, such as exclusive drilling rights in Bahrain along the Persian Gulf in 1990. Although deals such as this helped keep Harken in the financial news, the company was losing so much money its future was in jeopardy.

In the spring of 1990, Bush was considering selling some of his Harken stock to raise cash to participate in the purchase of the Texas Rangers baseball team. However, as he knew, he was required to obey federal laws that prohibit company insiders from profiting from private knowledge of a company. On May 17, Bush attended a special meeting of the Harken board of directors, in which the board was warned of Harken's looming crisis. On June 6, Bush, as a member of Harken's audit committee, received the company's so-called flash report, which predicted a $4 million loss. It is important to note, however, that Bush was not a member of the executive committee that had access to most of Harken's financial information.

WHAT IS "INSIDER TRADING"?

The U.S. Securities and Exchange Commission defines "insider trading" as follows:

"Insider trading" is a term that most investors have heard and usually associate with illegal conduct. But the term actually includes both legal and illegal conduct. The legal version is when corporate insiders—officers, directors, and employees—buy and sell stock in their own companies. When corporate insiders trade in their own securities, they must report their trades to the SEC. . . .

Illegal insider trading refers generally to buying or selling a security, in breach of a fiduciary duty or other relationship of trust and confidence, while in possession of material, nonpublic information about the security. Insider trading violations may also include "tipping" such information, securities trading by the person "tipped," and securities trading by those who misappropriate such information. . . .

Because insider trading undermines investor confidence in the fairness and integrity of the securities markets, the SEC has treated the detection and prosecution of insider trading violations as one of its enforcement priorities. The SEC adopted new Rules 10b5-1 and 10b5-2 to resolve two insider trading issues where the courts have disagreed.

- Rule 10b5-1 provides that a person trades on the basis of material nonpublic information if a trader is "aware" of the material nonpublic information when making the purchase or sale. The rule also sets forth several affirmative defenses or exceptions to liability. The rule permits persons to trade in certain specified circumstances where it is clear that the information they are aware of is not a factor in the decision to trade, such as pursuant to a pre-existing plan, contract, or instruction that was made in good faith.
- Rule 10b5-2 clarifies how the misappropriation theory applies to certain non-business relationships. This rule provides that a person receiving confidential information under circumstances specified in the rule would owe a duty of trust or confidence and thus could be liable under the misappropriation theory.

On June 8, Sutro & Company stockbroker Ralph Smith offered to purchase Bush's Harken shares on behalf of one of his clients. Bush promptly inquired of Harken's general counsel about the suitability of his selling Harken stock and was given a memorandum, "Liability for Insider Trading and Short-Term Swing Profits," which warned against any selling by insiders that could be in violation of insider-trading laws. On June 22, Bush sold 212,140 of his

317,152 shares of stock for $848,560—about $4.25 a share. Two months later on August 20, Harken announced an astronomical loss of $23 million for its second quarter. The price of its stock would soon fall to $1.25, a 75 percent decrease, although the stock would eventually rebound to the price at which it was sold at by Bush.

On April 5, 1991, the U.S. Securities and Exchange Commission (SEC) started an insider-trading investigation into the transaction, requesting several documents from Bush. Documents that were made public indicate that the SEC found that Bush was not well informed about the poor financial condition of Harken and, thus, did not sell his shares in anticipation of its pending losses. In addition, Bush had been approached first by Smith to sell his shares and he made no effort to conceal the transaction. Although Harken's price did fall 20 percent the day of the sale, it rebounded over the following days. Finally, Bush's failure to file certain SEC forms was found to be a minor violation. Thus, the SEC decided that it would not charge Bush with insider trading; and it would seem difficult in the light of the SEC investigation to claim that Bush violated the law. (The stock price of Harken would continue to fall over the following decade, and it lost hundreds of millions of dollars, eventually reaching penny stock status.)

IMPACT

Bush's sale of his Harken shares was perhaps the most important transaction of his business career to potentially threaten his political future. If the sale constituted insider trading, it could have resulted in criminal charges and would certainly have obstructed his presidential aspirations. The issue was raised again in the 2000 presidential campaign and during the early years of his presidency. The Enron scandal of 2001 raised issues of corporate greed and wrongdoing, and the Center for Public Integrity obtained numerous Harken and SEC documents relating to Bush's sale through the Freedom of Information Act of 1966. Bush's call for a new era of corporate integrity in the United States subjected his dealings to even closer scrutiny. With no official finding of wrongdoing, however, White House

press secretary Ari Fleischer was able to defend the sale in a July 5, 2002, press briefing, and the issue faded from public view.

Although it seems clear that Bush did not violate the law, his involvement with Harken Oil does raise questions in this age of corporate scandals in which public corporations are often accused of being run for the benefit of their executives, directors, and insiders at the expense of workers and shareholders. The SEC conclusion that Bush did not fully understand the financial condition of Harken does excuse him from criminal liability but also raises questions about the lavish consulting and directing fees that he received for his services. Even if Harken were paying Bush for his name and business contacts and not for his expertise, such an arrangement is legal if no improper influence is exerted.

Although Harken's loan of $180,000 to Bush is reminiscent of the loans Bernard Ebbers received from WorldCom and the Rigas family from Adelphia Communications Corporation in later corporate scandals, it is clear that Bush broke no law in borrowing from Harken. Although the SEC in January, 1991, compelled Harken to restate its losses for 1989 from $3.3 million as reported to the $12.6 million it actually suffered, this accounting irregularity reflects poorly on Harken management, not on Bush. Certainly, with Harken's stock price in long-term decline, Bush seems to have been one of the few shareholders to have profited from association with that relentlessly unsuccessful company. Whether the profits Bush accrued constitutes unscrupulous corporate conduct or shrewd business trading depends in the end on one's view of America's corporate culture of the last two decades.

—*Howard Bromberg*

FURTHER READING

Fleischer, Ari. *Taking Heat: The President, the Press, and My Years in the White House*. New York: William Morrow, 2005. President Bush's first press secretary defends the president's commitment to fighting corporate fraud and criticizes reporters trying to turn Bush's Harken sale into a scandal.

Ivins, Molly, and Lou Dubose. *Bushwhacked: Life in*

George W. Bush's America. New York: Random House, 2003. A chapter in this collection critical of Bush likens Harken to a miniature Enron scandal.

Kessler, Ronald. *A Matter of Character: Inside the White House of George W. Bush.* New York: Sentinel, 2004. In praising the strength of President Bush's character, Kessler defends Bush's relationship with Harken.

Minutaglio, Bill. *First Son: George W. Bush and the Bush Family Dynasty.* New York: Times Books, 1999. Includes the story of the Harken stock sale in the context of the business transactions of George H. W. Bush and George W. Bush.

Serwer, Andy. "W., President, Harken 38 [cents]." *Fortune*, August 12, 2002. An update on the dismal fortunes of Harken Oil from a leading financial magazine.

Unger, Craig. *House of Bush, House of Saud: The Secret Relationship Between the World's Two Most Powerful Dynasties.* New York: Scribner, 2004. An aggressive exposé by an investigative journalist of the financial relations between the Bush family and the Saudi oil princes. Unger finds shadowy links between Saudi Arabian interests and Harken business ventures.

SEE ALSO: Oct. 22, 1923: U.S. Senate Begins Hearings on Teapot Dome Oil Leases; Feb. 4, 1976: Lockheed Is Implicated in Bribing Foreign Officials; Nov. 13, 1986-May 4, 1989: Iran-Contra Weapons Scandal Taints Reagan's Administration; May 9, 2000: Former Louisiana Governor Edwin Edwards Is Convicted on Corruption Charges; Dec. 2, 2001: Enron Bankruptcy Reveals Massive Financial Fraud; Mar. 5, 2004: Martha Stewart Is Convicted in Insider-Trading Scandal; Sept. 8, 2004: *60 Minutes II* Reports on George W. Bush's Evasion of Wartime Duty.

July 26, 1991
COMEDIAN PEE-WEE HERMAN IS ARRESTED FOR PUBLIC INDECENCY

Actor Paul Reubens achieved fame as the comedian Pee-wee Herman and had been ending his run as the popular host of his own children's television show, Pee-wee's Playhouse, *when he was arrested for masturbating in an adult-movie theater in Sarasota, Florida. The incident attracted a great deal of media attention and condemnation of Reubens, which continued for more than a decade, but he later continued acting.*

LOCALE: Sarasota, Florida
CATEGORIES: Sex crimes; public morals; radio and television

KEY FIGURES
Paul Reubens (Paul Rubenfeld; b. 1952), television and film entertainer best known as "Pee-wee Herman"

Judy Goldman (fl. 1990's), Sarasota County judge
Ronald Dresnick (fl. 1990's), defense attorney
Don Hartery (fl. 1990's), Sarasota County prosecutor
Larry Goldman (fl. 1990), publicity agent

SUMMARY OF EVENT
Paul Reubens, born Paul Rubenfeld, grew up in Sarasota, Florida, where at the age of eleven he began acting in local plays. While attending college, he continued to act and eventually joined the Groundlings, an improvisation troupe. Reubens created the Pee-wee Herman character in 1978 as part of his Groundlings night club act. In 1986, he became the host of the CBS Saturday morning children's show *Pee-wee's Playhouse*, which subsequently won numerous Emmy Awards. By the summer of 1991, the same time Reubens was arrested,

765

however, the show had run its course, and CBS was airing the last of its reruns.

On the evening of July 26, 1991, Reubens, who was on a summer vacation visiting his parents in Sarasota, Florida, was suffering from boredom and decided to attend the screening of an X-rated movie at Sarasota's XXX-rated South Trail Cinema. During 1991, the Sarasota police had initiated a crackdown on "adult obscenity" intending to rid Sarasota of morality offenses. Detectives had been periodically visiting local adult movie theaters hoping to catch patrons indulging in indecent acts. While Reubens watched a porno film the Sarasota detectives were working undercover at the theater. As Reubens was exiting the Cinema at the conclusion of the movie the detectives arrested him for exposing his sexual organs in public.

Pee-wee Herman (Paul Reubens) in 1984. (Hulton Archive/Getty Images)

The indecent-exposure law allegedly violated by Reubens prohibited the exposure of sexual organs, except in places set aside for that purpose. Adult-movie theaters had not been designated as locations where sexual organs could be exposed. Local police claimed that Reubens had been caught masturbating during the porno film screening at the South Trail Cinema.

Reubens's mug shot depicts a scowling, long-haired, goateed figure wearing a tee shirt and shorts, the antithesis of the childlike and "nerdy" Pee-wee Herman character who was always nattily dressed in a too-small gray suit with a red bow tie, white socks, and slicked back hair. Reubens was released on $219 bail. Although local police may not at first have connected Reubens to Pee-wee Herman, Reubens told them who he was. The local media also figured out Reubens's identity through the police blotter. Soon, the national news media was in a frenzy over the star's arrest.

Media attention to the Reubens case created a chain reaction. Parents were concerned that their children had been exposed to immoral behavior watching *Pee-wee's Playhouse.* Moreover, adults did not know how to answer children's questions concerning the arrest of their beloved Pee-wee character. Many in the media and several celebrities supported Reubens and argued that the government had targeted Reubens because of his children's show. Several citizens in Sarasota publicly questioned whether prosecuting Reubens was the best use of taxpayers' money.

Despite claims by Reubens's publicity agent, Larry Goldman, that a videotape from a security camera in the theater would prove Reubens's innocence, no videotape evidence was ever produced. Reubens's defense attorney, Ronald Dresnick, also argued that the indecent exposure statute should not apply in adult-movie theaters, as exposure of sexual organs should be expected in such venues. Judy Goldman, the judge in the case, rejected the defense and ordered Reubens to face the charges.

Three and half months after Reubens's arrest, the actor entered a no contest plea on the charge of indecent exposure. (A no contest plea means that the person charged is neither admitting nor denying guilt.) Reubens also entered into a plea agreement with Sarasota County, which Judge Goldman reluctantly approved. Goldman decided that given the national media attention, which would increase with a trial, the wisest choice was to accept the plea and avoid further cost to the county. Had Reubens been found guilty of the misdemeanor charges, he could have been sentenced to one year in jail and received a one thousand dollar fine.

Reubens agreed to pay a $50 fine, $85.75 in court costs, and participate in community service by writing, producing, and paying for public service messages for the Partnership for a Drug-Free America. Judge Goldman believed that Reubens was receiving minor punishment and vowed to impose much harsher penalties if he failed to comply with the plea agreement. Reubens fulfilled the terms of the plea agreement, retired from the public stage, and maintained a low profile, but only for a time.

Sarasota County prosecutor Don Hartery also agreed to seal the legal documents in the case, which left Reubens with a clean criminal record, despite at least two previous arrests. During his younger years, Reubens had been arrested and charged with loitering near an adult theater and possessing marijuana. The loitering charge was later dropped, and a judge entered no finding of guilt in the marijuana possession case in exchange for two years' probation.

Reubens's legal troubles were not over, however. In 2002, he was charged in Los Angeles with a misdemeanor count for possession of material depicting children engaged in sex. Reubens was once again arrested—this time for a crime the prosecution claimed involved sexual exploitation of children. The material at issue included old magazines and photographs, some of nude persons, seized from Reubens's home in 2001. Reubens, who was out as gay, claimed the items seized were part of his vintage art collection and that he had legally purchased the nude pictures and magazine depictions that were now being labeled as child pornography.

Reubens's bail was set at twenty thousand dollars. He once again bargained to avoid a public trial and agreed to plead guilty to a misdemeanor obscenity charge. In 2004, the child pornography charges were dropped. He paid a fine of one hundred dollars and registered as a sex offender for three years.

IMPACT

The arrest of a children's show star for indecent exposure was big news in 1991. However, the media helped speed the demise of cult figure Pee-wee Herman, whose popularity had already begun to wane by the time of Reubens's 1991 arrest. After the arrest, CBS canceled the remaining reruns of *Pee-wee's Playhouse*, Disney canceled a short video of Pee-wee as part of its studio tours, and merchandisers discontinued the sale of Pee-wee Herman products. Reubens played the Pee-wee Herman character one more time at an MTV Music Video Awards show, and in 1988 he received a star on Hollywood's Walk of Fame.

Pee-wee Herman may have become the alter ego of Reubens, and Reubens may have been held to a higher standard because Pee-wee became the host of a children's show. Pee-wee, however, started out as an unusual, childlike character in a night club act, and Reubens never attempted to disguise Pee-wee's bad behavior, such as looking up women's dresses with mirrors glued to his shoes. In addition, as host of a children's show, Reubens, as Pee-wee, was never shy about poking fun at society's sexist and racial stereotypes.

Perhaps Reubens was singled out because of what he did—turn a childlike, adult entertainer into a beloved children's icon and use a children's show as a political platform. Supporters of Reubens believe that law enforcement targeted him to support its crackdown on adult obscenity through prosecutions and censorship. Reubens, however, may have the last word with the planned *Pee-wee's Playhouse: The Movie*.

—*Carol A. Rolf*

FURTHER READING

Buhle, Paul. *From the Lower East Side to Hollywood: Jews in American Popular Culture*. New York: Verso, 2004. Explores the contributions of Jewish entertainers to American film and television, including the work of Paul Reubens.
Ingraham, Laura. *Power to the People*. Washing-

1990's

ton, D.C.: Regnery, 2007. Examines Paul Reubens as one of America's bad boys who has been treated unfairly by law enforcement in its attempt to control obscenity.

Jenkins, Henry. *The Wow Climax: Tracing the Emotional Impact of Popular Culture.* New York: New York University Press, 2006. Considers the impact of vaudevillelike personae such as Pee-wee Herman, despite their deemed-vulgar behavior, on modern pop-culture audiences.

Woods, Paul A. *Tim Burton: A Child's Garden of Nightmares*, Medford, N.J.: Plexus, 2007. Discusses how the early collaboration between Reubens and director Tim Burton on the film *Pee-wee's Big Adventure* (1985) affected Burton's career.

SEE ALSO: Feb. 6, 1942: Film Star Errol Flynn Is Acquitted of Rape; Nov. 23, 1946: Tennis Star Bill Tilden Is Arrested for Lewd Behavior with a Minor; July 18, 1988: Actor Rob Lowe Videotapes Sexual Tryst with a Minor; June 27, 1995: Film Star Hugh Grant Is Arrested for Lewd Conduct; Sept. 22, 1997: Sportscaster Marv Albert Is Tried for Sexual Assault; Apr. 7, 1998: Pop Singer George Michael Is Arrested for Lewd Conduct; Dec. 18, 2003: Pop Star Michael Jackson Is Charged with Child Molestation; July 28, 2006: Actor Mel Gibson Is Caught Making Anti-Semitic Remarks; June 13, 2008: Singer R. Kelly Is Acquitted on Child Pornography Charges.

October 11-13, 1991
JUSTICE CLARENCE THOMAS'S CONFIRMATION HEARINGS CREATE A SCANDAL

The confirmation hearings of U.S. Supreme Court nominee Clarence Thomas took a dramatic turn when a law professor Anita Hill accused Thomas of sexual harassment. The nation was riveted by the sensational allegations, which became the focus of a Senate Judiciary Committee hearing broadcast to the nation on network television.

ALSO KNOWN AS: Hill-Thomas scandal

LOCALE: Washington, D.C.

CATEGORIES: Law and the courts; women's issues; racism; government; politics; sex; radio and television; social issues and reform; communications and media

KEY FIGURES

Clarence Thomas (b. 1948), associate justice of the United States, 1991-

Anita Hill (b. 1956), American attorney and law professor

George H. W. Bush (b. 1924), president of the United States, 1989-1993

SUMMARY OF EVENT

In 1967, Thurgood Marshall, the famed former civil rights lawyer for the National Association for the Advancement of Colored People (NAACP), became the first African American appointed to the position of justice of the United States. Marshall retired in 1991, leading Republican president George H. W. Bush to face a difficult political situation. While some within the Republican Party pressured him to continue Ronald Reagan's judicial legacy by nominating a conservative, the president did not want to be perceived as racist in denying the so-called black seat on the Court to an African American. As an opponent of racial quotas, however, Bush could not select someone solely on the basis of his or her race. However, Clarence Thomas, a jurist with solid conservative credentials, proved an ideal candidate; and he was black.

Bush believed Thomas's race would keep powerful civil rights groups from opposing the nomination. Furthermore, Thomas's ideology would satisfy the president's core constituency. On July 1,

Anita Hill testifies before the Senate Judiciary Committee on October 11, 1991. (AP/Wide World Photos)

1991, Bush nominated Thomas, indicating that race had "nothing to do" with his selection of Thomas.

Thomas was born into poverty, raised by his grandparents, and educated by Roman Catholic nuns in rural Pin Point, Georgia. He graduated with honors from Holy Cross College in 1971 and earned a law degree from Yale University in 1974. After a series of jobs with the federal government—including the Department of Education (DOE) and the Equal Employment Opportunity Commission (EEOC), where Thomas, as chairman, often found himself at odds with civil rights groups—he was appointed to the U.S. Court of Appeals for the District of Columbia Circuit in 1990.

The confirmation hearings began rather uneventfully before the Senate Judiciary Committee on September 10, 1991. The hearings, however, would not conclude that way. Thomas's supporters em-

phasized his rags-to-riches story, his career as a governmental employee, and most important, his belief that a judge's role was not to make decisions based upon personal opinions or interests, but rather to interpret and apply the choices made by the legislative and executive branches. Thomas's opponents decried his perceived lack of qualifications: a limited career in law practice—only five years—and even less judicial experience—a mere eighteen months. Twelve members of the American Bar Association (ABA) Standing Committee on the Federal Judiciary declared Thomas to be "qualified," two deemed him "not qualified," and one member abstained. No one on the committee believed him to be "well qualified." This was the lowest rating the committee had ever given a U.S. Supreme Court nominee.

Prominent interest groups criticized Thomas for failing to comprehend and appreciate the history and vestiges of racism. The NAACP, by a vote of 49-1, along with most civil rights organizations, formally opposed his nomination. Numerous senators disparaged him for his conservative judicial philosophy and affinity for natural law, to which, they believed, Thomas might subordinate constitutional principles. That philosophy, opponents feared, could result in a narrowing of abortion rights, affirmative action programs, and the constitutional role of the judiciary in relation to the elected branches of government.

During the hearings, Thomas ran from his record, playing down or disavowing previous statements on privacy rights, affirmative action, and other controversial topics. Though pressed repeatedly on abortion, Thomas claimed that he had "never" debated the 1973 case *Roe v. Wade*, one of the most controversial legal decisions of the twentieth century. For the most part, the administration's confirmation strategy—to keep the focus on his race and his rags-to-riches story—shielded the nominee from a more searching criticism of his judicial philosophy.

The Senate Judiciary Committee vote was divided 7-7 on the nomination, which was then forwarded to the full Senate without a recommendation. Nevertheless, Thomas appeared on his way to confirmation until October 6, when a lurid and explosive allegation surfaced—that the nominee had sexually harassed Anita Hill, an attorney, law professor, and former subordinate of Thomas at the DOE and the EEOC. (A Senate Judiciary Committee staff member had leaked to the press Hill's affidavit to the Department of Justice accusing Thomas of sexual harassment.) After Thomas requested a

delay so that the committee could investigate the allegations fully, the hearings reopened on October 11. This time, the Senate and the public paid serious attention to the hearings, which were broadcast nationally on network television.

Thomas testified first, categorically denying the allegations. Additionally, Thomas said that Hill had, after the alleged harassment, followed him from the DOE to the EEOC, asked him repeatedly for letters of recommendation, and contacted him by telephone on numerous occasions. Hill's testimony followed. She accused Thomas of pressuring her to accept his invitations to go out with him, and testified that while at work, Thomas would describe to her in detail acts he had seen in pornographic films, including women having sex with animals, group sex, rape scenes, and individuals with large penises and large breasts having sex. She testified that Thomas, in graphic detail, often would inform her of his "sexual prowess," which included a larger than average penis and a willingness to engage in oral sex.

Thomas responded the following day, once again denying the allegations. He characterized the accusations as resting on racial stereotypes, and described the committee hearings as a "circus," a "national disgrace," and a "high-tech lynching for uppity blacks."

A limited number of witnesses testified for both sides. Some supported Hill's testimony and others spoke in defense of Thomas, emphasizing his professionalism and integrity. In the end, the committee concluded the hearings without a determination as to the allegations. Regardless, the Senate confirmed Thomas by a vote of 52-48 on October 15, the closest vote ever for a successful Supreme Court nominee. Eleven Democrats joined forty-one Republicans in support of the nomination; two Republicans joined forty-six Democrats voting in opposition. On October 23,

THOMAS RESPONDS

At the evening session of the Senate Judiciary Committee hearing on the nomination of Clarence Thomas to the U.S. Supreme Court on October 11, 1991, Thomas responded to testimony that was presented against him by Anita Hill.

Senator, I would like to start by saying unequivocally, uncategorically, that I deny each and every single allegation against me today that suggested in any way that I had conversations of a sexual nature or about pornographic material with Anita Hill, that I ever attempted to date her, that I ever had any personal sexual interest in her, or that I in any way ever harassed her.

A second, and I think more important point, I think that this today is a travesty. I think that it is disgusting. I think that this hearing should never occur in America. This is a case in which this sleaze, this dirt, was searched for by staffers of members of this committee, was then leaked to the media, and this committee and this body validated it and displayed it at prime time over our entire nation. How would any member on this committee, any person in this room, or any person in this country, would like sleaze said about him or her in this fashion? Or this dirt dredged up and this gossip and these lies displayed in this manner? How would any person like it?

The Supreme Court is not worth it. No job is worth it. I'm not here for that. I'm here for my name, my family, my life, and my integrity. I think something is dreadfully wrong with this country when any person, any person in this free country would be subjected to this.

This is not a closed room. There was an FBI investigation. This is not an opportunity to talk about difficult matters privately or in a closed environment. This is a circus. It's a national disgrace. And from my standpoint as a black American, as far as I'm concerned, it is a high-tech lynching for uppity blacks who in any way deign to think for themselves, to do for themselves, to have different ideas, and it is a message that unless you kowtow to an old order, this is what will happen to you. You will be lynched, destroyed, caricatured by a committee of the U.S. Senate rather than hung from a tree.

Clarence Thomas, center, is sworn in as associate justice of the United States by Justice Byron White on October 23, 1991. (AP/Wide World Photos)

Thomas was sworn in as the 106th associate justice of the United States.

IMPACT

Public opinion on Thomas was closely divided even before Hill made her claims of sexual harassment. Nevertheless, it was widely believed that Thomas would be confirmed. Commentators speculated that some undecided senators, especially Democrats, would be reluctant to cast a vote against an African American who had lived a Horatio Alger-type life, achieving the American dream through hard work, determination, and education.

The allegations exacerbated an already existing division within the country and in the Senate. Supporters of Thomas were outraged at the media's stereotypical portrayal of him as a black man incapable of controlling his sexual appetite. Some depicted Hill as a vindictive, perhaps spurned, woman bent on destroying Thomas's career for personal, and perhaps even political, reasons. To Thomas's

opponents, the allegations supported their claim that the nominee was unqualified, both professionally and personally, for the position. Many applauded Hill for her strong stand against sexual harassment, a stand that increased the nation's consciousness of harassment in the workplace. Linguist Robin T. Lakoff, in an article analyzing the discourse of the hearings, wrote that Hill's testimony forced the nation to define sexual harassment, to face sexual harassment as a serious legal issue, and to acknowledge that women have every right to define and discuss male behavior before a public audience.

The hearings were among the most extraordinary in the history of nominations to the Court. No previous hearings had included so much lurid and personally explosive accusations; nor had any past hearing garnered such media attention. As a result of the scandal, senatorial access to Federal Bureau of Investigation reports of judicial nominees is now limited.

Additionally, the hearings turned out to be the opening salvo for a number of sexual exposés during the 1990's, including that of President Bill Clinton in the Monica Lewinsky scandal, with both parties utilizing personal accusations to harm political opponents.

Thomas became one of the most widely recognized justices on the Supreme Court. This is true not because of his conservative judicial philosophy or decisions on the bench but rather for the accusations of sexual harassment that surfaced during his confirmation hearings.

—Richard A. Glenn

FURTHER READING

Brock, David. *The Real Anita Hill*. New York: Free Press, 1993. Unsympathetic portrait of Thomas's accuser, concluding that she was not truthful in her testimony before the Senate Judiciary Committee. Author later recanted his research and thesis in this book, asserting that it was partially fabricated and meant to disgrace Hill.

Comiskey, Michael. *Seeking Justices: The Judging of Supreme Court Nominees*. Lawrence: University Press of Kansas, 2004. Comprehensive account of the nomination and confirmation process of presidential appointees to the Supreme Court. An entire chapter is devoted to Thomas's confirmation battle.

Forrell, Caroline A., and Donna M. Matthews. *A Law of Her Own: The Reasonable Woman as a Measure of Man*. New York: New York University Press, 2000. Study suggesting reforms that would take better account of women's experiences in defining sexual harassment and other such legal terms.

Lakoff, Robin Tolmach. "Sexual Harassment on Trial: The Anita Hill/Clarence Thomas Narrative(s)." In *Women's America: Refocusing the Past*, edited by Linda K. Kerber and Jane Sherron De Hart. 6th ed. New York: Oxford University Press, 2004. Lakoff, a linguistics professor, examines the wordplay of the Hill/Thomas hearing. A richly detailed analysis of the politics of language and the language of politics that helped define the hearing.

Mayer, Jane, and Jill Abramson. *Strange Justice: The Selling of Clarence Thomas*. Boston: Houghton Mifflin, 1994. Written by investigative reporters, an account of the distortions surrounding Thomas's nomination to the Supreme Court and the Bush administration's smear campaign to discredit Anita Hill. Concludes that Thomas lied when he denied Hill's accusations.

Thomas, Clarence. *My Grandfather's Son: A Memoir*. New York: Harper, 2007. Autobiography covering Thomas's life from his early days in poverty in rural Georgia to his investiture on the Supreme Court. Roughly one-third of the book is devoted to his nomination and confirmation.

SEE ALSO: Jan. 13, 1913: Federal Judge Is Impeached for Profiting from His Office; May 9, 1969: Supreme Court Justice Abe Fortas Is Accused of Bribery; Jan. 25, 1984: Jesse Jackson Calls New York City "Hymietown"; June 26, 1992: U.S. Navy Secretary Resigns in the Wake of Tailhook Sexual Assault Scandal; Aug. 21, 1994: Sex Scandal Forces Dismissal of NAACP Chief Benjamin Chavis; Dec. 11, 1997: HUD Secretary Henry Cisneros Is Indicted for Lying to Federal Agents; Jan. 17, 1998: President Bill Clinton Denies Sexual Affair with a White House Intern; Oct. 2, 2003: Newspaper Claims That Arnold Schwarzenegger Groped Women; June 2, 2004: U.N. Report Reveals That Secretary-General Kofi Annan Dismissed Sexual Harassment Charges; Oct. 13, 2004: Television Producer Files Sex Harassment Suit Against Bill O'Reilly.

WOODY ALLEN HAS AFFAIR WITH LOVER MIA FARROW'S ADOPTED DAUGHTER

For more than a decade, filmmaker Woody Allen was a romantic partner and artistic collaborator with actor Mia Farrow. In early 1992, Farrow learned that Allen had been having a romantic relationship with Soon-Yi Previn, her adopted daughter from a previous marriage. In the ensuing controversy, which led to a very public custody case, Farrow charged Allen, also, with molesting Dylan, Allen and Farrow's adopted daughter.

ALSO KNOWN AS: Allen-Farrow scandal
LOCALE: New York, New York
CATEGORIES: Sex; families and children; public morals; law and the courts; publishing and journalism

KEY FIGURES
Woody Allen (b. 1935), American filmmaker and actor
Mia Farrow (b. 1945), American film star
Soon-Yi Previn (b. 1970), Farrow's Korean-born adopted daughter

SUMMARY OF EVENT
Woody Allen and Mia Farrow were celebrated as a leading power couple throughout the 1980's. Though they never legally wed, they were so tightly linked together in the mind of the public, both on screen and off, that when their alliance ended in 1992, scandal was inevitable. Public shock was intensified by the degree of acrimony that the split-up engendered, and by its surprising cause.

By the time the scandal erupted, Woody Allen had been a household name for thirty years. He began his career as a gag writer for other humorists before embarking on a successful career of his own as a stand-up comedian. He began writing and appearing in various cinematic spoofs during the early 1960's and, by the end of the decade, had written and directed his first feature film: *Take the Money*

and Run (1969). A number of critical and popular successes followed, culminating in the bittersweet romantic comedy *Annie Hall* (1977), which garnered a number of Oscar nominations and is considered by many critics to be one of the best American comedic films. Early in his directorial career, Allen showed a tendency to emulate the renowned European directors whom he idolized, including Federico Fellini and Ingmar Bergman, by employing a repertory stable of actors film after film. He especially wanted a recurring female lead, and that lead often was his romantic partner. From 1980 through 1992, Farrow filled that dual role.

Farrow was a product of Hollywood—the daughter of actor Maureen O'Sullivan and agent John Farrow. She became a star as a teenager playing Allison McKenzie on the night-time soap opera *Peyton Place*, which led to an Oscar-nominated role as the protagonist in Roman Polanski's horror masterpiece *Rosemary's Baby* in 1968. Her love life drew attention throughout the 1960's and 1970's, when she wed singer Frank Sinatra and then, later, musician and conductor André Previn, both of whom were old enough to be her father. The marriage to Sinatra lasted only two years, but the marriage to Previn lasted a decade, during which the couple had three sons and adopted three daughters. Daughter Soon-Yi Previn had been abandoned in Korea as a child to a birth mother who might have been abusive to her.

Soon after Farrow and Previn divorced, Farrow met Allen, and they became inseparable. The two lovers had apartments near each other in New York, and Allen was frequently in the company of Farrow's children, whose number had by the end of the 1980's increased to include a child—Satchel—born to Allen and Farrow, and two children the couple had adopted: a boy named Moses and a girl named Dylan. (Farrow later changed the names of all three children.)

At some point around 1990, Allen and Previn,

Woody Allen kisses Soon-Yi Previn two days after the couple wed in Venice. (AP/Wide World Photos)

who by this time was twenty years old, became romantically involved. Farrow found out about the affair on the morning of January 13, 1992, when she let herself into Allen's apartment and discovered on his mantelpiece some nude photographs of her daughter. Farrow soon confronted Allen, who apparently tried to placate her by playing down what had happened as a brief lapse in propriety, but soon after the release of their last film together, *Husbands and Wives* (1992), the couple parted company. The cause of their separation made headlines around the world, as they began to feud publicly. Most of the initial sniping between the two amounted to little more than acidic remarks made to reporters until the question of the custody of their three children arose.

As the custody issue was going to court, Farrow made the stunning allegation that Allen, while visiting the children at her country home in Connecticut,

had sexually abused Dylan, causing the little girl to be terrified of her adoptive father. Allen responded that this claim was an untruth concocted by Farrow to punish him for his relationship with Previn. After listening to much debate between Allen's and Farrow's attorneys, a judge in Connecticut announced that the evidence was too inconclusive to charge Allen with molestation, but she sharply criticized him for his conduct with both Previn and Dylan. The judge awarded Farrow primary custody, with Allen getting rights to supervised visitation with the children.

During and after the court case in Connecticut, friends and family of Farrow and Allen took sides publicly, as did critics and commentators in the news and entertainment media. Those in Allen's camp argued that child molestation tends to be compulsive, repetitive, and patterned behavior, yet Allen had never before been suspected of such conduct, including during the decade in which he was frequently in the company of Farrow's numerous children. Farrow's supporters pointed to a common motif in a number of Allen's films, in which older men are attracted to young girls. These films include *Manhattan* (1979) and *Husbands and Wives*.

For years after the custody battle, Allen and Farrow continued to make caustic remarks about each other, but both resumed their respective careers. Allen and Previn began to appear in public frequently as a couple, and within five years they married, on Christmas Eve, 1997, in Venice, Italy. They later adopted two daughters of their own. Farrow and Previn have been estranged from each other since Previn's marriage to Allen.

IMPACT

The Farrow-Allen-Previn triangle is a textbook example of a public scandal from which no one emerged unscathed. Although much sympathy accrued to Farrow as the wronged lover and mother, questions arose about choices she had made in adopting numerous children, some with special needs, and then trying to bring them up in seemingly unorthodox, unstructured circumstances and with a partner who maintained a separate residence and adopted some but not all of the children. Also, some agreed with Allen's supporters that Farrow's sudden denunciation of Allen as a molester seemed ideally and theatrically timed, coming as it did after the discovery of his involvement with Previn and just before the custody hearings. Although Previn remained relatively quiet during and after the scandal, many saw her as a cruel, faithless, and ungrateful daughter.

It was Allen, though, whose reputation suffered the most. Apart from the wry humor, the most appealing aspect of his films had long been their compassionate portrayal of characters experiencing the disappointments, insecurities, and contradictions of everyday life. As soon as the news of his relationship with Previn hit the media, though, the public saw another facet of Allen, a cold and haughty one. He seemed insensitive and uncaring, wholly unconcerned with the pain he had caused a woman with whom he had shared twelve years of intimacy and fruitful artistic collaboration. Also, for a person who had spent most of his adult life in psychoanalysis, his take on his relationship with Farrow's children seemed simultaneously unsophisticated and naïve. He continued to stress that he had never really been a father figure to the children, meaning that there was nothing improper about his falling in love with Previn. While he might not have been a father figure to the Previn siblings, he was one to the younger children; Allen would have been the only stable male authority figure and role model in their young lives. If he truly refused to play such a role in their lives, he appears irresponsible at best; if he was simply denying his role as a father to excuse his affair with Previn, he appears selfish.

—*Thomas Du Bose*

FURTHER READING

Bailey, Peter J. *The Reluctant Film Art of Woody Allen*. Lexington: University Press of Kentucky, 2001. Comprehensive overview and analysis of all aspects of Allen's creative work, including articles, fiction, and his many films.

Ewing, Charles Patrick, and Joseph T. McCann. *Minds on Trial: Great Cases in Law and Psychology*. New York: Oxford University Press, 2006. An examination of some of the most historically significant legal cases involving a clear psychological element. Includes a chapter on the Allen-Farrow custody battle and charges of molestation against Allen.

Farrow, Mia. *What Falls Away: A Memoir*. New York: Doubleday, 1997. A detailed account of the scandal, including the day Farrow found out about Allen's affair with her daughter. Also includes fascinating recollections of Farrow's childhood in Hollywood and her experience during the 1950's with polio, which gave her special insight into the needs of children around the world.

Skoble, Aeon J., and Mark T. Conrad, eds. *Woody Allen and Philosophy*. Peru, Ill.: Open Court, 2004. Philosophical analyses of the ethos of Allen's work, interesting especially in light of the scandal, as it contains essays on integrity and morality as defined in his films.

SEE ALSO: Jan. 20, 1933: Hedy Lamarr Appears Nude in the Czech Film *Exstase*; Feb. 6, 1942: Film Star Errol Flynn Is Acquitted of Rape; May 27, 1949: Actor Rita Hayworth Marries Aly Khan After Adulterous Affair; Feb. 7, 1950: Swedish Film Star Ingrid Bergman Has a Child Out of Wedlock; Dec. 12, 1957: Rock Star Jerry Lee Lewis Marries Thirteen-Year-Old Cousin; Apr. 4, 1958: Actor Lana Turner's Daughter Kills Turner's Gangster Lover; 1978: Actor Joan Crawford's Daughter Publishes Damning Memoir, *Mommie Dearest*; Feb. 1, 1978: Roman Polanski Flees the United States to Avoid Rape Trial; Dec. 18, 2003: Pop Star Michael Jackson Is Charged with Child Molestation.

1990's

April 15, 1992
HOTEL TYCOON LEONA HELMSLEY ENTERS PRISON FOR TAX EVASION

Hotel tycoon Leona Helmsley once declared, "only the little people pay taxes," words that set off a scandal during her trial for federal tax evasion and other charges in 1989. She was convicted of underpaying taxes and, after losing her appeal, began her eighteen-month prison term in 1992. She died in 2007 and left the bulk of her multibillion-dollar estate to the care and welfare of dogs.

LOCALE: New York, New York
CATEGORIES: Law and the courts; corruption; business

KEY FIGURES

Leona Helmsley (1920-2007), hotel operator and real-estate investor
Harry Helmsley (1909-1997), real-estate and hotel investor

SUMMARY OF EVENT

Leona Helmsley came from immigrant roots. She was born to a Polish-Jewish hatmaker in Marbletown, New York. After she had experienced several unsuccessful marriages, she was courted in 1968 by millionaire real estate investor Harry Helmsley, who was married at the time. In 1970, she joined one of his brokerage firms, Brown, Harris & Stevens, and her troubles soon began. In late 1971, she was sued by several clients for forcing apartment tenants to buy condominiums, threatening eviction if they did not buy quickly. She lost the lawsuit and was ordered to pay the tenants and grant them three-year leases. Her real estate license was suspended as well.

In April, 1972, Helmsley married Harry and focused on running his empire of hotels. Together, the two expanded their real estate holdings, building the opulent Helmsley Palace Hotel with more than eleven hundred rooms and standing fifty-one sto-

ries on Madison Avenue in Manhattan, New York. The Helmsleys also acquired 230 Park Avenue, the Empire State Building, and the building that became the New York Helmsley Hotel, as well as holdings in other states. Helmsley was featured in advertisements that portrayed her as a demanding manager who worked to achieve only the best for her guests, although rumor maintained that in reality she was even meaner, firing employees over the slightest of infractions.

The Helmsleys also had a habit of disputing payments to contractors and vendors. In 1983, they had bought an eleven-million-dollar Greenwich, Connecticut, mansion to use as a weekend retreat. The mansion, Dunnellen Hall, was located on a twenty-six-acre estate. They disputed a portion of an eight-million-dollar remodeling bill, claiming that the work was inadequate and that they were overbilled by contractors. With the dispute over the overbilling came the question of having to pay taxes on the services as well. The Helmsleys balked. In the course of the resulting legal action in 1985, it was discovered that the remodeling work had been billed to Helmsley Hotels as a business expense. While this was not an uncommon business practice, it was an illegal one. Angry contractors sent overdue invoices to the *New York Post*, and the resulting story set off a federal investigation. U.S. agents discovered that more than four million dollars in personal expenses had been illegally billed to Helmsley subsidiaries.

In late 1988, the Helmsleys and two associates, Frank Turco and Joseph Licarci, were indicted on 188 counts of tax fraud as well as extortion and mail fraud. The trial was delayed by Helmsley's attorneys, who made the most of Harry's health issues, until midway through 1989. Harry had suffered a stroke and mental deterioration a few months before the trial and was ruled mentally and physically unfit to stand trial, leaving Leona Helmsley in the courtroom to face the charges. The trial finally began on June 26 in the court of Federal District judge John M. Walker, Jr.

Helmsley's reputation as a demanding ruler would end up working against her. The case was followed closely by the media, which dubbed Helmsley the Queen of Mean. Reporters interviewed her employees, uncovering hundreds of accounts of incidents where they had been threatened and verbally abused before being fired, often for slight infractions. Helmsley's staffers said that she extorted money and services from suppliers and employees and threatened to withdraw the income she provided them.

Her employees appeared in court as well. Elizabeth Baum, a former housekeeper, testified that Helmsley told her in 1983, "We [the rich] don't pay taxes. Only the little people pay taxes." Another staff member recalled being fired while Helmsley was being fitted for a dress. One executive was chased down a hallway after telling Helmsley he was quitting. Maids were screamed at and fired over leaving lint on a floor or leaving a lampshade out of alignment.

Helmsley's team of lawyers was led by Gerald A. Feffer, who was an expert in tax-fraud litigation. Assistant U.S. attorney James DeVita headed the prosecuting team. DeVita pointed to years of false invoices, tax fraud, extortion, and kickbacks on the part of the Helmsleys. Feffer claimed that Leona Helmsley had no knowledge of the falsified invoices, which had been created by Turco and Licarci because they wanted to pay the house-remodeling contractors without her knowledge. Turco's and Licarci's lawyers insisted at trial that Helmsley was indeed aware of the falsified invoices.

On August 30, 1989, Helmsley was acquitted of extortion. She was, however, convicted on one count to defraud the United States, three counts of tax evasion, three counts of filing false personal tax returns, sixteen counts of as-

sisting in filing false corporate and partnership tax returns, and ten counts of mail fraud for sending fraudulent invoices via the U.S. postal service. Overall, the convictions could have added up to more than one century in prison. Helmsley initially received a sentence of sixteen years but, eventually, all but eight charges were dropped. She was fined more than seven million dollars. Licarci received a sentence of thirty months in prison, three years probation, and a seventy-five million dollar fine, while Turco was sentenced to twenty-four months in prison and three years of probation and was fined fifty thousand dollars.

Helmsley collapsed outside the courthouse on the day the verdicts were read and was subsequently diagnosed with hypertension and a heart problem. She appealed to the New York State Supreme Court and succeeded in having her sentence minimized. She served eighteen months in a federal prison beginning on April 15 (tax day), 1992.

Helmsley died of congestive heart failure on August 20, 2007, at the age of eighty-seven and nearly

Leona Helmsley leaving court in New York City on February 8, 1990. (AP/Wide World Photos)

forgotten by the media and public. Former New York City mayor Edward I. Koch reportedly referred to her as the "wicked witch of the West," while entrepreneur Donald Trump said she was "the meanest woman in history." She was buried in Sleepy Hollow Cemetery in Westchester County, New York, near other public figures, such as Washington Irving and Andrew Carnegie, in a Greek-style mausoleum of thirteen-hundred square feet that features custom stained-glass windows of the New York skyline.

IMPACT

After her time in federal prison, Helmsley spent most of the rest of her life in isolation. Harry died in 1997, leaving to her his fortune of more than five billion dollars. In 2002, she was sued by a former employee, Charles Bell, who alleged that she had fired him because he is gay. A jury found in his favor and ordered Helmsley to pay him more than ten million dollars in damages, an amount later reduced by a judge to just over one-half million dollars.

In her later years, Helmsley was generous to charities, including the Red Cross in the aftermath of Hurricane Katrina in 2005, to African American churches that had been the victims of arsonists, and to numerous hospitals and medical centers. She donated twenty-five million dollars to New York's Presbyterian Hospital for medical research and contributed five million dollars to a fund for the families of firefighters killed following the terrorist attacks of September 11, 2001. Upon her death, the majority of her estate was left to a charitable trust, although twelve million dollars was reserved as a trust fund for her Maltese dog, Trouble. (This amount was later reduced to two million by the court.) In July, 2008, the Helmsley estate executors announced that Helmsley willed the bulk of her fortune, between five and eight billion dollars, to the care and welfare of dogs. She was far less generous with the majority of her family, with whom she had a long tumultuous relationship. She left fifteen mil-

lion for her brother and left nothing for two of her four grandchildren. The two left out subsequently received a few million by order of the courts.

—Catherine Rambo

FURTHER READING

Hammer, Richard. *The Helmsleys: The Rise and Fall of Harry and Leona*. New York: Signet, 1991. Describes the careers of the Helmsleys, the federal trial, and the trial's tribulations.

Moss, Michael. *Palace Coup: The Inside Story of Harry and Leona Helmsley*. New York: Doubleday, 1989. Written by a former employee of Leona Helmsley, this book describes events before and up to the time of the trial.

Pierson, Randall. *The Queen of Mean: Leona Helmsley*. New York: Bantam Books, 1989. Focuses on the people who had worked with Helmsley.

Randall, Stephen, ed. *The "Playboy" Interviews: Movers and Shakers*. Milwaukie, Oreg.: M Press, 2007. Includes a November, 1990, interview of Leona Helmsley by Glenn Plaskin. Revealing in its content. Part of the *Playboy* Interviews series.

Strom, Stephanie. "Helmsley Left Dogs Billions in Her Will." *The New York Times*, July 2, 2008. The news story about Helmsley leaving the majority of her estate to the care and welfare of dogs.

SEE ALSO: Sept. 10, 1981: *Chicago Sun-Times* Reports That Cardinal Cody Diverted Church Funds; Oct. 19, 1982: Car Manufacturer John De Lorean Is Arrested in a Drug Sting; May 2, 1984: E. F. Hutton Executives Plead Guilty to Fraud; Jan. 15, 1988: ZZZZ Best Founder Is Indicted on Federal Fraud Charges; Mar. 29, 1989: Financier Michael Milken Is Indicted for Racketeering and Fraud; Mar. 5, 2004: Martha Stewart Is Convicted in Insider-Trading Scandal.

May 6, 1992
Irish Bishop Eamonn Casey's Romantic Affair Leads to His Resignation

Bishop Eamonn Casey was an outspoken social and political reformist. In 1992, he admitted to having engaged in a romantic affair with a distant cousin in 1973 and that they had a child together. This revelation forced Casey's resignation from his see and led to his exile. Years later, an Irish woman alleged that Casey had sexually abused her. However, police determined the charges were groundless.

Locale: Ireland
Categories: Public morals; religion; sex; families and children

Key Figures
Eamonn Casey (b. 1927), bishop of Kerry, 1969-1976, and of Galway and Kilmacduagh, 1976-1992
Annie Murphy (b. 1949), Casey's former lover
Peter Murphy (b. 1974), Casey and Murphy's son

Summary of Event
Bishop Eamonn Casey, by all appearances a fairly typical Irish Roman Catholic Church administrator—though one who had more liberal views than most—was born in 1927 in the village of Firies in County Kerry, Ireland. He was the sixth child in a family of ten children. Choosing a religious vocation, he was ordained as a Catholic priest in 1951. After some eighteen years in the priesthood, Casey was consecrated bishop of Kerry, serving from 1969 through 1976. He was then translated to the diocese of Galway and Kilmacduagh and held the position of bishop until May 5, 1992.

Annie Murphy was an American who was related to Bishop Casey. Her mother was the bishop's distant cousin and her father, John Murphy, was a physician who practiced in New York. She had nearly been raped at the age of sixteen, had been sexually abused during a relationship, and was

abused by her husband. She had suffered a miscarriage and was divorced at the age of twenty-three. Troubled and depressed, she traveled, at the behest of her immediate family, to Ireland in April, 1973, to stay at her cousin Casey's residence in Inch, County Kerry. Shortly thereafter, Murphy and Casey embarked upon an intense love affair.

In November, Murphy discovered that she was pregnant. She and Casey disagreed about whether she should keep the child or put it up for adoption. Casey wanted her to have the baby at Coombe Maternity Hospital in Dublin, where unwed mothers routinely arranged for their children to be adopted. Instead, Murphy opted to stay at the Rotunda Hospital, also in Dublin, and to maintain custody. Their child, a boy who was christened Peter, was born on July 31, 1974. Continued disagreements over Peter's welfare culminated in Murphy's return to the United States with her son. It was agreed that the affair and their child would be kept secret and that the bishop would send monthly payments of $175 to Murphy and Peter—an amount that would eventually increase to $300 per month. Ultimately, Casey agreed to send a lump sum payment for Peter's education through their attorneys. The total was about $115,000 and was paid in 1990, from diocesan funds.

Casey had gained notoriety for his pronouncedly anticonservative stance on many issues. From an international point of view, he took a prominent role in the 1979 visit of Pope John Paul II to Ireland and in opposing the role of the United States in Central America. He had been a friend and ardent admirer of the reform-minded archbishop Oscar Romero of El Salvador and, after Romero's assassination in 1980, represented the Irish episcopate and clergy at Romero's funeral. He witnessed and reported on an ensuing riot, during which military forces loyal to the El Salvadoran government killed some fifty individuals.

779

In 1984, Casey pointedly refused to participate in the visit to Ireland of U.S. president Ronald Reagan because of his support of rightist regimes and of the counterrevolutionary guerrilla forces (the Contras) in Nicaragua. During the 1980's, Casey's opposition to apartheid in South Africa led him to openly support the strike and boycott campaign waged against the giant retailing chain Dunne's Stores by some of its own employees. He is credited as a cofounder of two major charitable organizations—Trocaire, an Irish-based charity dedicated to developing world relief projects, which he chaired from 1973 to 1992, and Shelter, established in England to assist the homeless, particularly among the Irish immigrant community.

In the years that followed Murphy's return to the United States, she continued to lead an unsettled life, becoming involved in two serious relationships. At one time she attempted suicide. The secret of her connection with Bishop Casey was suppressed for eighteen years. The situation began unraveling as Peter approached adulthood and expressed his desire for his father to publicly acknowledge him. Legal wrangling over a paternity declaration and a monetary settlement led to a breakdown in negotiations between Casey on one hand and Murphy, Peter, and Murphy's boyfriend, Arthur Pennell on the other. Murphy, urged on by her son and Pennell, leaked the story of her liaison with Casey to the *Irish Times*, which, after conducting investigations, discovered evidence for the large monetary payment made from diocesan funds in 1990 and confronted Casey with its findings. Casey, who was in Malta at the time, arranged to meet with reporters upon his return. Instead, however, the bishop flew to Rome, where he tendered his resignation as bishop, directly to the pope. Casey never met with the reporters.

On May 6, 1992, Casey announced his resignation. The *Irish Times* reported the resignation on May 7, adding financial details to the story. Shortly thereafter, Casey issued a statement admitting to the affair, acknowledged his son, and mentioned the misappropriation of funds that had, he added, been repaid by anonymous donors.

Immediately after his resignation, Casey, soon to be given the title bishop emeritus, flew to the United States and then Latin America. He spent the next six years as a missionary in Ecuador under the auspices of the Society of St. James the Apostle. In 1998, he left for southern England and served as pastor for St. Paul's Church in the village of Hayward's Heath, which was part of the diocese of Arundel and Brighton.

In November of 2005, a former female parishioner accused him of sexually molesting her during the mid-1970's while she was living in the Irish city of Limerick. The Irish woman's identity was never revealed. In December, Casey suspended his ministry at St. Paul's (he was never to return), while the Irish Gardai (police) investigated. By August of 2006, he was cleared of all charges. It was later revealed that the woman who made the accusations was a habitual accuser.

IMPACT

Rather than return to his parochial duties in England, Casey decided to retire. On February 5, 2006, before he was exonerated, he had returned to Ireland and taken up residence at the village of Shanaglish, County Galway. The bishop emeritus was granted permission to conduct his own private mass at his residence but, even though exonerated by civil authorities, he was denied authorization to celebrate mass at church pending completion of the Vatican's own investigation. Also in 2006, Casey, Murphy, and Peter reconciled.

The shock waves that emanated from the disgrace and sudden removal of the person who had been regarded as the most visible face of the Catholic hierarchy in Ireland signaled the first of a series of scandals involving the sexual abuse of minors by Catholic clerics around the Western world. Though these sex-abuse scandals have since made the Casey-Murphy affair (which was between consenting adults) seem mild in comparison, the revelations that led to Casey's resignation initiated a decline in the Catholic Church's prestige and political influence in the Republic of Ireland.

—*Raymond Pierre Hylton*

FURTHER READING

Brady, Conor. *Up with the Times.* Dublin: Gill & Macmillan, 2005. Provides background to *Irish Times* coverage of the Casey-Murphy scandal and its aftermath. Brady was editor of the *Irish Times* from 1986 to 2002.

Broderick, Joe. *Fall from Grace: The Life of Eamonn Casey.* Dingle, Ireland: Brandon House Press, 1992. Somewhat one-sided in that the author derived much from Annie Murphy's account of the affair, though lacking the florid detail of Murphy's own later work.

Murphy, Annie, with Peter de Rosa. *Forbidden Fruit: The True Story of My Secret Love Affair with Ireland's Most Powerful Bishop.* Boston: Little, Brown, 1993. A graphic and personalized account of the turbulent relationship. Murphy cites the controversy about whether or not to have Peter adopted as the major factor in her estrangement from Casey.

SEE ALSO: May 20, 1974: French Cardinal Daniélou Dies in a Prostitute's House; Oct. 31, 1975: Buddhist Teacher Orders His Students to Remove Their Clothes; Sept. 10, 1981: *Chicago Sun-Times* Reports That Cardinal Cody Diverted Church Funds; Mar. 19, 1987: Jim Bakker Resigns as Head of PTL Television Network; May, 1999: Civil Rights Leader Jesse Jackson Fathers a Child Out of Wedlock; Jan. 6, 2002: *Boston Globe* Reports on Child Sexual Abuse by Roman Catholic Priests.

May 19, 1992
AMY FISHER SHOOTS MARY JO BUTTAFUOCO

Later known as the Long Island Lolita, teenager Amy Fisher became infatuated with Joey Buttafuoco, a married auto-body shop owner. Fisher, wanting to marry Buttafuoco, with whom she was having an affair, shot and attempted to kill his wife, Mary Jo. The story became a sensation in the American media.

LOCALE: Massapequa, Long Island, New York

CATEGORIES: Communications and media; law and the courts; violence; families and children; psychology and psychiatry

KEY FIGURES

Amy Fisher (b. 1974), teenager who was having an affair with Joey Buttafuoco

Mary Jo Buttafuoco (Mary Jo Connery; b. 1955), wife of Joey Buttafuoco

Joey Buttafuoco (b. 1956), automobile shop owner

Peter Guagenti (b. c. 1972), Fisher's accomplice

SUMMARY OF EVENT

Amy Fisher apparently was a shy and insecure child who craved attention while growing up. She claimed that her father beat her as well as her mother. She also alleged that she was sexually abused by a family member while growing up as a young child in Long Island, New York, and that she was raped at the age of thirteen by a man working at her home.

In May, 1991, sixteen-year-old Fisher met thirty-five-year-old Joey Buttafuoco upon taking her car to Buttafuoco's auto-body shop for repair. At the time, Buttafuoco was married to Mary Jo Buttafuoco and had two children. Fisher quickly became infatuated with the auto mechanic and began hanging around his repair shop. By July, Fisher and Buttafuoco were sexually involved and carrying out their secret affair in Long Island hotels. By August, Fisher was still involved with Buttafuoco, and her attraction was becoming obsessive. Fisher finally told Buttafuoco he had to choose between her and

781

his wife. He chose to stay with Mary Jo, leading Fisher to break up with him.

Fisher became quite despondent. First, she made superficial cuts on her wrists, which may have been an attempt at suicide. She began dating other men, but she always wanted to get back together with Buttafuoco. By January, 1992, the two were once again together. Fisher came to believe that to keep Buttafuoco she would have to get rid of Mary Jo. Fisher later alleged that she and Buttafuoco discussed where to obtain a gun and how to shoot Mary Jo. Buttafuoco denied these claims.

On May 17, Fisher met the person who would supply her with a semiautomatic Titan .25 handgun: Peter Guagenti. Two days later, May 19, Fisher and Guagenti drove to the Buttafuoco home in Massapequa, New York. Before leaving, however, Fisher had replaced the license plates on Guagenti's car with stolen plates to ensure their car would not link

Amy Fisher. (AP/Wide World Photos)

them to the murder. Around 11:30 A.M., Fisher confronted Mary Jo on the front porch of the Buttafuoco home, gun in hand, and told her that Buttafuoco was having an affair with her (Fisher's) sister. Mary Jo told Fisher to get off her property, then turned away from her to reenter the house. Fisher then hit her on the head with the gun, and she fell to the ground. Fisher then shot her in the head.

Neighbors who heard the shots called 9-1-1 and tried to help Mary Jo, who was rushed to the local hospital and spent hours in surgery. By May 20 she was sufficiently conscious to speak with police. She told the officers that her attacker had held up a T-shirt she recognized from her husband's auto shop. Police immediately began to question Buttafuoco, who suggested that the shooter might have been Fisher. He said that she was obsessed with him. The police showed a photograph of Fisher to Mary Jo, and she identified Fisher as the person who shot her. The following day, with help from Buttafuoco, the police located and arrested Fisher for attempted murder in the second degree. Fisher also was charged with armed felony assault and criminal use of a firearm.

As the story began to unfold, it became clear that Buttafuoco also had some responsibility for the attempted murder of his wife, despite his repeated public denials of any relationship with Fisher. The media, which dubbed Fisher the Long Island Lolita, quickly picked up on the sex-charged and scandalous story. She became a cultural phenomenon, and her life story was broadcast on television and in the print media. Three television films documented her life.

Fisher's criminal case was docketed in the Nassau County, Long Island, court, where she initially pleaded not guilty. Her bail was set at $2 million, the highest bail ever set by the Nassau County court. Fisher was unable to pay the bail. She remained in jail until she sold the rights to her story to KLM Productions, using the money to post bail. Although New York state's Son of Sam law prevents criminals from making money based on the stories of their crimes, the law was not invoked in the Fisher case.

Fisher eventually agreed to a plea bargain in which she would plead guilty to aggravated assault and testify against Buttafuoco for statutory rape. In September, 1992, she was sentenced to five to fifteen years. In 1999, after serving seven years at New York's Albion Correctional Facility, she was paroled and released from prison after entering into a new plea bargain that carried a sentence of three to ten years. Mary Jo was behind the new plea-bargain agreement.

Buttafuoco was indicted on charges of statutory rape, endangering the welfare of a minor, and sodomy, based largely on the testimony of Fisher and evidence from one hotel receipt dated before Fisher's seventeenth birthday. In October, 1993, Buttafuoco pleaded guilty to statutory rape and entered a plea bargain that netted him four months in jail. Guagenti served a six-month sentence for supplying Fisher with the gun.

In 2003, Fisher married Louis Bellara, whom she had met online while she was in prison; he was twenty-four years older than Fisher. The couple had two children. Fisher also became a columnist for the *Long Island Press* and won a media award for her column in 2004. She left the newspaper in 2005. She also became an activist for prisoners' rights and prison reform, inspired in part by her experiences in prison, including an alleged rape by a correctional officer.

The Buttafuocos moved to California after the shooting and were divorced in 2003. He remarried in 2006. Buttafuoco's legal troubles continued, as he faced charges for soliciting a prostitute in 1995 and was fined and given probation; was convicted of auto insurance fraud in 2004, for which he pleaded guilty and served one year in jail; and pleaded no contest for illegal possession of ammunition in 2005, for which he served a few months in jail. Mary Jo changed her last name to Connery, her birth name, and founded a company that designs posters. Her injuries from the shooting, including permanent nerve damage and paralysis, blurred vision in her right eye, and hearing loss, have affected her life since.

IMPACT

The Amy Fisher story became an instant money-maker. Sex and scandal sells, and as long as the pub-

Mary Jo and Joey Buttafuoco. (AP/Wide World Photos)

lic is willing to pay, entrepreneurs will continue to make money from this and similar stories.

In addition to earning money from the television films about her life, Fisher wrote and published two tell-all books. A sex tape of Fisher appeared on the World Wide Web in the fall of 2007, leading her to sue Red Light District, a hard-core-sex film distribution company, for releasing the tape, which allegedly was sold to the company by her husband at the time. In 2008, Red Light District also began selling a video of Buttafuoco having sex with his wife, Evanka, at a party in 2004. Mary Jo Buttafuoco made money from the scandal as well, but she used the funds she earned to help defray her tremendous medical bills. Moreover, rumors persisted that Fisher and Buttafuoco were planning to launch a reality show.

Fisher and Buttafuoco were reunited at a coin toss for the so-called "Lingerie Bowl"—a heavily criticized pay-per-view alternative halftime show broadcast from Los Angeles on another station dur-

1990's

ing Super Bowl Sunday. In May, 2007, the two reportedly were seen together in Long Island. Also in 2007, their spouses filed for divorce, but Evanka Buttafuoco soon withdrew her petition.

—Carol A. Rolf

FURTHER READING

Dominguez, Pier. *Amy Fisher, Anatomy of a Scandal: The Myth, the Media, and the Truth Behind the Long Island Lolita Story*. Lincoln, Nebr.: Writers Club Press, 2001. Based on interviews, court documents, and archival research, this biography looks beyond the media accounts in presenting Amy Fisher's life story.

Eftimiades, Maria. *Lethal Lolita: A True Story of Sex, Scandal, and Deadly Obsession*. New York: St. Martin's Press, 1992. True-crime author Eftimiades presents a biographical account of Fisher before the scandal, outlines the details leading up to Fisher's shooting of Mary Jo Buttafuoco, and examines the criminal trial.

Fisher, Amy, with Sheila Weller. *Amy Fisher: My Story*. Reprint. New York: Pocket Books, 1994. Written soon after Fisher's conviction for attempted murder of Mary Jo Buttafuoco, Fisher and her mother attempt to explain and justify Fisher's criminal behavior.

Fisher, Amy, with Robbie Woliver. *If I Knew Then*. Lincoln, Nebr.: iUniverse, 2004. Fisher, now married with children, tells her own life story, including taking responsibility for her criminal actions.

Hornberger, Francine. *Mistresses of Mayhem: The Book of Women Criminals*. Indianapolis, Ind.: Alpha, 2002. A collection for general readers that includes a discussion of the Amy Fisher scandal.

SEE ALSO: June 25, 1906: Millionaire Heir Murders Architect Stanford White; Dec. 8, 1906: Former U.S. Senator Arthur Brown Is Murdered by Lover; July 27, 1917: Millionaire Socialite Dies Under Suspicious Circumstances; Apr. 4, 1958: Actor Lana Turner's Daughter Kills Turner's Gangster Lover; Sept. 5, 1967: Socialite Nancy Wakeman Shoots Her Politician-Husband; Mar. 21, 1976: Actor Claudine Longet Kills Ski Champion Vladimir Sabich; Mar. 10, 1980: Scarsdale Diet Doctor Is Killed by His Lover; Mar., 1990: Menendez Brothers Are Arrested for Murdering Their Parents; June 23, 1993: Lorena Bobbitt Severs Her Husband's Penis; June 12, 1994: Double Murder Leads to Sensational O. J. Simpson Trial.

June 26, 1992
U.S. NAVY SECRETARY RESIGNS IN THE WAKE OF TAILHOOK SEXUAL ASSAULT SCANDAL

H. Lawrence Garrett III, secretary of the U.S. Navy, was forced to resign after investigators looking into sexual assault charges at the 1991 Tailhook convention of naval aviators revealed that he was in attendance but did nothing to stop the assaults, harassment, and abuse of mostly female aviators and other women. As a result of the scandal, the Navy severed all ties to the Tailhook Association until 1999.

LOCALES: Las Vegas, Nevada; Washington, D.C.

CATEGORIES: Politics; military; government; women's issues; space and aviation; sex crimes

KEY FIGURES

H. Lawrence Garrett III (b. 1939), secretary of the U.S. Navy, 1989-1992

Frank B. Kelso, Jr. (b. 1933), Navy admiral, chief of naval operations, 1990-1994

Richard M. Dunleavy (b. 1933), Navy vice admiral and assistant chief of naval operations, 1989-1992

Paula Coughlin (b. 1963), Navy
   lieutenant and aviator
Derek Vander Schaaf (b. 1939),
   deputy inspector general, U.S.
   Department of Defense 1982-
   1996
John W. Snyder, Jr. (fl. 1990's),
   Navy rear admiral, commander
   of the Naval Air Test Center
Barbara S. Pope (b. 1951), assistant
   secretary of the Navy for
   Manpower and Reserve Affairs,
   1989-1993
J. Daniel Howard (b. 1944),
   undersecretary of the Navy,
   1989-1992

Summary of Event

Sponsors of the 1991 Tailhook Association Conference of naval aviators
at the Las Vegas Hilton Hotel in Nevada promised that year's gathering
would be special. The Tailhook Association, named for the hook that
aids an aviator in landing a jet or
other aircraft on the deck of an aircraft carrier, had been organizing an
annual event for more than thirty years; for two decades Las Vegas had been the conference's home.
Many U.S. Navy and U.S. Marine Corps aviators
from around the world converged on the city for
three days in September, ostensibly to attend professional seminars and examine the latest aviation
and war-fighting equipment displayed by vendors
who helped underwrite the conference.

Most aviators in attendance at Tailhook over the
years were men. Women had been excluded from
careers in naval aviation until the mid-1970's and
excluded as fighter pilots until 1993, thereby reducing the number of female aviators who would have
attended Tailhook. In practice, the convention had
become a place for attendees to let inhibitions run
wild—in other words, to party. While few wives or
female aviators attended Tailhook, women from the
Las Vegas area and other communities were lured
to the convention on the promise of being able to

*Former Navy lieutenant Paula Coughlin, right, in Las Vegas, Nevada, in
September, 1991.* (AP/Wide World Photos)

spend time with the aviators. The junior officers
routinely engaged in inappropriate behavior that included sexual misconduct and vandalism. Senior
officers seemed to tacitly approve the behavior, as
many did the same as junior officers, participating
in the annual series of pranks. Among attendees in
1991 were nearly three dozen senior officers, including the chief of Naval Operations, Admiral
Frank B. Kelso, Jr.; his assistant for air operations,
Vice Admiral Richard M. Dunleavy; and the secretary of the Navy, H. Lawrence Garrett III.

Among the more flamboyant rites at Tailhook
was the gauntlet, a cordon of aviators who made it a
practice of fondling, groping, or otherwise hassling
any woman who wandered down the hotel corridor
where they gathered. On September 7, Navy lieutenant Paula Coughlin, an aviator then working as
an aide to Rear Admiral John Snyder, commander
of the Naval Test Center in Patuxent, Maryland,

SEVERING TIES WITH TAILHOOK

On October 29, 1991, Secretary of the Navy H. Lawrence Garrett III wrote the following letter to Captain F. G. Ludwig, Jr., the president of the Tailhook Association, to sever the Navy's ties to the organization. Although Garrett claimed to be angered by the events that took place at the 1991 Tailhook convention, it was later revealed that he had attended the conference, and he was forced to resign as Navy secretary. The Navy reestablished ties with Tailhook in 1999.

Dear Captain Ludwig,

I am writing to you, and through you to your organization, to express my absolute outrage over the conduct reported to have taken place at the Tailhook Association symposium in September. . . .

Besides my anger, I am more than personally disappointed. The Tailhook Association has been, in the past, a source of great professionalism and esprit, an organization where productive dialogues and seminars have had a home. In particular, Tailhook '91 provided me with a superb forum to air some of the most serious issues that Naval Aviation has ever faced. But none of those attributes can make up for the personal abuses, behavioral excesses, and quite possibly criminal conduct that took place at Tailhook '91 and have now been reported to me.

There are certain categories of behavior and attitudes that I unequivocally will not tolerate. You know the phrase: "Not in my Navy, not on my watch." Tailhook '91 is a gross example of exactly what cannot be permitted by the civilian or uniformed leadership of the Navy, at any level. No man who holds a commission in this Navy will ever subject a woman to the kind of abuse in evidence at Tailhook '91 with impunity. And no organization which makes possible this behavior is in any way worthy of a naval leadership or advisory role.

Admiral Frank Kelso, our Chief of Naval Operations, and I have discussed this matter and, based upon his recommendation and with his full support, I am terminating, effective immediately, all Navy support in any manner whatsoever, direct or indirect, for the Tailhook Association.

Last April I sent a message to every command in the Navy about the progress of our women officers and sailors. I said then that I would reinforce a position of zero tolerance of sexual harassment, and I meant it. That policy was not new in April, nor when I became Secretary—but obviously it was as necessary then as it is now to reiterate just how strongly I feel about this matter. Also in April, with my strong concurrence, Admiral Kelso made specifically clear in a parallel message that a Navy free from sexual harassment or intimidation is a leadership issue. Together we made certain that the whole Navy knew: "Each of you, from the most junior sailor to the most senior officer, has a responsibility to build working and living spaces free from unprofessional conduct, fear, and prejudice." The Tailhook Association most certainly did not live up to that responsibility.

was forced to pass through the gauntlet and was assaulted by dozens of her male colleagues, despite her efforts to fight them off. Rather than ignore the incident, as many other women had done, Coughlin determined to see the perpetrators punished for what was nothing less than sexual assault.

The response to Coughlin's complaint by naval leadership was far from satisfactory. Although she reported the incident to Snyder the day after it occurred, he did nothing initially, telling her she should have expected such behavior under the circumstances. Coughlin pressed her case, going directly to the chief of Naval Operations for some resolution. Not until late October, however, did Secretary Garrett become aware of Coughlin's allegations. He decided some action was necessary. Within weeks, Snyder was relieved of his command, and separate investigations were launched by the Naval Investigative Service (NIS) and the Navy's Inspector General (IG).

During the months these investigations were underway, stories of Tailhook misdeeds began surfacing within the Navy and in the press, further escalating the gravity of the situation for Navy officials. There were calls from Congress members for the Navy to take this matter seriously, and legislators threatened to hold up all naval officer promotions until there were assurances that those nominated for promotion had not participated in illegal activities at Tailhook. These pressures notwithstanding, when the NIS and IG submitted their reports to Garrett, about two dozen possible victims were identified and only two officers were named as possible perpetrators. Furthermore, the reports recommended only mild reforms.

Assistant Secretary of the Navy Barbara S. Pope, the first woman to serve as assistant secretary in the Navy's history, urged Garrett to delve deeper into the matter, and he in turn asked the U.S. Department of Defense to launch a new investigation. Derek Vander Schaaf, a deputy inspector general at the Pentagon, headed up the new investigative team. The team would also look into the environment that allowed such behavior to occur with seeming impunity. Initially, Vander Schaaf's investigators met with a wall of silence, as most aviators refused to reveal any details of what they might have seen or done. Senior leaders were no more helpful. Nevertheless, as reports of junior officers' behavior continued to surface, people outside the Navy began arguing that high-ranking officers and others within the service—and not simply junior officers—should be held accountable for their behavior.

Meanwhile, an appendix to one of the Navy's investigations revealed that despite Garrett's assurances that he had not been near any inappropriate or illegal activities at Tailhook 1991, evidence shows that he was seen at a party adjacent to the location of the infamous gauntlet. This information was made public in June, 1992, the same month Coughlin told her story on national television. It was becoming apparent to members of the George H. W. Bush administration that Garrett was a liability. At the encouragement of officials in the White House, he submitted his resignation on June 26. Undersecretary of the Navy J. Daniel Howard was named acting secretary. He immediately issued a series of orders directing the Navy and Marine Corps to take more serious measures to address issues of sexual harassment and more fully integrate women into all positions within the services.

The release of Vander Schaaf's report later in the year made apparent the extent of the scandal. More than seventy women had been assaulted at Tailhook 1991, and more than one hundred male officers—and not only two, as the NIS and IG reports claimed—were suspected of participating in the assaults or other inappropriate activities. Moreover, the report was highly critical of senior Navy and Marine Corps leadership for condoning these activities—and in some cases encouraging them.

Secretary of the Navy H. Lawrence Garrett III. (U.S. Department of Defense)

Vander Schaaf also faulted the Navy for conducting what was essentially a whitewash of Coughlin's claims and for inhibiting his investigation out of a misguided sense of loyalty within the aviation community and the Navy and Marine Corps as a whole. Furthermore, his report made it clear that a hostile climate existed in both services for women wishing to pursue careers that could lead them to positions of responsibility equal to their male counterparts.

IMPACT

The Bush administration moved quickly to restore stability at the top of the Department of the Navy, naming Garrett's permanent replacement within a month of his departure. In the next eighteen months, Dunleavy, charged with having personal knowledge of the gauntlet and failing to do anything to halt it, was forced to retire at a reduced rank. Other officers were similarly pressured into retirement or reassigned from key positions into less prestigious ones. Although these changes at the top of the military chain of command had some immediate impact on the management of the service, the more significant impact of the Tailhook scandal on the Navy occurred through the next decade.

New regulations required full integration of women into the service, the establishment of an office to focus on women in the Navy, and the development of a series of programs to educate officers, sailors, and Marines in matters regarding appropriate treatment of women in uniform. All of these changes had some positive effect on working conditions for women in the Navy. Nevertheless, subsequent incidents of inappropriate behavior, including sexual assault, within the fleet and at the U.S. Naval Academy proved that the disrespect for and resistance to women in the Navy were far from being eliminated.

—*Laurence W. Mazzeno*

FURTHER READING

Donovan, Aine, et al., eds. *Ethics for Military Leaders*. Needham Heights, Mass.: Simon & Schuster Educational, 1998. Explores the ethical implications of the Tailhook scandal. Includes a chronology, excerpts from the Department of Defense investigative report on the scandal, and essays presenting opposing viewpoints regarding the Navy's conduct in handling the matter.

Ebbert, Jean, and Marie-Beth Hall. *Crossed Currents: Navy Women from World War I to Tailhook*. Washington, D.C.: Brassey, 1993. Describes the Tailhook scandal and the impact of the Navy's initial attempts to downplay the serious nature of the sexual harassment and assault charges.

Godson, Susan H. *Serving Proudly: A History of Women in the U.S. Navy*. Annapolis, Md.: Naval Institute Press, 2001. Comments on the Tailhook scandal in the context of women's struggle to be accepted as naval aviators and colleagues.

McMichael, William H. *The Mother of All Hooks: The Story of the U.S. Navy's Tailhook Scandal*. New Brunswick, N.J.: Transaction, 1997. Detailed analysis of the 1991 convention and its aftermath. Explores the impact of the various investigations of the Navy and the military in general. Provides mitigating evidence that exonerates some who were not directly involved in incidences of sexual harassment and assault.

Zimmerman, Jean. *Tailspin: Women at War in the Wake of Tailhook*. New York: Doubleday, 1995. Examines the implications of the Tailhook scandal for women in the military, focusing specifically on its impact on the potential for women to serve in combat alongside their male colleagues.

SEE ALSO: July 19, 1921: U.S. Senate Rebukes Navy in Homosexuality Investigation; Oct. 4, 1976: Agriculture Secretary Earl Butz Resigns After Making Obscene Joke; Apr. 28, 1994: U.S. Naval Academy Expels Midshipmen for Cheating; May 20, 1997: Air Force Prosecution of Female Officer for Adultery Reveals Double Standard; Jan. 2, 2003: E-mail Message Prompts Inquiry into Air Force Academy Sexual Assaults; June 2, 2004: U.N. Report Reveals That Secretary-General Kofi Annan Dismissed Sexual Harassment Charges; Oct. 13, 2004: Television Producer Files Sex Harassment Suit Against Bill O'Reilly; June 22, 2005: U.S. Air Force Investigates Religious Intolerance at Its Academy; Mar. 14, 2006: Duke Lacrosse Players Are Accused of Gang Rape.

August 23, 1992
Princess Diana's Phone Conversation with Her Lover Is Made Public

Princess Diana's taped conversation with her lover marked the first of two significant and embarrassing instances of the press getting a hold of tape-recorded talks between senior members of the British royal family and their lovers. The adultery scandal soon was overshadowed by allegations that members of British intelligence agencies had been involved in monitoring the princess's calls and that they leaked the tapes for her husband, Prince Charles. The royal couple was in the middle of a divorce battle.

ALSO KNOWN AS: Squidgygate; Dianagate
LOCALES: Sandringham, Norfolk, and
   Oxfordshire area, England
CATEGORIES: Communications and media;
   public morals; publishing and journalism;
   royalty; sex

KEY FIGURES

Diana, Princess of Wales (1961-1997), princess
   of Wales, married to Prince Charles
James Gilbey (b. 1956), Diana's lover and heir to
   the Gilbey's gin fortune
Charles, Prince of Wales (b. 1948), Diana's
   husband, heir to the British throne
Cyril Reenan (1922-2004), amateur radio
   enthusiast
Jane Norgrove (fl. 1990's), amateur radio
   enthusiast

SUMMARY OF EVENT

The August 23, 1992, headline on the front page of *The Sun* revealed the existence of tape recordings of a telephone conversation between Princess Diana and James Gilbey—apparently from New Year's Eve, 1989. The story was sensational in three respects. First, it represented a significant escalation of the willingness of the British media to publish material embarrassing to the royal family, even when a clear breach of privacy was involved. Sec-

ond, the story left no possible doubt that Diana and Gilbey were involved in a sexual relationship that was, technically, treasonous. Third, the story called attention to the apparent vulnerability to eavesdroppers of conversations on cell phones. (Diana was apparently speaking from Sandringham House on a regular phone, while Gilbey was using a mobile phone in his car.)

The revelation that Diana was an adulterer, although titillating, caused little surprise, and its shock value was brief. The continued erosion of the traditional diplomacy maintained by the British press in respect of royalty caused no surprise at all, and only vain protest. The third element of the scandal, cell phone breaches, kept the story going, maintained its newsworthiness for weeks, and continued to generate speculation and discussion for years.

The Sun reportedly received the tape from amateur radio enthusiast Cyril Reenan, a former manager of the Trustee Savings Bank. Reenan apparently constructed an elaborate listening post at his home in Abingdon, Oxfordshire, so that he could spend his time in retirement eavesdropping on noncommercial radio broadcasts. He claimed that he had recorded the conversation between Diana and Gilbey "at hazard," that is, he came across it by pure chance on January 4, 1990. This date was later shown to be false, however. The published story was subjected to extreme skepticism by other commentators, who immediately began searching for a motive to account for the tape's release.

In late 1989, Prince Charles and Princess Diana were involved in divorce negotiations, which were becoming increasing acrimonious. The public appetite for details was immense; Charles's younger brother, Prince Andrew, duke of York, and Diana's close friend, the duchess of York (the former Sarah Ferguson), had also separated a few months earlier. The tribulations of Queen Elizabeth II's children were beginning to resemble a soap opera.

For the first time, because of Diana's complex relationship with the press—who followed her everywhere—the media were willingly being employed as so-called heavy artillery in the developing battle between the prince and princess. Although not public knowledge at the time, Diana had been supplying journalist Andrew Morton with material for a book that would tell her side of the case. In the absence of this knowledge about Diana and Morton, the public soon pointed to Charles, and cooperating government security services—who had been monitoring Diana's calls—as the person who leaked the tape in an attempt to fight back on the same battleground.

On September 5, *The Sun* announced that the conversation had been recorded by a second eavesdropper, Jane Norgrove (also a resident of Oxford-

James Gilbey. (AP/Wide World Photos)

shire), who claimed that she came forward to clear up allegations regarding conspiracy theories and the possible involvement of the security services in the initial leak—a protestation that only served to add further fuel to such rumors. The rumors were boosted by an assertion made by a surveillance expert, William Parsons, that recording both sides of an intercepted telephone conversation with equal clarity would be almost impossible and that the tape must have been subject to sophisticated technical adjustment. *The Sunday Times* (London) commissioned security firm Audiotel International to analyze the tape. The subsequent report claimed that the tape contained pips (data bursts) that would normally have been edited out during transmission, and that there was a "background hum" that Reenan's equipment could not have recorded, suggestive of a tap on a land line. Two further tapes, of unknown origin, later surfaced in the offices of other newspapers.

The tape held by *The Sun* began during the middle of the Diana-Gilbey conversation, with Diana complaining about her depression and ill-treatment by the royal family, especially by Prince Charles, who was said to be making her life "torture." The discussion also touched on the television soap opera *EastEnders* and Diana's fascination with her own alleged clairvoyance and spiritual beliefs. The conversation's shock value, however, came from its intimate tone, enhanced by the fear expressed by Diana that she might be pregnant. At the time of the conversation, Gilbey was working as a car salesperson, but he was the heir to a family fortune made in the manufacture of Gilbey's gin. He had known Diana since childhood and dated her before she was selected as Charles's bride, so the intimate tone was not particularly unusual; nor was Gilbey's use, following common practice among the English upper classes, of the term "darling" fourteen times and by the use of a nickname, Squidgy, fifty-three times. The latter appellation, however, caught the public's attention. *The Sun* initially dubbed the affair Dianagate but soon renamed it Squidgygate. A special public phone line was set up by the newspaper for the entire thirty-minute conversation.

IMPACT

Speculation regarding the origins of the Squidgygate tape reached such a pitch that the British home secretary, Kenneth Clarke, issued a formal denial that the British security service MI5 (the equivalent of the U.S. Central Intelligence Agency) had been involved in the affair in any way, but his denial did not reduce popular suspicion. The affair inevitably added considerably to Diana's own suspicions, casting a dark shadow of paranoia over her subsequent conduct, including her behavior on the night of her death in a car crash in Paris in 1997.

In 2002, Diana's former protection officer, Ken Wharfe, claimed that his own investigation covered all the parties involved but that he was unable to reveal the details for legal reasons—although he did hint that Diana's suspicions that she was being spied on had merit—thus further fueling the elaborate conspiracy theories surrounding the sequence of events. The most striking consequence of the first tape's release, however, was the tit-for-tat release of another tape to *The Sun*'s rival tabloid, the *Daily Mirror*. This tape apparently was recorded on December 18, 1989, and included an intimate long-distance phone conversation between Prince Charles and his lover, and future wife, Camilla Parker Bowles. An Australian magazine, *New Idea*, published a transcript of the Charles-Bowles tape on January 13, 1993, and an international scandal was born.

Charles and Diana became increasingly desperate to manage media coverage after the release of the two tapes. Both gave high-profile television interviews to tell their sides of the story, but neither interview could be anything more than a futile exercise in damage limitation; the harm done to the image of the royal family was irreparable, and Diana's subsequent life was similarly blighted. Insofar as the private war between the two individuals, the photogenic Diana was always bound to win, in spite of the embarrassment caused by the first tape's release, but that she had to die to seal her victory completed the lesson delivered by Squidgygate regarding the deleterious effects of media scandal.

—Brian Stableford

FURTHER READING

Brown, Tina. *The Diana Chronicles*. New York: Doubleday, 2007. An attempt to definitively summarize Diana's life, by a high-profile journalist-editor and personal acquaintance of Diana who employs a sensationalistic tone throughout the book.

Jephson, Patrick. *Shadow of a Princess*. New York: HarperCollins, 2000. A glaring exception to the general run of hagiographic-style studies, written by Diana's one-time private secretary.

Levine, Michael. *The Princess and the Package: Exploring the Love-Hate Relationship Between Diana and the Media*. Los Angeles: Renaissance, 1998. A more cerebral account than the journalistic biographies, attempting to put Diana's dealings with the press into the context of a more general account of the contemporary production and negotiation of celebrity.

Morton, Andrew. *Diana: Her True Story, in Her Own Words*. New York: Simon & Schuster, 1997. The second, expanded version of a text initially published in 1992 as *Diana: Her True Story*, which had caused a scandal in its own right. This new version includes direct transcripts of Morton's own conversations with Diana, which prove that she indeed had given him the information contained in the 1992 version of the book.

Paxman, Jeremy. *On Royalty: A Very Polite Inquiry into Some Strangely Related Families*. New York: PublicAffairs, 2006. A serious exploration of the institution of royalty, with insightful attention to the late twentieth century problems plaguing the House of Windsor.

Smith, Sally Bedell. *Diana in Search of Herself: Portrait of a Troubled Princess*. New York: Times Books, 1999. A journalistic account with slightly more pretension to analytical acuity than most of its rivals.

Wharfe, Ken. *Diana: Closely Guarded Secret*. London: Michael O'Mara, 2002. The book in which Diana's former protection officer vaguely endorsed Diana's suspicions regarding her surveillance by British security and the source of the tape.

1990's

September 24, 1992
BRITISH CABINET MEMBER DAVID MELLOR RESIGNS OVER ROMANTIC AFFAIR

David Mellor, a member of British prime minister John Major's cabinet, became embroiled in scandal when actor Antonia de Sancha detailed her affair with Mellor in the popular tabloid newspaper The People. *Mellor's problems worsened when the press reported he received two free vacations, one from a daughter of an official of the Palestine Liberation Organization. Mellor resigned soon after the story broke.*

LOCALE: London, England
CATEGORIES: Sex; publishing and journalism; government; politics

KEY FIGURES
David Mellor (b. 1949), British politician and heritage minister
John Major (b. 1943), British prime minister, 1990-1997
Antonia de Sancha (b. 1961), British film actor

SUMMARY OF EVENT

When conservative politician John Major succeeded the equally conservative Margaret Thatcher as Great Britain's prime minister in 1990, he promoted arts minister David Mellor to a cabinet post, first as chief secretary to the treasury (1990-1992) then to the newly created National Heritage Department as its secretary in April, 1992. The British public was not sure of this new department's function, and when it became clear its responsibilities included sports and the leisure industry, Mellor was dubbed "minister for fun." One of his first actions was to try to curb press invasions of privacy. The popular press, therefore, became increasingly hostile toward him.

Mellor had graduated from Cambridge University and trained as a lawyer until 1972. He became a member of Parliament (MP) for Putney, London, in 1979, the same year Thatcher became Britain's first woman prime minister. He served in a number of junior ministerial posts under Thatcher, beginning in 1981, although unlike his friend and contemporary, Major, he never attained cabinet status in his appointments. Mellor's most important office was as arts minister in 1990.

The popular press around this time was beginning to sense an increasing hostility by the public toward politicians in power. Major, too, seemed above reproach, though events showed later that he was not. So the press began private investigations of many of the Conservative Party MPs, especially those with some office. During the next two years, more than twenty Conservative politicians were forced to resign over press allegations. A number of libel cases were contested, and several inquiries were set up to investigate various allegations, such as illegal arms sales to Iraq. Although some of the allegations were disproved, the period became known for "government sleaze," as it was termed.

Mellor was the first politician exposed in this series of scandals that, many have argued, erupted for several reasons. Some believed the prime minister was too lenient in cases of marital unfaithfulness. Others said the press was out of control in its intrusiveness. Still others said the public believed the Conservatives had been in power too long and were growing corrupt and out of touch with the people. Each argument had some merit. Certainly, though, the scandals showed that no longer could MPs expect their private lives to remain private.

In July, 1992, the prime minister was warned that the Sunday tabloid newspaper *The People* was about to unleash a well-documented account of Mellor having a romantic affair with a little-known film actor, Antonia de Sancha. The story ran on July 19. A reporter from the paper had convinced Sancha's landlord to bug her apartment, and the reporter was able to listen in on her telephone calls, which included calls with Mellor. *The People*'s editor Bill Hagerty defended the legality of the paper's action in the name of public interest, a defense Mellor had been working to limit. In fact, it proved to be perfectly legal to bug one's own property (as the landlord did). The actor reportedly was paid sixty thousand dollars for her story, and the details she supplied were sometimes quite lurid. Hagerty, following attacks on his professional integrity, would later say that Mellor's resignation was the first "decent thing" Mellor had accomplished for some time.

Prime Minister Major took the advice of his cabinet secretary, Robin Butler, who assured Major that no national security had been breached through the affair, and that the people most hurt were Mellor's own wife, Judith, and his children. Major, therefore, rejected all calls for firing Mellor. However, during the summer recess of Parliament, with little other interesting news, the popular press kept digging up Mellor's private life, and by September it had unearthed a few more details.

The first of these discoveries was that Mellor had received a Spanish holiday from Mona Bauwens, the daughter of Jaweed al-Ghussein, the treasurer of the Palestine Liberation Organization. The second discovery was Mellor's receipt of a similar holiday, paid for by the ruler of the United Arab Emirates state of Abu Dhabi. These gifts clearly were of national interest. Major again consulted Butler, but the 1922 committee, comprising Conservative backbench MPs and chaired by Sir Marcus Fox, already had met on the issue and insisted on Mellor's resignation. On September 24, Mellor handed in his resignation, which Major accepted with reluctance. Mellor's resignation letter avoided any mention of personal shame for past actions.

IMPACT

Mellor's reputation had been tarnished and his career ended because of not only his affair but also his acceptance of the travel gifts. Major's government was tarnished as well. The press, having sensed its own power along with Major's vulnerability, pursued a number of other government ministers. Despite Major's protestations that his administration, and his party, had a policy of decency, the press considered his administration hypocritical. Efforts to suppress the freedom of the press withered away because of this assumption of hypocrisy. It could be argued that the stunning defeat of the Conservative government five years later at the hands of Tony Blair's Labour Party took some of its origins from this seemingly insignificant incident involving Mellor.

Mellor himself failed to hold government office again and was finally defeated in the 1997 election, though he was asked to be part of the new Labour government's Football Task Force from 1997 to 1999. However, his legal career continued, as he had been named a Queen's Counsel in 1987. After Mellor left office, his interest in the arts and in sport led to radio jobs with the British Broadcasting Corporation and to journalistic work. Ironically, one of his jobs would be as a columnist with *The People*, the very newspaper that had discredited him five

1990's

years before. The public was then quite forgiving of him. However, his marriage came to an end in 1995.

The sexual improprieties of office-holding politicians remained under the unforgiving scrutiny of the popular press and the British general public from the time Mellor's affair came to light in 1992. Even Major could not resist commenting on the affairs of officeholders when he wryly quoted Jack Lang, a French minister of culture, who had said, "An affair with an actress! Why else does one become minister of culture?"

When Labour came to power, press interest shifted to Labour politicians. Psychologists also began to study the effect of overexposure to publicity, an effect that was found to lead to a sort of moral numbness. More cogently, perhaps, the separation of MPs from their families, their sense of power, and the attraction of alcohol and sex under these conditions have been described as likely reasons for the continuing improprieties of public officials. The scandals, in turn, led the media to expose private lives that, in the modern world of instant communication, are no longer private.

—David Barratt

FURTHER READING

Clark, Alan. *Diaries: In Power*. London: Weidenfeld & Nicholson, 2003. Clark's diaries recount the Thatcher and Major years of government and give intimate details into the affairs and indiscretions of a number of ministers.

Major, John. *The Autobiography*. New York: HarperCollins, 2000. Prime Minister Major's autobiography, which includes an account of Mellor's resignation. Also includes Major's opinion of the scandal and subsequent attacks on the Conservative Party.

Woodhouse, Diana. *Ministers and Parliament: Accountability in Theory and Practice*. New York: Oxford University Press, 1994. Woodhouse examines the resignation scandals of modern British politics, seeing patterns of responsibility and accountability. Mellor's case is studied in some detail.

SEE ALSO: July 10, 1934: Sex Scandal Forces Resignation of Alberta Premier Brownlee; Mar. 2-Sept. 25, 1963: John Profumo Affair Rocks British Government; Jan. 26, 1979: Former Vice President Nelson Rockefeller Dies Mysteriously; Oct. 14, 1983: British Cabinet Secretary Parkinson Resigns After His Secretary Becomes Pregnant; July 25, 1987: Novelist-Politician Jeffrey Archer Wins Libel Trial Against the *Daily Star*; Aug. 10, 1989: Japanese Prime Minister Sosuke Resigns After Affair with a Geisha; Dec. 18, 1989: Prince Charles's Intimate Phone Conversation with Camilla Parker Bowles Is Taped; Jan. 5, 1994: British Cabinet Member Resigns After Fathering a Child Out of Wedlock; Jan. 17, 1998: President Bill Clinton Denies Sexual Affair with a White House Intern; Sept. 28, 2002: British Politician Reveals Her Affair with Prime Minister John Major; Apr. 26, 2006: Britain's Deputy Prime Minister Admits Affair with Secretary.

June 23, 1993
LORENA BOBBITT SEVERS HER HUSBAND'S PENIS

Lorena Bobbitt cut off half of her abusive husband's penis while he was sleeping, then threw the penis into a field from her car window after she left their apartment. She was found not guilty of malicious wounding and was ordered to a psychiatric hospital for several weeks. John, whose penis was reattached by surgeons soon after the attack, was found not guilty of marital sexual assault. The case brought national attention to spousal rape and abuse, forced abortion, and battered woman, or person, syndrome.

LOCALE: Manassas, Virginia

CATEGORIES: Violence; psychology and psychiatry; women's issues; law and the courts

KEY FIGURES

Lorena Bobbitt (b. 1970), married to John Bobbitt

John Wayne Bobbitt (b. 1967), married to Lorena Bobbitt

David C. Reardon (b. 1956), expert witness for Lorena Bobbitt at her criminal trial

SUMMARY OF EVENT

Lorena Bobbitt, born in Bucay, Ecuador, married a U.S. Marine, John Wayne Bobbitt, on June 18, 1989. The marriage was the first for both, but it was not a happy one. On the evening of June 23, 1993, Bobbitt, at this time out of the Marine Corps, had been partying and returned home drunk to the couple's apartment in Manassas, Virginia. John demanded that Lorena have sex with him; she declined and he raped her. After John fell asleep, Lorena left the bedroom for some water in the kitchen. She testified that she saw an eight-inch carving knife on a counter and, wanting retribution against John for his continued abuse during the marriage, snapped, grabbed the knife, returned to the bedroom, and cut off half of John's penis while he was sleeping. According to media reports, she

had requested a restraining order against John just two days before her attack.

After severing John's penis, Lorena immediately left the apartment while clutching the organ in her hand. She drove a short distance before rolling down the car window and throwing the penis into a neighboring field. She then returned home and called 911 to report the incident. The police conducted an extensive search for the severed organ. Upon finding it in the field, they packed it in ice and brought it to the hospital, where John had been taken after the attack. After more than nine hours of surgery, two surgeons were able to reattach John's severed penis.

Lorena was charged with felony malicious wounding and could have been sentenced to twenty years in prison. Because the attack allegedly was in response to years of abuse by John, he, too, was charged with a crime—marital sexual assault. John was acquitted of the sexual assault in September, 1993, and Lorena entered a plea of not guilty by reason of insanity. During trial, she testified that her husband abused her physically and mentally, raped her, and was unfaithful. She also said that John forced her to have an abortion one year into their marriage, which left her emotionally scarred. Several witnesses testified on Lorena's behalf and confirmed her claims of abuse. She became one of the first to argue insanity as a defense in a case of battered woman syndrome (or battered person syndrome), whereby a battered person becomes unable to take action to stop repeated physical or psychological abuse, or both.

Despite its seeming popularity, the insanity defense is rarely used in criminal cases and is not likely to be successful. Meeting the legal definition of insanity is difficult in most states. Lorena, however, was successful in her case. A jury found her not guilty by reason of insanity based on the state of Virginia's irresistible impulse test. Irresistible impulse is a test of a person's volition (movement or action) and loss of control rather than his or her

Lorena Bobbitt and John Wayne Bobbitt. (AP/Wide World Photos)

cramps days before the attack on her husband, symptoms Reardon interpreted as characteristic of PTSD and likely caused by the forced abortion. Finally, he suggested that Lorena's fear that she would not be able to have children in the future because of the abortion also contributed to her temporary insanity and inability to control her behavior. He compared Lorena's forced abortion to sexual mutilation and testified that Lorena was seeking retribution against her husband by castrating him.

On January 21, 1994, Lorena was found not guilty by reason of insanity. Virginia law required that she be sent to a mental hospital for observation and diagnosis to determine if she should remain institutionalized or be released. She spent forty-five days in a state mental facility and, based on reports from the psychiatric hospital, was ordered released because she no longer posed a danger to herself or others. Lorena, however, was required to have weekly outpatient therapy and was forbidden to leave the state.

knowledge of right and wrong. Many state statutes provide that insanity is not a defense if the person committing the crime knows and understands the difference between right and wrong at the time the crime is committed. Lorena knew that what she did was wrong, and her insanity defense would have failed in most states. However, under Virginia's irresistible impulse test, Lorena only needed to show that she was unable to control her behavior because of a mental "defect."

Lorena's attorneys argued that at the time of the crime she was suffering from depression and post-traumatic stress disorder (PTSD), and that she believed she had to escape from her husband—and his penis—because of past abuse. Lorena's condition was supported by experts who claimed that her impulse to sever her husband's penis became irresistible after the rape that same evening.

One defense expert, David C. Reardon, testified that Lorena may have snapped because of her forced abortion from years earlier. Lorena told Reardon that she continued to have flashbacks about the abortion, and Reardon suggested that she was suffering from a mental condition known as postabortion trauma. Lorena also claimed that she had been having anxiety attacks and abdominal

IMPACT

Lorena and John Bobbitt were divorced in 1995 and Lorena resumed her birth name, Gallo. Although Lorena became a symbol for women's self-defense against domestic abuse, she continued to have legal problems. In 1997, she was charged with assaulting her mother with a punch while her mother was watching television. Four months after the incident, Lorena was found guilty of the assault.

About a year after having surgery to reattach his penis, John was declared fully recovered. Needing money to pay for his medical costs, he formed a musical band called the Severed Parts. The band was not successful, however, so he turned to making pornographic films, including *John Wayne Bobbitt Uncut* (1994) and *Frankenpenis* (1996). This venture failed as well. John has had various jobs since the attack, including bartender, mover, tow-truck operator, brothel employee, and chapel minister, and also had more legal problems. He was convicted of several crimes, including domestic abuse, assault and battery, and larceny, and he violated his parole.

The media sensationalized the Bobbitt case, and it became a humorist's treasure trove. New words were coined from the case, and the Bobbitt name, which became synonymous with male castration, has been mentioned in musical lyrics, books of fiction, and on television shows. One common motto following the scandal was "Lorena Bobbitt for Surgeon General." Even though Lorena used a violent method to defend herself against her husband, feminist and women's groups defended her, and she became a sort of hero.

The media's attention to the Bobbitt case brought to light domestic violence, the psychological impact of forced abortions, marital rape, and battered woman syndrome. All became topics of national debate and discussion. For many, Lorena's attack was an understandable act of self-defense, and it has since come to symbolize the anger, rage, and resentment felt by abused women and has come to justify their fighting back against their abusers.

—*Carol A. Rolf*

FURTHER READING

Davoli, Joanmarie. "Reconsidering the Consequences of an Insanity Acquittal." *New England Journal on Criminal and Civil Confinement* 31, no. 1 (Winter, 2005): 3-14. A journal article that examines the use of the insanity defense in light of studies of the effects of acquittals based on a person's claim of insanity.

Pershing, Linda. "His Wife Seized His Prize and Cut It to Size: Folk and Popular Commentary on Lorena Bobbitt." *National Women's Studies Association Journal* 8, no. 3 (Fall, 1996): 1-35. Contrary to this article's fun-and-games title, the discussion focuses on the academic topic of language use in popular culture in the aftermath of the Bobbitt scandal.

Ragle, Larry. *Crime Scene*. New York: Avon Books, 2002. Explores the collection of crime-scene evidence and the role of forensic science and medical technology in solving unusual crimes, including the Bobbitt case.

Walker, Lenore E. A. *The Battered Woman Syndrome*. 2d ed. New York: Springer, 2000. Walker explains the characteristics of battered woman syndrome, its relation to post-traumatic stress disorder, and its use in insanity-defense cases.

Westervelt, Saundra Davis. *Shifting the Blame: How Victimization Became a Criminal Defense*. New Brunswick, N.J.: Rutgers University Press, 1998. Discussion of the insanity defense, as employed by abuse victims, including Lorena Bobbitt. Also discusses verdicts of not guilty by reason of insanity in cases of spousal abuse.

SEE ALSO: Apr. 4, 1958: Actor Lana Turner's Daughter Kills Turner's Gangster Lover; Mar. 13, 1964: Kitty Genovese Dies as Her Cries for Help Are Ignored; Mar. 10, 1980: Scarsdale Diet Doctor Is Killed by His Lover; Dec. 22, 1984: Subway Vigilante Bernhard Goetz Shoots Four Black Youths; Mar., 1990: Menendez Brothers Are Arrested for Murdering Their Parents; May 19, 1992: Amy Fisher Shoots Mary Jo Buttafuoco; June 12, 1994: Double Murder Leads to Sensational O. J. Simpson Trial.

1990's

January 5, 1994
BRITISH CABINET MEMBER RESIGNS AFTER FATHERING A CHILD OUT OF WEDLOCK

Tim Yeo, a Conservative member of the British parliament who publicly espoused traditional family values, fathered a child out of wedlock. The child's mother was a local Conservative politician and attorney, Julia Stent, who told the media that Yeo was the father of her child. The scandal led to Yeo's resignation as a government minister, but he remained a member of Parliament. The scandal was a major blow to Prime Minister John Major's conservative agenda.

LOCALES: London and Suffolk, England
CATEGORIES: Politics; sex; government; public morals; families and children

KEY FIGURES

Tim Yeo (b. 1945), Conservative member of British parliament from Sudbury South, 1983-
Julia Stent (b. 1960), attorney and council member for Hackney, London
Aldine Horrigan (b. 1936), mayor of Haverhill, Suffolk, and local Conservative Party branch chair
John Major (b. 1943), British prime minister, 1990-1997

SUMMARY OF EVENT

Tim Yeo was a popular member of John Major's Conservative government in Great Britain, fully backing Major's so-called Back to Basics agenda. News of his affair with a London attorney and politician, and the subsequent birth of their child, brought his government career to a temporary halt. For the Conservative government, the revelation was a major embarrassment because it had been stressing traditional values, responsibility, and fidelity, especially in family life. Yeo also was a vocal proponent of this agenda.

Yeo was born in Lewisham, a suburb in southeastern London, in 1945. He was educated at the prestigious private school Charterhouse in Godalming, Surrey, and then went on to Emmanuel College, Cambridge, where he was active in student politics and earned a master's degree in history in 1968. He gained a position with the Bankers Trust Company in London, and from 1970 to 1973 was an assistant treasurer there. In 1970, he married Diane Helen Pickard, with whom he had a son and a daughter. In 1975, he became a director of the Worcester Engineering Company, a position he retained until 1986. In 1980, he was appointed chief executive of a major British charity, the Spastics Society, or Scope. He held the post until his parliamentary career began in 1983.

Yeo had tried unsuccessfully to enter Parliament in 1974 as a Conservative Party candidate for the constituency of Bedwelty, Wales, a safe Labour Party seat. He was looking for a more winnable seat when Aldine Horrigan, chairman of the Sudbury South local Conservative Party, backed him to run as the candidate in her constituency, even though a sitting Conservative member of Parliament already was seated. A redrawing of boundaries gave Horrigan the excuse to push for a new candidate in what was technically a new constituency. Yeo was their candidate, and he ran for office in the 1983 election. The Conservative government of Prime Minister Margaret Thatcher was then at the height of its influence and power, and Yeo was easily elected.

Yeo's first experience in government office came in 1988, when he was appointed private parliamentary secretary to Foreign Secretary Douglas Hurd. After Major defeated Thatcher to become prime minister, subsequently winning the next election, Yeo got his first major appointment, as minister of the environment and countryside, in 1992. Major was launching a new Conservative Party manifesto, called Back to Basics, which emphasized traditional values and public morality, among other things. Yeo committed to this manifesto and

798

even spoke out against increases in benefits for single-parent families.

However, while working in London away from his family in 1992 and 1993, Yeo had struck up a sexual liaison with Julia Stent, a young attorney in her early thirties, through her involvement with Hackney Borough Council as a Conservative councillor. Stent became pregnant, and she had a child in July, 1993. The affair and child were hushed up at the time, but finally came to the attention of Horrigan on the day after Christmas, 1993. Horrigan believed Yeo had betrayed the Back to Basics campaign and called a meeting of the constituency committee to discuss the matter, hoping to censure Yeo.

Inevitably, the story broke, and in a short time made sensational national headlines, especially with the popular, tabloid press. Yeo admitted he had been "foolish" over the affair, but at first stated he saw no reason to resign. He did not feel his stand on family values was compromised. Although his fellow government ministers uttered general support for him, there was a feeling that if the local party did not back him, he would need to leave office. Several previous ministers, including David Mellor and Michael Mates, were forced to resign in similar circumstances, even though Prime Minister Major had supported them.

Debate was confused at this point. Major insisted his Back to Basics program was not about private morality but rather about methods of delivery. Stent refused to comment on what she considered a private matter. On the other hand, the archbishop of York had weighed in, accusing political leaders of moral and spiritual bankruptcy, and Labour Party leader John Smith accused the government of being in retreat on its own manifesto. Plenty of earlier statements by Conservative leaders showed that they did indeed include private morality and family responsibility in their campaign. Sir Norman Fowler, the party leader, was accused of letting the affair drift out of control.

Above all, the deafening silence of the local constituency party and its failure to publicly support Yeo at its meeting on January 4 forced Yeo's resignation from his government position the following day. However, the call to deselect him altogether as a local MP failed at a branch meeting held on January 14, and he retained his seat in Parliament.

IMPACT

For Major's government, the Yeo-Stent affair and Yeo's subsequent resignation were major blows to its Conservative agenda. The prime minister had to enter into a damage-limitation exercise, redefining what the term Back to Basics meant. In the end, however, this attempt only trivialized the campaign, and it was scrapped.

The Yeo affair became one of a long list of resignations forced on government ministers because of sexual affairs and other indiscretions. When this later became compounded by internal divisions over the European Union, Major's government was considered ineffective and weak. In the 1997 elections, the Conservatives suffered a landslide defeat, as a victorious Labour Party swept in under the youthful new prime minister, Tony Blair.

Yeo suffered much less than he might have. He retained his seat in the safe Suffolk constituency and was appointed by the new Conservative Party leader, William Hague, as spokesperson on environment, transport, and the regions. Under the next party leader, Iain Duncan Smith, Yeo was made a member of the shadow cabinet, as shadow secretary of state from trade and industry. In 2001, as shadow minister of agriculture, he played a leading role in exposing the Labour government's mishandling of the foot-and-mouth disease epidemic. In 2003, under new leader Michael Howard, he became shadow education and health secretary. In the leadership contest following the party's defeat in the general election, Yeo was briefly considered as a possible candidate. In fact, in the new Parliament he became chairman of the House of Commons environmental audit select committee. His career diversified as well as he became a writer on agricultural topics and a business speaker.

—*David Barratt*

FURTHER READING

Clark, Alan. *Diaries: In Power*. London: Weidenfeld & Nicholson, 2003. Clark's diaries recount the Thatcher and Major years of government and give intimate details into the affairs and indiscretions of a number of ministers.

Major, John. *The Autobiography.* New York: HarperCollins, 2000. Contains Major's perspectives on Yeo's resignation, putting it in context of the wider Back to Basics campaign.

The Times, London, January 5-6, 1994. Gives a restrained view of the breaking scandal of Yeo's affair.

Woodhouse, Diana. *Ministers and Parliament: Accountability in Theory and Practice.* New York: Oxford University Press, 1994. Woodhouse examines the resignation scandals of modern British politics, seeing patterns of responsibility and accountability.

SEE ALSO: Dec. 10, 1936: King Edward VIII Abdicates to Marry an American Divorcée; Mar. 2-Sept. 25, 1963: John Profumo Affair Rocks British Government; Aug. 4, 1978: British Politician Jeremy Thorpe Is Charged with Attempted Murder; Oct. 14, 1983: British Cabinet Secretary Parkinson Resigns After His Secretary Becomes Pregnant; July 25, 1987: Novelist-Politician Jeffrey Archer Wins Libel Trial Against the *Daily Star*; Dec. 18, 1989: Prince Charles's Intimate Phone Conversation with Camilla Parker Bowles Is Taped; Aug. 23, 1992: Princess Diana's Phone Conversation with Her Lover Is Made Public; Sept. 24, 1992: British Cabinet Member David Mellor Resigns over Romantic Affair; May, 1999: Civil Rights Leader Jesse Jackson Fathers a Child Out of Wedlock; Sept. 28, 2002: British Politician Reveals Her Affair with Prime Minister John Major; Jan. 21, 2006: British Politician Resigns After Gay-Sex Orgy; Apr. 26, 2006: Britain's Deputy Prime Minister Admits Affair with Secretary.

April 28, 1994
U.S. NAVAL ACADEMY EXPELS MIDSHIPMEN FOR CHEATING

A number of cadets at the U.S. Naval Academy had been expelled from the institution in the wake of a widespread cheating scandal. A backlash to the sanctions, believed to have been unequally doled out, led to further investigations by outside agencies, who looked into the cheating, the integrity of the Naval Academy, and the integrity of U.S. service academies as a whole. The scandal also affected the academy's tradition of policing its own based on its honor code.

LOCALE: Annapolis, Maryland

CATEGORIES: Education; corruption; military; government; ethics

KEY FIGURES

Thomas C. Lynch (b. 1942), U.S. Navy rear admiral and Naval Academy superintendent, 1991-1994

John H. Dalton (b. 1941), secretary of the U.S. Navy, 1993-1998

Frank B. Kelso, Jr. (b. 1933), U.S. Navy admiral, chief of Naval Operations, 1990-1994

Charles R. Larson (b. 1936), U.S. Navy admiral, commander in chief of the Pacific Command, 1991-1994

SUMMARY OF EVENT

On April 28, 1994, twenty-four midshipmen were expelled from the United States Naval Academy for cheating on an electrical engineering examination more than one year earlier, marking the culmination of a series of investigations that had demoralized students and brought to light serious problems at the military institution. In the fall of 1992 a number of midshipmen, students at the college, obtained information about the contents of a test being administered in an electrical engineering course. Some of

THE U.S. NAVAL ACADEMY'S HONOR CONCEPT

Midshipmen are persons of integrity: They stand for that which is right.

They tell the truth and ensure that the full truth is known. They do not lie.

They embrace fairness in all actions. They ensure that work submitted as their own is their own, and that assistance received from any source is authorized and properly documented. They do not cheat.

They respect the property of others and ensure that others are able to benefit from the use of their own property. They do not steal.

these students shared the information with others enrolled in the course. Shortly thereafter, news of the cheating ring was brought to the attention of academy officials. Several dozen midshipmen were identified for cheating, among them at least eight members of the academy's football team.

While the punishment for cheating varies widely among colleges and universities in the United States, any form of cheating at a military service academy is considered a serious breach of that institution's honor code. Normally, determination of guilt or innocence is made by an honor board consisting of fellow students, who either exonerate their fellow midshipman or recommend to the superintendent that a violator be immediately expelled. Hence, when word of this new cheating scandal spread among members of the brigade of midshipmen, most expected that all who had cheated would be dismissed. Rear Admiral Thomas C. Lynch, the academy superintendent, did not see the situation in such simple terms. It became apparent quickly that quite a few students were involved in the case and subject to expulsion. The media would be eager to publicize such a story, given that just two years had passed since the academy was embroiled in a sexual harassment scandal. The new cheating incident threatened to further damage the institution's already tarnished reputation with the American public.

Nevertheless, in December, 1992, Admiral Lynch launched an investigation, enlisting the assistance of the Navy's Criminal Investigative Service, or

CIS. Its involvement suggested to many academy students that the theft of the examination was being treated as a criminal offense. The effect of the inquiry on campus was chilling. At the same time, rumors began circulating that the superintendent was unwilling to dismiss certain offending students, especially members of the football team. The initial investigation was completed in the spring of 1993. Twenty-eight midshipmen were implicated. Only six, however, stood before honor boards and were recommended for expulsion, which were upheld by Admiral Lynch. The expelled students then appealed his decision to the secretary of the Navy.

Admiral Frank B. Kelso, Jr., a graduate of the Naval Academy, was serving as acting secretary of the Navy at the time the investigation was completed. He was concerned by the allegations of mismanagement and of favoritism within the investigation, so he directed a new inquiry to be headed by the Navy's inspector general. More than one dozen investigators spent months interviewing the students who had taken the electrical engineering examination. The scope of the cheating became apparent as the inquiry progressed, and investigators learned that some midshipmen even sold classmates copies of the examination in advance of testing. Also of concern was the widespread disregard for the honor code on which the institution had relied for years as a means of self-policing among midshipmen.

Meanwhile, newspapers such as *The Washington Post*, *Baltimore Sun*, and *The New York Times* carried detailed accounts of the proceedings during the sixteen months between the initial discovery of the cheating and outcome of the investigations. The media also paid special attention to the fate of the former Navy football players whose involvement as ringleaders in the cheating scandal allegedly sparked the controversy.

By the time the lengthy inquiry was completed in the spring of 1994, 134 midshipmen, by this time all

1990's

seniors, had been implicated. A special honor panel consisting of three Navy admirals reviewed the inspector general's findings and made recommendations to the new secretary of the Navy, John H. Dalton, regarding each case. Dalton, also a Naval Academy graduate, understood the gravity of the situation and wanted to be certain he dealt evenhandedly with each of the accused. After reviewing the evidence, he ordered the expulsion of twenty-four midshipmen and retained forty-two. Because the decisions were handed down just weeks before the implicated midshipmen were scheduled to graduate, the press zeroed in on the incident. Reporters were concerned that a considerable amount of taxpayers' money had been spent on the investigation. They also focused on the fate of expelled midshipmen, who under current regulations could have been forced to pay back the cost of their education or enter the Navy not as commissioned officers but as enlisted personnel. Dalton waived both requirements.

The U.S. Department of Defense took immediate steps to restore integrity and trust in academy leadership. Admiral Charles R. Larson, a former academy superintendent who in 1994 was commander in chief of the Pacific Command, was asked to return to the academy to lead the institution. Given that Larson was under consideration at the time for appointment as chairman of the Joint Chiefs of Staff and as chief of naval operations, it was obvious that he was held in high esteem. The designation of a senior admiral to a position normally held by an officer of lower rank was an immediate signal that Defense Department officials considered the situation at the academy a top priority.

IMPACT

The cheating scandal at the Naval Academy was devastating to the institution as a whole. The cheating was demoralizing in itself, but the generally held belief that the superintendent had shown favoritism in dealing with alleged offenders and had tried to minimize the incident and cover up details was especially harmful to students who had rightly assumed that their leaders were persons of fairness and integrity. The incident ended the career of Admiral Lynch, who decided to retire.

The academy's honor code was affected as well. Because outsiders such as Navy CIS and the Navy's Office of the Inspector General entered the investigation, the time-honored tradition of allowing midshipmen to enforce the honor code themselves was violated. Also, the cheating scandal—coupled with reports of continuing sexual harassment at Annapolis and the Army academy at West Point, New York, and the U.S. Air Force Academy at Colorado Springs, Colorado—led the U.S. Congress to initiate hearings on the state of operations at all the service academies. Congress wanted to ensure that appropriate steps were taken to protect the rights of all individuals involved. Outside review and direction, even from Congress, altered the Naval Academy's freedom to establish its own rules for dealing with internal matters, that is, for taking care of its own.

—*Laurence W. Mazzeno*

FURTHER READING

Fleming, Bruce. *Annapolis Autumn: Life, Death, and Literature at the U.S. Naval Academy*. New York: New Press, 2005. Examines the cheating scandal from the perspective of a academy faculty member. Discusses the personal reactions of a number of midshipmen involved in the incident.

Gantar, Jeffrey, and Tom Patten. *A Question of Honor*. Grand Rapids, Mich.: Zondervan, 1996. Personal account of the scandal by a midshipman accused of cheating. Provides details of actions taken by officials at the Naval Academy and the reaction of midshipmen to the charges and subsequent investigations.

Gelfland, H. Michael. *Sea Change at Annapolis: The United States Naval Academy, 1949-2000*. Chapel Hill: University of North Carolina Press, 2006. Brief assessment of the cheating scandal in light of the many changes and challenges facing both the students and faculty at the Naval Academy in the second half of the twentieth century.

Valentine, Paul. "Two Dozen Expelled in Naval Academy Cheating Scandal." *The Washington Post*, April 28, 1994. Describes the outcome of the Naval Academy's probe of the scandal, detailing facts uncovered during the sixteen-month investigation.

SEE ALSO: Apr. 4, 1976: West Point Cadets Are Caught Cheating on Exams; June 26, 1992: U.S. Navy Secretary Resigns in the Wake of Tailhook Sexual Assault Scandal; May 20, 1997: Air Force Prosecution of Female Officer for Adultery Reveals Double Standard; Jan. 2, 2003: E-mail Message Prompts Inquiry into Air Force Academy Sexual Assaults; June 22, 2005: U.S. Air Force Investigates Religious Intolerance at Its Academy; Feb. 18, 2007: *Washington Post* Exposes Decline of Walter Reed Army Hospital.

June 1, 1994
CONGRESSMAN DAN ROSTENKOWSKI IS INDICTED IN HOUSE POST OFFICE SCANDAL

As part of the House post office scandal, long-time U.S. representative Dan Rostenkowski, a Washington, D.C., power player, was indicted on charges that included exchanging postal stamps purchased for official House business for cash, buying expensive gifts for friends and family with government funds, and witness tampering. He was found guilty on some charges, served fifteen months in a federal white-collar-crime prison camp, and saw the end of an otherwise illustrious, influential career.

LOCALE: Washington, D.C.
CATEGORIES: Corruption; government; politics; hoaxes, frauds, and charlatanism; law and the courts

KEY FIGURES
Dan Rostenkowski (b. 1928), U.S. representative from Illinois, 1959-1995, and chairman of the House Ways and Means Committee
Robert V. Rota (fl. 1990's), former House postmaster
Carl Rauh (b. 1940), Rostenkowski's attorney
Robert S. Bennett (b. 1939), Rostenkowski's attorney

SUMMARY OF EVENT
Dan Rostenkowski was born in Chicago, Illinois, in 1928 and elected to the U.S. House of Representatives in 1958. In 1964 he became a member of the House Ways and Means Committee, which writes most tax legislation, and served as the committee's chairman from 1981 to 1994.

During this thirteen-year-period as chairman, Rostenkowski controlled the tax-writing committee with an iron fist. He played a significant part in the tax and trade policy formation during the Ronald Reagan administration of the 1980's. In particular, he helped push through the 1986 Tax Reform Act, which lowered taxes and simplified the rather complex and confusing tax code. He had established himself as one of the most dominant members of the House of Representatives and was expected to play a crucial role in numerous legislative battles for the Bill Clinton administration of the 1990's, battles that would include health care, tax reform, trade provisions, and welfare policy. However, Rostenkowski's reputation and political career quickly collapsed in the spring of 1994 when he was charged with more than one dozen counts of fraud and political corruption involving the House post office.

Rostenkowski had attended the prestigious St. John's Military Academy in Delafield, Wisconsin, for high school from 1942 to 1946. After graduation, he entered the U.S. Army's 7th Infantry Division and served in Korea from 1946 to 1948. After his military service he opted to continue his education at Loyola University in Chicago, where he attended from 1948 to 1951. After college, Rostenkowski began his political career as an Illinois state senator at the young age of twenty-four.

Rostenkowski's political roots date back to the early 1930's, when his father, Joseph P. Rostenkowski, served as a ward alderman and committee member for more than two decades between 1936 and 1961. His father's years of service to the Democratic Party provided his son with a strong political foundation on which to begin and, essentially, flourish. Eventually, the young Rostenkowski would follow in his father's footsteps. During his early years as a state senator, Rostenkowski cultivated a strong political friendship with Chicago mayor Richard Daley. Daley became Rostenkowski's mentor and helped him get elected to the U.S. House of Representatives in 1958. Thirty-five years after becoming a Congress member, his lengthy, successful career would come to an end.

On June 1, 1994, a federal grand jury indicted Rostenkowski on seventeen criminal corruption charges, including misuse of public and government funds, fraud, conspiracy, and concealing material facts. U.S. attorney Eric H. Holder, Jr., said at a news conference following the indictment,

> The allegations contained in today's indictment represent a betrayal of the public trust for personal gain. In essence, this indictment alleges that Congressman Rostenkowski used his elective office to perpetuate an extensive fraud on the American people.

Rostenkowski's schemes allegedly cost taxpayers more than $500,000. Charges included witness tampering, mail fraud, and wire fraud. Between January, 1978, and April, 1991, he allegedly took at least $50,000 in cash disguised as purchases of stamps from the House post office. His coconspirator, former House postmaster Robert V. Rota, who also pleaded guilty to embezzlement, said that during a six-year period, Rostenkowski traded in postal vouchers for over $20,000, had taken stamps, and then sold those for cash. The investigation into Rostenkowski's illegal activities began in 1991, after Rota and his employees were being monitored for criminal activities in the House post office as well. Those investigations began in what came to be called the House post office scandal.

Rostenkowski also was accused of a kickback scam dating back to 1971. He had hired fourteen individuals to work for him, yet their work amounted to menial tasks such as mowing his lawn at his summer home and taking wedding photographs for his daughters. Some of his hires did no work. Those who did no work allegedly collected a substantial monthly paycheck and kicked back a portion of their salaries to Rostenkowski as a sign of gratitude for being hired. These employees would submit their government paychecks to Rostenkowski's Chicago office manager, who would then distribute the cash to the "ghost" employees for less than the actual value of their original paychecks.

From April, 1988, to January, 1992, Rostenkowski also allegedly used approximately $40,000 in office funds to buy expensive gifts for family and friends. Furthermore, he used more than $100,000 in House funds and over $70,000 in political-campaign funds to buy and rent automobiles for the personal use of his family members and his friends. Additionally, the most serious of the charges—witness tampering—occurred in September, 1993. After learning of the federal investigation into his past illicit activities, Rostenkowski also attempted to discourage a federal prosecution witness, an engraver who had inscribed plaques for crystal sculptures that he was giving as gifts to friends. Rostenkowski had billed these engravings to his government expense account at the House stationery shop but neglected to pay for them. This charge of witness tampering was by far the most severe allegation, bringing with it a possible criminal sentence of ten years in federal prison.

As the corruption unfolded and the federal investigation continued, Rostenkowski lost his leadership roles and lost his bid for reelection to the House. The first deal offered to Rostenkowski by the U.S. attorney, one that the Congress member publicly rejected, would have sent him to jail for six months and required him to pay a fine of roughly $38,000. Based on the advice of his high-profile defense attorneys, Carl Rauh and Robert S. Bennett, Rostenkowski accepted a plea agreement the following year that reduced the total number of criminal charges from seventeen to two—for mail fraud only. Finally, in April, 1996, he was sentenced to seventeen months in a federal white-collar-crime prison camp and was fined $100,000.

In May, before entering prison, Rostenkowski had successful prostate cancer surgery. On July 22, he began serving his sentence at the Federal Medical Center Rochester (in Minnesota) for white-collar prisoners. Following a full recovery from his cancer treatment, he was transferred to a federal minimum-security prison camp in Oxford, Wisconsin, which was near Chicago. The camp is known as a recreational house of reform for former crooked politicians and elderly mobsters. After serving fifteen months, Rostenkowski was given

Dan Rostenkowski outside the federal courthouse in Washington, D.C., following his arraignment on corruption charges on June 10, 1994. (Hulton Archive/Getty Images)

the chance to serve his last two months at a Salvation Army halfway house in Chicago until his formal release on October 15, 1997.

Rostenkowski was granted a full federal pardon in 2000 by President Bill Clinton, who pardoned more than seventy white-collar offenders in his last days in office. In the years following his release from prison, Rostenkowski worked as a political commentator, adjunct college professor, and chief executive officer of Danross Associates, Inc., a legislative consulting firm specializing in governmental affairs.

IMPACT

After more than three decades in Congress and as one of the nation's most powerful Democratic Party leaders, Rostenkowski saw his political career collapse almost instantaneously. The extent of his known illegal activities cost the American public close to half a million dollars and inadvertently brought attention to the many misuses of authority and power carried out by those persons who are elected to serve their constituents and represent them in Congress.

The U.S. Department of Justice's response to the myriad illicit activities carried out by Rostenkowski offered some hope that criminal and unethical acts carried out by politicians will not be tolerated. Although he was granted a full presidential pardon, the fact remains that Rostenkowski was caught, indicted, convicted, and imprisoned for his crimes. However, the public witnessed once again how political power, greed, and success breed crime and corruption. Politicians continue to cross moral and legal boundaries. Ultimately, Rostenkowski's greed destroyed his career, but it also further strained the public's fragile trust and faith in their elected officials.

—*Paul M. Klenowski*

FURTHER READING

Cohen, Richard. *Rostenkowski: The Pursuit of Power and the End of the Old Politics*. Chicago: Ivan R. Dee, 2000. This work provides a detailed look at the rise and fall of one of Washington's most powerful members of Congress.

Merriner, James. *Mr. Chairman: Power in Dan Rostenkowski's America*. Carbondale: Southern Illinois University Press, 2002. An unauthorized biography of Rostenkowski, highlighting both the positive and negative aspects of his career as a politician.

1990's

805

Roberts, Robert North. *Ethics in U.S. Government: An Encyclopedia of Investigations, Scandals, Reforms, and Legislation.* Westport, Conn.: Greenwood Press, 2001. A comprehensive encyclopedia documenting political scandals, ethical controversies, and investigations in the United States between 1775 and 2000.

Williams, Robert. *Political Scandals in the United States: America in the Twentieth Century.* New York: Routledge, 1998. This book gives a detailed history of American political scandal during the twentieth century, making special note of Rostenkowski's illicit crimes as a member of Congress.

SEE ALSO: Jan. 23, 1904: Senator Joseph R. Burton Is Convicted of Bribery; Jan. 13, 1913: Federal Judge Is Impeached for Profiting from His Office; May 12, 1924: Kentucky Congressman John W. Langley Is Convicted of Violating the Volstead Act; Nov. 16, 1951: Federal Tax Official Resigns After Accepting Bribes; Mar. 1, 1967: Adam Clayton Powell, Jr., Is Excluded from Congress; June 23, 1967: Senator Thomas J. Dodd Is Censured for Misappropriating Funds; Oct. 7, 1974: Congressman Wilbur D. Mills's Stripper Affair Leads to His Downfall; Oct. 11, 1979: Senate Denounces Herman E. Talmadge for Money Laundering; Feb. 2, 1980: Media Uncover FBI Sting Implicating Dozens of Lawmakers; Sept. 23, 1987: Plagiarism Charges End Joe Biden's Presidential Campaign; Aug. 5, 1994: Kenneth Starr Is Appointed to the Whitewater Investigation; Dec. 11, 1997: HUD Secretary Henry Cisneros Is Indicted for Lying to Federal Agents.

June 12, 1994
DOUBLE MURDER LEADS TO SENSATIONAL O. J. SIMPSON TRIAL

The discovery of the bodies of Nicole Brown Simpson and Ronald Goldman marked the beginning of one of the most notorious scandals and criminal trials in American history. Brown Simpson's former husband, O. J. Simpson, was charged with the crime and found not guilty, but he was found responsible for the murders in a civil trial. Simpson moved to Florida to avoid payments to the Brown and Goldman families on the civil judgment of $33.5 million.

LOCALE: Los Angeles, California
CATEGORIES: Murder and suicide; publishing and journalism; radio and television; law and the courts; racism

KEY FIGURES
Nicole Brown Simpson (1959-1994), former wife of O. J. Simpson
Ronald Goldman (1968-1994), waiter, who was a friend of Nicole Brown Simpson
O. J. Simpson (b. 1947), retired professional football player

SUMMARY OF EVENT
On the night of June 12, 1994, a couple walking their dogs came upon the dog of their neighbor, Nicole Brown Simpson. The Akita, wandering the streets, had what appeared to be blood stains on its fur. The neighbors, knowing that Brown Simpson's dog was not allowed to run loose, brought the dog to her condominium on Bundy Drive. Upon reaching the entry gate to the complex, they saw a ghastly, macabre scene and immediately notified police.

The police found the bodies of thirty-five-year-old Brown Simpson and her acquaintance, twenty-six-year-old Ronald Goldman. The two had been stabbed and slashed to death. The bruising on Brown

Simpson's face and head showed that she was punched and bludgeoned into unconsciousness and was stabbed several times in her neck. She was nearly decapitated from a deep cut across her throat. Her body lay at the foot of a short flight of steps, and her blood ran down the tiles of the walkway. It appeared that she was unable to fight her attacker.

Goldman appeared to have struggled with his attacker. He received several defensive wounds and several shallow stab wounds and deep knife wounds to a thigh and to his aorta and neck. He also caused his murderer to lose a large leather glove, which would play a part in the criminal trial of the suspect in his and Brown Simpson's murder. Goldman was a waiter at a nearby restaurant, where Brown Simpson and her family had dined earlier that evening. After his shift, he returned Brown Simpson's mother's eyeglasses, which she had forgotten at the restaurant, to Brown Simpson.

The exact circumstances of the murder remains unknown, but the forensic reconstruction of the crime scene suggests the following: Brown Simpson was the primary target and Goldman was a secondary, or even situational, target. Evidence on their bodies and at the crime scene suggests that Brown Simpson was bludgeoned and stabbed into unconsciousness before Goldman was attacked and killed. The attacker returned to Brown Simpson, grabbed her hair, pulled her head back to expose her throat, and made a fatal knife slash.

The murders, for the most part, were unremarkable as common domestic homicides. They were, however, exceptionally violent and brutal, suggesting a crime of passion. The sole suspect in the case, O. J. Simpson, the former husband of Brown Simpson and a former star professional football player, made this case remarkable. Although he was retired from football, Simpson kept himself in the public eye by limited acting and by promoting products on

O. J. Simpson, in an infamous court scene, is unable to put on the leather gloves the prosecution claimed he wore as he allegedly murdered Nicole Brown Simpson and Ronald Goldman. (AP/Wide World Photos)

television. He also was noted by the media for his golf games with the rich and famous. His celebrity status made this domestic homicide case a different case altogether. The criminal evidence made him the only suspect.

Although the police investigation and interrogation were less than illustrious, the evidence against Simpson was overwhelming. His blood (from a deep finger cut) was found at the crime scene. Blood from both victims and from the suspect was found in or near Simpson's Ford Bronco and on a glove found near the crime scene. Hair from Goldman and fibers from the Bronco were found on that same glove, and the matching glove was found on Simpson's property. The glove type was uncommon, yet Simpson owned a pair. Furthermore, Simpson had received promotional knives from a manufacturer, any number of which could have been used in the murders.

Most usually, brutal murders are precipitated by an emotionally significant event in the life of the perpetrator. On the day of the murders, Simpson had been embarrassed in public after Brown Simpson failed to save a seat for him at his daughter's recital. In a packed auditorium, he was forced to wander up and down the aisles to find a seat. Also, his girlfriend at the time testified that she had broken up with him the day of the murders.

Simpson's murder trial was a media sensation. Every aspect of the trial was filmed, reported upon, discussed in print and on the air, and remarked upon by media-appointed experts. Major debate about race, racism, and domestic violence surfaced not only among commentators but also a divided public, and Simpson's defense relied heavily upon issues of race and racism as factors in the investigation and trial. The prosecution focused heavily on domestic violence and violence against women during the trial.

On October 3, 1995, Simpson was found not

"IF IT DOESN'T FIT, YOU MUST ACQUIT"

In his closing statement at the criminal trial of O. J. Simpson, lead defense attorney Johnnie Cochran, with folksy rhetoric, appealed to the jury's sense of obligation to acquit Simpson if the evidence does not make sense.

The Defendant, Mr. Orenthal James Simpson, is now afforded an opportunity to argue the case, if you will, but I'm not going to argue with you, ladies and gentlemen. What I'm going to do is to try and discuss the reasonable inferences which I feel can be drawn from this evidence. . . .

From the very first orders issued by the LAPD so-called brass, they were more concerned with their own images, the publicity that might be generated from this case than they were in doing professional police work. . . . Because of their bungling, they ignored the obvious clues. . . . We think if they had done their job as we have done, Mr. Simpson would have been eliminated early on. . . .

And so as we look then at the time line and the importance of this time line, I want you to remember these words. Like the defining moment in this trial, the day [assistant prosecutor Christopher] Darden asked Mr. Simpson to try on those gloves and the gloves didn't fit, remember these words; if it doesn't fit, you must acquit. . . .

And when you are back there deliberating on this case, you're never going to be ever able to reconcile this time line and the fact there's no blood back there. . . . They don't have any mountain or ocean of evidence. It's not so because they say so. That's just rhetoric. We this afternoon are talking about the facts. And so it doesn't make any sense. It just doesn't fit. If it doesn't fit, you must acquit. . . .

guilty of murdering Brown Simpson and Goldman. Jury members, who had deliberated only four hours, later stated that prosecutors failed to prove Simpson's guilt beyond a reasonable doubt.

It is commonly believed that the incompetence of key professionals in the murder investigation and trial compounded the injustice against the victims, their families, and the people of the state of California. Prosecutors, a criminal-trial court judge, and police investigators performed their professional duties with incredible incompetence, and Simpson was freed as a result.

IMPACT

Finding little closure for their losses in the verdict in the criminal case, the Brown and Goldman families responded by suing Simpson for wrongful death. On February 5, 1997, a civil court awarded $33.5 million to the Brown and Goldman families. Publicly vowing never to pay the victims' families anything, Simpson sought refuge against the civil judgment by moving to Florida, where his earnings, house, and pension would be protected to some degree from seizure.

The Simpson trial and media coverage had far-reaching social impact. The outcome of the criminal trial led to further public distrust of the criminal justice and legal systems, concluding that justice is differentially investigated and distributed based upon a defendant's race, socioeconomic status, and fame. The murder trial also solidified the belief that hero-worship stymies justice. A large percentage of those persons involved in the murder investigation and trial appeared star struck in Simpson's presence. The jury, along with onlookers, seemingly ignored the overwhelming evidence against Simpson and determined in favor of the celebrity. Also, the principals in the case, including key witnesses, prosecutors, defense attorneys, and the judge, were made into celebrities as well.

In hindsight, it became clear that the media invented and repeated "facts" that first were embraced by a public obsessed by the case. For example, in every major city, the news media, also obsessed with the case, found experts (most of whom had dubious credentials) to speak on the case and predict the outcome of the trial. These so-called talking heads became the mainstay of trial coverage for many, if not most, media outlets. As the trial progressed, however, many viewers began to question the veracity of these news reports and commentaries, casting doubt on news reporting as a whole.

Perhaps most significant, though, was the not-guilty verdict in the murder trial, which polarized the public along racial lines on a scale not seen since the 1950's and 1960's, the height of the Civil Rights movement in the United States. The trial was interpreted by both blacks and whites as having been overwhelmingly about race.

—*Edward J. Schauer*

FURTHER READING

Bugliosi, Vincent T. *Outrage: The Five Reasons Why O. J. Simpson Got Away with Murder.* New York: W. W. Norton, 1996. A study of the Nicole Brown Simpson and Ronald Goldman murders by a successful felony prosecutor, and an explanation as to how the abundant and quality evidence points solely to Simpson as the murderer. Examines in detail how the murder trial went wrong.

Clark, Marcia, and Teresa Carpenter. *Without a Doubt.* New York: Viking Press, 1997. Critical appraisal of all major actors and happenings in the Simpson trial by the deputy district attorney who led the prosecution.

The Family of Ron Goldman, with William Hoffer and Marilyn Hoffer. *His Name Is Ron: Our Search for Justice.* New York: William Morrow, 1997. Discusses the impact of the murder of Ronald Goldman on his family. Also looks at Goldman's life, little discussed by the media.

Fuhrman, Mark. *Murder in Brentwood.* Washington, D.C.: Regnery, 1997. Foreword by Vincent Bugliosi. Fuhrman, one of the heavily criticized police investigators in the case, presents a careful analysis and critique of the crime-scene investigation, the follow-up investigation, the weight of the evidence, and the murder trial itself.

Goldman Family. *If I Did It: Confessions of the Killer.* New York: Beaufort Books, 2007. Contains the original manuscript of Simpson's fictional tell-all book *If I Did It*, which was never published. This edition, which includes the chapter "He Did It"—pointed commentary by the Goldman family—also includes an afterword by murder-victims advocate Dominick Dunne.

Hunt, Darnell. *O. J. Simpson, Facts, and Fictions: News Rituals in the Construction of Reality.* New York: Cambridge University Press, 1999. A scholarly study of the differences across racial lines in the public perception of the Simpson trial, including the way the media used these perceptions to shape its coverage of the trial.

Newton, Michael, and John L. French. *Celebrities and Crime.* New York: Chelsea House, 2008. Written especially for younger readers, this book examines the intersection of celebrity and crime. Discusses how law enforcement handles celebrities accused of criminal acts, and celebrities victimized by crime. Includes a chapter on the Simpson case.

Toobin, Jeffrey. *The Run of His Life: The People v. O. J. Simpson.* New York: Random House, 1996. An excellent account of the Simpson trial by a knowledgeable criminal attorney and accomplished journalist. Toobin, a former prosecutor, covered the trial for *The New Yorker.*

SEE ALSO: June 25, 1906: Millionaire Heir Murders Architect Stanford White; Mar. 10, 1980: Scarsdale Diet Doctor Is Killed by His Lover; Mar., 1990: Menendez Brothers Are Arrested for Murdering Their Parents; May 19, 1992: Amy Fisher Shoots Mary Jo Buttafuoco; June 23, 1993: Lorena Bobbitt Severs Her Husband's Penis; June 24, 1994: *Time* Magazine Cover Uses Altered O. J. Simpson Photo; Nov. 20, 2006: News Corp Abandons Plan to Publish O. J. Simpson's Book.

1990's

June 24, 1994
TIME MAGAZINE COVER USES ALTERED O. J. SIMPSON PHOTO

In 1994, retired football star O. J. Simpson was charged with the murder of his former wife, Nicole Brown Simpson, and her friend, Ronald Goldman. In its coverage of the story, Time *magazine used an altered version of the Los Angeles Police Department booking photograph of Simpson on its cover. The altered photo made Simpson appear "blacker" than in the original photo and caused an uproar amid accusations that* Time *engaged in editorial manipulation and encouraged racist stereotypes.*

LOCALE: New York, New York
CATEGORIES: Forgery; publishing and journalism; communications and media; racism; ethics; social issues and reform

KEY FIGURES

O. J. Simpson (b. 1947), former football star and actor
Matt Mahurin (b. 1959), freelance illustrator, artist, and film director
James R. Gaines (b. 1947), journalist, *Time* magazine editor, and author
Nancy Kearney (fl. 1990's), spokesperson for *Time* magazine

SUMMARY OF EVENT

On June 12, 1994, Nicole Brown Simpson, the former wife of O. J. Simpson, and her friend, Ronald Goldman, were found murdered outside her condominium. Simpson was arrested and charged with their murders. On June 17, a Los Angeles Police Department photographer produced a mug shot of Simpson; this photo was released to the media. Both *Time* and *Newsweek* magazines used this mug shot on the cover of their respective issues of June 24. *Newsweek* published the photo in its original form but *Time* altered the photo in ways that made Simpson appear "blacker" and, therefore, more guilty.

As was reported widely in the media, Matt Mahurin, the freelance artist who worked on the photo for *Time*, altered the original picture so that Simpson appeared unshaven and with a darker complexion. Also, Mahurin made the mug shot identification number smaller and added the caption "An American Tragedy" to the photo. The alterations might not have been noticed had *Time* and *Newsweek* not published the photo on their covers on the same day, which allowed readers to see the two issues side by side and, thereby, compare the photos.

Critics strongly objected to the photo alterations. The controversy was discussed in newspapers, on television, and in the electronic media. Critics argued that *Time*, in making Simpson appear more black, was perpetuating racist stereotypes that black men are dangerous by nature, and that the magazine manipulated these fears to influence readers perceptions of Simpson's guilt or innocence prior to trial. Sheila Stainback, vice president of the National Association of Black Journalists, asked, rhetorically, "Why did [Simpson] have to be darker? I think that it plays into the whole menacing black-male portrayal."

Nancy Kearney, a spokesperson for *Time*, responded to the criticism by denying that *Time* intended to manipulate or mislead readers. She added that it was insulting to the magazine and to the artist to cast the photo as sinister or racist and that the artist's intent was to create a "visually compelling" image for the magazine's cover.

As the outcry continued and amid charges of poor editorial judgment, *Time* magazine's managing editor, James R. Gaines, was forced to respond to critics. First, he posted a message on a computer bulletin board stating that "no racial implication was intended, by *Time* or by the artist." Ultimately, in a letter in the July 4 issue of *Time*, Gaines apologized to readers who were offended by the altered Simpson cover and reiterated that it was not his or the artist's intent to offend readers or to influence their perceptions of Simpson's guilt or innocence.

In the published apology, he reiterated that there were "no racial implications" in the reworking of the photo but that *Time* should have been more sensitive to the racial issues implied by the cover.

IMPACT

The controversy did not end with the public apologies. The issue of the negative portrayal of ethnic and racial minorities, as well as women, by the media continues as a topic in academic and political circles. For example, Greg Dickinson and Karrin Vasby Anderson (2004) compared the altered *Time* cover photo of Simpson with an altered photo of Hillary Rodham Clinton that the magazine used during its coverage of the Whitewater controversy during the early 1990's.

The *Time* cover scandal also revealed the ethical dilemmas of altering photographs that are part of the documentary record. Indeed, Simpson's celebrity, along with the racial dimensions of the scandal, added public interest to the problem of photo manipulation, and it is true that photographs have been altered since the beginning of photography during the early nineteenth century. One of the more infamous cases of photo manipulation was Joseph Stalin's "disappearing" of people from official photos. This practice is well documented in a 1997 book by David King. However, what is different now is the digital retouching of images—also called "photoshopping" in reference to the popular software editing program Adobe Photoshop. The alteration of Simpson's photo was a mere precursor to what was soon to come.

The *Time* photo scandal prompted early calls for new rules and frameworks to guide editors deciding on whether a photo or other image should be altered or enhanced. John Long, as ethics cochairman and past president of the National Press Photographers Association (NPPA) in the United States, created the resource "Ethics in the Age of Digital Photography" in 1999. In this ethical guide for journalists, he uses as an example the 1994 *Time* cover of Simpson. Long and, by association the NPPA, takes the position that all photo manipulation is lying if it changes the content of a photo; that is, if it transforms a photo from a document or direct account of

reality into an editorial statement. The NPPA's position is that this kind of manipulation undermines the credibility of the press. The *Time* magazine cover of Simpson continues to stand as one of the most significant and negative examples of editorialized photo manipulation.

—*Carmen James Schifellite*

FURTHER READING

Barak, Gregg, ed. *Media, Criminal Justice, and Mass Culture.* Monsey, N.Y.: Criminal Justice Press, 1999. Nineteen essays that explore the O. J. Simpson murder trial and its verdict. Focuses on media representations of crime and justice in the United States.

Dickinson, Greg, and Karrin Vasby Anderson. "Fallen: O. J. Simpson, Hillary Rodham Clinton, and the Re-centering of White Patriarchy." *Communication and Critical/Cultural Studies* 1, no. 3 (September, 2004): 271-296. Analysis of two *Time* magazine cover images: Simpson after his arrest for murder and Clinton during the Whitewater controversy.

Hawkins, Billy. "The Dominant Images of Black Men in America: The Representation of O. J. Simpson." In *African Americans in Sport: Contemporary Themes*, edited by Gary A. Sailes. New Brunswick, N.J.: Transaction, 1998. Analyzes negative images of black men, including Simpson, that predominate in the American mass media.

King, David. *The Commissar Vanishes: The Falsification of Photographs and Art in Stalin's Russia.* New York: Metropolitan Books, 1997. Chronicles the removal of political undesirables from the photo record in Stalin's Soviet Union by juxtaposing the original and altered photos.

Morrison, Toni, and Claudia Brodsky Lacour, eds. *Birth of a Nation'hood: Gaze, Script, and Spectacle in the O. J. Simpson Case.* New York: Pantheon Books, 1997. Eleven articles that focus on the significance of the O. J. Simpson case as a media spectacle.

Reaves, Sheila. "The Unintended Effects of New Technology (And Why We Can Expect More)." *News Photographer* 50, no. 7 (1995): 11-24. Ar-

1990's

gues that new digital technologies and an increasing focus on pseudo-events and celebrity news encourage more photo manipulation. Encourages editors to guard against the unintended affects of photo alteration.

SEE ALSO: July 23, 1984: Vanessa Williams Is the First Miss America to Resign; June 12, 1994: Double Murder Leads to Sensational O. J. Simpson Trial; Nov. 20, 2006: News Corp Abandons Plan to Publish O. J. Simpson's Book.

June 30, 1994
TONYA HARDING IS BANNED FROM SKATING AFTER ATTACK ON RIVAL

At the 1994 U.S. Figure Skating Championships, an unknown assailant clubbed skater Nancy Kerrigan on her knee after a practice session. Although Kerrigan had to withdraw from the event, she was still named to the U.S. Olympic team. The former husband of 1994 champion Tonya Harding claimed that he had hired Kerrigan's assailant, touching off a heavily publicized scandal. Harding competed in the Olympics but was later stripped of her national title and banned from sanctioned skating events.

LOCALE: Detroit, Michigan
CATEGORIES: Sports; corruption; violence; law and the courts

KEY FIGURES
Tonya Harding (b. 1970), professional figure skater
Nancy Kerrigan (b. 1969), professional figure skater
Jeff Gillooly (fl. 1990's), Harding's former husband
Shane Stant (b. 1971), bounty hunter and former convict
Shawn Eckardt (1967-2007), Harding's bodyguard

SUMMARY OF EVENT
The 1994 U.S. Figure Skating Championships, held at the Joe Louis Arena in Detroit, Michigan, was a qualifying event for the coming Winter Olympics in

Lillehammer, Norway. The United States had qualified to send two skaters for the ladies skating event, so the top two finishers at the championships would receive automatic spots on the U.S. Olympic team. Nancy Kerrigan, a bronze medalist at the 1992 Olympics in Albertville, France, and the reigning U.S. national champion, was the favorite to win the event for the second year in a row. Tonya Harding, the 1991 U.S. national champion and second-place finisher in the 1991 World Championships, was her main rival.

At approximately 2:35 P.M. on January 6, 1994, Kerrigan stepped behind a curtain separating the ice rink from a back hallway leading to the locker rooms after a practice session at nearby Cobo Arena. She stopped briefly to speak with a reporter when a then-unknown assailant rushed by and struck her on the right knee with a blunt baton similar to those used by police officers. Kerrigan fell to the ground crying, as reporters and skating personnel gathered around. Her attacker disappeared in the confusion. Kerrigan was taken to nearby Hutzel Hospital, where she was diagnosed with severe muscle and tissue bruising. She was forced to withdraw from the competition. Harding won the event and Michelle Kwan won second place. The U.S. Figure Skating Association (USFSA) named Kerrigan to the team, along with Harding, and named Kwan the alternate. The attack on Kerrigan received widespread publicity, and speculation began immediately as to who was behind the attack.

Harding's bodyguard, Shawn Eckardt, was arrested in Portland, Oregon, on January 13. He informed the Federal Bureau of Investigation (FBI) that Harding's former husband, Jeff Gillooly, had orchestrated the attack. Also arrested in the conspiracy was Derrick B. Smith. Shane Stant, a bounty hunter and former convict, was charged with the actual attack on Kerrigan and surrendered to police in Phoenix, Arizona, on January 14. Gillooly surrendered to Portland police on January 19.

Questions about Harding's role in the attack grew with every passing day. She held a press conference in Portland on January 27, admitting that she learned of the conspiracy to attack Kerrigan after the fact and failed to report what she knew to investigators. She maintained that she had no prior knowledge of the attack and did not help in its planning. On February 1, Gillooly pleaded guilty to his role in the conspiracy and reached a plea bargain. He confessed to racketeering charges only. In ex-

change, he promised authorities that he would implicate Harding.

The negative publicity and allegations against Harding led the U.S. Olympic Committee (USOC) to seek a way to keep her from participating in the Olympics. She appeared before the USOC's administrative board to respond to charges that she violated its athletic code, but the board ultimately voted to let her skate because she had not been formally charged with a crime. She also threatened to sue the committee if it prohibited her participation.

The Olympics began in mid-February, and both Harding and Kerrigan stayed in the Olympic Village during their time away from the ice arena. Both skaters were hounded by the media as they skated at the same practice sessions. Further drama erupted on February 17, when Kerrigan arrived at practice wearing the same white lace practice dress she had

Tonya Harding, left, and Nancy Kerrigan at a training session at the 1994 Winter Olympics in Norway. (Hulton Archive/ Getty Images)

1990's

been wearing when she was attacked. On February 25, she had a nearly flawless performance and won the silver medal behind Ukrainian skater Oksana Baiul in a controversial 5-4 split of the nine-judge panel. Harding finished a disappointing eighth after tearfully requesting that the judges let her restart her program when one of the laces on her skate broke.

After the Olympics, Harding pleaded guilty in Portland to conspiracy to hinder prosecution for her role in covering up the attack. She was not charged with helping to plan the attack and has always maintained her innocence. She received a fine, probation, and orders to perform community service, but no jail sentence. On June 30, the USFSA stripped Harding of her 1994 national title and banned her for life from USFSA-sanctioned events. She could still skate in professional events, but many of the top professional skaters would not skate with her. She would later take up the sport of professional boxing. Gillooly, Eckardt, and Stant would all serve prison sentences for their roles in the attack. Kerrigan became a professional skater, married, and had two sons.

IMPACT

The scandal tarnished figure skating's image, but at the same time it greatly increased its popularity. Television ratings for skating events soared, resulting in new skating shows, competitions, and television specials. Increased advertising revenue and ticket sales brought new money into the sport that could be invested in its development. Rising skating stars such as Kwan built on the popularity brought by the scandal. Sports reporter Christine Brennan once joked that all skaters should send a thank-you card to Harding for the benefits they have reaped in the scandal's aftermath. The publicity also exposed the inner, competitive world of figure skating and led many to question the treatment of Harding as a skater before the attack; she did not fit the traditional stereotype of the female skater as an "ice princess."

The attack on Kerrigan came less than one year after tennis star Monica Seles was stabbed in the back by an obsessed "fan" during a break in an April, 1993, match in Germany. Although Seles recovered physically, the stabbing was a tragedy that, like the Harding-Kerrigan case, helped to raise awareness about the need for heightened security at all athletic events.

—Marcella Bush Trevino

FURTHER READING

Baughman, Cynthia, ed. *Women on Ice: Feminist Essays on the Tonya Harding/Nancy Kerrigan Spectacle.* New York: Routledge, 1995. Examines the scandal from the perspective of gender politics. Discusses how mass media stereotypes of female ice skaters affected how the media covered the scandal and the public's image of Tonya Harding, who did not fit the stereotype of the traditional, ultrafeminine figure skater.

Brennan, Christine. *Inside Edge: A Revealing Journey into the Secret World of Figure Skating.* New York: Scribner, 1996. A longtime sports reporter's detailed account of backstage politics during the 1994 and 1995 skating seasons. Includes discussion of the Kerrigan attack and its aftermath.

Kerrigan, Nancy. *Nancy Kerrigan: In My Own Words.* New York: Hyperion Books, 1996. A work written especially for young readers. Provides the skater's firsthand account of the attack and surrounding media scandal as well as a retelling of her life and career.

Prouse, Linda D. *The Tonya Tapes: The Tonya Harding Story In Her Own Words.* New York: World Audience, 2008. Based on several interviews with Harding, this tell-all book explores Harding's life from her younger years through her life following professional figure skating. An authorized biography.

Rowe, David. "Apollo Undone: The Sports Scandal." In *Media Scandals*, edited by James Lull and Stephen Hinerman. New York: Columbia University Press, 1998. Examines the social impact of sports scandals, such as the Kerrigan attack, which receive much media attention.

SEE ALSO: Sept. 26, 2000: Gymnast Andreea Răducan Loses Her Olympic Gold Medal Because of Drugs; Feb. 11, 2002: French Judge Admits Favoring Russian Figure Skaters in Winter Olympics; Mar. 17, 2005: Former Baseball Star Mark McGwire Evades Congressional Ques-

tions on Steroid Use; July 26, 2006: Tour de France Is Hit with a Doping Scandal; Aug. 20, 2007: Football Star Michael Vick Pleads Guilty to Financing a Dogfighting Ring.

July 1, 1994
SOCCER STAR DIEGO MARADONA IS EXPELLED FROM WORLD CUP

Diego Maradona, generally regarded as one of the greatest soccer players of the modern era, was a national hero in his native Argentina, for which he helped win the 1986 World Cup. In later years, he developed a drug dependency. At the 1994 World Cup competition in the United States, he tested positive for ephedrine doping and was sent home. He claimed that the International Federation of Association Football had expelled him for innocently using a weight-loss drug that contained traces of ephedrine.

LOCALE: Dallas, Texas

CATEGORIES: Drugs; medicine and health care; sports

KEY FIGURES

Diego Maradona (b. 1960), Argentine soccer star

Daniel Cerrini (b. 1968), Argentine body builder and weight-loss trainer

Carlos Menem (b. 1930), president of Argentina, 1989-1999

SUMMARY OF EVENT

Even among the greatest of modern soccer players—Pelé, Franz Beckenbauer, Johann Cruiff, Roberto Baggio, Alfredo Di Stéfano, Zico—Diego Maradona was a unique presence. His skill at the world's most popular sport was unrivaled. Like these other great offensive players, he rose to his best in the World Cup final matches, held every four years and watched by hundreds of millions of fans.

Likewise, Maradona's play so dominated his national team that he became inextricably associated

with Argentina's image and was the most famous Argentine in the world. However, unlike his peers, who felt a certain obligation thereby to represent their nations in a dignified manner, Maradona at times gave the appearance that he believed that international soccer existed for his benefit. Off the field—and sometimes on as well—he was often embroiled in controversy and seemed but one step from scandal.

Maradona was born on October 30, 1960, in a shanty town outside Buenos Aires. He began playing soccer at the age of three. By the age of twelve he was already well known for his soccer skills and tricks. Starring for several professional soccer clubs, Maradona played in his first World Cup competition in 1982. In 1986, as team captain, he led Argentina to victory at the Mexico World Cup with a brilliant tournament.

The most memorable game of the 1986 cup was the June 22 quarterfinal match between Argentina and England, two countries that had been at war over the Falkland Islands off the coast of Argentina. The two goals that Maradona scored in Argentina's 2-1 victory are among the most famous in World Cup history. The first goal was the infamous hand of God goal, in which Maradona was accused of illegally knocking the ball into the English net with his hand (the "hand of God," Maradona claimed). The second goal is considered by many fans to be the greatest in soccer history and has been dubbed the goal of the century. Maradona dribbled the ball 55 yards past five of England's fabled defenders before shooting it past the superb goalkeeper Peter Shilton. In 1990, Argentina lost the final-round World Cup match to the champion Italian team.

By the 1990's, however, Maradona was struggling with both a cocaine addiction and a tendency to gain weight. Playing for a Naples, Italy, soccer club, he was under the spotlight of European tabloids for his unruly personal life and under investigation by the Italian police for drug use and Mafia connections. On March 17, 1991, a random drug test revealed the presence of cocaine in his body. He was banned from professional soccer for fifteen months. When Maradona returned to professional soccer in 1992, he was overweight, depressed, and a diminished presence on the soccer field. His fans—and he himself—saw the 1994 World Cup, to be played over the summer in the United States, as an opportunity for Maradona to restore his tarnished reputation, both on and off field.

Diego Maradona is mobbed by reporters one day before being expelled from World Cup competition for failing a drug test. (Hulton Archive/Getty Images)

In the summer of 1993, Maradona had begun training with Argentine personal trainer and body builder Daniel Cerrini, who prescribed a regimen of intense exercise, rigorous dieting, supplements of vitamins and minerals, and energy-boosting drugs. Soon, Maradona had lost fifteen kilograms (thirty-three pounds) and felt ready for the World Cup. He arrived in the United States during the summer of 1994. Cerrini joined Maradona's long-time fitness trainer, Fernando Signorini, for the trip as well. During the first two qualifying games, Maradona performed well. He led his team to a 4-0 victory over Greece on June 21 and a well-played 2-1 win against Nigeria four days later. One of the few players of international renown, he was cheered by the American fans in Boston.

Cerrini and Signorini were still disputing Maradona's ideal weight. Maradona weighed 76.8 kilograms (169 pounds) at the start of the tournament, which was acceptable to Signorini, but Cerrini wanted him at 70 kilograms (154 pounds) and continued to prescribe him diet supplements. Apparently, the team physician, Ernesto Ubalde, was not involved in the diet regimen.

On June 25, during half-time in the Argentina-Nigeria match, two urine samples were collected from Maradona, pursuant to the new random drug-testing policy of the Fédération Internationale de Football Association (FIFA), which called for testing players during the qualifying rounds. On July 1, the World Cup organizing committee announced that Maradona's urine test revealed the presence of the stimulant ephedrine and four other substances prohibited by FIFA doping control regulations. Maradona, waiting in Dallas for Argentina's game against Bulgaria, was immediately suspended from further play. In addition, an investigation was launched into his use of drugs. After his suspension he took a lucrative position as commentator on the games for Argentine television.

On August 24, the organizing committee announced the results of the investigation. Although Maradona was found not to have taken drugs to enhance his performance, and was in fact not even aware of the contents of the drug, he nevertheless was in breach of FIFA regulations. Ultimate responsibility for the infraction was assigned to Cerrini, but FIFA did take into account Maradona's previous history of drug abuse in holding him partly responsible. Both Maradona and Cerrini were banned from participation in all soccer events for fifteen months and fined twenty thousand Swiss francs. With Maradona off the team, Argentina was soon eliminated from the 1994 World Cup tournament.

The outcry in response to Maradona's suspension was worldwide. In Dharka, more than twenty thousand Bangladeshis demonstrated in protest. American newspapers, many of which were sympathetic to Maradona, compared the scandal to the one seared in the consciousness of American sports fans—the Black Sox baseball scandal of 1919. In Argentina, fans were devastated. Argentine president Carlos Menem wrote FIFA a five-page letter pleading for clemency for Maradona. Nevertheless, the committee affirmed its decision, recommending that in the future all players' medical treatments should be under the exclusive supervision of the team physician.

IMPACT

Maradona garnered much sympathy because of his heroic training regimen for the World Cup. By all accounts, his conditioning level was the best it had been in years and he recovered playing skills. When told of his suspension, he said, "They have sawed off my legs."

Moreover, there is little reason to doubt Maradona's contention—confirmed by the organizing committee—that the drug infraction was the by-product of his attempt to stabilize his weight, not to enhance his performance. In his 2000 autobiography, published in English in 2007, Maradona claimed that Cerrini had made an innocent mistake. Maradona had run out of his usual supplement, Ripped Fast. Cerrini had substituted the over-the-counter product Ripped Fuel, not knowing that it contained a small amount of ephedrine.

FIFA was required to act on the matter. By expelling Maradona, FIFA took overdue measures against the proliferation of stimulants in soccer, a problem that was increasingly plaguing all sports.

While Maradona's explanation for the accidental presence of ephedrine was plausible, there is no denying its potential for stimulating athletic energy.

The 1994 games would be tragically marred as well by the combination of illegal drug money and the importance of soccer in Latin American culture. When the Colombian defender Andres Escobar returned home after making a well-publicized mistake in the game with the United States, he was gunned down on the crime- and drug-plagued streets of Medellín, Colombia.

Maradona retired from soccer a few years after the doping affair. His drug addiction continued and he eventually had a heart attack in 2004 following a cocaine overdose. Maradona appeared to change after this, becoming free of weight concerns and cocaine addiction.

—*Howard Bromberg*

FURTHER READING

Burns, Jimmy. *Hand of God: The Life of Diego Maradona*. Guilford, Conn.: Lyons Press, 2003. A harsh look at Maradona that discusses the 1994 scandal as an example of Maradona's indulgence, narcissism, and rebelliousness.

Lisi, Clemente Angelo. *A History of the World Cup: 1930-2006*. Lanham, Md.: Scarecrow Press, 2007. A journalistic history of the world's most popular sports event. Chapter 6, "The Hand of God," explores the career of Maradona.

Maradona, Diego, with Daniel Arcucci and Ernesto Bialo. *Maradona: The Autobiography of Soccer's Greatest and Most Controversial Star*. New York: Skyhorse, 2007. Maradona's candid recollection of his life and career in international soccer, first published in 2000, displays his legendary egotism.

Radnedge, Keir. *The Complete Encyclopedia of Soccer*. Rev. ed. London: Carlton Books, 2007. Photo-rich survey of modern soccer. Ranks Maradona as the greatest soccer player of the 1980's and early 1990's.

SEE ALSO: Apr. 2, 1915: Players Fix Liverpool-Manchester United Soccer Match; Sept. 26, 2000: Gymnast Andreea Răducan Loses Her

1990's

Olympic Gold Medal Because of Drugs; Jan. 27, 2005: German Soccer Referee Admits to Fixing Games for Money; Mar. 17, 2005: Former Baseball Star Mark McGwire Evades Congressional Questions on Steroid Use; May 4, 2006: Me-

dia Uncover Match-Fixing in Italian Soccer; July 26, 2006: Tour de France Is Hit with a Doping Scandal; Oct. 5, 2007: Olympic Champion Marion Jones Admits Steroid Use.

August 5, 1994

KENNETH STARR IS APPOINTED TO THE WHITEWATER INVESTIGATION

A three-judge panel appointed Kenneth Starr as independent counsel to investigate whether U.S. president Bill Clinton broke any laws in a real estate project in Whitewater, Arkansas. For the next five years, Starr aggressively directed an investigation that moved well beyond Whitewater and into allegations that the president lied under oath about his sexual relationship with former White House intern Monica Lewinsky.

LOCALE: Washington, D.C.
CATEGORIES: Law and the courts; politics; government; sex; corruption

KEY FIGURES
Kenneth Starr (b. 1946), White House independent counsel
Bill Clinton (b. 1946), governor of Arkansas, 1979-1981 and 1983-1992, and president of the United States, 1993-2001
Hillary Rodham Clinton (b. 1947), First Lady, 1993-2001, U.S. senator from New York, 2001-2009, and Secretary of State, 2009-
Robert B. Fiske (b. 1930), special prosecutor
David B. Sentelle (b. 1943), Court of Appeals justice in Washington, D.C.
Jim McDougal (1940-1998), co-owner of Whitewater Development Corporation and Madison Guaranty Savings & Loan
Susan McDougal (b. 1955), co-owner of Whitewater Development Corporation and Madison Guaranty Savings & Loan

SUMMARY OF EVENT
From 1979 to 1989, Bill and Hillary Rodham Clinton were business associates with Jim and Susan McDougal in the Whitewater Development Corporation, a failed real estate venture in Arkansas that resulted in the 1989 bankruptcy of the McDougal's financial firm Madison Guaranty Savings & Loan and a federal government bailout of sixty million dollars. The Clintons claimed to have done nothing improper in the matter, suffering personal losses of more than forty thousand dollars.

In late 1993, David Hale, a banker who was under indictment for fraud, claimed that U.S. president Bill Clinton, while governor of Arkansas, pressured him into making an illegal $300,000 loan to Susan McDougal. Hearing of Hale's claim, *The Washington Post* called for an investigation, but one without the U.S. Department of Justice, to establish whether Clinton had been a part of the Whitewater venture.

In January, 1994, Clinton's advisers convinced him to ask U.S. attorney general Janet Reno to appoint a special prosecutor. For the task, Reno appointed Robert B. Fiske, a moderate Republican lawyer. On the last day in June, Fiske issued two reports: The first report concluded that the 1993 suicide of White House counsel Vincent Foster, a former law partner of Hillary Clinton, was not related to Whitewater, and the second report concluded that the evidence for Hale's allegations was insufficient to bring criminal charges against anyone in the White House. Some Republicans criticized Fiske for not being sufficiently aggressive in the investigations.

As the Fiske reports were being issued, the U.S. Congress passed a bill reestablishing the Office of Independent Counsel (OIC). President Clinton reluctantly signed the bill into law. (Hillary Clinton had recommended that he veto the legislation.) Like the earlier law that had been in effect from 1978 to 1992, the new statute conferred the OIC with almost unlimited powers to investigate, subpoena, and prosecute persons having a relationship to any matter under investigation. The statute further provided that the independent counsel would be appointed by a panel of three U.S. Court of Appeals judges, and the panel was to be selected by the chief justice of the United States, at this time William H. Rehnquist. To lead the three-judge panel, Rehnquist selected Judge David B. Sentelle, who had close connections to U.S. senator Jesse Helms of North Carolina and other conservative politicians highly critical of the president.

The panel dismissed Fiske and replaced him with Kenneth Starr on August 5. Sentelle explained that a change was desirable because Fiske's appointment by the attorney general gave the appearance of a conflict of interest. Starr, the new appointee, was a former U.S. Court of Appeals judge who had left the bench to serve as the solicitor general. His appointment initially received favorable comment from most journalists and informed observers. The Clintons, who were familiar with his past work, were suspicious that Starr would be extremely assertive and probably motivated by partisan zeal. Hillary Clinton and Democratic adviser James Carville even recommended a campaign against the appointment. White House Counsel Lloyd Cutler, however, argued that Starr was highly professional and would conduct a fair investigation.

Starr assembled a large OIC staff of aggressive, experienced lawyers. The OIC expanded the Whitewater investigation to target any person having had any direct or indirect relationship to the venture. Upon finding evidence of illegal acts, Starr offered the person in ques-

tion a reduced penalty in exchange for testimony against one of the Clintons. In December, Webster Hubbell, a former Arkansas associate attorney general who had worked with Hillary Clinton on Whitewater matters, pleaded guilty to tax evasion and mail fraud in connection with his billing practices. In 1996, Starr obtained convictions of Jim McDougal and Arkansas governor Jim Guy Tucker for fraud. Susan McDougal, claiming that Starr was pressuring her to lie about the president, refused to answer questions before a federal grand jury and was sentenced to eighteen months in prison for contempt of court.

Despite their best efforts, Starr and his OIC team were unable to obtain sufficient proof to indict the Clintons. However, the OIC did discover items that turned out to be embarrassing to the Clintons. Hil-

Kenneth Starr at a news conference in 1997 in Washington, D.C., announcing that he will remain lead counsel with the Whitewater investigation. (AP/Wide World Photos)

819

lary Clinton's lost billing records were finally located, revealing that she had done sixty hours of legal work on Whitewater-related business, even though she had earlier told investigators she could not recall working on the project. Furthermore, Starr requested and received approval to investigate allegations that she had given false testimony to a U.S. Senate committee about her role in the firing of employees at the White House Travel Office. After 125 subpoenas, the OIC concluded that there was insufficient evidence to establish beyond a reasonable doubt that she perjured herself before the committee.

By January, 1998, the OIC had been investigating claims of improprieties well beyond its initial Whitewater mandate. It also discovered credible allegations that President Clinton, in a lawsuit filed by Paula Jones against Clinton for sexual harassment, had lied under oath when he denied having had a sexual encounter with former White House intern Monica Lewinsky. Starr also found evidence that Clinton had encouraged Lewinsky to lie under oath. After the three-judge panel granted Starr permission to pursue the matter, Starr discovered that the allegations against Clinton were true. Starr's report of September, 1998, which dealt primarily with the Lewinsky scandal, resulted in Clinton's impeachment by the U.S. House of Representatives. The majority of the Senate, however, voted to acquit him on February 12, 1999, and he continued his term in office. Starr officially resigned from the OIC in October and was replaced by Robert W. Ray.

IMPACT

By the time of Starr's resignation, the majority of Democratic and Republican leaders had serious questions about the fairness and efficacy of the OIC. With the June, 1999, demise of the bill that created the office came a reluctance by many members of Congress to okay its reauthorization. Although five in-process investigations continued, the OIC, without reauthorization, would not get a new independent counsel. Acting under statutory authority, Attorney General Reno drew up new regulations for conducting independent investigations

of misconduct by public officials under the supervision of the Justice Department.

Many Americans, especially Democratic supporters of the president, have been highly critical of Starr for his zeal in pursuing the Lewinsky scandal. His detractors tend to describe him as a scandal-obsessed fanatic with a disdain for liberal politicians. Many argue that the president's sexual behavior, as detailed in the Starr Report, is a matter of private morality, not public policy. Other critics point to the large amount of money—more than fifty million dollars—spent during the five years that Starr directed OIC investigations. Only one other independent counsel—Lawrence E. Welsh—had spent more money on an investigation. His mandate had been to look into the Iran-Contra scandal of the 1980's.

Others, however, defended Starr's direction of OIC investigations. His supporters argued that he was a serious prosecutor seeking truth according to the law, and that he successfully prosecuted several individuals who had committed criminal acts in the Whitewater project. They also emphasized that the Starr Report proved that President Clinton had given false testimony, a crime, in a civil suit. In January, 2000, Starr's successor, Ray, reached an agreement with the president. To avoid prosecution, Clinton had to acknowledge that he lied under oath, agree to a suspension of his law license for five years, and pay a fine of $25,000.

—*Thomas Tandy Lewis*

FURTHER READING

Carville, James. *And the Horse He Rode in On: The People v. Kenneth Starr*. New York: Simon & Schuster, 1998. A partisan, one-sided polemic against Starr as well as those who accused the president of wrongdoing.

Clinton, William Jefferson. *My Life*. New York: Alfred A. Knopf, 2004. The former president denounces Starr and accuses his opponents of falsehoods, but he also neglects to mention certain historical facts.

Johnson, Charles, and Danette Brickman. *Independent Counsel: The Law and the Investigations*. Washington, D.C.: CQ Press, 2001. A well-written summary of the twenty investigations by independent counsels starting with Watergate during the early 1970's through Whitewater and Kenneth Starr in 1999.

Schmidt, Susan, and Michael Weisskopf. *Truth at Any Cost: Ken Starr and the Unmaking of Bill Clinton.* New York: HarperCollins, 2000. A detailed account by two journalists who sympathize with Starr and are critical of Clinton.

Starr, Kenneth W. *The Starr Report: The Findings of Independent Counsel Kenneth W. Starr on President Clinton and the Lewinsky Affair.* New York: PublicAffairs, 1998. The controversial document by Starr that was the basis for Clinton's impeachment.

Toobin, Jeffrey. *A Vast Conspiracy: The Real Story of the Sex Scandal That Nearly Brought Down a President.* New York: Simon & Schuster, 2000. A lively account of the Lewinsky scandal that is highly critical of Starr's investigation.

Wittes, Benjamin. *Starr: A Reassessment.* New Haven, Conn.: Yale University Press, 2002. Argues that Clinton is a pathological liar and Starr is a person of integrity who, nonetheless, was the "wrong man" for the investigation into Whitewater because of his moralistic theories of prosecution.

SEE ALSO: Mar. 1, 1967: Adam Clayton Powell, Jr., Is Excluded from Congress; June 13, 1971: *New York Times* Publishes the Pentagon Papers; June 17, 1972-Aug. 9, 1974: Watergate Break-in Leads to President Nixon's Resignation; Oct. 10, 1973: Spiro T. Agnew Resigns Vice Presidency in Disgrace; June 1, 1994: Congressman Dan Rostenkowski Is Indicted in House Post Office Scandal; Dec. 11, 1997: HUD Secretary Henry Cisneros Is Indicted for Lying to Federal Agents; Jan. 17, 1998: President Bill Clinton Denies Sexual Affair with a White House Intern; Dec. 5, 2002: Senator Trent Lott Praises Strom Thurmond's 1948 Presidential Campaign; Sept. 8, 2004: *60 Minutes II* Reports on George W. Bush's Evasion of Wartime Duty.

August 21, 1994
SEX SCANDAL FORCES DISMISSAL OF NAACP CHIEF BENJAMIN CHAVIS

Benjamin Chavis, executive director of the NAACP, lost his job for agreeing to an out-of-court monetary settlement to be paid to his assistant, Mary E. Stansel, to forestall a sexual harassment and sex discrimination lawsuit against him and the NAACP. He had paid Stansel using NAACP funds without the permission or the knowledge of the organization. A court later ruled that the NAACP would not have to pay any part of the original settlement, and it ordered Stansel to return the funds she already received.

LOCALE: Baltimore, Maryland
CATEGORIES: Law and the courts; sex crimes; women's issues

KEY FIGURES
Benjamin Chavis (b. 1948), director of the National Association for the Advancement of Colored People
Mary E. Stansel (fl. 1990's), Chavis's executive secretary

SUMMARY OF EVENT
Benjamin Chavis was appointed executive director of the National Association for the Advancement of Colored People (NAACP) in April, 1993. Seventeen months later he was dismissed as director when it was discovered that he had agreed to an out-of-court settlement with his former executive assistant, Mary E. Stansel, to keep her from suing both

Chavis and the NAACP for sexual harassment, sex discrimination, and violating her civil rights. Chavis agreed to pay Stansel more than $80,000 from NAACP funds without the knowledge of its board or general counsel. On August 21, 1994, the NAACP board overwhelmingly voted to dismiss Chavis, concluding that his actions were inimical to the best interests of the organization. In turn, Chavis called his ouster a "lynching."

While Chavis may have been within his powers as executive director to settle a suit against the NAACP, it remains questionable whether he should have used the organization's funds to settle the accusations against himself. The settlement between Chavis and Stansel, signed on November 12, 1993, consisted of cash and an agreement that Chavis would find her another job outside the NAACP. In late July, 1994, the NAACP found out about the agreement. Stansel, who had been Chavis's executive assistant for less than two months, filed suit against Chavis and the NAACP on June 30 for breach of contract. In court papers, she indicated that she already had received around $77,000, most of that from NAACP coffers, of an agreed-upon $80,000. Furthermore, Chavis had agreed to pay her an additional $250,000 were he to fail in finding her another job paying a salary of at least $80,000 within six months. Stansel sued when the deal fell through.

Chavis, an African American civil rights and religious leader, was born to educators and civil rights activists and was an activist from an early age. He was involved with the Southern Christian Leadership Conference (SCLC) and school desegregation in North Carolina. In 1976, he was convicted, with nine other desegregationists known collectively as the Wilmington Ten, for arson, firebombing, and conspiracy to commit assault. Chavis was sentenced to thirty-four years in prison and the others to ten years. After a lengthy battle that made international headlines, all ten were exonerated and released in 1980.

Chavis attended college while in prison and wrote the books *An American Political Prisoner Appeals for Human Rights in the United States of America* (1978) and *Psalms from Prison* (1983). He earned a bachelor of arts degree in chemistry from the University of North Carolina, a master of divinity degree from Duke University, and a doctor of ministry degree from Howard University. He also completed the course requirements for a doctor of philosophy degree from Union Theological Seminary. He was a youth coordinator in North Carolina for the Reverend Martin Luther King, Jr., and the SCLC and then returned to Oxford, North Carolina, and taught at the all-black Mary Potter High School. He was a minister in the United Church of Christ during the 1980's and led the church's Commission for Racial Justice. Chavis is credited with coining the term "environmental racism," a form of discrimination whereby, to take one example, a disproportionate number of toxic and hazardous materials waste sites and facilities are located within neighborhoods with many ethnic and racial minorities. His influential study *Toxic Waste and Race in the United States of America* was published in 1986.

According to his lawyer, Chavis agreed to the settlement with Stansel under duress. He wanted to avoid bad publicity and questions about his credibility. Other concerns about Chavis's tenure at the NAACP might have contributed to his dismissal. He was already under fire from some board members for his unorthodox practices, including reaching out to the Nation of Islam and to gang members. There was concern about how he handled NAACP finances. The organization was facing mounting debt and declining membership, and many within the NAACP believed Chavis's legal troubles had been affecting donations. Chavis, however, maintained that membership was growing, despite all the evidence to the contrary. Some of the larger contributors and supporters, such as the Ford Foundation, began to question the effectiveness of the NAACP. Some also believed that Chavis's unorthodox methods were leading the organization away from its original goals.

As the board was meeting to determine Chavis's future with the NAACP, Susan Tisdale, who had worked as a secretary for Chavis's wife, Martha, sent a memo to the board, indicating that she was initiating a sexual harassment suit against Chavis. However, Tisdale dropped the matter, saying the accusation of sexual harassment was a misunderstanding. Nevertheless, Chavis was dismissed by the board on August 21, 1994.

IMPACT

Being dismissed as head of the NAACP did not affect Chavis's career. He became the executive director of the National African American Leadership Summit in 1995 and was appointed national director of the Million Man March on Washington, D.C., in October, 1995. Two years later, in 1997, he became a member and a minister of the Nation of Islam, changed his surname to Muhammad, and soon was named the organization's East Coast regional minister. He organized the Million Family March in 2000. In 2001, he became the cochairman and chief executive officer of the Hip-Hop Summit Action Network (HHSAN) in collaboration with entrepreneur Russell Simmons. The HHSAN is a coalition of community members and activists and hip-hop artists dedicated to fighting for justice and against poverty among African Americans.

Stansel had sued both Chavis and the NAACP as responsible parties, but a Washington, D.C., court ruled that the NAACP was not financially liable for any part of the settlement between Stansel and Chavis. The court ordered Stansel to return the money she had already received from the organization.

The NAACP sought to recover from the Chavis scandal and its own mounting debt. Organization leaders pledged to restore the NAACP's reputation. Myrlie Evers-Williams, a civil rights activist and the wife of slain NAACP field secretary Medgar Evers, was elected chair, thereby becoming the first woman to head the organization. Kweisi Mfume, a U.S. representative from Maryland, was appointed the new executive director. A Democrat, Mfume gave up his congressional seat in 1996 to take the position at the NAACP, which was on the verge of bankruptcy. With Evers-Williams and Mfume at the helm, the NAACP managed to pull itself out of debt but still suffered some image problems.

—*Judy L. Porter*

FURTHER READING

Jonas, Gilbert. *Freedom's Sword: The NAACP and the Struggle Against Racism in America, 1909-1969*. New York: Routledge, 2005. A comprehensive history of the beginnings of the NAACP up to 1969. The author, a member of the NAACP for more than fifty years, is a journalist and civil rights activist. Includes a foreword by civil rights leader Julian Bond.

Marshall, Anna-Maria. *Confronting Sexual Harassment: The Law and Politics of Everyday Life*. Burlington, Vt.: Ashgate, 2005. Examines law, social change, and the politics of workers' everyday lives. Also provides a framework for studying issues of everyday life, especially in the workplace.

Russell-Brown, Katheryn. *Protecting Our Own: Race, Crime, and African Americans*. Lanham, Md.: Rowman & Littlefield, 2006. Law professor Russell-Brown explores ideas of "black protectionism" and "linked fate" among African Americans during times of scandal involving black public figures, including Benjamin Chavis, and media focus on crimes committed by blacks. Argues that protectionism extends to all races.

SEE ALSO: Jan. 13, 1913: Federal Judge Is Impeached for Profiting from His Office; May 9, 1969: Supreme Court Justice Abe Fortas Is Accused of Bribery; Oct. 11-13, 1991: Justice Clarence Thomas's Confirmation Hearings Create a Scandal; Dec. 11, 1997: HUD Secretary Henry Cisneros Is Indicted for Lying to Federal Agents; Jan. 17, 1998: President Bill Clinton Denies Sexual Affair with a White House Intern; Jan. 2, 2003: E-mail Message Prompts Inquiry into Air Force Academy Sexual Assaults; June 2, 2004: U.N. Report Reveals That Secretary-General Kofi Annan Dismissed Sexual Harassment Charges; Oct. 13, 2004: Television Producer Files Sex Harassment Suit Against Bill O'Reilly.

1990's

February 28, 1995
FORMER MEXICAN PRESIDENT CARLOS SALINAS'S BROTHER IS ARRESTED FOR MURDER

In an unprecedented action, Mexican president Ernesto Zedillo ordered the arrest of Raúl Salinas, the brother of his predecessor and political ally Carlos Salinas, for murdering the Salinas's brother-in-law. Raúl Salinas was convicted and sentenced but was later acquitted of the murder and released. The ensuing scandal led to breaks in tradition, the exposure of widespread government corruption, political reform, and a shift toward democracy in Mexico.

LOCALE: Mexico City, Mexico
CATEGORIES: Corruption; drugs; government; politics; law and the courts; murder and suicide

KEY FIGURES
Raúl Salinas de Gortari (b. 1946), brother of former Mexican president Carlos Salinas de Gortari
Ernesto Zedillo Ponce de Léon (b. 1951), president of Mexico, 1994-2000
José Francisco Ruiz Massieu (1946-1994), Mexican politician, member of the Institutional Revolutionary Party
Carlos Salinas de Gortari (b. 1948), president of Mexico, 1988-1994
Luis Donaldo Colosio (1950-1994), politician and presidential candidate in 1994

SUMMARY OF EVENT
Carlos Salinas de Gortari served as president of Mexico from 1988 to 1994, as Mexico's constitution limits the number of terms for a president to one. However, because the Partido Revolucionario Institucional (Institutional Revolutionary Party), or PRI, had won all of the presidential elections since its founding in 1929, each president traditionally picked the candidate who would succeed him. Luis Donaldo Colosio, who had been Salinas's campaign manager in 1988 and served as social development secretary in Salinas's cabinet since 1992, appeared to be the chosen successor.

Colosio, however, was not having a successful campaign, and there were rumors that he would be replaced by Manuel Camacho, who had attracted public attention for his negotiations with the guerrillas of the Ejército Zapatista de Liberacíon Nacional (Zapatista Army of National Liberation). Salinas publicly stated his support for Colosio, and Camacho declared he would not be a candidate. Then, on March 23, 1994, Colosio was killed at a campaign rally in Tijuana. Camacho was first blamed for the murder; others were then accused, including members of organized crime and, finally, Salinas. Apparently, Colosio had given a speech in which he had angered Salinas by speaking of the leader's hope for justice and a good future.

The PRI almost was left without a candidate. Any person who had held a public office six months before an election was not eligible to run for the presidency. This requirement eliminated most of the potential replacements. Salinas chose Ernesto Zedillo Ponce de Léon, who had some time earlier resigned his office to serve as campaign manager for Colosio, as the candidate.

On September 28, Salinas's brother-in-law, José Francisco Ruiz Massieu, was shot and killed in downtown Mexico City, about one block from the Paseo de la Reforma. Massieu was slated to become the PRI majority leader in the chamber of deputies at the time he was assassinated. The assassin, Daniel Aguilar, a farmworker hired to kill Ruiz Massieu, was quickly arrested and revealed the names of a number of coconspirators.

The assassination caused pandemonium in Mexico. President Salinas immediately ordered an investigation. Ruiz Massieu's brother, Mario Ruiz Massieu, was the head prosecutor. On November 15, Ruiz Massieu accused the PRI of hindering the investigation. This caused distrust within Mexico and led major foreign investors to withdraw from the country. On November 23, Ruiz Massieu resigned and left Mexico. It was later discovered that he had seven million dollars deposited in a Texas bank, arousing suspicions that he was hiding the identity of the person responsible for his brother's death.

Pablo Chapa Bezanilla replaced Ruiz Massieu as head prosecutor. He initiated a series of interviews with José's family members. He discovered that a bitter feud existed between José and Raúl Salinas de Gortari, President Salinas's brother, since the time José had divorced Adriana Salinas, their sister, in 1978. Further investigations revealed that all references to Raúl Salinas had been removed from the testimony given by the conspirators.

The investigation continued through the end of Salinas's term as president and into the term of Zedillo. All of the evidence pointed to Raúl Salinas as the architect of the murder. Zedillo was stunned. He regarded Carlos Salinas as his friend and mentor. Moreover, the Mexican president was protective of his predecessor. However, the law demanded that Raúl Salinas be brought to trial. Zedillo had to make a choice: remain loyal to Carlos Salinas and his family or uphold the law. He chose to obey the law and arrest Raúl Salinas.

On February 28, 1995, Raúl Salinas was arrested for ordering the murder of his former brother-in-law. The investigation further corroborated Raúl Salinas's involvement. Carlos Salinas strongly objected to the proceedings and insisted that it was a slander campaign against his family. In November, as Raúl Salinas's trial continued, his wife, Paulina Castañon, and her brother, Antonio, attempted to withdraw about $84 million from an account in a Swiss bank. The account was under a fictitious name. They were arrested. Investigations began in Switzerland and implicated Raúl Salinas in money laundering and drug trafficking. The Swiss accounts were frozen. Meanwhile, Raúl Salinas remained in the maximum-security prison he had been in since his arrest.

In 1998, the prosecution rested its case. On October 16, 1998, the Mexican attorney-general asked that Raúl Salinas receive a maximum sentence of fifty years in prison for the murder of Ruiz Massieu. On January 22, 1999, he received that sentence. He had insisted that he was innocent during the long

trial and appealed the sentence. The Mexican appeals court reduced the sentence to twenty-seven and one-half years.

On June 14, 2005, Raúl Salinas was released from prison after being acquitted of the murder. His release, however, also cost him financially. He had to pay a three-million-dollar bond because he was under investigation for corruption, money laundering, and drug trafficking. He was exonerated of all these charges, however. The only misdeed he admitted to was obtaining a false passport, which he used in Switzerland.

IMPACT

The Salinas scandal was far-reaching—involving murder, corruption, and unethical political practices—and had serious consequences for Mexico

A police mug shot of Raúl Salinas de Gortari after his arrest for murder. (Hulton Archive/Getty Images)

1990's

825

and Mexican politics. Political crisis ensued, and even tradition was tarnished when President Zedillo arrested Raúl Salinas.

The arrest and trial of Raúl Salinas fully exposed the opportunities for corruption that were inherent in Mexico's political system, a strong one-party system that controlled the elections and the government. The power of tradition afforded to an outgoing president—allowed to choose his successor—provided a safe, unquestioned atmosphere for unethical political practices. The public notoriety given to Raúl Salinas for masterminding a murder and for his roles in money laundering and drug trafficking played a significant part in bringing about political reform and a shift toward democracy in Mexico.

Furthermore, because the Salinas brothers were known to share a close relationship—Raúl had been part of Carlos's government, serving as his aide and as a government food distribution officer—Raúl's arrest for murder threw suspicion on Carlos as well. Rumors already existed that Carlos Salinas was involved in the murder of Colosio. The family scandal, coupled with blame for economic problems in Mexico, led to Carlos Salinas's self-imposed exile from Mexico. He moved to Ireland, where he remained for several years.

The PRI also lost its hold on the presidency in the next election. Vicente Fox, an opposition party candidate, defeated the PRI candidate, Francisco Labastida, in the 2000 election. For the first time since its founding in 1929, the PRI could not elect its candidate to the presidency.

—Shawncey Webb

FURTHER READING

Camp, Roderic Ai. *Politics in Mexico: The Democratic Transformation*. New York: Oxford University Press, 2002. Examines the significance of the leadership of Carlos Salinas and Ernesto Zedillo, and the arrest of Raúl Salinas, in pushing Mexico toward democratic government. Also looks at the administration of Zedillo's successor, Vicente Fox, who received business training in the United States.

Fabre, Guilhem. *Criminal Prosperity: Drug Trafficking, Money Laundering, and Financial Crises After the Cold War*. New York: Routledge-Curzon, 2003. A study of international crime as a means to a nation's prosperity following the Cold War era. Chapter 5 examines the problem of drug trafficking in Mexico and the possible involvement of Raúl Salinas in that trafficking.

Oppenheimer, Andres. *Bordering on Chaos: Mexico's Roller Coaster Journey Toward Prosperity*. Boston: Back Bay Press, 1998. Discusses Carlos Salinas's presidency, Zedillo's election, and the unrest caused by the arrest of Raúl Salinas in the context of Mexico's attempts to become a capitalist democracy.

SEE ALSO: Oct. 29, 1965: Moroccan Politician Mehdi Ben Barka Disappears in Paris; Feb. 3, 1975: Honduras's "Bananagate" Bribery Scandal Leads to Executive's Suicide; Aug. 21, 1983: Filipino Opposition Leader Aquino Is Assassinated on Return Home; Jan. 12 and May 11, 1987: Media Reports Spark Investigation of Australian Police Corruption; Jan., 1997: Pyramid Investment Schemes Cause Albanian Government to Fall; Dec. 23, 1998: Prominent Belgians Are Sentenced in Agusta-Dassault Corruption Scandal; Oct. 22, 2006: Chilean Politicians Use Community Funds for Personal Campaigns.

June 27, 1995
FILM STAR HUGH GRANT IS ARRESTED FOR LEWD CONDUCT

Los Angeles police officers arrested film star Hugh Grant for lewd conduct in public and also arrested Divine Brown for prostitution after the two were caught having oral sex in a parked car in Hollywood. The incident generated much gossip and attention in the media but did not harm Grant's career. The publicity also earned for Brown more than one million dollars for telling her story to British tabloids and television and radio shows in the United States and for posing for the adult magazine Penthouse.

LOCALE: Los Angeles, California

CATEGORIES: Prostitution; sex crimes; public morals; law and the courts; publishing and journalism; Hollywood

KEY FIGURES

Hugh Grant (b. 1960), British film star
Divine Brown (b. 1969), American prostitute
Elizabeth Hurley (b. 1965), British model and actor

SUMMARY OF EVENT

Hugh Grant's brush with scandal came at a time in his career that could have meant disaster for him. However, if anything, the incident in which police caught the debonair English actor with a prostitute in Los Angeles left him relatively unscathed and gave the prostitute he paid fifty dollars for fellatio a chance for fame and fortune.

Grant had begun acting in films just before graduating from Oxford University during the early 1980's. Of his early films, the two that drew the most attention from press and public both had sexuality as a major theme. In *Maurice* (1987), a prestigious adaptation of E. M. Forster's novel about a young gay man's coming of age in early twentieth century England, Grant played the title character's first lover. In the Australian production *Sirens*

(1994), Grant played an Anglican priest who learns to let go of his inhibitions while frolicking in the Outback with an artist's gorgeous and often naked models. However, it was the film he made directly after *Sirens*, the wildly popular comedy *Four Weddings and a Funeral* (1994), which put him on the edge of superstardom.

One of the biggest hits of the 1990's and also one of the highest-grossing films ever produced in the United Kingdom, *Four Weddings and a Funeral* focused on a handsome young Englishman who has had dozens of girlfriends but cannot commit for long to any of them and who becomes obsessed with a somewhat promiscuous American woman even as she prepares to marry another man. Critics praised Grant's comic flair for both verbal and physical humor, and audiences were impressed with his good looks and abundant charm. He had just arrived in the United States to begin work on his first big-budget Hollywood film, *Nine Months* (1995), when he solicited Divine Brown on a street corner on Sunset Boulevard in Hollywood.

Divine Brown's background could not have contrasted more markedly from that of Grant. Whereas Grant had grown up amid upper-middle-class affluence in London, Brown had come of age in one of the poorest, most crime-ridden neighborhoods of Oakland, California. Following in the footsteps of her friends, she turned to prostitution in her late teen years as a way to pay the bills. She acquired a pimp, who called himself Gangster Brown, and with whom she had two daughters. Under his guidance she began to work regularly on the streets of San Francisco and Oakland. On June 27, 1995, the night that she was solicited by Grant, she was a new arrival to Los Angeles, just as Grant had only recently come to California to try his luck in Hollywood. Grant agreed to pay Brown fifty dollars for oral sex. Before the sex act could be completed, however, two police officers interrupted the pair and arrested them. Brown was booked for prostitution and Grant for lewd conduct in public. Within twenty-four hours, their mug shots were in newspapers around the United States, with accompanying copy detailing their encounter.

However brief their time together, the names Hugh Grant and Divine Brown were inextricable in print, on television, and in the minds of the public. Comedians found the incident irresistible, as did newspaper cartoonists. Brown and Grant were repeatedly featured on late-night television news and were the topic of many talk-show jokes. Grant's longtime companion Elizabeth Hurley made a public statement about the hurt and humiliation she was experiencing because of her lover's infidelity and the surrounding media circus, and the media covered her statement with the sort of deadpan seriousness usually afforded presidents or the chairs of important committees.

Just as the frenzy began to die down, Grant's attorneys appeared in a Los Angeles court on July 11 to answer to the charges leveled against their client, rekindling media and public interest in the affair even though Grant did not attend the hearing personally. Through his lawyers, he pleaded no contest to the charge of lewd conduct in public. The judge ordered Grant to pay a fine of $1,180 and to take a course in HIV-AIDS awareness. He also placed Grant on two years' probation.

Even after the settling of Grant's court case, the public—and the principals—did not stop talking about the events of June 27. While his attorneys represented him in court, Grant appeared on one of the most widely watched television programs in the United States, *The Tonight Show with Jay Leno*. If the audience expected to hear far-fetched rationalizations, contempt for the police, disparaging remarks about Brown, or expressions of self-pity, they were surprised. Grant simply, clearly, even somewhat humbly admitted that he had done what he had been accused of, that it had been wrong, and that he was sorry. Both the studio audience and host Jay Leno were obviously impressed with his straightforward mea culpa, and Grant went on to make more or less the same statements again and again on other programs, including *Larry King Live*

and *Live with Regis and Kathie Lee*. Though the names of Grant, Brown, and Hurley continued to be bandied about in the media for months to come, the scandal was effectively diffused by Grant's appearance on *The Tonight Show*.

IMPACT

Because of Grant's ready openness about the incident, the scandal had little effect on his career. *Nine Months* proved to be a modest hit and Grant's career proceeded without a hitch. His work has included popular and critical favorites such as *Notting Hill* (1999), *Bridget Jones's Diary* (2001), and *About a Boy* (2002). His relationship with Hurley did not fare as well. Though they managed to stay together for some time, they announced their split in May, 2000.

The effect the scandal had on Brown was perhaps more startling. She is rumored to have made more than one million dollars from her few minutes with Grant. Much of the money came from British tabloids, such as *News of the World*, which paid lavishly for her recollections of that night in June. Brown also appeared on a wide array of American television programs, including the two most notorious talk shows of the decade, *The Jerry Springer Show* and *The Howard Stern Show*. She also posed for adult magazines such as *Penthouse* and even starred in a pornographic video re-creating her and Grant's encounter. At some point, she also recorded a music album.

An ethicist might suggest that Grant survived the Brown scandal purely because of his honesty and openness. Certainly it could be argued that if the incident had any impact at all on the public as a whole, it provided an exemplar for how to deal with one's own wrongdoing: Admit the mistake openly and apologize. However, as admirable as Grant was in taking responsibility for his actions, the scandal did not harm his career mostly because of changing times.

By the final years of the twentieth century, a young actor's consorting with a prostitute simply was not as shocking or damaging to his public image as it would have been in previous decades. The sexual encounter between Grant and Brown, albeit involving an exchange of money, was consensual and between adults. Furthermore, Grant was an actor who played in films geared toward adults. His actions would have fared differently had he been a celebrity such as Paul Reubens (Pee-wee Herman), who was charged with public indecency in 1991 and whose work was geared toward children.

—*Thomas Du Bose*

FURTHER READING

Bowyer, Alison. *Liz Hurley Uncovered*. London: Andre Deutsch, 2003. In its coverage of the scandal, this work favors the viewpoint of Elizabeth Hurley over Hugh Grant and traces the couple's long relationship until its end in the wake of the Divine Brown scandal.

Bracewell, Michael. *The Nineties: When Surface Was Substance*. London: Flamingo, 2002. Insightful examination of the decade in which the scandal occurred. Hugh Grant is mentioned as a prototypical celebrity of the period.

Neal, Sarah. "Populist Configurations of Race and Gender: The Case of Hugh Grant, Liz Hurley, and Divine Brown." In *Thinking Identities: Ethnicity, Racism, and Culture*, edited by Avtar Brah, Mary J. Hickman, and Maírtín Mac an Ghaill. New York: St. Martin's Press, 1999. A sociological look at the intersections of ethnicity, race, and culture in the case of the Hugh Grant-Divine Brown sex scandal.

Parish, James Robert. *Hollywood Bad Boys: Loud, Fast, and Out of Control*. Chicago: Contemporary Books, 2002. A revealing collection of biographies of Hollywood male celebrities, including Hugh Grant, who are known for extremes of behavior.

Tresidder, Jody. *Hugh Grant: The Unauthorized Biography*. New York: St. Martin's Press, 1996. Published soon after the sex scandal. Offers insights and observations fresh from the time.

SEE ALSO: Jan. 20, 1933: Hedy Lamarr Appears Nude in the Czech Film *Exstase*; Summer, 1936: Film Star Mary Astor's Diary Becomes a Public Sensation; Feb. 6, 1942: Film Star Errol Flynn Is Acquitted of Rape; Aug. 31, 1948: Film Star Robert Mitchum Is Arrested for Drug Possession; Feb. 1, 1978: Roman Polanski Flees the United States to Avoid Rape Trial; July 19, 1985: Mayflower Madam Pleads Guilty to Promoting Prostitution; July 18, 1988: Actor Rob Lowe Videotapes Sexual Tryst with a Minor; July 26, 1991: Comedian Pee-wee Herman Is Arrested for Public Indecency; Sept. 22, 1997: Sportscaster Marv Albert Is Tried for Sexual Assault; Apr. 7, 1998: Pop Singer George Michael Is Arrested for Lewd Conduct; Dec. 18, 2003: Pop Star Michael Jackson Is Charged with Child Molestation; July 28, 2006: Actor Mel Gibson Is Caught Making Anti-Semitic Remarks.

1990's

829

November 18, 1995
FORMER CANADIAN PREMIER BRIAN MULRONEY IS EXPOSED IN AIRBUS SCANDAL

In 1995, Canadian police began investigating former prime minister Brian Mulroney and his adviser, Frank Moores, for taking kickbacks in the sale of Airbus Industrie planes to government-owned Air Canada in 1988. The news media had been reporting on the Airbus investigation for more than one year until finally connecting Mulroney to the scandal in November, 1995. Mulroney eventually was exonerated, but not without controversy.

ALSO KNOWN AS: Schreiber affair; Air Canada scandal; Airbus affair
LOCALE: Canada
CATEGORIES: Publishing and journalism; corruption; government; trade and commerce; business; space and aviation

KEY FIGURES
Philip Mathias (fl. 1990's), reporter with the *Financial Post*
Brian Mulroney (b. 1939), prime minister of Canada, 1984-1993
Frank Moores (1933-2005), adviser for Mulroney, lobbyist, and premier of Newfoundland, 1972-1979
Karlheinz Schreiber (b. 1934), German-Canadian businessman, lobbyist, and consultant for Airbus Industrie
Giorgio Pelossi (b. 1938), Swiss accountant and Schreiber's former partner at International Airline Leasing

SUMMARY OF EVENT
Air Canada, owned by the Canadian government, signed a $1.8 billion contract in 1988 to purchase thirty-four A-320 medium-range passenger airliners from the European business consortium Airbus Industrie, comprising four companies: Aèrospatiale of France; British Aerospace; Messerschmitt-Bölkow-Blohm of West Germany; and CASA of Spain. American aerospace giant Boeing lost out in the bidding. Speculation circulated that there were improprieties in awarding the contract to Airbus, but early investigations by the Royal Canadian Mounted Police (RCMP) and the Federal Bureau of Investigation (FBI) did not find any wrongdoing.

Years later, on September 29, 1995, the senior counsel of the Canadian Department of Justice (DOJ), on behalf of the RCMP, sent Swiss government officials a letter of request asking for help in obtaining access to banking records that might implicate former Canadian prime minister Brian Mulroney and Ottawa lobbyist and former Newfoundland premier Frank Moores in accepting kickbacks from German-Canadian businessman Karlheinz Schreiber. Schreiber had been a fund-raiser for Mulroney, was an associate of Moores, and was a Canadian representative for Airbus. Moores was chairman of the lobbying firm Government Consultants International (GCI) and a board member of Air Canada.

The DOJ was investigating Mulroney, Moores, and Schreiber on charges of defrauding the Canadian government. One of the bad deals involved Messerschmitt-Bölkow-Blohm's sale of helicopters to the Canadian coast guard and the other deal involved a failed attempt to launch a German armored-vehicle factory in Canada. All of the deals involved Schreiber. The letter to the Swiss authorities also requested that the alleged bank accounts of Moores and Mulroney be frozen and that the RCMP be given the right to access account information.

Later that fall, someone leaked the letter's existence to the media; many claim it was Schreiber. On November 18, *Financial Post* reporter Philip Mathias broke the story that Mulroney, Moores, and Schreiber were being investigated. Even though the media had been reporting on the Airbus contract controversy for some time, the article by

Mathias was the first to connect Mulroney's name with the scandal. Mathias's article included portions of the letter of request as well. The media indicated that the letter acknowledged possible schemes to receive illegal payments involving the sale of the thirty-four A-320 aircraft to Air Canada. The reports claimed that money was likely transferred from Airbus to Schreiber's company, International Aircraft Leasing (IAL), and then transferred into two Swiss bank accounts set up for Moores and Mulroney.

Mulroney responded to the investigations and news reports by filing a $50 million libel suit— $25 million in damages and an additional $25 million in punitive damages—against the DOJ and the RCMP. The DOJ insisted that it had followed normal investigative procedures in writing the letter and that details of the investigation had to be included to ensure Swiss authorization of the request. Mulroney denied claims of misconduct, rejected ownership of bank accounts outside Canada, and refuted claims of having close ties with Moores during the time in question. Moores also denied claims that he lobbied Airbus for the contract and that he had any direct contact with GCI or any of the partners of the consortium. Mulroney and his lawyers argued that the disclosure and publication of excerpts from the letter from the DOJ was defamatory, based on false allegations, and that the excerpts led to worldwide criticism of Mulroney.

In July, 1996, Schreiber filed his own lawsuit, contending that the letter of request was tantamount to undue search and seizure. A Canadian federal court ruled that prior judicial approval of the letter to Swiss authorities was needed and, therefore, any evidence gathered as a result of the letter's requests was unusable in court. In May, 1998, Canada's supreme court overruled the lower court's finding.

The key informant against Schreiber was Giorgio Pelossi, Schreiber's former accountant-book-keeper at IAL. Pelossi worked with both the RCMP and Swiss authorities to provide evidence against Schreiber. Pelossi told investigators that he had attended a meeting in which Schreiber and Moores opened bank accounts in Switzerland. He claimed Schreiber said that one of the accounts was for Mulroney, but Pelossi also acknowledged he had no evidence that Mulroney was aware of the account or that it had been used.

Mulroney's lawsuit against the Canadian government was scheduled to start in Quebec superior court on January 6, 1997. Shortly before the appointed date, Mulroney agreed to settle the case in exchange for an apology for the letter of request and for payment of his legal fees. Mulroney received his apology, which noted that officials had not found evidence of "wrongdoings." Moores and Schreiber also received letters of apology, but their letters did not mention a lack of conclusive evidence against them. The settlement, however, did not preclude the RCMP from conducting further investigations.

Brian Mulroney. (Hulton Archive/Getty Images)

New information about Schreiber's and Mulroney's questionable relationship was revealed after the settlement between Mulroney and the Canadian agencies, furthering the Airbus scandal. In 1993, after resigning as prime minister but while still a member of the House of Commons—as well as on two succeeding dates during the next eighteen months—Mulroney had met with Schreiber and received three separate $100,000 cash payments. Mulroney allegedly received these payments to help Schreiber promote other businesses, but the former prime minister failed to report these funds on his tax forms at that time. Years later, in 1999, he voluntarily filed a tax disclosure of $225,000.

In September, 1997, German investigators issued an arrest warrant for Schreiber, seeking details from him about several allegations, including tax evasion, fraud, and the Airbus affair. Canadian officers arrested Schreiber in Toronto two years later, on August 27, 1999. He was ordered to be extradited to Germany, but he was released on bail while he appealed the order.

IMPACT

On April 22, 2003, after nine years of costly investigations and a lack of evidence, the RCMP announced an end to the Airbus inquiry. In May, 2004, the Ontario superior court concurred with a lower court's decision to extradite Schreiber, and the Ontario court of appeals followed suit in March, 2006. Early in 2007, Schreiber's bail bond expired, and he was taken back into custody. Two months later, Schreiber sued Mulroney for failure to deliver services after he paid the former prime minister $300,000 in 1993 and 1994.

In June, 2007, the federal court of Canada agreed with the lower courts regarding Schreiber's extradition. Schreiber once more appealed the extradition order, but he failed in the Ontario court of appeals in November and remained in jail in Toronto. Schreiber still feared extradition to Germany, where he was wanted for several corruption charges, including his connection to a fraud investigation involving Helmut Kohl, the former German chancellor. In March, 2008, he lost his last chance to be tried in Canada when the supreme court ruled that he

should be extradited, but only after the completion of a public inquiry into his business dealings with Mulroney.

The Airbus affair ranks as one of the worst political scandals in Canadian history. The time-consuming investigation consumed money as well: Canadian citizens had to pay millions of dollars over the course of the inquiry, creating much cynicism about politics when the investigation became widely known by the public.

The vague and uncorroborated aspects of the Airbus affair and the subsequent scandalous business dealings between Mulroney and Schreiber still mystify many people, and there remains much speculation about whether or not Mulroney deserved exoneration. Some believe he should return the settlement monies he received for the cost of his legal fees. Mulroney has vacillated between publicly welcoming further inquiry in hopes of improving his reputation to arguing that there is no sense in wasting even more taxpayer money on further investigations.

—*Cynthia J. W. Svoboda*

FURTHER READING

Cameron, Stevie. *On the Take: Crime, Corruption, and Greed in the Mulroney Years.* Toronto, Ont.: Macfarlane Walter & Ross, 1994. A scathing examination of the corruption and crime that plagued Mulroney's term as prime minister of Canada.

Cameron, Stevie, and Harvey Cashore. *The Last Amigo: Karlheinz Schreiber and the Anatomy of a Scandal.* Toronto, Ont.: Macfarlane Walter & Ross, 2001. A detailed analysis of the Airbus scandal, mostly focusing on the workings of businessman Karlheinz Schreiber.

Kaplan, William. *Presumed Guilty: Brian Mulroney, the Airbus Affair, and the Government of Canada.* Toronto, Ont.: McClelland & Stewart, 1999. Kaplan investigates the widespread presumptions that defined the Airbus affair and Mulroney's role in the scandal. Also examines how Mulroney worked to gain his own exoneration.

_____. *A Secret Trial: Brian Mulroney, Stevie*

Cameron, and the Public Trust. Ithaca, N.Y.: McGill-Queen's University Press, 2004. A comprehensive account of the Airbus scandal with much attention paid to the role of journalist Stevie Cameron in revealing the affair to the public.

SEE ALSO: Mar. 4, 1966: Munsinger Sex and Spy Scandal Rocks Canada; Sept. 17, 1985: Media Allege Canadian Officials Allowed Sale of Rancid Tuna; May 7, 1999-Mar. 2, 2001: Ethics Counselor Exonerates Canadian Prime Minister Jean Chrétien.

February 4, 1996

WHISTLE-BLOWER REVEALS TOBACCO INDUSTRY CORRUPTION

Former Brown & Williamson researcher Jeffrey Wigand revealed on the CBS news program 60 Minutes *that his former employer added chemicals such as ammonia to cigarettes to increase nicotine's addictiveness. The scandal and its fallout created an ethical and legal earthquake that shook the underpinnings of the tobacco industry, led to a new consumer awareness of the dangers of tobacco products, and rattled investigative journalism.*

LOCALE: New York, New York

CATEGORIES: Radio and television; corruption; medicine and health care; environmental issues; business; publishing and journalism

KEY FIGURES

Jeffrey Wigand (b. 1942), former vice president for research, development, and environmental affairs at Brown & Williamson

Mike Wallace (b. 1918), CBS television correspondent

Lowell Bergman (b. 1945), CBS television producer and investigative reporter

SUMMARY OF EVENT

Jeffrey Wigand, a biochemist and former vice president for research, development, and environmental affairs at Brown & Williamson (B&W) in Louisville, Kentucky, became a big-tobacco whistle-blower after confronting his former employer by claiming on national television that the company was guilty of illegal and unethical activities. Wigand, who as a B&W employee also was deeply involved in the corrupt practices, alleged that B&W attempted to systematically conceal the adverse health risks of smoking and consciously introduced injurious toxins (a practice he referred to as "impact boosting") into cigarettes to enhance their appeal and addictive qualities. The revelation also evolved into a major journalistic scandal when *60 Minutes*, a prime-time CBS news program, initially chose to delay airing its interview with Wigand before finally opting to air a heavily edited version of his confession.

Wigand was born in Pleasant Valley, New York, on December 17, 1942. After a brief stint in the military, he received a doctorate from State University of New York, Buffalo, and subsequently worked as a marketer and manager at several pharmaceutical companies, including Pfizer and Johnson & Johnson, before going to work for B&W in January, 1989. Although his formal title at B&W was researcher and developer, his job more specifically involved investigative processes including fire safety, ignition propensity, and tobacco additives. He later disclosed that he thought he would have the opportunity to make a difference at B&W by working on a safer cigarette, or cigarettes that would be less harmful. According to Wigand, however, the company blocked most of his proposed studies. He was fired on March 24, 1993.

Former Brown & Williamson researcher Jeffrey Wigand, accompanied by attorneys, arrives for a deposition in Pascagoula, Mississippi, in November, 1995. (AP/Wide World Photos)

his confidentiality agreement with the company. Attorney Richard Scruggs agreed to represent Wigand pro bono. Wigand agreed to the deal, and CBS set up his interview with *60 Minutes* correspondent Mike Wallace.

In the August 3, 1995, interview, Wigand explained the practice of impact boosting, a harmful chemical process that ensures nicotine is absorbed more quickly by the lungs, which, in turn, affects the brain and central nervous system. He also discussed B&W's target market—youths—and the company's refusal to develop a safer cigarette. He further claimed that additives in tobacco were known carcinogens, and he referred to cigarettes as mere delivery devices for highly addictive nicotine. Wigand also claimed that B&W legal counsel edited the results of some of his studies to exclude references to the hazardous effects of cigarettes.

Following the *60 Minutes* interview, which had yet to be broadcast, Wigand began to receive death threats, which he naturally attributed to his conflict with B&W. He confessed to writer Marie Brenner in a 1996 *Vanity Fair* magazine interview that his children had received death threats and his reputation was under systematic attack through a B&W smear campaign. Someone broke into his Louisville apartment on at least one occasion.

Meanwhile, as the Wigand interview moved forward at CBS, a legal settlement between ABC and the companies Philip Morris and R. J. Reynolds developed out of fear that ABC's airing of its own program about big tobacco would prove damaging to all parties. CBS took note of the case, and although Lowell, Wallace, and *60 Minutes* executive producer Don Hewitt understood the significance of the Wigand interview, other CBS executives, fearing that a potential lawsuit would cost billions of dollars, opted to shelve the broadcast. Producers

Upon his termination, Wigand initially honored his confidentiality agreement with B&W, denying any illegal practices on the part of his former employer. In the spring of 1994, however, Wigand was approached by and cooperated with CBS producer Lowell Bergman, who was seeking advice (mostly involving Wigand's work in developing the self-extinguishing cigarette) about a Philip Morris cigarette-safety program *60 Minutes* was preparing to air. At the same time, Wigand, along with former Philip Morris chemist William Farone, became the lead informant in a U.S. Food and Drug Administration investigation into the tobacco industry's use of genetically altered plants to increase nicotine levels in cigarettes.

Lowell understood that Wigand's insider knowledge was important, but Wigand himself remained concerned about the legal and personal consequences of going public. After expressing such doubts, CBS, in exchange for Wigand's complete forthrightness as their informant, agreed to help him legally if he were sued by B&W for violating

834

also feared CBS could be charged with tortious interference for persuading Wigand to break his confidentiality agreement with B&W. On November 12, CBS agreed to air a redacted version of the interview and the allegations against B&W, but the network did so without naming Wigand as its source. Almost immediately, *The New York Times*, media critics, and others condemned the decision as journalistic cowardice. Wallace, too, went on record condemning the executive decision. Only after someone at CBS leaked a transcript of the interview to the *New York Daily News* and after the threat of a lawsuit passed did the network decide to broadcast a revised version of the interview that included Wigand. The program aired on February 4, 1996.

As expected, B&W sent a message to future whistle-blowers by suing Wigand for breach of contract. By this time, however, the damage had been done. B&W's lawsuit against Wigand garnered little public or media sympathy. Now, few could trust the word of a big tobacco company, or support its claims. *The Wall Street Journal* and other publications expressed popular sentiment when they concluded that most of the serious allegations against Wigand were unfounded. Though he escaped a possible prison sentence, economic ruin, and attacks on his personal integrity, Wigand emerged from the incident with his credibility and positive public image largely intact.

Wigand's story was adapted for film. *The Insider* (1999), directed by acclaimed filmmaker Michael Mann, was adapted by Mann and screenwriter Eric Roth from Brenner's *Vanity Fair* article "The Man Who Knew Too Much" (1996). The celebrated cast includes Russell Crowe as Wigand, Al Pacino as Bergman, and Christopher Plummer as Wallace. Ultimately, *The Insider* not only popularized the Wigand-B&W scandal but also garnered popular appeal and critical praise. The film received seven Academy Award nominations in 2000, including Best Picture, Best Director, and Best Actor for Crowe, and five Golden Globe nominations.

The film, however, was not without controversy. Mann was accused of using excessive dramatic license. Several persons at CBS (including Wallace) claimed that Bergman attempted to negotiate the film deal while the real-life events were still unfolding. Some also alleged that Bergman was on the phone with Mann during a number of CBS meetings. Wallace was alarmed as well, arguing that Mann's film portrayed him in an unflattering way.

B&W also claimed Mann had distorted the facts. The company primarily was concerned about scenes in the film in which Wigand receives death threats and is being following by menacing figures. However, according to Brenner's article (on which the film is based), additional death threats had been made against Wigand, most of which were not addressed in the film. As a public-relations safety measure, the company sent representatives to screenings of the film to answer questions. B&W also purchased a full-page advertisement in *The Wall Street Journal* to respond to the film's promotional campaign (particularly the public appearances of Wigand) and to maintain its innocence.

IMPACT

In the months following Wigand's *60 Minutes* interview, a succession of big tobacco whistle-blowers came forward, including three from industry giant Philip Morris.

Wigand became a standard-bearer for a grassroots crusade against big tobacco, and his name is now synonymous with corporate whistle-blowing, the tobacco wars, and the government's attempt to regulate the fifty billion dollar tobacco industry.

More generally, the Wigand scandal led to a broad shift in protocol for investigative media. It also led to changes in the public-relations strategies of tobacco companies but also to a more cynical public. The case also represents a critical moral transformation in the battle against cigarette manufacturers. With the public disclosure of what was previously internal knowledge, tobacco companies began to face new ethical impediments, and the industry's earsplitting denials of the dangers of tobacco went unheard in the wake of overwhelming evidence to the contrary. Likewise, whistle-blowing and investigative journalism proved to be exceptional partners for an informed consumer society.

The whistle-blowing scandal also affected Wigand personally: After moving to Mt. Pleasant,

1990's

Michigan, he began working as a lecturer and consultant on various tobacco issues. Perhaps most important, he also became deeply involved in teaching adolescents about the dangers of using tobacco, forming Smoke-Free Kids, Inc., his own nonprofit organization.

—*Matthew E. Stanley*

FURTHER READING

Brandt, Allan M. *The Cigarette Century: The Rise, Fall, and Deadly Persistence of the Product That Defined America.* New York: Basic Books, 2007. An authoritative and superbly researched history of cigarettes, smokers, and the tobacco industry in the twentieth century.

Brenner, Marie. "The Man Who Knew Too Much." *Vanity Fair*, May, 1996. Brenner's illuminating article broke much of the Wigand story and was the basis for the screenplay to Michael Mann's film *The Insider.*

Kessler, David. *A Question of Intent: A Great American Battle with a Deadly Industry.* New York: PublicAffairs, 2001. Kessler, former head of the FDA, was faced with a simple question upon starting his job with the agency in 1990: "Why doesn't the FDA regulate the consumer product that is the nation's number-one killer?" This book looks at the FDA's role in regulating the giant tobacco industry.

Tate, Cassandra. *Cigarette Wars: The Triumph of the "Little White Slaver."* New York: Oxford University Press, 2000. Provides an all-purpose overview of the history of cigarettes and their use. Pays particular attention to the trajectory of various movements against tobacco use and successfully ties the movements into the broader historical and social context of reform history.

SEE ALSO: Sept.-Oct., 1937: Prescription Elixir Causes More than One Hundred Deaths; Summer, 1974: Dalkon Shield Contraceptive Is Removed from the Market; Oct. 20, 1978: Firestone Recalls Millions of Defective Car Tires; Sept. 26, 1979: Love Canal Residents Sue Chemical Company; May 29, 1981: Court Finds That Ford Ignored Pinto's Safety Problems; Sept. 17, 1985: Media Allege Canadian Officials Allowed Sale of Rancid Tuna; Nov. 26, 1997: Canadian Health Commissioner Releases Report on Tainted Blood; July, 2002: Journalist Alleges Release of Genetically Modified Corn Seeds in New Zealand; Aug., 2002: Immunologist Resigns After Being Accused of Falsifying Research; Summer, 2006-Mar. 16, 2007: Manufacturer Recalls Pet Food That Killed Thousands of American Pets; Sept. 18, 2006: *Newsweek* Reveals That Hewlett-Packard Spied on Its Own Board.

Spring, 1996
PHYSICIST PUBLISHES A DELIBERATELY FRAUDULENT ARTICLE

Concerned about a perceived misuse of scientific vocabularies and theories by postmodernist critics, American physicist Alan Sokal parodied postmodern criticism in a journal article he later acknowledged was a hoax. The incident provoked widespread debate about intellectual integrity, academic publishing, postmodern criticism, and cultural studies.

ALSO KNOWN AS: Sokal hoax; Sokal affair
LOCALE: United States
CATEGORIES: Hoaxes, frauds, and charlatanism; publishing and journalism; education

KEY FIGURES

Alan Sokal (b. 1955), American physicist
Andrew Ross (b. 1956), Scottish cultural theorist and editor
Bruce Robbins (b. 1949), American historian, literary theorist, and editor
Stanley Aronowitz (b. 1933), American sociologist and editor
Jean Bricmont (b. 1953?), Belgian theoretical physicist

SUMMARY OF EVENT

Physicist Alan Sokal, distressed by what he considered was a retreat from a responsible concern with evidence in both academics and leftist politics influenced by postmodernism, conducted an experiment that would ignite a firestorm of controversy in academia and the press. "Transgressing the Boundaries: Toward a Transformative Hermeneutics of Quantum Gravity," a brilliant parody of the jargon and attitudes of faddish leftist academic scholarship, was the outcome of that experiment. The essay, which Sokal submitted to the respected critical and cultural studies journal *Social Text*, was filled with what Sokal considered characteristically ill-defined claims having little but their fashionable-

ness to recommend them. Those with knowledge of mathematical set theory, for example, could only chuckle at the following Sokal line, taken from a footnote in the controversial work.

> [L]iberal (and even some socialist) mathematicians are often content to work within the hegemonic Zermelo-Fraenkel framework (which, reflecting its nineteenth century liberal origins, already incorporates the axiom of equality) supplemented only by the axiom of choice. But this framework is grossly insufficient for a liberatory mathematics, as was proven long ago.

Journal editors published Sokal's essay in the Spring/Summer, 1996, "Science Wars" issue of *Social Text*.

Sokal acknowledged his deception in "A Physicist Experiments with Cultural Studies," published in the May/June, 1996, issue of the popular academic magazine *Lingua Franca*. He then submitted a second essay to *Social Text* to explain his motives for the deception, but the journal declined to publish the piece. That second essay, "Transgressing the Boundaries: An Afterword," was published in the fall, 1996, issue of the political journal *Dissent* and in slightly different form in the October, 1996, issue of the journal *Philosophy and Literature*.

Intense debate ensued. Sokal's "Transgressing the Boundaries" was full of exaggerated and absurd science, nonsensical claims, ungrounded assertions, and vocabulary considered politically correct and fashionably flattering. Two editors of *Social Text*, Andrew Ross and Bruce Robbins—and various sympathizers—explained how the article came to be accepted, but the reasons they offered cast an even less flattering light on the viewpoints they represented.

Social Text founding editor Stanley Aronowitz defended the journal's decision to publish the essay. He took issue with Sokal's belief that, as

ACADEMIC PARODY

Physicist Alan Sokal parodied the appropriation of scientific theory by cultural theorists in an admittedly fraudulent journal article he had published in a leading cultural studies journal. An excerpt from his article appears here.

Can the boundary be transgressed (crossed), and if so, what happens then? Technically this is known as the problem of "boundary conditions." At a purely mathematical level, the most salient aspect of boundary conditions is the great diversity of possibilities: for example, "free b.c." (no obstacle to crossing), "reflecting b.c." (specular reflection as in a mirror), "periodic b.c." (re-entrance in another part of the manifold), and "antiperiodic b.c." (re-entrance with 180° twist). The question posed by physicists is: Of all these conceivable boundary conditions, which ones actually occur in the representation of quantum gravity? Or perhaps, do *all* of them occur simultaneously and on an equal footing, as suggested by the complementarity principle?

Source: Social Text, nos. 46/47 (Spring/Summer, 1996).

Aronowitz put it, "proper scientific method filters out social and cultural influences in the process of discovery." Others also questioned the belief that scientific method is clear and that only error can be explained in terms of cultural factors. Literary theorist Stanley Fish argued, in an op-ed piece in *The New York Times* ("Professor Sokal's Bad Joke," May 21, 1996), that Sokal's deception undermined the basic trust and collegiality relied on by scientific investigation.

To many others, however, Sokal's experiment demonstrated the incompetence (at best) or dishonesty (at worst) of those who had been deceived. More generally, the hoax seemed a decisive demonstration of the intellectual bankruptcy of trendy postmodernism in its various guises.

Some of those sympathetic to postmodernism's virtues embraced dismissive explanations or changed the subject to Sokal's own motivations, and a few misunderstood the hoax as a right-wing entry in the debate over political correctness (either to revile or salute it). Indeed, Sokal did not conceal his own leftist political sympathies. Others argued that Sokal had caricatured postmodernist philosophy and oversimplified the history of science. Mathe-

matician Gabriel Stolzenberg, for example, critiqued Sokal's work in a series of articles emphasizing "the failure of my professional colleagues, the science warriors, to recognize the limits of their competence to read and reason intelligently about certain texts that are outside their professional domains." Philosopher and historian of science Mara Beller argued that "astonishing statements, hardly distinguishable from those satirized by Sokal, abound in the writings of [famous physicists such as] Bohr, Heisenberg, Pauli, Born and Jordan."

With many additional examples on hand of the (apparent) misuse of science by nonscientists, mostly collected during the preparation of the parody, Sokal wrote a book, in French (*Impostures intellectuelles*, 1997), with his Belgian colleague, Jean Bricmont. Published later in the United States as *Fashionable Nonsense: Postmodern Intellectuals' Abuse of Science* (1999), the work offers detailed criticism of the scientific faux pas of a number of French intellectuals who had influenced American academics. A new firestorm was ignited.

Undeterred, Sokal continued what he considered was his second career: defender of an evidence-based, scientific approach to social issues. In later work, he explored the ways in which pseudoscience shares intellectual weaknesses with postmodernism. Sokal argues that pseudoscience and postmodernism encourage a self-serving scientific gullibility. He also turned his attention to the ways in which the political left's postmodernist vices facilitated the conservative distortion of science during the administration of U.S. president George W. Bush, a distortion based on the vested interests of big corporations and religious fundamentalists. Sokal's criticism culminated in the book *Beyond the Hoax: Science, Philosophy, and Culture* (2008).

IMPACT

The Sokal hoax provoked international debate, especially in the United States and France, about the meanings of science, rationality, and intellectualism, and about the academy in general. According to scholar Patricia Clough, the hoax and ensuing debate help to explain why the so-called culture wars became the so-called science wars. In assessing the long-term effects of the hoax, Clough laments that "cultural studies of science have been turned over to disciplinary studies," meaning that the social sciences and humanities have themselves formed their own science-studies specializations (within their respective fields), "as if to assure the disciplinary and methodological rigor of those engaged in science studies." That shift, she suggests, had the effect of limiting or restricting criticism: Questions about the legitimacy of science and reason had been "quieted," Clough argues, and the relationship of such questions to various differences (of race, gender, and class) has "ceased to be central to social criticism." Sokal himself rejoiced that among the academic left, "pronouncements of extreme relativism have subsided significantly in recent years."

Even assuming that such changes in scholarship and focus were made, their connection to the hoax remains uncertain. Nonetheless, there can be little doubt that Sokal's engaging criticism of the abuse of science played a major role in focusing attention on these issues. Some even would contend that because postmodernist attitudes are so impervious to reasoned criticism, effective refutation ironically had to employ more than merely argumentative means. Arguably, it was scandal alone—the scandal of appearing (and, in fact, being) gullible—that affected the selective skepticism and convenient relativism of academics at the end of the twentieth century.

—Edward Johnson

FURTHER READING

Bell, Mara. "The Sokal Hoax: At Whom are We Laughing?" *Physics Today* 51, no. 9 (September, 1998). Bell argues that it was "the great quantum physicists," and not modern cultural critics, "in whose writings we find roots of the postmodernist excesses of today."

Clough, Patricia Ticineto. "Technoscience, Global Politics, and Cultural Criticism." *Social Text* 22, no. 3 (Fall, 2004): 1-23. Introduction to an issue examining the impact of Sokal's parody. The authors "think about technoscience not only as an object of social criticism" but also "as a resource of thought for social criticism."

Mooney, Chris, and Alan Sokal. "Can Washington Get Smart About Science?" *Los Angeles Times*, February 4, 2007. A brief discussion of the ways in which right-wing corporate and fundamentalist science abuse in Washington, D.C., has supplanted leftist postmodernist science abuse in the academy.

Sokal, Alan D. *Beyond the Hoax: Science, Philosophy, and Culture*. New York: Oxford University Press, 2008. A reconsideration of his own 1996 hoax and an extension of its lessons to right-wing abuses of science. Includes a reprint of the parody, with explanatory footnotes.

Sokal, Alan D., and Jean Bricmont. *Fashionable Nonsense: Postmodern Intellectuals' Abuse of Science*. New York: Picador, 1999. Originally published in French in 1997, this detailed criticism of the postmodernist thought of French intellectuals examines a broad range of texts discovered in the course of Sokal's preparation of his parody. Includes a reprint of the parody and its later-published afterword.

The Sokal Hoax: The Sham that Shook the Academy. Lincoln: University of Nebraska Press, 2000. An anthology by the editors of *Lingua Franca*. Surveys the impact of the hoax (the original parody, Sokal's "confession," and numerous commentaries).

Stolzenberg, Gabriel. "Reading and Relativism: An Introduction to the Science Wars." In *After the Science Wars*, edited by Keith Ashman and Philip Baringer. New York: Routledge, 2001. One of several essays in which Stolzenberg makes his case that the Sokal-style criticism of postmodernist and other philosophical thought frequently misreads texts, argues simplistically, and generally overreaches its limits of competence.

1990's

SEE ALSO: 1928-1929: Actor Is Suspected of Falsely Claiming to Be an American Indian;

August 16, 1996

BELGIAN MEDIA REVEAL HOW POLICE BUNGLED SERIAL MURDER CASE

Belgian police investigating an alleged kidnaper and serial killer named Marc Dutroux missed evidence of a basement dungeon containing two kidnapped teenagers. Charges of police corruption and incompetence soon followed, leading to a major reorganization of Belgian law enforcement.

LOCALE: Brussels, Belgium

CATEGORIES: Murder and suicide; violence; corruption; law and the courts; families and children

KEY FIGURES

Marc Dutroux (b. 1956), Belgian serial killer

Michel Nihoul (b. 1941), Dutroux's accomplice

Bernard Weinstein (1955-1995), Dutroux's accomplice

Sabine Dardenne (b. 1983), one of Dutroux's last two victims

Laetitia Delhez (b. 1981), one of Dutroux's last two victims

SUMMARY OF EVENT

A Belgian parliamentary committee investigating the Marc Dutroux serial killing case determined that the abductions, torture, rape, and murders of at least two girls could have been prevented had police not made numerous mistakes during its investigation of Dutroux prior to his arrest in August, 1996. Police had neglected to follow a tip about missing teenage girls, leading to a public scandal that began when the news media reported on the investigation the day after police raided Dutroux's home. Two days later, he confessed to the killings and abductions.

On August 15, after deciding to act on the tip about missing girls, police found two teenage girls locked in a soundproof concrete dungeon inside Dutroux's house. The youngest girl, twelve-year-old Sabine Dardenne, was kidnapped on May 28 and kept in the basement by Dutroux for more than two months. Fourteen-year-old Laetitia Delhez was abducted on August 9. Both girls reported being sexually assaulted by Dutroux.

A few days later police exhumed the bodies of Julie Lejeune and Mélissa Russo, two eight-year-old girls who disappeared in June, 1995. They were found in the backyard of one of Dutroux's seven homes. Also found were the remains of an accomplice—Bernard Weinstein—who Dutroux insisted was at fault for the girl's deaths. Dutroux said Weinstein kidnapped the children and failed to feed them while Dutroux was jailed for several months for vehicle theft. Dutroux admitted to drugging Weinstein and burying him alive next to the girls.

Police had searched Dutroux's home in Charleroi during a separate investigation into stolen cars before his arrest, but they failed to notice a dungeon in the basement of the house; Dardenne and Delhez were in that dungeon. Further investigations revealed rampant government and police corruption and incompetence in the months before the arrest. In 1993, police ignored a tip from an informant who told them that Dutroux offered him the equivalent of about five thousand U.S. dollars to kidnap young girls and that Dutroux was selling girls into prostitution. Police also ignored a tip that came from Dutroux's mother. She had contacted prosecutors to report that her son was keeping young girls in the basements of his unoccupied houses. Despite these disturbing, detailed tips, the police did nothing, and more girls disappeared.

The scandal would bring more surprises. Additional accomplices, including Dutroux's second wife, Michelle Martin, were arrested, and the media revealed that Dutroux had been convicted in 1989 for the rape and abuse of five young girls. He received a thirteen-year prison sentence but was released for good behavior after serving only three years. Shortly after his release, young girls began to disappear around the neighborhoods where Dutroux's homes were located.

The public was outraged at the news that the girls were murdered at the hands of a convicted rapist and child abuser who had been released early from prison. The public also condemned police for not acting on the tips from informants about Dutroux's activities after his release from prison.

Investigators also uncovered evidence of a related child-sex ring and arrested a number of people connected with Dutroux, including Michel Nihoul, Michel Lelièvre, and nine police officers. Nihoul was a businessman who admitted to arranging orgies at a Belgian château that catered to government and police officials. Lelièvre was identified as an accomplice in the kidnapping of two girls.

In October, 1996, Jean-Marc Connerotte, the investigative judge in the Dutroux case, was dismissed. The supreme court of Belgium removed him because he was involved in fund-raising for programs that helped search for missing children, particularly children who had been kidnapped by Dutroux. The court ruled that Connerotte lacked objectivity.

Connerotte's dismissal, and the incompetence of the police and government in handling the case, led to the largest peacetime marches in Belgium since World War II. About 300,000 people marched throughout the city of Brussels, demanding serious reforms of the political and judicial system. Suspicion of a government cover-up was high. The protests and heightened scrutiny led to a parliamentary committee investigation into how law enforcement and the courts handled—and mishandled—the case. The committee's final report was clear: The young girls who were murdered might have lived had police properly investigated the tips they received. The official inquiry demanded a change in laws, including a reinstatement of the death penalty in Belgium.

To further complicate matters, the case dragged on in the legal system, reinforcing suspicions of a

Accused serial murderer Marc Dutroux being led into a Belgian court in 1998. (Hulton Archive/Getty Images)

1990's

cover-up. Dutroux and his accomplices were scheduled for trial in 2000, but the trial did not begin until 2004. On the third day of the proceedings, Dutroux testified that two Belgian police officers helped him kidnap two of his victims. He also blamed his accomplices in the deaths of some of the victims and hinted that he was merely one part of a large pedophile network led by codefendant Nihoul. Dutroux also claimed the case involved other prominent Belgians, including bankers, members of the royal family, and high-ranking government officials. Investigations into these claims did not go far, however, because the accusations lacked accompanying evidence.

Dismissed judge Connerotte testified that he received death threats during his investigation of the case, and that the inquiry was severely hampered by the government's protection of suspects. Finally, on June 17, 2004, the jury reached a verdict. Dutroux was found guilty of six counts of kidnapping and rape and three counts of murder. His accomplices were found guilty on offenses that included kidnapping and murder. Dutroux received a sentence of life in prison and his codefendants received sentences ranging from five to thirty years.

IMPACT

The notoriety of the Dutroux abduction and murder case brought worldwide attention to Belgium, and Dutroux became the most despised person in that small nation. The incompetence of the police force and its bungled investigations brought scorn from around the world.

The Belgian parliament's inquiry into the bungled case led to court hearings, which then led to discussions of critical government and police reform. However, it was not until after Dutroux escaped for three hours in April, 1998, after overpowering a police officer that the government finally agreed to take action and restructure the justice system. The 1998 escape also prompted the resignation of three officials, including the justice and interior ministers.

—*Jesus F. Gonzalez*

FURTHER READING

Bisin, Sandra. "Belgium: The Pedophilia Files." In *Abuse Your Illusions: The Disinformation Guide to Media Mirages and Establishment Lies*, edited by Russ Kick. New York: Disinformation, 2003. Collection of essays on cover-ups and conspiracies. Bisin's essay on the Marc Dutroux case provides a general overview and coverage of police incompetence.

Dardenne, Sabine, with Marie-Therese Cuny and Penelope Dening. *I Choose to Live*. London: Virago Press, 2005. Excellent memoir by Dutroux abductee Sabine Dardenne, who describes her eight-day ordeal in the dungeon.

Sarre, Rick. "The Belgian Disease: Dutroux, Scandal, and System Failure in Belgium." In *Policing Corruption: International Perspectives*, edited by Rick Sarre, Dilip K. Das, and H. J. Albrecht. Lanham, Md.: Lexington Books, 2005. In this collection of essays on criminal investigations, the chapter by Sarre focuses on investigative failures and government and police misconduct and incompetence in the Dutroux case.

SEE ALSO: Mar. 2, 1906: Psychoanalyst Ernest Jones Is Accused of Molesting Mentally Disabled Children; May 20, 1974: French Cardinal Daniélou Dies in a Prostitute's House; July 23, 1978: Utah Millionaire Is Murdered by His Grandson; Aug. 12, 1983-July 27, 1990: McMartin Preschool Is Embroiled in Child-Abuse Case; Jan. 12 and May 11, 1987: Media Reports Spark Investigation of Australian Police Corruption; Mar., 1990: Menendez Brothers Are Arrested for Murdering Their Parents; Dec. 23, 1998: Prominent Belgians Are Sentenced in Agusta-Dassault Corruption Scandal; Dec., 2000: Sexual Abuse of Children in France Leads to the Outreau Affair; Jan. 30, 2001: Liverpool Children's Hospital Collects Body Parts Without Authorization; Dec. 18, 2003: Pop Star Michael Jackson Is Charged with Child Molestation.

November 3, 1996
CAR CRASH REVEALS DEPTH OF GOVERNMENT CORRUPTION IN TURKEY

A former chief of the Istanbul police, a leader of the Grey Wolves right-wing terrorist group, and a model turned assassin were killed in a car crash that marked the start of the Susurluk scandal in Turkey. Documents in the car revealed connections between Turkish politicians and military forces and organized crime groups, a revelation that came as no surprise to many who already suspected deep government corruption.

LOCALE: Susurluk, near Istanbul, Turkey
CATEGORIES: Corruption; drugs; organized crime and racketeering; politics; violence

KEY FIGURES

Hüseyin Kocadağ (d. 1996), former deputy chief of the Istanbul police special operations department
Sedat Bucak (b. 1960), True Path Party deputy, leader of the Kurdistan Workers' Party
Abdullah Çatli (1956-1996), leader of the Grey Wolves terrorist group and a convicted fugitive
Gonca Us (d. 1996), former model who became a hired assassin
Mehmet Ağar (b. 1951), former government interior minister, True Path Party member, 2002-2007
Tansu Ciller (b. 1946), former prime minister of Turkey, 1993-1996

SUMMARY OF EVENT

The Susurluk scandal was born from the remains of a traffic accident in Susurluk, Turkey, on November 3, 1996. The identities of the passengers in one of the crashed vehicles revealed a connection between criminal organizations and Turkish politicians, police, and military officials and confirmed suspicions of what was known as the deep state in Turkey. The deep state is an alleged coalition of antidemocratic officials and organized criminals believed to be enmeshed within the Turkish state (a

state within a state). The scandal led to the resignation of a major political figure, numerous arrests of police and government officials, several convictions, and increased tensions and distrust between Turkish citizens and the national government.

Three of four passengers in an automobile were killed after a truck driver, later charged with reckless driving, hit the car, a Mercedes. Inside the car at the accident scene, police discovered fake passports and gun licenses, pistols, sniper rifles, submachine guns, silencers, ammunition, explosives, narcotics, and cash. The discovery of this arsenal was not as shocking and frightening to the public as was the identities of the four passengers riding in the car.

The only survivor from the car was Sedat Bucak, a True Path Party deputy of the Turkish parliament and leader of the Kurdistan Workers' Party (a militant Kurdish organization seeking independence from Turkey). Bucak was taken from the vehicle with serious injuries. Hüseyin Kocadağ, a former deputy chief of the special operations department with the Istanbul police, was killed in the crash. The other two passengers killed in the crash were Mehmet Özbay and his girlfriend, Gonca Us, a Turkish former model who turned hired assassin. During the police investigation of the accident, it was discovered that Özbay was an alias for a convicted international fugitive named Abdullah Çatli, the leader of a right-wing terrorist organization called the Grey Wolves (also known as the Commandos or the Nationalist Action Party). The Grey Wolves were known for torturing, bombing, massacring, and assassinating left-wing political figures and supporters and had been held responsible for many of the unexplained bombings and deaths throughout Turkey's civil war between the Turkish military and Kurdish separatists. The group was responsible, particularly, for many of the killings during the war's peak during the 1970's. Çatli was an international fugitive sought after by Interpol (the International Criminal Police Organization) for his 1982

1990's

843

Former interior minister Mehmet Ağar in November, 1996. (AP/Wide World Photos)

escape from a prison where he was serving time for drug trafficking and murder.

The tragedy of the crash muted Turkish citizens' fear and anger as many questioned why these four people of varying backgrounds were in the same car. For many, the connection solidified fears that Turkey was a deep state in which government officials collaborated with criminal organizations to secure political interests through terrorism and murder while overlooking the organizations' own illicit activities, such as drug trafficking. The police weapons and false passports—particularly those signed by Mehmet Ağar, Turkey's interior minister and a member of the True Path Party—found inside the Mercedes fueled speculation that the deep-state government was protecting wanted criminals.

After details of the crash surfaced, Ağar insisted that Kocadağ and Çatli were in the same car because Kocadağ had captured Çatli. However, evidence that the four passengers had been staying at the same hotel for several days contradicted Ağar's

claims. Ağar resigned from his position as interior minister, citing that the government was involved in confidential security operations in connection with the accident and that he could not provide further details.

On November 12, a parliamentary commission was created to investigate the possible connection between government and security officials and criminal organizations. Bucak and several special-police officers were suspended for their possible involvement in illegal operations. The commission hearings began on December 24 and both Bucak and Ağar declared their innocence and used parliamentary immunity to exempt them from testifying—or being convicted. In February, 1997, nonviolent protests that included blackouts, flashing lights, and honking car horns poured out across Turkey because of the diplomatic immunity of Ağar and Bucak and the lack of information given to citizens regarding the incident. The protests eased at the end of March in anticipation of the commission's Susurluk Report, which was released in early April.

Instead of assuaging the public's distrust and anger, the report produced more questions, infuriated those who demanded that Bucak's and Ağar's immunity be removed, and disappointed many who expected a purge of Turkey's government, police, and military to sever criminal connections. The suspected government cover-up led to further protests.

The Susurluk investigation was hampered by the commission's inability to access government documents and by the numerous refusals by officials to testify, including former prime minister Tansu Ciller, who also was suspected of being involved with the deep state. The report called for the removal of Bucak's and Ağar's immunities and that they be tried; it also cited how such diplomatic protection had exacerbated the corruption of politicians. The report speculated that the passengers of the Mercedes had been planning or were about to perform an illegal act prior to the crash. The report concluded that politicians such as Ciller and Ağar had organized a criminal network in conjunction with Turkish security forces to protect the nation's interests against separatists, and that the security operations grew out of control when terrorists such as Çatli executed political opponents, distributed drugs, and committed other crimes. The report blamed individual politicians and not the state for dealing with criminal organizations.

The Susurluk trial concluded on September 19 and was met with a mix of protests from Turks and praise from Kurdish separatists. A majority of the defendants were released because of insufficient evidence. Only a few defendants, mainly special police, who confessed to their involvement were convicted and sentenced. Following the defendants' release, Ciller demanded an official apology from the state. In response to public protests, the commission annulled Bucak's and Ağar's immunities in December and charged them with organizing and participating in criminal enterprises.

The commission's final report was released in January, 1998, which reiterated previous findings, urged the immediate removal of politicians found to be involved in criminal activities, and suggested an immediate crackdown on drug trafficking. The commission's investigation of Bucak's and Ağar's involvement in Susurluk was deferred when they were reelected to Parliament in February, 1999.

In 2001, the convictions of security officials previously found guilty in Susurluk were overturned because of an inadequate investigation; a retrial was ordered. On November 3, 2002, Bucak's trial resumed after he failed to be reelected. Bucak was found innocent on June 26, 2003; however, the Turkish supreme court annulled the verdict on February 28, 2004, demanded that Bucak be charged as the head of a criminal organization, and ordered a retrial (which began on January 17, 2006). Bucak was found guilty on November 14 and sentenced to one year and fifteen days in prison. Ağar's trial resumed on February 14, 2008, after he also lost his bid for reelection.

IMPACT

The Susurluk scandal rocked the political and social foundations of Turkey but offered the chance for the formation of a movement against government corruption. However, many citizens believe that Turkey remains a deep state and that the government was able to bury much of its involvement in Susurluk and avoid accountability. The open wound left in Turkey's political system by the scandal forced many to question the state's legitimacy and its ability to rid the country of corruption and terrorism and to protect its citizens. On March 21, 2008, scandal again struck the country as several politicians, legal officials, and military personnel were apprehended for their involvement with a criminal group known as the Ergenekon network.

—Sheena Garitta

FURTHER READING

Gunter, Michael M. "Susurluk: The Connection Between Turkey's Intelligence Community and Organized Crime." *International Journal of Intelligence and Counter Intelligence* 11, no. 2 (June, 1998). An examination of the individuals and events involved in the Susurluk scandal, the contents of the parliamentary commission report on Susurluk, and the history of Turkey's internal corruption, deep state, and civil war.

Meyer, James H. "Politics as Usual: Ciller, Refah, and Susurluk: Turkey's Troubled Democracy." *East European Quarterly* 32, no. 4 (January, 1999): 489-502. Examines corruption in Turkey's political system, especially the corruption that helped define the Susurluk scandal.

Yoruk, Zafer. "Gangs of Ankara: A 'Deep History.'" *Kurdish Globe*, May 29, 2008. Provides a detailed historical narrative of how the deep state has for generations embedded itself within the political structure of Turkey.

SEE ALSO: May 3, 1950: U.S. Senate Committee Begins Investigating Organized Crime; Feb. 2, 1980: Media Uncover FBI Sting Implicating Dozens of Lawmakers; May 23, 1981: Italian Justice Minister Resigns Because of Crime Connection; Aug. 6, 1982: Banco Ambrosiano Collapses Amid Criminal Accusations; Dec. 23, 1998: Prominent Belgians Are Sentenced in Agusta-Dassault Corruption Scandal; Oct. 22, 2006: Chilean Politicians Use Community Funds for Personal Campaigns.

1990's

January, 1997
PYRAMID INVESTMENT SCHEMES CAUSE ALBANIAN GOVERNMENT TO FALL

After the fall of communism in Albania, numerous investment companies with little capital backing began to appear in the country. Some of these companies were actually pyramid schemes that took advantage of desperate times. The schemes collapsed, however, leading to riots approaching civil war and the fall of the corrupt government.

LOCALE: Albania
CATEGORIES: Hoaxes, frauds, and charlatanism; government; corruption; violence; business

KEY FIGURES
Sali Berisha (b. 1944), president of Albania, 1992-1997
Aleksander Meksi (b. 1939), prime minister of Albania, 1992-1997
Fatos Lubonja (b. 1951), cofounder of the Albanian Forum for Democracy

SUMMARY OF EVENT
When the communist regimes of Eastern Europe began falling between 1989 and 1991, Albania smoothly introduced democratic rule into the country. However, Albania was still the poorest country in Europe. With the economy in dismal shape, Albanians looked for a quick fix. They thought they found it in what ultimately turned into a series of pyramid schemes. The plans, given the low level of the Albanian economy, were unprecedented in their scope and audacity, and their eventual collapse was monumental as well. At its height the nominal value of the investments reached almost half the country's gross national product. Almost 70 percent of the population had stock in the fraudulent companies.

The schemes were fed by the lack of stable and historic Albanian financial institutions and markets and the failure of the government to regulate the economy, much of which was handled through in-

formal markets. Albania lacked private banks, and the three state banks that existed established strict credit policies after bad loans mounted in their portfolios. Private loans from family members and unregulated lenders filled the gaps. Some of these private lending companies invested depositors' funds in the pyramids.

A banking act of February, 1996, put the lending institutions under the authority of the Bank of Albania, but the bank was unable to exercise control because the government continued to support the pyramid companies and prevented closure of the rogue banks. Some of the highest government leaders, including prime minister Aleksander Meksi, were closely associated with these banks, which gave large contributions to the ruling Democratic Party.

Some of the companies involved were pure pyramids, attracting investors by promising huge returns from the investments of later depositors. The companies themselves had no intrinsic value nor did they engage in any enterprise to raise profits, except seeking more investors. As more investors became involved, it was impossible to keep up with the promised returns, and when investors wanted to pull their monies, they discovered that the companies were in fact frauds.

Some of the companies fell into a more gray area: investing in enterprises. Three of the largest of these companies—VEFA, Gjallica, and Kamberi—had investments in illegal activities that included smuggling contraband into Bosnia. These companies, too, dissolved into pyramids in 1996, when their liabilities far outstripped their assets.

The road to ruin began in late 1995. United Nations sanctions against Yugoslavia ended the lucrative smuggling activities of the companies, but the corruption continued. At the beginning of 1996, the companies increased their promised interest rates to attract more investors. Taking into account that Albania's runaway inflation rate was 17 percent at the time—triple what it had been the previous year—the promised annual rate of return amounted to almost 100 percent and, during the year, that rate continued to rise. Two new pyramid companies, Xhafferi and Populii, joined in with even greater promises. One of the pure pyramid companies, Sude, offered rates that were double those of the others.

More investors entered the pyramids. VEFA had the largest number of liabilities, with eighty-five thousand depositors. Xhafferi and Populii attracted two million depositors between them. (Albania had a population of only 3.5 million.) A war of inflated promises began. Kamberi promised 10 percent per month; Populii promised 30 percent. In November, Xhafferi promised a 300 percent increase after a three-month period. Sude countered with a promise of doubling the depositor's investment in two months. Pyramid liabilities rose to $1.2 billion. Albanians sold their homes and farmers sold their cattle.

The population, initially, paid little attention to the rumors of fraudulent dealings. There was an expectation that the government would take care of things, a feeling perhaps stemming from the decades under communist rule. If the money was the fruit of some shady dealing, the investors did not care. They happily put all their expendable income, and some income they could not afford, into the investments.

Meanwhile, the government remained idle. Only in October did it warn the public against the risky investments, but it attacked only the pure pyramid companies. Albanian president Sali Berisha defended the companies, but the International Monetary Fund (IMF) warned the government of the danger of the schemes. Berisha responded by accusing the IMF of interfering in Albania's internal affairs. Under external pressure, he established a commission to investigate the companies, but that commission never met.

On November 19, Sude defaulted, and like a house of cards the pyramids began to tumble. Sude's failure led to a lack of confidence in the rest of the companies. Some tried to restore confidence by offering more reasonable rates on deposits, but

the public would reject the attempts. In January, 1997, Sude and Gjallica declared bankruptcy. Soon, the other companies stopped making their payments as well. The government refused to compensate the investors for their losses, which made possible national economic recovery but did not appease the investors.

The government moved against the pure pyramids, freezing the assets of Xhafferi and Populii, but it still took no action against those that had investments, especially the largest ones, even after the parliament enacted a law against pyramids in February. The Bank of Albania, on its own, limited the amount of money that could be withdrawn at any one time to prevent the depletion of resources.

Greek soldiers patrol Durres, Albania, in the spring of 1997. The soldiers were part of a United Nations peacekeeping force in Albania to restore order and distribute humanitarian aid following rioting and other violence. (AP/Wide World Photos)

1990's

By the spring of 1997 the government lost control of the country. Soldiers and police officers deserted, allowing many people to loot the national armories for rifles. Foreigners were evacuated by their home countries and Albanians fled the country. The government resigned, and a caretaker government faced a hopeless situation. Rioting led to the deaths of two thousand people, and the economy collapsed. Anarchy ruled through most of the nation. The rioters burned customs and tax offices, and state revenues dwindled. Industries closed, trade stopped, and prices rose close to 30 percent in the first six months of the year. The lek (the national currency) fell 40 percent in value. Still, the largest pyramid companies claimed to be solvent and clung to their existing assets.

In Vlora, angry crowds threw stones at police trying to restore order. The mob beat some police and stripped off their uniforms, burning them with their weapons and equipment in bonfires. The police fired in the air and retaliated with stones from rooftops. In Tirana, thirty-five thousand rioters attacked the police and forced them to retreat. The police returned with water cannons and police dogs to quell the mob, but the rioters continued, setting government buildings afire. Berisha called a state of emergency on March 2, and on March 28, thousands of U.N. peacekeeping troops entered the country.

IMPACT

With international assistance the caretaker government began to restore order. The economic effects of the schemes affected the economy in the short term only. The political and social effects were more damaging, however. Much of the population lost its meager savings, and confidence in the new democracy was severely shaken. Some of the pyramid leaders were tried and convicted.

Fatos Lubonja, cofounder of the Albanian Forum for Democracy, told an American political scientist after the crisis that the government corruption destroyed Albania's infrastructure and, far worse, destroyed the people's faith in the new Albania. Lubonja hoped that those who fled would return and rebuild the country.

The development of a new Albanian constitution led to reform in politics and the economy, but although democracy and the rule of law took hold, government corruption persisted. In 2005, Berisha, who had defended the pyramid companies, returned to public office as prime minister of Albania.

—Frederick B. Chary

FURTHER READING

Bezemer, Dirk J., ed. *On Eagle's Wings: The Albanian Economy in Transition.* New York: Nova Science, 2006. A collection of articles by authors with academic, business, and policy backgrounds. Includes a chapter on the pyramid schemes. Bibliography.

Jarvis, Christopher. "The Rise and Fall of Albania's Pyramid Schemes." *Finance and Development* 37, no. 1 (March, 2000). Jarvis, an economist, examines the Albanian financial and economic crisis in detail. Offers solutions to prevent such economic collapse.

Prifti, Peter R. *Unfinished Portrait of a Country.* Boulder, Colo.: East European Monographs, 2005. A survey of Albania by a leading expert. Examines the pyramid companies and the aftermath of the scheme. Includes bibliography.

Vaughan-Whitehead, Daniel. *Albania in Crisis: The Predictable Fall of the Shining Star.* Northampton, Mass.: Edward Elgar, 1999. One of the best studies of the pyramid schemes by an academic expert. Contains a bibliography.

Vickers, Miranda, and James Pettifer. *Albania: From Anarchy to a Balkan Identity.* Rev. ed. New York: New York University Press, 2000. An excellent study by two specialists focusing on the postcommunist period in Albania. Examines the pyramid schemes but does not include discussion of the rioting and violence.

SEE ALSO: 1919-1920: Ponzi Schemes Are Revealed as Investment Frauds; Oct. 22, 1923: U.S. Senate Begins Hearings on Teapot Dome Oil Leases; Jan. 8, 1934-Jan. 17, 1936: Stavisky's Fraudulent Schemes Rock French Government; Mar. 29, 1962: Billie Sol Estes Is Arrested for Corporate Fraud; May 2, 1984: E. F. Hutton Executives Plead Guilty to Fraud; May 7, 1985: Banker Jake Butcher Pleads Guilty to Fraud; Nov. 13, 1986-May 4, 1989: Iran-Contra Weapons Scandal Taints Reagan's Administration; Jan. 15, 1988: ZZZZ Best Founder Is In-

dicted on Federal Fraud Charges; Mar. 29, 1989: Financier Michael Milken Is Indicted for Racketeering and Fraud; Dec. 23, 1998: Prominent Belgians Are Sentenced in Agusta-Dassault Corruption Scandal.

February 26, 1997
TEACHER MARY KAY LETOURNEAU IS ARRESTED FOR STATUTORY RAPE

In 1996, a thirty-four-year-old married schoolteacher named Mary Kay Letourneau became sexually involved with a thirteen-year-old student named Vili Fualaau. Initially released on a suspended sentence, she violated the terms of her parole by seeing the boy again and was sentenced to more than seven years in prison. She had two children with Fualaau and married him in 2005.

LOCALE: Seattle, Washington
CATEGORIES: Law and the courts; families and children; sex crimes; public morals

KEY FIGURES
Mary Kay Letourneau (b. 1962), teacher at Shorewood Elementary School in Burien, Washington
Vili Fualaau (b. 1983), student at Shorewood Elementary School

SUMMARY OF EVENT
Mary Kay Letourneau, who was thirty-four years old, a wife, and a mother of four children, became the source of tabloid fodder and instant scandal when it became known that she had been having an affair with a thirteen-year-old student. She was sent to prison in 1997 for statutory rape.

Letourneau grew up in Southern California and was one of seven children of John and Mary Schmitz. John G. Schmitz was a member of the conservative John Birch Society and had political aspi-

rations. He served in the California state senate and was a U.S. representative. After an unsuccessful bid to run for president on the American Independent Party ticket in 1972, Schmitz moved his family to Corona del Mar, California. Two years later, Letourneau's three-year-old brother, Philip, drowned in the family pool. Letourneau insists that this tragic event in her family's life did not have any long-term effects on her.

In 1982, Schmitz's political career was cut short by revelations that he was having an affair with Carla Stuckle, a former college student and Republican campaign volunteer, and had fathered two of her children. During the scandal, Letourneau sided with her father. In November, 1983, Letourneau met Steve Letourneau, a baggage handler for Alaska Airlines. Four months into their relationship, Letourneau became pregnant. While Letourneau was not in love with her husband, her strict Roman Catholic parents insisted that she and Steve marry; they did so on June 30, 1984. The couple moved to Anchorage, Alaska, then Seattle, Washington.

Letourneau finished her teaching degree at Seattle University in 1989 and got a job at the Shorewood Elementary School located in Burien, Washington, a suburb of Seattle. Initially assigned to second-grade classes, she first encountered Vili Fualaau when he was eight years old and in the second grade. By all accounts a talented artist, Fualaau made an impression on his teachers and was among Letourneau's circle of favorite students. Fualaau

Mary Kay Letourneau. (AP/Wide World Photos)

was raised in a large, extended Samoan family. His father was in prison for armed robbery and his mother worked in a bakery. Letourneau, in spite of her own increasing money worries, helped nurture his abilities by buying him art supplies.

The year 1995 was a particularly stressful time for Letourneau. She was a busy mother of four and was now teaching fifth and sixth graders. Her marriage woes were compounded by her and Steve's financial situation. Letourneau's father was diagnosed with cancer and she miscarried a fifth child just a few months later. The Letourneaus were forced to declare bankruptcy. At this time, the relationship between Letourneau and Fualaau grew closer. He was a constant presence in the home and even accompanied the Letourneaus on their family vacation. The unusual relationship between teacher and student did not go unnoticed among Steve's family members.

During the summer of 1996, Letourneau and Fualaau had sexual relations for the first time.

Fualaau would boast to friends that he and his teacher had sex more than four hundred times that summer, and had done so in every room of the Letourneau home. While making last-minute preparations for the fall semester, Letourneau discovered she was pregnant. As she and Steve had stopped having sex, she had no doubt whose child it was. Steve, who suspected Letourneau was having an affair with Fualaau, found a shoe box of letters in the linen closet of their home. Steve moved out of the house and started divorce proceedings.

Steve's cousin made an anonymous call to Letourneau's employer to reveal the affair. On February 26, 1997, she was arrested for statutory rape of an unnamed minor. She was released later that night and told not to go near Fualaau. Letourneau's mother took charge of the children. When counseled by her attorney, David Gehrke, Letourneau admitted that she was carrying the child of the boy she was accused of raping. As the trial approached, Letourneau underwent a series of court-ordered exams. Psychiatrist Julia Moore noted Letourneau's rapid mood swings during her interview and diagnosed her as having bipolar disorder. At her trial in November, Letourneau pleaded guilty to two counts of rape of a child in the second degree.

At her hearing, a seemingly repentant Letourneau told the judge, "I give you my word . . . it will not happen again." Judge Linda Lau of the King County Superior Court accepted Letourneau's plea. The judge took into consideration that Letourneau had no criminal record and sentenced her to three months in jail and ordered her to enroll in a sexual deviancy treatment program. Letourneau and Fualaau's child, Audrey, who had been born in May, would be placed in the care of Fualaau's mother, Soona Vili. Under the terms of her release, Letourneau was forbidden to have contact with Fualaau.

The court-ordered restriction did not stop Letourneau from seeing Fualaau again. Upon her release in January, 1998, the two resumed their relationship. On February 3, during a routine late-night neighborhood patrol, a police officer noticed a parked car with two people inside. When he ran the car's license plates he discovered that the owner was Letourneau, now a registered sex offender. Inside the car was sixty-five hundred dollars in cash, baby clothes, and a passport. The officer recognized Letourneau immediately and arrested her for violating the terms of her parole. Fualaau's name was publicly linked to Letourneau's after his mother, Soona, agreed to a series of interviews with the tabloids.

Judge Lau harshly admonished Letourneau, saying, "This case is not about a flawed system . . . it is about an opportunity that you foolishly squandered." Letourneau's original maximum sentence of 7.5 years was reinstated, and she entered the Washington Correction Center for Women in Gig Harbor, forty miles south of Seattle. Upon her incarceration, a medical exam revealed that she was pregnant. In October, 1998, she gave birth to another daughter, Alexis, who would be placed in the care of Fualaau's mother.

Defiant even behind bars, Letourneau attempted to smuggle notes to Fualaau in violation of court orders and was placed in solitary confinement for six months for doing so. In January, 2001, Letourneau's father died of cancer. Her request to attend his funeral was denied. Letourneau served her full sentence and was released on August 2, 2004. Two days later, Fualaau filed a motion to vacate a court order that barred Letourneau from contacting him upon her release. Letourneau, never wavering from her belief that she and Fualaau from the beginning were deeply in love and meant to be together, married her twenty-one-year-old former student on May 20, 2005. Letourneau, now Mary Fualaau, would remain a registered sex offender for the rest of her life, regardless of the couples' legal status as husband and wife, unless a court order allows her to unregister.

Impact

The Letourneau-Fualaau affair unleashed a media frenzy that inspired a made-for-television film and at least two privately published accounts of the scandal. More important, it prompted discussion about gender bias in statutory rape cases. In 2004, a U.S. Department of Education study found that 40 percent of educators who had been reported for sex-

ual misconduct were women. The well-publicized incidents of female teachers having sex with their underage students led to renewed interest in the controversy surrounding age of consent and teacher-student sexual relations. These cases reflect a decline in the double standard of treating male authority figures more harshly than female authority figures in cases involving the abuse of a minor.

—Robin Imhof

Further Reading

Denove, Myriam S. "The Myth of Innocence: Sexual Scripts and the Recognition of Child Sexual Abuse by Female Perpetrators." *Journal of Sex Research* 40, no. 3 (August, 2003): 303-314. Reviews existing data regarding the prevalence of sex offending by women, placing specific emphasis on the ways in which conventional sexual scripts preclude official recognition of female sexual offending as a problem.

Dress, Christina, Tama-Lisa Johnson, and Mary Kay Letourneau. *Mass with Mary: The Prison Years*. Victoria, B.C.: Trafford, 2004. Dress, a close friend and former cell mate of Letourneau, chronicles Letourneau's experiences behind bars.

Letourneau, Mary, and Vili Fualaau, with Bob Graham. *Une Seule Crime: L'amour* (Only One Crime: Love). Paris: Robert Laffront, 1998. This collection of interviews with Letourneau, Fualaau, and Soona Vili was ghost-written by Bob Graham. Capitalizes on the sympathetic belief held by many Europeans that Letourneau and Fualaau were victims of puritanical and outdated U.S. laws.

Olsen, Gregg. *If Loving You Is Wrong: The Shocking True Story of Mary Kay Letourneau*. New York: St. Martin's Press, 1999. True-crime writer Olsen's investigative account of the Letourneau-Fualaau affair includes testimonies from friends of the family and belated interview material from Letourneau herself.

See also: Nov. 23, 1946: Tennis Star Bill Tilden Is Arrested for Lewd Behavior with a Minor; Dec. 12, 1957: Rock Star Jerry Lee Lewis

1990's

Marries Thirteen-Year-Old Cousin; Feb. 1, 1978: Roman Polanski Flees the United States to Avoid Rape Trial; July 20, 1982: Conservative Politician John G. Schmitz Is Found to Have Children Out of Wedlock; July 20, 1983: Con-

gress Members Censured in House-Page Sex Scandal; May 19, 1992: Amy Fisher Shoots Mary Jo Buttafuoco; Sept. 29, 2006: Congressman Mark Foley Resigns in Sex Scandal Involving a Teenage Page.

March 12, 1997
PRIZE-WINNING ABORIGINE NOVELIST REVEALED AS A FRAUD

In 1997, the Australian literary establishment was rocked by the revelation that a critically acclaimed prize-winning female author of the aboriginal autobiographical novel My Own Sweet Time *was actually a white man. The scandal led to questions of literary and cultural authenticity, gender and race, sexism and racism, national identity, publishing practices, and the intellectual property rights of indigenous peoples.*

ALSO KNOWN AS: Wanda Koolmatrie hoax
LOCALES: Sydney and Adelaide, Australia
CATEGORIES: Hoaxes, frauds, and charlatanism; literature; racism; publishing and journalism; social issues and reform; cultural and intellectual history

KEY FIGURES

Leon Carmen (b. 1949?), Australian writer
John Bayley (b. 1949), Australian literary agent
Ava Hubble (fl. 1990's), reporter for the Sydney *Daily Telegraph*
Andrew Stevenson (fl. 1990's), reporter for the Sydney *Daily Telegraph*

SUMMARY OF EVENT

Wanda Koolmatrie's first novel, *My Own Sweet Time* (1994), was hailed by noted Australian playwright, author, and critic Dorothy Hewett as the start of a new genre. In 1996, Koolmatrie's autobiographical novel was short-listed for the New South

Wales Premier's Award and it won the Nita May Dobbie National Award for the best first novel written by a woman. *My Own Sweet Time* became required reading for high school students sitting for their exit exams (and to obtain their higher school certificates) in New South Wales in 1996.

My Own Sweet Time depicts the life of an aboriginal woman born in 1949 who was raised by white foster parents in the suburbs. The novel's author, Koolmatrie, it turned out, was a pseudonym for Leon Carmen, a white man. Carmen later claimed in an interview that he believed he could get published only if he were nonwhite and female. He claimed that the Australian literary establishment discriminated against white men when considering who to publish.

A former school friend of Carmen, John Bayley, agreed to be his literary agent. (Some believe that Bayley, and not Carmen, wrote the book.) Bayley submitted Carmen's manuscript to three publishers: the University of Queensland Press, Reed Books, and Magabala Books. Magabala Books, a government-subsidized publisher specializing in works written by aboriginal authors, agreed to publish the work, and it was launched in Sydney, Australia, during the Sydney Writers Festival on January 25, 1995. Neither Koolmatrie (Carmen) nor Bayley attended the launch. Indigenous author and poet Roberta Sykes launched the book on behalf of the "absent" Koolmatrie.

The defense of using an assumed identity in literature is not new. Carmen argued that he would not have been published without the symbolic currency of his chosen identity. Other writers, especially women, have chosen an assumed identity (most often another gender). These writers include George Eliot (Mary Anne Evans), Henry Handel Richardson (Ethel Richardson), and Miles Franklin (Stella Maria Sarah Miles Franklin), women whom Carmen claimed presented "only a short step to Wanda, our mythical female author." (Bayley was a fan of writer Thomas Chatterton, who created a fifteenth century priest-poet called Thomas Rowley.)

For many writers, the motivation behind adopting a gender-bending nom de plume is twofold. First, as Carmen himself argued, the motivation is purely artistic ("bookish," as he called it); that is, to compromise one's real identity to garner readers of their work of literature. Second, as confirmed by the first argument, the motivation is implicitly commercial: One compromises his or her true identity to exploit the book market—to sell books.

Carmen claimed that he and Bayley had to accept Magabala's advance against royalties to avoid potentially awkward questions arising about the book's (fictional) author. The pair accepted the five thousand dollars prize money for the Nita Dobbie Award. Soon, Bayley sent Magabala a copy of Carmen's sequel to *My Own Sweet Time*, the book *Door to Door*, which Magabala published in 1998. Before this, however, Magabala representatives became suspicious when they could not speak with Koolmatrie personally. It was not long before Carmen admitted to the hoax, and the scandal broke.

Reporters Ava Hubble and Andrew Stevenson of Sydney's *Daily Telegraph* newspaper broke the story, "My Sweet Hoax," on March 12, 1997. The news report came within weeks of two other newsworthy hoaxes: those of Ukrainian writer Helen Demidenko (Helen Darville) and aboriginal painter Eddie Burrup (Irish-born Elizabeth Durack). Bayley, though, claims in his book *Daylight Corroboree* (2004) that he confessed his part in the Koolmatrie hoax to Adelaide *Advertiser* columnist Tony Baker months before the hoax came to light in the *Daily Telegraph*.

The New South Wales Fraud Enforcement Agency targeted Bayley for arrest and prosecution because he made "a false and misleading statement involving the author Wanda Koolmatrie who was a fictitious person invented by Leon Carmen and Mr. Bayley." It appears that criminal charges materialized only because Bayley had accepted the Nita Dobbie Award cash prize on behalf of Koolmatrie. Consequently, his house was raided on May 8. Officers entered the premises, but Bayley was not home; he was en route from Melbourne. They seized the contents of his computer hard drive and his working journals. Interestingly, Bayley's appearance at Sydney's Downing Centre magistrates court on March 12, 1998, came one year to the day after the *Daily Telegraph* broke the story of the Koolmatrie hoax. Magistrate Geoff Brad presided over the case.

To many observers, Bayley was the one who defrauded Magabala Books, and he was the one charged with a crime. Critics were bewildered when the magistrate dismissed the fraud charge against Bayley because there was no prima facie case to substantiate the allegations of fraud. However, evidence seems to prove a prima facie case did exist. First, Bayley falsely claimed that he accepted the Nita Dobbie Award on Koolmatrie's behalf because Koolmatrie was in England. Also, in *Daylight Corroboree*, Bayley admits to indicating "yes" on a declaration sent to him by Magabala Books before

---

YOUNG WANDA REFLECTS

Leon Carmen, better known by the pseudonym Wanda Koolmatrie, opens his controversial autobiographical novel My Own Sweet Time *(1994) with his protagonist, Wanda, reflecting on her days as a black child growing up with white parents in a white neighborhood.*

By six years old I'd picked up a handful of stunts—bawling out for milk and porridge, recognizing animals and visitors, responding to my parents with coyness, indifference, enthusiasm, whatever. Cause and effect were tumbling into a pattern. One thing puzzled me though. Mum and Dad and the few people who came to the house were all white. I knew no other children. I was certainly growing, but I stayed black. Would I fade, or what?

publication of *My Own Sweet Time* that included the question "Is the author of aboriginal or Torres Strait Islander descent?"

IMPACT

One of the most significant aspects of the Koolmatrie hoax was the extent to which it mobilized a range of critical opinion. For instance, while the hoax still inspires much debate about the politics of nonindigenous writers assuming a nonwhite racial identity, according to some critics the incident highlights the existence of antiwhite bias within the Australian culture industry. Such critics argue that the hoax gave credibility to the opinion that white men experience prejudice within a culture defined by a prevailing fascination with minority culture, namely indigenaity, or indigenousness. Critics also argue the hoax legitimated claims of the existence of special privileges for indigenous Australians. Others argue that because the 1990's saw a series of identity poachers exposed in Australian literary and artistic circles as frauds, the trend is symptomatic of a cultural downturn in white-Anglo privilege. Others claim the fraud was artfully contrived in that Carmen and Bayley specifically approached Magabala Books, a government-financed publisher of works written by aboriginal authors especially.

By extension, some critics claim the hoax exposed the urgent need for the Australian government to recognize, formalize, and protect aboriginal intellectual property rights. Even more critics claim the incident exposed the inherent tensions in postmodern approaches to written works. These critics argue that while postmodern understandings of written works created the very space in which Koolmatrie was heard—as a culturally marginalized voice—the hoax itself raised important postmodern questions regarding authorial intent, authenticity in writing, and the blurring lines between factual and fictional Australian national identity.

—*Nicole Anae*

FURTHER READING

Bayley, John. *Daylight Corroboree: A First-hand Account of the Wanda Koolmatrie Hoax.* Sydney: Eidolon Press, 2004. Bayley's personal account of his and Carmen's motivation behind the hoax. Includes reflections on the hoax's cultural consequences.

Hosking, Sue. "The Wanda Koolmatrie Hoax: Who Cares? Does It Matter? Of Course It Does!" *Adelaidean* (University of Adelaide), April 21, 1997. Hosking's article asks many questions about the hoax and concludes that Carmen's assumption of an aboriginal identity was purely in self-interest.

Morrissey, Philip. "Stalking Aboriginal Culture: The Wanda Koolmatrie Affair." *Australian Feminist Studies* 18, no. 42 (2003): 299-307. Morrissey, who wrote a reader's report of the book *My Own Sweet Time* before the Koolmatrie hoax was exposed, offers his personal account of the hoax in this informative journal article.

Nolan, Maggie, and Carrie Dawson, eds. *Who's Who? Hoaxes, Imposture, and Identity Crises in Australian Literature.* St. Lucia: University of Queensland Press, 2004. A wide-ranging examination of literary hoaxes and scandals specific to Australian literature. Includes discussion of the Koolmatrie hoax.

SEE ALSO: 1928-1929: Actor Is Suspected of Falsely Claiming to Be an American Indian; June 5, 1944: Australian Poets Claim Responsibility for a Literary Hoax; Jan. 28, 1972: Clifford Irving Admits Faking Howard Hughes Memoirs; 1978: *Roots* Author Alex Haley Is Sued for Plagiarism; Apr. 25, 1983: German Magazine Publishes Faked Hitler Diaries; Apr., 1998: Scottish Historian Is Charged with Plagiarism; July 24, 2007: University of Colorado Fires Professor for Plagiarism and Research Falsification.

May 20, 1997
AIR FORCE PROSECUTION OF FEMALE OFFICER FOR ADULTERY REVEALS DOUBLE STANDARD

The first woman in the U.S. Air Force qualified to fly the B-52 bomber, Kelly Flinn was charged with adultery for having sex with an enlisted woman's husband and then lying to superiors about it and ignoring direct orders to desist. The threat that Flinn, an accomplished and respected pilot, would face imprisonment for consensual sex suggested a double standard for female service members, outraging many, including members of Congress. Instead of being court-martialed, Flinn received a general discharge from the Air Force.

LOCALE: Minot, North Dakota

CATEGORIES: Military; women's issues; sex crimes; law and the courts; space and aviation; politics

KEY FIGURES

Kelly Flinn (b. 1970), U.S. Air Force pilot, first lieutenant

Marc Zigo (b. 1972?), Flinn's civilian lover

Sheila Widnall (b. 1938), secretary of the U.S. Air Force

Ronald R. Fogelman (fl. 1990's), Air Force chief of staff

SUMMARY OF EVENT

First Lieutenant Kelly Flinn was no stranger to publicity or U.S. Air Force regulations when she became the focus of a military sex scandal in 1996-1997. The youngest of five children, Flinn grew up in Missouri and Georgia as an exemplar of the so-called all-American tomboy. At the age of sixteen, after attending Space Camp in Huntsville, Alabama, she decided on an aviation career. Following high school, she won appointment to the U.S. Air Force Academy in Colorado Springs, Colorado, in 1989. The rigorous training, discipline, and male-oriented ethos at the academy came as a shock to her, yet she persisted and became a top-ranking cadet. She also won two coveted overseas training assignments before graduating. During postacademy flight training, her first choice of aircraft for permanent assignment was the B-52 bomber, a massive plane equipped to carry nuclear payloads.

During the 1990's, the U.S. armed forces was under intense pressure to incorporate women into combat support roles. Flinn's assignment to fly B-52s was widely publicized as part of this new direction for the military. Flinn reported for duty at Minot Air Force Base in North Dakota, the B-52 fleet's home base, in October, 1995. The base is on a remote, desolate prairie, and there were few amenities either on base or in the nearby town. According to Flinn's autobiography *Proud to Be* (1997), she arrived in Minot with the hope of making a life for herself there, and to meet a special man with whom to develop a serious relationship. Even though she had spent the prior few years studying and working in a mostly male environment, Flinn had tried to be "one of the guys," developing only a few buddy-type friendships. She probably was less prepared than most twenty-four-year-old single women for the hazards and duplicities of the dating scene.

Unfortunately, social life at Minot seemed to revolve around drinking and sexual games. At least that was the impression that Flinn received. There were certainly few other recreations available for single, action-oriented young adults. Flinn fell into one dubious situation when she threw a wine-cellar party. At the party she had a sexual encounter with Colin Thompson, a senior enlisted airman. Both were apparently drunk at the time. The Uniform Code of Military Justice prohibits fraternization, that is, relations between an officer and an enlisted person, even if the persons in question come from different commands. Afterward, Flinn mostly shrugged off her encounter with Thompson (an encounter that would be included as part of the charges against her).

Most of Flinn's leisure time, however, was devoted to soccer. An avid soccer player since childhood, she joined the base soccer team, which was coached by a civilian named Marc Zigo. (He had claimed college and professional soccer experience, which later proved false.) Zigo was charming and smooth and Flinn fell for him. He seemed to be equally smitten. Zigo was at Minot with his wife, Gayla, who was an enlisted airman at the base. Zigo told Kelly that the two were now legally separated. Although that remark was not true, the marriage was stormy. Gayla threw her husband out of their house after she found some of Flinn's letters to him. Zigo threatened suicide, and he pleaded with Flinn to let him stay with her, as he had nowhere else to go.

Meanwhile, base security police began investigating both Flinn and Zigo, based on reports of their relationship from a lieutenant against whom Flinn had testified in an unrelated case. Flinn and Zigo were called in separately and questioned. Flinn denied any sexual component to their relationship.

Air Force first lieutenant Kelly Flinn before a pretrial hearing at Minot Air Force Base, North Dakota, in May, 1997. (AP/Wide World Photos)

Shortly afterward she regretted this denial. Following protocol, she told Lieutenant Colonel Ted LaPlante, her commanding officer, that she wanted to revise her statement to police. LaPlante knew nothing about the charges but refused to listen to Flinn, saying he might eventually be called on to adjudicate the case. Flinn would remain on record as having lied in an official investigation. Two days after Zigo moved into her place, Flinn was handed a written order forbidding her from any contact with Zigo, even if through a third party. Disobeying the order would have left her homeless.

Flinn followed LaPlante's advice to seek legal counsel, but both Air Force attorneys who took her case were stationed elsewhere and unable to devote time to the issue. Meanwhile, Flinn was slowly realizing that Zigo was moody, dishonest, and manipulative—the classic profile of an abusive man. She was still partly in love with him, and he played on her sympathies, keeping her from making a clean break from him. The fall of 1996 started out full of promise for Flinn, with her piloting achievements drawing additional plaudits from superiors and the public. Now things were changing drastically, moving faster than she realized. Despite the mounting charges against her, Flinn assumed that she would be able to negotiate for an Article 15 administrative punishment. Adultery cases usually led to Article 15 reprimands. This would stall her career but allow her to remain flying.

In a shocking twist of events, the *St. Louis Post Dispatch*, on February 21, 1997, published a news story about Flinn facing court-martial. Flinn knew nothing of the pending action, nor did her commanding officer and most others on base. Flinn now realized she was facing a lengthy prison sentence. She hired a civilian attorney to work with her military lawyers, who released Flinn's side of the story to the press. Congressional hearings were called, and several lawmakers expressed the opinion that the Pentagon needed, in U.S. senator Trent Lott's words, to "get real" about fraternization. Zigo had long since moved out of Flinn's home, and the explosive case was working its way up to the secretary of the Air Force, Sheila Widnall. Flinn asked her superiors for an honorable discharge instead of going through a court-martial. The court-martial convened on May 20.

The prosecution came prepared with copious documentation, but Flinn's lawyers obtained a delay in the proceedings until Widnall decided on Flinn's discharge request. In testimony to the U.S. Congress, Air Force chief of staff Ronald R. Fogelman argued forcefully that the case was not about sex but rather about lying, disobeying orders, and conduct unbecoming an officer. Widnall denied the honorable discharge request. Flinn wanted to fight her case in the court-martial, convinced that with the overdrawn charges and Zigo's many lies, she would be exonerated. The consensus of her family and attorneys was that the cards would be stacked against her in a trial. After a tearful vigil, she took their advice and requested a general discharge, which was granted. Flinn's ordeal was over, but so was her career in the Air Force.

IMPACT

The U.S. military did not emerge unscathed from the controversy. The most immediate effect was upon the fortunes of General Joseph Ralston, who had been up for appointment as chairman of the Joint Chiefs of Staff at the time of Flinn's court-martial. On June 5, 1997, stories appeared in major newspapers about Ralston's reported affair with a civilian woman about thirteen years earlier. Ralston was separated from his wife prior to divorce at the time of the affair, and his lover was a civilian. The House of Representatives' Women's Caucus argued that confirming Ralston would confirm a double standard in the military. General Ralston withdrew his nomination and retired.

The case also called attention to military standards for personal behavior that were increasingly at odds with sociocultural attitudes outside the service. Adultery seldom is prosecuted, even in states

FLINN RESIGNS HER COMMISSION

U.S. Air Force pilot Kelly Flinn sent a letter of resignation to Air Force secretary Sheila Widnall just days before her court-martial was to begin on May 20, 1997. That letter, made public by Flinn, is excerpted here.

It is extremely difficult, if not impossible to put into words my love for the Air Force and devotion to the Air Force. It is with heartfelt agony and the deepest sadness I have ever felt that I submit my resignation from the Air Force. . . .

I did not turn to anyone for help when I should have. Instead, I decided to handle the threats of a detestable man, and live in fear of him and his possible actions. . . .

I have dedicated my life to becoming an Air Force pilot. I have endured comments, videos ridiculing my arrival at Minot AFB [Air Force Base], sexual molestation, and harassing comments, just to fly. I never wanted to be treated as something special, I just wanted the chance, as my counterparts have, to fly for the Air Force as a trained combat pilot. If there was anyway to undo all the wrongs, I would. Unfortunately, at this point, I can only learn from my mistakes and move forward with my life.

I would never wish my ordeal upon my worst enemy. Deep in my heart, I believe that no punishment the Air Force renders will every compare to the public humiliation I have suffered, the loss of my trust, and the loss of my innocence. Before this happened, I never dreamed that people like Marc Zigo existed. Perhaps that was my first mistake. Secondly, I myself, should have researched the legalities of the situation, instead of trusting his word. However, hindsight is 20/20. Looking back, I should have done many things differently. Lying was the worst possible action, yet I did not have the courage then to admit my faults and shortcomings. I now recognize them. I just wanted a chance to reconcile this situation and perhaps have the opportunity to redeem myself in the eyes of the Air Force. . . .

1990's

where it remains a crime. Widespread acceptance of marital separation and divorce also has blurred definitions of adultery by putting those waiting for a final divorce decree into a sort of limbo of marital status. Efforts like General Fogelman's to convince the public that the case was really about "good order and discipline" went awry. The phrase meant little to civilians. While command status—actual or potential—does impose certain responsibilities, the Air Force failed to make the case that Flinn's behavior posed a danger to the nation. The military did not change its rules afterward, but its inept handling of the case resulted in a public relations fiasco. The gap between military and civilian views of sex and sexuality thus persisted, to surface again in the future over related issues.

—*Emily Alward*

FURTHER READING

Bumiller, Elisabeth. "Flying Solo." *Good Housekeeping*, January, 1998. Based on an interview with Flinn, who is depicted as wary and unsettled after her ordeal but also as a person trying to build a new life.

Burke, Carol. *Camp All-American, Hanoi Jane, and the High-and-Tight: Gender, Folklore, and Changing Military Culture.* Boston: Beacon Press, 2004. Study of how conflict arises from the integration of women into previously all-male military units.

"Double Standards, Double Talk." *The New York Times*, June 6, 1997. An editorial denouncing the Air Force's plan to court-martial Kelly Flinn as a

double standard against female service members charged with adultery.

Flinn, Kelly. *Proud to Be: My Life, the Air Force, the Controversy.* New York: Random House, 1997. Flinn's own life story and apologia that includes a focus on her career with the Air Force.

Fogelman, Ron. "A Question of Trust, Not Sex." *Newsweek*, November 24, 1997. The Air Force's position on Flinn's case is presented by the Air Force chief of staff in this magazine article.

SEE ALSO: July 19, 1921: U.S. Senate Rebukes Navy in Homosexuality Investigation; June 26, 1992: U.S. Navy Secretary Resigns in the Wake of Tailhook Sexual Assault Scandal; Apr. 28, 1994: U.S. Naval Academy Expels Midshipmen for Cheating; Jan. 2, 2003: E-mail Message Prompts Inquiry into Air Force Academy Sexual Assaults; June 22, 2005: U.S. Air Force Investigates Religious Intolerance at Its Academy.

June 25, 1997
SWISS BANKS ADMIT TO HOLDING ACCOUNTS OF HOLOCAUST VICTIMS

Investigations revealed that Swiss banks contained hundreds of millions of dollars in cash and valuables of Holocaust victims who had hidden their assets from the Nazis. Swiss banks admitted to holding the accounts, which led to shock, outrage, and an international scandal that forced the banks and the Swiss government into reparations.

LOCALE: Switzerland

CATEGORIES: Banking and finance; atrocities and war crimes; international relations; corruption; public morals; social issues and reform; government

KEY FIGURES

Paul Volcker (b. 1927), chairman of the Federal Reserve System, 1979-1987, and chairman of Volcker Commission, 1996-2000

Christophe Meili (b. 1968), Swiss security guard at Union Banque Suisse

Stuart Eizenstat (b. 1943), U.S. undersecretary of commerce for international trade, 1993-2001

Arnold Koller (b. 1933), federal councilor, 1986-1999, and president of Switzerland, 1990, 1997

Thomas Borer (b. 1957), Swiss ambassador at large

SUMMARY OF EVENT

Switzerland was a neutral nation during World War II, so it was common practice for European Jews to open accounts with Swiss banks. In 1994, Elan Steinberg, the executive director of the World Jewish Congress (WJC), charged that Swiss banks still held between ten and twenty thousand dormant accounts containing the assets of Jewish victims of the Nazi Holocaust. Twenty thousand far exceeded the number of accounts the banks had admitted to in the past.

On May 2, 1996, a memorandum of understanding announced by the World Jewish Restitution Organization, the WJC, and the Swiss Bankers Association (SBA) led to the formation of the Independent Committee of Eminent Persons (ICEP). Paul Volcker, the former chairman of the Federal Reserve System, was asked to form the commission to audit wartime accounts. The ICEP was instrumental in leading the banks finally to admit that thousands of accounts lay dormant in their vaults. On June 25, 1997, a claims resolution process was announced jointly by the SBA, the Swiss Federal Banking Commission, and the ICEP.

Thomas Borer, a Swiss diplomat and chairman of Switzerland's own investigating commission, established in December, 1996, announced that the Swiss government would release all information it had on unclaimed bank accounts belonging to Holocaust victims. The revelation brought Switzerland great embarrassment, and the United States issued swift condemnation. The U.S. Senate introduced a bill requiring the U.S. government to divest its $300 million in investments in Swiss companies and to cease doing business with Switzerland until reparations were made. A commission headed by Stuart Eizenstat, the U.S. undersecretary of commerce for international trade, castigated Switzerland for not taking action in the case and also blamed the U.S. government for not insisting the Swiss take action.

The Eizenstat commission's May, 1997, report noted that the Swiss received $400 million in gold (worth ten times as much by 1997 standards) from Germany during the war, gold that was deposited with Union Banque Suisse (Union Bank of Switzerland, or UBS) or sent to other countries to pay for war materials. The report denounced the Swiss for their complicity with Germany, denounced their attitudes toward victims of Nazi oppression during the war, and claimed that Switzerland's dealings in German gold prolonged the conflict. The Swiss argued, in turn, that they should be judged on their present actions in trying to compensate the victims and not for what they did or did not do before and during World War II.

Further information on the banking scandal had come to light on January 8, 1997, when Christophe Meili, working as a security guard at UBS, came across during his rounds two carts filled with "very old documents and books" that were scheduled for shredding, including two thick books, with "1945-1965" marked on their covers. Meili testified at a later hearing (May 6) before the U.S. Senate that he returned to the room because he remembered press reports concerning bank documents and records from World War II. He believed the items set for the shredder belonged in the national archives and that it would have been illegal had they been destroyed. As he found out the following day when he returned to the shredding room, most already had been destroyed. He also testified that he did not want harm to come to either the Jews or the Swiss, who certainly would be blamed for the illegal shredding. Meili brought what he could of the remaining documents to the Israeli Cultural Association, who handed them over to the police.

Meili was treated as a pariah in Switzerland. He was fired from his job and unable to find new employment. He was threatened by an anonymous caller who said he would kidnap his children and that he could collect the ransom money "from the Jews." Meili complained that the Swiss police would not investigate the case and asked for political asylum in the United States. The WJC offered him employment. Meile also has received awards from Jewish organizations as well as aid to help with his legal fees.

The ICEP, in its final report of December 6, 1999, found no proof that the banks were acting together to destroy account records nor was there proof of a concerted effort to use the funds from these dormant accounts for illicit purposes. The commission did conclude, however, that some individual banks were unethical in handling the dormant accounts.

A plan to give billions of Swiss francs to victims of the Holocaust as a humanitarian measure was presented before the Swiss parliament, but Borer stated that the continued public accusations against Switzerland hindered passage of the measure because many Swiss believed the country was being

1990's

treated unfairly. Switzerland cherished its strict neutrality during World War II, and allegations that it abetted Nazi dictator Adolf Hitler remained a critical concern for the country. The Swiss eventually agreed to some reparations from the government.

On February 26, the SBA announced the establishment of a $67 million humanitarian fund by the banks, and on March 5, Switzerland's president, Arnold Koller, announced the government's Swiss Foundation for Solidarity (SFS) to help victims of poverty, disasters, and human tragedy, such as genocide. He proposed that Swiss banks contribute $4.7 billion from their gold reserves, and the interest, several hundred million dollars per year, be used for aid, including for those persons (and their families) who survived the Holocaust. Koller's announcement marked an official acknowledgment that the banks held deposits of gold owned by Jewish account holders. The conservative opposition in the Swiss parliament opposed the plan, claiming that it acknowledged Swiss guilt. The government proposed raising the money by the sale of gold over a ten-year period so that the sale would not affect the price of the precious metal or harm the Swiss economy by undermining its currency. Furthermore, tax money would not be used.

Moshe Fogel of the Israeli Press Office said Jerusalem welcomed the funds. Avraham Burg, the head of the Jewish Agency for Israel, said it marked a victory for the moral stand the agency had taken in championing the reparations.

IMPACT

The Union Bank of Switzerland, Swiss Bank Corp., and Credit Suisse admitted to having thousands of dormant accounts from the time before and during World War II, accounts that totaled $200 million. The Central Bank of Switzerland, which received most of the Nazi gold, did not participate in the banks' humanitarian fund. The humanitarian fund and SFS, the Swiss government foundation, helped repair some of the damage Switzerland incurred for denying its role in keeping the dormant accounts secret.

At the end of 1998, more than 100,000 Holocaust survivors in Eastern Europe received from five hun-

dred to twelve hundred dollars each. Payments were then made to survivors in Western Europe in February, 1999. An agreement was reached in March to reimburse $1.25 billion to American and Israeli victims for their economic losses. The banks, however, refused to admit liability.

German companies also charged with exploiting Holocaust victims looked at the Swiss model to settle their own lawsuits. In July, 1998, Volkswagen, which had used slave labor during the war, agreed to a reparations plan. In 1999, the German government agreed to set up a fund similar to that of Switzerland to compensate victims exploited by German companies in the Nazi era.

—*Frederick B. Chary*

FURTHER READING

Braillard, Philippe. *Switzerland and the Crisis of Dormant Assets and Nazi Gold.* New York: Kegan Paul International, 2000. An analysis of the dormant accounts scandal by an economist, with emphasis on the scandal's effect on Switzerland as a nation.

Eizenstat, Stuart. *Imperfect Justice: Looted Assets, Slave Labor, and the Unfinished Business of World War II.* New York: PublicAffairs, 2003. An account by an American official and diplomat about efforts to raise funds for reparations from various governments, including Switzerland.

Vincent, Isabel. *Hitler's Silent Partners: Swiss Banks and Nazi Gold and the Pursuit of Justice.* New York: William Morrow, 1997. An award-winning Canadian journalist examines the Swiss accounts scandal, starting with the case of a Holocaust survivor in Canada and her efforts for reparations.

Ziegler, Jean. *The Swiss, the Gold, and the Dead.* New York: Harcourt Brace, 1998. An account by a Swiss sociologist, who lays much blame on the greed of the Swiss banks for cooperating with the Nazis and covering up the story.

SEE ALSO: Nov., 1929: Banque Oustric et Cie Failure Prompts French Inquiry; Apr. 22, 1942: French Prime Minister Pierre Laval Wants Germany to Win World War II; Aug. 14, 1945: French War Hero Pétain Is Convicted of Nazi Collaboration; Feb. 23, 1963: Play Accuses Pope Pius XII of Complicity in the Holocaust; May 23, 1981: Italian Justice Minister Resigns Because of Crime Connection; Aug. 6, 1982: Banco Ambrosiano Collapses Amid Criminal Accusations.

August 31, 1997

PRINCESS DIANA DIES IN A CAR CRASH

The death of Diana, princess of Wales, in a car crash in Paris led to international mourning, controversy, and scandal. The British royal family, especially Queen Elizabeth II, was severely criticized for its seemingly cold response to Diana's death. The crash also raised several questions, including the following: What circumstances placed Diana in the car with Dodi al-Fayed, the son of an Egyptian billionaire? Was the driver of Diana's and Fayed's car drunk? Was Diana's death an assassination? Did a cover-up hamper later investigations of the accident? What role did the paparazzi play in the crash?

LOCALE: Paris, France

CATEGORIES: Communications and media; law and the courts; publishing and journalism; royalty

KEY FIGURES

Diana, Princess of Wales (1961-1997), British princess and former wife of Prince Charles, heir to the British throne

Dodi al-Fayed (1955-1997), son of an Egyptian billionaire and Princess Diana's companion

Henri Paul (1956-1997), driver for Diana and Fayed, who crashed the car in which they were riding

Trevor Rees-Jones (b. 1968), Fayed's bodyguard

Mohamed al-Fayed (b. 1929), Dodi al-Fayed's father

Scott Baker (b. 1937), British coroner

SUMMARY OF EVENT

Diana, the princess of Wales, was an extremely popular international figure, beloved around the world for her philanthropy, and for her beauty. Many believe that she was the world's most photographed woman. This public fascination often put her at odds with the British royal family, which tried to observe royal protocol and procedures when in public, and with the press and paparazzi, who followed her incessantly.

Diana and her husband, Charles, prince of Wales, had divorced in 1996. The media followed Diana everywhere after the divorce. Being a humanitarian, she often was in the public spotlight, working on issues such as HIV-AIDS and unexploded land mines. The media was following her as well when she died in a car crash in Paris on August 31, 1997. The accident fueled a number of conspiracy theories, as many unusual circumstances and facts in the case remain unclear and unresolved.

In mid-1997, Diana was romantically linked to Dodi al-Fayed, who also died in the Paris crash. They had been seen together in public a number of times, and they even bought a ring together in Paris on the afternoon before the crash. Their relationship fueled rumors that they would become engaged the following day, September 1. Another rumor, later proven untrue, was that Diana was pregnant at the time of the crash and that Fayed was the father. Paparazzi followed Diana and Fayed everywhere, and reportedly harassed them to get photos of the famous couple.

Fayed's father, Mohamed al-Fayed, owned the Ritz Hotel in Place Vendôme Paris, where Diana and Fayed had stopped after having spent nine days on the elder Fayed's yacht. The Fayed family also owned an apartment on rue Arsène Houssaye, which is located near the Ritz Hotel and close to the Champs-Élysées. Diana and Fayed were planning to return to the apartment from the hotel. Henri Paul, the acting head of security for the hotel, was concerned about the number of paparazzi in front of the hotel, waiting for the couple to emerge. To elude the media, Paul planned for a decoy vehicle to leave from the front of the hotel. Diana and Fayed would leave the hotel from the rear entrance, with Paul serving as the chauffeur for their car, a Mercedes-Benz S280. Evidence would later show that Paul had been drinking alcohol at the hotel before the crash.

Diana, Fayed, Paul, and Trevor Rees-Jones, Fayed's bodyguard, departed the Ritz Hotel at 12:20 A.M. Fayed and Diana were seated in the rear of the Mercedes, while Paul and Rees-Jones were seated in the front. Upon leaving the hotel, Paul drove to an embankment road that runs beside the Seine River to enter the Pont d'Alma tunnel. The posted speed limit for the tunnel was 50 kph (31 mph). The Mercedes then entered the tunnel about 12:23 A.M., at high speed. Paul lost control of the vehicle, causing it to veer left and strike the thirteenth pillar, which was not protected by a metal rail guard. The car was traveling at an estimated speed of about 118 kph (73 mph) before it struck the pillar.

Fayed and Paul died at the scene of the crash. Diana was critically injured but conscious. Photographers, who had followed the Mercedes into the underpass, were looming over the destroyed car. Pictures taken at the scene remain controversial, especially because Diana was alive after the crash. One of the photographers tried to help her out of the car but was unable to remove her. She reportedly uttered the words "oh my God" and later said "leave me alone" to the paparazzi when the emergency crew arrived at 12:32 A.M. A number of paparazzi were arrested when the police arrived; some of the photographers had been standing on the car taking pictures. Rees-Jones also was conscious and had suffered numerous facial wounds. He was the only survivor of the crash.

Diana was taken away from the scene by ambulance. To administer emergency treatment, the ambulance stopped for about one hour, only a few hundred meters from the Pitié-Salpêtrière Hospital in Paris. The emergency vehicle did not arrive at the hospital until 2:06 A.M., with the princess still alive. She died two hours later from fatal heart and lung injuries.

Conspiracy theories emerged quickly after the death of Princess Diana. Investigations into the driver's background showed that he had many bank accounts and had quietly accumulated extensive savings. He also was deemed negligent for driving drunk—his blood alcohol level was three times the legal limit—and he was

Officials at the scene of the car crash that killed Princess Diana and two others in Paris on August 31, 1997. (AP/Wide World Photos)

The coffin bearing the body of Princess Diana is taken into Westminster Abbey in London for funeral services. Standing watch are, from left and with backs turned, Prince Charles, Prince Harry, Earl Charles Spencer, Prince William, and Prince Philip. (AP/Wide World Photos)

speeding. Other theories alleged that Diana and Fayed were targeted for assassination because the British royal family did not want Fayed, a Muslim, to marry Diana. Even Fayed's father alleged that the husband of Queen Elizabeth II, Prince Philip, orchestrated his son's murder. Others contend that the British secret services and intelligence had Diana murdered to protect the royal family. Still others believe that Fayed was the target because his father had crossed others in failed business deals. All of these theories, along with many others, have been dismissed through subsequent investigations. Al-

though conspiracy theories continue to surround the crash, none yet have been supported by the facts of the case.

A number of detailed investigations, the first of which was conducted by French authorities, determined that the crash was an accident. A second investigation was initiated in 2004 by the coroner of the queen's household, Michael Burgess. The inquest was continued by London's Metropolitan Police and headed by Commissioner Lord Stevens, who looked into several conspiracy theories about the crash. London police published the results of its investigation as the *Paget Report* on December 14, 2006. The report said there was no evidence of a conspiracy.

It is clear, however, that driver Paul had an excessive amount of alcohol in his system and was speeding at the time of the crash. Furthermore, investigations determined that none of the passengers in the car were wearing seatbelts when the Mercedes hit the pillar. According to investigation documents, all could have survived the crash had they been wearing their seatbelts.

Another inquest began on January 8, 2007, with discovery and continued in London's High Court on October 2. It was led by Coroner Scott Baker. On April 7, 2008, the inquest jury returned its verdict: Princess Diana and Fayed were "unlawfully killed" due to the gross negligence—and drunk driving—of driver Paul as well as the actions of the paparazzi. The jury of six women and five men also confirmed that the failure of Diana, Fayed, and Paul to wear seatbelts contributed to their deaths.

IMPACT

Princess Diana's death had immediate significance. Millions around the world mourned her death, watched her funeral on television, and witnessed an outpouring of donations. Bouquets of flowers by the hundreds of thousands were placed in front of Kensington Palace, Diana's home in London. Tens of thousands more bouquets were taken to her family's estate in Althorp.

The public clamored for Queen Elizabeth to comment on the loss of Diana, but the royal response was not fast enough. Many believed the queen was not expressing compassion. Elizabeth finally spoke about Diana on September 5, when she expressed the nation's shock at the loss and gave her personal tribute to the princess. The public mourning continued at her funeral on September 6, when an estimated crowd of more than three million gathered in the area around Westminster Abbey, and hundreds of millions of people around the world watched the funeral on television.

Princess Diana touched people near and far with her personal charm and humanitarianism. Many of her efforts continue through the Diana, Princess of

Wales Memorial Fund, which was initially started with money left by mourners at Kensington Palace and other locations. Diana's sons, Princes William and Harry, have assisted in this memorial effort, and they sponsored a concert on July 1, 2007, to mark the tenth anniversary of Diana's death. Some of the funds raised went to the memorial fund.

—*Douglas A. Phillips*

FURTHER READING

Andersen, Christopher. *After Diana: William, Harry, Charles, and the Royal House of Windsor.* New York: Hyperion, 2007. Provides details on the Scotland Yard-Metropolitan Police probe called Operation Paget, which investigated Diana's death in Paris.

Botham, Noel. *The Murder of Princess Diana.* London: Metro Books, 2007. Written by an investigative reporter who believes that Diana was murdered by a hit squad. Examines circumstances that were covered up during the investigations.

Brown, Tina. *The Diana Chronicles.* New York: Doubleday, 2007. This book reveals the complex life and personality of Diana and includes a chapter on the tunnel crash in Paris.

Davies, Nicholas. *Diana: The Killing of a Princess.* Brighton, England: Pen Press, 2006. Provides interesting questions about circumstances before Diana's death that may have contributed to her demise.

King, Jon, and John Beveridge. *Princess Diana: The Hidden Evidence.* New York: S. P. I. Books, 2001. Examines the surveillance of Diana by the U.S. Central Intelligence Agency and British secret service. Claims the two security agencies were involved in her murder. Discusses other suspicious circumstances surrounding her death.

Levine, Michael. *The Princess and the Package.* Los Angeles: Renaissance Books, 1998. Explores the love-hate relationship that existed between Princess Diana and the media, primarily the paparazzi.

Rees-Jones, Trevor, with Moira Johnston. *The Bodyguard's Story: Diana, the Crash, and the Sole Survivor.* New York: Warner Books, 2000. A detailed account of the night of the crash by the only survivor of the accident, Fayed's body-guard, Trevor Rees-Jones.

SEE ALSO: Dec. 10, 1936: King Edward VIII Abdicates to Marry an American Divorcée; Dec. 18, 1989: Prince Charles's Intimate Phone Conversation with Camilla Parker Bowles Is Taped; Aug. 23, 1992: Princess Diana's Phone Conversation with Her Lover Is Made Public; Jan. 21, 2006: British Politician Resigns After Gay-Sex Orgy; Apr. 26, 2006: Britain's Deputy Prime Minister Admits Affair with Secretary.

September 22, 1997
SPORTSCASTER MARV ALBERT IS TRIED FOR SEXUAL ASSAULT

Veteran sportscaster Marv Albert was tried for assault and battery, including violent biting, and forcible sodomy against a woman with whom he had a long-term sexual relationship. His criminal trial turned into a scandal as intimate details of his unconventional sexual life, including rough sex and threesomes, became public knowledge.

LOCALE: Arlington, Virginia
CATEGORIES: Law and the courts; sex crimes; radio and television; popular culture

KEY FIGURES
Marv Albert (Marvin Philip Aufrichtig; b. 1941), television sportscaster
Vanessa Perhach (b. 1955), former hotel telephone operator
Roy Black (b. 1945), Albert's defense attorney

SUMMARY OF EVENT
In 1997, Marv Albert was the voice of New York sports, a role established over a period of more than three decades. His energetic and informed play-by-play calls, first in radio and later on television, as the voice of Madison Square Garden—most prominently in basketball (for the New York Knicks) and hockey (for the New York Rangers)—had defined him as one of the most influential sports announcers in the United States. He is especially known for his signature (and often imitated) catch-phrase "yessss."

It was a peripatetic lifestyle that may have contributed to the allegations against Albert in the spring of 1997. Vanessa Perhach, a forty-two-year-old former hotel telephone operator from Miami, Florida, had maintained an on-again, off-again sexual relationship with Albert for more than ten years (much of it through phone sex), during which Albert was married and then, after his 1992 divorce, engaged. According to Perhach's later testimony, she and Albert regularly met in different cities to engage in his preference for kinky sex, including threesomes (with a second man), rough sex, and his wearing of women's lingerie.

Albert, born Marvin Philip Aufrichtig, grew up in poverty in Brooklyn, New York, the son of a grocer. The young Albert had a passion for both New York and its sports franchises, called games in his bedroom for an imagined radio station, and got his humble start as a ball boy at the storied Madison Square Garden in Manhattan. As his career blossomed, he maintained close to a year-round commitment to sports broadcasting and established himself as something of a hip celebrity, appearing more than one hundred times on *The David Letterman Show* with his trademark sports-blooper videos.

The specific charges against Albert involved a sexual liaison on February 12 at the Ritz-Carlton Hotel near Washington, D.C., after Albert had called a Knicks game in Landover, Maryland. According to Perhach, Albert had expected a third participant for sex that night at the hotel. After finding out that Perhach did not make the arrangements, he became extremely agitated and threw Perhach face down on the bed. In a frenzy, he then began to bite her back (eighteen to twenty times, according to medical reports, one sufficiently deep enough to draw blood). Despite her repeated requests to stop, Albert insisted that rough sex was what she liked, and so continued. He allegedly sodomized her as well. Forcible sodomy and assault and battery are crimes punishable by life imprisonment.

DNA tests in August showed that the bite marks on Perhach's back were indeed made by Albert. At the criminal trial in northern Virginia, which began on September 22, 1997, Albert's attorney, Roy Black, a high-profile defense lawyer notable for securing the acquittal in 1991 of William Kennedy Smith, who had been tried for rape, argued that Perhach was a troubled woman who could not bear the idea of Albert ending their relationship (he was engaged to marry Heather Falkiner, a producer for the sports network ESPN).

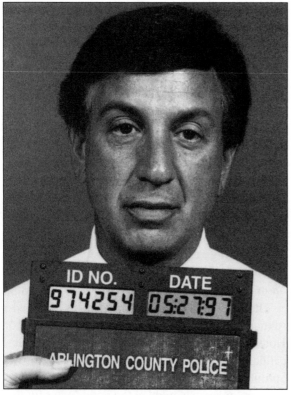

Marv Albert's booking photograph from May 27, 1997. Albert was arrested by Arlington County (Virginia) police on assault and forcible sodomy charges. (AP/Wide World Photos)

Citing the film *Fatal Attraction*, Black portrayed Perhach as vindictive and desperate to destroy Albert. Virginia state shield laws prevented Black from introducing testimony that would have discussed Perhach's previous relationships (including with an abusive former husband) and evidence that Perhach had pursued sexual relationships with other celebrities. Black was able to suggest in court that Perhach had a six-week stay in a mental hospital in late 1996 after she attempted suicide. Also, Black argued that the sodomy between Albert and Perhach not only was consensual but also at her suggestion because she was not on birth control at the time.

After Perhach's emotional testimony on September 23 (during which Albert maintained a stoic demeanor, supported in court by his fiancée, his father, and his children), Black played an audiotape in which Perhach appeared to coach a Washington, D.C., taxi driver who had picked up Albert the night of the alleged attack to testify that Albert had been agitated and had vehemently requested the third participant. Although this damaged Perhach's credibility, the prosecution then introduced a surprise witness, another woman who testified that between 1993 and 1994, Albert had made similar requests for rough sex, had bitten her twice, and tried to forcibly sodomize her. The surprise witness's testimony proved devastating, as it established a pattern of behavior.

Black moved quickly in response. First, he petitioned (successfully) to have the more serious charge, forcible sodomy, dismissed (it was impossible to determine consent legally) and then advised Albert to plead guilty to the misdemeanor charge of assault and battery, thus ending what had become a carnival atmosphere in the media.

Albert was given a relatively light twelve-month suspended sentence, extensive counseling, and a guarantee that his record would be expunged if he refrained from similar sexual activities in that time. He also received no fine.

Albert, fifty-six years old and with his career and reputation in shambles, apologized during a brief posttrial statement, saying he never imagined Perhach was not a willing participant. Within hours,

Albert was fired by NBC, even after the network had stood by its broadcaster throughout the long summer after the grand jury brought the initial charges against him. He then resigned from his announcer position at Madison Square Garden.

Women's rights activists vehemently denounced Albert's light sentence, arguing that the lack of jail or prison time sent the wrong message: that once again, the American legal system sided with a male perpetrator, turning him into a victim, and instead allowed the female victim to be portrayed as the victimizer. However, the reality was far less dramatic. Although Perhach's relationship history was not permitted in court (Black later would say that decision had cost his defense nearly 90 percent of its material), the decision to move to a plea agreement was made because Black recognized the only way to counter the second woman's testimony would have been to put Albert on the stand. Doing so would have cleared the way for potentially damaging (and humiliating) questions by the prosecution. The plea agreement was Black's only legal option to avoid jail or prison time for his client.

IMPACT

It is difficult to shape Albert into a conventional cautionary figure. The same year he could have been imprisoned for life, he also was elected to the Basketball Hall of Fame for outstanding media contribution to the sport. Less than one year after his plea agreement—and with an expunged record—a contrite Albert was rehired by Madison Square Garden to call Knicks games on radio, where he remained until a dispute over the direction of the team led to his termination. When Madison Square Garden management initially rehired Albert, it cited not only his stellar credentials and loyal fan base but also his successful year of therapy. After the Garden, he joined the prestigious sports division of cable television network TNT. His sportscasting career continued unabated.

Feminist groups were outraged at the lack of condemnation against Albert after his conviction, citing a system that destroys the lives and careers of women but allows male perpetrators to return to their careers unscathed. Albert quickly reestablished himself as one of basketball's most informed and charismatic broadcasters (indeed, media critics argued the notoriety only increased his value in a market driven by celebrity). In June, 2008, he was a television commentator for the postseason games of the National Basketball Association, calling the finals' series between the Los Angeles Lakers and Boston Celtics.

Little is known of what happened to Perhach after the trial. She intimated, through her attorney, that she might pursue a civil lawsuit against Albert, but none was ever filed.

In the long term, the Albert sex scandal reveals that such scandals in a media age do not, in fact, have long runs. Whatever impact the case had on Albert's career was a short one, and it was soon forgotten, or simply disregarded. For the tawdry celebrity trials that followed, the Albert trial became a template with the following characteristics: extravagant media scrutiny, the blurring of the line between tabloid news and respectable press coverage, a focus on a marginal celebrity whose eccentric private life was deemed suitable for public investigation, a clash of high-profile attorneys, and a lurid mix of sex and power. In the aftermath, the beloved scandals that are celebrity trials offer irrefutable evidence of a contemporary culture's inability to sustain either its curiosity or its outrage.

—*Joseph Dewey*

1990's

FURTHER READING

Langer, John. *Tabloid Television: Popular Journalism and the "Other News."* New York: Routledge, 1997. Examines the definitions of "news" and how tabloids and celebrity trials have altered that definition. Also looks at how pretrial coverage trivializes the justice system by creating heroes and villains before the system renders its verdict.

Orth, Maureen. *The Importance of Being Famous: Behind the Scenes of the Celebrity-Industrial Complex.* Farmingdale, N.Y.: Owl Books, 2005. A journalist's analysis of the celebrity-driven tabloid era that includes the Albert trial. Argues the trial was part of a growing public fascination with the salacious details of the private lives of celebrities.

Schickle, Richard. *Intimate Strangers: The Culture of Celebrity.* Chicago: Ivan R. Dee, 2000. A scathing indictment of tabloid journalism by a respected media critic. Argues that media renderings of the distinctions between public and private make those distinctions virtually meaningless and in turn trivializes disturbing behavior.

Turner, Graeme. *Understanding Celebrity.* Thousand Oaks, Calif.: Sage, 2004. A theoretical investigation with numerous examples of how the treatment of contemporary celebrities, particularly in entertainment and sports, inevitably creates consumer boredom and the forgetting of scandalous behavior.

SEE ALSO: Feb. 6, 1942: Film Star Errol Flynn Is Acquitted of Rape; Feb. 1, 1978: Roman Polanski Flees the United States to Avoid Rape Trial; July 28, 1980: Magazine Reveals Baseball Star Steve Garvey's Marital Problems; July 26, 1991: Comedian Pee-wee Herman Is Arrested for Public Indecency; June 27, 1995: Film Star Hugh Grant Is Arrested for Lewd Conduct; Apr. 7, 1998: Pop Singer George Michael Is Arrested for Lewd Conduct; July 1, 2003: Basketball Star Kobe Bryant Is Accused of Rape; Early Nov., 2003: Paris Hilton Sex-Tape Appears on the Web; Dec. 18, 2003: Pop Star Michael Jackson Is Charged with Child Molestation; June 13, 2008: Singer R. Kelly Is Acquitted on Child Pornography Charges.

November 26, 1997

CANADIAN HEALTH COMMISSIONER RELEASES REPORT ON TAINTED BLOOD

During the 1980's, blood tainted with the human immunodeficiency virus, or HIV, and hepatitis C entered the Canadian blood supply. Justice Horace Krever led a commission in 1993 that began an inquiry into the tainted blood and the Canadian government's response to the emergency. The resulting document, the Krever Report, was released in 1997.

ALSO KNOWN AS: Health Management Associates scandal

LOCALE: Canada

CATEGORIES: Drugs; medicine and health care; government; law and the courts; business

KEY FIGURES

Horace Krever (fl. 1990's), Ontario Court of Appeals justice, 1986-1999, and chairman of the Krever Commission, 1993-1997

Roger Perrault (b. 1937), national director of the Canadian Red Cross Society, 1974-1991

John Furesz (fl. 1990's), director of Canada's Bureau of Biologics, 1974-1992, and member of the Canadian Blood Committee

SUMMARY OF EVENT

During the late 1970's and throughout the 1980's, Canada faced a massive outbreak of human immunodeficiency virus, or HIV, and hepatitis C cases among hemophiliacs and blood-transfusion recipients. In response, a Canadian House of Commons committee authorized an inquiry into the possible contamination of the blood supply and requested recommendations for policies to maintain a safe and efficient supply of blood.

Ontario Court of Appeals justice Horace Krever, one of the country's foremost experts on the confidentiality of health records, was appointed to lead the Royal Commission of Inquiry on the Blood System in Canada, or the Krever Commission. Public hearings began on November 22, 1993. The commission heard testimony from those infected and from doctors, officials of the Canadian Red Cross Society (CRCS), and organizations responsible for blood collection and distribution. The hearings ended in December, 1995, after testimony from close to five hundred persons and a cost of millions of dollars.

The CRCS, founded in 1896, was responsible for the majority of blood and blood-components coordination, collection, and distribution. The Canadian government did not regulate the CRCS because of the organization's excellent reputation. The Canadian Blood Committee (CBC) was established in 1981 to financially manage the blood supply system throughout Canada. The blood system as a whole was uncoordinated and inefficient, with no clear line of authority, so that the agencies involved could not respond quickly to a widespread emergency. Until 1989, the federal Canadian government had no legal control over whole blood and its components.

During the 1970's, more than 200,000 Canadians received blood or blood products annually, including approximately twenty-three hundred hemophiliacs, those who have a blood-clotting disorder. By 1971, testing was available to detect hepatitis B, and the CRCS no longer collected blood from prisons, where the hepatitis rate was higher than in the general population. By 1974, the first cases of hepatitis C (originally called non-A and non-B hepatitis) were identified and found to be transmitted through blood transfusions. Hepatitis C can lie dormant for up to twenty-five years and cause liver cancer and cirrhosis. Effective tests were available by 1986, but the CRCS did not begin testing until 1990, and unscreened plasma was given to patients through 1992.

By March, 1983, the United States was screening all persons considered part of a higher-risk group for acquired immunodeficiency syndrome (AIDS), an autoimmune disease that develops from HIV. Persons no longer allowed to donate blood included gay men, Haitians, intravenous-drug users, and their sexual partners. The U.S. Food and Drug Administration (FDA), however, allowed the export of tainted plasma from prisons in Arkansas and Louisiana to Canada during the 1980's. By this time, the

FDA already had ruled that prisoners' plasma was too unsafe for the manufacture of blood products in the United States. Health Management Associates (HMA), the company that ran the Arkansas prisoners' plasma program from 1978 to 1994 and bought prisoners' plasma from Louisiana, purchased most of the tainted plasma from the Cummins Unit, a correctional facility in Arkansas. The Arkansas Department of Corrections sold the inmates' blood to HMA, which then sold it to North American Biologics, a subsidiary of Continental Pharma Cryosan, a blood broker in Montreal. Cummins was known to have used dirty needles and for failing to test donors for AIDS and hepatitis C. The FDA accused the prison of numerous violations during the early 1980's and ordered its closure, but HMA continued to sell inmates' blood to Connaught Laboratories, a Canadian company.

Even though potential donors were being screened in the United States in early 1983, Roger Perrault, national director of the CRCS, implemented a policy of asking members of higher-risk groups to not donate, but to refrain voluntarily. Especially in the face of a severe shortage of blood, it would be poor policy to question potential donors, who were being generous by donating. To question them showed distrust. In August, 1982, John Furesz, director of Canada's Bureau of Biologics, which was responsible for regulating blood products, asked the CRCS to report new cases of HIV and AIDS. The request was rejected because the CRCS believed that hemophiliacs were not at risk of HIV infection and that such risk was exaggerated and inconclusive.

The CRCS began screening Canadian blood donations for the HIV antibody in November, 1985. Potential donors were given health-related information and asked if they were in good health, but they were not asked about sexual activities or drug use until 1986. The Bureau of Biologics did not insist that blood donors be informed about AIDS symptoms or asked if they had symptoms of AIDS, nor were they asked if they were in a higher-risk group. The bureau also did not require that higher-risk groups be excluded from donating blood.

The Krever Commission released an interim report on February 15, 1995, containing forty-three recommendations. The report called for a comprehensive, effective program to provide transfusion recipients with information about the risks of HIV. Other major recommendations included that hospitals notify all patients who had transfusions between 1978 and 1985 about the risk of developing AIDS, and to notify all patients who received blood or blood products between 1978 and 1990 about the risk of hepatitis C.

By the time the final report was released on November 26, 1997, many of the recommendations from the interim report had been enacted. The Krever Report found misconduct at every level. Among the findings were that the CBC failed to create a national blood policy and regulate donations; it also failed to provide quality blood products to hemophiliacs. The report found that the CRCS failed to oversee and provide resources for the blood system, to recognize HIV transmission by blood, and to implement donor screening, and that the CRCS underestimated the risk of HIV transmission.

IMPACT

The tainted blood scandal was the worst preventable public health disaster in Canadian history. The Krever Report of 1997 highlighted numerous problems with Canada's blood system, and Canadian governmental bodies began working to establish a new blood system to improve safety.

In September, 1998, the blood-related tasks of the CRCS were taken over by the newly formed Canadian Blood Services (CBS). CBS had the authority to oversee and integrate services and provide accountability. In addition, the federal government tightened regulations for improving manufacturing standards, reporting adverse drug reactions, and sharing information on transfusion risks. CBS also would provide national control over the blood system. Also in 1998, provincial and federal governments began authorizing compensation for those infected by tainted blood and blood products.

THE KREVER REPORT

The Krever Commission, which was formed to investigate the tainted Canadian blood supply, released its report on November 26, 1997. In that report, Chairman Horace Krever includes a statement he made on the first day of hearings in 1993, ensuring people that the purpose of the hearings was to find facts, and not to condemn.

On 22 November 1993, the first day of public hearings, in the course of my introductory comments about the Inquiry, I made the following statement about its purpose: It is not and it will not be a witch hunt. It is not concerned with criminal or civil liability. I shall make findings of fact. It will be for others, not for the commission, to decide what actions if any are warranted by those findings.

I shall not make recommendations about prosecution or civil liability. I shall not permit the hearings to be used for ulterior purposes, such as a preliminary inquiry, or Examination for Discovery, or in aid of existing or future criminal or civil litigation.

As I interpret the terms of reference, the focus of the Inquiry is to determine whether Canada's blood supply is as safe as it could be and whether the blood system is sound enough that no future tragedy will occur. For those purposes it is essential to determine what caused or contributed to the contamination of the blood system in Canada in the early 1980's.

We intend to get to the bottom of that issue, let there be no mistake about that.

Source: Library and Archives Canada, July, 2008.

In April, 2001, the Supreme Court of Canada ruled that the CRCS was negligent in managing the blood system. In November, 2002, the CRCS and four physicians, including Perrault and Furesz, were charged with criminal negligence. In May, 2005, the CRCS was fined five thousand dollars for its role in the tainted blood scandal, a small amount, but the maximum amount allowed for the charge of distributing a contaminated product. Six other criminal charges were dropped. In October, 2007, after an eighteen-month trial, all the physicians were acquitted of criminal negligence charges.

The cost in terms of human suffering and death was substantial. By 1985, about eight hundred hemophiliacs were infected with HIV. Approximately

1,148 cases of AIDS were attributed to transfusions received between 1978 and 1985, and 627 of these persons were dead by 1993. Since infected recipients and donors were not identified, located, and treated, the number of people actually infected was higher because it included family members infected through sexual and maternal transmission. Between 1986 and 1990, 28,600 people were infected with hepatitis C by blood transfusion, even though heat-treated products and AIDS screening tests were available. Eighty-six percent of the infections could have been prevented had adequate screening techniques been introduced in 1986, the year they first became available. Approximately 95 percent of the hemophiliacs who received blood products before 1990 contracted hepatitis C. The Krever Report estimated that as many as twenty thousand Canadians contracted AIDS and more than sixty thousand had been infected with hepatitis C.

With multiple layers of testing and screening, the blood supply by 2007 was considered safe. More funding boosted safeguards at laboratories and other health facilities and helped to increase the monitoring of international trends and other related health concerns.

—Virginia L. Salmon

FURTHER READING

DeMont, John. "A Harsh Rebuke: The Krever Report Dissects the Tainted Blood Scandal." *Maclean's*, December 8, 1997. Magazine article that lists examples of negligence and error, describes the current state of blood donation, and discusses changes made with new blood system.

Gilmore, Norbert, and Margaret A. Somerville. "From Trust to Tragedy: HIV/AIDS and the Canadian Blood System." In *Blood Feuds: AIDS, Blood, and the Politics of Medical Disaster*, edited by Eric A. Feldman and Ronald Bayer. New York: Oxford University Press, 1999. Overview and discussion of Canada's blood system and the tainted blood scandal. Points out numerous failures to act that resulted in tragedy.

Sillars, Les. "Bureaucratic Serial Killers: (Horace) Krever's Tainted-Blood Inquiry Lays Bare in Meticulous Detail the Death Toll from Political Correctness." *Alberta Report*, December 15, 1997. Highlights results of the Krever Report and examines the inaction of the Canadian health system to protect the blood supply. Provides statistics and some personal accounts.

Starr, Douglas. *Blood: An Epic History of Medicine and Commerce*. New York: Alfred A. Knopf, 1998. An exposé of the global business of human blood, namely the "blood-services complex." Discussion includes the distribution of blood in the context of the rise of HIV and AIDS during the early 1980's.

"Tainted Blood: Poison from the Prisons." *The Economist*, March 13, 1999. Brief magazine article discussing the sale to Canada of contaminated prisoners' plasma from the United States during the 1980's.

SEE ALSO: Mar. 21, 1928: Alberta Government Sterilizes Thousands Deemed Genetically and Mentally Unfit; Sept.-Oct., 1937: Prescription Elixir Causes More than One Hundred Deaths; 1956-1962: Prescription Thalidomide Causes Widespread Birth Disorders; July 25, 1972: Newspaper Breaks Story of Abuses in Tuskegee Syphilis Study; Sept. 17, 1985: Media Allege Canadian Officials Allowed Sale of Rancid Tuna; Feb. 4, 1996: Whistle-Blower Reveals Tobacco Industry Corruption; Mar. 4, 1999: Quebec Offers Support for Abused Duplessis Orphans; Sept., 2000: American Scientists Are Accused of Starting a Measles Epidemic in the Amazon; Jan. 30, 2001: Liverpool Children's Hospital Collects Body Parts Without Authorization; Aug., 2002: Immunologist Resigns After Being Accused of Falsifying Research; Summer, 2006-Mar. 16, 2007: Manufacturer Recalls Pet Food That Killed Thousands of American Pets; Feb. 18, 2007: *Washington Post* Exposes Decline of Walter Reed Army Hospital.

1990's

December 11, 1997
HUD SECRETARY HENRY CISNEROS IS INDICTED FOR LYING TO FEDERAL AGENTS

U.S. Housing and Urban Development secretary Henry Cisneros, a rising star in the Democratic Party and a successful businessman and respected community leader, broke the public trust when he was indicted for conspiracy, lying, and obstructing justice by trying to hide facts regarding money he provided to a former mistress. He was convicted but served no prison time. The scandal ended his political career but not his business career.

LOCALE: Washington, D.C.
CATEGORIES: Law and the courts; politics; corruption; government; sex

KEY FIGURES

Henry Cisneros (b. 1947), mayor of San Antonio, Texas, 1981-1989, and head of the U.S. Department of Housing and Urban Development, 1993-1996
Linda Jones Medlar (b. 1948), Cisneros's former campaign aide and former mistress
David M. Barrett (b. 1936 or 1937), White House independent counsel

SUMMARY OF EVENT

Henry Cisneros, the nominee for U.S. secretary of Housing and Urban Development (HUD) in late 1992, was under scrutiny by the Federal Bureau of Investigation (FBI) for misrepresenting facts about payments he made to his former campaign aide and mistress, Linda Jones Medlar. Cisneros never denied paying Medlar, and he even met with representatives of the transition team for president-elect Bill Clinton to discuss both his relationship with Medlar and his payments. However, what remained unclear to investigators was how much he paid her and for how long. What led to scandal was his failure to tell the truth to the FBI.

Cisneros, who was the first Latino mayor of a major U.S. city, had ended the affair with Medlar near the end of 1989 and reconciled with his wife, who had filed for divorce. He made a verbal agreement with Medlar to pay her $4,000 per month until she could find a job or until her daughter completed college. Cisneros admitted his payments were inconsistent and that he could no longer afford them once he became HUD secretary in January, 1993; he did continue to pay her some money for about one more year. In July, 1994, Medlar sued Cisneros for $256,000 for breach of contract. She maintained in the suit that he promised to pay her for emotional distress and loss of livelihood following their affair and that he publicly disclosed private information about her without her knowledge and consent.

On September 12, Medlar appeared on the television show *Inside Edition* and claimed that Cisneros had lied to the FBI during its background check of the nominee. *Inside Edition* also broadcast excerpts from audiotapes Medlar recorded without Cisneros's knowledge. The tapes included statements made by Cisneros that contradicted what he told the FBI about the payments to Medlar. The U.S. Justice Department began its investigation in March, 1995, as U.S. attorney general Janet Reno requested an independent counsel to investigate the matter. David M. Barrett was appointed for that job in May. Soon after Barrett's appointment, Cisneros settled Medlar's 1994 lawsuit for $49,000. Barrett then granted Medlar immunity from prosecution in exchange for her cooperation in building a case against Cisneros. In January, 1997, Cisneros resigned as HUD secretary, stating that he needed to be with his family.

Close to one year later, on December 11, Cisneros was indicted by a federal grand jury on eighteen counts of conspiracy, making false statements to the FBI, and obstructing justice. The indictment charged that Cisneros made frantic efforts prior to, during, and after his confirmation as HUD secretary to ensure that Medlar did not reveal the true nature of the love affair, which began in 1987, and the actual amount of money she received from him.

Cisneros denied the grand jury's allegation that his payments to Medlar amounted to hush money. He said the payments were humanitarian in nature. The grand jury also maintained that Medlar had threatened to publicly expose the affair and payoff.

In June, 1999, Cisneros's lawyers attacked Medlar's credibility. One of Medlar's former attorneys testified that Medlar had been lying, especially about more than thirty conversations with Cisneros that she had secretly taped between 1990 and 1994. Medlar claimed that she taped her conversations so that she would have a record of Cisneros's promises of financial assistance. When payments ceased, Medlar took the tapes to her lawyers. She also claimed her lawyers told her to edit the tapes to remove any portions that could suggest she was threatening Cisneros. In September, 1996, an analysis of the tapes verified that they were altered.

Medlar would soon be charged in a case involving bank fraud in Texas and was sentenced to three and a half years in prison. Nevertheless, prosecutors agreed to seek a reduced sentence for the bank fraud conviction in return for her full cooperation in the Cisneros case. The subsequent hearings focused on the admissibility of the tapes after Medlar reaffirmed that she edited several of them. Prosecutors argued that the tapes, which contained discussions by Cisneros of ways to mislead investigators, were critical to the case, and the court agreed. Had the tapes not been allowed as evidence, the prosecution would have had to rely on Medlar's testimony alone and on a complicated trail of financial records.

Cisneros pleaded guilty in September, 1999, to a single misdemeanor charge of lying to the FBI about the money. He had pleaded not guilty in January, 1998, to a felony charge of lying to the FBI about the payments. As part of a plea agreement, Cisneros admitted to lying to federal agents and paid a $10,000 fine. However, he was spared a prison sentence or probation and thus was free to seek elected office if he so desired.

Difficult issues affected both sides of the case. Barrett had to convince a jury that Cisneros committed a crime. Doing so was complicated because Cisneros had earlier acknowledged both the affair and the payments; his crime was understating the amount of money involved by lying to the FBI. Cisneros risked the embarrassment of having his private life made public. Both sides concluded that the plea agreement was the appropriate way to handle the case.

IMPACT

The payments controversy affected not only Cisneros's personal life but also his professional life, and his prosecution confirmed the consequences of lying to the FBI. First, the Cisneros scandal was one in a line of controversies involving President Clinton's cabinet. Others who were investigated by independent counsels include former agriculture secretary Mike Espy, commerce secretary Ronald H. Brown, interior secretary Bruce Babbitt, and labor secretary Alexis M. Herman.

Barrett would continue his investigation for several years after Cisneros was convicted, believing the Internal Revenue Service and the Department of Justice were blocking his inquiries. This investigation ended in early 2006 at a cost to taxpayers of about $22 million.

Second, the aggressive nature of the FBI's investigation of Cisneros for lying to agents reflects the bureau's insistence on maintaining its integrity and on investigating perjurers, even those in high government office. Third, the indictment and conviction changed Cisneros's career plans. He had been a rising star in politics, but after the scandal, his plans did not include politics. He moved from San Antonio, severing deep family roots there, to Los Angeles to engage in new business ventures, but he reportedly returned to San Antonio. He was pardoned by President Clinton in 2001.

—Victoria Price

FURTHER READING

Henry, Christopher E. *Henry Cisneros*. Langhorne, Pa.: Chelsea House, 1994. One of a series of books on Latinos of achievement. Extols the qualities that made Cisneros an outstanding success in local politics.

Locy, Toni. "Ex-Housing Chief Cisneros Indicted." *The Washington Post*, December 12, 1997. The leading newspaper of record in Washington,

D.C., reports on Cisneros's indictment for perjury, conspiracy, and obstructing justice.

Miller, Bill. "Cisneros Pleads Guilty to Lying to FBI Agents." *The Washington Post*, September 8, 1999. The local news report on Cisneros's plea in the federal case against him.

Roberts, Robert North. *Ethics in U.S. Government: An Encyclopedia of Investigations, Scandals, Reforms, and Legislation*. Westport, Conn.: Greenwood Press, 2001. A comprehensive encyclopedia documenting political scandals, ethical controversies, and investigations in the United States between 1775 and 2000.

Romero, Maritza. *Henry Cisneros: A Man of the People*. New York: PowerKids Press, 2001. A brief biography of Cisneros, written to inspire young readers.

SEE ALSO: Mar. 2, 1923: U.S. Senate Investigates Veterans Bureau Chief for Fraud; Sept. 22, 1958: President Eisenhower's Chief of Staff Resigns for Influence Selling; Feb. 7, 1960: President Kennedy's Romantic Affair Links Him to Organized Crime; May 9, 1969: Supreme Court Justice Abe Fortas Is Accused of Bribery; Oct. 7, 1974: Congressman Wilbur D. Mills's Stripper Affair Leads to His Downfall; May 23, 1976: *Washington Post* Exposes Congressman Wayne L. Hays's Affair; Oct. 4, 1976: Agriculture Secretary Earl Butz Resigns After Making Obscene Joke; Sept. 21, 1977: Carter Cabinet Member Resigns over Ethics Violations; Sept. 24, 1992: British Cabinet Member David Mellor Resigns over Romantic Affair; June 1, 1994: Congressman Dan Rostenkowski Is Indicted in House Post Office Scandal; Aug. 5, 1994: Kenneth Starr Is Appointed to the Whitewater Investigation; Aug. 21, 1994: Sex Scandal Forces Dismissal of NAACP Chief Benjamin Chavis.

January 17, 1998
PRESIDENT BILL CLINTON DENIES SEXUAL AFFAIR WITH A WHITE HOUSE INTERN

Allegations of having lied under oath about an inappropriate sexual relationship with White House intern Monica Lewinsky led to the impeachment of U.S. president Bill Clinton by the House of Representatives but his exoneration by the Senate.

ALSO KNOWN AS: Lewinsky affair; Zippergate; Monicagate
LOCALE: Washington, D.C.
CATEGORIES: Sex; government; politics; publishing and journalism

KEY FIGURES

Bill Clinton (b. 1946), president of the United States, 1993-2001
Monica Lewinsky (b. 1973), former White House intern

Kenneth Starr (b. 1946), White House independent counsel
Linda Tripp (b. 1949), long-time federal employee
Hillary Rodham Clinton (b. 1947), First Lady, 1993-2001, U.S. senator from New York, 2001-2009, and Secretary of State, 2009-

SUMMARY OF EVENT

Even before Bill Clinton was elected U.S. president in November, 1992, his campaign was troubled by rumors of improprieties. Opponents questioned his role in the failure of the Whitewater Development Corporation, a real estate firm, while he was governor of Arkansas, and he was accused of at least one extramarital affair, all claims that brought his character into question. First Lady Hillary Rodham Clinton, later U.S. senator from New York and a

Democratic presidential candidate, made it clear that she had forgiven her husband for the affair and considered the matter closed.

Clinton's administration progressed, but rumors continued to emerge, claiming repeated infidelities by the president. Arkansas state police officers reportedly had procured women for Clinton while he was governor and allegedly were fired if considered a political liability. Such rumors gained a certain believability in 1993 when news of the firing of several employees at the White House Travel Office was leaked to the press. Questions of financial improprieties also arose during this time, but White House independent counsel Kenneth Starr could not find evidence of wrongdoing by the president or First Lady.

However, the image of an administration riddled with scandal persisted, and it became an issue in the 1996 presidential election. Campaign contributions from persons connected with the People's Republic of China raised serious questions about foreign influence upon elections in the United States and led to reconsideration of the laws governing campaign contributions. Still, Clinton was reelected for a second term as president.

During Clinton's second term, questions of sexual misconduct came to the fore. Two women alleged that Clinton had made inappropriate sexual advances toward them while he was governor of Arkansas. However, neither allegation had been proven in court, and in the case of one woman, the statute of limitations had long since expired, making it impossible to bring the case to trial. All the same, Starr would come to consider the allegations reason to look more deeply into Clinton's sexual conduct.

Starr's investigations led him to Paula Jones, a former Arkansas state employee who had sued Clinton for sexual harassment in connection with an encounter in a hotel room in Little Rock, Arkansas. Her story was a textbook case of sexual harassment: She had been summoned to the room on the pretext that she needed to take care of some job-related business. However, when she arrived, Clinton (then governor) allegedly propositioned her and suggested that things could go badly for her if she did

Monica Lewinsky. (AP/Wide World Photos)

not acquiesce. She subsequently claimed that she was as surprised by the crudity of his advance as by the act itself and had expected a man as handsome and intelligent as Clinton to have better pick-up lines. Jones's suit was ultimately dismissed because she was unable to prove damages for refusing Clinton's request for sexual favors.

Linda Tripp, a staff member in the Pentagon's public affairs office and a former White House administrative assistant, was the next person to enter the developing scandal. In September, 1997, Tripp began to secretly record telephone conversations she had with Pentagon coworker Monica Lewinsky, a former White House intern. According to Tripp, Lewinsky (before being taped) told her about having had sex with the president. In the secretly recorded conversations, in which Lewinsky elaborates on her relations with the president, Lewinsky tells Tripp that she kept as a memento a blue dress with evidence (semen stains) that the relationship with Clinton had been a physical one. On January 7, 1998, Lewinsky declared in a signed affidavit for the Jones case that she had never had sex with the

1990's

president. Tripp learned of the affidavit and, believing Lewinsky lied, gave the tapes to Starr on January 12.

On January 17, Clinton was deposed in the Jones case and swore that he never had "sexual relations" with Lewinsky. Four days later, the *Los Angeles Times*, *The Washington Post*, and *ABC News* reported that Starr was investigating the president's sexual ties to Lewinsky. In interviews with the press later that day, Clinton further denied extramarital relations. Months later, when confronted with evidence from the Federal Bureau of Investigation that his DNA (deoxyribonucleic acid) matched the sample taken from Lewinsky's dress, Clinton admitted to having had "inappropriate intimate contact" with Lewinsky but also equivocated about the precise meaning of the term "sexual relations." Although technically his attempt to restrict the term to vaginal intercourse had some grounds, it did not match with the intuitive definition held by many people. He insisted as well that he did not lie in his January deposition.

BILL CLINTON'S CONFESSION

On August 17, 1998, following his grand jury testimony, U.S. president Bill Clinton spoke to the American people and admitted to his affair with White House intern Monica Lewinsky. He urged the nation to focus its attention on urgent matters of public concern.

This afternoon in this room, from this chair, I testified before the Office of Independent Counsel and the grand jury. I answered their questions truthfully, including questions about my private life, questions no American citizen would ever want to answer. Still, I must take complete responsibility for all my actions, both public and private. And that is why I am speaking to you tonight.

As you know, in a deposition in January, I was asked questions about my relationship with Monica Lewinsky. While my answers were legally accurate, I did not volunteer information. Indeed, I did have a relationship with Ms. Lewinsky that was not appropriate. In fact, it was wrong. It constituted a critical lapse in judgment and a personal failure on my part for which I am solely and completely responsible.

But I told the grand jury today and I say to you now that at no time did I ask anyone to lie, to hide or destroy evidence or to take any other unlawful action. I know that my public comments and my silence about this matter gave a false impression. I misled people, including even my wife. I deeply regret that....

It is time to stop the pursuit of personal destruction and the prying into private lives and get on with our national life. Our country has been distracted by this matter for too long, and I take my responsibility for my part in all of this. That is all I can do. Now it is time—in fact, it is past time—to move on. We have important work to do—real opportunities to seize, real problems to solve, real security matters to face.

And so tonight, I ask you to turn away from the spectacle of the past seven months, to repair the fabric of our national discourse, and to return our attention to all the challenges and all the promise of the next American century.

Some considered the media's continual focus on the precise nature of Clinton's extramarital activities, rather than upon whether his denial of them in a sworn deposition constituted perjury and obstruction of justice, to be far more inappropriate than the acts themselves. By focusing so intensely upon sexual details, critics argued, the media was appealing to the prurient interest of its readership rather than to the very serious questions about rule of law.

On September 10, Starr delivered his report to the House of Representatives. The report was released to the public the following day. By December 19, the House passed articles of impeachment against President Clinton, making him only the second U.S. president to be impeached (Andrew Johnson was impeached over his conduct of Reconstruction; Richard Nixon resigned before articles of impeachment could be passed against him for his role in Watergate). Because this act followed a congressional election that had significantly shifted the composition of the House in favor of the Democrats, some commentators felt that it was a last-ditch effort by outgoing Republicans to attack a president they despised. Thus, it was in a heavily partisan atmosphere that the U.S. Senate's impeachment trial began on January 7, 1999.

As provided by the U.S. Constitu-

Bill Clinton speaks after his impeachment by the House of Representatives on December 19, 1998. From left is Representative Richard Gephardt, Clinton, Vice President Al Gore, and First Lady Hillary Rodham Clinton. (AP/Wide World Photos)

tion, the trial was presided over by U.S. Supreme Court chief justice William H. Rehnquist. Thirteen members of Congress served as managers of the trial, the functional equivalent of prosecutors. They were led by Senator Henry Hyde of Illinois, who was notable for his insistence that the focus must be kept upon the questions of perjury and obstruction of justice and not on Clinton's extramarital affairs per se, which were better left a private matter between the president and First Lady. After nearly a month of testimony, on February 12, the Senate returned verdicts of not guilty on both counts.

IMPACT

Although Clinton was formally acquitted of the charges against him by the Senate and, thus, continued in office until the end of his term on January 20, 2001, he was subsequently cited for contempt of court by a federal district judge for his refusal to fully cooperate in the Paula Jones case. As a result of his citation and fine, he was disbarred (stripped of his license to practice law) by the Arkansas Supreme Court, which led to his suspension from the bar of the U.S. Supreme Court.

Although many people believe the media had discredited itself by its excessive focus on the president's sexual conduct, even comparing reputable news outlets to supermarket tabloids, the question of honesty and moral character weighed heavily in the 2000 presidential election. Vice President Al Gore's personal connection to Clinton was a strike against him, while Texas governor George W. Bush's squeaky-clean image of prosaic devotion to his wife, Laura Bush, promised an administration that would not be riddled with sexual scandals.

Years later, as Hillary Clinton began her campaign for the 2008 presidential election, the shadow of the Lewinsky scandal hung over her candidacy.

More than a few people feared that having Hillary Clinton in the White House would mean four years of a womanizing Bill Clinton in the White House as well.

—*Leigh Husband Kimmel*

FURTHER READING

Apostolidis, Paul, and Juliet A. Williams, eds. *Public Affairs: Politics in the Age of Sex Scandals.* Durham, N.C.: Duke University Press, 2004. A study of politics and political culture in the context of sex scandals. Includes three chapters on Clinton and the Lewinsky affair and scandal.

Bennett, William J. *The Death of Outrage: Bill Clinton and the Assault on American Ideals.* Thorndike, Maine: G. K. Hall, 1998. Bennett, a conservative, considers the lack of moral outrage about Clinton's behavior.

Berlant, Lauren, and Lisa Duggan, eds. *Our Monica, Ourselves: The Clinton Affair and the National Interest.* New York: New York University Press, 2001. Collection of articles by mostly liberal academics and intellectuals examining the sociopolitical assumptions, implications, and consequences of the Clinton-Lewinsky affair.

Clinton, Bill. *My Life.* New York: Alfred A. Knopf, 2004. Memoir includes discussion of Clinton's perspective on the events surrounding his impeachment.

Dershowitz, Alan M. *Sexual McCarthyism: Clinton, Starr, and the Emerging Constitutional Crisis.* New York: Basic Books, 1998. Famed Harvard law professor Dershowitz discusses the issues at the height of the scandal.

Kalb, Marvin. *One Scandalous Story: Clinton, Lewinsky, and Thirteen Days That Tarnished American Journalism.* New York: Free Press, 2001. Focuses on the role of the media in the scandal, particularly its focus on sex rather than law.

Morton, Andrew. *Monica's Story.* New York: St. Martin's Press, 1999. Authorized biography that explores not only Lewinsky's time in the White House but also how the impeachment trial affected her and her family. Based on interviews with Lewinsky.

Posner, Richard A. *An Affair of State: The Investigation, Impeachment, and Trial of President Clinton.* Cambridge, Mass.: Harvard University Press, 1999. Presents a definitive assessment of the Clinton impeachment process, from its beginning to the acquittal.

Toobin, Jeffrey. *A Vast Conspiracy: The Real Story of the Sex Scandal That Nearly Brought Down a President.* New York: Random House, 1999. General, popular account of the scandal and the subsequent impeachment of Clinton.

SEE ALSO: 1927: President Warren G. Harding's Lover Publishes Tell-All Memoir; Feb. 7, 1960: President Kennedy's Romantic Affair Links Him to Organized Crime; May 19, 1962: Marilyn Monroe Sings "Happy Birthday, Mr. President"; July 18, 1969: Senator Edward Kennedy's Driving Accident Kills Mary Jo Kopechne; Oct. 7, 1974: Congressman Wilbur D. Mills's Stripper Affair Leads to His Downfall; May 23, 1976: *Washington Post* Exposes Congressman Wayne L. Hays's Affair; Sept., 1976: Jimmy Carter Admits Committing Adultery in His Heart; Jan. 26, 1979: Former Vice President Nelson Rockefeller Dies Mysteriously; Aug. 10, 1989: Japanese Prime Minister Sosuke Resigns After Affair with a Geisha; Aug. 5, 1994: Kenneth Starr Is Appointed to the Whitewater Investigation; Apr. 30, 2001: Washington Intern Chandra Levy Disappears; Oct. 2, 2003: Newspaper Claims That Arnold Schwarzenegger Groped Women; Apr. 26, 2006: Britain's Deputy Prime Minister Admits Affair with Secretary; Sept. 29, 2006: Congressman Mark Foley Resigns in Sex Scandal Involving a Teenage Page; Mar. 12, 2008: New York Governor Eliot Spitzer Resigns in Prostitution Scandal.